COLLECTED WHEEL PUBLICATIONS

VOLUME 15

NUMBERS 216 – 230

BPE

BPS Pariyatti Editions

BPS Pariyatti Editions
An imprint of Pariyatti Publishing
www.pariyatti.org

Copies of this book for sale in the Americas only. Although this is an American edition, we have left any British spelling of words unchanged.

First BPS Pariyatti Edition, 2025
ISBN: 978-1-68172-180-4 (Print)
ISBN: 978-1-68172-181-1 (PDF)
ISBN: 978-1-68172-182-8 (ePub)
ISBN: 978-1-68172-183-5 (Mobi)
LCCN: 2018940050

Contents

WH 216 The Buddhist Attitude to Other Religions
K. N. Jayatilleke 1

WH 217 to 220 An Analysis of the Pāli Canon
Russell Webb 29

WH 221 to 224 Kamma and Its Fruit
Leonard A. Bullen, Nina van Gorkom, Bhikkhu Ñāṇajīvako, Nyanaponika Thera, Francis Story 163

WH 225 Buddhism and Sex
M. O'C. Walshe 253

WH 226 to 230 A Technique of Living
Leonard A. Bullen 277

Key to Abbreviations

A	Aṅguttara Nikāya	Paṭis	Paṭisambhidamagga
Ap	Apadāna	Peṭ	Peṭakopadesa
Bv	Buddhavaṃsa	S	Saṃyutta Nikāya
Cp	Cariyāpiṭaka	Sn	Suttanipāta
D	Dīgha Nikāya	Th	Theragātha
Dhp	Dhammapada	Thī	Therigātha
Dhs	Dhammasaṅgaṇī	Ud	Udāna
It	Itivuttaka	Vibh	Vibhaṅga
Ja	Jātaka verses and commentary	Vin	Vinaya-piṭaka
Khp	Khuddakapāṭha	Vism	Visuddhimagga
M	Majjhima Nikāya	Vism-mhṭ	Visuddhimagga Sub-commentary
Mil	Milindapañha	Vv	Vimānavatthu
Nett	Nettipakaraṇa	Nidd	Niddesa

The above is the abbreviation scheme of the Pali Text Society (PTS) as given in the *Dictionary of Pali* by Margaret Cone.

The commentaries, *aṭṭhakathā*, are abbreviated by using a hyphen and an "a" ("-a") following the abbreviation of the text, e.g., *Dīgha Nikāya Aṭṭhakathā* = D-a. Likewise the sub-commentaries are abbreviated by a "ṭ" ("-ṭ") following the abbreviation of the text.

The sutta reference abbreviation system for the four Nikāyas, as is used in Bhikkhu Bodhi's translations is:

AN	Aṅguttara Nikāya	DN	Dīgha Nikāya
MN	Majjhima Nikāya	Sn	Saṃyutta Nikāya
J	Jātaka story	Mv	Mahāvagga (Vinaya Piṭaka)
Cv	Cullavagga (Vinaya Piṭaka)	SVibh	Suttavibhaṅga (Vinaya Piṭaka)

The Buddhist Attitude to Other Religions

by

K. N. Jayatilleke

WHEEL PUBLICATION NO. 216

The Buddhist Attitude to Other Religions

The Buddhist attitude to other religions has from its very inception been one of critical tolerance. But what is significant is that it was able to combine a missionary zeal with this tolerant outlook. Not a drop of blood has been shed throughout the ages in the propagation and dissemination of Buddhism in the many lands to which it spread; religious wars either between the schools of Buddhism or against other religions have been unheard of. Very rare instances of the persecution of heretical opinions are not lacking, but they have been exceptional and atypical. Buddhism has also shown a remarkable degree of adaptability in the course of its historical expansion.

A student of Buddhism, a professor of philosophy, who made a special study of this aspect of Buddhism, has observed: "I refer to its remarkable elasticity and adaptability. Wherever Buddhism has gone it has manifested this characteristic, and manifested it in a superlative and unique degree. I do not think there is another religion that possesses so much of it. Buddhism has been emphatically a missionary religion. Its transplanting to new lands has been accomplished never through conquest or through migration but solely by the spread of ideas. Yet almost everywhere it has gone, it has so completely adapted itself to the new people and the new land as to become practically a national religion. This has been partly due to the tolerance and liberality of its thought, to which I have already referred, a tolerance which it has exhibited both within and without. With the most extremely rare exceptions, Buddhism has held no heresy trials and has carried on no persecutions. With a daring catholicity that approaches foolhardiness it has recognized every form of rival as a possessor of some degree of truth."[1]

Speaking of the relevance for modern times of Buddhism and the cultural milieu in which it arose, namely Hinduism, Prof. Arnold J. Toynbee says: "Co-existence is mankind's only alternative to mass-suicide in the Atomic Age; and mankind means to save itself from committing mass-suicide if it can find a way. One open

---

1. J. B. Pratt, *The Pilgrimage of Buddhism*, London, 1928, p. 719.

way is the Indian way; and it might therefore seem probable that, in the Atomic Age, the spirit of Indian religion and philosophy will receive a welcome in the Western half of the world."[2] In one of his earlier works, Toynbee speaks of the religions of Southern and Eastern Asia as "Buddhaic religions" in contrast to the Judaic religions of Judaism, Christianity and Islam. He says: "There are three Buddhaic religions: the Hīnayāna Buddhism of Ceylon and South-East Asia; the Mahāyāna Buddhism of East Asia, Tibet and Mongolia; and the post-Buddhaic Hinduism of India."[3]

Perhaps what Toynbee had in mind in calling post-Buddhistic Hinduism a "Buddhaic religion" is the fact that Hinduism was deeply influenced by Buddhism, so much so that Hindus have claimed to have absorbed Buddhism rather than to have discarded it. Vaishṇavite Hindus have deified the Buddha and consider him the last (ninth) avatar (incarnation) of Vishnu. Saṃkara, one of the greatest philosophers of Hindu Vedānta, was so profoundly affected by Buddhist thought that he has been called a "concealed Buddhist" (*pracchanna-bauddha*), and the influence of Buddhism on recent Indian leaders like Mahātma Gandhi and Jawaharlal Nehru has been no less profound. Besides, millions of the so-called depressed classes, following their late leader Ambedkar, have consciously embraced Buddhism, attracted by its doctrine of social and spiritual equality. It is therefore worthwhile to examine the nature as well as the basis of the tolerant attitude of Buddhism towards other religions, despite its missionary zeal.

If we go into the historical origins of Buddhism, we note that Buddhism arose at a time when there was an interminable number of mutually conflicting theories about the nature and destiny of man in the universe. Some of them first arose as a result of the free speculations among the brahmins of the Āraṇyaka period, just prior to about 800 BCE, when knowledge came to be highly valued. Later, speculation on these and other matters spread in non-Brahmanical circles as well. It was from about this time that "dialectics" (*vākovākya*) became a separate branch of study among the Brahmins and the habit of debating religious and metaphysical topics in public became a recognised institution.

---

2. A. J. Toynbee, *America and the World Revolution*, London, 1962, p. 49.
3. A. J. Toynbee, *An Historian's Approach to Religion*, London, 1956, p. 272.

These theories are recorded or referred to in the Upaniṣadic and Jain texts. The Buddha summarizes the main views of his predecessors and contemporaries in the *Brahmajāla Sutta*, one of the oldest and most authentic of suttas in the Pāli Canon. It is one of the few suttas to which the Buddha has given a title at the end and the only one for which several such titles are given. The Buddha says: "You may remember this exposition as the 'net of aims,' the 'net of doctrines,' the 'supreme net,' the 'net of religio-philosophic theories,' and 'the glorious victory in the war (of ideologies)'" (D I 46). The sutta and the doctrines contained in it are referred to elsewhere in the early portion of the Canon, the Nikāyas themselves (e.g. S II 227f; Sn 538), and a brief account of the circumstances in which it was preached is given in the proceedings of the First Council, reported in the *Vinaya Piṭaka*. The *Brahmajāla Sutta* is found in the Chinese *Āgamas* as well and may be presumed to belong to the common core of early doctrine.

I think that one of the reasons why Buddhism adopted a non-dogmatic attitude was that at its very inception it had to face a plurality of contending religio-philosophic theories about the nature and destiny of man. As a result, scepticism was rampant and the Buddha could not assume the truth of any particular religious philosophy in addressing the intellectual elite (*viññū-purisa*) of his age. A claim to authority would not have been seriously considered or accepted.

A Jain commentator, Sīlāñka of the ninth century, speaks in the following vein of the reasons for the growth of the sceptical schools of thought during the time of Mahāvīra, who was the senior contemporary of the Buddha: "The sceptics say that those who claim knowledge cannot be making factual claims since their statements are mutually contradictory, for even with regard to the category of the soul, some assert that the soul is omnipresent and others that it is not omnipresent, some say it is of the size of a digit, others that it is of the size of a kernel of a grain of millet, some say it both has form and is formless, some that it resides in the heart and others that it is located in the forehead, etc. In respect of every category there is no uniformity in their assertions; there is no one with an outstanding intellect whose statements may be regarded as authoritative; even if such a person existed, he cannot be discovered by one with a limited vision according to the maxim that 'one who is not omniscient does not know everything,' for it is said 'how can one desiring to know that a certain person is omniscient at a certain time do so if he is devoid of that person's intellect, his knowledge and his consciousness.'"[4]

The very presence of such a variety of religio-philosophic theories at that time is a tribute to the tolerance of Hinduism in this period. The Vedic tradition at this time stressed the importance of knowledge (*jñāna*) whatever the form it may take, whether it be empirical, rational or intuitive, as the key to power or salvation. This was, no doubt, opposed by those who stressed the claims of social action and ritual (*karma-mārga*) as the way to salvation, but so long as the *jñāna-vādins* gave a nominal allegiance to the Vedic tradition they were not suppressed.

The *Āraṇyakas* for the first time proclaimed that what was important was not the actual performance of the various Vedic sacrifices but the understanding of their meaning and symbolism, which came to be interpreted to mean the understanding of the meaning of life. Eventually, in the *Upaniṣads* it is shown that there is no greater "sacrifice" (*yajña*) than that of understanding the meaning of life and living accordingly. The *Chāndogya Upaniṣad* says: "Now, what people call sacrifice (*yajña*) is really the religious life (*brahmacarya*), for only through the religious life does one who is a knower find that world" (8.5.1).

We may recall that when the Brahmin Kūṭadanta comes to the Buddha and wants to be instructed by him as to how to perform a really valuable sacrifice (Pāli *yañña*, Skr. *yajña*), the Buddha explains that it would be a waste of valuable resources and a needless destruction of animals to perform a ritualistic sacrifice; he points out that the true "sacrifice" consists in leading the Buddhist way of life and adds: "There is no sacrifice that man can celebrate, O brahmin, higher and sweeter than this" (D I 147).

The thinkers of the *Āraṇyakas* and the *Upaniṣads* were not propounding one theory but a multiplicity of mutually contradictory theories about the nature and destiny of man in the universe. According to the independent attestation of the Buddhist scriptures, the Brahmins during this period were cultivating a "skill in metaphysics and logic," a branch of study which was known as

4. See K. N. Jayatilleke, *Early Buddhist Theory of Knowledge*, London, 1963.

lokāyata, a word which at this time meant "theories pertaining to the cosmos" but which later came to mean "materialist theories." Among these cosmological theories, which were being put forward by these Brahmins, according to the Buddhist texts, were the following:

(1) that everything exists (*sabbaṃ atthi*);
(2) that nothing exists (*sabbaṃ natthi*);
(3) that the world is a unity (*sabbaṃ ekattaṃ*); and
(4) that the world is a plurality (*sabbaṃ puthuttaṃ*)
(S II 77).

The fact that they were putting forward and debating mutually contradictory views based on reasoning did not seem to have bothered orthodoxy at the time. Of the above theories, the first and the third are generally in keeping with Vedic assumptions, whereas the second and the fourth are characterized as materialist theories in the Buddhist commentarial tradition and would appear to contradict these assumptions. But it was agreed that evolving such diverse theories and living in accordance with them constituted worship of Brahman and complete intellectual freedom was thus allowed.

The above evidence is from Buddhist sources but it is confirmed from what we find in the Vedic tradition. The *Bhagavadgītā* speaks of "some who worship with offerings of knowledge, with (theories) of unity as well as of plurality" (*jñāña-yajñena cā'pyanye ... upāsate ekatvena pṛthaktvena*) (IX.15). As far as the Vedic scriptural tradition went, an idealistic monistic theory was apparently considered to be on the same footing as a materialist pluralistic theory.

We referred to the theory that "nothing exists" as a materialist theory. In the Buddhist canonical texts too one of the several materialist schools is said to hold that "neither this world existed nor the world beyond" (*natthi ayani loko, natthi paro loko*) (D I 55). It should appear strange that a materialist school of thought should deny the reality of this world, though it is understandable that it should deny the reality of the world beyond. The publication in 1940 of a work by Jayarāsi Bhaṭṭa called the *Tattvopaplavasiṃha*[5] has now settled our doubts. It is the only extant text of a materialist

5. Eds., S. Sanghavi and E. C. Parikh, *Gaekwad Oriental Series*, No. 87, Baroda, 1940.

school hitherto discovered. It argues that even sense-perception (which was accepted by most materialist schools as the only valid means of knowledge) cannot be trusted, but that out of purely pragmatic considerations we must act on the assumption that there are only material things and values, though in actual fact even the reality of this world cannot be proved. This remarkable breadth of outlook on the part of the pre-Buddhist Vedic traditionalists, who permitted the widest degree of speculation within its fold, did not, however, last very long. Such absolute and untrammeled freedom of thought and expression was considered to be somewhat dangerous for orthodoxy; soon curbs and restrictions were believed to be necessary. Soon after the impact of Buddhism the *Maitrī Upaniṣad* states: "There are those who love to distract the believers in the Veda by the jugglery of false arguments, comparisons and paralogisms: with these one should not associate ... The world, bewildered by a doctrine that denies the self (*nairātmya-vāda*), by false comparisons and proofs, does not discern the difference between the wisdom of the Vedas and the rest of knowledge ... They say that there should be attention to a (new) Dharma, which is destructive of the teaching of the Vedas and the other scriptures ... Therefore what is set forth in the Vedas, that is the truth. On what is said in the Vedas, on that wise men live their life. Therefore a Brahmin should not study what is not of the Veda" (*Maitrī Up.* 7.8.10).

The *Lokāyata* speculations, likewise, led to the propagation of materialist theories of man and the universe in Brahmin circles and these were considered to undermine the Vedic tradition. The *Manusmṛti* therefore lays down the rule: "The Brahmin who despises the roots of the Vedic tradition because of his dependence on the science of reasoning should be expelled by the good Brahmins as a nihilist, who scorns the Vedas" (*Manusmṛti* II.11). After this, *Lokāyata* as a branch of study was taboo to Brahmin orthodoxy and the word survived to denote the materialist theories, which were once nurtured within the orthodox fold itself.

The free atmosphere for speculation and controversy generated by the pre-Buddhist Vedic tradition, however, had caused a hundred flowers to bloom both within as well as without the Brahmin intellectual circles. The variety of religio-philosophic views, which included several sceptical theories, as well as the unbounded freedom of thought and expression permitted at the time, no doubt left their mark on Buddhism.

This does not mean that the dawn of the Buddhist era was not without its dogmatists. In the welter of mutually contending theories, there were bound to be those who tried to peddle their own wares with dogmatic insistence. The *Suttanipāta* refers to "all those people who tenaciously cling to their respective religio-philosophical theories and argue, 'Here alone is the truth!'" (*ye kec'ime diṭṭhi paribbassānā, 'idam eva saccan' ti vivādayanti*) (Sn 896). There is also a reference to people who claimed to dispense salvation: "'Here alone is salvation'—thus do they proclaim; they do not grant salvation in the religions of others" (*idh'eva suddhi' iti vādiyanti, nāññesu dhammesu visuddhim āhu*) (Sn 824).

The question of survival is central to religion, for unless there is some concept of survival after death the concept of salvation would be meaningless and we might as well dispense with religion. It would therefore be pertinent to illustrate the variety of views held on topics pertaining to religion by reference to the several solutions put forward at this time regarding this question. It will show the difference of the Buddhist point of view, with which some of these discarded theories are even today identified. Logically there are four possible points of view that we can adopt with regard to this question. We may say: (a) that we survive death in the form of discarnate spirits, i.e. a single after-life theory; (b) that we come back to subsequent earth-lives or lives on other similar planets, i.e. a rebirth theory; (c) that we are annihilated with death, i.e. a materialist theory; and (d) that we are unable to discover a satisfactory answer to this question or there is no satisfactory answer, i.e. a sceptical, agnostic or positivist theory.

The Buddhist texts record several variants of each of the above types. The *Brahmajāla Sutta* classifies the single after-life theories as follows:

It says that there are religious teachers, who assert that the soul after death is (a) conscious (*saññī*), (b) unconscious (*asaññī*) or (c) superconscious, lit. neither conscious nor unconscious (*nevasaññīnāsaññī*). There are sixteen variants of the conscious-theory and eight each of the other two. The following are the sixteen:

I. Variations regarding the form of the soul:

- (i) has a subtle material form;
- (ii) has no such form;
- (iii) has a subtle material form for some time and then has no such form;
- (iv) intrinsically has no such form but has the power of manifesting such a form.

II. Variations regarding the duration of the soul:

- (i) comes to an end, e.g. the theory of "second death" in the Brāhmaṇas;
- (ii) is of eternal duration;
- (iii) changes its state after some time and becomes eternal;
- (iv) does not exist in time.

III. Variations regarding the nature and extent of consciousness:

- (i) consciousness of unity;
- (ii) consciousness of diversity;
- (iii) of limited consciousness;
- (iv) of unlimited consciousness.

IV. Variations regarding the hedonic tone of experiences:

- (i) extremely happy;
- (ii) extremely unhappy;
- (iii) both happy and unhappy;
- (iv) not experiencing happiness or unhappiness.

Only variations I (i)–(iv) and II (i)–(iv) are considered applicable to those who held that the soul was (b) unconscious or (c) superconscious after death.

It would not be difficult to find instances of the above theories of survival put forward by religious teachers and philosophical thinkers of East and West. On first glance the above list looks artificial, but the fact that many of these theories can be traced to the pre-Buddhist literature proves that it is not. Thus Prajāpati held, on the basis of rational and metaphysical speculation, that the soul was "conscious and having its own form after death" (*Chāndogya Up.*, 8.12), i.e. (a)(I)(i).

Uddālaka held that the soul was "unconscious and without form" after death, i.e. (b)(I)(ii). The *Taittirīya Upaniṣad* asserts that the soul has a subtle material form for some time and then ceases to have such a material form (*Taittirīya Up.* 3.10.5), i.e. (a)(I)(iii). Yājñavalkya tries to show that the soul is "neither conscious nor unconscious after death" and has no form, i.e. (c)(I)(ii). Just as much as there are several single after-life theories, there are several rebirth theories in the pre-Buddhist traditions of the Upaniṣads, the Ājīvikas and Jains. They range from those who assert that the soul is reborn even as "herbs and trees" (*Chāndogya Up.* 5.10.6) to those who hold that the soul betters its status at each successive stage of rebirth, taking on "another newer and more beautiful form".[6]

On the other hand the several schools of materialists denied survival altogether. Seven such schools are referred to in the *Brahmajāla Sutta.* One of them, the most extreme, held that there is no mind or soul apart from the body, which is entirely a hereditary product of one's parents. What we call "mind" is the patterns of movement in our bodies. Another school held that the mind is an emergent product, which has a material basis, and its condition is determined by the food we eat. They argued that just as much as when we mix up certain chemicals in certain proportions there emerges the intoxicating power of liquor, even so the material particles of the body and the food we eat go to form the mind, which is an emergent by-product. This would be similar to a Marxist materialist conception of the mind. This emergent mind, however, was deemed to disintegrate on the dissolution of the body at death. There were also schools of mystic materialists, who believed in the possibilities of the expansion of consciousness but argued that since such forms of consciousness are dependent on the condition of the body, there is no survival after death.

The dialectical opposition between the soul-theorists, who asserted survival, and the various schools of materialists, who denied it, led to scepticism with regard to the question of survival and other such matters as well. The *Kaṭha Upaniṣad* says: "This doubt there is with regard to a man deceased—'he exists' say some; 'he exists not' say others" (*Kaṭha Up.* I.20). The sceptics adopted scepticism on the basis of various intellectual or pragmatic grounds

6. *Bṛhadāraṇyaka Up.*, 4.4.4.

or both. Some held that our experiences are subjective since they are based on our own individual perspective and that no objectivity in knowledge was possible since we cannot have any insight into the minds of others. Others held that on these matters one is led by one's prejudices for (*chanda, rāga*) or against (*dosa, paṭigha*) and that we are therefore unjustified in coming to definite conclusions. Yet others were of the opinion that in dogmatically accepting a theory of survival or denying it, we get involved with the theory and that such "involvement" is a source of mental unrest. Others found that we could argue rationally for or against survival and that therefore we are none the wiser. Sañjaya appears to have been of the view that the question of survival and similar questions are beyond verification and it is immaterial as to what we believe.

It would divert us from our task to give a detailed account of the Buddhist theory of survival and the grounds on which it is based. Suffice it to say, as it would appear to be evident from the above, that the Buddhist theory of survival was taught by the Buddha after examining all the alternative possible theories with regard to the question of survival. According to the information of the earliest texts, he did so after he was convinced of it on the basis of his capacity to recall his past lives and also to read by means of his clairvoyance the past lives of others. He trained several of his disciples to acquire these faculties and realise the truth of his discoveries for themselves.

It is a belief of many people today that religious dogmas cannot be empirically verified but have to be accepted on the basis of faith. It is therefore necessary to add that rebirth, which forms part of the Buddhist theory of re-becoming (*punabbhava*), is no longer in the realm of superstition and religious dogma. It is one thing which distinguishes Buddhism from other religions with the possible exception of certain forms of Hinduism. Rebirth has become philosophically respectable even to a modern logical analyst, who has expressly come out in favour of a concept of rebirth without a soul, which is exactly the Buddhist form of the doctrine. This professor of philosophy, A. J. Ayer, states his position as follows in one of his recent works: "I think that it would be open to us to admit the logical possibility of reincarnation merely by laying down the rule that if a person who is physically identified as living at a later time does have the extensible memories and character of a person who is physically identified as living at an earlier time, they are to be counted as one person and not two."[7]

There are three sorts of empirical evidence for rebirth: the evidence from age-regression experiments conducted with subjects who allegedly recall minute historical details of experiences in prior lives without having obtained such information in this life, the evidence from authentic instances of the spontaneous cases of recall mostly on the part of children even from countries in which they are not predisposed to believe in rebirth, and finally evidential clairvoyance.

A psychologist refers to some of the case records of a psychiatrist, Dr Blanche Baker, in one of which the subject was regressed "through a total of forty-seven lives (twenty-three as a man and twenty-four as a woman)" and says, "literally hundreds of details of these lives have been verified in historical reference books. 'Coincidence' is the stock explanation offered by sceptics for these occurrences, but the explanation is at best inadequate in view of the frequency with which they occur."[8] Dr Ian Stevenson selected forty-four cases in which there have been "apparent recollections of specific people, places and events in the life of a definitely identified other person, who died prior to the birth of the subject." He states his conclusion as follows after trying to account for the data in terms of several alternative normal and paranormal hypotheses: "I will say, therefore, that I think reincarnation the most plausible hypothesis for understanding cases of this series."[9] The best attested case of evidential clairvoyance is that of Edgar Cayce, who gave detailed and accurate medical diagnoses of the illnesses of patients, some of whom he had not even seen. Later, when questions were put to him about the nature and destiny of man in the universe, he claimed to see and read the prior lives of himself as well as of others.[10]

---

7. A. J. Ayer, *The Concept of a Person*, London, 1963, p. 127.
8. Gina Cerminara, *The World Within*, New York, 1957, p. 28f.
9. *The Evidence for Survival from Claimed Memories of Former Incarnations*, Essex, 1964, p. 84.
10. Thomas Sugrue, *There Is a River*, New York, 1943, and G. Cerminara, *Many Mansions*, New York, 1960.

Rebirth is not a well-established scientific hypothesis universally accepted by psychologists as yet, but it is significant that it should be considered by at least some psychologists as "the most plausible hypothesis" to account for the empirical data.[11] I have digressed from my main theme in order to show that the Buddhist theory of rebirth can today be subjected to experimental investigation, and it would therefore be incorrect to say that it is a doctrine which has to be either accepted or rejected on mere faith.

To get back to my subject, I took this question of survival after death merely to illustrate the diversity of views regarding it prevalent at the time of the Buddha. Had I taken any other problem pertinent to religion, such as the problem of free will vs. determinism, moral responsibility vs. amoralism, theism vs. atheism, it would have been possible to illustrate a similar diversity of views prevalent at the time. At no other time in human history, unless it be in the present, was such a variety of views on matters pertaining to religion present together in the same epoch. No wonder that the Buddha referred to them as a "thicket of views, a wilderness of views, a tangle of views" (*diṭṭhi-gahanaṃ, diṭṭhi-kantāraṃ, diṭṭhi-visūkaṃ*) (M I 8). The opening verse of the *Visuddhimagga*, quoted from the Pāli Canon, gives a beautiful and apt description of the plight of thinking men in that age:

The inner tangle and the outer tangle—
This generation is entangled in a tangle.
And so I ask of Gotama this question:
Who succeeds in disentangling this tangle?

(*Path of Purification* I.1)

To have adopted a dogmatic attitude and to have accepted one or more of these views uncritically from one of the prevailing Vedic or non-Vedic traditions would have been self-defeating. So with those who were bewildered by the variety of religio-philosophical theories offered them during this age, the Buddha advocated a critical outlook, recommending that they test the validity of any particular religion or philosophy that appeals to them in the light

11. For a careful analysis of the evidence, see C. J. Ducasse, *A Critical Examination of the Belief in a Life after Death*, Springfield, Illinois, 1961, pp. 207–307.

of their personal experience. The sceptics had already taught that a man may be led by his prejudices for (*chanda*) or against (*dosa*) accepting or rejecting a theory. The Buddha showed them how one should examine things dispassionately without being led by attachment (*chanda*), hatred (*dosa*), ignorance (*moha*) or fear (*bhaya*) (D II 133). The following oft-quoted passage, which is not always accurately translated, contains the essence of the attitude recommended by the Buddha in choosing between conflicting ideologies as a basis for living:

> "There are certain religious teachers who come to Kesaputta. They speak very highly of their own theories, but oppose, condemn and ridicule the theories of others. At the same time there are yet other religious teachers who come to Kesaputta and in turn speak highly of their own theories, opposing, condemning and ridiculing the theories of these others. We are now in a state of doubt and perplexity as to who out of these venerable recluses spoke the truth and who spoke falsehood."
>
> "O Kālāmas, you have a right to doubt or feel uncertain, for you have raised a doubt in a situation in which you ought to suspend your judgement. Come now, Kālāmas, do not accept anything on the grounds of revelation, tradition or report or because it is a product of mere reasoning or because it is true from a standpoint or because of a superficial assessment of the facts or because it conforms with one's preconceived notions or because it is authoritative or because of the prestige of your teacher. When you, Kālāmas, realise for yourselves that these doctrines are evil and unjustified, that they are condemned by the wise, and that when they are accepted and lived by they conduce to ill and sorrow, then you should reject them ..." (A I 189).

This critical attitude should be focused on Buddhism itself:

> "If anyone were to speak ill of me, my doctrine or my Order, do not bear any ill will towards him, be upset or perturbed at heart; for if you were to do so, it would only cause you harm. If, on the other hand, anyone were to speak well of me, my doctrine and my Order, do not be overjoyed, thrilled or elated at heart; for if you were to do so, it would only be an obstacle in the way of forming a realistic judgment as

to whether the qualities praised in us are real and actually found in us" (D I 3).

The later tradition often underlines this attitude. The following verse attributed to the Buddha is to be found in a Sanskrit Buddhist text called the *Tattvasaṃgraha* and a Tibetan work called the *Jñānasamuccayasāra*:

> "Just as the experts test gold by burning it, cutting it, and applying it on a touchstone, my statements should be accepted only after critical examination and not out of respect for me."

This does not, however, mean that faith is no requirement at all in Buddhism. Far from it. One cannot test a theory unless one accepts it at least tentatively as one's basis of life. The Buddhist accepts the "right philosophy of life" (*sammā-diṭṭhi*) as the basis of his living because he finds it reasonable and in fact more reasonable than any other way of life. Such faith which eventually culminates in knowledge is called a "rational faith" (*ākāravatī saddhā*) as opposed to a blind or "baseless faith" (*amūlikā saddhā*).

Going along with this critical outlook is the causal conception of nature, which is conceived of as a causal system in which there operate physical laws (*utu-niyāma*), biological laws (*bīja-niyāma*), psychological laws (*citta-niyāma*) as well as moral and spiritual laws (*kamma-dhamma-niyāma*). These laws are said to operate whether a Buddha comes into existence or not, and all that the Buddha does is to discover them and reveal to us those which are of relevance to the moral and spiritual life, which is both possible and desirable in the universe in which we live. It is said:

> "Whether Tathāgatas arise or not, this order exists, namely, the fixed nature of phenomena, the regular pattern of phenomena or conditionality. This the Tathāgata discovers and comprehends; having discovered and comprehended it, he points it out, teaches it, lays it down, establishes, reveals, analyses, clarifies it and says, "Look!"" (S II 25).

This dispassionate and impartial but critical outlook (the causal conception of the universe and the conception of the Buddha as a being who discovers the operation of certain moral and spiritual laws and reveals them to us) may be said to be the first plank on which Buddhist tolerance rests. A scientist does not ask a fellow scientist to accept a theory on faith, though his fellow scientist must have enough faith in the theory on his preliminary examination of it before he thinks of testing it out. In the same way, the Buddha shows us the way but we have to do the hard work of treading it before we can get anywhere—*tumhe hi kiccaṃ ātappaṃ akkhātāro tathāgata*. The Dhamma is well-proclaimed (*svākkhāto*), *it* produces results without delay in this very life (*sandiṭṭhiko akāliko*), it invites anyone to verify it for himself (*ehipassiko*), it leads to the desired goal (*opanayiko*), and it is to be realised by the wise, each person for himself (*paccattaṃ veditabbaṃ viññūhi*). It looks as if the Buddha was addressing a modern mind of the twentieth century, for the outlook that the Buddha recommends is what we today call the scientific outlook, except for the fact that it does not make a dogma of materialism.

The concept of the Buddha as one who discovers the truth rather than as one who has a monopoly of the truth is clearly a source of tolerance. It leaves open the possibility for others to discover aspects of the truth or even the whole truth for themselves. The Buddhist acceptance of Pacceka-Buddhas, who discover the truth for themselves, is a clear admission of this fact. Referring to certain sages (*munayo*), who had comprehended the nature of their desires and had eliminated them, crossing over the waves of saṃsāric existence, the Buddha says: "I do not declare that all these religious men are sunk in repeated birth and decay" (*nāhaṃ bhikkhave sabbe samaṇa brahmaṇāse jātijarāya nivutā ti brūmi*) (Sn 1082). Yet, as it is pointed out, the Dhamma is to be preached to all beings, though all beings may not profit by it, just as much as all sick people are to be treated, although some may get well or succumb to their illnesses despite the medicines given (A I 120f). This is because there are beings who would profit only from the Dhamma.

This assertion of the possibility of salvation or spiritual growth outside Buddhism does not mean that Buddhism values all religions alike and considers them equally true. It would be desirable to determine the Buddhist use of the word for religion before examining this question. In early Buddhism, a religious doctrine was denoted by the word *dhamma*. *Diṭṭhi* was a "religio-philosophical theory" and for it the word *darsana* was later used in Indian thought. But for "religion," which includes both beliefs as well as practises, the word used was *dhamma-vinaya,* which literally means "doctrine and discipline." But the term which was common to the Vedic tradition as well was *brahmacarya,* which literally means the "religious life." It was used in a very wide sense, because of the intellectual tolerance of the Vedic tradition at this time, to denote any "ideal life." It could be interpreted to mean any way of life that was considered to be the ideal as a result of one accepting a certain view of life concerning the nature and destiny of man in the universe. In this sense, the way of life of a materialist is also an ideal life from his point of view.

Indian thought has been accused of failing to divorce religion from philosophy. The accusation is unjustified. For what happened in the history of Indian thought is that the theoretical aspect of each religion was considered its philosophy, whereas its practical aspect was the religion. Every philosophy including materialism thus had both a view of life as well as a way of life, and consistency was demanded not only in each sphere (i.e. within each "view of life" and within each "way of life"), but also between both. A materialist philosopher who did not live in accordance with material values was thus considered inconsistent. The Buddha claimed that there was consistency between his theory and practise (*yathāvādī tathākārī*). Western classical metaphysics on the other hand latterly came to be divorced from living. It was for this reason that existentialism had to come in to fill the void. In Indian thought, however, every philosophical system had its theory as well as its practise and a philosophy was not entertained in isolation from its practical bearing on life. Today we call those non-theistic philosophies (which have a practical bearing on life and often claim the sole allegiance of an individual) religion-surrogates since they take the place of traditional religions and act as substitutes for religion. Humanism, certain forms of existentialism not related to traditional religions and certain materialist philosophies like Marxism, which have a practical bearing on life, may be considered such religion-surrogates. Buddhism considers some of those religion-surrogates on the same footing as practical religions (*brahmacariya-vāsa*) in stating its attitude to various types of religion. In the *Sandaka Sutta* Ānanda, reporting the ideas of the Buddha, says that there are four pseudo-religions (*abrahmacariya-vāsā*) or false religions in the world and four religions which are unsatisfactory (lit. *anassāsikaṃ*, unconsoling) but not necessarily false.

The pseudo-religions are: first, materialism, which asserts the reality of the material world alone and denies survival; second, a religious philosophy which recommends an amoral ethic; third, one which denies free will and moral causation and asserts that beings are either miraculously saved or doomed; and fourth, deterministic evolutionism, which asserts the inevitability of eventual salvation for all (M I 515–18).

The four unsatisfactory but not necessarily false religions are presumably those which in some sense recognise the necessity for a concept of survival, moral values, freedom and responsibility and the non-inevitability of salvation. The first is one in which omniscience is claimed for its founder in all his conscious and unconscious periods of existence. The second is a religion based on revelation or tradition; the third a religion founded on logical and metaphysical speculation; and the fourth is one which is merely pragmatic and is based on sceptical or agnostic foundations.

We note here that the relativist valuation of religion in early Buddhism does not presuppose or imply the truth of all religions or religion-surrogates. Some types of religion are clearly condemned as false and undesirable, while others are satisfactory to the extent to which they contain the essential core of beliefs and values central to religion, whatever their epistemic foundations may be. Those based on claims to omniscience on the part of the founder, revelation or tradition, metaphysical speculation or pragmatic scepticism, are unsatisfactory insofar as they are based on uncertain foundations.

Revelations and revelational traditions contradict each other and it is said that they may contain propositions which may be true or false. In the case of religions based on metaphysical arguments and speculations, "the reasoning may be valid or invalid and the conclusions true or false" (*sutakkitaṃ pi hoti duttakkitaṃ pi hoti tathā pi hoti aññatha pi hoti*) (M I 520). Buddhism is, therefore, by implication a religion which asserts survival, moral values, freedom and responsibility, and the non-inevitability of salvation. It is also verifiably true.

I do not propose here to examine any of the specific doctrines of another religion and compare or contrast them with Buddhism, but it will be observed that the definition of the Buddhist "right view of life" (*sammā-diṭṭhi*) comprehends the basic beliefs and values of the higher religions. The definition reads as follows: "There is value in alms, sacrifices and oblations; there is survival and recompense for good and evil deeds; there are moral obligations, and there are religious teachers who have led a good life and who have proclaimed with their superior insight and personal understanding the nature of this world and the world beyond" (M III 72). This "right view of life" (*sammā-diṭṭhi*) is said to be of two sorts: (a) one of which is mixed up with the inflowing impulses (*sāsavā*), and (b) the other not so mixed up. These impulses are the desire for sensuous gratification (*kāmāsavā*), the desire for self-centred pursuits and for continued existence in whatsoever form (*bhavāsavā*), and illusions (*avijjāsavā*). Thus a right view of life mixed up with a desire for personal immortality in heaven or a belief in sensuous heavens would be a *sāsava-sammā-diṭṭhi.*

The above summary of the right philosophy of life, it may be observed, is comprehensive enough to contain, recognise and respect the basic truths of all higher religions. All these religions believe in a Transcendent, characterised as Nibbāna, which is beyond time, space and causation in Buddhism, as an impersonal monistic principle such as Brahman or Tao in some religions, and as a personal God in others. They all assert survival, moral recompense and responsibility. They all preach a "good life," which has much in common and whose culmination is communion or union with or the attainment of this Transcendent. The early Buddhist conception of the nature and destiny of man in the universe is, therefore, not in basic conflict with the beliefs and values of the founders of the great religions so long as they assert some sort of survival, moral values, freedom and responsibility and the non-inevitability of salvation. But at the same time it is not possible to say that in all their phases of development, and in all their several strands of belief in varying social contexts, they have stood for this central core of beliefs and values. This applies to Buddhism as well, particularly when we consider some of the developments in Tantric Buddhism.

One of the last questions put to the Buddha was by the wandering ascetic Subhadda. He wanted to know whether the leading philosophies and religions proclaimed in his day by the six outstanding teachers, who each had a large following were all true, all false or whether some were true and some false. The Buddha did not give a specific answer to this question since he generally avoided making specific criticisms of particular religions unless he was invited or challenged to do so. He says, however, that any religion is true to the extent to which it would incorporate the Noble Eightfold Path: "In whatever religion the Noble Eightfold Path is not found, that religion would not have the first saint, the second, the third, and the fourth; in whatever religion the Noble Eightfold Path is found, that religion would have the first, second, third and fourth saints. Void are these other religions of true saints. If these monks were to live righteously, the world would never be devoid of saints" (D II 151). The first saint, the stream-enterer or *sotāpanna*, is the person who has given up preconceptions about a soul to be identified with or located within aspects or the whole of his psycho-physical personality, is convinced that no permanent and secure existence is possible within the cosmos of becoming (i.e. has given up *sakkāya-diṭṭhi* or personality belief), has by study and understanding cleared his doubts about the Buddha, Dhamma and the saintly Sangha (i.e. has got rid of *vicikicchā*), has given up obsessional attachments to religious virtues and observances (i.e. has discarded *sīlabbata-parāmāsa*), and leads a pure moral life. As such he is not likely to fall below the level of human existence in any of his future births (*avinipāta-dhammo*) and is assured of final realization. The third saint[12] is the person who, in addition to the above, tends to act out of selfless charity (*cāga*), compassion (*karuṇā*) and understanding (*vijjā*) rather than out of greed (*lobha*), hatred (*dosa*) and ignorance (*moha*). Ignorance comprises all the erroneous beliefs and illusions we entertain about the nature and destiny of man in the universe. Hatred is the source of our aggressive (*vibhava-taṇhā*) tendencies and greed includes the desire for sensuous gratification (*kāma-taṇhā*) as well as the desire for self-centred pursuits (*bhava-taṇhā*), such as the desire for power,

12. The non-returner to the world of sensuality (*anāgāmi*). He has fully eliminated the fetters of sensuous desire and ill will, which are still present, though weakened, in the second saint (once-returner), who is not mentioned in this text. (Editor)

fame, etc. The fourth saint, the *arahant*, is the person who attains final realization in this life itself.[13]

Leaving out Nigaṇṭha Nātaputta, the founder of Jainism, the other five outstanding teachers in the day of the Buddha represent standard types of philosophies or religions. In Sañjaya, we have the sceptic or agnostic or positivist who argued that questions pertaining to survival, moral responsibility and values, spiritual beings and transcendent existence were beyond verification. Ajita Kesakambalī was a materialist who denied any value in religious activities, denied survival, moral recompense and moral obligations, and denied that there were any religious teachers who had led a good life and who have proclaimed with their superior insight and understanding the nature of this world and the world beyond. His view was that the fools and the wise alike were annihilated at death. Makkhali Gosāla has been called a theist (*issara-kāraṇa-vādi*); as a theist who believed in God he seemed to have argued that salvation is eventually predestined for all. Everything is preplanned and takes place in accordance with the fiat of God; it is like the unraveling of a ball of thread thrown on the ground. Fools and wise alike evolve in various forms of existence, high and low, in the course of which they gather experience under the impact of diverse forces, living in accordance with the sixty-two philosophies of life in different lives. Man himself has no will of his own since everything is predetermined by the divine will, which guarantees final salvation for all.

The theism of Makkhali is severely criticized since it gives a false sense of security to people and encourages complacency by denying free will, the value of human effort and ensuring eventual salvation. The Buddha says that he knows of no other person than Makkhali born to the detriment and disadvantage of so many people, comparing him to a fisherman casting his net at the mouth of a river for the destruction of many fish (AN 1:18/A I 33).

There are two arguments against belief in such a personal God (*īsvara*) mentioned in the Buddhist scriptures. The first is that the truth of theism entails a lack of man's final responsibility

---

13. The *arahant* has fully eliminated all the remaining five fetters: desire for fine-material and immaterial existence, conceit, restlessness and ignorance. (Editor)

for his actions: "If God designs the life of the entire world—the glory and the misery, the good and the evil acts—man is but an instrument of his will and God is responsible" (J-a V 238). The other is that some evils are inexplicable if we grant the truth of such a theism: "If God is the lord of the whole world and creator of the multitude of beings, then why has he ordained misfortune in the world without making the whole world happy? For what purpose has he made a world that has injustice, deceit, falsehood and conceit? The lord of the world is unrighteous in ordaining injustice where there could have been justice" (J-a VI 208).

The fact that such a theistic philosophy is severely criticized does not mean that all forms of theism are condemned. A theistic religion and philosophy which: (1) stresses the importance of human freedom, responsibility and effort; (2) encourages the cultivation of moral and spiritual values and the attainment of moral perfection; and (3) offers the hope of fellowship with God (Brahmā), who is represented as a perfect moral being (wise and powerful but not omniscient or omnipotent); is to be commended on pragmatic grounds. Addressing some personal theists among the Brahmins, the Buddha describes the path to fellowship (*sahavyatā,* lit. companionship) with God (Brahmā) and speaks of the necessity of cultivating selflessness, compassion, freedom from malice, purity of mind and self-mastery for this purpose:

> "Then you say, too, Vāseṭṭha, that the Brahmins bear anger and malice in their hearts and are impure in heart and uncontrolled, whilst God is free from anger and malice, pure in heart and has self-mastery. Now can there be concord and harmony between the Brahmins and God?"
>
> "Certainly not, Gotama!"
>
> "Very good, Vāseṭṭha. That those Brahmins versed in the Vedas and yet bearing anger and malice in their hearts, sinful and uncontrolled, should after death, when the body is dissolved, attain fellowship with God, who is free from anger and malice, pure in heart and has self-mastery—such a state of things can in no way be" (Tevijja Sutta, D I 247–8).

Whatever the basis of the theistic myth they believed in, so long as these Brahmins could be persuaded to cultivate these virtues grounded in their faith in God, it was a step in the right direction. Thus on pragmatic grounds the belief in a personal God is not discouraged insofar as it is not a hindrance but an incentive for moral and spiritual development. At the same time we must not forget that, even according to the Buddhist conception of the cosmos, such a heaven had a place in the scheme of things, though the God who ruled in it, worshipped as the Almighty, was only very wise, powerful and morally perfect, though not omniscient and omnipotent.

It will be worthwhile drawing attention to this conception of the cosmos in order to clarify this statement. The early Buddhist description of the cosmos, as far as the observable universe goes, is claimed to be based on extrasensory clairvoyant perception. It is remarkably close to the modern conception of the universe:

> As far as these suns and moons revolve shedding their light in space, so far extends the thousand-fold universe. In it there are thousands of suns (*sahassānaṃ suriyānaṃ*), thousands of moons, thousands of inhabited worlds of varying sorts ... thousands of heavenly worlds of varying grades. This is the thousand-fold minor world system (*cūlaṇikā loka-dhātu*). Thousands of times the size of the thousand-fold minor world system is the twice-a-thousand middling world system (*majjhimika loka-dhātu*). Thousands of times the size of the middling world system is the thrice-a-thousand great cosmos (*mahā loka-dhātu*) (A I 227–28).

This conception of the universe as consisting of hundreds of thousands of clusters of galactic systems containing thousands of suns, moons and inhabited worlds is not to be found in the Hindu or Jain scriptures and was much in advance of the age in which it appears. In later Theravāda it gets embedded in and confused with mythical notions about the universe. In the Mahāyāna, the conception is magnified and there are references to the "unlimited and infinite number of galactic systems (*loka-dhātu*) in the ten quarters" (*Sukhāvatī-vyūha,* I), but the original conception of a "sphere of million millions of galactic systems" (*Vajracchedikā,* XXX) survives. Brahmā occupies a place in the highest of heavens, and although he is morally perfect, he is still within the cosmic scheme of things and his knowledge does not extend as far as that of a Buddha.

In the *Brahmajāla Sutta*, the Buddha points out that the origins of some forms of theistic religion and philosophy are to be traced to the religious teachings of beings from this heaven, who are born on earth and lead a homeless life preaching a doctrine which leads to fellowship with Brahmā. It is said that in the ages past Sunetta (Fair-Eyed) and five other such teachers taught the path to heaven and fellowship with God (A III 371). Such teachings are commended since they help man in bettering his condition.

On the other hand, when the Buddha addressed materialists, sceptics, determinists or indeterminists, who denied survival, freedom and responsibility, he does not presuppose the truth of these latter concepts but uses a "wager argument" reminiscent of Pascal. This shows that on pragmatic grounds it is better to base one's life on the assumptions of survival, freedom and responsibility; for, otherwise, whatever happens, we stand to lose whereas on the other alternative we stand to gain (*Apaṇṇaka Sutta,* MN 60).

It would be possible for scholars and students of Buddhism to take these texts in isolation and, ignoring the rest of the material in the Canon, argue that either the Buddha was a theist or an agnostic, a sceptic or a materialist, as the case may be. There seem to be even "Buddhists" who, on the basis of the erroneous belief that the doctrine of *anattā* (no-soul) precludes any possibility of a belief in survival, argue that the Buddha could not have entertained any belief in survival. This would make Buddhism a form of materialism, perhaps a dialectical materialism with the emphasis on the doctrine of impermanence (*anicca*) or a scepticism, doctrines from which Buddhism has been clearly distinguished in all its phases of expansion. It has even been said that rebirth is not taught in the First Sermon, which no one dared tamper with, whereas even this sermon quite clearly refers to "the desires which tend to bring about rebirth or re-becoming" (*taṇhā ponobhavikā*). So does the last sermon to Subhadda emphasize the Noble Eightfold Path, whose first member is "the right view of life," which underlines the reality of this world as well as the world beyond (*atthi ayaṃ loko, atthi paro loko*).

Likewise, on the question of theism, we find that a scholar like Mrs. Rhys Davids latterly believed that Buddhism was no different in principle from a theistic religion, making the Buddha a personal theist. Radhakrishnan saw in the Buddha an impersonal theist or implicit monist. For Keith, the Buddha was an agnostic and for Stcherbatsky an atheist. In actual fact none of these labels is adequate to describe Buddhism, which transcends them all. It is important to distinguish Buddhism from all of them, for the Buddhist attitude to other religions would depend on the view we take of Buddhism itself.

It is important to distinguish Buddhism on the one hand from personal theism and on the other hand from atheistic materialism, although Buddhism has common ground with both. The Buddha was quite emphatic about this. He referred to the former as *bhava-diṭṭhi*, "the personal immortality view," and the latter as *vibhava-diṭṭhi*, "the annihilation view." Distinguishing Buddhism from both these views, which he says are found in the world and are mutually opposed to each other, the Buddha states: "These religious teachers who do not see how these two views arise and cease to be, their good points and their defects, and how one transcends them in accordance with the truth are under the grip of greed, hate and ignorance ... and will not attain final redemption from suffering" (M I 65).

We have already talked about the common ground that Buddhism has with some forms of theism in urging the validity of moral and spiritual values and of a transcendent reality. It will be worthwhile summarizing the common ground that Buddhism has with some forms of materialism. The Buddha refused to preach to a hungry man. What Buddhism requires of man in society is the pursuit of one's material as well as spiritual well-being (such a quest being practicable), where one's wealth is righteously earned and spent for one's good and that of others, without squandering or hoarding it. The man who is valued is the person who "possesses the capacity to acquire wealth that he could not acquire before and also to increase it and at the same time possesses that insight which makes it possible for him to distinguish good and evil" (*Puggalapaññatti*, III). Buddhism upholds the reality of this world as well as the next, and the Buddha speaks of the happiness of the average man as deriving from economic security (*atthi sukha*), the enjoyment of one's wealth (*bhoga-sukha*), freedom from debt (*anaṇa-sukha*), and a blameless moral and spiritual life (*anavajja-sukha*). All forms of asceticism that mortify the flesh are condemned even for monks since a strong and healthy body is necessary for both material and spiritual endeavours.

The Buddha was the first to proclaim the equality of man in the fullest sense of the term. There are differences of species, points out the Buddha, among plants and animals, but despite differences in the colour of the skin, the shape of the nose or the form of the hair, mankind is biologically one species (*Vāseṭṭha Sutta, Suttanipāta*). There was absolute spiritual equality as well for man, for anyone could aspire to become a Brahmā or a Buddha; there are no chosen castes, chosen churches or chosen individuals.

The Buddha gives a dynamic conception of society and holds that the economic factor is one of the main determinants of social change. Social disintegration and the division of the world into the haves and the have-nots, resulting in tensions, the loss of moral values in human society and destructive wars, originate from the misdistribution of goods: "As a result of goods not accruing to those bereft of goods, poverty becomes rampant; poverty becoming rampant, stealing becomes rampant ..." (D III 65). Tracing the cause of this poverty, which leads to such dire consequences, it is said that the mistake that the kings made was to consider that their task was merely to preserve law and order without developing the economy; the king "provided for the righteous protection and security of his subjects but neglected the economy" (*dhammikaṃ rakkhāvaraṇaguttiṃ saṃvidahi, no ca kho adhanānaṃ dhanaṃ anuppadāsi*) (D III 65). The ideal state was one in which there was both freedom as well as economic security. This freedom embraces the recognition of human rights, the freedom to propagate any political or religious doctrine, as well as freedom for "birds and beasts" (*migapakkhīsu*) to live without being wantonly attacked by humans.

In advising a king, the Buddha says that the best way to ensure peace and prosperity in one's kingdom is not by wasting the country's resources in performing religious sacrifices but by ensuring full employment and thereby developing the economy (see D I 135). The Emperor Asoka, who was imbued with these ideals, has been credited with being the first king in history to conceive of a welfare state. Imbued with these same ideals Sinhalese kings set up tremendous irrigation works for the welfare of man. It was King Parākramabāhu who said: "Truly in such a country not even a little water that comes from the rain must flow into the ocean without being made useful to man ... for a life of enjoyment of what one possesses, without having cared for the welfare of the people, in no wise befits one like myself."[14]

I think these few observations will suffice to show how strongly Buddhism stresses the importance of the material realities of life and how practical the advice has been. Both freedom as well as economic security are necessary ingredients for man's material and spiritual advancement. And freedom includes the freedom to criticise each others' political or religious philosophies without rancour or hatred in our hearts.

I said earlier that the dispassionate and impartial quest for truth, the causal conception of the universe and the conception of the Buddha as a discoverer and proclaimer of truth were some of the planks of Buddhist tolerance. Another has been compassion. We cannot force the truth on others. All we can do is to help them to discover it, and the greatest help we can give others especially in imparting spiritual truth is to try not to speak out of greed, hatred and ignorance but out of unselfishness, compassion and wisdom.

Truth is immortal speech—this is the eternal law.

Saccaṃ ve amatā-vācā—esa dhammo sanantano.

Hatred does not cease by hatred—hatred ceases by love.
This is the eternal law.

Na hi verena verāni—sammantīdha kudācanaṃ
Averena ca sammanti—esa dhammo sanantano.

14. See Wilhelm Geiger, *The Cūḷavaṃsa*, Colombo, 1953, p. 277.

An Analysis of the Pāli Canon

Edited by

Russell Webb

WHEEL PUBLICATION NO. 217/218/219/220

Preface

An Analysis of the Pāli Canon was originally the work of A.C. March, the founder-editor of *Buddhism in England* (from 1943, *The Middle Way*), the quarterly journal of The Buddhist Lodge (now The Buddhist Society, London). It appeared in the issues for Volume 3 and was later offprinted as a pamphlet. Finally, after extensive revision by I.B. Horner (the late President of the Pali Text Society) and Jack Austin, it appeared as an integral part of *A Buddhist Student's Manual*, published in 1956 by The Buddhist Society to commemorate the thirtieth anniversary of its founding. The basic analysis of the Tipiṭaka appeared in *The Maha Bodhi*, 37:19–42 (Calcutta 1929), and was reprinted in K.D.P. Wickremesinghe's *Biography of the Buddha* (Colombo 1972).

In the present edition, the basic analysis of the Canon has been left in its original state although some minor corrections had to be made. However, it has been found possible to fully explore the Saṃyutta and Aṅguttara Nikāyas together with three important texts from the Khuddaka Nikāya: Udāna, Itivuttaka, and Suttanipāta. It was deemed unnecessary to give similar treatment to the Dhammapada, as this popular anthology is much more readily accessible. The Paṭisambhidāmagga has also been analysed.

The index (except for minor amendments) was originally prepared by G.F. Allen and first appeared in his book *The Buddha's Philosophy*. In this edition it has been simplified by extensive substitution of Arabic for Roman numerals.

The Bibliography, a necessary adjunct in view of the reference nature of the whole work, has, however, been completely revised as a consequence of the vast output of books on the subject that have come on to the market over the past few decades. Indeed, it was originally intended to make this an exhaustive section of Pāli works in the English language, past and present. A number of anthologies, however, include both *suttas* in their entirety and short extracts from the texts. In such cases the compiler has, where the works in question appear, only indicated the complete *suttas*, as it is hardly likely that brief passages in such (possibly out-of-print) books will be referred to by the student who can now so easily turn to complete texts. Moreover, to keep the Bibliography to a manageable size, it was also necessary to omit a number of anthologies which include selected translations available from other, more primary sources.

It is thus hoped that this short work will awaken in the reader a desire to study the original texts themselves, the most authoritative Buddhist documents extant. Space has precluded a detailed study of the Tipiṭaka from the standpoints of language and chronology, but the source books mentioned in the Bibliography will more than compensate for this omission.

Russell Webb
March 1991

I. Textual Analysis

The Pāli Canon, also called the Tipiṭaka or "Three Baskets" (of doctrine), is divided into three major parts:

a) Vinaya Piṭaka: The Collection of Disciplinary Rules.
b) Sutta Piṭaka: The Collection of the Buddha's Discourses.
c) Abhidhamma Piṭaka: The Collection of Philosophical Treatises.

A. Vinaya Piṭaka—the Collection of Disciplinary Rules

Bhikkhu and Bhikkhunī Pātimokkha

The monastic code of the *bhikkhu* (Buddhist monk) contains 220 rules and 7 legal procedures, consisting of eight classes:

Four rules, if infringed, entail expulsion from the Order (*pārājika*).

These are sexual intercourse, theft, taking a human life or inciting another to commit suicide, and falsely boasting of supernormal attainments.

Thirteen rules entailing initial and subsequent meetings of the Sangha (*saṅghādisesa*). These include masturbation, lustful physical and verbal contact with a woman, creating a schism, etc.

Two rules are indefinite (*aniyata*). Whether the being alone with a woman is a *pārājika*, *saṅghādisesa* or *pācittiya* offence.

Thirty rules entail expiation with forfeiture (*nissaggiya pācittiya*). Rules dealing with improper possession of requisites such as robes.

Ninety-two rules entail expiation (*pācittiya*). Rules dealing with wrong conduct such as lying, damaging plants, possessing gold and silvers, etc.

Four rules require confession (*pāṭidesanīya*).

Seventy-five rules are concerned with etiquette and decorum (*sekhiya*).

Seven procedures are for the settlement of legal processes (*adhikaraṇasamatha*).

This section is followed by another called the *Bhikkhunīvibhaṅga*, providing similar guidance for nuns.

The monastic code of the *bhikkhunī* (Buddhist nun) contains 304 rules and 7 legal procedures, consisting of seven classes:

a) Eight rules, if infringed, entail expulsion from the Order (*pārājika*).
b) Seventeen rules entailing initial and subsequent meetings of the Sangha (*saṅghādisesa*).
c) Thirty rules entail expiation with forfeiture (*nissaggiya pācittiya*).
d) Hundred sixty-six rules entail expiation (*pācittiya*).
e) Eight rules require confession (*pāṭidesanīya*).
f) Seventy-five rules are concerned with etiquette and decorum (*sekhiya*).
g) Seven procedures are for the settlement of legal processes (*adhikaraṇasamatha*).

1. Suttavibhaṅga

The analysis of the *Sutta* or *Pātimokkha*. Each *Pātimokkha* rule is treated by way of an origin story (*nidāna*) leading up to the laying down of the rule, the rule, a word analysis (*padabhājanīya*) of the rule, and (usually) modifications of the rule and exceptions.

2. Khandhaka, subdivided into Mahāvagga and Cūḷavagga

Rules, regulations and procedures which are not part of the *Pātimokkha*. The first chapter of the *Mahāvagga* contains a lengthy biography of the Buddha from his *sambodhi* up to the going forth of Sāriputta and Moggallāna. The last two chapters of the *Cūḷavagga* are accounts of the first and second councils.

(a) Mahāvagga

1. Rules for admission to the Order.
2. The *Uposatha* meeting and recital of the *Pātimokkha* (code of rules).
3. Residence during the rainy season (*vassa*).

4. The ceremony concluding the retreat (*pavāraṇa*).
5. Rules for articles of dress and furniture.
6. Medicine and food.
7. The annual distribution of robes (*kaṭhina*).
8. Rules for sick Bhikkhus, sleeping, and robe-material.
9. The mode of executing proceedings by the Order.
10. Proceedings in cases of schism.

(b) Cūḷavagga (or Cullavagga)

1. Rules for dealing with offences that come before the Order.
2. Procedures for putting a Bhikkhu on probation.
3. Procedures for dealing with accumulation of offences by a Bhikkhu.
4. Rules for settling legal procedures in the Order.
5. Miscellaneous rules for bathing, dress, etc.
6. Rules for dwellings, furniture, lodging, etc.
7. Rules for schisms.
8. Classes of Bhikkhus, and duties of teachers and novices (*sāmaṇera*).
9. Rules for exclusion from the *Pātimokkha*.
10. Rules for the ordination and instruction of Bhikkhunīs.
11. Account of the First Council, at Rājagaha.
12. Account of the Second Council, at Vesālī.

3. Parivāra

Summaries and classification of the rules of the Vinaya arranged as a kind of catechism for instruction and examination purposes.

B. Sutta Piṭaka—the Collection of the Buddha's Discourses

The Sutta Piṭaka, the second main division of the Tipiṭaka, is divided into five sections or collections (*nikāyas*) of discourses (*suttas*).

Dīgha Nikāya: the Collection of Long Discourses.
Majjhima Nikāya: The Collection of Middle Length Discourses.
Saṃyutta Nikāya: The Collection of Connected Discourses.
Aṅguttara Nikāya: The Collection of Numerical Discourses.
Khuddaka Nikāya: The Collection of Small Books.

1. Dīgha Nikāya

The Collection of Long Discourses is arranged in three *vaggas* or sections:

(a) *Sīlakkhanda Vagga*

1. Brahmajāla Sutta: "The Net of Brahmā" or the Perfect Net, in which are caught all the 62 heretical forms of speculation concerning the world and the self taught by the Buddha's contemporaries.
2. Sāmaññaphala Sutta: "The Fruits of the Homeless Life." The Buddha explains to King Ajātasattu the advantages of joining the Buddhist Order and renouncing the life of the world.
3. Ambaṭṭha Sutta: Pride of birth and its fall. A dialogue with Ambaṭṭha on caste. Contains reference to the legend of King Okkāka, the traditional founder of the Sakya clan.
4. Soṇadaṇḍa Sutta: Dialogue with the brahmin Soṇadaṇḍa on the characteristics of the true brahmin.
5. Kūṭadanta Sutta: Dialogue with the brahmin Kūṭadanta condemning animal sacrifice.
6. Mahāli Sutta: Dialogue with Mahāli on deva-like vision and hearing, and the attainment of full enlightenment.
7. Jāliya Sutta: On the nature of the life-principle as compared with the body.
8. Kassapasīhanāda Sutta: A dialogue with the naked ascetic Kassapa against self-mortification.
9. Poṭṭhapāda Sutta: A discussion with Poṭṭhapāda on the nature of the soul, in which the Buddha states the enquiry to be irrelevant and not conducive to enlightenment.

10. Subha Sutta: A discourse, attributed to Ānanda, on conduct, concentration, and wisdom.
11. Kevaḍḍha Sutta: The Buddha refuses to allow a Bhikkhu to perform a miracle. Story of the monk who visited the devas (deities) to question them.
12. Lohicca Sutta: Dialogue with the brahmin Lohicca on the ethics of teaching.
13. Tevijja Sutta: On the futility of a knowledge of the Vedas as means to attaining companionship with Brahmā.

(b) *Mahā Vagga*

14. Mahāpadāna Sutta: The Sublime Story of the Buddha Gotama and his six predecessors. Also, the Discourse on the Buddha Vipassi, describing his descent from the Tusita heaven to the commencement of his mission.
15. Mahānidāna Sutta: On the "chain of causation" and theories of the soul.
16. Mahāparinibbāna Sutta: The Great Discourse that records the passing of the Tathāgata into Parinibbāna.
17. Mahāsudassana Sutta: The Great King of Glory. The story of a previous existence of the Buddha, as King Sudassana, told by the Buddha on his deathbed.
18. Janāvāsabha Sutta: The Buddha relates the story of the *yakkha* (demon) Janāvāsabha to the people of Nādikā.
19. Mahāgovinda Sutta: The heavenly musician Pañcasikha relates the story of Mahāgovinda to the Buddha, who states that he himself was Mahāgovinda.
20. Mahāsamaya Sutta: The devas of the Pure Abode and their evolution.
21. Sakkapañha Sutta: Sakka, the lord of devas, visits the Buddha, and learns from him that everything that originates is also subject to dissolution.
22. Mahāsatipaṭṭhāna Sutta: Discourse on the Foundations of Mindfulness on the body, feelings, thoughts, and states of mind. With a commentary on the Four Noble Truths.
23. Payāsi Sutta: Kumārakassapa converts Payāsi from the heresy that there is no future life or reward of actions.

(c) *Pāṭika Vagga*

24. Pāṭika Sutta: Story of the disciple who follows other teachers because the Buddha does not work miracles or teach the origin of things.
25. Udumbarikasīhanāda Sutta: The Buddha discusses asceticism with the ascetic Nigrodha.
26. Cakkavattisīhanāda Sutta: Story of the universal king, the corruption of morals and their restoration, and the coming of the future Buddha Metteyya.
27. Aggañña Sutta: A discussion on caste, and an exposition on the origin of things (as in No.24) down to the origin of the four castes.
28. Sampasādanīya Sutta: A dialogue between the Buddha and Sāriputta, who describes the teaching of the Buddha and asserts his faith in him.
29. Pāsādika Sutta: The Delectable Discourse. Discourse of the Buddha on the perfect and the imperfect teacher.
30. Lakkhaṇa Sutta: The 32 marks of a Great Man.
31. Sigālovāda Sutta: The Sigāla homily on the duties of the householder to the six classes of persons.
32. Āṭānāṭiya Sutta: On the Four Great Kings and their spell for protection against evil.
33. Saṅgīti Sutta: Sāriputta outlines the principles of the teaching in ten numerical groups.
34. Dasuttara Sutta: Sāriputta outlines the doctrine in tenfold series.

2. Majjhima Nikāya

This division consists of 152 *suttas* of medium length arranged in 15 *vaggas*, roughly classified according to subject matter.

(a) *Mūlapariyāya Vagga*

1. Mūlapariyāya Sutta: How states of consciousness originate.
2. Sabbāsavā Sutta: On the elimination of the cankers.
3. Dhammadāyāda Sutta: Exhorting the Bhikkhus to realise the importance of the Dhamma and the unimportance of their physical wants.

4. Bhayabherava Sutta: On braving the fears and terrors of the forest. Also the Buddha's account of his enlightenment.
5. Anaṅgaṇa Sutta: A dialogue between Sāriputta and Moggallāna on the attainment of freedom from depravity.
6. Ākaṅkheyya Sutta: On those things for which a Bhikkhu may wish.
7. Vatthūpama Sutta: The parable of the soiled cloth and the defiled mind.
8. Sallekha Sutta: On the elimination of self and false views. How to efface defilements.
9. Sammādiṭṭhi Sutta: A discourse by Sāriputta on right views.
10. Satipaṭṭhāna Sutta: The same as DN 22, but without the detailed explanation of the Four Noble Truths.

(b) *Sīhanāda Vagga*

11. Cūḷasīhanāda Sutta: See No. 12 below.
12. Mahāsīhanāda Sutta: The short and the long "challenge" *suttas*. The futility of ascetic practices.
13. Mahādukkhakkhandha Sutta: See No. 14 below.
14. Cūḷadukkhakkhandha Sutta: The long and the short discourses on the suffering inherent in sensual pleasures.
15. Anumāna Sutta: By Moggallāna, on the value of introspection. (There is no reference to the Buddha throughout.)
16. Cetokhila Sutta: On the five mental bondages.
17. Vanapattha Sutta: On the advantages and disadvantages of the forest life.
18. Madhupiṇḍika Sutta: The Buddha gives a brief outline of his teaching, which Kaccāna amplifies.
19. Dvedhāvitakka Sutta: The parable of the lure of sensuality. Repetition of the Enlightenment as in No. 4.
20. Vitakkasaṇṭhāna Sutta: Methods of meditation to dispel undesirable thoughts.

(c) *Tatiya Vagga*

21. Kakacūpama Sutta: The simile of the saw. On the control of the feelings and the mind under the most severe provocation.
22. Alagaddūpama Sutta: Simile of the water snake. Holding wrong views of the Dhamma is like seizing a snake by the tail.

23. Vammika Sutta: The simile of the smouldering anthill as the human body.
24. Rathavinīta Sutta: Puṇṇa explains the purpose of the holy life to Sāriputta.
25. Nivāpa Sutta: Parable of Māra as a sower or hunter laying baits for the deer.
26. Ariyapariyesana Sutta: The Noble Quest. The Buddha's account of his renunciation, search, and attainment of enlightenment.
27. Cūḷahatthipadopama Sutta: The short "elephant's footprint" simile, on the Bhikkhu's training.
28. Mahāhatthipadopama Sutta: The long "elephant's footprint" simile, on the Four Noble Truths.
29. Mahāsāropama Sutta: On the dangers of gain, honour and fame. Said to have been delivered when Devadatta left the Order.
30. Cūḷasāropama Sutta: Development of the preceding *sutta*. On attaining the essence of the Dhamma.

(d) *Mahāyamaka Vagga*

31. Cūḷagosiṅga Sutta: A conversation of the Buddha with three Bhikkhus, who speak on harmonious living and relate their attainments to him.
32. Mahāgosiṅga Sutta: A conversation between six Bhikkhus who discuss what kind of monk makes the forest beautiful.
33. Mahāgopālaka Sutta: On the eleven bad and good qualities of a herdsman and a monk.
34. Cūḷagopālaka Sutta: Simile of the foolish and wise herdsman crossing the river.
35. Cūḷasaccaka Sutta: A discussion between the Buddha and the debater Saccaka on the nature of the five aggregates and other topics.
36. Mahāsaccaka Sutta: The account of the Buddha's asceticism and enlightenment, with instructions on right meditation.
37. Cūḷataṇhāsaṅkhaya Sutta: Sakka asks the Buddha about freedom from craving and satisfactorily repeats his reply to Moggallāna.
38. Mahātaṇhāsaṅkhaya Sutta: Refutation of the wrong view of a Bhikkhu who thinks that it is consciousness that transmigrates.

39. Mahā-assapura Sutta: See No. 40 below.
40. Cūḷa-assapura Sutta: The great and the small discourses given at Assapura on the duties of an ascetic.

(e) *Cūḷayamaka Vagga*

41. Sāleyyaka Sutta: A discourse to the brahmins of Sālā. Why some beings go to heaven and some to hell.
42. Verañjaka Sutta: The same discourse repeated to the householders of Verañjā.
43. Mahāvedalla Sutta: A psychological discourse by Sāriputta to Mahākoṭṭhita.
44. Cūḷavedalla Sutta: A psychological discourse by the Bhikkhunī Dhammadinnā to the lay-devotee Visākha.
45. Cūḷadhammasamādāna Sutta: See No. 46 below.
46. Mahādhammasamādāna Sutta: The short and long discourses on the results of good and bad conduct.
47. Vīmaṃsaka Sutta: On the right methods of investigation of the Buddha.
48. Kosambiya Sutta: A discourse to the Bhikkhus of Kosambi on the evil of quarrelling.
49. Brahmanimantanika Sutta: The Buddha converts Baka the Brahmā from the heresy of permanency.
50. Māratajjanīya Sutta: Moggallāna admonishes Māra.

(f) *Gahapati Vagga*

51. Kandaraka Sutta: Discourse on the four kinds of personalities, and the steps to liberation.
52. Aṭṭhakanāgara Sutta: A discourse by Ānanda on the ways of attainment of Nibbāna.
53. Sekha Sutta: The Buddha opens a new meeting hall at Kapilavatthu, and Ānanda discourses on the training of the disciple.
54. Potaliya Sutta: The Buddha explains to Potaliya the real significance of the abandonment of worldliness.
55. Jīvaka Sutta: The Buddha explains the ethics of meat-eating.
56. Upāli Sutta: The conversion of Upāli the Jain.
57. Kukkuravatika Sutta: A dialogue on *kamma* between the Buddha and two ascetics.

58. Abhayarājakumāra Sutta: The Jain Nātaputta sends Prince Abhaya to question the Buddha on the condemnation of Devadatta.
59. Bahuvedanīya Sutta: On different classifications of feelings and the gradation of pleasure.
60. Apaṇṇaka Sutta: On the "Certain Doctrine," against various heresies.

(g) *Bhikkhu Vagga*

61. Ambalaṭṭhikarāhulovāda Sutta: The discourse on falsehood given by the Buddha to Rāhula.
62. Mahārāhulovāda Sutta: Advice to Rāhula on contemplation, stressing mindfulness of breathing.
63. Cūḷamāluṅkya Sutta: Why the Buddha does not answer certain types of speculative questions.
64. Mahāmāluṅkya Sutta: On the five lower fetters.
65. Bhaddāli Sutta: The confession of Bhaddāli, and the Buddha's counsel.
66. Laṭukikopama Sutta: Advice on renunciation of the world.
67. Cātuma Sutta: Advice to boisterous Bhikkhus at Cātuma.
68. Nālakapāna Sutta: The Buddha questions Anuruddha concerning certain points of the Dhamma.
69. Gulissāni Sutta: Rules for those who, like Gulissāni, live in the forest.
70. Kīṭāgiri Sutta: The conduct to be followed by various classes of Bhikkhus.

(h) *Paribbājaka Vagga*

71. Tevijjavacchagotta Sutta: The Buddha visits the ascetic Vacchagotta and claims that he is called *tevijja* (possessing the three-fold knowledge) because he has recollection of his previous lives, supernormal vision, and knowledge of the way to the elimination of the taints (*āsava*).
72. Aggivacchagotta Sutta: The danger of theorising about the world, etc.
73. Mahāvacchagotta Sutta: Further explanation to Vacchagotta on the conduct of lay disciples and Bhikkhus.

74. Dīghanakha Sutta: The Buddha refutes the ascetic Dīghanakha. Sāriputta attains Arahatship.
75. Māgandiya Sutta: The Buddha relates his renunciation of the life of the senses, and speaks on the abandonment of sensual desires.
76. Sandaka Sutta: Ānanda refutes various wrong views in discussion with the ascetic Sandaka.
77. Māhasakuludāyi Sutta: On the five reasons why the Buddha is honoured.
78. Samaṇamaṇḍika Sutta: On the qualities of perfect virtue.
79. Cūḷasakuludāyi Sutta: The Jain leader Nātaputta, and the way to true happiness.
80. Vekhanassa Sutta: A repetition of part of the preceding *sutta*, with additional matter on the five senses.

(i) *Rāja Vagga*

81. Ghaṭīkāra Sutta: The Buddha tells Ānanda of his previous existence as Jotipāla.
82. Raṭṭhapāla Sutta: The story of Raṭṭhapāla, whose parents endeavoured in vain to dissuade him, from entering the Sangha.
83. Makhādeva Sutta: The story of the Buddha's previous life as King Makhādeva.
84. Madhurā Sutta: A discourse given after the Buddha's decease by Kaccāna to King Avantiputta on the real meaning of caste.
85. Bodhirājakumāra Sutta: The Buddha tells the story of his renunciation and enlightenment as in nos. 26 and 36 above.
86. Aṅgulimāla Sutta: Story of the conversion of Aṅgulimāla, the robber chief.
87. Piyajātikā Sutta: The Buddha's counsel to a man who has just lost a son, and the dispute between King Pasenadi and his wife thereon.
88. Bāhitika Sutta: Ānanda answers a question on conduct put by Pasenadi who presents him with his cloak.
89. Dhammacetiya Sutta: Pasenadi visits the Buddha and extols the holy life.
90. Kaṇṇakatthala Sutta: A conversation between the Buddha and Pasenadi on caste, the devas, and Brahmā.

(j) *Brāhmaṇa Vagga*

91. Brahmāyu Sutta: On the thirty-two marks of a Great Man, the Buddha's daily routine, and the conversion of the brahmin Brahmāyu.
92. Sela Sutta: The brahmin Sela sees the thirty-two marks of a Buddha and is converted (the same story is related in Suttanipāta 3:7).
93. Assalāyana Sutta: The brahmin Assalāyana discusses caste with the Buddha. An important presentation of the Buddha's teaching on this subject.
94. Ghoṭamukha Sutta: The brahmin Ghoṭamukha questions the monk Udena on the value of the life of renunciation, and builds an assembly hall for the Sangha.
95. Caṅkī Sutta: Discourse on brahmin doctrines, and the Buddha's way to realisation of ultimate truth.
96. Esukāri Sutta: Discourse on caste and its functions.
97. Dhānañjāni Sutta: Sāriputta tells the brahmin Dhānañjāni that family duties are no excuse for wrongdoing.
98. Vāseṭṭha Sutta: A discourse, mostly in verse, on the nature of the true brahmin (this recurs in Suttanipāta 3:9).
99. Subha Sutta: On whether a man should remain a householder or leave the world.
100. Saṅgārava Sutta: The brahmin woman who accepted the Dhamma, and a discourse on the holy life. Also repetition of parts of nos. 24 and 34 above.

(k) *Devadaha Vagga*

101. Devadaha Sutta: The Buddha discourses on the attainment of the goal by the living of a skilful life.
102. Pañcattaya Sutta: On five theories of the soul, and that the way of release (Nibbāna) does not depend on any of them.
103. Kinti Sutta: Rules for Bhikkhus who dispute about the Dhamma and who commit transgressions.
104. Samāgama Sutta: After the death of Nātaputta, the Buddha's discourse on dispute and harmony.
105. Sunakkhatta Sutta: The simile of extracting the arrow of craving.

106. Āneñjasappāya Sutta (or: Ānañjasappāya Sutta): Meditations on impassibility, the attainments, and true release.
107. Gaṇakamoggallāna Sutta: A discourse to Gaṇakamoggallāna on the training of disciples.
108. Gopakamoggallāna Sutta: After the decease of the Buddha, Ānanda explains to Vassakāra that the Dhamma is now the only guide.
109. Mahāpuṇṇama Sutta: The Buddha answers the questions of a Bhikkhu concerning the *khandhas*.
110. Cūḷapuṇṇama Sutta: A discourse on the untrue and true man.

(l) *Anupada Vagga*

111. Anupada Sutta: The Buddha praises Sāriputta and his analysis of mind.
112. Chabbisodhana Sutta: On the questions to ask a Bhikkhu who declares he has attained Arahantship.
113. Sappurisa Sutta: On the good and bad qualities of a Bhikkhu.
114. Sevitabbāsevitabba Sutta: Sāriputta expounds the right way to live the holy life.
115. Bahudhātuka Sutta: Lists of elements and principles in a dialogue between the Buddha and Ānanda.
116. Isigili Sutta: The Buddha on Paccekabuddhas.
117. Mahācattārīsaka Sutta: Exposition of the Noble Eightfold Path.
118. Ānāpānasati Sutta: Mindfulness of breathing.
119. Kāyagatāsati Sutta: Meditation on the body.
120. Saṅkhārupapatti Sutta: On the development of the five qualities enabling a Bhikkhu to determine the conditions of his rebirth.

(m) *Suññata Vagga*

121. Cūḷasuññata Sutta: Meditation on emptiness.
122. Mahāsuññata Sutta: Instruction to Ānanda on the practice of meditation on emptiness.
123. Acchariyabbhūtadhamma Sutta: On the marvellous life of a Bodhisatta. A repetition of part of DN 14, but applied to the Buddha himself.

124. Bakkula Sutta: Bakkula converts his friend Acelakassapa.
125. Dantabhūmi Sutta: By the simile of elephant training, the Buddha shows how one should instruct another in the Dhamma.
126. Bhūmija Sutta: Bhūmija answers the questions of Prince Jayasena.
127. Anuruddha Sutta: Anuruddha explains emancipation of mind to the householder Pañcakaṅga.
128. Upakkilesa Sutta: The Buddha appeases the quarrels of the Bhikkhus of Kosambi and discourses on right meditation.
129. Bālapaṇḍita Sutta: On rewards and punishments after death.
130. Devadūta Sutta: On the fate of those who neglect the messengers of death.

(n) *Vibhaṅga Vagga*

131. Bhaddekaratta Sutta: A poem of four verses, with a commentary on striving.
132. Ānandabhaddekaratta Sutta: Ānanda's exposition of the same poem.
133. Mahākaccanabhaddekaratta Sutta: Mahākaccāna expounds the same poem.
134. Lomasakaṅgiyabhaddekaratta Sutta: The Buddha expounds the same poem to Lomasakaṅgiya.
135. Cūḷakammavibhaṅga Sutta: The Buddha explains the various results of different kinds of *kamma*.
136. Mahākammavibhaṅga Sutta: The Buddha refutes those who deny the operation of *kamma*.
137. Saḷāyatanavibhaṅga Sutta: The analysis of the six senses.
138. Uddesavibhaṅga Sutta: Mahākaccāna speaks on an aspect of consciousness.
139. Araṇavibhaṅga Sutta: The middle path between two extremes, and the opposite courses that lead to conflicts and to their cessation.
140. Dhātuvibhaṅga Sutta: The story of Pukkusāti who recognises the Master by his teaching. The analysis of the elements.
141. Saccavibhaṅga Sutta: Statement of the Four Noble Truths. A commentary thereon by Sāriputta.
142. Dakkhiṇavibhaṅga Sutta: On gifts and givers.

(o) *Saḷāyatana Vagga*

143. Anāthapiṇḍikovāda Sutta: The death of Anāthapiṇḍika, his rebirth in the Tusita heaven, and his appearance to the Buddha.
144. Channovāda Sutta: Story of the Thera Channa who, when sick, was instructed by Sāriputta, but finally committed suicide.
145. Puṇṇovāda Sutta: The Buddha's instruction to Puṇṇa on bearing pleasure and pain.
146. Nandakovāda Sutta: Nandaka catechises Mahāpajāpatī and 500 Bhikkhunīs on impermanence.
147. Cūḷarāhulovāda Sutta: The Buddha takes Rāhula to the forest and questions him on impermanence. The devas come to listen to the discourse.
148. Chachakka Sutta: On the six sixes (of the senses).
149. Mahāsaḷāyatanika Sutta: On the right knowledge of the senses.
150. Nagaravindeyya Sutta: The Buddha's instruction on the kinds of ascetics and brahmins who are to be honoured.
151. Piṇḍapātapārisuddhi Sutta: Instruction to Sāriputta on the training of the disciple.
152. Indriyabhāvanā Sutta: The Buddha rejects the methods of the brahmin Pārāsariya for subduing the senses, and expounds his own method.

3. Saṃyutta Nikāya

This is the "grouped" or "connected" series of *suttas* which either deal with a specific doctrine or devolve on a particular personality. There are fifty-six *saṃyuttas* divided into five *vaggas* containing 2,889 *suttas*.

(a) *Sagātha Vagga*

1. *Devata Saṃyutta*: Questions of devas.
2. *Devaputta Saṃyutta*: Questions of the sons of devas.
3. *Kosala Saṃyutta*: Anecdotes of King Pasenadi of Kosala.
4. *Māra Saṃyutta*: Māra's hostile acts against the Buddha and disciples.
5. *Bhikkhunī Saṃyutta*: Māra's unsuccessful seduction of nuns and his arguments with them.

6. *Brahma Saṃyutta*: Brahmā Sahampati requests the Buddha to preach the Dhamma to the world.
7. *Brāhmaṇa Saṃyutta*: Bhāradvāja brahmin's encounter with the Buddha and his conversion.
8. *Vaṅgīsa Saṃyutta*: Vaṅgīsa, the foremost poet among the Bhikkhus, tells of his eradication of lust.
9. *Vana Saṃyutta*: Forest deities direct undeveloped Bhikkhus on the right path.
10. *Yakkha Saṃyutta*: Demons' encounters with the Buddha and with nuns.
11. *Sakka Saṃyutta*: The Buddha enumerates the qualities of Sakka, King of the Gods.

(b) *Nidāna Vagga*

12. *Nidāna Saṃyutta*: The explanation of Paṭiccasamuppāda (the doctrine of dependent origination).
13. *Abhisamaya Saṃyutta*: The encouragement to attain penetration of the Dhamma.
14. *Dhātu Saṃyutta*: The description of physical, mental, and abstract elements.
15. *Anamatagga Saṃyutta*: On the "incalculable beginning" (of *saṃsāra*).
16. *Kassapa Saṃyutta*: Exhortation of Kassapa.
17. *Lābhasakkāra Saṃyutta*: "Gains, favours and flattery."
18. *Rāhula Saṃyutta*: The instructing of Rāhula.
19. *Lakkhaṇa Saṃyutta*: Questions of Lakkhaṇa on *petas* (ghosts).
20. *Opamma Saṃyutta*: Various points of Dhamma illustrated by similes.
21. *Bhikkhu Saṃyutta*: Admonitions of the Buddha and Moggallāna to the Bhikkhus.

(c) *Khandha Vagga*

22. *Khandha Saṃyutta*: The aggregates, physical and mental, that constitute the "individual."
23. *Rādha Saṃyutta*: Questions of Rādha.
24. *Diṭṭhi Saṃyutta*: Delusive views arise from clinging to the aggregates.

25. *Okkantika Saṃyutta*: Entering the Path through confidence (*saddhā*) and through wisdom (*paññā*).
26. *Uppāda Saṃyutta*: Arising of the aggregates leads to *dukkha*.
27. *Kilesa Saṃyutta*: Defilements arise from the sixfold sense base and sense-consciousness.
28. *Sāriputta Saṃyutta*: Sāriputta answers Ānanda's question concerning the calming of the senses.
29. *Nāga Saṃyutta*: Enumeration of four kinds of *nāga* (serpents).
30. *Supaṇṇa Saṃyutta*: Enumeration of four kinds of *garuda* (magical birds).
31. *Gandhabbakāya Saṃyutta*: Description of the *gandhabbas* (celestial musicians).
32. *Valāhaka Saṃyutta*: Description of the cloud spirits.
33. *Vacchagotta Saṃyutta*: Vacchagotta's metaphysical questions.
34. *Samādhi Saṃyutta*: Enumeration of the four types of practisers of the *jhānas* (meditative absorptions).

(d) *Saḷāyatana Vagga*

35. *Saḷāyatana Saṃyutta*: The sixfold sense base and the correct attitude towards it.
36. *Vedanā Saṃyutta*: The three kinds of feeling and the correct attitude towards them.
37. *Mātugāma Saṃyutta*: The destinies of women according to their qualities.
38. *Jambukhādaka Saṃyutta*: Questions of the wanderer Jambukhādaka to Sāriputta.
39. *Sāmaṇḍaka Saṃyutta*: Questions of the wanderer Sāmaṇḍaka to Sāriputta.
40. *Moggallāna Saṃyutta*: Moggallāna explains the *jhānas* to the Bhikkhus.
41. *Citta Saṃyutta*: Senses and sense-objects are not intrinsically evil, only the unwholesome desires that arise through contact with them.
42. *Gāmaṇi Saṃyutta*: The definitions of "wrathful" and "kindly."
43. *Asaṅkhata Saṃyutta*: The Unconditioned (Nibbāna).
44. *Avyākata Saṃyutta*: Speculative questions put by King Pasenadi to Khema, Anuruddha, Sāriputta, and Moggallāna.

(e) *Mahā Vagga*

45. *Magga Saṃyutta*: The Noble Eightfold Path.
46. *Bojjhaṅga Saṃyutta*: The seven factors of enlightenment (mindfulness, investigation, energy, happiness, calm, concentration, and equanimity).
47. *Satipaṭṭhāna Saṃyutta*: The four foundations of mindfulness.
48. *Indriya Saṃyutta*: The five faculties (confidence, energy, mindfulness, concentration, and wisdom).
49. *Sammappadhāna Saṃyutta*: The four right efforts.
50. *Bala Saṃyutta*: The five powers (as for the faculties above).
51. *Iddhipāda Saṃyutta*: The four psychic powers (will, energy, thought, and investigation).
52. *Anuruddha Saṃyutta*: Supernormal powers attained by Anuruddha through mindfulness.
53. *Jhāna Saṃyutta*: The four *jhānas*.
54. *Ānāpāna Saṃyutta*: Mindfulness of breathing.
55. *Sotāpatti Saṃyutta*: Description of a "Stream-Enterer."
56. *Sacca Saṃyutta*: The Four Noble Truths.

4. Aṅguttara Nikāya

In the Aṅguttara Nikāya, the division is a purely numerical one. There are eleven classified groups (*nipātas*), the subject of the first being single items, followed by groups of two items, and so on, to the final group of eleven items. Each *nipāta* is divided into *vaggas,* each of which contains ten or more *suttas,* there being 2,308 *suttas* in all.

1. Ekaka Nipāta: The mind: Concentrated/unconcentrated, trained/untrained, cultivated/uncultivated; exertion; diligence; the Buddha, Sāriputta, Moggallāna, Mahākassapa; views: Right/wrong; concentration: Right/wrong.

2. Duka Nipāta: Two kinds of *kamma* (either producing results in this life or leading to rebirth); cause of origin of good and evil; hopes and desires; gain and longevity; two kinds of gifts (that of material things and that of Dhamma); two assemblies of Bhikkhus: Those who have realised/not realised the Four Noble Truths, and those who live/do not live in harmony.

3. Tika Nipāta: Three offences of body, speech, and mind; three praiseworthy acts: Generosity, renunciation, maintenance

of parents; exertion of checking growth of unarisen evil states, developing unarisen good states, removing arisen evil states; heretical views, i.e., that pleasant and painful and neither-pleasant-nor-painful experiences are caused by previous actions, that these experiences are providential, that these experiences are causeless.

4. Catukka Nipāta: Undisciplined persons lack conduct, concentration, insight, emancipation; the ignorant increase demerit by praising the unworthy, blaming the worthy, rejoicing when one should not rejoice, not rejoicing when one should rejoice; four kinds of persons: Neither wise nor pious, not wise but pious, wise but impious, both wise and pious; Bhikkhus should remain content with their robes, alms, dwelling-places and medicines; four kinds of happiness: Living in a suitable environment, association with a well-developed man, self-realisation, accumulated merit in the past; the four "divine abodes": Loving-kindness, compassion, sympathetic joy and equanimity; four qualities guarding a Bhikkhu against lapsing: Observation of *sīla*, control of the sense-doors, moderation in eating, constant mindfulness; four ways of self-concentration: For a happy condition in this life, for knowledge and insight, for mindfulness and self-possession, for destruction of the defilements; four persons fostering hatred, hypocrisy, gains and honours other than connected with the Dhamma; four mistaken views: Impermanence for permanence, pain for pleasure, non-self for self, impurity for purity; four faults of ascetics and brahmins: Drinking fermented liquor, addiction to sense pleasures, accepting money, earning their livelihood by unethical means; four fields of merit-bringing happiness: Rightly believing the Buddha as fully enlightened, the Dhamma as well expounded, the Sangha as well-established, the disciples as being free from impurities; four ways of living together: The vile with the vile, the vile with the good, the good with the vile, the good with the good; offering food gives the recipient: Long life, beauty, happiness, physical strength; four conditions for worldly prosperity: Persistent effort, protecting one's earnings, good friendship, balanced livelihood; four conditions for spiritual prosperity: Confidence, morality, charity, wisdom; four families of snakes to whom one should extend loving-kindness; four right efforts; four unthinkables: The sphere of a Buddha, the *jhānas*, *kamma* and result, speculating over the origin of the world; four pilgrimages: To the sites of the

Buddha's birth, enlightenment, first sermon and decease; four kinds of beneficial/non-beneficial speech: Truthfulness/lying, non-backbiting/backbiting, gentle/harsh, thoughtful/frivolous; four essential qualities: Morality, concentration, wisdom and emancipation; four faculties: Confidence, energy, mindfulness, concentration; the four elements; four persons worthy of monuments: The Buddha, Paccekabuddhas, Arahants, "Wheel-turning" kings; Bhikkhus should not retire to the forest if given to: Lust, malice, envy, or lacking commonsense.

5. Pañcaka Nipāta: Five good characteristics of a disciple: Reverence, modesty, abstinence from unskilful acts, energy, wisdom; five mental hindrances: Sensual lust, ill will, sloth, restlessness and worry, sceptical doubt; five objects of meditation: The impure, non-self, death, disagreeableness of food, not finding delight in the world; five evil qualities: Not free from passion, hatred, delusion, hypocrisy, malice; five good acts: Loving actions of body, speech and mind, observance of virtue, and holding to right views.

6. Chakka Nipāta: Sixfold duty of a Bhikkhu: Abstaining from distracting work, arguments, sleep and company; humility; association with the wise.

7. Sattaka Nipāta: Seven kinds of wealth: Reverence, good conduct, modesty, abstinence from unskilful acts, learning, renunciation, wisdom; seven kinds of attachment: Requesting favours, hatred, mistaken confidence, doubt, pride, worldly existence, ignorance.

8. Aṭṭhaka Nipāta: Eight causes of mindfulness/almsgiving/earthquakes.

9. Navaka Nipāta: Nine contemplations: Impurity, death, disagreeableness of food, indifference to the world, impermanence, suffering resulting from impermanence, non-self, renunciation, equanimity; nine kinds of persons: Those who have trod the four paths to Nibbāna and experience the "fruits" together with the worldling, etc.

10. Dasaka Nipāta: Ten contemplations: Impermanence, non-self, death, disagreeableness of food, indifference to the world, bone, and four stages of a decomposing corpse: Worm-infested, black with decay, fissured through decay, bloated; ten kinds of purification through right knowledge, right liberation, and the eight steps of the Noble Eightfold Path.

11. Ekadasaka Nipāta: Eleven kinds of happiness/ways to Nibbāna/good and bad characteristics of a herdsman and a Bhikkhu.

5. Khuddaka Nikāya

This is the division of the shorter books of the Sutta Piṭaka, the "Division of Small Books," as Buddhaghosa called it. This Nikāya appears to have grown up generally after the older Nikāyas were closed and probably was incorporated into the Canon later. There are fifteen main divisions:

Khuddakapāṭha: The "Text of Small Passages" contains:

(1) *Saraṇattaya*: The thrice-repeated "Refuge Formula" for all Buddhists.
(2) *Dasasikkhāpada*: The Ten Precepts binding on Sāmaṇeras (novices).
(3) *Dvattiṃsakāra*: List of the 32 constituents of the body.
(4) *Kumārapañhā*: Catechism of ten questions for Sāmaṇeras.
(5) *Maṅgala Sutta*: A poem on the "greatest blessings" (*maṅgala*).
(6) *Ratana Sutta*: A poem on the Three Jewels: Buddha, Dhamma, and Sangha.
(7) *Tirokuḍḍa Sutta* (or: Tirokuṭṭa Sutta): A poem on the offerings to be made to the ghosts of departed relatives.
(8) *Nidhikaṇḍa Sutta*: A poem on the storing up of true treasure.
(9) *Mettā Sutta*: A poem on loving-kindness.

Dhammapada: The Dhamma Path. It consists of 423 verses arranged in 26 *vaggas*.

Udāna: A collection, in eight *vaggas*, of eighty *udānas* or "inspired utterances" of the Buddha. They are mostly in verse and each is accompanied by a prose account of the circumstances which called it forth:

(1) *Bodhi Vagga*: Describes certain events following the Buddha's enlightenment, including the famous discourse to Bāhiya which stresses living in the present moment.

(2) *Mucalinda Vagga*: This *vagga* is named after the Nāga king who shielded the Buddha with his (cobra) hood.

(3) *Nanda Vagga*: The Buddha convinces his half-brother, Nanda, of the hollowness of worldly existence. Also contains admonitions to the Sangha.

(4) *Meghiya Vagga*: Ignoring the advice of the Buddha, Meghiya retires to a mango grove to practise meditation but his mind is soon assailed with unhealthy thoughts. On returning to the Buddha, he is told that five factors should be cultivated by one with an undeveloped mind: good friendship, morality, profitable conversation, determination, and insight. Also contains the stories of Sundarī and the assault on Sāriputta by a *yakkha*.

(5) *Soṇathera Vagga*: Contains a visit of King Pasenadi to the Buddha, the discourse to the leper Suppabuddha, the elucidation of the eight characteristics of the Sāsana, and the first year of the Bhikkhu-life of Soṇa.

(6) *Jaccandha Vagga*: Contains the Buddha's hint at his passing away, Pasenadi's dialogue, and the story of the king who caused men, blind from birth, to each feel and describe an elephant (illustrative of partial realisation of truth).

(7) *Cūḷa Vagga*: Contains minor episodes, mainly concerning individual Bhikkhus.

(8) *Pāṭaligāma Vagga*: Contains the famous definition of Nibbāna as being unborn, unbecome, unmade, uncompounded; the Buddha's last meal and his admonition to Ānanda over Cunda; and the visit to Pāṭaligāma where the Buddha enunciated the five advantages of leading a pure life and the five disadvantages of not doing so.

Itivuttaka: A collection of 112 short *suttas* in four *nipātas*, each accompanied with verses. The collection takes its name from the words usually introducing each set of verses: *iti vuccati*, "thus it is said." The work comprises the ethical teachings of the Buddha:

(1) *Ekaka Nipāta*: Three *vaggas*. Lust, ill will, delusion, wrath, spite, pride, ignorance, craving, schism, lying, stinginess, are condemned; mindfulness, association with the wise, concord, mental peace, happiness, diligence, generosity and loving-kindness are praised.

(2) *Duka Nipāta*: Two *vaggas*. Elucidates guarding of the sense-doors and moderation in eating, skilful actions, healthy habits and correct views, serenity and seclusion, shame and dread, the two kinds of Nibbāna, and the virtues of leading an energetic ascetic life.
(3) *Tika Nipāta*: Five *vaggas*. Categorises factors which are threefold: evil roots, elements, feelings, thirsts, cankers, etc., and proclaims the ideal life of a Bhikkhu.
(4) *Catukka Nipāta*: Categorises factors which are fourfold: Bhikkhus' necessities, Noble Truths, etc., and emphasises purity of mind for a Bhikkhu.

Suttanipāta: "Collection of Suttas." This comprises five *vaggas* containing 70 *suttas* in all. The *suttas*, each containing from eight to fifty verses, are in verse with introductions in either verse or prose.

(a) *Uragavagga*

1. Uraga Sutta: The Bhikkhu who discards all human passions (anger, hatred, craving, etc.) and is free from delusion and fear, is compared to a snake which has shed its skin.
2. Dhaniya Sutta: The complacent "security" of a worldling is contrasted with the genuine security of the Buddha.
3. Khaggavisāṇa Sutta: The wandering life of a Bhikkhu is praised. Family and social ties are to be avoided in view of their *saṃsāric* attachments, excepting the "good friend" (*kalyāṇamitta*).
4. Kasībhāradvāja Sutta: Socially useful or mundane labour is contrasted with the no less important efforts of the Buddha striving for Nibbāna.
5. Cunda Sutta: The Buddha enumerates four kinds of *samaṇas*: a Buddha, an Arahant, a conscientious Bhikkhu, and a fraudulent Bhikkhu.
6. Parābhava Sutta: The "causes of personal downfall" in the moral and spiritual domains are enumerated.
7. Vasala or Aggika Bhāradvāja Sutta: In refutation of the charge "outcast," the Buddha explains that it is by actions, not lineage, that one becomes an outcast or a brahmin.
8. Mettā Sutta: The constituents of the practice of loving-kindness towards all beings.

9. Hemavata Sutta: Two yakkhas have their doubts about the qualities of the Buddha resolved by him. The Buddha continues by describing the path of deliverance from death.
10. Āḷavaka Sutta: The Buddha answers the questions of the *yakkha* Āḷavaka concerning happiness, understanding, and the path to Nibbāna.
11. Vijaya Sutta: An analysis of the body into its (impure) constituent parts, and the mention of the Bhikkhu who attains Nibbāna through understanding the body's true nature.
12. Muni Sutta: The idealistic conception of a *muni* or sage who leads a solitary life freed from the passions.

(b) *Cūḷavagga*

13. Ratana Sutta: A hymn to the Three Jewels: Buddha, Dhamma and Sangha.
14. Āmagandha Sutta: Kassapa Buddha refutes the Brahmanic view of defilement through eating meat and states that this can only come about through an evil mind and corresponding actions.
15. Hiri Sutta: A dissertation on the nature of true friendship.
16. Mahāmaṅgala Sutta: Thirty-eight blessings are enumerated in leading a pure life, starting with basic ethical injunctions and culminating in the realisation of Nibbāna.
17. Sūciloma Sutta: In reply to the threatening attitude of the *yakkha* Sūciloma, the Buddha states that passion, hatred, doubt, etc., originate with the body, desire and the concept of self.
18. Dhammacariya Sutta: A Bhikkhu should lead a just and pure life and avoid those of a quarrelsome nature and those who are slaves of desire.
19. Brāhmaṇadhammika Sutta: The Buddha explains to some old and wealthy brahmins the high moral standards of their ancestors and how they declined, following greed for the king's wealth. As a result they induced the king to offer animal sacrifice, etc., in order to acquire wealth and thus lost knowledge of the Dhamma.
20. Nava Sutta: Taking heed of the quality of the teacher, one should go to a learned and intelligent man in order to acquire a thorough knowledge of Dhamma.

21. Kiṃsīla Sutta: The path of a conscientious lay disciple, Dhamma being one's first and last concern.
22. Uṭṭhāna Sutta: An attack on idleness and laziness. Pierced by the arrow of suffering, one should not rest until all desire is eliminated.
23. Rāhula Sutta: The Buddha advises his son, the novice Rāhula, to respect the wise man, associate with him, and live up to the principles of a recluse.
24. Vaṅgīsa Sutta: The Buddha assures Vaṅgīsa that his late teacher, Nigrodhakappa, attained Nibbāna.
25. Sammāparibbājanīya Sutta: The path of a conscientious Bhikkhu disciple: non-attachment, eradication of the passions, and understanding the nature of *saṃsāra*.
26. Dhammika Sutta: The Buddha explains to Dhammika the respective duties of a Bhikkhu and layman, the latter being expected to keep the five precepts and observe *Uposatha* days.

(c) *Mahāvagga*

27. Pabbajjā Sutta: King Bimbisāra of Magadha tempts the Buddha with his material resources and asks after his lineage. The Buddha states the fact of his birth amongst the Sakyans of Kosala and that he has seen through the illusive nature of sensual pleasures.
28. Padhāna Sutta: The graphic description of Māra's temptations immediately prior to the Buddha's Enlightenment.
29. Subhāsita Sutta: The language of Bhikkhus should be well-spoken, pleasing, correct, and true.
30. Sundarikabhāradvāja Sutta: The Buddha explains to the brahmin Sundarika, how one becomes worthy of the honour of receiving an offering.
31. Māgha Sutta: The Buddha explains the above to the layman Māgha, and elucidates the various kinds of blessings from offerings.
32. Sabhiya Sutta: Sabhiya, a wandering ascetic, could not obtain answers to his questions from the six famous teachers of the time. Hence he approaches the Buddha and becomes a disciple after obtaining satisfactory answers to his questions.
33. Sela Sutta: A brahmin, Sela, converses with the Buddha and is converted with his three hundred followers.

34. Salla Sutta: Life is short and all are subject to death, but the wise, who understand the nature of life, have no fears.
35. Vāseṭṭha Sutta: Two young men, Bhāradvāja and Vāseṭṭha, discuss a question regarding brahmins. The former states that one is a brahmin by birth, the latter that one becomes one only through actions. The Buddha subsequently confirms the latter view as being correct.
36. Kokāliya Sutta: Kokāliya falsely ascribes evil desires to Sāriputta and Moggallāna, and subsequently comes to a painful end through death and rebirth in one of the hells. The Buddha then enumerates the different hells and describes the punishment for slandering and backbiting.
37. Nālaka Sutta: The sage Asita's prophecy concerning the future Buddha Gotama. His sister's son, Nālaka, has the highest state of wisdom explained to him by the Buddha.
38. Dvayatānupassana Sutta: Suffering arises from substance, ignorance, the five aggregates, desire, attachment, effort, food, etc.

(d) *Aṭṭhakavagga*

39. Kāma Sutta: To avoid the unpleasant effects, sensual pleasures should be avoided.
40. Gūhaṭṭhaka Sutta: In addition to the above, physical existence also should not be clung to if one is keen on attaining deliverance from *saṃsāra*.
41. Duṭṭhaṭṭhaka Sutta: One who praises his own virtue and is tied to dogmatic views (that differ from man to man and sect to sect) lives a restricted life. The sage, however, remains self-effacing and independent of philosophical systems.
42. Suddhaṭṭhaka Sutta: Knowledge of philosophical systems cannot purify one and there is the tendency to chop and change, never attaining inward peace. The wise, however, are not misled by passion and do not cling to anything in *saṃsāra*.
43. Paramaṭṭhaka Sutta: One should not engage in philosophical disputations. A true brahmin does not and thereby attains Nibbāna.
44. Jara Sutta: From selfishness come greed and regrets. The ideal Bhikkhu, a "homeless one," is independent and does not seek purification through others.

45. Tissa Metteyya Sutta: The Buddha elucidates the kinds of undesirable effects that follow from sensual contacts.
46. Pasura Sutta: The folly of debates where both sides insult or deride each other. If defeated they become discontented. Therefore purification cannot result.
47. Māgandiya Sutta: Again, the Buddha emphasises to Māgandiya, a believer in purity through philosophy, that purity can result only from inward peace.
48. Purābheda Sutta: The conduct and characteristics of a true sage: freedom from craving, anger, desire, passion, and attachment; and he is always calm, thoughtful, and mentally equipoised.
49. Kalahavivāda Sutta: Arguments and disputes arise from deeply felt objects, etc.
50. Cūḷaviyūha Sutta: A description of the different schools of philosophy, all contradicting one another without realising that Truth is one.
51. Mahāviyūha Sutta: Philosophers only praise themselves and criticise others but a true brahmin remains indifferent to such dubious intellectual attainment and is thus calm and peaceful.
52. Tuvaṭaka Sutta: The Bhikkhu should sever the root of evil and cravings, learn the Dhamma, be calm and meditative, avoid talking, indolence, etc., and strictly follow his prescribed duties.
53. Attadaṇḍa Sutta: The sage should be truthful, undeceitful, sober, free from greed and slander, energetic, and without desire for name and fame.
54. Sāriputta Sutta: Again, this time in answer to Sāriputta's enquiry, the Buddha lays down the principles that should govern the life of a Bhikkhu.

(e) *Pārāyanavagga*

This section consists of sixteen dialogues (*pucchā*) between the Buddha and sixteen brahmins. They all stress the necessity of eradicating desire, greed, attachment, philosophical views, sensual pleasures, and indolence, and of remaining aloof, independent, calm, mindful, and firm in the Dhamma in order to attain Nibbāna:

55. Ajita.
56. Tissa Metteyya.
57. Puṇṇaka.
58. Mettagū.
59. Dhotaka.
60. Upasīva.
61. Nanda.
62. Hemaka.
63. Todeyya.
64. Kappa.
65. Jatukaṇṇī.
66. Bhadrāvudha.
67. Udaya.
68. Posāla.
69. Mogharāja.
70. Piṅgiya.

Vimānavatthu: The "Stories of Celestial Mansions," being 85 poems in seven *vaggas* on merit and rebirth in the heavenly worlds.

Petavatthu: This comprises 51 poems in four *vaggas* on rebirth as wandering ghosts (*petas*) through demeritorious actions.

Theragātha: "Verses of the Elders" (*theras*), containing 107 poems (1,279 *gāthas*).

Therīgāthā: "Verses of the Elder Nuns" (*therīs*), containing 75 poems (522 *gāthas*).

Jātaka: The Jātaka or Birth Stories is a collection of 547 stories purporting to be accounts of former lives of the Buddha Gotama. The Nidānakathā, or "Story of the Lineage," is an introductory commentary which details the life of the Buddha up to the opening of the Jetavana monastery at Sāvatthī, and also his former lives under preceding Buddhas.

Niddesa:

Mahāniddesa: A commentary/gloss on the *Aṭṭhakavagga* of the Suttanipāta; and

Cūḷaniddesa: A commentary/gloss on the *Pārāyanavagga* and the *Khaggavisāṇa Sutta,* also of the Suttanipāta.

The Niddesa is itself commented on in the *Saddhammapajjotikā* of Upasena and is there attributed to Sāriputta.

Paṭisambhidāmagga: A detailed analysis of concepts and practices already mentioned in the Vinaya Piṭaka and Dīgha, Saṃyutta and Aṅguttara Nikāyas. It is divided into three *vaggas*, each containing ten topics (*kathā*):

Mahā Vagga: Knowledge of impermanence and *dukkha* of compoundedthings, the Four Noble Truths, dependent origination, four planes of existence, false views, the five faculties, three aspects of Nibbāna, *kamma-vipāka,* the four paths to Nibbāna.

Yuganaddha Vagga: The seven factors of enlightenment, four foundations of mindfulness, four right efforts; four powers (will, energy, thought, investigation), the Noble Eightfold Path, four fruits of the monk's life (*patticariyā*) and Nibbāna; 68 potentialities.

Paññā Vagga: Eight kinds of conduct (*cariya*); postures (walking, sitting, standing, lying down), sense organs, mindfulness; concentration (the *jhānas*), the Four Noble Truths, the four paths to Nibbāna, the four fruits of a monk's life, and for the promotion of the world's welfare.

Apadāna: Tales in verse of the former lives of 550 Bhikkhus and 40 Bhikkhunīs.

Buddhavaṃsa: "The History of the Buddhas," in which the Buddha relates the account of his forming the resolve to become a Buddha and gives the history of the twenty-four Buddhas who preceded him.

Cariyāpiṭaka: Thirty-five tales from the Jātakas in verse illustrating seven out of the Ten Perfections (*pāramīs*): generosity, morality, renunciation, wisdom, energy, patience, truthfulness, determination, loving-kindness, and equanimity.

C. Abhidhamma Piṭaka—the Collection of Philosophical Treatises

The Abhidhamma Piṭaka is the third main division of the Pāli Canon. It consists of seven works which are systematic expositions of the doctrine from a strict philosophical point of view. They deal especially with the psychological analysis of phenomenal existence.

1. **Dhammasaṅgaṇī**: Enumeration of the *dhammas* or factors of existence. The work opens with a *mātikā*, a "matrix" or schedule of categories which classifies the totality of phenomena into a scheme of twenty-two triads (*tika*), sets of three terms, and a hundred dyads (*duka*), sets of two terms. The *mātikā* also includes a Suttanta matrix, a schedule of forty-two dyads taken from the *suttas*. The *mātikā* serves as a framework for the entire Abhidhamma, introducing the diverse perspectives from which all phenomena are to be classified. The body of the Dhammasaṅgaṇī consists of four parts:

1. "States of Consciousness," which analyses all states of consciousness into their constituent factors, each of which is elaborately defined.
2. "Matter," which enumerates and classifies the various types of material phenomena.
3. "The Summary," offering concise explanations of all the terms in both the Abhidhamma and Suttanta matrixes.
4. "The Synopsis," offering more condensed explanations of the Abhidhamma matrix but not the Suttanta matrix.

2. **Vibhaṅga**: "Distinction or Determination." Continued analysis of the foregoing. The Vibhaṅga contains eighteen chapters, dealing in turn with the following: aggregates, sense bases, elements, truths, faculties, dependent arising, foundations of mindfulness, supreme efforts, means to accomplishment, factors of enlightenment, the eightfold path, *jhānas*, illimitables (or *brahma-vihāras*), training rules, analytical knowledges, kinds of knowledge, defilements, and "the heart of the doctrine" (a concise overview of the Buddhist universe).

3. **Dhātukathā**: "Discussion of Elements." This book discusses all phenomena with reference to the three schemes of aggregates, sense bases and elements. It attempts to determine whether, and

to what extent, they are included or not included in them, and whether they are associated with them or dissociated from them.

4. Puggalapaññatti: The body of this work provides formal definitions of different types of individuals. It has ten chapters: the first deals with single types of individuals, the second with pairs, the third with groups of three, etc.

5. Kathāvatthu: Discussion of the points of controversy between the early "Hīnayāna" sects, and the defence of the Theravada viewpoint. Attributed to Moggaliputta Tissa, the president of the 3rd council, which was convened at Patna by the Emperor Asoka in the middle of the 3rd century BCE.

6. Yamaka: This book has the purpose of resolving ambiguities and defining the precise usage of technical terms. It is called the "Book of Pairs" because it employs throughout pairs of questions which approach the subject under investigation from converse points of view. For example, the first pair of questions runs thus: "Are all wholesome phenomena wholesome roots? And are all wholesome roots wholesome phenomena?" The book contains ten chapters: roots, aggregates, sense bases, elements, truths, formations, latent dispositions, consciousness, phenomena, and faculties.

7. Paṭṭhāna: The "Book of Relations." Causation and the mutual relationship of phenomena are examined. The special contribution of the Paṭṭhāna is the elaboration of a scheme of twenty-four conditional relations (*paccaya*) for plotting the causal connections between different types of phenomena. The body of the work applies these conditional relations to all the phenomena included in the Abhidhamma matrix. The book has four great divisions: origination according to the positive method, origination according to the negative method, origination according to the positive-negative method, and origination according to the negative-positive method. Each of these in turn has six subdivisions: origination of triads, dyads, dyads and triads combined, triads and dyads combined, triads and triads combined, and dyads and dyads combined. In the Burmese-script Sixth Council edition of the Pāli Canon, the Paṭṭhāna comprises five volumes totalling 2500 pages. Because of its great size as well as its philosophical importance, it is also known as the Mahāpakaraṇa, "the Great Treatise."

II. Index to the Canon

This index lists the principal sections and *suttas* of the Pāli Canon.

The number in the third column refers to the unit of analysis mentioned in the first column. Thus Khandha Saṃyutta SP SN 22 refers to the Sutta Piṭaka, Saṃyutta Nikāya, Saṃyutta No. 22, while Khandha Vagga SP SN 3 refers to the Sutta Piṭaka, Saṃyutta Nikāya, Vagga No. 3. When the number in the third column contains two parts separated by a colon, the first figure refers to the larger unit (*vagga* or *saṃyutta*), the second figure to the *sutta* within that unit.

Abhayarājakumāra Sutta	SP	MN 58
Abhidhamma Piṭaka	3rd of the 3	Piṭakas
Abhisamaya Saṃyutta	SP	SN 13
Acchariya-abbhūtadhamma Sutta	SP	MN 123
Aggañña Sutta	SP	DN 27
Aggi(ka) Bhāradvāja Sutta	SP	KN Sn 7
Aggivacchagotta Sutta	SP	MN 72
Ajitamāṇava Pucchā	SP	KN Sn 55
Ākaṅkheyya Sutta	SP	MN 6
Alagaddūpama Sutta	SP	MN 22
Āḷavaka Sutta	SP	KN Sn 10
Āmagandha Sutta	SP	KN Sn 14
Ambalaṭṭhikarāhulovāda Sutta	SP	MN 61
Ambaṭṭha Sutta	SP	DN 3
Anupada Vagga	SP	MN
Anamatagga Saṃyutta	SP	SN 15
Ānandabhaddekaratta Sutta	SP	MN 132
Anaṅgaṇa Sutta	SP	MN 5
Āneñjasappāya Sutta	SP	MN 106
Ānāpāna Saṃyutta	SP	SN 54
Ānāpānasati Sutta	SP	MN 118
Anāthapiṇḍikovāda Sutta	SP	MN 143
Anattalakkhaṇa Sutta	SP	SN 22:59
Aṅgulimāla Sutta	SP	MN 86
Aṅguttara Nikāya	SP	4th Nikāya
Anumāna Sutta	SP	MN 15
Anupada Sutta	SP	MN 111

Anupada Vagga	SP	MN
Anuruddha Saṃyutta	SP	SN 52
Anuruddha Sutta	SP	MN 127
Apadāna	SP	KN
Apaṇṇaka Sutta	SP	MN 60
Appamāda Vagga	SP	KN Dhp 2
Arahanta Vagga	SP	KN Dhp 7
Araṇavibhaṅga Sutta	SP	MN 139
Ariyapariyesana Sutta	SP	MN 26
Asaṅkhata Saṃyutta	SP	SN 43
Assalāyana Sutta	SP	MN 93
Āṭānāṭiya Sutta	SP	DN 32
Atta Vagga	SP	KN Dhp 12
Attadaṇḍa Sutta	SP	KN Sn 53
Aṭṭhakanāgara Sutta	SP	MN 52
Aṭṭhaka Nipāta	SP	AN 8
Aṭṭhakavagga	SP	KN Sn
Avyākata Saṃyutta	SP	SN 44
Bāhitika Sutta	SP	MN 88
Bahudhātuka Sutta	SP	MN 115
Bahuvedanīya Sutta	SP	MN 59
Bakkula Sutta	SP	MN 124
Bala Saṃyutta	SP	SN 50
Bala Vagga	SP	KN Dhp 5
Bālapaṇḍita Sutta	SP	MN 129
Bhaddāli Sutta	SP	MN 65
Bhaddekaratta Sutta	SP	MN 131
Bhadrāvudhamāṇava Pucchā	SP	KN Sn 66
Bhayabherava Sutta	SP	MN 4
Bhikkhu Saṃyutta	SP	SN 21
Bhikkhu Pātimokkha	VP	
Bhikkhu Vagga	SP	MN
Bhikkhu Vagga	SP	KN Dhp 25
Bhikkhunī Saṃyutta	SP	SN 5
Bhikkhunī Pātimokkha	VP	
Bhūmija Sutta	SP	MN 126
Bodhi Vagga	SP	KN Ud 1
Bodhirājakumāra Sutta	SP	MN 85
Bojjhaṅga Saṃyutta	SP	SN 46

Brahma Saṃyutta	SP	SN 6
Brahmajāla Sutta	SP	DN 1
Brāhmaṇa Vagga	SP	MN
Brāhmaṇa Saṃyutta	SP	SN 7
Brāhmaṇa Vagga	SP	KN Dhp 26
Brāhmaṇadhammika Sutta	SP	KN Sn 19
Brahmanimantanika Sutta	SP	MN 49
Brahmāyu Sutta	SP	MN 91
Buddha Vagga	SP	KN Dhp14
Buddhavaṃsa	SP	KN
Cakkavattisīhanāda Sutta	SP	DN 26
Caṅkī Sutta	SP	MN 95
Cariyāpiṭaka	SP	KN
Catukka Nipāta	SP	AN 4
Catukka Nipāta	SP	KN It 4
Cātuma Sutta	SP	MN 67
Cetokhila Sutta	SP	MN 16
Chabbisodhana Sutta	SP	MN 112
Chachakka Sutta	SP	MN 148
Chakka Nipāta	SP	AN 6
Channovāda Sutta	SP	MN 144
Citta Saṃyutta	SP	SN 41
Citta Vagga	SP	KN Dhp 3
Cūḷa-assapura Sutta	SP	MN 40
Cūḷadhammasamādāna Sutta	SP	MN 45
Cūḷadukkhakkhandha Sutta	SP	MN 14
Cūḷagopālaka Sutta	SP	MN 34
Cūḷagosiṅga Sutta	SP	MN 31
Cūḷahatthipadopama Sutta	SP	MN 27
Cūḷakammavibhaṅga Sutta	SP	MN 135
Cūḷamāluṅkya Sutta	SP	MN 63
Cūḷaniddesa	SP	KN Nidd
Cūḷapuṇṇama Sutta	SP	MN 110
Cūḷarāhulovāda Sutta	SP	MN 147
Cūḷasaccaka Sutta	SP	MN 35
Cūḷasakuludāyi Sutta	SP	MN 79
Cūḷasāropama Sutta	SP	MN 30
Cūḷasīhanāda Sutta	SP	MN 11
Cūḷasuññata Sutta	SP	MN 121

Cūḷataṇhāsaṅkhaya Sutta	SP	MN 37
Cūḷavagga	VP	Kha
Cūḷavagga	SP	KN Ud 7
Cūḷavagga	SP	KN Sn 2
Cūḷavedalla Sutta	SP	MN 44
Cūḷaviyūha Sutta	SP	KN Sn 50
Cūḷayamaka Vagga	SP	MN
Cunda Sutta	SP	KN Sn 5
Dakkhiṇavibhaṅga Sutta	SP	MN 142
Daṇḍa Vagga	SP	KN Dhp 10
Dantabhūmi Sutta	SP	MN 125
Dasaka Nipāta	SP	AN 10
Dasa Sikkhāpadā	SP	KN Khp 2
Dasuttara Sutta	SP	DN 34
Devadaha Sutta	SP	MN 101
Devadaha Vagga	SP	MN
Devadūta Sutta	SP	MN 130
Devaputta Saṃyutta	SP	SN 2
Devata Saṃyutta	SP	SN 1
Dhamma Sutta[1]	SP	KN Sn 18
Dhammacakkappavattana Sutta	SP	SN 56:11
Dhammacariya Sutta	SP	KN Sn 18
Dhammacetiya Sutta	SP	MN 89
Dhammadāyāda Sutta	SP	MN 3
Dhammapada	SP	KN
Dhammasaṅgaṇi	AP	1st book of AP
Dhammaṭṭha Vagga	SP	KN Dhp 19
Dhammika Sutta	SP	KN Sn 26
Dhanañjāni Sutta	SP	MN 97
Dhaniya Sutta	SP	KN Sn 2
Dhātukathā	AP	3rd book of AP
Dhātu Saṃyutta	SP	SN 14
Dhātuvibhaṅga Sutta	SP	MN 140
Dhotakamāṇava Pucchā	SP	KN Sn 59
Dīgha Nikāya	SP	1st Nikāya
Dīghanakha Sutta	SP	MN 74
Diṭṭhi Saṃyutta	SP	SN 24

1. This is an alternate title for the Nava Sutta.

Duka Nipāta	SP	AN 2
Duka Nipāta	SP	KN It 2
Duṭṭhaṭṭhaka Sutta	SP	KN Sn 41
Dvattiṃsakāra	SP	KN Khp 3
Dvayatānupassana Sutta	SP	KN Sn 38
Dvedhavitakka Sutta	SP	MN 19
Ekaka Nipāta	SP	AN 1
Ekaka Nipāta	SP	KN It 1
Ekadasaka Nipāta	SP	AN 11
Esukāri Sutta	SP	MN 96
Gahapati Vagga	SP	MN
Gāmaṇi Saṃyutta	SP	SN 42
Gaṇakamoggallāna Sutta	SP	MN 107
Gandhabbakāya Saṃyutta	SP	SN 31
Ghaṭīkāra Sutta	SP	MN 81
Ghoṭamukha Sutta	SP	MN 94
Gopakamoggalāna Sutta	SP	MN 108
Gūhaṭṭhaka Sutta	SP	KN Sn 40
Gulissāni Sutta	SP	MN 69
Hemakamāṇava Pucchā	SP	KN Sn 62
Hemavata Sutta	SP	KN Sn 9
Hiri Sutta	SP	KN Sn 15
Iddhipāda Saṃyutta	SP	SN 51
Indriya Saṃyutta	SP	SN 48
Indriyabhāvanā Sutta	SP	MN 152
Isigili Sutta	SP	MN 116
Itivuttaka	SP	KN
Jaccandha Vagga	SP	KN Ud 6
Jāliya Sutta	SP	DN 7
Jambukhādaka Saṃyutta	SP	SN 38
Janāvāsabha Sutta	SP	DN 18
Jara Sutta	SP	KN Sn 44
Jara Vagga	SP	KN Dhp 11
Jātaka	SP	KN
Jatukaṇṇimāṇava Pucchā	SP	KN Sn 65
Jhāna Saṃyutta	SP	SN 53
Jīvaka Sutta	SP	MN 55
Kakacūpama Sutta	SP	MN 21
Kalahavivāda Sutta	SP	KN Sn 49

Kāma Sutta	SP	KN Sn 39
Kandaraka Sutta	SP	MN 51
Kaṇṇakatthala Sutta	SP	MN 90
Kapila Sutta	SP	KN Sn 18
Kappamāṇava Pucchā	SP	KN Sn 64
Kasībhāradvāja Sutta	SP	KN Sn 4
Kassapa Saṃyutta	SP	SN 16
Kassapasīhanāda Sutta	SP	DN 8
Kathāvatthu	AP	5th book of AP
Kāyagatāsati Sutta	SP	MN 119
Kāyavicchandanika Sutta[2]	SP	KN Sn 11
Kevaḍḍha Sutta	SP	DN 11
Khaggavisāṇa Sutta	SP	KN Sn 3
Khandha Saṃyutta	SP	SN 22
Khandha Vagga	SP	SN 3
Khandhaka	VP	
Khuddaka Nikāya	SP	5th Nikāya
Khuddakapāṭha	SP	KN
Kilesa Saṃyutta	SP	SN 6
Kiṃsīla Sutta	SP	KN Sn 21
Kinti Sutta	SP	MN 103
Kīṭāgiri Sutta	SP	MN 70
Kodha Vagga	SP	KN Dhp 17
Kokāliya Sutta	SP	KN Sn 36
Kosala Saṃyutta	SP	SN 3
Kosambiya Sutta	SP	MN 48
Kukkuravatika Sutta	SP	MN 57
Kumārapañhā	SP	KN Khp 4
Kūṭadanta Sutta	SP	DN 5
Lābhasakkāra Saṃyutta	SP	SN 17
Lakkhaṇa Saṃyutta	SP	SN 19
Lakkhaṇa Sutta	SP	DN 30
Laṭukikopama Sutta	SP	MN 66
Lohicca Sutta	SP	DN 12
Loka Vagga	SP	KN Dhp 13
Lomasakaṅgiyabhaddekaratta Sutta	SP	MN 134
Madhupiṇḍika Sutta	SP	MN 18

2. This is an alternate title for the Dhammacariya Sutta.

Madhura Sutta	SP	MN 84
Māgandiya Sutta	SP	MN 75
Māgandiya Sutta	SP	KN Sn 47
Magga Saṃyutta	SP	SN 45
Magga Vagga	SP	KN Dhp 20
Māgha Sutta	SP	KN Sn 31
Mahā-assapura Sutta	SP	MN 39
Mahācattārīsaka Sutta	SP	MN 117
Mahādhammasamādāna Sutta	SP	MN 46
Mahādukkhakkhandha Sutta	SP	MN 13
Mahāgopālaka Sutta	SP	MN 33
Mahāgosiṅga Sutta	SP	MN 32
Mahāgovinda Sutta	SP	DN 19
Mahāhatthipadopama Sutta	SP	MN 28
Mahākaccānabhaddekaratta Sutta	SP	MN 133
Mahākammavibhaṅga Sutta	SP	MN 136
Mahāli Sutta	SP	DN 6
Mahāmāluṅkya Sutta	SP	MN 64
Mahāmaṅgala Sutta	SP	KN Khp
Mahānidāna Sutta	SP	DN 15
Mahāniddesa	SP	KN Nidd
Mahāpadāna Sutta	SP	DN 14
Mahāparinibbāna Sutta	SP	DN 16
Mahāpuṇṇama Sutta	SP	MN 109
Mahārāhulovāda Sutta	SP	MN 62
Mahāsaccaka Sutta	SP	MN 36
Mahāsakuludāyi Sutta	SP	MN 77
Mahāsaḷāyatanika Sutta	SP	MN 149
Mahāsamaya Sutta	SP	DN 20
Mahāsamaya Sutta[3]	SP	KN Sn 25
Mahāsāropama Sutta	SP	MN 29
Mahāsatipaṭṭhāna Sutta	SP	DN 22
Mahāsīhanāda Sutta	SP	MN 12
Mahāsudassana Sutta	SP	DN 17
Mahāsuññata Sutta	SP	MN 122
Mahātaṇhāsaṅkhaya Sutta	SP	MN 38
Mahāvacchagotta Sutta	SP	MN 73

3. This is an alternate title for the Vijaya Sutta.

Mahāvagga	VP	Kha
Mahāvagga	SP	DN
Mahāvagga	SP	SN
Mahāvagga	SP	KN Sn
Mahāvagga	SP	KN Paṭis
Mahāvedalla Sutta	SP	MN 43
Mahāviyūha Sutta	SP	KN Sn 51
Mahāyamaka Vagga	SP	MN
Majjhima Nikāya	SP	2nd Nikāya
Makhādeva Sutta	SP	MN 83
Mala Vagga	SP	KN Dhp 18
Maṅgala Sutta[4]	SP	KN Khp 5
Maṅgala Sutta[5]	SP	KN Sn 16
Māra Saṃyutta	SP	SN 4
Māratajjanīya Sutta	SP	MN 50
Mātugāma Saṃyutta	SP	SN 37
Meghiya Vagga	SP	KN Ud 4
Mettā Sutta	SP	KN Khp 9
Mettā Sutta	SP	KN Sn 8
Mettagūmāṇava Pucchā	SP	KN Sn 58
Moggallāna Saṃyutta	SP	SN 40
Mogharājamāṇava Pucchā	SP	KN Sn 69
Moneyya Sutta[6]	SP	KN Sn 37
Mucalinda Vagga	SP	KN Ud 2
Mūlapariyāya Sutta	SP	MN 1
Mūlapariyāya Vagga	SP	MN
Muni Sutta	SP	KN Sn 12
Nagaravindeyya Sutta	SP	MN 150
Nāga Saṃyutta	SP	SN 29
Nāga Vagga	SP	KN Dhp 23
Nālaka Sutta	SP	KN Sn 37
Nālakapāna Sutta	SP	MN 68
Nanda Vagga	SP	KN Ud 3
Nandakovāda Sutta	SP	MN 146
Nandamāṇava Pucchā	SP	KN Sn 61

4. This is an alternate title for the Sammāparibbājanīya Sutta.
5. This is an alternate title for the Mahāmaṅgala Sutta.
6. This is an alternate title for the Nālaka Sutta.

Nava Sutta	SP	KN Sn 20
Navaka Nipāta	SP	AN 9
Nidāna Saṃyutta	SP	SN 12
Nidāna Vagga	SP	SN
Niddesa	SP	KN
Nidhikaṇḍa Sutta	SP	KN Khp 8
Nigrodhakappa Sutta[7]	SP	KN Sn 24
Niraya Vagga	SP	KN Dhp 22
Nivāpa Sutta	SP	MN 25
Okkantika Saṃyutta	SP	SN 25
Opamma Saṃyutta	SP	SN 20
Opamma Vagga	SP	MN 3
Pabbajjā Sutta	SP	KN Sn 27
Padhāna Sutta	SP	KN Sn 28
Pakiṇṇaka Vagga	SP	KN Dhp 21
Pañcaka Nipāta	SP	AN 5
Pañcattaya Sutta	SP	MN 102
Paññā Vagga	SP	KN Paṭis
Paṇḍita Vagga	SP	KN Dhp 6
Pāpa Vagga	SP	KN Dhp 9
Paramaṭṭhaka Sutta	SP	KN Sn 43
Parābhava Sutta	SP	KN Sn 6
Pārāyanavagga	SP	KN Sn
Paribbājaka Vagga	SP	MN
Parivāra	VP	
Pāsādika Sutta	SP	DN 29
Pasūra Sutta	SP	KN Sn 46
Pāṭaligāma Vagga	SP	KN Ud 8
Pāṭika Sutta	SP	DN 24
Pāṭika Vagga	SP	DN
Pāṭika Vagga	SP	M
Paṭisambhidāmagga	SP	KN
Paṭṭhāna	AP	7th book of AP
Pāyāsi Sutta	SP	DN 23
Petavatthu	SP	KN
Piṇḍapātapārisuddhi Sutta	SP	MN 151
Piṅgiyamāṇava Pucchā	SP	KN Sn 70

7. This is an alternate title for the Vaṅgīsa Sutta.

Piya Vagga	SP	KN Dhp 16
Piyajātika Sutta	SP	MN 87
Posālamāṇava Pucchā	SP	KN Sn 68
Potaliya Sutta	SP	MN 54
Poṭṭhapāda Sutta	SP	DN 9
Puggalapaññatti	AP	4th book of AP
Puṇṇakamāṇava Pucchā	SP	KN Sn 57
Puṇṇovāda Sutta	SP	MN 145
Puppha Vagga	SP	KN Dhp 4
Purābheda Sutta	SP	KN Sn 4:10
Pūraḷāsa Sutta[8]	SP	KN Sn 30
Rādha Saṃyutta	SP	SN 23
Rāhula Saṃyutta	SP	SN 18
Rāhula Sutta	SP	KN Sn 23
Raja Vagga	SP	MN
Ratana Sutta	SP	KN Khp 6
Ratana Sutta	SP	KN Sn 13
Rathavinīta Sutta	SP	MN 24
Raṭṭhapāla Sutta	SP	MN 82
Sabbāsava Sutta	SP	MN 2
Sabhiya Sutta	SP	KN Sn 32
Sacca Saṃyutta	SP	SN 56
Saccavibhaṅga Sutta	SP	MN 141
Sagātha Vagga	SP	SN
Sahassa Vagga	SP	KN Dhp 8
Sakkapañha Sutta	SP	DN 21
Sakka Saṃyutta	SP	SN 11
Saḷāyatana Saṃyutta	SP	SN 35
Saḷāyatana Vagga	SP	MN
Saḷāyatana Vagga	SP	SN
Saḷāyatana-vibhaṅga Sutta	SP	MN 137
Sāleyyaka Sutta	SP	MN 41
Salla Sutta	SP	KN Sn 34
Sallekha Sutta	SP	MN 8
Samādhi Saṃyutta	SP	SN 34
Samāgama Sutta	SP	MN 104
Samaṇamaṇḍika Sutta	SP	MN 78

8. This is an alternate title for the Sundarikabhāradvāja Sutta.

Sāmaṇḍaka Saṃyutta	SP	SN 39
Sāmaññaphala Sutta	SP	DN 2
Sammādiṭṭhi Sutta	SP	MN 9
Sammāparibbājanīya Sutta	SP	KN Sn 25
Sammappadhāna Saṃyutta	SP	SN 49
Sampasādanīya Sutta	SP	DN 28
Saṃyutta Nikāya	SP	3rd Nikāya
Sandaka Sutta	SP	MN 76
Saṅgārava Sutta	SP	MN 100
Saṅgīti Sutta	SP	DN 33
Saṅkhārupapatti Sutta	SP	MN 120
Sappurisa Sutta	SP	MN 113
Saraṇattaya	SP	KN Khp 1
Sāriputta Saṃyutta	SP	SN 28
Sāriputta Sutta	SP	KN Sn 54
Sātāgira Sutta[9]	SP	KN Sn 9
Satipaṭṭhāna Saṃyutta	SP	SN 47
Satipaṭṭhāna Sutta	SP	MN 10
Sattaka Nipāta	SP	AN 7
Sekha Sutta	SP	MN 53
Sela Sutta	SP	MN 92
Sela Sutta	SP	KN Sn 33
Sevitabbāsevitabba Sutta	SP	MN 114
Sigālovāda Sutta	SP	DN 31
Sīhanāda Vagga	SP	MN
Sīlakkhandha Vagga	SP	DN
Soṇadaṇḍa Sutta	SP	DN 4
Soṇathera Vagga	SP	KN 5
Sotāpatti Saṃyutta	SP	SN 55
Subha Sutta	SP	DN 10
Subha Sutta	SP	MN 99
Subhāsita Sutta	SP	KN Sn 29
Sūciloma Sutta	SP	KN Sn 17
Suddhaṭṭhaka Sutta	SP	KN Sn 42
Sukha Vagga	SP	KN Dhp 15
Sunakkhatta Sutta	SP	MN 105
Sundarikabhāradvāja Sutta	SP	KN Sn 30

9. This is an alternate title for the Hemavata Sutta.

Suññata Vagga	SP	MN
Supaṇṇa Saṃyutta	SP	SN 30
Suttanipāta	SP	KN
Sutta Piṭaka	SP	2nd of the 3 Piṭakas
Suttavibhaṅga	VP	
Taṇhā Vagga	SP	KN Dhp 24
Tatiya Vagga	SP	M
Tevijja Sutta	SP	DN 13
Tevijjāvacchagotta Sutta	SP	MN 71
Theragāthā	SP	KN
Therapañha Sutta[10]	SP	KN Sn 54
Therīgāthā	SP	KN
Tika Nipāta	SP	AN 3
Tika Nipāta	SP	KN 3
Tirokuḍḍa Sutta	SP	KN Khp 7
Tissametteyya Sutta	SP	KN Sn 45
Tissametteyyamāṇava Pucchā	SP	KN Sn 56
Todeyyamāṇava Pucchā	SP	KN Sn 63
Tuvaṭaka Sutta	SP	KN Sn 52
Udāna	SP	KN
Udayamāṇava Pucchā	SP	KN Sn 67
Uddesavibhaṅga Sutta	SP	MN 138
Udumbarikasīhanāda Sutta	SP	DN 25
Upakkilesa Sutta	SP	MN 128
Upāli Sutta	SP	MN 56
Upasīvamāṇava Pucchā	SP	KN Sn 60
Uppāda Saṃyutta	SP	SN 26
Uraga Sutta	SP	KN Sn 1
Uraga Vagga	SP	KN Sn
Uṭṭhāna Sutta	SP	KN Sn 22
Vacchagotta Saṃyutta	SP	SN 33
Valāhaka Saṃyutta	SP	SN 32
Vammika Sutta	SP	MN 23
Vanapattha Sutta	SP	MN 17
Vana Saṃyutta	SP	SN 9
Vaṅgīsa Saṃyutta	SP	SN 8
Vaṅgīsa Sutta	SP	KN Sn 24

10. This is an alternate title for the Sāriputta Sutta.

Vasala Sutta	SP	KN Sn 7
Vāseṭṭha Sutta	SP	MN 98
Vāseṭṭha Sutta	SP	KN Sn 35
Vatthūpama Sutta	SP	MN 7
Vedanā Saṃyutta	SP	SN 36
Vekhanassa Sutta	SP	MN 80
Verañjaka Sutta	SP	MN 42
Vibhaṅga	AP	2nd book of AP
Vibhaṅga Vagga	SP	MN
Vijaya Sutta	SP	KN Sn 11
Vīmaṃsakā Sutta	SP	MN 47
Vimānavatthu	SP	KN
Vinaya Piṭaka	VP	1st of the 3 Piṭakas
Vitakkasaṇṭhāna Sutta	SP	MN 20
Yakkha Saṃyutta	SP	SN 10
Yamaka	AP	6th book of AP
Yamaka Vagga	SP	KN Dhp 1
Yuganaddha Vagga	SP	KN Paṭis 2

III. Bibliography

1. Translated Texts

The Pali Text Society (founded in 1881) has published English translations of the Pāli texts from 1909. To date (2006) only the Niddesa and Apadāna from the Khuddaka Nikāya and Yamaka from the Abhidhamma Piṭaka remain untranslated out of the entire Canon. Apart from their own series (PTS, and SBB— *Sacred Books of the Buddhists*), there are five others of note: *Sacred Books of the East* (SBE—reprinted from the 1960s by UNESCO via Motilal Banarsidass, Delhi); *The Wheel* and *Bodhi Leaf* series of the Buddhist Publication Society (BPS); The Maha Bodhi Society in either India or Sri Lanka (MBS); the (now defunct) Bauddha Sahitya Sabha (Buddhist Literature Society—BSS); and the Buddhist Missionary Society (BMS) of Kuala Lumpur. In addition, a few individual texts have appeared from Sinhalese, Indian, Burmese, Thai, English, and American publishers.

(To avoid the tedium of indicating the years of reprints of those works that have run into several editions, only the years of the first and latest editions have been shown. In the case of BPS publications, however, because these are normally kept in print, only the year of initial publication is shown.)

A. Vinaya Piṭaka

I.B. Horner (tr.) *The Book of the Discipline.* PTS:

1. Suttavibhaṅga, 1938, 1992.
2. Suttavibhaṅga, 1940, 1993.
3. Suttavibhaṅga, 1942, 1993.
4. Mahāvagga, 1951, 1993.
5. Cullavagga, 1952, 1993.
6. Parivāra, 1966, 1993.

T.W. Rhys Davids and H. Oldenberg (tr.) *Vinaya Texts.* SBE:

1. Pātimokkha, Oxford 1881, Delhi 1975, 2003.
2. Mahāvagga, 1882, 1975, 2003.
3. Cullavagga, 1885, 1975, 2003.

P.V. Bapat & A. Hirakawa, *Shan-Chien-P'i-P'o-Sha, A Chinese Version by Saṅghabhadra of Samantapāsādika,* Poona 1970. Despite the English subtitle, it is not identical with the *Samantapāsādikā,* but perhaps with one of its sources or a parallel version of another, non-Mahāvihāra Theravādin lineage; see Ananda W. Guruge, "*Shan-jian-lu-piposha* as an Authentic Source on the Early History of Buddhism and Asoka", in *Dhamma-Vinaya,* SLABS, Colombo 2005, pp. 91–110. Bapat thinks that the Chinese translator has adapted the *Samantapāsādikā* to fit the Vinaya of the Dharmaguptaka tradition.

Herbert Baynes, "A Collection of Kammavâcâs (monastic confessionals)", JRAS 1892, pp. 53–75.

J.F. Dickson (tr.), "The Upasampadā Kammavācā, being the Buddhist Manual of the Form and Manner of Ordering Priests and Deacons", Monastero di San Lazzaro degli Armeni, Venice 1875 and JRAS, N.S. VII, 1875, reprinted in Warren, *Buddhism in Translations*, Harvard 1896, and Piyadassi, *Ordination in Theravada Buddhism*, BPS 1963.

—"The Pātimokkha, being the Buddhist Office of the Confession of Priests", JRAS, N.S. VIII, 1876, reprinted *ibid.*

Ñāṇamoli (ed. and tr.), *The Pātimokkha.* Bangkok 1966, 1969.

Ñānatusita Bhikkhu, *A Translation and Analysis of the Pātimokkha,* text, translation and analysis of the Pātimokkha. Kandy 2011.

W. Pachow, "A Comparative Study of the Prātimokṣa on the basis of its Chinese, Tibetan, Sanskrit and Pali versions." *Sino-Indian Studies* 4 (1951), pp. 18–46, 51–114, 115–93; 5 (1955), 1–45. Offprinted Delhi 2000.

William Pruitt (ed.) and K.R. Norman (tr.), *The Pātimokkha.* PTS 2001.

Thanissaro (tr.), *The Buddhist Monastic Code I.* Valley Center (CA) 1996, rev. ed., 2007; *II*, *ibid.*, 2002, rev. ed., 2007.

U Thumana (tr.), *Pārājika Pāḷi.* Yangon [Rangoon] 2001.

Mohan Wijayaratna, "Bhikkhunī-Pātimokkha" (translation and text), Appendix 1/2, in *Buddhist Nuns: The Birth and Development of a Women's Monastic Order.* Colombo 2001, Kandy 2010.

B. Sutta Piṭaka

Dīgha Nikāya

T.W. and C.A.F. Rhys Davids (tr.), *Dialogues of the Buddha.* SBB:

1. Suttas 1–13, 1899, 1995.
2. Suttas 14–23, 1910, 1995.
3. Suttas 24–34, 1921, 1995.

Maurice Walshe (tr.), *Thus Have I Heard: The Long Discourses of the Buddha.* London 1987.

Partial translations

P. Anatriello, *The Long Discourses of the Buddha.* Bognor Regis 1986. Comprises a selection with narrative themes.

A.A.G. Bennett (tr. 1–16), *Long Discourses of the Buddha.* Bombay 1964.

Bhikkhu Bodhi (tr.), *Discourse on the All-Embracing Net* of *Views: The Brahmajāla Sutta and its Commentarial Exegesis.* BPS 1978, rev. ed. 2007. Partial offprint: *A Treatise on the Pāramīs.* BPS 1996.

—*The Great Discourse on Causation: The Mahānidāna Sutta and its Commentaries.* BPS 1984, rev. ed., 2000, 2010.

—*The Discourse on the Fruits of Recluseship: The Sāmaññaphala Sutta and its Commentaries.* BPS 1989, rev. ed., 2008.

Acharya Buddharakkhita, *Satipaṭṭhāna System of Meditations.* Bangalore 1980. Pali text and tr. of Mahāsati-paṭṭhāna Sutta (DN 22).

—*The Buddha, the Arahats and the Gods.* Bangalore 1989. Pali text and translation of Mahāsamaya Sutta (DN 20).

—*Invisible Protection.* Bangalore 1990. Pali text and tr. of Āṭānāṭiya Sutta (DN 32).

Burma Piṭaka Association (tr.), *Ten Suttas from Dīgha Nikāya* (DN 1, 2, 9, 15, 16, 22, 26, 28, 29, 31). Rangoon 1984, Sarnath 1987, Delhi 1999.

Steven Collins, "The Discourse on What is Primary (Aggañña-Sutta). An Annotated Translation." *Journal of Indian Philosophy* 21.4 (Dordrecht 1993), pp. 301–93. Offprinted, New Delhi 2001.

Albert J. Edmunds (tr. DN4), *A dialogue on former existence and on the marvellous birth and career of the Buddhas, between Gotamo and his monks.* Philadelphia 1899.

S.N. Goenka *et al.* (ed.), *Mahā Satipaṭṭhāna Sutta.* Igatpuri 1985. Repr. as *Mahāsatipaṭṭhāna Sutta. Great Discourse on the Establishing of Awareness.* Seattle 1996, Onalaska (WA) 2005.

—and Patrick Given-Wilson, *Satipaṭṭhāna Sutta Discourses.* Igatpuri and Seattle 1998. Talks from a course in Mahāsatipaṭṭhāna Sutta.

Trevor Ling, *The Buddha's Philosophy of Man.* London 1981. Revised versions of Rhys Davids' translations of DN 2, 4, 5, 9, 12, 16, 22, 26, 27, 31.

Usha McNab et al. (tr. 32), The Suttanta on the Marks. Samatha Trust (Powys, Wales) 1996.

Mahāsi Sayādaw, *Discourse on Sakkapañha Sutta.* Rangoon 1980.

T.W. Rhys Davids (tr.), *Tevijja Sutta.* London 1891. BPS 1963.

—*Kūṭadanta Sutta*, BPS 1968.

—*Sigālovāda Sutta.* Colombo 1972.

—(tr.15 and 22), *Two Dialogues from Dialogues of the Buddha.* New York 1972.

Sīlācāra (tr. 2), *The Fruit of the Homeless Life.* London 1917.

U Sīlānanda (tr. 22), *Four Foundations of Mindfulness.* Boston 1990.

S. Sumaṅgala (tr.), *Saṅgīti Sutta.* MBS, Colombo 1904. Repr.in *The Mahā Bodhi,* 12–13, 2 parts, Calcutta 1905.

Ṭhānissaro Bhikkhu (tr.), *Handful of Leaves. Volume One: An Anthology from the Dīgha and Majjhima Nikāyas.* Santa Cruz (CA) 2002, rev.ed, 2004. Includes DN 2, 11, 12, 15, 16 (5 and 6), 21 (excerpt), 22.

—*Volume Five: An Anthology from the Five Nikāyas.* 2007. Includes DN 9.

Union Buddha Sāsana Council (tr.), *Brahmajāla Sutta.* Rangoon 1958.

—*Sāmaññaphala Sutta.* Rangoon 1958.

Sister Vajirā (tr. 21), *Sakka's Quest.* BPS 1959.

Sister Vajirā and Francis Story (tr. 16), *Last Days of the Buddha.* BPS 1964, rev. ed. 1988, 2007.

Majjhima Nikāya

Lord Chalmers (tr.), *Further Dialogues of the Buddha*. SBB:
1. Suttas 1–76, 1926, Delhi 1988.
2. Suttas 77–152, 1927, Delhi 1988.

I.B. Horner (tr.), *The Middle Length Sayings*. PTS:
1. Suttas 1–50, 1954, 1995.
2. Suttas 51–100, 1957, 1994.
3. Suttas 101–152, 1959, 1993.

Bhikkhu Ñāṇamoli and Bhikkhu Bodhi (tr.), *The Middle Length Discourses of the Buddha*. Boston 1995, 2005.

Partial translations

Egerton C. Baptist, *The Conversion of Saccaka*. Galle, no date. Narrative versions of MN 35 and 36.

Bhikkhu Bodhi (tr.), *The Discourse on the Root of Existence: The Mūlapariyāya Sutta and its Commentarial Exegesis*. BPS 1980, rev. ed., 2006.

Acharya Buddharakkhita (tr. 2), *Mind Overcoming its Cankers*. Bangalore 1978, BPS 2005.

Burma (Myanmar) Piṭaka Association (tr.), *Twenty-Five Suttas from Mūlapaṇṇāsa*. (repr.) Delhi 1990.

—*Twenty-Five Suttas from Majjhimapaṇṇāsa*. *Ibid.*, 1991.

—*Twenty-Five Suttas from Uparipaṇṇāsa*. *Ibid.*[11]

David Evans (tr.), *The Discourses of Gotama the Buddha, Middle Collection*. London 1992.

K. Sri Dhammānanda (ed. and tr. 10), *Satipaṭṭhāna Sutta: The Foundations of Mindfulness*. BMS 1982.

Jotiya Dhirasekera (tr. 22), "Parable of the Snake." *Encyclopaedia of Buddhism*, Research Studies Series 1. Colombo 1983.

11. N.B. The Association was founded in Rangoon 1980 and the Foreword to the first translation (by U Htin Fatt, above) was dated 16.11.86. However, the first reprint in 2003 appeared under the authority of the Department for the Promotion and Propagation of the Sāsana (Ministry of Religious Affairs) and distributed by the Department of Research & Compilation, Sītagū International Buddhist Academy, Sagaing Hills, Sagaing (Myanmar). A further reprint was printed in Kuala Lumpur and published by Selangor Buddhist Vipassanā Meditation Society in 2004.

I.B. Horner (tr. 107 & 125), *Taming the Mind*. BPS 1963.
—(tr. 26), *The Noble Quest*. BPS 1974.
Mahāsi Sayādaw, *A Discourse on the Sallekha Sutta*. Rangoon 1981.
—*Cullavedalla Sutta or Discourse on Various Aspects of the Buddha's Dhamma*. Rangoon 1981.
—*Vammika Sutta*. Rangoon 1982, Selangor 1994.
Ñāṇamoli (tr. 90 *suttas*, ed. Khantipālo), *A Treasury of the Buddha's Discourses*. 3 vols, Bangkok 1980.
—(tr. 122), *The Greater Discourse on Voidness*. BPS 1965.
—(tr. 82), *Raṭṭhapāla Sutta*. BPS 1967.
—(tr. 41, 57, 135, 136), *The Buddha's Words on Kamma*. BPS 1977.
—(tr. 139), *The Exposition of Non-Conflict*. BPS 1979.
—(tr. 9 and commentary), *The Discourse on Right View*. BPS 1991.
Ñāṇananda (tr. 131), *Ideal Solitude*. BPS 1973.
Nārada and Mahinda (tr. 51, 54), *Kandaraka and Potaliya Suttas*. BPS 1965.
—(tr. 60, 63, 56), *Apaṇṇaka, Cūla Māluṅkya and Upāli Suttas*. BPS 1966.
Thich Nhat Hanh (tr. 10), *Transformation and Healing. Sutra on the Four Establishments of Mindfulness*. Berkeley 1990. Includes essay and translations from Chinese Tripiṭaka versions of *sutta* as well.
—(tr. 118), *Breathe! You are Alive: Sutra on the Full Awareness of Breathing*. Berkeley 1990.
—(tr. 131), *Our Appointment with Life*. Berkeley 1990. Includes essay based on Bhaddekaratta Sutta.
—(tr. Chinese equivalent of 22), *Thundering Silence. Sutra on Knowing the Better Way to Catch a Snake*. Berkeley 1993.
Nyanaponika (tr. 61, 62, 147), *Advice to Rāhula*. BPS 1961.
—(tr. 22), *The Discourse on the Snake Simile*. BPS 1962.
—(tr. 7, 8), *The Simile of the Cloth and the Discourse on Effacement*. BPS 1964.
—(tr. 28), *The Greater Discourse on the Elephant footprint Simile*. BPS 1966.
Nyanasatta (tr. 10), *The Foundations of Mindfulness*. BPS 1960.
Sīlācāra (tr.), *The First Fifty Discourses*. Breslau-London 1912, Munich 1924, Delhi 2005.
Soma (tr. 10 and commentary), *The Way of Mindfulness*. Kandy 1941, Colombo 1949, BPS 1967, 2003.

—(tr. 9 and commentary), *Right Understanding*. BSS 1946.
—(tr. 10), *Foundations of Mindfulness*. Colombo 1956, Dehiwela 1962.
—(tr. 20), *The Removal of Distracting Thoughts*. BPS 1960.
—(tr. 27), *The Lesser Discourse on the Elephant-footprint Simile*. BPS 1960.
—(tr. 35), *An Old Debate on Self*. BPS 1962.
S. Sumaṅgala (tr.), *Mūlapariyāya Sutta*. MBS, Colombo 1908.
Ṭhānissaro Bhikkhu (tr.), *Handful of Leaves. Volume One: An Anthology from the Dīgha and Majjhima Nikāyas*. Santa Cruz (CA) 2002, rev. ed., 2004. Includes MN 1, 2, 4, 18–20, 21 (excerpt), 24, 36 (excerpt), 44, 45, 58, 61, 63, 72, 75 (excerpt), 82 (excerpt), 87, 95 (excerpt), 105, 106, 108, 109, 110, 117–119, 121, 126, 131, 135, 138, 140, 146, 148, 149, 152.
—*Volume Five: An Anthology from the Five Nikāyas*. 2007. Includes MN 9, 13, 14, 22, 26–28, 53, 54 (excerpt), 66, 70, 78, 82 (excerpt), 86, 90, 101, 122, 137, 143.

Saṃyutta Nikāya

The Book of the Kindred Sayings. PTS, reprinted Delhi 2005:

1. Saṃyuttas 1–11, tr. C.A.F. Rhys Davids, 1917, 1993.
2. Saṃyuttas 12–21, tr. C.A.F. Rhys Davids and F.L. Woodward, 1922, 1990.
3. Saṃyuttas 22–34, tr. F.L. Woodward, 1927, 1995.
4. Saṃyuttas 35–44, 1927, 1993.
5. Saṃyuttas 45–56, 1930, 1994.

Partial translations

Bhikkhu Bodhi (tr.), *The Connected Discourses of the Buddha*. 2 vols, Boston 2000.
—(tr. 12:23), *Transcendental Dependent Arising*. BPS 1980. A translation and exposition of the Upanisa Sutta, from the Nidānasaṃyutta.
Buddharakkhita (tr. 56:11), *Setting in Motion the Wheel of Truth*. Bangalore 1990.
Burma (Myanmar) Piṭaka Association (tr.), *Nidāna Saṃyutta*. Delhi 1993.
—*Khandha Saṃyutta*. Delhi 1996.

U Hla Maung (tr.), *Saḷātanavagga Saṃyutta: Division of Discourses with Verses*. Yangon 1998.

John D. Ireland (tr.), *Saṃyutta Nikāya: An Anthology I*. BPS 1967.

U Ko Lay (tr.), *Mahāvagga Saṃyutta: Division of Discourses with Verses*. Yangon 1998.

Mahāsi Sayādaw (tr. 22:22), *Bhāra Sutta or Discourse on the Burden of Khandha*. Rangoon 1980.

—(tr. 56:11), *Discourse on the Wheel of Dhamma*. Rangoon 1981.

—(tr. 22:122), *Discourse on Silavanta Sutta*. Rangoon 1982.

—(tr. SN 35:95), *Mālukyaputta Sutta*. Rangoon 1981, Selangor 1992.

—(tr. 22:59), *Anattalakkhaṇa Sutta or Great Discourse on Not Self*. Rangoon 1983, Bangkok 1996.

N.K.G. Mendis (ed. and tr. 22:59), *On the No-Self Characteristic*. BPS 1979.

Ñāṇamoli (tr. 22:59, 35:28, 56:11), *Three Cardinal Discourses of the Buddha*. BPS 1960.

—(tr. 10:60), *The Girimānanda Sutta: Ten Contemplations*. BPS 1972.

Ñāṇananda (tr.), *Saṃyutta Nikāya: An Anthology II*. BPS 1972.

Nārada (tr.), *The First Discourse of the Buddha*. Colombo 1972.

Nyanaponika (tr. Vedanā-Saṃyutta), *Contemplation of Feeling*. BPS 1983, 2008.

Nyanasatta (tr. 35:197, 200—abridged), *Two Buddhist Parables*. BPS 1958.

Soma (ed. and tr.), *Dhammacakkappavattana Sutta*. BPS 1960, 2011.

Ṭhānissaro Bhikkhu (tr.), *Handful of Leaves. Volume Two: An Anthology from the Saṃyutta Nikāya*. Santa Cruz (CA) 2003, rev. ed., 2006. Comprises 189 suttas.

—*Volume Five: An Anthology from the Five Nikāyas*. 2007. Includes 74 suttas.

U Tin U (tr.), *Sagāthavagga Saṃyutta: Division of Discourses with Verses*. Yangon 1998, Delhi 2004.

Sister Vajirā (tr.), *Dhammacakkapavattana Sutta*. MBS, Sarnath 1944, 1952.

M.O'C. Walshe (tr.), *Saṃyutta Nikāya: An Anthology III*. BPS 1985.

Aṅguttara Nikāya

The Book of the Gradual Sayings. PTS, reprinted Delhi 2006:

1. Nipātas 1–3, tr. F.L. Woodward, 1932, 1993.
2. Nipāta 4, 1933, 1990.
3. Nipātas 5–6., tr. E. M. Hare, 1934, 1995.
4. Nipātas 7–9, 1935, 1993.
5. Nipātas 10–11, tr. F.L. Woodward, 1936, 1994.

Partial translations

Bhikkhu Bodhi (tr.), *Numerical Discourses of the Buddha. An Anthology of Suttas from the Aṅguttara Nikāya*. Walnut Creek (CA) 1999.

E.R.J. Gooneratne (tr. 1–3), *Aṅguttara Nikāya*. Galle 1913.

E. Hardy (ed.), *Aṅguttara-Nikāya V*. PTS 1900, 1958. Appendix I. Analytical Table of the eleven Nipātas.

A.D. Jayasundera (tr. IV), *The Book of the Numerical Sayings*. Adyar 1925.

Susan Elbaum Jootla (tr. 9:20), *The Scale of Good Deeds: The Message of the Velāma Sutta*. BPS 1990.

Mahāsi Sayādaw, *Discourse on Ariyāvāsa Sutta* (4:28). Rangoon 1980.

Ñāṇananda, *The Magic of the Mind*. BPS 1974. An exposition of the Kālakārāma Sutta (4:24).

Nyanaponika (tr.), *Aṅguttara Nikāya: An Anthology II*. BPS 1972, rev. ed. by Bhikkhu Bodhi, 2007.

Soma (tr. 3:56), *Kālāma Sutta: The Buddha's Charter of Free Enquiry*. BPS 1959. Repr. in Nyanaponika (ed.) *The Road to Inner Freedom*. BPS 1982.

Ṭhānissaro Bhikkhu (tr.), *Handful of Leaves. Volume Three: An Anthology from the Aṅguttara Nikāya*. Santa Cruz (CA) 2003. Comprises 194 suttas.

—*Volume Five: An Anthology from the Five Nikāyas*. 2007. Includes 67 suttas.

U Thein Maung (tr.), *Ekaka & Duka Nipāta Pāḷi*. Yangon 2001.

—*Tika Nipāta Pāḷi*. *Ibid.*

Saber Uddiyan (tr. & commentary), *Kalama Sutta: The Buddha's Charter of Free Enquiry*. Kathmandu 2010.

Khuddaka Nikāya

Khuddakapāṭha

Bhadragaka, *Khuddaka-Pāṭha or Short Buddhist Recitations*. Bangkok 1953

N.K. Bhagwat (tr.). Bombay 1931.

Acharya Buddharakkhita, *Khuddaka Pāṭha*. Bangalore 1980.

Robert Caesar Childers, "*Khuddaka Pāṭha*", JRAS, N.S. IV (1870), pp. 309–39.

Ñāṇamoli, *Minor Readings*. PTS 1960, 1991.

Pe Maung Tin (tr.). Rangoon 1913.

C.A.F. Rhys Davids, *The Text of the Minor Sayings*. SBB 1931, 1997.

Sangharakshita (v–ix) serialised in *The Mahā Bodhi* 58, Calcutta 1950, reprinted in *The Enchanted Garden*. FWBO, London 1978, 1980.

Ṭhānissaro Bhikkhu (tr.), *Handful of Leaves. Volume Four: An Anthology from the Khuddaka Nikāya*. Santa Cruz (CA) 2003, rev. ed., 2006.

F.L. Woodward in *Some Sayings of the Buddha*. London 1925, 1960, New York 1973.

Dhammapada

Translated under the following titles if different from Dhammapada:

E.W. Adikaram (tr.). Colombo 1954.

Bhikkhu Ānandajoti (ed.), *A Comparative Edition of the Dhammapada*. Battaramulla 2007. Pali text with parallels from Sanskritised Prakrit, edited together with a study of the Dhammapada collection.

B. Ānanda Maitreya (tr.), serialised in *Pali Buddhist Review* 1 and 2, London 1976–77, and offprinted as *Law Verses*. Colombo 1978, rev. ed., New York 1988.

Anon, comp. or tr. for The Cunningham Press, Alhambra (CA) 1955. Repr. by The Theosophical Society, Bombay 1957, 1965.

J. Austin (comp.). The Buddhist Society, London 1945, 1978.

Irving Babbitt (tr.). New York 1936, 2009.

Anne Bancroft (comp.). Rockport (MA), Shaftesbury and Brisbane 1997.
N.V. Banerjee (ed. and tr.). New Delhi 1989, 2000.
Bhadragaka (comp.), *Collection of Verses on the Doctrine of the Buddha*. Bangkok 1952 (printed 1965).
N.K. Bhagwat (tr.). Bombay 1931, Hong Kong 1968.
Srikrishna Datta Bhatta (tr.), *nava saṃhita*. Varanasi 1972. Text 'rearranged' by Vinoba.
S. Brahmachari (ed. Devanagari text & tr.). Bodhgaya 1980.
A.P. Buddhadatta (ed. and tr.). Colombo 1954, Bangkok 1971.
Acharya Buddharakkhita (tr.). MBS, Bangalore 1966, Buddhayoga Meditation Society, Fawnskin (CA), Syarikat Dharma, Kuala Lumpur 1984, BPS 1985, 2007.
E.W. Burlingame (tr. incl. commentary). *Buddhist Legends*. 3 vols, Harvard 1921, PTS 1979. Selected and rev. by Khantipālo for *Buddhist Stories*. 4 vols, BPS 1982–88.
Thomas Byrom (comp.). London 1976.
John Ross Carter and Mahinda Palihawadana (ed. and tr.). New York and Oxford 1987, 1998; without the commentary, 2000.
Thomas Cleary (tr.). New York and London 1995.
J.P. Cooke and O.G. Pettis (tr.). Boston 1898.
Department of Pali, University of Rangoon, *Dhammapada Commentary*. Rangoon 1966.
U. Dhammajoti (tr.). MBS, Benares 1944.
Eknath Easwaran (tr.). Blue Mountain Center, Berkeley 1986, London 1987.
Albert J. Edmunds (tr.), *Hymns of the Faith*. La Salle (IL) 1902.
Anthony Elenjimittam, *Buddha's Teachings*. Allahabad 1975.
David Evans (tr.), *The Dhamma Way*. Leeds 1988.
Gil Fronsdal (tr.). Boston 2005.
D.J. Gogerly (tr. vaggas 1–18) in *The Friend IV*, Colombo 1840. Repr. in *Ceylon Friend*, Colombo 1881 and in his collected works, *Ceylon Buddhism II*, London 1908.
James Gray (tr.). Rangoon 1881, Calcutta 1887.
K. Gunaratana (tr.). Penang 1937.
Norton T.W. Hazeldine (tr.), *The Dhammapada, or the Path of Righteousness*. Denver 1902.
Amara Hewamadduma (ed.), *Dhammapada, Pali-Sinhala-Tamil-English Version*. Colombo 1994.

Raghavan Iyer (ed. and tr.). Santa Barbara 1986.

U.D. Jayasekera (ed. and tr.). Dehiwela 1992.

David J. Kalupahana (ed. and tr.), *A Path of Righteousness*. Lanham 1986.

Suzanne Karpeles (? tr.), serialised in *Advent*. Pondicherry 1960–65. Repr. in *Questions and Answers, Collected Works of the Mother 3*. Pondicherry 1977.

Harischandra Kaviratna (ed. and tr.), *Wisdom of the Buddha*. Theosophical University Press, Pasadena 1980.

Khantipālo (tr.), *Growing the Bodhi Tree*. Bangkok 1966; *The Path of Truth*. Bangkok 1977. Repr. as *Verses of the Buddha's Teaching*. Kaohsiung 1989.

Ravindra Kumar (tr. into Hindi and English), *Gautama Buddha and the Dhammapada*. New Delhi 2007.

C. Kunhan Raja (ed. Devanāgarī text & tr.), *Dhammapada, holy text of the Buddhists.* Adyar 1956, Madras 1984.

P. Lal (tr.). New York 1967.

Geri Larkin, *The Still Point Dhammapada: living the Buddha's essential teachings*. New York and San Francisco 2003.

T. Latter (tr.). Moulmein 1850.

Wesley La Violette (free rendering and interpretation). Los Angeles 1956.

Jack Maguire, Woodstock (VT) 2005.

G.P. Malalasekera (tr. unpublished by PTS). Colombo 1969.

Juan Mascaro (tr.). Harmondsworth 1973.

F. Max Müller (tr.). London 1870. SBE, Oxford 1881, New York 1887, Delhi 2004, St. Petersburg, FL 2008. Included in: John B. Alphonso-Karkala, *An Anthology of Indian Literature* (selection only) Harmondsworth 1971; Lewis Browne, *The World's Greatest Scriptures* (selection only) New York 1945, 1961; E.A. Burtt, *The Teachings of the Compassionate Buddha* New York 1955, 1963; Allie M. Frazier, *Readings in Eastern Religious Thought II* (selection only) Philadelphia 1969; C.H. Hamilton, *Buddhism, a Religion of Infinite Compassion* New York 1952; Charles F. Horne, *The Sacred Books and Early Literature of the East X* New York 1917, Delhi 1987; Raymond van Over, *Eastern Mysticism I* (selection only) New York 1977; Lin Yutang, *The Wisdom of China and India* New York 1942 and *The Wisdom of India* London 1944, Bombay 1966.

Mya Tin (tr.). Rangoon 1986, Yangon 1990 (verses, stories), Delhi 1990, Yangon 1993 (verses only), Sagaing 2003, Selangor 2004.
Nārada (ed. and tr.). Kandy 1940, London 1954, 1972, Saigon 1963, Calcutta 1970, Colombo and New Delhi 1972, BMS 1978, Taipei 1993, Dehiwela 2000, and, with summary of commentary to each verse by K. Sri Dhammānanda, BMS 1988; tr. incl. in *The Path of Buddhism*, Colombo 1956.
K.R. Norman (tr.), *The Word of the Doctrine*. PTS 1997, 2000.
Piyadassi (tr.), *Selections from the Dhammapada*. Colombo 1974.
Piyadassi (tr. incl. Commentary), *Stories of Buddhist India*. 2 vols, Moratuwa 1949, 1953.
Swami Premananda (tr.), *The Path of the Eternal Law*. Self-Realisation Fellowship, Washington (DC) 1942.
S. Radhakrishnan (ed. and tr.). Oxford 1950, 1991, Madras 1968, 1997, Delhi 1980; incl. in S. Radhakrishnan and Charles A. Moore (ed.), *A Source Book in Indian Philosophy*. Princeton and Oxford 1957, and *The Buddhism Omnibus*. New Delhi and New York 2004.
P. Sri Ramachandrudu (ed. Devanagari text & tr.), Hyderabad 1976.
C.A.F. Rhys Davids (ed. and tr.), *Verses on Dhamma*. PTS 1931, 1997.
Valerie J. Roebuck (tr.), London 2010.
Sangharakshita (tr. vaggas 1–12) serialised in *FWBO Newsletter*, London 1969 ff.
W. Sarada (Mahāthera), *Treasury of Truth: Illustrated Dhammapada*. Singapore 1994. Pali text, explanatory translation of the verses with commentary.
K.T.S. Sarao (ed. & tr.), *The Dhammapada. A Translator's Guide*. New Delhi 2009.
S.E.A. Scherb (tr.), "The golden verses of the Buddha". A selection for the *Christian Register*, Boston 1861.
Karma Yonten Senge (Lawrence R. Ellyard), *Everyday Buddha. A Contemporary Rendering of the Buddhist Classic, The Dhammapada*. New Alresford (Hampshire) 2005.
Mahesh Kumar Sharan (ed. and tr.). New Delhi 2006.
Sīlācāra (tr.), *The Way of Truth*. The Buddhist Society of Great Britain and Ireland, London 1915.
Sīlānanda (ed. and tr.), *The Eternal Message of Lord Buddha*. Calcutta 1982.

B. Siri Sivali (tr.). Colombo 1954, 1961.
W. Somalokatissa (tr.). Colombo 1953, 1969.
Ṭhānissaro Bhikkhu (Geoffrey DeGraff, tr.). Barre (MA) 1998.
Roger Tite (comp.—unpublished). Southampton 1974.
P.L. Vaidya (tr.). Poona 1923, 1934.
W.D.C. Wagiswara and K.J. Saunders (tr.), *The Buddha's Way of Virtue*. London 1912, 1927.
Glenn Wallis (tr.), *Verses on the Way*. New York 2004.
Sathienpong Wannapok (tr.), *The Buddha's Words*. Bangkok 1979, 1988
S.W. Wijayatilake (tr.), *The Way of Truth*. Madras 1934.
F.L. Woodward (tr.), *The Buddha's Path of Virtue*. Adyar 1921, 1949.

Udāna

Bhadragaka (tr.), *80 Inspiring Words of the Buddha*. Bangkok 1954.
John D. Ireland (tr.), *The Udāna: Inspired Utterances of the Buddha*. BPS 1990. Reprinted as *The Udāna and Itivuttaka*. BPS 2007.
Peter Masefield (tr.), *The Udāna*. PTS 1994.
D.M. Strong (tr.), *The Solemn Utterances of the Buddha*. London 1902.
Ṭhānissaro Bhikkhu, *Handful of Leaves. Volume Four* (*op. cit.*). Excluding I.4, 5, 7–9; II.8; III.6, 9; IV.2, 5, 8; V.8; VI.1, 10; VII.5, 7, 8; VIII.5–7.
F.L. Woodward (tr.), *Verses of Uplift*. SBB 1935, 1948.

Itivuttaka

John D. Ireland (tr.), *The Itivuttaka: The Buddha's Sayings*. BPS 1991. Repr. as *The Udāna and Itivuttaka*. BPS 2007.
J.H. Moore (tr.), *Sayings of the Buddha*. New York 1908, 1965, New Delhi 1981.
Peter Masefield (tr.), *The Itivuttaka*. PTS 2000.
Ṭhānissaro Bhikkhu (tr.), *This Was Said by the Buddha*. Barre (MA) 2001. Also in *Handful of Leaves. Volume Four* (*op. cit.*).
F.L. Woodward (tr.), *As it was Said*. SBB 1935, 1948.

Sutta-Nipāta

G.F. Allen (tr. 4), *Aṭṭhaka*. Bambalapitiya 1958. Repr. in G.F. Allen *The Buddha's Philosophy*. London 1959.

Lord Chalmers (ed. and tr.), *Buddha's Teachings*. Cambridge (MA) 1932, 1999, Delhi 2000.

Sir Muthu Coomaraswamy (tr. 1, 2, 3:7–9, 4:1), *Dialogues and Discourses of Gotama Buddha*. London 1874.

V. Fausböll (tr.), *A Collection of Discourses*. SBE, Oxford 1880, Delhi 1988.

E.M. Hare (tr.), *Woven Cadences of Early Buddhists*. SBB 1945, 1947.

John D. Ireland (tr. selection), *The Discourse Collection*. BPS 1965.

N.A. Jayawickrama, *Suttanipāta: Text and Translation*. Post-Graduate Institute of Pali and Buddhist Studies, Colombo. 2001.

(Mom Chao) Upalisan Jumbala (tr. 5), *The Solasapañha*. Bangkok 1956

Mahāsi Sayādaw, *A Discourse on Hemavata Sutta*. Rangoon 1980.

—*Sammā Paribbājaniya Sutta*. Rangoon 1981.

—*Tuvataka Sutta*. Rangoon 1982.

—*Purābheda Sutta or The Dhamma One Should Accomplish Before Death*. Rangoon 1983.

K.R. Norman (tr.) with alternative translations by I.B. Horner and Walpola Rāhula, *Group of Discourses* I. PTS 1984; repr. as *The Rhinoceros Horn and other Early Buddhist Poems*. PTS 1985; rev. tr. with introduction and notes by K.R. Norman, PTS 1992, repr. with corrections, PTS 2006.

Nyanaponika (ed. and tr. 1:1), *The Worn-Out Skin*. BPS 1977.

Piyasīlo (tr.), *Book of Discourses I*. Petaling Jaya 1989.

H. Saddhātissa (tr.), *The Sutta-Nipāta*. London 1985.

Ṭhānissaro Bhikkhu (tr.) *Handful of Leaves. Volume Four* (*op. cit.*). Excluding I.6, 7, 9; II.2, 5–7, 11–14; III.4–7, 9, 10; IV.5.

U Tin Oo (tr.), Sagaing and Selangor 2002.

Sister UK Vajira (and SL Dhammajoti) (tr.), *Suttanipāta* I. Uragavagga MBS, Sarnath 1941; II. Cūlavagga (ib. 1942).

Vimānavatthu and Petavatthu

Henry S. Gehman (tr.), *Stories of the Departed.* SBB 1942, 1993.
I.B. Horner (tr.), *Stories of the Mansions.* SBB 1993.
U Htin Fatt (tr. Vimānavatthu), Sagaing and Selangor 2002; (tr. Petavatthu), Sagaing 2003, Selangor 2004.
Jean Kennedy (tr.), *Stories of the Mansions.* SBB 1942.
B.C. Law (summaries), *The Buddhist Conception of Spirits.* Calcutta 1923, Varanasi 1974, Delhi 1997, New Delhi 2005.
—*Heaven and Hell in Buddhist Perspective.* Calcutta 1925, Varanasi 1973, Delhi 2005.
P. Masefield (tr.), *Vimāna Stories.* PTS 1990.

Thera-Therīgāthā

V.F. Gunaratana (tr. selection), *The Message of the Saints.* BPS 1969.
Edmund Jayasuriya, *Thera-Therigatha. Inspired Utterances of Buddhist Monks and Nuns* (based on the translations by C.A.F. Rhys Davids and K.R. Norman). Dehiwela 1999.
Khantipālo (tr. verses of Tālapuṭa Thera, with commentary), *Forest Meditations.* BPS 1977.
Susan Murcott, *The First Buddhist Women.* Berkeley 1991. Translation and commentary of Therīgāthā.
K.R. Norman (tr.), *The Elders' Verses.* 2 vols, PTS 1969/71, 2007; I. *Poems of Early Buddhist Monks*, 1997; II. *Poems of Early Buddhist Nuns*, 1997.
Damayanthi Ratwatte (tr.), *Selected Translations of the Theri Gatha: Songs of Buddhist Nuns.* Kandy 1983.
C.A.F. Rhys Davids (tr.), *Psalms of the Brethren.* PTS 1913, 1994.
—*Psalms of the Sisters.* PTS 1909; repr. with Norman II as *Poems of Early Buddhist Nuns.* PTS 1997.
Both Rhys Davids vols. repr. as *Psalms of the Early Buddhists*, PTS 1980, and *Sacred Writings of the Buddhists*, 3 vols, New Delhi 1986.
C.A.F. Rhys Davids (tr. selection), *Poems of Cloister and Jungle.* London 1941.
Andrew Schelling and Anne Waldman (tr. selection), *Songs of the Sons and Daughters of Buddha.* Boston 1996.
Soma (tr. verses of Tālapuṭa Thera), *His Last Performance.* Kandy 1943.

Ṭhānissaro Bhikkhu (tr.), *Handful of Leaves. Volumes Four* and *Five* (*op. cit.*). Includes selections from Thag-Thīg.

Jātaka

Ellen C. Babbit, *Jataka Tales*. New York 1912. Retellings.
Ethel Beswick, *Jātaka Tales*. London 1956. 35 tales based on Cowell's tr.
W.B. Bollée (ed. and tr.), *Kuṇāla Jātaka*. SBB 1970.
E.B. Cowell (tr.), *Jātaka Stories*. 6 vols, Cambridge 1895–1905; repr. in 3 vols, PTS 1972, 1981, Delhi 1990, 2008. The only complete translation of the Jātakas.
L.H. Elwell (tr.), *Nine Jātakas*. Boston 1886.
Fausböll (tr.), *Five Jātakas*. Copenhagen and London 1861.
—*The Dasaratha-jātaka, being the Buddhist story of King Rāma. Ibid.*, 1871.
—*Ten Jātakas. Ibid.*, 1872, Whitefish (MT) 2007.
—*Two Jātakas* (33 and 20). JRAS N.S. V (1871).
H.T. Francis (tr.), *The Vedabbha Jātaka*. Cambridge 1884.
H.T. Francis and E.J. Thomas (tr.), *Jātaka Tales*. Cambridge 1916, Bombay 1970. Comprises 114 tales.
Richard Gombrich and Margaret Cone (tr. *Vessantara Jātaka*), *The Perfect Generosity of Prince Vessantara*. Oxford 1977.
I.B. Horner (ed. and tr.), *Ten Jātaka Stories*. London 1957, Bangkok 1974. Designed to illustrate each of the Ten Perfections.
N.A. Jayawickrama, *The Story of Gotama Buddha*. PTS 1990, 2002. Translation of *Jātaka-nidāna*.
C.S. Josson, *Stories of Buddha's Births: A Jātaka Reader*. New York 1976.
Ken and Visakha Kawasaki, *Jātaka Tales of the Buddha: An Anthology*. Three volumes. BPS 2010. A retelling based on Cowell (*op. cit.*).
Rafe Martin, *The Hungry Tigress: Buddhist Legends and Jātaka Tales*. Berkeley 1990. A free retelling of selected Jātakas and other Buddhist stories.
R. Morris (tr.), "Jātaka Tales from the Pali." *Folklore Journal* II–IV, London 1887.
Piyasīlo, *Jātaka Stories*. Petaling Jaya, Selangor 1983. A free adaptation of the last ten Jātakas.
C.A.F. Rhys Davids (tr.), *Stories of the Buddha*. London 1929, New York 1989. Comprises 47 tales.

T.W. Rhys Davids (tr.), *Buddhist Birth Stories.* London 1880; rev. ed. by C.A.F. Rhys Davids, 1925, and Leiden and Delhi 1973, 2004. Comprises the *Nidāna-Kathā* and the first 40 Jātakas.

Sarah Shaw (tr.), *The Jātakas: Birth Stories of the Bodhisatta.* Delhi and New York 2006. Comprises 26 tales.

E. Wray, C. Rosenfield and D. Bailey, *Ten Lives of the Buddha. Thai temple paintings and Jātaka tales.* New York 1972.

Paṭisambhidāmagga

Ñāṇamoli (tr.), *The Path of Discrimination.* PTS 1982, 1997.

Apadāna

Jonathan S. Walters (tr.), "Gotami's Story." *Buddhism in Practice,* ed. Donald S. Lopez. Princeton 1995, pp. 113–38.

Buddhavaṃsa

I.B. Horner (tr.), *Chronicle of Buddhas.* SBB 1975.

B.C. Law (tr.), *The Lineage of the Buddhas.* SBB 1938.

Meena Talin (tr.), *The Genealogy of the Buddhas.* Bombay 1969.

Vicittasārābhivaṃsa (Mingun Sayādaw), *The Great Chronicle of Buddhas.* Rangoon 1994, Selangor 1997. Translation of the Burmese edition of the Buddhavaṃsa in 6 vols and 8 books. Including copious explanations by the Mingun Sayādaw.

Cariyāpiṭaka

I.B. Horner (tr.), *Basket of Conduct.* SBB 1975.

B.C. Law (tr.), *Collection of Ways of Conduct.* SBB 1938.

C. Abhidhamma Pitaka

Dhammasaṅgaṇī: U Kyaw Khine (tr.), *The Dhammasangini: Enumeration of Ultimate Realities.* Yangon 1996; 2 vols., Delhi 1999.

—C.A.F. Rhys Davids (tr.), *A Buddhist Manual of Psychological Ethics.* RAS, London 1900, Delhi 1975, 1996. PTS reprint 1974, 1993.

Vibhaṅga: U Thittila (tr.), *The Book of Analysis.* PTS 1969,1988.

Dhātukathā: U Nārada (tr.), *Discourse on Elements.* PTS 1962, 1995.

Puggalapaññatti: B.C. Law (tr.), *A Designation of Human Types*. PTS 1922, 1992.
Kathāvatthu: S.Z. Aung and C.A.F. Rhys Davids (tr.), *Points of Controversy*. PTS 1915, 1993.
Yamaka I (I–V): U Nārada and U Kumārābhivaṃsa (tr.), *The Book on Pairs*. Penang 1998.
Paṭṭhāna (part of the Tikapaṭṭhāna): U Nārada (tr.), *Conditional Relations*. PTS I. 1969, 1992, II. 1981, 1993.

2. Anthologies

G.F. Allen, *Buddha's Words of Wisdom*. London 1959, Dehiwela 2002. Sayings for each day of the year compiled from SP, mainly Sn.

Herbert Baynes (tr.), *The Way of the Buddha*. London 1906, New York 1913. Including Dhp XX–The Way.

Stephan Beyer (tr.), *The Buddhist Experience: Sources and Interpretations*. Belmont 1974.

Bhikkhu Bodhi (ed.), *In the Buddha's Words. An Anthology of Discourses from the Pāli Canon*. Boston 2005. Large collection organised on the scheme of the three benefits of practice of the Dhamma.

E.M. Bowden, *The Imitation of Buddha*. London 1891, Delhi 1989. Quotations from mainly Pāli texts for each day of the year.

E.H. Brewster, *The Life of Gotama the Buddha*. London 1926, Varanasi 1975. Compiled exclusively from the Pāli Canon as tr. by the Rhys Davids.

Kerry Brown and Joanne O'Brien (eds.), *The Essential Teachings of Buddhism*. London 1989. Includes I. Theravada: 1. Thailand–daily readings from SP compiled by Ajahn Tīradhammo; 2. Sri Lanka–same, by W. G. Weeraratna and Dhanapala Samarasekara.

Buddhist Lodge, The, *Selected Buddhist Scriptures from the Pāli Canon of the Theravāda School*. London 1930.

E.W. Burlingame (tr.), *Buddhist Parables*. New Haven 1922, Delhi 2004. Comprises over 200 allegories, anecdotes, fables and parables from VP, SP, AN, Dhp Commentaries, and Mil.

—*The Grateful Elephant and Other Stories*. New Haven 1923. 26 stories extracted from *Buddhist Parables*.

E.A. Burtt (ed.), *The Teachings of the Compassionate Buddha*. New York 1955, 1963. Includes selections from Mahāvagga and Thera-Therīgāthā (Rhys Davids), Dhp (Max Müller), Sn (Chalmers), etc.

Paul Carus, *The Gospel of Buddha*. LaSalle (IL) 1894, London 1943, 1974, Tucson (AZ) 1972, New Delhi 1981, Varanasi 2006. Selection offprinted as *Sayings of Buddha*. New York 1957.

Edward Conze (ed.), *Buddhist Texts through the Ages*. Oxford 1954, New York 1964, New Delhi 2008. Includes I.B. Horner (tr.) selection mainly from VP and SP.

—(tr.), *Buddhist Scriptures*. Harmondsworth 1959, 1971.

—*The Way of Wisdom: The Five Faculties*. BPS 1964. Illustrated from MN, SN, Mil and Vism.

A.K. Coomaraswamy and I.B. Horner (tr.), *The Living Thoughts of Gotama the Buddha*. London 1948, Bombay 1956, New Delhi 1982, Delhi 1999, Louisville (KY) 2001. Includes extracts from VP and SP (and Commentaries), Mil and Vism.

S. Dhammika (ed. & tr.), *Gemstones of the Good Dhamma*. BPS 1987. A short selection of verses from SP and Mil, Pāli and English on facing pages.

—(comp.), *Buddha Vacana, Daily Readings from Sacred Literature of Buddhism*. Singapore 1989.

Sudhakar Dikshit, *Sermons and Sayings of the Buddha*. Bombay 1958, 1977. A selection from VP and SP.

Albert J. Edmunds, "Gospel Parallels from Pali Texts." *The Open Court* XIV-XVI, 1900–1902. A collection of excerpts from the Pāli canon, presented to show their thematic relation to Christian scriptures.

David Evans, *The Buddha Digest: Modern verses based on ancient texts* (published privately). Leeds 2000.

—*The Buddha Digest: Modern transcriptions of Pali texts. Ibid.*, 2004.

The Five Nikāyas: Discourses of the Buddha I. Rangoon 1978. Offprints from *The Light of the Dhamma*, including the Pātimokkha, DN 1–3, MN 21, 26, 33, 44, 55, 67, 118, 129, 135, SN 12:1, 62, 70; 22:56, 57, 59, 86; 35:132, 197, 241; 55:7; 56:11; AN 1:1–50; 3:55, 61; 4:53; 5:33, 145, 171, 174, 180; 6:63; 8:30, 34, 41; Khp 7, Sn II:2 and *suttas* selections from the Vibhaṅga and Dhp Commentary.

N. Gangulee, *The Buddha and His Message*. Bombay 1957.

Rupert Gethin (tr.), *Sayings of the Buddha*. Oxford 2008. Includes DN 2, 16, 17, 27, 31; MN 10, 20, 22, 63, 85, 136; and selections from SN and AN.

Dwight Goddard (ed.), *A Buddhist Bible*. New York 1932, Boston 1970. Includes DN 13, MN 118, all of Nyanatiloka's *Word of the Buddha*.

C.H. Hamilton, *Buddhism, a Religion of Infinite Compassion*. New York 1952. Includes selections from SP in standard early translations.

John J. Holder (tr.), *Early Buddhist Discourses*. Indianapolis 2006. Comprises new translations of DN 9, 13, 15, 22, 26, 31, MN 18, 22, 26, 38, 58, 63, 72, 93, Kālāma Sutta and extracts from SN.

I.B. Horner (tr. from SP), *Early Buddhist Poetry*. Colombo 1963.

Christmas Humphreys, *Thus Have I Heard*. The Buddhist Society, London 1948. A reprint of *Selected Buddhist Scriptures ...*, *op. cit.*

Khantipālo, *The Splendour of Enlightenment*. 2 vols, Bangkok 1976. A life of the Buddha extracted from Pāli (PTS Translation Series) and early Buddhist Sanskrit texts.

—*Buddha, My Refuge: Contemplation of the Buddha based on the Pali Suttas*. BPS 1990. Texts on the Buddha from SP, arranged by way of the nine Buddha-virtues (*Buddhaguṇa*).

David Maurice (tr.), *The Lion's Roar*. London 1962, New York 1967. Anthology mostly from SP, includes Pātimokkha.

Ñāṇamoli, *The Practice of Loving kindness*. BPS 1959. Comprises the Karaṇīyametta Sutta and short extracts from texts on this subject.

—*Mindfulness of Breathing*. BPS 1964. Includes MN 118 and related passages.

—(tr.), *The Life of the Buddha*. BPS 1972, 2006 (Seattle 2001). Compiled from VP and SP. Partial offprint as *The Buddha's Teaching in His Own Words*. BPS 1998.

Nārada (tr.), *The Life of Buddha (in his own words)*. Adyar 1931.

—(tr.), *Everyman's Ethics*. BPS 1959. Comprises DN 31, AN 8:54, Sn 1:6, 2:4. Republished in *A Constitution for Living*. BPS 2007.

Nyanaponika (tr.), *The Five Mental Hindrances*. BSS 1947, BPS 1961. Selected passages from the Canon and Commentaries.

—*The Four Nutriments of Life*. BPS 1967. A selection mainly from SN and its Commentary.

—*The Roots of Good and Evil*. BPS 1978. Extracts mainly from AN.

Nyanatiloka (tr.), *Word of the Buddha*. Rangoon 1907, London 1950, Santa Barbara (CA) 1950, 18th English ed., BPS 2001. The first really systematic exposition of the entire teachings of the Buddha presented in the Master's own words as found in the Sutta Piṭaka in the form of the Four Noble Truths.

—(tr.), *The Buddha's Path to Deliverance*, in its Threefold Division and Seven Stages of Purity. BSS 1952, BPS 1982. Compiled from SP.

Geoffrey Parrinder, *The Wisdom of the Early Buddhists*. London 1977. 108 extracts mainly from DN (Rhys Davids) and MN (Horner), reprinted as *The Sayings of the Buddha*. London 1991.

S. Radhakrishnan and Charles A. Moore (ed.), *A Source Book in Indian Philosophy*. Princeton-Oxford 1957. Includes MN 141 (Chalmers), Dhp (Radhakrishnan), extracts from the Udāna and Itivuttaka (Woodward), etc.

T.W. Rhys Davids (tr.), *Buddhist Suttas*. SBE 1881, New York 1969, London 2001, Delhi 2003. Comprises DN 13, 16, 17; MN 2, 6, 16; SN 56:11.

Stanley Rice, *The Buddha Speaks Here and Now, Fundamental Buddhist Scriptures interpreted in Contemporary Idiom*. BPS 1981. Reformulations of DN 2, MN 10, 20, 22, 43, 131; several other suttas from SN, AN, and Sn.

K.J. Saunders, *The Heart of Buddhism. An Anthology of Buddhist Verse*. Oxford 1915, Varanasi 1998.

Sayings of the Buddha. Singapore 1993. (Author unknown.)

Peter Skilling (ed.), *Beyond Worldly Conditions*. Bangkok 1999. Translations and commentaries on the Lokadhamma Sutta and related texts.

Lucien Stryk (ed.), *World of the Buddha*. New York 1968, 1982. Includes extracts from SP, Mil and Vism (Warren).

J. Subasinha, *Buddhist Rules for the Laity*. Madras 1908, Delhi 1997. Comprises DN 31 and AN 8:54.

Sugatananda (Francis Story), *Saṅgīti*. Rangoon 1954. Includes synopses of DN 1, 13, 27, MN 98, Sn I-7,8, III-3, IV-1,7.

—*Taming the Mind*. BPS 1963. Short passages from SP.

Luang Suriyabongs (comp.), *A Buddhist Anthology*. Bangkok 1956. Extracts from VP and SP on the subjects of the Buddha, Dhamma, Sangha and Lay Disciple.

Ṭhānissaro Bhikkhu (tr.), *Handful of Leaves, Volume Five: An Anthology from the Five Nikāyas*. Redwood City (CA) 2004.

—*That the True Dhamma Might Last a Long Time: Readings Selected by King Asoka*. *Ibid.*, 1996. Suttas which King Asoka selected as representative of the essence of the Dhamma.

J. Thomas (tr.), *Buddhist Scriptures*. London 1913.

—*Early Buddhist Scriptures*. London 1935, New York 1974, New Delhi 1996. Contains a wide selection from SP.

—*The Road to Nirvana*. London 1950, Rutland (VT) 1992. Selected texts.

Vajirañāṇavarorasa *Dhammavibhāga: Numerical Sayings of Dhamma*. 2 vols, Bangkok 1968–70.

Glenn Wallis (tr.), *Basic Teachings of the Buddha. A New Translation and Compilation, with a Guide to Reading the Texts*. New York 2007. 16 suttas including DN 13, 22, MN 63, 118.

E. Ward, *Light from the East, being Selections from the Teachings of the Buddha*. London 1905.

Henry Clarke Warren (tr.), *Buddhism in Translations*. Harvard 1896, New York 1972, 2005, Delhi 2007. Also reprinted as *Buddhist Discourses* (Delhi 1980) and *A Buddhist Reader. Selections from the Sacred Books* (New York 2004). Comprises selections from VP, SP, Jātakas, DN Commentary, Mil and Vism.

—See also *Buddhism: Pali Text with English Translation*, ed. N.C. Panda, rev. & enl. ed., 2 vols, Delhi 2008.

—*The Life of the Buddha*. Harvard 1923, New Delhi 2003, Delhi 2005. Compiled from relevant sections of the above work. Rev. ed., *Everyman's Life of the Buddha*. Conesville 1968. A further selection appeared as *The Wisdom of Buddha*. New York 1968.

F.L. Woodward (tr.), *Some Sayings of the Buddha*. London 1925, 1974, New York 1973, New Delhi 2002. Short passages from VP and SP. Repr. as *The Wisdom of Buddha*. Gurgaon 2005.

3. Devotional Manuals (romanised Pāli texts and translations)

Ānandajoti Bhikkhu, *Safeguard Recitals*. Kandy, 2004. An edition and translation of the *Catubhāṇavārapāḷi* or *Mahāparitta*.

Herbert Baynes (ed. & tr.), "The Mirror of Truth, or Bauddha Confession of Faith." *Wiener Zeitschrift für die Kunde des Morgenländes* X, 1896, pp. 242–51.

Acharya Buddharakkhita, *Buddhist Manual for Everyday Practice*. Bangalore 1986.

K. Sri Dhammananda, *Handbook of Buddhists*. BMS 1965—*Daily Buddhist Devotions*. BMS 1991, 1993.

B. Dhammaratana, *Aura of the Dhamma*. Singapore 1979.

S.N. Goenka, *The Gem Set in Gold*. Onalaska (WA) 2006. Dhamma chanting with Pāli and Hindi texts.

Khantipālo, *Buddhist Texts for Recitation*. BPS 1974.

—*Namo: Chanting Book*. Wisemans Ferry, NSW (Australia) 1988.

Khantipālo and Jotimano, *Book of Chants (a compilation, being the romanised edition of the Royal Thai Chanting Book)*. Bangkok 1975.

Mahamakuta Educational Council, *Excerpts from the Book of Recitations*. Bangkok 1957.

Rāngphim Mahāmakutrātchamitthayālai (comp.), *Pali Chanting, with Translations*. Bangkok 1974, 1983.

Nārada and Kassapa, *The Mirror of the Dhamma. Colombo,* 1926, BPS 1963, Dehiwela 2005.

Pe Maung Tin, *Buddhist Devotion and Meditation*. SPCK, London 1964.

B. Pemaratana, *Way to the Buddha*. Penang 1964, 1970.

D.G. Ariyapala Perera, *Buddhist Paritta Chanting Ritual*. Dehiwela 2000.

Piyadassi, *The Book of Protection*. BPS 1975. Translation of the *paritta* book.

Piyasīlo, *The Puja Book: Paritta, Plainchant, and Rites of Passage*. 4 vols, Petaling Jaya 1990–92.

Rewata Dhamma, *Mahā Paritta. The Great Protection*. Birmingham Buddhist Vihara 1996.

H. Saddhātissa, *Handbook of Buddhists*. MBS, Sarnath 1956, 1973.

—and Russell Webb, *A Buddhist's Manual*. MBS, London 1976.

—and Ven. Pesala, *ibid.* 2nd rev. ed., 1990.
H.L. St. Barbe (tr.), "The Namakkāra (stanzas of praise/ worship)." JRAS N.S. XV, 1883, pp. 213–20.
U Sīlāndābhivaṃsa (tr. 11 protective *suttas*), *Paritta Pāli and Protective Verses.* Rangoon 2000.
Sao Htun Hmat Win, *Eleven Holy Discourses of Protection.* Mahā Paritta Pāli, including the apocryphal *Pubbaṇha Sutta.* Rangoon 1981.
—*Basic Principles of Burmese Buddhism.* Rangoon 1985.
Somboon Siddhinyano, *Romanization of the Pāli Chanting Book.* Bangkok 1985, Wolverhampton Buddha Vihara 1987.
Jandamit Vorasak (comp.), *Pali Recitations, with English Versions.* Bangkok 1989.
K. Wimalajothi, *Buddhist Chanting.* Dehiwela 2003.

4. Post-Canonical and Commentarial Literature

A. The Commentaries (in English translation)

U Ba Kyaw and P. Masefield, *Peta-Stories.* (*Paramatthadīpanī*, Dhammapāla's commentary on the Petavatthu.) SBB 1980.
Mabel Bode, "Women Leaders of the Buddhist Reformation." (From the *Manorathapurāṇī*, Buddhaghosa's commentary on the Aṅguttara Nikāya.) JRAS 1893, pp. 517–66, 763–98.
Acharya Buddharakkhita, *An Unforgettable Inheritance.* (Commentary on Dhp I and II.) 4 volumes. MBS, Bangalore 1973–89.
E.W. Burlingame, *Buddhist Legends.* (Buddhaghosa's *Dhammapadaṭṭhakathā.*) 3 volumes, Harvard 1921, PTS 1995, Delhi 2005.
P. Godahewa, *Samanta-pāsādikā* (*Bāhira Nidāna Vaṇṇanā*). (Introduction to the *Samantapāsādika*, Buddhaghosa's commentary on the Vinaya Piṭaka.) Ambalangoda 1954.
I.B. Horner, *Clarifier of the Sweet Meaning.* (*Madhuratthavilāsinī*, Buddhadatta's commentary on the Buddhavaṃsa.) SBB 1978.
N.A. Jayawickrama, *The Inception of Discipline and the Vinaya Nidāna.* (As for Godahewa.) SBB 1962.
—*Story of Gotama Buddha.* (*Nidānakathā* of the *Jātakaṭṭhakathā.*) PTS 1990.

—"The Exegesis of the Sabbāsavasutta" (tr. M2 from the *Papañcasūdanī*) in *Buddhist and Pali Studies in Honour of The Venerable Professor Kakkapalliye Anuruddha*, ed. K.L. Dhammajoti and Y. Karunadasa. Hong Kong 2009, pp. 1–41.

Khantipālo, *Buddhist Stories.* (Selected and revised from Burlingame, *op. cit.*) 4 parts, BPS 1982–88.

B.C. Law, *The Debates Commentary.* (Buddhaghosa's *Kathāvatthuppakaraṇaṭṭhakathā*, part of the *Pañcappakaraṇa-ṭṭhakathā.*) PTS 1940, 1988.

Peter Masefield, *Elucidation of the Intrinsic Meaning so Named.* (Dhammapāla's commentary on the Vimānavatthu.) SBB 1989.

—*Itivuttaka Commentary.* 2 vols, PTS 2008–9.

—*Udāna Commentary.* 2 vols, PTS 1994–95.

Ñāṇamoli, *Illustrator* (from *Minor Readings and Illustrator*). (*Paramatthajotikā*, Buddhaghosa's commentary on the Khuddakapāṭha.) PTS 1960, 1991.

—*The Dispeller of Delusion.* (*Sammohavinodanī*, Buddhaghosa's commentary on the Vibhaṅga.) SBB I, 1987, II, 1991.

Nyanaponika (ed.), *Stories of Old.* BPS 1963. An anthology from the Commentaries.

Andrew Olendzki, "Guhatthaka-suttaniddeso. Upon the Tip of a Needle" (excerpt from the *Mahāniddesa*). Retrieved from www.accesstoinsight.org/tipitaka/kn/nm/nm.2.04.olen.html

Pe Maung Tin, *The Expositor.* (*Atthasālinī*, Buddhaghosa's commentary on the Dhammasaṅgaṇī.) 2 vols, PTS 1920–21, 1976.

William Pruitt, *The Commentary on the Verses of the Theris.* PTS 1998.

Junjirō Takakusu, "Pāli Elements in Chinese Buddhism. A Translation of Buddhaghosa's Samantapāsādika, a Commentary on the Vinaya, found in the Chinese Tripiṭaka." *Journal of the Royal Asiatic Society* NS 28, 1898, pp. 415–39.

Yang-Gyu An, *The Buddha's Last Days. Buddhaghosa's Commentary on the Mahāparinibbāna Sutta.* PTS 2003.

B. Pāli Exegeses (in English translation)

Abhidhammatthasaṅgaha

S.Z. Aung and C.A.F. Rhys Davids, *Compendium of Philosophy*. PTS 1910, 1995, Whitefish (MT) 2003.
Egerton C. Baptist, *Abhidhamma for the Beginner*. Colombo 1959, Dehiwela 2004.
Bhikkhu Bodhi (ed. and tr.), *A Comprehensive Manual of Abhidhamma*. BPS 1993, 2006.
C.L.A. de Silva, *A Treatise on Buddhist Philosophy or Abhidhamma*. Colombo 1937, Delhi 1997.
Huyen-Vi, *The Four Abhidhammic Reals*. Linh-Son, Joinville-le-Pont (Paris) 1982.
Jagdish Kashyap, *The Abhidhamma Philosophy I*. Benares 1942, Patna 1954, Delhi 1982.
Nārada, *A Manual of Abhidhamma*. Colombo 1956, BPS 1968, Rangoon 1970; rev. ed. BPS 1975.
R.P. Wijeratne and Rupert Gethin (tr., and *Abhidhammavibhāvinī*), *Summary of the Topics* and *Exposition of the Topics of Abhidhamma*. PTS 2002.

Milindapañhā

R. Basu, *A Critical Study of the Milindapañha*. Calcutta 1978.
I.B. Horner, *Milinda's Questions*. 2 vols, SBB 1963–64, 1990–91.
N.K.G. Mendis (ed.), *The Questions of King Milinda—An Abridgement of the Milindapañha*. BPS 1993, 2007. Introduction by Bhikkhu Bodhi.
Minh Chau, *Milindapañha and Nāgasenabhikshusūtra*. Calcutta 1964. A comparative study.
Bhikkhu Pesala, *The Debate of King Milinda* [abridged]. Delhi 1991.
C.A.F. Rhys Davids, *The Milinda-Questions*. London 1930, Delhi 1997, Richmond (Surrey) 2000. *An inquiry into its place in the history of Buddhism with a theory as to its author.*
T.W. Rhys Davids, *The Questions of King Milinda*. 2 vols, SBE 1890–94, New York 1969, Delhi 2005.
V. Trenckner, *Pali Miscellany*. London 1879. Edition and translation of a "specimen of Milindapañha".

Nettippakaraṇa

Ñāṇamoli, *The Guide*. PTS 1962, 1977.

George D. Bond, "The Netti-Ppakaraṇa: A Theravādin Method of Interpretation." *Buddhist Studies in honour of Walpola Rahula*, ed. S. Balasooriya *et al.*, London 1980, pp. 16–28.

Peṭakopadesa

Ñāṇamoli, *Piṭaka-Disclosure*. PTS 1964, 1979.

Rūpārūpavibhāga

B.N. Chaudhury, *Abhidhamma Terminology in the Rūpārūpavibhāga*. Calcutta 1983.

Robert Exell, "The Classification of Forms and Formless Things." *Visākha Puja*, Bangkok 1964, JPTS XVII, 1992, pp. 1–12.

D.K. Barua (ed. & tr.), *Rūpārūpa-vibhāga of Ācariya Buddhadatta Thera*. Calcutta 1995.

Vimuttimagga

Anālayo, "The Treatise on the Path to Liberation and the *Visuddhimagga*." *Fuyan Buddhist Studies* 2009. 4, pp. 1–15.

N.R.M. Ehara, Soma and Kheminda, *The Path of Freedom*. Colombo 1961, BPS 1977, 1995.

T. Hayashi, "The *Vimuttimagga* and Early Post-Canonical Literature." 3 parts, *Bukkyō Kenkyū* 31, 2003, pp. 91–122; 32, 2004, pp. 59–82; 34, 2006, pp. 5–33.

Lalen Kumar Jha, *The Vimuttimagga, a critical study*. Delhi 2008.

Makoto Nagai, "The *Vimutti-Magga*, the 'Way to Deliverance'. The Chinese Counterpart of the Pāli *Visuddhi-magga*." JPTS, 1919, pp. 69–80.

Visuddhimagga

Jion Abe, *Saṅkhepatthajotani Visuddhimaggacullaṭīkā Sīla-Dhutaṅga: A study of the first and second chapters of the Visuddhimagga and its Commentaries*. Poona 1981.

P.V. Bapat, *Vimuttimagga and Visuddhimagga: A Comparative Study*. Poona 1937, BPS 2010.

Edward Conze, *Buddhist Meditation*. London 1956, Abingdon 2008. Includes extensive passages from Vism.

U Dhammaratana, *Guide through Visuddhimagga*. MBS, Varanasi 1964, Colombo 1980.
Damien Keown, "Morality in the *Visuddhimagga*." *Journal of the International Association of Buddhist Studies* 6, 1983, pp. 61–75.
Baidyanath Labh, *Paññā in Early Buddhism, with special reference to Visuddhimagga*. Delhi 1991.
Robert Mann and Rose Youd, *Buddhist Character Analysis* (based on Vism). Bradford-on-Avon 1992.
Ñāṇamoli, *The Path of Purification*. Colombo 1956, BPS 1975, 1999, 2010; 2 vols, Berkeley 1976, Singapore and Taipei 2003.
Pe Maung Tin, *The Path of Purity*. PTS, 3 vols, 1922–1931; 1 vol, 1975.
Vyañjana, *Theravāda Buddhist Ethics with special reference to Visuddhimagga*. Calcutta 1992.

C. Non-Indian Pāli Literature

Burma (Myanmar from 1989)

Chester Bennett (tr. *Mālālaṅkāravatthu*), "Life of Gaudama." *Journal of the American Oriental Society* III, New York 1853. Revised by Michael Edwardes as *A Life of the Buddha*. London 1959.
Paul Bigandet (tr. *Tathāgata-udāna*), *The Life or Legend of Gaudama*. 2 vols, Rangoon 1858, London 1911–12
Mabel H. Bode, *The Pali Literature of Burma*. London 1909, 1966.
Asha Das, *The Glimpses of Buddhist Literature*. Calcutta 2000. A critical study and translation of the Gandhavaṃsa.
Dorothy H. Fickle, "An Historical and Structural Study of the Paññāsa Jātaka". Ph.D. diss., Pennsylvania 1978.
Emil Forchhammer, *Report on the Pali Literature of Burma*. Calcutta 1879.
James Gray (ed. and tr.), *Buddhaghosuppatti or Historical Romance of the Rise and Career of Buddhaghosa*. London 1892, 2001; New Delhi 1999.
Ann Appleby Hazelwood (tr.), "*Pañcagatidīpanī*." JPTS XI, 1987, pp. 133–59.
Mahāsi Sayadaw, *The Progress of Insight*. BPS 1965. A contemporary Pali treatise on *satipaṭṭhāna* meditation, with translation by Nyanaponika.

Sri Lanka (Ceylon)

Acharíya Buddharakkhita, *Halo'd Triumphs*. Bangalore 2001. Pāli text, translation and explanation of the Jayamaṅgala Gāthā.

James D'Alwis, *A Descriptive Catalogue of Sanskrit, Pali and Sinhalese Literary Works of Ceylon*. 3 vols, Colombo 1870.

C. Duroiselle (tr.), *Jinacarita or "The Career of the Conqueror"*. London 1906, Delhi 1982, Whitefish (MT) 2007.

D.J. Gogerly, "Buddhism". *The Orientalist* I, 1884, pp. 204–5. A detailed summary of the *Rasavāhinī*.

R.F. Gombrich (ed. and tr.), *"Kosalabimbavaṇṇanā."* In *Buddhism in Ceylon and Studies in Religious Syncretism in Buddhist Countries*, ed. Heinz Bechert, Göttingen 1978.

James Gray (tr.), *Jinālaṅkāra or "Embellishments of Buddha"*. London 1894, SBB 1981.

Charles Hallisey, "Devotion in the Buddhist Literature of Medieval Sri Lanka." Ph.D. diss., Chicago 1988.

—(ed.), "*Tuṇḍilovāda*: an Allegedly Non-Canonical Sutta." JPTS XV, 1990, pp. 155–95.

—(tr.), "The Advice to Layman Tuṇḍila." *Buddhism in Practice*, ed. Donald S. Lopez. Princeton 1995, pp. 302–13.

N.A. Jayawickrama, "Literary Activity in Pali." *Pali Buddhist Review* 5, 1980, pp. 76–88. Repr. from *Education in Ceylon* I, ch.7, Min. of Education and Cultural Affairs, Colombo 1969.

Ann Appleby Hazelwood (tr.), *Saddhammopāyana*. JPTS XII, 1988, pp. 65–168.

B.C. Law (tr. *Telakaṭāhagāthā*), "Verses on Oil-Pot." *Indian Culture* V. Calcutta 1938–39.

—(tr. *Saddhammasaṅgaha*), *A Manual of Buddhist Historical Records*. Calcutta 1963, Delhi 1999.

G.P. Malalasekera, *The Pali Literature of Ceylon*. London 1928, Colombo 1958, BPS 1994.

Junko Matsumura, *The Rasavāhinī of Vedeha Thera Vaggas V and VI: Migapotaka-Vagga and Uttaroḷiya-Vagga*. Osaka 1992.

—"Remarks on the Rasavāhinī and the Related Literature." JPTS XXV, 1999, pp. 155–72.

—"Materials for the Rasavāhinī: a reconsideration of the Sahassavatthaṭṭhakathā and its relationship to the Rasavāhinī." *Indogaku Bukkyōgaku Kenkyū* 52.1, 2003, pp. 455–58.

Maung Tin (tr.), "Abhisambodhi Alaṅkāra: The Embellishments of Perfect Knowledge." *Journal of the Burma Research Society* I-III, Rangoon 1912-13.

Primoz Pecenko, "Sāriputta and his works." JPTS XXIII, 1997, pp. 159-79.

—"*Līnatthapakāsinī* and *Sāratthamañjūsā*: The *Purānaṭīkās* and the *Ṭīkās* on the Four Nikāyas." JPTS XXVII, 2002, pp. 61-113.

—"The Ṭīkās on the Four Nikāyas: Līnatthapakāsinī and Sāratthamañjūsā." *Indologica Taurinensia* XXX, 2004, pp. 201-27.

Widurupola Piyatissa (ed. and tr.), *Kāmalañjali: With Folded Hands.* Colombo 1952; repr. in P. Sugatānanda, *Sangīti.* Rangoon 1954. A modern devotional poem.

William Pruitt (tr.), "*Anāgatavaṃsa*, The Chronicle of the Future Buddha" in Sayagyi U Chit Tin, *The Coming Buddha, Ariya Metteyya.* BPS 1992, pp. 49-61; rev.tr. by K.R. Norman, "The Chronicle of the Future [Buddha]." JPTS XXVIII, 2006, pp. 19- 32; *Collected Papers VIII.* PTS 2007, pp. 224-60.

Telwatte Rāhula (ed. and tr.), "*Rasavāhinī: Jambudīpuppattivatthu.*" Ph.D. diss., ANU (Canberra) 1981.

—"The *Rasavāhinī* and the *Sahassavatthu*: A comparison." *Journal of the International Association of Buddhist Studies* 7, 1984, pp. 169-84.

S.K. Rāmachandra Rao (ed. and tr. *Telakaṭāhagāthā*), "Song in the Cauldron of Oil." *Quarterly Journal of the Mythic Society* XLVII, Bangalore 1957.

W.H.D. Rouse (tr.), "Jinacarita." JPTS 1905, pp. 1-65, repr. Oxford 1978, New Delhi 1985.

H. Saddhātissa (ed.), *Upāsakajanālankāra* (with English synopsis of the "Adornment of the Buddhist Laity"). PTS 1965.

—(tr. and ed.), *The Birth Stories of the Ten Bodhisattas and the Dasabodhisattuppattikathā.* SBB 1976.

—(tr. *Khema's Nāmarūpasamāso*), "The Summary of Mind and Matter." JPTS XI ,1987, pp. 5-31.

C. Sameresingha (tr. *Telakaṭāhagāthā*), "The Dying Rahat's Sermon." *The Buddhist Ray*, Santa Cruz (CA) 1889-90; repr. in *Pali Buddhist Review* 2, London 1977.

Laksmana Sāstri (tr. from the *Rasavāhinī*), "Buddhist Legends of Asoka and his Times." *Journal of the Asiatic Society of Bengal.* N.S. 6, 1910, pp. 52-72

H.C. Warren (partial tr. of the *Anāgatavaṃsa*), "The Buddhist Apocalypse" (describing the disappearance of the Buddha's Teaching). *Buddhism in Translations* (*op. cit.*), pp. 481–87.
Thailand (Siam).

Steven Collins, "The Story of the Elder Māleyyadeva." JPTS XVIII, 1993, pp. 65–96.

Kate Crosby, "A Theravāda Code of Conduct for Good Buddhists: The *Upāsakamanussavinaya*." *Journal of the American Oriental Society* 126 (2006), pp. 177–87.

Oscar von Hinüber, "Pāli Manuscripts of Canonical Texts from North Thailand. A Preliminary Study." *Journal of the Siam Society* 71, 1983, pp. 75–88.

—"On Some Colophons of Old Lānnā Pāli Manuscripts." *Proceedings of the 4th International Conference on Thai Studies* IV, Kunming 1990, pp. 56–77.

—"Chips from Buddhist Workshops. Scribes and Manuscripts from Northern Thailand." JPTS XXII, 1996, pp. 35–57.

—"Lān2 Nā as a Centre of Pāli Literature During the Late 15th Century." JPTS XXVI, 2000, pp. 119–37.

Padmanabh S. Jaini, "*Akāravattārasutta*: An 'Apocryphal' Sutta from Thailand." *Indo-Iranian Journal 35,* 1992, pp. 192–223.

(Bh.) P.L. Likhitananta, "History of Buddhism in Thailand." Ph.D. diss., Magadh Univ., Patna 1970. Part I:4. Introduction of Theravāda and Pāli Literature; Part II (pp. 208–344): 1. The Golden Age of Pāli Scholarship in Northern Thailand, 2. The Pāli Literature in Fifteenth and Sixteenth Century, 3. The Pāli Literature in Seventeenth, Eighteenth and Nineteenth Century, 4. Literary Contributions of Thai Scholars.

Bunyen Limsawaddi (tr.), "Stanzas on the Ten Perfections" in *The Wisdom Gone Beyond*. Bangkok 1966.

Hans Penth, "Buddhist Literature of Lān Nā on the History of Lān Nā's Buddhism." JPTS XXIII, 1997, pp. 43–81.

H. Saddhātissa, "Pāli Literature of Thailand." *Buddhist Studies in Honour of I.B. Horner,* ed. L.S. Cousins *et al.*, Dordrecht 1974, pp. 211–25.

—"A Survey of the Pāli Literature of Thailand." *Amalā Prajñā (Professor P.V. Bapat Felicitation Volume)*, ed. N.H. Samtani and H.S. Prasad, Delhi 1989, pp. 41–46.

—Both articles repr. in *Pāli Literature of South-East Asia*. Singapore 1992, Dehiwela 2004, pp. 11–31, 61–68.

Peter Skilling, "The Sambuddha verses and later Theravādin Buddhology." JPTS XXII, 1996, pp. 151–83.

Daniel M. Veidlinger, *Spreading the Dhamma: Writing, Orality, and Textual Transmission in Buddhist Northern Thailand*. Honolulu 2006.

Kenneth E. Wells, *Thai Buddhism: Its Rites and Activities*. Bangkok 1940, 1975. A comprehensive survey which includes (in translation) all the Pāli stanzas recited on all religious, social and state occasions.

Cambodia and Laos

Jacqueline Filliozat and Peter Masefield, "Two Indo-Chinese Pali Versions of the Petavatthu." *Mahachulalongkorn Journal of Buddhist Studies* 1, 2008, pp. 11–18.

Charles Hallisey, "The Sutta on Nibbāna as a Great City." *Buddhist Essays. A Miscellany*, ed. P. Sorata Thera et al. London 1992, pp. 38–67. Repr. as "*Nibbānasutta*: an allegedly non-canonical sutta on *Nibbāna* as a Great City". JPTS XVIIII, 1993, pp. 97–130.

Peter Masefield, "Indo-Chinese Pali." *Mahachulalongkorn Journal of Buddhist Studies* 1, 2008, pp. 1–9.

—"Petavatthu Translation." *Ibid.*, pp. 19–25.

H. Saddhātissa, "Pāli Studies in Cambodia." *Buddhist Studies in honour of Walpola Rāhula,* ed. S. Balasooriya et al., London 1980, pp. 242–50.

—"Pāli Literature in Cambodia." JPTS IX, 1981, pp. 178–97.

—"Pāli Literature from Laos." *Studies in Pali and Buddhism. A Memorial Volume in Honor of Bhikkhu Jagdish Kashyap*, ed. A.K. Narain, Delhi 1979, pp. 327–40.

—All three articles repr. in *Pāli Literature of South-East Asia*. Singapore 1992, Dehiwela 2004, pp. 69–126.

5. Studies from Pāli and Related Sources

A. General Studies

Oliver Abeynayake, "Sri Lanka's Contribution to the Development of the Pali Canon." *Buddhism for the New Millenium*, London 2000, pp. 163–83.

E. W. Adikaram, *The Early History of Buddhism in Ceylon*. Colombo 1946.

G.F. Allen, *The Buddha's Philosophy*. London 1959, 2008.

Mark Allon, "The Oral Composition and Transmission of Early Buddhist Texts." *Indian Insights: Buddhism, Brahmanism and Bhakti*, ed. P. Connoly, London 1997, pp. 39–61.

Roy C. Amore, "The Concept and Practice of Doing Merit in Early Theravāda Buddhism." Ph.D. diss., Columbia (NY) 1970.

Carol S. Anderson, *Pain and its Ending. The Four Noble Truths in the Theravāda Buddhist Canon*. Richmond (Surrey) 1999, Delhi 2001.

Anālayo, "The Vicissitudes of Memory and Early Buddhist Oral Transmission." *Canadian Journal of Buddhist Studies* 5, 2009, pp. 5–19.

—"The Influence of Commentarial Exegesis on the Transmission of Āgama Literature in Translating Buddhist Chinese." *Problems and Prospects*, ed. K. Meisig, Wiesbaden 2010, pp. 1–20.

—*The Genesis of the Bodhisattva Ideal*, Hamburg, 2010.

K. Anuruddha, "Studies in Buddhist social thought as documented in the Pali tradition." Ph.D. diss., Lancaster 1972.

Harvey B. Aronson, *Love and Sympathy in Theravada Buddhism*. Delhi 1980, 1986. A survey based on the four main Nikāyas, their Commentaries and Vism.

Arnold Aronroff, "Contrasting Modes of Textual Classification: The Jātaka Commentary and its Relationship to the Pali Canon." Ph.D. diss., Chicago 1982.

A.J. Bahm, *Philosophy of the Buddha*. London 1958, New York 1969. A basic introduction extracted from the texts.

Biswanath Banerjee and Sukomal Chaudhuri (ed.), *Buddha and Buddhism*. Kolkata (Calcutta) 2005.

S.C. Banerji, *An Introduction to Pali Literature*. Calcutta 1964.

P.V. Bapat (ed.), *2500 Years of Buddhism*. Delhi 1956, 1987. Includes a survey of VP, SP and Dhp.

Egerton C. Baptist, *In the Footsteps of the Sākyamuni* (Ānupubbi-Kathā). Colombo 1962. The Buddha's gradual method of teaching.

A. Barua, "The editing of the *Peṭakopadesa*, with critical apparatus and commentary." Ph.D. diss., London 1933.

Heinz Bechert, "The Writing Down of the Tripiṭaka in Pāli." *Wiener Zeitschrift für die Kunde Südasiens* 36, pp. 45–53.

V. Bhattacharya, *Buddhist Texts as recommended by Asoka*. Calcutta 1948.

Anne M. Blackburn, *Buddhist Learning and Textual Practice in the Eighteenth-Century Lankan Monastic Culture*. Princeton 2001. Based on her doctoral dissertation (Chicago 1996), "The Play of the Teaching in the Life of the Sāsana".

Kathryn R. Blackstone, *Women in the Footsteps of the Buddha. Struggle for Liberation in the Therigatha*. London 1998.

Mabel H. Bode, "The legend of Raṭṭhapāla in the Pali Apadāna and Buddhaghosa's Commentary." *Mélanges d'Indianisme* [Sylvain Lévi felicitation volume], Paris 1911, pp. 183–92

S. Bodhesako, *Beginnings, Collected Essays*. BPS 2008. The 1st essay, "Beginnings: The Pali Suttas", on the authenticity of the Pāli Canon, was published by the BPS in 1987; the 2nd essay, "Change: An Examination of Impermanence in Experience" was originally published as *Change*, Colombo 1988.

Bhikkhu Bodhi, *The Noble Eightfold Eightfold Path*. BPS 1984.

Mathieu Boisvert, *The Five Aggregates: Understanding Theravāda Psychology and Soteriology*. Waterloo (Ontario) 1995, Delhi 1997.

George D. Bond, *The Word of the Buddha*. Colombo 1982. On the Tipiṭaka and its interpretation in Theravāda Buddhism.

Acharya Buddharakkhita, *Mettā: The Philosophy & Practice of Universal Love*. BPS 1989.

John B. Buescher, "The Buddhist Doctrine of Two Truths in the Vaibhāṣika and Theravāda Schools." Ph.D. diss., Virginia, Charlottesville 1983.

John Bullitt, *Beyond the Tipitaka. A Field-Guide to Post-canonical Pali literature* (2002). Retrieved from www.accesstoinsight.org/lib/index.html

Siddhi Butr-Indr, *The Social Philosophy of Buddhism*. Bangkok 1973.

Marie B. Byles, *Footprints of Gautama the Buddha*. London 1957, Wheaton (IL) 1967. The biography of the Buddha related by Yasa, based on texts from VP and SP.

Dennis Candy, *Peace in the Buddha's Discourses, A Compilation and Discussion*. BPS 2008.

John Ross Carter (ed.), *The Threefold Refuge in the Theravāda Buddhist Tradition*. Chambersburg (PA) 1982.

W.D. Chandima-Wijebandara, "A study of early Buddhism as a critique of its contemporary religio-philosophic milieu." Ph.D. diss., Lancaster 1974.

Pratap Chandra, *Metaphysics of Perpetual Change. The Concept of Self in Early Buddhism*. Bombay 1978.

Heramba Nath Chatterji, *Comparative Studies in Pāli and Sanskrit Alaṅkāras*. Calcutta 1960.

P. Cholvarn, "Nibbāna as Self or Not Self: Some Contemporary Thai Discussions." M.Phil. diss., Bristol 2007.

Angraj Choudhary, *Essays in Buddhism and Pali Literature*. Delhi 1994.

Steven Collins, *Selfless Persons: Imagery and thought in Theravāda Buddhism*. Cambridge 1982, 1994. Based on his doctoral dissertation (Oxford 1982), "Personal Continuity in Theravāda Buddhism".

—"On the very idea of the Pali Canon." JPTS XV, 1990, pp. 89–126. Repr. in *Buddhism. Critical Concepts in Religious Studies* I, ed. Paul Williams, Abingdon 2005, pp. 72–95.

—"Notes on Some Oral Aspects of Pāli literature." *Indo-Iranian Journal* 35, 1992, pp. 121–35.

H.S. Cooray, "The Origin and Development of Navaṅga in Buddhist Literature." M.A. thesis, Univ. of Ceylon, 1964.

L.S. Cousins, "Pali Oral Literature." *Buddhist Studies. Ancient and Modern*, ed. Philip Denwood and Alexander Piatigorsky. London 1983, pp. 1–11. Repr. in *Buddhism. Critical Concepts in Religious Studies* I, ed. Paul Williams, Abingdon 2005, pp. 96– 104.

Mary Cummings, *The Lives of the Buddha in the Art and Literature of Asia*. University of Michigan, Ann Arbor 1982. Includes a selection from the Jātakas.

Sally Cutler [Mellick], "A Critical Edition, with translation, of selected portions of the Pāli Apadāna." Ph.D. diss., Oxford 1993.

James D'Alwis, *Buddhism: its Origins, History and Doctrines, its Scriptures and their Language, Pali*. Colombo 1862, JPTS 1883, repr. 1978.

Asha Das, *A Literary Appraisal of Pali Poetical Works*. Calcutta 1994.

Subas Chandra Dash, *Bibliography of Pali and Buddhism*. Poona 1994.

G.V. Davane, *Pali Language and Literature: A Systematic Survey and Historical Study*. New Delhi 1994.

—*Language: History and Structure; Literature: Canonical Pali Texts*. New Delhi 1998.

—*Literature: Non-canonical Pali Texts. Ibid.*

C. de Saram, *The Pen Portraits of Ninety-Three Eminent Disciples of the Buddha*. Colombo 1971.

Nalini Devdas, *Cetanā and the Dynamics of Volition in Theravāda Buddhism*. Delhi 2008.

M.G. Dhadhale, *Some Aspects of Buddhist Literary Criticism, as gleaned from Pali sources*. Bombay 1975.

—*Synonymic Collocations in the Tipiṭaka: A Study*. Poona 1980.

Mark Wesley Earl, "The idea of salvation in the Vinaya and Sutta Piṭakas." MA thesis, Birmingham 1959.

James Egge, *Religious Giving and the Invention of Karma in Theravāda Buddhism*. Richmond (Surrey) 2002.

Toshiichi Endo, *Dāna: The Development of Its Concept and Practice*. Colombo 1987.

—"The Aṭṭhakathā as Source-material of the Pāli Commentaries." *Dhamma-Vinaya: Essays in Honour of Venerable Professor Dhammavihari (Jotika Dhirasekera)*, ed. Asanga Tilakaratne, *et al*. Peradeniya 2005.

—"The *Mahā-aṭṭhakathā-s*: Some Observations on the Date of of Their Compilation." *Buddhist and Pali Studies in Honour of The Venerable Professor Kakkapalliye Anuruddha*, ed. K.L. Dhammajoti and Y. Karunadasa. Hong Kong 2009, pp. 169–81.

Jan T. Ergardt, *Faith and Knowledge in Early Buddhism*. Leiden 1977. An analysis of the contextual structures of an Arahant-formula in the Majjhima Nikāya.

J. Evola, *The Doctrine of Awakening. A study on the Buddhist Ascesis.* London 1951, Rochester (Vermont) 1995. Illustrated from the four main Nikāyas, Dhp and Sn, this work remains the most radical interpretation of the subject.

P.L. Farkas, "The fourth noble truth: a study in Buddhist ethics." Ph.D. diss., Aberdeen 1931.

Rein Fernhout, *Canonical Text Bearers of Absolute Authority. Bible, Koran, Veda, Tipiṭaka: A Phenomenological Study.* Amsterdam 1994.

Ellison Banks Findly, *Dana: giving and getting in Pali Buddhism.* Delhi 2003.

Ralph Flores, *Buddhist Scriptures as Literature: Sacred Rhetoric and the Uses of Theory.* New York 2008.

Michael Freedman, "The Characterization of Ānanda in the Pali Canon of the Theravāda: A Hagiographic Study." Ph.D. diss., McMaster (Ontario) 1977.

Oliver Freiberger, "The Buddhist Canon and the Canon of Buddhist Studies." *Journal of the International Association of Buddhist Studies* 27, 2004, pp. 261–83.

(Lt.Col.) G.E. Fryer, *Note on the Pali Grammarian Kaccāyana.* Calcutta 1882.

Paul Fuller, *The Notion of Diṭṭhi in Theravāda Buddhism.* Richmond (Surrey) 2004.

Aruna K. Gamage, "Some Observations on the Exegetical Elaborations on the Pāli Canon in the Aṭṭhakathā-s". *Buddhist and Pali Studies ... Anuruddha, op. cit.*, pp. 603–16.

Wilhelm Geiger, *Pali Literature and Language.* Calcutta 1943, Delhi 1968, New Delhi 1996. Rev. by K.R. Norman as *Pāli Grammar.* PTS 1994.

Rupert Gethin, "The Five Aggregates in the Nikāyas and Early Abhidhamma." M.A. thesis, Manchester 1982.

—*The Buddhist Path to Awakening. A Study of the Bodhi-Pakkhiyā Dhammā.* Leiden 1992. Based on his doctoral dissertation, Manchester 1987.

—*The Foundations of Buddhism.* Oxford 1998.

—"Mythology as Meditation: from the Mahāsudassana Sutta to the Sukhāvatīvyūha Sūtra." JPTS XXVIII, 2006, pp. 63–112.

A.R. Giles, "Dukkha in Theravāda and Early Mahāyāna Buddhism." M.Th. thesis, King's College, London 1976.

Helmuth von Glasenapp, *Vedanta and Buddhism*. BPS 1958.
—*Buddhism and Christianity*. BPS 1959.
—*Buddhism, a Non-Theistic Religion*. New York 1966, London 1970. Includes extensive references to *devas* in the Pāli Canon.
Richard Gombrich, *How Buddhism Began: The Conditioned Genesis of the Early Teachings*. London and Atlantic Highlands (NJ) 1996, Richmond (Surrey) 2000.
—*What the Buddha Thought*. London and Oakville (CT) 2009.
L.R. Goonesekere, *Buddhist Commentarial Literature*. BPS 1967.
L. Grey, *Concordance of Buddhist Birth Stories*. PTS 1990, 2000.
Georg Grimm, *The Doctrine of the Buddha: The Religion of Reason and Meditation*. Leipzig 1926, East Berlin 1958, Delhi 1973. Despite the controversial nature of this classic tome, the author claimed that "he has built up his work exclusively on the Sutta Piṭaka."
G. Grönbold *Die Worte des Buddha in den Sprachen der Welt/The Words of the Buddha in the Languages of the World. Tipiṭaka-Tripiṭaka-Dazangjing-Kanjur*. Munich 2005.
Henepola Gunaratana, *The Path of Serenity and Insight: Explanation of the Buddhist Jhānas*. Delhi 1985, New Delhi 1995. (The American Univ., WA-DC 1980.) Based on his doctoral dissertation "A Critical Analysis of the Jhānas in Theravāda Buddhist Meditation."
Mirisse Gunasiri, *The Buddha and His Ethics*. Colombo 1962, 1965. Includes some popular *suttas* in condensed form.
R.A.L.H. Gunawardana, *Robe and Plough, Monasticism and Economic Interest in Early Medieval Sri Lanka*. Tucson 1979. Discusses the transmission and origin, etc., of several Pāli texts.
Ānanda W.P. Guruge, *Buddhism: The Religion and Its Culture*. Madras 1975, rev. ed., Colombo 1984. Includes a concise analysis of Buddhist Literature (Ch. V) together with an anthology from SP (Ch. VI).
Edith (Ludowyk-) Gyömröi, "The Role of the Miracle in Early Pali Literature." University of Ceylon doctoral dissertation, 1944.
J.R. Halder, *Early Buddhist Mythology*. New Delhi 1977. A comprehensive study based mainly on the Vimānavatthu, Petavatthu and Buddhavaṃsa.

Sue Hamilton, *Identity and Experience: The Constitution of the Human Being According to Early Buddhism.* London 1996. Based on her doctoral dissertation, Oxford 1992.

—*Early Buddhism: A New Approach.* London 2000.

Peter Harvey, "The concept of the person in Pāli Buddhist literature." Ph.D. diss., Lancaster 1982.

—*An Introduction to Buddhism: Teachings, History and Practices.* Cambridge 1990, Delhi 1990

—*The Selfless Mind: Personality and Consciousness, and Nirvana in Early Buddhism.* Richmond (Surrey) 1995.

—*An Introduction to Buddhist Ethics.* Cambridge 2000.

K.L. Hazra, *History of Theravāda Buddhism in South-East Asia.* New Delhi 1982.

—*Studies on Pali Commentaries.* New Delhi 1991.

—*Pāli Language and Literature.* 2 vols, New Delhi 1994.

—*Rise and Decline of Buddhism in India.* New Delhi 1998.

—*Buddhist Annals and Chronicles of South-East Asia.* New Delhi 2002.

Hellmuth Hecker, *Lives of the Disciples I.* BPS 1967. Contains "The Upāsaka Citta," "The Bhikkhu Citta," and "Father and Mother Nakula".

—*Life of Mahā Moggallāna.* BPS 1979.

—*Ānanda: The Guardian of the Dhamma.* BPS 1980.

—*Life of Aṅgulimāla.* BPS 1984.

—*Anāthapiṇḍika: The Great Benefactor.* BPS 1986.

—*Mahā Kassapa: Father of the Sangha.* BPS 1987.

—*Anuruddha: Master of the Divine Eye.* BPS 1989.

Oscar von Hinüber, *Selected Papers.* PTS 1995.

—*A Handbook of Pāli Literature.* Berlin, New York, New Delhi 1996.

Frank J. Hoffman, *Rationality and Mind in Early Buddhism.* Delhi 1987.

—and Deegalle Mahinda (ed.), *Pāli Buddhism.* Richmond (Surrey) 1996.

I.B. Horner, *Women under Primitive Buddhism.* London 1930, Delhi 1973, Amsterdam 1975.

—*The Early Buddhist Theory of Man Perfected. A Study of the Arahant.* London 1936, Amsterdam 1975, New Delhi 1979.

—*The Basic Position of Sīla.* BSS 1950.

—*Women in Early Buddhist Literature*. BPS 1961.
—*Early Buddhism and the Taking of Life*. BPS 1967.
Huyen-Vi, *A Critical Study of the Life and Works of Sāriputta Thera*. Saigon 1972, Linh-So'n Buddhist Association, Paris 1989.
Soon-Il Hwang, *Metaphor and Literalism in Buddhism. The Doctrinal History of Nirvāṇa*. Abingdon 2006.
John D. Ireland, *Comments on the Buddha Word*. BPS 1963.
—*The Buddha's Practical Teaching*. BPS 1965.
Louise Ireland-Frey, *The Blossom of Buddha. A novel on the life of Gautama based on the Pali Canon and other Buddhist scriptures.* Nevada City 2008.
K.N. Jayatilleke, *Early Buddhist Theory of Knowledge*. London 1963, Delhi 2004, Abingdon 2008. Based on his doctoral dissertation (London 1961), "The epistemological basis of thought of the Pali Canon, with special reference to the Nikāyas."
—"The Principles of International Law in Buddhist Doctrine." *Recueil des Cours*, Vol.120, The Hague 1967, pp. 441–567. Offpr. as *Dhamma, Man and Law*. Singapore 1988. Included in *Facets of Buddhist Thought, Collected Essays*, BPS 2010.
—*The Message of the Buddha* (ed. and intro. by Ninian Smart). London 1975, BPS 2000. Included in *Facets of Buddhist Thought, Collected Essays*, BPS 2010.
S. Jayawardhana, *Handbook of Pali Literature*. Colombo 1994.
N.A. Jayawickrama, "*Papañcasūdanī*: The Commentary to the *Majjhimanikāya*." *Journal of Buddhist Studies* (Sri Lanka) 1, 2003, pp. 73–119; 2, 2004, pp. 1–57.
Rune E.A. Johansson, *The Psychology of Nirvana*. London 1969, New York 1970. The goal of Buddhism clarified by means of SP.
—*The Dynamic Psychology of Buddhism*. London 1983. A study of *paṭiccasamuppāda* from SP.
Susan Elbaum Jootla, *Inspiration from Enlightened Nuns*. BPS 1988. An essay based on the Therīgāthā and Bhikkhunī Saṃyutta.
T. Kariyawasam, "The development of Buddhology in the early Mahāyāna and its relation to the Pali Nikāyas." Ph.D. diss., Lancaster 1974.
W.S. Karunaratne, *The Theory of Causality*. Nugegoda 1988. Based on his doctoral dissertation (London 1956), "The development of the theory of causality in early Theravāda Buddhism".

S.M. Katre, "Early Buddhist Ballads and their relation to the older Upanishadic Literature." Ph.D. diss., London 1931.

Damien Keown, *The Nature of Buddhist Ethics*. Basingstoke 1996, 2001.

Khantipālo, *Pointing to Dhamma*. Bangkok 1973. Thirty discourses based on Pāli texts.

—*Banner of the Arahants*. BPS 1979, 2008. A detailed history and account of the Bhikkhu- and Bhikkhunī-Saṅgha.

Hegoda Khemananda, *Logic and Epistemology in Theravāda*. Colombo 1993.

Kheminda, *Path Fruit and Nibbāna*. Colombo 1965. The path to Nibbāna illustrated from Pāli sources.

—*The Way of Buddhist Meditation (Serenity and Insight according to the Pali Canon)*. Colombo 1982.

Winston L. King, *In the Hope of Nibbana: The Ethics of Theravada Buddhism*. LaSalle (IL) 1964, Seattle 2001. Based on VP and SP.

Ria Kloppenborg, *The Paccekabuddha*. Leiden 1974, abridged ed. BPS 1983. A study of asceticism from canonical and commentarial literature, including a translation of Sn 1:3.

Ko Lay, *Guide to Tipiṭaka*. Rangoon 1986, Delhi 1990, Bangkok 1993, Dehiwela 1998.

Tse-fu Kuan, *Mindfulness in Early Buddhism. New Approaches through Psychology and Textual Analysis of Pāli, Chinese and Sanskrit Sources*. Abingdon 2007.

Baidyanath Labh, *Paññā in Early Buddhism*. Delhi 1991. A philosophical analysis with special reference to Vism.

Étienne Lamotte, "The Assessment of Textual Authenticity in Buddhism." *Buddhist Studies Review* 1, 1984, pp. 4–15.

—"The Assessment of Textual Interpretation in Buddhism." *Ibid.* 2, 1985, pp. 4–24.

—Both articles repr. in *Buddhism. Critical Concepts in Religious Studies* I, ed. Paul Williams, Abingdon 2005, pp. 188–213.

Bimala Churn Law, *The Life and Work of Buddhaghosa*. Calcutta 1923, Bombay 1946, Delhi 2005.

—"Non-Canonical Pali Literature." *Annals of the Bhandarkar Oriental Research Institute* (Poona) XIII, Part II (1930–31), pp. 97– 143.

—*A History of Pali Literature*. 2 vols, London 1933, Varanasi 2002. Vol. I comprises a detailed analysis of SP.

Ledi Sayadaw:[12]

1. *Bodhipakkhiya Dīpanī: The Requisites of Enlightenment.* BPS 1971, 2007.
2. *Catusacca Dīpanī: Manual of the Four Truths.*
3. *Maggaṅga Dīpanī: Manual of the Constituents of the Noble Path.* Rangoon 1961, Abingdon 1984. Rev. ed., *The Noble Eightfold Path and its Factors Explained.* BPS 1977, 1998.
4. "Sammādiṭṭhi Dīpanī: Manual of Right Understanding." *The Light of the Dhamma* N.S. II, 1982.
5. *Vipassanā Dīpanī: Manual of Insight.* Mandalay 1915, BPS 1961.
6. *Paṭṭhānuddesa Dīpanī: Buddhist Philosophy of Relations.* BPS 1986.
7. *Niyama Dīpanī: Manual of Cosmic Order.* Mandalay 1921.
8. *Alin-Kyan and Vijjāmagga Dīpanī: The Manual of Light and The Manual of the Path to Higher Knowledge.* BPS 2007.
9. *Ānāpānasati Dīpanī: Manual of Mindfulness of Breathing.* BPS 1999.
10. *Uttamapurisa Dīpanī: A Manual of the Excellent Man.* BPS 2000.

T.O. Ling, *Buddhism and the Mythology of Evil.* London 1962. A comprehensive survey of all references to Māra in the Pāli Canon.

Friedgard Lottermoser, "Quoted Verse Passages in the Works of Buddhaghosa. Materials towards the study of the Sīhaḷāṭṭhakathā." Ph.D. diss., Göttingen 1979.

James P. McDermott, *Development in the Early Buddhist Concept of Kamma/Karma.* New Delhi 1984

Joseph G. McKeon, "Faith in Early Buddhist Teachings." Ph.D. diss., Fordham (NY) 1978.

Bandu W. Madanayake, "The Concept of Saññā in Theravāda Buddhism." M.A. thesis, Toronto 1978.

12. N.B. Manuals 1 to 7 and part of 8 (*Alin*-Kyan, partially) also appeared in the first series of The Light of the Dhamma (Rangoon 1950s-60s) and were offprinted, minus manual 7, in one volume entitled The Manuals of Buddhism. Rangoon 1965, Bangkok 1978, Delhi 1997; Manuals of Dhamma, Igatpuri 1999.

—"The Study of Saṅkhāras in Early Buddhism." Ph.D. diss., Toronto 1987.

T. Magness, *Sammā Diṭṭhi. A Treatise on Right Understanding.* Bangkok circa 1960.

Mahāsi Sayadaw, *On the Nature of Nibbāna.* Rangoon 1981, Subang Jaya 1992.

—*Brahmavihāra Dhamma.* Rangoon, 1985. On the 4 Divine Abidings.

—*A Discourse on Dependent Origination.* Bangkok 1999.

Peter Masefield, *Divine Revelation in Pali Buddhism.* Colombo 1986, Abingdon 2008. Based on his doctoral dissertation (Lancaster 1980), "Thus They Once Heard: Oral Initiation in the Pali Nikāyas".

Bruce Matthews, *Craving and Salvation: A Study in Buddhist Soteriology.* Waterloo (Ontario) 1983. Based on his doctoral dissertation (McMaster 1974), "The Concept of Craving in Early Buddhism".

Junko Matsumura, "The Sumedhakathā in Pāli Literature: Summation of Theravāda-tradition versions and proof of linkage to the Northern textual Tradition." *Indogaku bukkyōggaku kenkyū* 56, 2008, pp. 1086–94. Enlarged ed., "The *Sumedhakathā* in Pāli Literature and Its Relation to the Northern Buddhist Textual Tradition", *Journal of the International College for Postgraduate Buddhist Studies* XIV, 2010, pp. 101–33.

Veerachart Nimanong, "*Theravāda* Methods of Interpretation on Buddhist Scriptures." *International Journal of Buddhist Thought & Culture* 6, Seoul 2006, pp. 77–120.

Sodo Mori, *Studies of the Pali Commentaries.* Niza 1989.

—"The Origin and History of the Bhānaka Tradition." *Ananda A. W. Guruge Felicitation Volume*, ed. Y. Karunadasa, Colombo 1990, pp. 123–29.

Supaphan Na Bangchang, "A Critical Edition of the Mūlapariyāyavagga of Majjhimanikāya-aṭṭhakathāṭīkā." Ph.D. diss., Peradeniya 1981.

Sunthorn Na Rangsi, *The Buddhist Concepts of Karma and Rebirth.* Bangkok 1976. With special reference to the Pāli Canon. Chapter IV on rebirth and the planes of existence has been reprinted as *The Four Planes of Existence in Theravāda Buddhism.* BPS 2006

Muni Shri Nāgarajji, *Āgama and Tripiṭaka: A Comparative Study I, Historical Background.* New Delhi 1986.
Hajime Nakamura, *Gotama Buddha.* Los Angeles-Tokyo 1977.
—*Indian Buddhism. A Survey with Bibliographical Notes.* Osaka 1980, Delhi 1987.
Ñāṇananda, *Concept and Reality in Early Buddhist Thought.* BPS 1971. An essay on *papañca* and *papañca-saññā-saṅkha.*
H. Ñāṇavāsa, "The development of the concept of Buddha in Pali Literature." Ph.D. diss., Univ. of Ceylon, 1964.
Ñāṇavīra Thera, *Notes on Dhamma,* 1st edition, Colombo 1963. 2nd edition, Nieuwerkerk a/d IJssel 2011. Repr. together with collected letters as *Clearing the Path,* Colombo 1987, Nieuwerkerk a/d IJssel 2011. Republished in two parts, Colombo 2001-02. Notes and essays, often polemical, arguing for a "one life" interpretation of *paṭicca-samuppāda,* etc.
—*Seeking the Path: Early Writings of Ñāṇavīra Thera (1954-1960),* Nieuwerkerk a/d IJssel 2011.
Ñāṇatusita Bhikkhu, *Reference Table of Pali Literature.* Kandy 2008. A comprehensive table listing all known Pāli texts with references.
Nārada, *The Life of Venerable Sāriputta.* Ratnapura 1929.
—*The Bodhisatta Ideal.* Colombo 1963. The Ten Perfections illustrated from the Jātakas.
—*The Buddha and His Teachings.* Saigon 1964, Colombo 1973, BMS 1977, BPS 1980.
K.R. Norman, *Pali Literature.* Wiesbaden 1983.
—"On Translating from Pāli." *One Vehicle.* Singapore 1984, pp. 77–87; *Buddhist Essays. A Miscellany. A Memorial Volume in Honour of Venerable Hammalawa Saddhātissa,* ed. P. Sorata Thera, *et al.* London 1992, pp. 1–25; *Collected Papers III.* PTS 1992, pp. 60–81.
—"The Pāli Language and Scriptures." *The Buddhist Heritage,* ed. Tadeusz Skorupski. Tring 1989, pp. 29–53; *Collected Papers IV.* PTS 1993, pp. 92–123.
—*A Philological Approach to Buddhism.* SOAS, London 1997, PTS 2006.
—"On Translating Literally." JPTS XXX, 2009, pp. 81-97.
Nyanaponika, *The Heart of Buddhist Meditation.* Colombo 1954, London 1962, 1983, New York 1969, BPS 1992, 2005, York Beach (ME) 1996. Includes MN 10 and related texts.

—*Anatta and Nibbāna.* BPS 1959, repr. in *Pathways of Buddhist Thought.* London 1971.

—*Buddhism and the God-Idea.* BPS 1962.

—*The Life of Sāriputta.* BPS 1966.

—*Contemplation of Feelings.* BPS 1993, 2008. Including a translation of the Vedanā Saṃyutta.

—*The Vision of Dhamma: Buddhist Writings of Nyanaponika Thera.* London 1986, BPS 2007.

Nyanaponika and H. Hecker, *Great Disciples of the Buddha.* Boston 1997, BPS 2007.

(Somdet Phra) Nyanasamvara (formerly Phra Sasana Sobhana). *Contemplation of the Body.* Bangkok 1974. The transcription of 19 talks on mindfulness of the body.

C. Nyanasatta, *Basic Tenets of Buddhism.* Colombo 1965.

Hermann Oldenberg, *Buddha: His Life, His Doctrine, His Order.* London 1882, Delhi 1971. The first major exposition of Buddhism in the West based entirely on the Pāli Canon.

A.R. Olendzki, "Interdependent origination and cessation: the paticca-samuppāda as an early Buddhist model of liberation." Ph.D. diss., Lancaster 1987.

G.C. Pande, *Studies in the Origins of Buddhism.* Allahabad University 1957, Delhi 1974, 2006. Includes a comprehensive analysis of the four main Nikāyas.

Lakshuman Pandey, "Buddhist Conception of Omniscience." Ph.D. diss., McMaster (Ontario) 1972.

P.A. Payutto, *A Constitution for Living.* Bangkok 1979, rev. ed., BPS 2007. A code of lay ethics based on the Sigālovāda Sutta and other suttas.

—*Good, Evil and Beyond.* Bangkok 1993. On kamma in the Buddha's Teaching.

—*Dependent Origination.* Bangkok 1994.

—*The Pali Canon. What a Buddhist Must Know.* Bangkok 2003.

Primoz Pecenko, "The History of the Nikāya Subcommentaries (*ṭīkās*) in Pāli Bibliographic Sources." JPTS XXX, 2009, pp. 5–32.

Hans H. Penner, *Rediscovering the Buddha. The Legends and Their Interpretations.* New York 2009. In Part One, classic stories of the Buddha are "drawn from various texts of Theravāda Buddhism".

T.H. Perera, *The Four Cankers*. BPS 1967. Illustrated from SP.
Joaquin Perez-Remon, *Self and Non-Self in Early Buddhism*. The Hague 1980.
Ole Holten Pind, "Buddhaghosa—His Works and Scholarly Background." *Bukkyō Kenkyū* 21, 1992, pp. 135–56.
Piyadassi, *The Buddha. His Life and Teaching*. BPS 1961. Illustrated from VP and SP.
—*The Buddha's Ancient Path*. London 1964, BPS 1974. A detailed analysis of the Four Noble Truths and Noble Eightfold Path.
Ilkka Pyysäinen, *Beyond Language and Reason. Mysticism in Indian Buddhism*. Helsinki 1993.
Walpola Rāhula, *What the Buddha Taught*. Bedford 1959, New York 1962, Dehiwela 2006. Includes a short anthology from SP.
R. Rajapaksa, "A philosophical investigation of the ethical hedonism and the theory of self implicit in the Pali Nikāyas." Ph.D. diss., London 1975.
Rajesh Rañjan, *Exegetical Literature in Pali: Origin and Development*. Delhi 2005.
Niharranjan Ray, *Theravāda Buddhism in Burma*. Calcutta, 1946, Chieng Mai 2002.
Noble Ross Reat, "The origins of Buddhist psychology." Ph.D. diss., Lancaster 1980.
C.A.F. Rhys Davids, *Buddhist Psychology*. London 1914, New Delhi 2002. An inquiry into the analysis of mind in Pāli literature. Rewritten as *The Birth of Indian Psychology and its Development in Buddhism*. London 1936.
T.W. Rhys Davids, *Buddhism: Its History and Literature*. New York 1896, Calcutta 1962, Varanasi 1975—Lecture II from *The Hibbert Lectures 1881*. London 1891. Includes probably the earliest accurate analysis of the Pāli Canon.
—*Buddhist India*. New York 1903, Calcutta 1957.
Alec Robertson, *The Triple Gem and the Uposatha*. Colombo 1971. "An analysis of the cardinal doctrinal teachings and observances associated with the Full-Moons", extensively illustrated from canonical and post-canonical sources.
R. H. Robinson & W. L. Johnson, *The Buddhist Religion: A Historical Introduction*. Belmont 1996.
H. Saddhātissa, *Buddhist Ethics: Essence of Buddhism*. London 1970, 1987.

—*The Buddha's Way*. London 1971. Includes selected suttas.
—*The Life of the Buddha*. London 1976. Includes the salient features of the Buddha's teaching mission based on VP and SP.
Pragati Sahni, *Environmental Ethics in Buddhism*. Abingdon 2007.
E.R. Saratchandra, *Buddhist Psychology of Perception*. Colombo 1958, Dehiwela 1994.
K.J. Saunders, *Gotama Buddha*. New York 1922. A biography based on the canonical account.
Juliane Schober (ed.), *Sacred Biography in the Buddhist Traditions of South and Southeast Asia*. Honolulu 1997.
Martin Seeger, "Thai Buddhist Studies and the Authority of the Pali Canon." *Contemporary Buddhism* 8, 2007, pp. 1–18.
—"Phra Payutto and Debates 'On the Very Idea of the Pali Canon' in Thai Buddhism." *Buddhist Studies Review* 26, 2009, pp. 1–31.
Ved Seth, *Study of Biographies of the Buddha based on Pali and Sanskrit sources*. New Delhi 1992.
Sarah Shaw, *Buddhist Meditation*. Richmond (Surrey) 2006, Abingdon 2008. Includes DN 2 and MN 10.
Sīlācāra, *Lotus Blossoms*. Adyar 1914, 1968. Essays on the Four Noble Truths illustrated from SP.
Sheo Kumar Singh, *History and Philosophy of Buddhism*. Patna 1982. Based mainly on Pāli canonical and exegetical literature.
K.P. Sinha, *Nairatmya-Vada: The Buddhist Theory of Not-Self.* Calcutta 1985.
L. Siridhamma, "The Theory of Kamma in Early Theravāda Buddhism." D.Phil. diss., Oxford 1976.
Peter Skilling and Santi Pakdeekham, *Pali Literature Transmitted in Central Siam*. 2 vols, PTS 2002 & 2004.
Harcharan Singh Sobti, *Nibbāna in Early Buddhism*. Delhi 1985. Based on Pāli sources from 6th BCE to 5th CE.
K.D. Somadasa, *Catalogue of the Nevill Collection of Sinhalese Manuscripts in The British Library*. 5 vols, PTS 1987–1995. Nevill's notes, etc., provide information about numerous Pāli texts.
G.A. Somaratne, "Intermediate Existence and the Higher Fetters in the Pāli Nikāyas." JPTS XXV, 1999, pp. 121–54.
R.L. Soni, *The Only Way to Deliverance*. Boulder 1980. Includes DN 22.

Susan C. Stalker, "A Study of Dependent Origination: Vasubandhu, Buddhaghosa, and the Interpretation of Pratītya-samutpāda." Ph.D. diss., Pennsylvania 1987.

John S. Strong, *The Experience of Buddhism: Sources and Interpretations*. Belmont 1995.

Bhikkhu Sujāto, *A Swift Pair of Messengers: Calm with Insight from the Buddha's Lips*. Penang 2001.

—*A History of Mindfulness: How Insight worsted Tranquility in the Satipaṭṭhāna Sutta*. Taipei 2005.

M. Sumanatissa, "Kamma and Kamma-Vipāka in the Nikāyas." M.A. thesis, Manchester 1974.

Donald K. Swearer, *A Guide to the Perplexed: The Satipaṭṭhāna Sutta*. BPS 1973.

A. Syrkin, "Notes on Pāli Canonic Style." *Pali Buddhist Review* 6, 1981–82, pp. 69–87.

S. Tachibana, *The Ethics of Buddhism*. Oxford 1926, BSS 1961, London and Totowa (NJ) 1981, Richmond (Surrey) 1995. A study from the SP.

Meena Talin, *Women in Early Buddhist Literature*. Bombay University 1972. Includes *Bhikkhunī Pātimokkha*.

Serena Tennekoon, *An Introduction to Three Sociologically Significant Buddhist Concepts; Kamma, Dāna, Dhamma*. Colombo 1981.

N. Tetley, "The Doctrine of Rebirth in Theravāda Buddhism." D.Phil. diss., Bristol 1990.

Vijay Kumar Thakur, *Social Dimensions of Buddhism*. Varanasi 2001.

Ṭhānissaro Bhikkhu (tr.), *The Mind Like Fire Unbound: An Image in Early Buddhist Discourses*. Barre (MA) 1993, rev. ed., 1999. On the use of fire imagery in early Buddhism to describe Nibbāna.

—*The Wings to Awakening*. Barre 1996. On the *bodhipakkhiyā dhammā*.

—*Noble Strategy: Essays on the Buddhist Path*. Valley Center (CA) 1999.

—*Refuge: an introduction to the Buddha, Dhamma Sangha*. *Ibid.*, 2001.

—*Purity of Heart: Essays on the Buddhist Path*. *Ibid.*, 2006.

—"Computerization of the Buddhist Scriptures for the Twenty-First Century." *Buddhism for the New Millenium*, London 2000, pp. 217–30.

E.J. Thomas, *The Life of Buddha as Legend and History*. London 1927, 1975, Delhi 2003.

—*The History of Buddhist Thought*. London 1933, Richmond (Surrey) 1997. Includes a short analysis of the Pāli Canon (pp. 266–76).

Asanga Tilakaratne, *Nirvana and Ineffability*. Postgraduate Institute of Pali and Buddhist Studies, Colombo 1993.

H.H. Tilbe, *Pali Buddhism*. Rangoon 1900, New Delhi 1979.

Mahesh Tiwary, *Sīla, Samādhi and Prajñā: The Buddha's Path of Purification*. Patna 1987.

Entai Tomomatsu, *Lectures on the Dhammapada*. Tokyo 1956–59.

—*Lectures on the Saṃyutta Ratha*. Tokyo 1960.

Tran Hoan Tru'o'ng, "A Study in the Ethics of Theravāda Buddhism." Ph.D. diss., Magadh Univ., Patna 1972.

H. Vinita Tseng, "The *Nidānavagga* of *Sāratthappakāsinī*." D.Phil. diss., Oxford 2001.

Paravahera Vajirañāṇa, *Buddhist Meditation in Theory and Practice*. Colombo 1962, BMS 1975. 'A General Exposition according to the Pali Canon of the Theravada School'.

Nina van Gorkom, *Buddhism in Daily Life*. Bangkok 1977. Illustrated by relevant passages from SP.

Tilmann Vetter, *The Ideas and Meditative Practices of Early Buddhism*. Leiden 1988. Includes conference paper, "Mysticism in the Aṭṭhakavagga".

—*The 'Khandha Passages' in the Vinayapiṭaka and the four main Nikāyas*. Vienna 2000.

A.K. Warder, *Indian Buddhism*. Delhi 1970, rev. ed. 1980.

K.S. Warnasuriya, "Social philosophy of Buddhism." Ph.D. diss., Lancaster 1975.

David Webster, *Philosophy of Desire in the Buddhist Pali Canon*. London 2005, Abingdon 2010.

W.G. Weeraratne, "The role of the individual in Buddhism according to Buddhist teachings." Ph.D. diss., Lancaster 1975. Published privately, Colombo 19--.

R.G. de S. Wettimuny, *The Buddha's Teaching: It's Essential Meaning*. Colombo 1969. Based on Ñāṇavira's radical interpretation of the earliest Nikāya material.

—*The Buddha's Teaching and the Ambiguity of Existence*, Colombo 1978.

K.D.P. Wickremesinghe, *The Biography of the Buddha*. Colombo 1972. A detailed narrative interspersed with extracts from VP and SP.

Chandima Wijebandara, *Early Buddhism, its religious and intellectual milieu*. Postgraduate Institute of Pali and Buddhist Studies, Colombo 1993.

O.H. de A. Wijesekera, *The Three Signata*. BPS 1960. Essay on *anicca, dukkha* and *anattā* illustrated from SP.

D.M. Williams, "The nature and function of the Paṭiccasamuppāda within the Theravāda canon." Ph.D. diss., Manchester 1971.

Martin Wiltshire, *Ascetic Figures before and in Early Buddhism*. Berlin 1990. Based on his doctoral dissertation (Lancaster 1980), "The Origins of the Paccekabuddha Concept".

B. Wimalaratana, "The Concept of the Mahāpurisa in Buddhist Literature and Iconography." Ph.D. diss., Lancaster 1980.

M. Winternitz, *History of Indian Literature II*. Calcutta 1933, New York 1971, New Delhi 1972.

Alexander Wynne, "The Oral Transmission of Early Buddhist Literature". *Journal of the International Association of Buddhist Studies* 27, 2004, pp. 97–127.

—"The Historical Authenticity of Early Buddhist Literature: A Critical Evaluation." *Wiener Zeitschrift für die Kunde Südasiens* XLIX, 2005, pp. 35–70.

Yashpal, *A Cultural Study of Early Pali Tipiṭakas*. 2 vols., Delhi 1998.

Ryudo Yasui, *Theory of Soul in Theravāda Buddhism*. Calcutta 1994.

Paul Younger, *The Indian Religious Tradition*. Varanasi 1970. "Studies in the concept of *duḥkha* or suffering".

Stefano Zacchetti, "Some Remarks on the '*Peṭaka* Passages' in the *Da zhidu lun* and their Relation to the Pāli *Peṭakopadesa*." *Annual Report of the International Research Institute for Advanced Buddhology at Soka Universityfor the Academic Year 2006*, Tokyo 2007, pp. 67–85.

—"An early Chinese translation corresponding to Chapter 6 of the *Peṭakopadesa*. An Shigao's *Yin chi ru jing* T 603 and its Indian original: a preliminary survey." *Bulletin of the School of Oriental and African Studies* 65, 2002, pp. 74–98.

B. Vinaya Studies

Bhikkhu Ariyesako, *The Bhikkhus' Rules: A Guide for Laypeople.* Kallista (Victoria, Australia) 1998. The Theravādin Buddhist Monk's Rules compiled and explained.

Subhra Barua, *Monastic Life of the Early Buddhist Nuns.* Calcutta 1997.

D.N. Bhagavat, *Early Buddhist Jurisprudence.* Poona 1939. A study of the Vinaya.

Anne M. Blackburn, "Looking for the *Vinaya*: Monastic Discipline in the Practical Canons of the Theravāda." *Journal of the International Association of Buddhist Studies* 22, 1999, pp. 281–309.

William M. Bodiford, *Going Forth. Visions of Buddhist Vinaya.* Honolulu 2005.

Torkel Brekke, "The Skandhaka of the Vinayapiṭaka and its Historical Value." *Wiener Zeitschrift für die Kunde Südasiens* XLII, 1998, pp. 23–40.

Jotiya Dhirasekera, *Buddhist Monastic Discipline.* Colombo 1982. Based on his doctoral dissertation (Univ. of Ceylon, 1964), "Buddhist Monastic Discipline: a study of its origin and development in relation to the Sutta and Vinaya Piṭakas".

Antony Fernando, "Buddhist Monastic Life according to the Vinaya Piṭaka and the Commentaries." Ph.D. diss., Gregorian Univ., Rome 1961.

—"Buddhist Monastic Attire." Ph.D. diss., Vidyalankara 1978.

Erich Frauwallner, *The Earliest Vinaya and the Beginnings of Buddhist Literature.* Rome 1956.

Charles Hallisey, "Apropos the Pāli Vinaya as a Historical Document." JPTS XV, 1990, pp. 197–208.

R. Spence Hardy, *Eastern Monachism*, 'An account of the origins, laws, discipline, sacred writings, religious ceremonies and present circumstances of the order of mendicants founded by Gotama Buddha.' Compiled from Sinhalese Pali manuscripts, etc. London 1850, Delhi 1989.

O.v. Hinüber, *The Oldest Pāli Manuscript. Four Folios of the Vinaya-Piṭaka from the National Archives, Kathmandu.* Untersuchungen zur Sprachgeschichte und Handschriftenkunde des Pāli II, Akademie der Wissenschaften und der Literature, Mainz. Stuttgart 1991.

—"Buddhist Law According to the Theravāda-Vinaya." *Journal of the International Association of Buddhist Studies* 18.1, 1995, pp. 7-45.
—*Ibid.*, "II: Some Additions and Corrections." *Ibid.*, 20.2, 1997, pp. 87-92.
—"Structure and Origin of the Pātimokkhasutta of the Theravādins." *Acta Orientalia Hungaricae* 51, 1998, pp. 257–65.
John C. Holt, *Discipline: The Canonical Buddhism of the Vinayapiṭaka*. Delhi 1981. Based on his doctoral dissertation, Chicago 1977.
Ute Husken, "The Legend of the Establishment of the Buddhist Order of Nuns in the Theravāda Vinaya-Piṭaka." JPTS XXVI, 2000, pp. 43–69.
Jinananda, "A study of the Pali Vinaya Mahāvagga in comparison with the corresponding sections of the Gilgit manuscripts." Ph.D. diss., London 1953.
Prince Jinavarasirivaḍḍhana, *Sāmaṇerasikkha—the Novice's Training*. Bangkok 1967.
Chatsumarn Kabilsingh, *A Comparative Study of Bhikkhunī Pātimokkha*. Varanasi 1984.
—*The Bhikkhunī Pātimokkha of the Six Schools*. Bangkok 1991.
Edith Nolot, "Studies in Vinaya Technical Terms I-III." JPTS XXII, 1996, pp. 73–150; *IV-X*. JPTS XXV, 1999, pp. 1–111.
Patrick Olivelle, *The Origin and Early Development of Buddhist Monachism*. Colombo 1974.
Maulichand Prasad, *A Comparative Study of Abhisamācārikā: Abhisamācārikā-Dharma-Vinaya of the Arya Mahāsghika-Lokottaravādins and Pali Vinaya of the Theravādins*. Patna 1984.
Charles S. Prebish, *A Survey of Vinaya Literature*. Taipei 1994, London 1996.
Ṭhānissaro Bhikkhu (Geoffrey de Graff), *The Buddhist Monastic Code I and II*. Valley Center (CA) (rev. ed.) 2007. Extensive explanation of the *Pātimokkha and Suttavibhaṅga* rules (Part I) and the *Khandhaka* regulations and rules (Part II).
Chandrika Singh Upasak, *Dictionary of Early Buddhist Monastic Terms*. Varanasi 1975, Patna 2001.
Vajirañāṇavarorasa, *Ordination Procedure*. Bangkok 1963, rev. 1990. Includes chapters explaining the basis of Vinaya.

—(tr. *Vinayamukha*), *The Entrance to the Vinaya*. 3 volumes, Bangkok 1970–83. An introduction to the Vinaya including an explanation of the *pātimokkha* rules.

—*Navakovāda. Instructions for Newly Ordained Bhikkhus and Sāmaṇeras*. Bangkok 1971. Explains basic rules to be observed.

Malcolm B. Voyce, "Aspects of the Nature of the Responsa." (An introduction to the Vinaya.) M.A. thesis, London 1977.

—"The Legal Aspects of Early Buddhist Vinaya." Ph.D. diss., London 1982.

Mohan Wijayaratna, *Buddhist Monastic Life According to the Texts of the Theravāda Tradition*. Cambridge 1990.

—*Buddhist Nuns. The Birth and Development of a Women's Monastic Order*. Colombo 2001, BPS 2010.

C. Sutta Studies

Oliver Abeynayake, *A Textual and Historical Analysis of the Khuddaka Nikāya*. Colombo 1984.

Chizen Akanuma, *The Comparative Catalogue of Chinese Āgamas & Pāli Nikāyas*. Nagoya 1929, Tokyo 1958, Delhi 1990.

Mark Allon, *Style and Function. A study of the dominant stylistic features of the prose portions of Pali canonical sutta texts and their mnemonic function*. Tokyo 1997.

—*Three Gāndhārī Ekottarikāgama-Type Sūtras*. Seattle 2001.

Anālayo, *Satipaṭṭhāna, the Direct Path to Realization*. Birmingham and BPS 2003. A detailed textual study of the Satipaṭṭhāna Sutta including its translation.

—"Some Pali Discourses in the Light of Their Chinese Parallels." 2 parts, *Buddhist Studies Review* 22, 2005, pp. 1–14, 93–105.

—"Mindfulness in the Pāli Nikāyas." *Buddhist Thought and Applied Psychological Research*, ed. K. Nauriyal, Abingdon 2006, pp. 229–49.

—(with Rod Bucknell) "Correspondence Table for Parallels to the Discourses of the Majjhima Nikāya: Toward a Revision of Akanuma's Comparative Catalogue." *Journal of the Centre for Buddhist Studies* 4, 2006, pp. 215–43.

—"Who Said It? Authorship Disagreements between Pāli and Chinese Discourses." *Festschrift für Michael Hahn*, ed. Konrad Klaus and Jens-Uwe Hartmann, Vienna 2007, pp. 25–38.

—"The Vekhanassa-sutta and its Madhyama-āgama Parallel—A Case Study in the Transmission of the Pāli Discourses." *Journal of the Centre for Buddhist Studies, Sri Lanka* 5, 2007, pp. 89–104.
—"Comparative Notes on the Madhyama-āgama." *Fuyuan Buddhist Studies* 2, 2007, pp. 33–56.
—"Oral Dimensions of Pāli Discourses: Pericopes, other Mnemonic Techniques, and the Oral Performance Context." *Canadian Journal of Buddhist Studies* 3, 2007, pp. 5–33.
—"The Verses on an Auspicious Night, Explained by Mahākaccāna—A Study and Translation of the Chinese Version" [of the Mahākaccānabhaddekaratta-sutta]. *Ibid.*, 4, 2008, pp. 5–29.
—"The Vicissitudes of Memory and Early Buddhist Oral Transmission." *Ibid.*, 5, 2009.
—"The Chinese Madhyama-āgama and the Pāli Majjhima-nikāya—In the Footsteps of Thich Minh Chau." *The Indian International Journal of Buddhist Studies* 9, 2008, pp. 1–21.
—"Reflections on Comparative *Āgama* Studies." *Chung-Hwa Buddhist Journal* 21, 2008, pp. 3–22.
—*From Craving to Liberation—Excursions into the Thought-world of the Pāli Discourses*, Part 1. New York 2009. Collection of revised articles originally published in the *Encyclopaedia of Buddhism*.
—*From Grasping to Emptiness—. . .*, Part 2. *Ibid.*, 2010. *Ibid.*
—"*Views and the Tathāgata*—A Comparative Study and Translation of the *Brahmajāla* in the Chinese *Dīrgha-āgama*." *Buddhist and Pali Studies in Honour of The Venerable Professor Kakkapalliye Anuruddha*, ed. K.L. Dhammajoti and Y. Karunadasa. Hong Kong 2009, pp. 183–234.
—"The Development of the Pāli *Udāna* Collection." *Bukkyō Kenkyū* 37, 2009, pp. 39–72.
—"Karma and Liberation—The *Karajakāya-sutta* (AN 10.208) in the Light of its Parallels." *Pāsādikadānaṃ. Festschrift für Bhikkhu Pāsādika*, ed. Martin Straube *et al.*, Marburg 2009, pp. 1–24.
—"Qualities of a True Recluse (*Samaṇa*)—According to the *Samaṇamaṇḍikā-sutta* and its *Madhyama-āgama* Parallel." *Journal of the Centre for Buddhist Studies* VII, 2009, pp. 153–84.
—"The *Āneñjasappāya-sutta* and its Parallels on Imperturbability and on the Contribution of Insight to the Development of Tranquillity." *Buddhist Studies Review* 26, 2009, pp. 177–95.

—"The *Bahudhātuka-sutta* and its Parallels on Women's Inabilities." *Journal of Buddhist Ethics* 16, 2009, pp. 136–90.

—"The Buddha's Truly Praiseworthy Qualities According to the *Mahāsakuludāya-sutta* and its Chinese Parallel." JPTS XXX, 2009, pp. 137–60.

—"Structural Aspects of the Majjhima-nikāya." *Bukkyō Kenkyū* 38, 2010, pp. 35–70.

—"Saccaka's Challenge—A Study of the Saṃyukta-āgama Parallel to the Cūḷasaccaka-sutta in Relation to Notion of Merit Transfer." *Chung-Hwa Buddhist Journal* 23, 2010, pp. 39–70.

—"Teachings to Lay-Disciples: The *Saṃyukta-āgama* Parallel to the *Anāthapiṇḍika-sutta*." *Buddhist Studies Review* 27, 2010, pp. 3–14.

—"Once again on Bakkula." *The Indian International Journal of Buddhist Studies* 11, 2010, pp. 1–28

Masaharu Anesaki, "Traces of Pali Texts in a Mahāyāna Treatise" (Mahāprajñāpāramitāśāstra). *Le Muséon* VII, Louvain 1906, pp. 33–45.

—*The Four Buddhist Āgamas in Chinese. A Concordance of their parts and of the corresponding counterparts in the Pāli Nikāyas.* Tokyo 1908.

Naomi Appleton, *Jātaka Stories in Theravāda Buddhism. Narrating the Bodhisatta Path.* Farnham and Burlington (VT) 2010.

B.P. Bapat, "The Different Strata in the Literary Material of the Dīgha Nikāya." *Annals of the Bhandarkar Oriental Research Institute* VIII, 1926, pp. 1–16.

D.K. Barua, *An Analytical Study of Four Nikāyas.* Calcutta 1971, New Delhi 2003. An outline of DN, MN, SN and AN.

Marcus Bingenheimer, "The *Suttas* on Sakka in *Āgama* and *Nikāya* Literature—With Some Remarks on the Attribution of the Shorter Chinese *Saṃyukta-āgama*." *Buddhist Studies Review* 25, 2006, pp. 149–73.

Kathryn Rennie Blackstone, *Women in the Footsteps of the Buddha.* Richmond (Surrey) 1998. Based on her M.A. thesis (McMaster, Ontario, 1990), "The Struggle for Liberation in the Therīgāthā".

Bodhesako, *Beginnings: The Pali Suttas.* BPS 1984. Reprinted in *Beginnings: Collected Papers of S. Bodhesako*. BPS 2008.

Roderick S. Bucknell, "The Structure of the *Sagātha-Vagga* of the *Saṃyutta-Nikāya*." *Buddhist Studies Review* 24, 2007, pp. 7–34.

Grace G. Burford, *Desire, Death and Goodness. The Conflict of Ultimate Values in Theravāda Buddhism*. New York 1991. Based on the Aṭṭhakavagga, Mahāniddesa and Paramatthajotikā II.

Burma Piṭaka Association, *Ten Suttas from Dīgha Nikāya. Three Fundamental Concepts and Comments on Salient Points in each Sutta*. Rangoon 1985.

Choong Mun-keat, *The Notion of Emptiness in Early Buddhism*. Singapore 1995, Delhi 1999. Based on his M.A. thesis, Univ. of Queensland 1994.

—*The Fundamental Teachings of Early Buddhism. A comparative study based on the Sūtrāṅga portion of the Pāli Saṃyutta-Nikāya and the Chinese Saṃyuktāgama*. Wiesbaden 2000. Based on his doctoral dissertation, Univ. of Queensland 1998.

—*Annotated Translation of Sūtras from the Chinese Saṃyuktāgama relevant to the Early Buddhist Teachings on Emptiness and the Middle Way*. Penang 2004.

—"A comparison of the Pali and Chinese versions of the *Kosala Saṃyutta*, an early Buddhist discourse on King Pasenadi of Kosala." *The Indian International Journal of Buddhist Studies* 7, 2006, pp. 21–35.

—"*A Comparison of the Pāli and Chinese Versions of the Bhikkhu Saṃyutta*, a Collection of Early Buddhist Discourses on Monks." *Buddhist Studies Review* 23, 2006, pp. 61–70.

—"A Comparison of the Pāli and Chinese Versions of the *Vaṅgīsa-thera Saṃyutta*, a Collection of Early Buddhist Discourses on the Venerable Vaṅgīsa." *Ibid.*, 24, 2007, pp. 35–45.

—"A Comparison of the Pāli and Chinese Versions of the Brāhmaṇa Saṃyutta, a collection of Early Buddhist Discourses on the priestly Brāhmaṇas." *Journal of the Royal Asiatic Society* 19, 2009, pp. 371–82.

Nissim Cohen, "A Note on the Origin of the Pāli Dhammapada Verses." *Buddhist Studies Review* 6, 1989, pp. 130–52.

Sally Mellick Cutler, "The Pāli Apadāna Collection." JPTS XX, 1994, pp. 1–42.

—"A Critical Edition with Selected Portions of the Pāli Apadāna (Yasodharāpadāna)." Ph.D. diss., Oxford 1997.

Gokuldas De, *Significance and Importance of Jātakas with special reference to Bharhut*. University of Calcutta 1951.

Bh. K. Dhammajoti, "The Mahāpadāna Suttanta and the Buddha's Spiritual Lineage." *Sri Lanka Journal of Buddhist Studies* I, 1987, pp. 187–96.

—"The Origin and Development of the Dharmapada." *Ibid.*, IV, 1994, pp. 49–68.

Nalinaksha Dutt, "The Brahmajāla Sutta." *Indian Historical Quarterly* 8, 1932, pp. 706–46.

Stephen Evans, "Doubting the *Kālāma Sutta*: Epistemology, Ethics, and the Sacred." *Buddhist Studies Review* 24, 2007, pp. 91–107.

—"Epistemology of the *Brahmajāla Sutta.*" *Ibid.*, 26, 2009, pp. 67–84.

Leon Feer, *A Study of the Jātakas, analytical and critical.* Calcutta 1963.

Mavis Fenn, "The *Kūṭadanta Sutta*: Tradition in Tension." *Buddhist Studies from India to America: essays in honor of Charles S. Prebish*, ed. Damien Keown. Abingdon and New York 2005, pp. 78–88.

Ernesto Fernandez, *A Guide to the Udāna*. (based on John D. Ireland *The Udāna*, op. cit.). Retrieved on 31.3.2011 from http://www.bps.lk/other library/guide to the udana.pdf.

Peter G. Friedlander, "Dhammapada: Translations and Recreations." *One Word, Many Versions*, ed. R. Palapathwala and A. Karickam. Tiruvalla-1 (Kerala) 2007, pp. 54–76.

—"Dhammapada Traditions and Translations." *Journal of Religious History* 33, 2009, pp. 218–37.

Sean Gaffney, "The Pāli *Nidānakathā* and its Tibetan Translation: Its Textual Precursors and Associated Literature." *The Buddhist Forum* IV, ed. Tadeusz Skorupski, SOAS, London 1996, pp. 75–91.

Rupert Gethin, "What's in a Repetition? On Counting the Suttas of the Saṃyutta-nikāya." JPTS XXIX, 2007, pp. 365–87.

Andrew Glass, *Four Gāndhārī Saṃyuktāgama Sūtras.* Seattle 2007.

P. Gnanarama, *The Mission Accomplished: A Historical Analysis of the Mahāparinibbāna Sutta of the Dīgha Nikāya of the Pāli Canon.* Singapore 1997.

—*Aspects of Early Buddhist Sociological Thought.* Singapore 1998.

Richard Gombrich, "The Buddha's Book of Genesis?". *Indo-Iranian Journal* 35, 1992, pp. 159–78. Repr. in *Buddhism.*

– *Critical Concepts in Religious Studies* I, ed. Paul Williams, Abingdon 2005, pp. 129–46.

Ronald M. Green, "Buddhist Economic Ethics: A Theoretical Approach." *Ethics, Wealth and Salvation*, ed. Russell F. Sizemore and Donald K. Swearer, Columbia 1990: "The Aggañña Sutta", pp. 227–34.

Devaprasad Guha, "Relative Antiquity of the Khuddakanikāya Texts—A Suggestion." *Journal of the Dept. of Pali* 3, Univ. of Calcutta, 1985–86, pp. 86–98.

K. Gunaratana, *Maṅgala Sutta Vaṇṇana*. Penang 1952. A commentary on the Maṅgala Sutta.

Hellmuth Hecker, *Similes of the Buddha*. BPS 2009. A description of the similes in the Pali Canon.

I.B. Horner, "Mahā- and Cūḷa-Vaggas and Suttas in the Majjhima-Nikāya." *University of Ceylon Review* XI.3–4, 1953, pp. 1–6. Repr. in *Indianisme et Bouddhisme. Mélanges offerts à Mgr Étienne Lamotte*, Louvain-la-Neuve 1980, pp. 191–6.

—"Some Notes on the *Buddhavaṃsa* Commentary (*Madhuratthavilāsinī*)." *Buddhist Studies in honour of Walpola Rahula*, ed. S. Balasooriya *et al.*, London 1980, pp. 73–83.

John D. Ireland, "The Significance of the Sutta Nipāta in Buddhism." *The Buddhist* [The Sangha Association, London], October 1965, pp. 240–47.

—"The Kosambi Suttas." *Pali Buddhist Review* 1, 1976, pp. 105–21.

N.A. Jayawickrama, "A Critical Analysis of the Pali Sutta-Nipāta." Serialised in *University of Ceylon Review* VI–IX, 1948– 51, and *Pali Buddhist Review* 1-3, London 1976–78. Based on his doctoral dissertation (London 1947), "A critical analysis of the Pali Sutta-Nipāta illustrating its gradual growth".

—"The Exegesis of the Sabbāsavasutta." *The Journal of the Centre for Buddhist Studies [Sri Lanka]* 3, 2005, pp. 42–84.

John Garrett Jones, *Tales and Teachings of the Buddha. The Jātaka Stories in relation to the Pali Canon*. London 1979.

David J. Kalupahana, *Causality: The Central Philosophy of Buddhism*. Honolulu 1975. Based on his doctoral dissertation (London 1967), "A critical analysis of the early Buddhist theory of causality as embodied in the Pali Nikāyas and the Chinese Āgamas".

—"A Buddhist tract on empiricism." *Philosophy East and West* XIX.1, 1969, pp. 65–67. Texts and translations of SN IV 15 (Sabba Sutta) and its Chinese recension.

Kassapa, *The Simpler Side of the Buddhist Doctrine*. BPS 1960. Extracts from SP with commentary.

Nathan Katz, *Buddhist Images of Human Perfection. The Arahant of the Sutta Piṭaka compared with the Bodhisattva and the Mahāsiddha*. Delhi 1982.

Khantipālo, "Where's that Sutta? A guide to the Discourses in the Numerical Collection (Aṅguttara-nikāya) listing subjects, similes, persons and places." JPTS X, 1985, pp. 37–153.

Gisela Krey, "Remarks on the Two Suttas: *Cūḷavedalla-Sutta* and *Khemā (Therī)-Sutta*" (from "On Women as Teachers in Early Buddhism: Dhammadinnā and Khemā"). *Buddhist Studies Review* 27, 2010, pp. 23–38.

Tse-fu Kuan, "Annotated Translation of the Chinese Version of the *Kāyagatāsati Sutta*." *The Indian International Journal of Buddhist Studies* 8, 2007, pp. 175–94.

Étienne Lamotte, "Khuddakanikāya and Kṣudrakapiṭaka." *East and West* VII, 1957, pp. 341–48.

M.T. Lwin, "A Study of Pali-Burmese *nissaya*, with Special Reference to the Mahāparinibbāna-sutta." M.A. thesis, London 1961.

Larry G. McClury, "The 'Vessantara Jātaka': Paradigm for a Buddhist utopian ideal." Ph.D. diss., Princeton 1975.

Leslie Clifford McTighe, "Mentoring in the 'Majjhima Nikāya': a study of the canonical Buddha's instruction of the laity." Ph.D. diss., Northwestern, Evanston 1988.

Joy Manné, "Categories of Sutta in the Pāli Nikāyas." JPTS XV, 1990, pp. 29–87.

—"The Dīgha Nikāya Debates." *Buddhist Studies Review* 9, 1992, pp. 117–36.

—"On a Departure Formula and its Translation." *Ibid.*, 10, 1993, pp. 27–43.

—"Case Histories from the Pāli Canon I: The Sāmaññaphala Sutta Hypothetical Case History." JPTS XXI, 1995, pp. 1–34; II: "*Sotāpanna, Sakadāgāmin, Anāgāmin, Arahat*—The Four Stages Case History." *Ibid.*, pp. 35–128.

—"*Sīhanāda*—The Lion's Roar." *Buddhist Studies Review* 13, 1996, pp. 7–36.

Konrad Meisig, "Chung Têh King. The Chinese Parallel to the Soṇadaṇḍa-Sutta." *Kalyāṇa-Mitta. Professor Hajime Nakamura Felicitation Volume*, ed. V.N. Jha, Delhi 1991, pp. 51–62.

—"On the Archetype of the Ambāṣṭasūtra." *Wiener Zeitschrift für Kunde Südasiens—Supplementband*, 1993, pp. 229–37.

—"On the Precanonical Shape of the *Kevaddha-sutta* as Compared with the *Kien-ku-King*." *Premier Colloque Étienne Lamotte*, Louvain-la-Neuve 1993, pp. 63–70.

—"A Translation of the Chinese Kevaddhasutta Together with the Critical Apparatus of the Pāli Text." *Festschrift Dieter Schlingloff*, ed. Friedrich Wilhelm, Reinbek 1996, pp. 187–200.

—"A Stratification of the Śoṇatāṇḍyasūtra." *Studia Tibetica et Mongolica (Festschrift Manfred Taube)*, ed. Helmut Eimer *et al.*, Swisttal-Odendorf 1999, pp. 217–24.

Minh Chau, *The Chinese Mādhyama Āgama and Pāli Majjhima Nikāya*. Saigon 1964, Delhi 1991.

Hōjun Nagasaki, "The Khaggavisāṇa-sutta and the Pacceka-buddha". *The Buddhist Seminar* 55, 1993, pp. 1–14.

—"The Rhinoceros Sūtra." *Nyāya-Vasiṣṭha. Felicitation Volume of Prof. V.N. Jha*, Kolkata 2006, pp. 279–84.

U Ñāṇadicca, *The Thirty-Eight Blessings for World Peace*. A translation of and word-for-word commentary on the Maṅgala Sutta.

N.P. Nimalasuria (tr.) and Mahāgoda Nyāṇissara (rev.), *Dhamma Hadaya Vibhaṅga Sutta* (from the apocryphal Sutta-saṅgaha). Colombo (?) 1910.

K.R. Norman, "Notes on the Sutta-nipāta." *Sri Lanka Journal of Buddhist Studies I*, 1987, pp. 100–16; *Collected Papers III*. PTS 1992, pp. 137–56.

—"The Dhaniya-Sutta of the Sutta-nipāta." *Journal of the Department of Pali*. University of Calcutta IV, 1987–88, pp. 10- 18; *Collected Papers IV*. PTS 1993, pp. 146–54.

—"On Translating the Dhammapada." *Buddhist Studies Review* 6, 1989, pp. 153–65.

—"The Aṭṭhakavagga and early Buddhism." *Jainism and Early Buddhism. Essays in Honor of Padmanabh S. Jaini*, ed. Olle Qvarnström, Fremont (CA) 2003, pp. 511–22; *Collected Papers VIII*. PTS 2007, pp. 167–82.

—"The structure of the Sādhu-sutta" [SN I, 20–22]. *Śemuṣi. Padmabhūṣaṇa Professor Baladeva Upādhyāya Birth Centenary Volume*, Varanasi 2004, pp. 660–63; *Collected Papers VIII*. PTS 2007, pp. 216–23.

—"On Translating the Suttanipāta." *Buddhist Studies Review* 21, 2004, pp. 69–84.

U Nu, *What are Maṅgalas?* Rangoon 1962. A commentary on the Maṅgala Sutta.

Hermann Oldenberg, "The Sutta Nipāta, a Collection of Old Buddhist Poems." *The Buddhist Review II* [The Buddhist Society of Great Britain and Ireland, London], pp. 243–68.

P. Oliver, "A critical analysis of the Pali Khuddaka Nikāya in a historical and literary perspective." Ph.D. diss., Lancaster 1972.

W. Pachow, *Comparative Studies in the Mahāparinibbāna Sutta and its Chinese Versions*. Shantiniketan 1946.

Sudharma Pandita, "The Role of Similes in the Pali Nikāyas." *Buddhist Philosophy and Culture. Essays in Honour of N.A. Jayawickrema*, ed. David J. Kalupahana and W.G. Weeraratne, Colombo 1987, pp. 279–85.

Bh. M. Paññāsiri, "Sigālovada-Sutta." *Visva-Bharati Annals* III, Shantiniketan 1950, pp. 150–228. Annotated translation of the four Chinese recensions of this text

Bh. Pāsādika, "The Madhyamāgama Parallel to the Rathavinīta Sutta of the Majjhimanikāya." *Buddhism for the New Millenium*, London 2000, pp. 193–205.

—"The *Ekottarāgama* Parallel to *Aṅguttaranikāya* III, 57–62 (V.50). Translated from the Chinese Version." *Jaina-Itihāsa-Ratna. Festschrift für Gustav Roth zum 90. Geburtstag*, ed. Ute Hüsken *et al.*, Marburg 2006, pp. 397–406.

—"The *Ekottarāgama* Parallel to the *Mūlapariyāyasutta.*" *The Indian International Journal of Buddhist Studies* 9, 2008, pp. 141–49.

W. Pemaratana, "An Introduction to [the] Aggaññasutta." *Essays in Honour of Professor Lily de Silva*. Peradeniya 2001.

L.P.N. Perera, "An Analysis of the Sela Sutta of the Sutta Nipāta." *Pali Buddhist Review* 4, 1979, pp. 66–70. Repr. from *University of Ceylon Review* VIII.3, 1950.

Piyasīlo, *Translating Buddhist Sutras* (sic). Petaling Jaya 1989.

Chandra Shekhar Prasad, "Some Reflections on the Relation between the Āgamas and the Nikāyas." *Proceedings and Papers of the Second Conference of the International Association of Buddhist Studies*, Nalanda 1985, pp. 131–40.

P.D. Premasiri, *The Philosophy of the Aṭṭhakavagga*. BPS 1972. An elucidation of the themes in Sn 4.

Christopher D.C. Priestley, *A Study of the Pāli and Chinese Versions of the Mahānidānasuttanta*. Toronto 1966.

Vijitha Rajapakse, "Therigāthā: On Feminism, Aestheticism and Religiosity in an early Buddhist verse anthology." *Buddhist Studies Review* 12, 1995, pp. 7–26, 135–55. Offprinted as *The Therīgāthā*. BPS 2000.

Richard Salomon, *A Gāndhārī Version of the Rhinoceros Sūtra*. Seattle 2000.

Jampa Samten, "Notes on the Study of [the] Pali Version and Tibetan Translation of [the] *Mahāparinirvāṇasūtra*." *Mahayana Buddhism. History and Culture*, ed. Darrol and Susan Bryant, New Delhi 2008, pp. 101–10.

Sadhanchandra Sarkar, *A Study on the Jātakas and the Avadānas*. Calcutta 1981.

B.C. Sen, *Studies in the Buddhist Jātakas*. Calcutta 1930, 1974.

Eviatar Shulman, "Mindful Wisdom: The Satipaṭṭhāna-sutta on Mindfulness, Memory and Liberation." *History of Religions* 49, 2010, pp. 393–420.

Peter Skilling, "Jātaka and Paññāsa-jātaka in Southeast Asia." JPTS XXVIII, 2006, pp. 113–73.

R.L. Soni, *Life's Highest Blessing*. Mandalay 1956, BPS 1978. A commentary on the Maṅgala Sutta.

Ajahn Sucitto, *Turning the Wheel of Truth. Commentary on the Buddha's First Teaching*. Boston 2010.

A. Syrkin, "On the First Work in the Sutta-Piṭaka: the Brahmajāla-Sutta." *Buddhist Studies Ancient and Modern*, ed. Philip Denwood and Alexander Piatigorsky, London 1983, pp. 153–66. (Thich) Thiên Thanh, "A comparative study of the Pāli Dīgha-Nikāya and Chinese Dīrghāgama." Ph.D. diss., Magadh Univ., Patna 1976.

Susunaga Weeraperuma, *The First and Best Buddhist Teachings: Sutta Nipāta, Selections and Inspired Essays*. Delhi 2006.

Raymond B. Williams, "Historical Criticism of a Buddhist Scripture: The Mahāparinibbāna Sutta." *Journal of the American Academy of Religion* 38, 1970, pp. 156–67.

Alexander Wynne, "How old is the Suttapiṭaka?" (2003). Retrieved on 32.3.2011 from http://www.buddhanet.net/budsas/ebud/ebsut056.htm.

D. Abhidhamma Studies

Alka Barua, *Kathāvatthu: A Critical and Philosophical Study*. Delhi 2006.

Amal K. Barua, *Mind and Mental Factors in Early Buddhist Psychology*. New Delhi 1990.

N.K. Bhagwat, *The Buddhistic Philosophy of the Theravada School, as embodied in the Pali Abhidhamma*. Patna University 1929.

Lance Cousins, "The Paṭṭhāna and the Development of the Theravādin Abhidhamma." JPTS IX, 1981, pp. 22–46. Repr. in *Buddhism. Critical Concepts in Religious Studies* IV, ed. Paul Williams, Abingdon 2005, pp. 52–70.

S.N. Dube, *Cross Currents in Early Buddhism*. Delhi 1980. A critical analysis of the Kathāvatthu.

Erich Frauwallner, "The Abhidharma of the Pali School." *Abhidharma Literature and the Origins of Buddhist Philosophical Systems*, New York 1995, pp. 39–95.

Rupert Gethin, "The *Mātikas*: memorization, mindfulness and the list." *In the Mirror of Memory. Reflections on Mindfulness and Rembrance in Tibetan Buddhism*, ed. Janet Gyatso. Albany (NY) 1992, pp. 149–72.

—"On the Nature of dhammas." *Buddhist Studies Review* 22, 2005, pp. 175–94. Review article on Noa Ronkin (see below).

Nina van Gorkom, *Abhidhamma in Daily Life*. Bangkok 1975.

—*Cetasikas*. Bangkok 1977.

—*Conditionality of Life. An Outline of the Twenty-Four Conditions as Taught in the Abhidhamma*. London 2010.

Lama Anāgārika Govinda, *The Psychological Attitude of Early Buddhist Philosophy—and its Systematic Representation according to the Abhidhamma Tradition*. London 1961.

Herbert V. Guenther, *Philosophy and Psychology in the Abhidharma*. Delhi 1974.

David J. Kalupahana, "The Philosophy of Relations in Buddhism" (a study of the Paṭṭhāna). M.A. thesis, Univ. of Ceylon, 1961.

Y. Karunadasa, *Buddhist Analysis of Matter*. Colombo 1967.

—*The Dharma Theory, Philosophical Cornerstone of the Abhidhamma*. BPS 1996.
—*The Theravada Abhidhamma*. Hong Kong, 2010.
Jagdish Kashyap, *The Abhidhamma Philosophy II*. Benares 1943, Patna 1954, Delhi 1982, New Delhi 1996. Comprises an analysis of this Piṭaka.
Ledi Sayadaw, *Paṭṭhānuddesa Dīpanī: Manual of the Philosophy of Relations*. Rangoon 1935. Reprinted as *The Buddhist Philosophy of Relations*. BPS 1986.
U Nārada, *Guide to Conditional Relations I*. PTS 1979, *II* Rangoon 1986.
Nyanaponika, *Abhidhamma Studies*. Dodanduwa 1949, BPS 1965, 2007. Essays mainly based on the Dhammasaṅgaṇī and Atthasālinī.
Nyanatiloka, *Guide through the Abhidhamma Piṭaka*. BSS 1938, BPS 1971, 2008.
Aloysius Pieris, s.j., *Studies in the Philosophy and Literature of Pali Abhidhammika Buddhism*. Colombo 2007.
Karl H. Potter (ed.), *Encyclopedia of Indian Philosophy VII*: Abhidhamma Buddhism to 150 A.D. New Delhi 1996.
Noa Ronkin, *Early Buddhist Metaphysics. The Making of a Philosophical Tradition*. Richmond (Surrey) 2005.
G.D. Sumanapala, *An Introduction to Theravāda Abhidhamma*. Singapore 1998.
—*Reality and Expression, A Study on the Conception of Paññatti in the Theravāda Abhidhamma*. Kadugannawa 1999.
Chandra B. Varma, *A Concise Encyclopaedia of Early Buddhist Philosophy based on the study of the Abhidhammatthasaṅgaha-sarūpa*. Delhi 1992.
—*Methodology for editing and translating a source material on history of science and the text of the Abhidhammathasaṅgahasarūpa*. Delhi 1995.
Alfonsa Verdu, *Early Buddhist Philosophy in the Light of the Four Noble Truths*. Delhi 1985. Based primarily on the Abhidharmakośa and Vism.
(Paṭṭhān Sayadaw) U Visuddha and Myanaung U Tin, *An Approach to Paṭṭhāna*. Rangoon 1956.
Fumimaro Watanabe, *Philosophy and its Development in the Nikāyas and Abhidhamma*. Delhi 1981.

Alexander Wynne, "The Buddha's 'Skill in Means' and the Genesis of the Five Aggregate Teaching." (Focussing on MN 22.) *Journal of the Royal Asiatic Society* 20, 2010, pp. 191–216.

6. Journals

Innumerable popular Buddhist magazines and academic periodicals of the Royal Asiatic Society (JRAS), European, American, Indian, Sri Lankan and Thai University Oriental faculties and learned societies publish translations from the Pāli Canon together with studies of the language and later or related literature in their periodicals. Invaluable studies are recorded in the journals of the Pali Text Society (JPTS 1882–1927, reprinted 1978, and revived in 1981). However, four journals should be singled out for special mention:

The Blessing, ed. Cassius A. Perera (later Kassapa Thera), published by the Servants of the Buddha, Bambalapitiya, Sri Lanka. This appeared in ten issues during 1925 and contained, almost exclusively, translations from the SP (notably MN 51–70) by Nārada and Mahinda.

The Light of the Dhamma, ed. David Maurice for the Union Buddha Sāsana Council, Rangoon 1952–63. Apart from containing (on average) two *suttas* in each issue, this quarterly provided the first popular outlet for the writings of Ledi Sayadaw, Ñāṇamoli, Nyanaponika, Nyanasatta, Nyanatiloka, Francis Story and other leading Theravādins. Many of their translations and essays subsequently appeared in *The Wheel* series of the Buddhist Publication Society, Kandy.

Pali Buddhist Review, ed. Russell Webb for the Pali Buddhist Union, Ilford, Essex (later London) 1976–82. This appeared thrice yearly and included translations and exegeses.

Buddhist Studies Review, the successor of the *Pali Buddhist Review*, ed. Russell Webb and Sara Boin-Webb from 1983 to 2004 (from 1998 on behalf of the UK Association for Buddhist Studies).

Sridhar Tripathi (ed), *Encyclopaedia of Pali Literature*. 20 vols, Pune 2008.

7. Encyclopedias

B. Baruah and N.K. Singh, *Encyclopaedic Dictionary of Pali Literature*. 2 vols, Delhi 2003.
Robert E. Buswell (ed.), *Encyclopaedia of Buddhism*. 2 vols, New York 2004.
Ian C. Harris, *Illustrated Encyclopaedia of Buddhism*. London 2009.
Edward A. Irons, *Encyclopaedia of Buddhism*. New York 2008.
Damien Keown *et al.*, *A Dictionary of Buddhism*. Oxford 2003.
Damien Keown and Charles S. Prebish (ed.), *Encyclopaedia of Buddhism*. Abingdon 2007.
T.O. Ling, *A Dictionary of Buddhism*. New York 1972, Calcutta 1996.
Stephan Schuhmacher and Gert Woerner (ed.), *The Rider Encyclopaedia of Eastern Philosophy and Religion*. London 1989, 1999. The sections on Buddhism were offprinted as *The Shambhala Dictionary of Buddhism and Zen*. Boston 1991.

Encyclopaedia of Buddhism

G.P. Malalasekera et al., *Encyclopaedia of Buddhism*. Colombo 1961–2009. The most informative and relevant entries comprise the following. References to DN, MN and It reflect the *sutta* no. in each collection and Sn according to suttas within each *vagga*. However, as regards SN and AN, the suttas are numbered according to their provenance in the *saṃyuttas* and *nipātas* respectively. In AN I, e.g., the PTS Translation Vol.I (The Book of the Ones) has each of Chapters I–XIII (pp. 1–15) including the specific number of suttas for each section followed by Chapter XIV divided into sections (a) to (g). For the purposes of achieving a continuous sequence of suttas, I have calculated that the first thirteen chapters comprise 177 suttas and have counted those sections in Ch.XIV as seven suttas, numbering the succeeding suttas accordingly.

Abhabba Sutta (AN 10:76), Fasc. A–Aca, 1961, p.10
Abhaya S. (SN 46:56; AN 4:184), *ibid.*, 33–34
Abhayarājakumāra S. (MN 58), *ibid.*, 32
Abibhū S. (AN 3:80, 8:65), *ibid.*, 36–37
Abhidhamma, *ibid.*, 37–49
Abhidhammatha-Saṅgaha, *ibid.*, 50–51

Abhidhammāvatāra, *ibid.*, 52–53
Abhidharma Literature, *ibid.*, 64–68, 75–80
Abhijāna S. (SN 22:24), *ibid.*, 90
Abhinandamāna S. (SN 22:64), *ibid.*, 93–94
Abhiññā S. (AN 4:25), *ibid.*, 102–03
Abhisamaya Saṃyutta (SN 13), *ibid.*, 119–20
Abhisambodhi-Alaṅkāra, *ibid.*, 120–21
Abhisanda Sutta (SN 55:31–33, 41–43; AN 4:51–52, 5:51, 8:39), *ibid.*, 121–22
Acchariya-Abbuta-Dhamma S. (MN 123; AN 4:127–30), Fasc. Acala–Ākaṅ, 1963, pp. 171–72
Acela S. (SN 12:17, 41:9), *ibid.*, 178
Acelaka Vagga (*Book of the Discipline* II, pp. 347–81; AN 3), *ibid.*, 177
Adanta Vagga (AN 1 iv), *ibid.*, 189
Addha Vagga (SN 1:61–70), *ibid.*, 193
Adhamma Sutta (AN 10:113), *ibid.*, 193–95
Adhamma Vagga (AN :140–49), *ibid.*, 195
Adhammika Sutta (AN 4:70), *ibid.*
Adhicitta S. (AN 3:100, Vv 11–15), *ibid.*, 196–97
Adhimutti S. (AN 10:21), *ibid.*, 204
Ādhipateyya S. (AN 3:40), *ibid.*, 205
Ādittapariyāya S. (SN 35:28), *ibid.*, 225–26
Āditta S. (SN 1:41, 35:194), *ibid.*, 226
Āditta Vagga (SN 1:41–50), *ibid.*
Ādiya Sutta (AN 3:41), *ibid.*, 227–28
Agārava S. (AN 5:8–10, 21–22), *ibid.*, 254–55
Agati S. (AN 4:17–19), *ibid.*, 255–56
Aggañña S. (DN 27), *ibid.*, 258–60
Aggappas-da S. (It. 90), *ibid.*, 260
Aggavati-Parisā S. (AN 3:93), *ibid.*, 260–61
Aggi S. (SN 46:53; AN 5:219, 7:43–44), *ibid.*, 265–66
Aggika S. (SN 7:9), *ibid.*, 263
Aggikkhandhopama S. (AN 7:68), *ibid.*, 263–64
Aggi-Vacchagotta S. (MN 72), *ibid.*, 266
Āghāta S. (AN 5:161–62, 9:29–30), *ibid.*, 268
Āhara S. (SN 12:11, 46:51), *ibid.*, 283–84
Āhara Vagga (SN 12:11–20), *ibid.*, 284
Ahirikamūlaka S. (SN 14:23ff), *ibid.*, 293

Āhuneyya S. (AN 6:1–7, 8:57–60, 9:10, 10:16), *ibid.*, 296
Ājāniya S. (AN 3:94–96), *ibid.*, 299–300
Ājañña S. (AN 4:256–57, 8:13), *ibid.*, 300
Ajita S. (AN 10:113–16), *ibid.*, 328–29
Ajitamāṇava-Pucchā (Sn V), *ibid.*, 327
Ājīvaka S. (AN 3:72), *ibid.*, 330
Ākaṅkheyya S. (MN 6; AN 10:71), *ibid.*, 336
Ākāsa S. (SN 28:5, 36:12, 40:5, 45:155), Fasc. Ākaṅkheyya S [*sic*]-Anabhirati, 1964, p.348
Akkhaṇa S. (AN 8:29), *ibid.*, 354–55
Akkosa S. (SN 7:2; AN 5:211), *ibid.*, 358
Akkosa Vagga (AN 10:41–50), *ibid.*
Akkosaka Vagga (AN 5:211–20), *ibid.*, 357–58
Akusalamūla Sutta (AN 3:69), *ibid.*, 369
Alagaddūpama S. (MN 22), *ibid.*, 370
Āḷavaka S. (AN 3:34; Sn I 10), *ibid.*, 381
Āmagandha S. (Sn II 2), *ibid.*, 401–02
Amata S. (SN 43:12, 47:41; AN 9:54), *ibid.*, 413
Amata Vagga (SN 47:41–50), *ibid.*, 414
Ambalapāli Sutta (SN 47:1, 52:9), *ibid.*, 419
Ambalapāli Vagga (SN 47:1–10), *ibid.*, 419–20
Ambaṭṭha Sutta (DN 3), *ibid.*, 424
Anabhirati S. (SN 46:70), *ibid.*, 504
Anabhisamaya S. (SN 33:1), Fasc.4, 1965, p.505
Anāgāmi S. (AN 6:65), *ibid.*, 509
Anāgata S. (AN 5: 79), *ibid.*, 514
Anāgatavaṃsa, 515
Anālaya Sutta (SN 43:44), *ibid.*, 518
Anamata Saṃyutta (SN 15), *ibid.*, 527–28
Ananaka Sutta (AN 4:62), *ibid.*, 528
Ānañcāyatana S. (AN 3:114), *ibid.*
Ānanda S. (SN 8:4, 9:5, 22:21,37,38,83, 44:10, 51:29,30, 54:13,14, 55:13; AN 3:32, 4:174, 5:106, 6:51, 9:37, 10:5,82), *ibid.*, 543–44
Anaṅgana S. (MN 5), *ibid.*, 545–46
Āneñjasappāya S. (MN 106), *ibid.*, 546
Anantavā S. (SN 24:18), *ibid.*, 556
Ananussuta S. (AN 5:11), *ibid.*, 557
Ānāpāna Saṃyutta (SN 54), *ibid.*, 558
Ānāpāna Sutta (SN 46:66), *ibid.*, 561–62

Ānāpāna Vagga (SN 46:57–66), *ibid.*, 562
Ānāpānasati Sutta (MN 118), *ibid.*, 561
Anāsava S. (SN 43:22), *ibid.*, 562–63
Anāthapiṇḍika S. (SN 56:26–28), *ibid.*, 566
Anāthapiṇḍikakovāda S. (MN 143), *ibid.*, 566–67
Anatta-Lakkhaṇa S. (*Book of the Discipline* IV, pp. 20–21; SN 22:59), *ibid.*, 576–77
Anatta S. (SN 22:14,29,33,70, 35:3,6,10–12,32), *ibid.*, 578
Andhakāra S. (SN 56:46; It.87), *ibid.*, 606
Andhakavibda S. (SN 6:13; AN 5:114), *ibid.*, 609
Andhakavinda Vagga (AN 5:111–20), *ibid.*
Aṅga, ibid., 616–17
Aṅgāni Sutta (AN 5:28, 10:12), *ibid.*, 622
Aṅgika S. (AN 5:28), *ibid.*, 625
Aṅguttara-Nava-Ṭīkā, *ibid.*, 629
Aṅguttara Nikāya, *ibid.*, 629–55
Anicca Sutta (SN 22:15,16, 23:13,23–34, 35:1–10,53, 46:76, 48:39; AN 7:16), *ibid.*, 663–64
Aniccatā S. (SN 22:45,46,102), *ibid.*, 664
Ānisaṃsa S. (AN 6:97), *ibid.*, 678
Ānisaṃsa Vagga (AN 6:96–106, 10:1–10), *ibid.*
Āṇī Sutta (SN 20:7), *ibid.*, 678–79
Anna S. (SN 1:42,43, 2:23; AN 4:87), *ibid.*, 702
Añña S. (SN 47:36), *ibid.*
Aññatara-Bhikkhu S. (SN 45:6,7), *ibid.*, 702–03
Aññatara-Brahma S. (SN 1:5), *ibid.*, 703
Aññatara S. (SN 12:46), *ibid.*
Aññatitthiya S. (SN 12:24; AN 3:68), *ibid.*, 703–04
Aññatitthiya Vagga (SN 45:41–48), *ibid.*, 704
Aññatra Sutta (SN 56:102ff), *ibid.*
Anodhi S. (AN 6:102–04), *ibid.*, 712
Anottāpī S. (SN 16:2), *ibid.*, 721
Anottappamūlaka S. (SN 14:23–25), *ibid.*, 722
Anta S. (SN 22:103, 43:14–43), *ibid.*, 737–38
Antavā S. (SN 24:37–44), *ibid.*, 738
Antevāsī S. (SN 35:150), *ibid.*, 740
Anudhamma S. (SN 22:39–42), *ibid.*, 740–41
Anukampaka S. (AN 5:235), *ibid.*, 742–43
Anumāna S. (MN 15), *ibid.*, 746

Anupada S. (MN 111), *ibid.*, 750
Anupada Vagga (MN 111-20), *ibid.*
Anurādha Sutta (SN 22:86, 44:2), *ibid.*, 765-66
Anuruddha Saṃyutta (SN 52), *ibid.*, 772
Anuruddha Sutta (MN 127; SN 9:6; AN 3:128, 8:30,9:46), *ibid.*, 772-74
Anusaya S. (SN 18:21, 35:58,59, 45:42-48, 48:64, 54:20), *ibid.*, 777- 78
Anusota S. (AN 6:6), *ibid.*, 778
Anussati S. (AN 6:25), *ibid.*, 779
Anuttariya S. (AN 6:11,12), *ibid.*, 784
Anuttariya Vagga (AN 6:21-30), *ibid.*
Anuvattanā Sutta (AN 5:132), *ibid.*, 784-85
Apadāna, Fasc. II, 1, 1966, pp. 2-3
Apaṇṇaka Sutta (MN 60; AN 3:115), *ibid.*, 6
Apaṇṇakatā S. (AN 3:16), *ibid.*, 6-7
Apaṇṇaka Vagga (AN 2:71-80), *ibid.*, 7
Aparihāniya Sutta (AN 6:22,32), *ibid.*, 16
Āpatti S. (AN 4:241), *ibid.*, 23-24
Āpatti Vagga (AN 4:241-50), *ibid.*, 24
Āpāyika Vagga (AN 3:111-20), *ibid.*, 26
Appamāda Sutta (SN 3:17,18, 12:83ff, 45:63-69; AN 4:116, 6:53, 7:31, 10:15; It.23), *ibid.*, 29-30
Appamāda Vagga (SN 46:89-98), *ibid.*, 30
Appamatta Vagga (AN 1:140-49), *ibid.*, 31
Appasuta Sutta (SN14:14-22), *ibid.*, 32-33
Aputtaka S. (SN 3:19,20), *ibid.*, 39
Ārabbhavatthu S. (AN 8:80), *ibid.*
Ārabhati S. (AN 5:142), *ibid.*
Arahaṃ S. (SN 1:25, 22:110, 48:4,5, 51:8, 56:23; AN 6:66), *ibid.*, 40
Arahanta S. (SN22:76,77), *ibid.*, 55
Arahā S. (SN 23:8, 48:27,28,33), *ibid*
Arahatta S. (SN 38:1; AN 6:76), *ibid.*
Arahatta Vagga (SN 22:63-72; AN 6:75-84), *ibid.*
Araka Sutta (AN 7:70), *ibid.*, 58
Ārammaṇa S. (SN 34:14,15), *ibid.*, 62
Araṇavibhaṅga S. (MN 139), *ibid.*, 62-63
Araṇi S. (SN 48:39), *ibid.*, 63-64
Āraññа S. (SN 1:10; AN 4:259, 5:98,110), *ibid.*, 65-66

Āraññа Vagga (AN 5:181–90), *ibid.*, 66
Arati Sutta (SN 8:2; AN 6:113), *ibid.*, 70
Ariyamagga S. (AN 10: 145), *ibid.*, 82
Ariyamagga Vagga (AN 10: 145–54), *ibid.*
Ariyapariyesana Sutta (MN 26), *ibid.*, 83
Ariyasāvaka S. (SN 12:49,50), *ibid.*, 88
Ariya S. (SN 46:19, 47:17, 51:3), *ibid.*, 88–89
Ariyavāsa S. (AN 10:19,20), *ibid.*, 93
Aruka S. (AN 3:25), *ibid.*, 101
Asaddhamūlaka S. (SN 14:23–27), *ibid.*, 123
Asallakkhaṇā S. (SN 33:26–30), *ibid.*, 125
Asamapekkhaṇā S. (SN 33:41–45), *ibid.*
Asaṅkhata Saṃyutta (SN 43), *ibid.*, 150–51
Āsaṇkhata Sutta (SN 43:12–44), *ibid.*, 151
Asappurisa S. (SN 45:31,32), *ibid.*, 153
Āsavakkhaya S. (SN 45:45, 48:64, 54:20, 56:25; AN 5:69), *ibid.*, 155
Āsava S. (AN 6:58, 10:126; It. 56,57), *ibid.*
Āseva S. (AN 1:51–60), *ibid.*, 169
Āsevitabba S. (AN 3:26), *ibid.*
Āsīvisa S. (SN 35:197; AN 4:110), Fasc. II, 2 (1967), p.177
Āsīvisopama S. (ibid.), *ibid.*, 177–78
Assalāyana S. (MN 93), *ibid.*, 219–20
Assutavā S. (SN 12:62), *ibid.*, 228
Assutavata S. (SN 12:61), *ibid.*
Asubha S. (SN 46:67; AN 4:163; It. 85), *ibid.*, 282–83
Asura Vagga (AN 4:91–100), *ibid.*, 291
Āṭānāṭiya S. (DN 32), *ibid.*, 302
Ātappa S. (SN 12:89; AN 3:49), *ibid.*, 303
Ātītānāgatapaccuppana S. (SN 22:9–11), *ibid.*, 315–16
Atītena S. (SN 35:19–36), *ibid.*, 316
Attadaṇḍa S. (Sn 4:15), *ibid.*, 322–23
Attadīpa S. (SN 22:43), *ibid.*, 323
Attakāra S. (AN 6:38), *ibid.*, 324
Attantāpa S. (AN 4:198), *ibid.*, 327
Atta S. (SN 45:64–69), *ibid.*, 328
Aṭṭhakanāgara S. (MN 52; AN 11:17), *ibid.*, 334
Aṭṭhaka Nipāta (AN 8), *ibid.*
Aṭṭhaka Sutta (SN 36:17,18), *ibid.*, 334–35
Aṭṭhakathā, *ibid.*, 335–52

Aṭṭhaka Vagga (Sn 4), *ibid.*, 352; contd. in Fasc. II, 3 (1967), p.353
Aṭṭhaṅgika Sutta (SN 14:28; AN 4:205), Fasc.II, 3, 363–64
Aṭṭhaṅgika-Magga S. (SN 43:11), *ibid.,* 363
Aṭṭhapuggala S. (AN 8:59,60), *ibid.*, 365
Atthasālinī, *ibid.*, 366–68
Atthasata S. (SN 36:22), *ibid.*, 369
Atthavasa Vagga (AN 2:280–84), *ibid.*, 369–70
Atthirāga Sutta (SN 12:65), *ibid.*, 371
Āvaraṇa-Nīvaraṇa S. (SN 46:37), *ibid.*, 428
Āvaraṇa S. (AN 5:51), *ibid.*
Avijjā S. (SN 22:49,50,113, 35:53, 38:9, 45:1, 56:17), *ibid.*, 459–60
Avyākata S. (AN 7:51–60), *ibid.*, 466–67
Āyācana Vagga (AN 2:130–42), *ibid.*, 468
Āyu Sutta (SN 4:9,10), *ibid.*, 483
Āyussa S. (AN 5:125,126), *ibid.*
Bahudhātuka S. (MN 115), Fasc. II, 4 (1968), *p.497*
Bahukāra S. (AN 3:24), *ibid.*, 497–98
Bahūpakāra S. (AN 5:234; It.107), *ibid.*, 499–500
Bahuvedanīya S. (MN 59), *ibid.*, 505
Baka-Brahmā S. (SN 6:4), *ibid.*, 509
Balām S. (AN 4:151–55), *ibid.*, 519
Bālapaṇḍita S. (MN 129; SN 12:19), *ibid.*, 519–20
Bala Saṃyutta (SN 50), *ibid.*, 520
Bala Sutta (SN 43:12.xxvi–xxx, 45:149; AN 4:58, 5:204, 6:4, 7:3,4, 8:27,28, 10:90), *ibid.*, 520–21
Bala Vagga (SN 50:1–12,55–66; AN 5:11–20), *ibid.*, 521
Bāla Sutta (AN 2:31–40,98–117, 3:1–10), *ibid.*, 521–22
Bandhanā S. (SN 1:65, 3:10, 22:117), *ibid.*, 538
Bhaddāli S. (MN 65), *ibid.*, 625–26
Bhaddekaratta S. (MN 131), *ibid.*, 628–29
Bhaddiya [S.] (AN 4:193), *ibid.*, 630
Bhadra S. (SN 42:11), *ibid.*, 643
Bhaṇḍagāma Vagga (AN 4:1–10), *ibid.*, 690–91
Bhaṇḍana Sutta (AN 3:122, 5:212, 10:50), *ibid.*, 691
Bhāra S. (SN 22:22), *ibid.*, 695
Bhāvanā S. (SN 47:34, 51:20; AN 7:67), Fasc. III, 1 (1971), pp. 16– 17
Bhava S. (SN 38:13, 45:164; AN 3:76, 6:105), *ibid.*, 21
Bhaya S. (SN 55:29; AN 3:62, 4:119–21, 6:23, 8:56), *ibid.*, 24–25
Bhaya Vagga (AN 4:121–30), *ibid.*, 25

Bhayabherava Sutta (MN 4), *ibid.*, 24
Bhikkhu Saṃyutta (SN 21:1–12), *ibid.*, 48
Bhikkhu Sutta (SN 12:28, 17:30, 19:17, 22:35,36,113,114, 35:81, 36:20,23, 47:3, 51:7,23,29,30, 54:15,16, 55:29,46; AN 7:21), *ibid.*, 48–50
Bhikkhunī Saṃyutta (SN 5:1–10), *ibid.*, 47
Bhikkhunī Sutta (SN 19:18; AN 4:159), *ibid.*
Bhikkhunīvāsaka S. (SN 47:10), *ibid.*
Bhoga S. (AN 5:227), *ibid.*, 63
Bhojana S. (AN 4:59, 5:37), *ibid.*, 67
Bhūmicāla S. (AN 8:70), *ibid.*, 81
Bhūmija S. (MN 126; SN 12:25), *ibid.*, 81–82
Bīja S. (SN 22:54, 45:150, 56:78; AN 1:225–34, 10:104), *ibid.*, 111–12
Bodhirājakumāra S. (MN 85), Fasc. III, 2 (1972), p.220
Bojjhaṅga Saṃyutta (SN 46), *ibid.*, 272
Bojjhaṅga Sutta (SN 43:10, 54:2; AN 4:236), *ibid.*, 272–73
Brahmajāla S. (DN 1), *ibid.*, 310–11
Brāhmaṇadhammika S. (Sn 2:7), *ibid.*, 316
Brāhmaṇa Saṃyutta (SN 6), *ibid.*, 317–18
Brāhmaṇa Sutta (SN 45:4, 47:25, 51:15, 55:12; AN 3:53, 9:38; It.100), *ibid.*, 318–19
Brāhmaṇa Vagga (AN 3:51–60, 5:191–200), *ibid.*, 320–21
Brāhmanimantanika S. (MN 49), *ibid.*, 321
Brahmañña S. (SN 45:37,38, 56:69), *ibid.*, 329
Brahma Saṃyutta (SN 6), *ibid.*, 331
Brahma Sutta (SN 47:18, 48:57), *ibid.*, 332
Brahmāyu S. (MN 91), *ibid.*, 337
Buddhavaṃsa, *ibid.*, 465
Cakkānuvatta S. (AN 5:131,132), Fasc. III, 4 (1977), pp. 568–69
Cakka S. (AN 4:31), *ibid.*, 569–70
Cakka Vagga (AN 4:31–40), *ibid.*, 570
Cakkavattisīhanāda S. (DN 26), *ibid.*, 570–72
Cakkavatti S. (SN 46:42; AN 3:14), *ibid.*, 572
Cakkavatti Vagga (SN 46:41–50), *ibid.*
Cakkhu Sutta (SN 18:1, 25:1, 26:1, 27:1; It.51), *ibid.*, 575
Caṅkī S. (MN 95), *ibid.*, 663
Cāpāla Vagga (SN 51:1–10), *ibid.*, 666
Cara Sutta (AN 4:11), *ibid.*, 669
Cara Vagga (AN 4:11–20), *ibid.*

Carita Sutta (AN 4:148,149; It.64,65), *ibid.*, 672
Catukka Nipāta (AN 4), *ibid.*, 705–06
Cātuma Sutta (MN 67), *ibid.*, 706
Dhammacakkappavattana S. (*Book of the Discipline* IV, pp. 15–18; SN 56:11), Fasc. IV, 3 (1988), pp. 472–78
Dhammapada, Fasc.IV, 4 (1989), pp. 488–94
Dhammasaṅgaṇī, *ibid.*, 505–08
Dhātukathā, *ibid.*, 575
Dīgha-Nikāya, *ibid.*, 610–13
Esukāri Sutta (MN 96), Fasc. V, 1 (1990), p.137
Etadagga Vagga (AN 1:168–74), *ibid.*, 137–41
Iṇa Sutta (AN 6:45), Fasc. V, 4 (1993), pp. 541–42
Indriya-Bhāvanā S. (MN 152), *ibid.*, 563–64
Itivuttaka, *ibid.*, 604–05
Jātaka, Fasc. VI,1 (1996), pp. 2–23
Kakacūpama Sutta (MN 21), *ibid.*, 81
Kālāma S. (AN 3:65), *ibid.*, 84–89
Kandaraka S. (MN 51), *ibid.*, 127–28
Kathāvatthu, Fasc. VI, 2 (1999), pp. 155–60
Khuddaka-Nikāya, *ibid.*, 207–11
Khuddakapāṭha, *ibid.*, 211–13
Kīṭāgiri Sutta (MN 70), *ibid.*, 226–27
Kūṭadanta S. (DN 5), *ibid.*, 263–64
Lakkhaṇa S. (DN 30), *ibid.*, 272–74
Madhuratthavilāsinī (Buddhavaṃsa Commentary), Fasc. VI, 3 (2002), pp. 362–63
Mahāparinibbāna Sutta (DN 16), *ibid.*, 461–67
Majjhimanikāya, Fasc. VI, 4 (2002), pp. 564–77
Maṅgalasutta (Sn 2:4), *ibid.*, 607–08
Manorathapūraṇī (AN Commentary), *ibid.*, 624–26
Milindapañha, *ibid.*, 688–92
Milinda-Ṭīkā, *ibid.*, 693–94
Mūlapariyāyasutta (MN 1), Fasc. VII, 1 (2003), pp. 52–55
Nettippakaraṇa, *ibid.*, 156–59
Niddesa, *ibid.*, 168–70
Nikaya, *ibid.*, 173–75
Nissaggiya-Pācittiya, *ibid.*, 179–81
Pāli, Fasc. VII, 2 (2004), pp. 265–79
Papañcasūdanī (MN Commentary), *ibid.*, 303–04

Paramatthadīpanī (Khuddakanikāya Commentary), *ibid.*, 307–09
Paramatthajotikā (*ibid.*), *ibid.*, 309–11
Paramatthamañjusā (Visuddhimagga sub-commentary), *ibid.*, 311–12
Pārāyanavagga (Sn 5), *ibid.*, 314–15
Pātimokkha, *ibid.*, 363–65
Pātimokkhuddesa, *ibid.*, 365–67
Paṭisambhidāmagga, *ibid.*, 373–75
Peṭakopadesa, *ibid.*, 395–96
Petavatthu, *ibid.*, 397–403
Puggalapaññatti, Fasc. VII, 3 (2005), pp. 451–52
Ratana Sutta (Khuddakapāṭha 6; Sn 2:1), *ibid.*, 513
Rathavinīta S. (MN 24), *ibid.*, 518–20
Sabbāsava S. (MN 2), *ibid.*, 567–70
Saddhammapajjatikā (Niddesa Commentary), *ibid.*, 605–06; Fasc. VII, 4 (2006), p.607
Saddhammappakāsinī (Paṭisambhidāmagga Commentary), *ibid.*, 607–08
Sāmaññaphala Sutta (DN 2), *ibid.*, 665–67
Samantapāsādikā (Vinaya Commentary), *ibid.*, 669–73
Sammohavinodanī (Vibhaṅga Commentary), *ibid.*, 681–82
Saṃyuttanikāya, *ibid.*, 687–90
Sārasaṅgaha (medieval Sinhalese Pāli treatise), *ibid.*, 761–62
Sāratthadīpanī (Samantapāsādikā sub-commentary), *ibid.*, 762–63
Sāratthamañjusā (Manorathapūraṇī sub-commentary), *ibid.*, 763–64
Sāratthasamuccaya (Catubhānavāra [*paritta*] Commentary), *ibid.*, 766
Sāsanavaṃsa, *ibid.*, 791–92
Satipaṭṭhāna Sutta (MN 10), Fasc. VIII, 1 (2007), pp. 15–18
Scripture, *ibid.*, 26–29
Sigālovāda Sutta (DN 31), *ibid.*, 86–90
Sumaṅgalavilāsinī (DN Commentary), *ibid.*, 187–91
Suttanipāta, *ibid.*, 205–14
Suttapiṭaka, *ibid.*, 214
Tevijja-Vacchagotta Sutta (MN 71), Fasc. VIII, 2 (2008), pp. 302–03
Thera-Therī-Gāthā, *ibid.*, 306–12
Ṭīkā Literature, *ibid.*, 350–58
Tirokuḍḍa Sutta (Khuddakapāṭha 7), *ibid.*, 358–60
Udāna, *ibid.*, 375–84

Uddesavibhaṅga Sutta (MN 138), *ibid.*, 389–90
Upakkilesa S. (MN 128), *ibid.*, 420–22
Upāsakajanālaṅkara, *ibid.*, 435–38
Vammika Sutta (MN 23), Fasc. VIII, 3 (2009), p.494
Vāsettha S. (MN 98; Sn 3:9), *ibid.*, 494–96
Vatthūpama S. (MN 7), *ibid.*, 512–13
Vīmaṃsaka S. (MN 47), *ibid.*, 609–10
Vimānavatthu, *ibid.*, 397–403
Vimativinodanī Ṭīkā, *ibid.*, 610–11
Vimuttimagga, *ibid.*, 622–32
Vinayapiṭaka, *ibid.*, 650–58
Vinayavinicchaya, *ibid.*, 658–59
Visuddhimagga, *ibid.*, 706–12
Vitakkasaṇṭhāna Sutta (MN 20), *ibid.*, 717–18
Yodhājīva S. (SN 42:3), *ibid.*, 798–99
Yuganaddha S. (AN 4:170), *ibid.*, 815–17

8. Pāli Grammars and Dictionaries

Chizen Akanuma, *A Dictionary of Buddhist Proper Names*. Delhi 1994. Translation of *Indo Bukkyō Koyūmeishi Jiten. Genshkihen* ("A Dictionary of Indian Buddhist Proper Names. Primitive Period"), Nagoya 1930–31.

Bhikkhu Ānandajoti, *An Outline of the Metres in the Pāḷi Canon* (3rd rev. ed.), 2006. Retrieved on 31.3.2011 from http:// www. ancient-buddhist-texts.net/Textual-Studies/Outline/ index.htm

Balangoda Ānanda Maitreya, *Pali Grammar and Composition*, lessons 1–29 out of 34 serialised in *Pali Buddhist Review* 2–6. London 1977–82.

—*Pali Made Easy*. Shizuoka 1993, Dehiwela 1997.

Dines Andersen, *A Pāli Reader*. Copenhagen, London and Leipzig: Part I, 1901, Glossary, 1904–07; Kyoto 1968. Repr. as *A Pāli Reader and Pāli Glossary*. 2 vols, New Delhi 1996.

Kakkapalliye Anuruddha, *A Guide to the Study of Pali: The Language of Theravada Buddhism*. Hong Kong, 2010.

Arayankhura Prayuddha, *Students Thai-Pali-English Dictionary of Buddhist Terms*. Bangkok 1963.

S.C. Banerji, *A Companion to Middle Indo-Aryan Literature*. Calcutta 1977. A dictionary of Buddhist and Jaina texts.

P.V. Bapat and R.D. Vadekar, *A Practical Pali Dictionary for the use of students in High Schools and Colleges*. Poona 1940.

A. Barua, *Introduction to Pali*. Varanasi 1965, Delhi 1977. Pāli terms in Devanāgarī script.

D.L. Barua, *Pali Grammar*. Board of Secondary Education, W. Bengal, Calcutta 1956.

A.P. Buddhadatta, *Tribhasharatnakara*. "A handbook of Pali conversation, with Sinhalese and English versions." Ambalangoda 1928.

—*New Pali Course I*. Colombo 1937, 1962; *II*. 1938, 1974; combined ed., Dehiwela 2006.

—*Concise Pali-English Dictionary*. Colombo 1949, 2000, New York 1992, Delhi 2002 (repr. by another Delhi publisher as *Pāli-English Dictionary*. 1999).

—*Aids to Pali Conversation and Translation*. Colombo 1950.

—*The Higher Pali Course for Advanced Students*. Colombo 1951, repr. as *New Pali Course III*. Dehiwela 2005.

—*English-Pali Dictionary*. Colombo 1955, New York 1992, PTS 1995, Delhi 2007.

—*English to Pali Dictionary*. New Delhi 2008.

—*Palipāthāvalī*. (A supplementary reader to the *New Pali Course*.) Dehiwela 2003.

N. Cakravarti and M.K. Ghose, *Pali Grammar*. Repr. Delhi 1983.

K.K. Chandaburinarunath, *Pali-Thai-Sanskrit-English Dictionary*. Bangkok 1969, 1977.

Binayendra Nath Chaudhury, *Dictionary of Buddhist Doctrinal and Technical Terms* (based on Pāli and Sanskrit Buddhist literature). Kolkata (Calcutta) 2005.

R.C. Childers, *A Dictionary of the Pali Language*. London 1872–75, Rangoon 1974, Kyoto 1976, Delhi 2003, New Delhi 2005.

—*A Pali Grammar for Beginners*. (Repr?) New Delhi 1999.

Benjamin Clough (tr. Bālāvatāra), *A Compendious Pali Grammar with a copious vocabulary in the same language*. Colombo 1824, 1832.

Steven Collins, *A Pali Grammar for Students*. Chiang Mai 2006.

Margaret Cone, *A Dictionary of Pāli*. Part I—A-Kh. PTS 2001.

James D'Alwis, An Introduction to Kachchayana's Grammar of the Pali Language. Colombo 1863.

Dhammakitti, tr. L. Lee, *Bālāvatāra*, a grammar, *The Orientalist* II, Kandy 1892; tr. H.T. de Silva and K. Upatissa, rev. F.L. Woodward, Pegu 1915.

Lily de Silva, *Pali Primer*. Igatpuri 1995.

W.A. de Silva, *A vocabulary to aid to speak the Hindu and Pali languages*. Colombo 1903.

Harsha V. Dehejia (ed.), *The English-Pali Glossary*. Delhi 1999.

—*A Pali-English Glossary*. *Ibid.*

Mahesh A. Deokar, *Technical Terms and Techniques of the Pali and the Sanskrit Grammars*. Varanasi 2008.

B. Devarakkhita (alias Don Andris de Silva Batuwantudawe, ed. & tr.), *Kaccāyana's Dhātumañjūsā*. Colombo 1872.

Charles Duroiselle, *A Practical Grammar of the Pali Language*. Rangoon 1907, 1921.

—*School Pali Series*—I. Reader, II. Vocabulary. Rangoon 1907–8.

Ernest John Eitel, *Handbook of Chinese Buddhism, being a Sanskrit-Chinese Dictionary with vocabularies of Buddhist terms in Pali, Singhalese, Siamese, Burmese, Tibetan, Mongolian and Japanese*. 2nd rev. & enl. ed., Hong Kong 1888, Delhi 1981.

T.Y. Elizarenkova and V.N. Toporov, *The Pali Language*. Moscow 1976.

K.C. Fernando, *A Student's Pali-English Dictionary*. Colombo 1950. Pāli terms in Sinhala script.

Oscar Frankfurter, *Handbook of Pali*. London-Edinburgh 1883. An elementary grammar.

James W. Gair and W.S. Karunatilaka, *Introduction to Reading Pali*. Cornell University 1975. Repr. as *A New Course in Reading Pali*. New Delhi 1998, Delhi 2001.

Ron Geaves, *Key Words in Buddhism*. Georgetown (WA-DC) 2006. "A basic useful glossary of explanations of important Buddhist terms".

Wilhelm Geiger, *Pāli Literature and Language*. Calcutta 1943, Delhi 1968. Rev. by K.R. Norman as *Pāli Grammar*. PTS 1994.

(Rev.) David C. Gilmore, *A Brief Vocabulary to the Pali Text of Jatakas I–XL for the use of students preparing for the first examination in arts in Calcutta University*. Rangoon 1895.

James Gray, *Pāli Primer*. Adapted for schools in Burma. Moulmein 1879.

—*First Lessons in Pāli.* 3rd ed., Rangoon 1882.
—*Elements of Pāli Grammar.* Rangoon 1883. Pāli terms in Burmese script.
—*Pāli Courses.* 3 parts, including translations of stories 13–31 in D. Andersen, *A Pāli Reader*, *op. cit.*
—*Pāli Prose.* 2 parts, including translations of portions of D. Andersen, *Pāli Reader*, *op. cit.*
—*Elementary Pāli Grammar.* 2nd Pāli course. Calcutta 1905.
—*Pāli Poetry.* Calcutta 1909.
—*First Pāli Course.* Calcutta 1913.
—*First Pāli Delectus.* Companion reader to his Pāli course. *Ibid.*
K. Manohar Gupta, *Linguistics in Pāli.* New Delhi 2003.
—*Linguistic Approach to Meaning in Pāli.* New Delhi 2006.
K. Higashimoto, *An Elementary Grammar of the Pali Language.* Tokyo 1965.
P. Holler, *The Student's Manual of Indian Vedic-Sanskrit-Prakrit-Pali Literature.* Rajahmundri 1901.
Peter A. Jackson, *A Topic Index of the Sutta Piṭaka.* Bangkok 1986. Pāli technical terms in Roman and Thai scripts with brief English and Thai translations cross-referred to the books/sections of SP.
Rune E.A. Johansson, *Pali Buddhist Texts explained to beginners.* Copenhagen 1973, London 1976, Richmond (Surrey) 1998.
C.V. Joshi, *A Manual of Pali.* (Pāli terms in Devanāgari.) Poona 1916, 1964, Delhi 2005.
J.R. Joshi, *Introduction to Pali.* Pune 1985.
I.Y. Junghare, *Topics in Pāli Historical Phonology.* Delhi 1979.
D.G. Koparkar, *English Guide to C.V. Joshi's Manual of Pali.* Poona 1942.
D. Kosambi and C.V. Rajwade, *Pali-Reader.* Two parts, Poona 1914–16.
K. Krishna Murthy, *A Dictionary of Buddhist Terms and Terminologies.* Delhi 1991, Calcutta 1999.
B.C. Law, *M.A. Pali Course.* Calcutta 1941.
Lionel Lee (tr.), "The Bālāvatāra, a Pāli Grammar." 4 parts, *The Orientalist II–III.* Kandy 1885–90.
Lim Teong Aik, *A Glossary of Buddhist Terms in Four Languages—English, Chinese, Pāli and Sanskrit.* Penang 1960.
G.P. Malalasekera, *Dictionary of Pāli Proper Names.* 2 volumes,

London 1937, 3 volumes, PTS and New Delhi 2007.
Lynn Martineau (ed.), *Pāli Workbook*. Seattle (WA) 1998. Pāli vocabulary from the ten-day courses of S.N. Goenka.
Francis Mason, *Pali Grammar on the Basis of Kachchayano*. Toungoo-London 1866, Delhi 1984.
Ministry of Religious Affairs, *A Dictionary of Buddhist Terms*. Yangon (Rangoon) 1996. Pāli terms in Burmese script.
Madhusudan Mishra, *Comparative and Historical Pali Grammar*. New Delhi 1986.
J. Minayeff (I.P. Minaev), *Pali Grammar, a phonetic and morphological sketch of Pali Language, with introductory essay on its form and character*. Moulmein 1882, New Delhi 1990.
E. Müller, *A Simplified Grammar of the Pali Language*. London 1884, Varanasi 1967, Delhi 1995. Repr. as *Pali Grammar* (Delhi 2003) and *The Pali Language: A Simplified Grammar* (? 2005).
—*A Glossary of Pali Proper Names*. Offprint from JPTS 1888 (repr. 1978), Delhi 1989.
Ñāṇamoli *A Pali-English Glossary of Buddhist Technical Terms*. BPS 1994, 2006.
Medagama Nandawansa, *Abhidhānappadīpikā: A Study of the Text and Its Commentary*. Pune 2001.
Nārada, *An Elementary Pali Course*. Colombo 1941, 1953.
Nyanatiloka, *Buddhist Dictionary*. Dodanduwa 1950, Colombo 1972, New York 1983, Taipei 1987, BPS 1988, 2004.
—*Buddha-Vacanam*. (Texts for *The Word of the Buddha*.) BPS 1968.
Thomas Oberlies, *Pāli. A Grammar of the Language of of the Theravāda Tipiṭaka*. Berlin 2001.
Madihe Paññāsīha (ed.), *Pali Dictionary I*. 1: A-Akkhabhañjana. Mahārāgama 1975. Pāli in Sinhala and Roman scripts with Sinhalese and English translations.
Pe Maung Tin, *A Pali Primer*. Rangoon 1914, Delhi 2003.
—*A Pali Reader*. 2nd ed., Rangoon 1920.
—*The Student's Pali-English Dictionary*. Rangoon 1920.
V. Perniola, *A Grammar of the Pali Language*. Colombo 1958. Rev. as *Pāli Grammar*. PTS 1997.
John Powers, *A Concise Encyclopaedia of Buddhism*. Oxford 2000.
Widurupola Piyatissa, *The English-Pali Dictionary*. Colombo 1949. Pāli terms in Sinhala script.
Rajavaramuni, *Pali-English Dictionary of Buddhist Terms*. Bangkok

1963, 1969.
—*Thai-Pali-English Dictionary of Buddhism*. 3rd ed., Bangkok 1970.
—*A Dictionary of Buddhism*. Bangkok 1976, 1985. Pāli terms in Thai script.
T.W. Rhys Davids and W. Stede *Pali-English Dictionary*. PTS 1921–25, 1999; repr. New York 1989, New Delhi 1997, Delhi 2007.
U Sīlananda, *Pāli Roots in the Saddanīti*. Publ. by Centro Mexicano del Buddhismo Theravada, Jilotepec, 2002.
W. Subhūti (ed.), *Abhidhānappadīpikā*. (Dictionary of the Pāli language by Moggallāna.) Colombo 1865, 1938. English and Sinhalese interpretations. Pāli terms in Sinhala script.
S. Sumaṅgala, *A Graduated Pali Course*. Colombo 1913, Dehiwela 1994.
J. Takakusu, *A Pali Chrestomathy*. Tokyo 1900.
Tha Do Oung, *A Grammar of the Pali Language*. 4 volumes, Akyab 1899–1902.
H.H. Tilbe, *Pali First Lessons*. Rangoon 1902.
—*Pali Grammar*. Rangoon 1899.
V. Trenckner, D. Andersen, H. Smith *et al.* (ed.), *Critical Pāli Dictionary*. Copenhagen: I. 1924–48, II.1960.
Tick Twon, A Short Dictionary of Buddhist Hybrid Pali. Kalimpong 1969.
Udornganādhikāra (Javinda Sragam), *Pali-Thai-English Dictionary*. 8 vols, Bangkok 1962.
A.C.G. Vidyabhūsan, *Selections from Pali*. Calcutta 1911.
N.C. Vidyabhusan and M.K. Ghose, *A Pali Grammar*. Calcutta 1982.
S.C. Vidyabhūsan, *Kaccāyana's Pali Grammar*. Calcutta 1901.
S.C. Vidyabhūsan and Swami Punnanand (ed. and tr.), *Bālāvatāra: An Elementary Pali Grammar*. Calcutta University 1916, 1935.
J. Wade, *A Dictionary of Boodhism and Burman Literature*. Moulmein 1862, Rangoon 1911.
M.O'C. Walshe, *Pali and the Pali Canon*. English Sangha Trust, London 1968.
A.K. Warder, *Introduction to Pali*. PTS 1963, rev. ed., 1995, 2001. (The PTS also distributes a companion audio recording.)
—*Pali Metre*. PTS 1967.
O.H. de A. Wijesekera, *Syntax of Cases in the Pāli Nikāyas*. Colombo 1993. Doctoral dissertation, London 1951.
U Wimala, *A New Elementary Pali Grammar*. Rangoon n.d.

F.L. Woodward, E.M. Hare, K.R. Norman, A.K. and N. Warder, H. Saddhātissa, I. Fisher (ed.), *Pāli Tipiṭaka Concordance*. PTS, I (A-O)1955; II (K-N) 1973, 1995; III 1993.

9. Online Texts and Resources

New websites with various materials on Buddhism and other resources, often copied from existing websites, are continuously appearing (and disappearing). The following list is an overview of the most useful ones. If the link is broken, then search for the site's name instead.

Ancient Buddhist Texts. Studies on Pali prosody, etc. www.ancient-buddhist-texts.net/Textual-Studies/TS-index.htm.

Association for Insight Meditation. Includes some books by Ledi Sayadaw as well as Pāli fonts. www.aimwell.org

Beyond the Tipitaka. A Field Guide to Post-canonical Pali Literature (John Bullitt). www.accesstoinsight.org/lib/authors/bullitt/fieldguide.html

Bibliography of Indian Philosophies, by Karl H. Potter (ed.). Part I *Texts Whose Authors Can Be Dated. Authors Listed Chronologically before the Christian Era through 4th century*: faculty.washington.edu/kpotter/xtxt1.htm Part IV *Secondary Literature: Abhidharma, especially Theravāda Buddhism*: faculty.washington.edu/kpotter/xb.htm#[AB]

Bibliography to the Buddhist Religion: A Historical Introduction, by R. H. Robinson, and W. L. Johnson. Extensive bibliography. Section 5.3 deals with Pāli texts, etc. here-and-now.org/buddrel/directory.html.

Buddhanet Ebook Library with Nārada's *Manual of Abhidhamma*, etc. www.buddhanet.net/ebooks_s.htm

Buddhasāsana—English Section. www.saigon.com:8081/ ~ anson/ebud/ebidx.htm Library.

Buddhism—Buddhist Studies—Academic Info. www.academicinfo.net/buddhism.html

Buddhism in Myanmar. http://www.triplegem.plus.com/# Translations of suttas, articles, etc.

Buddhism Today: Readings in Theravāda and Mahāyāna Buddhism with emphasis on contemporary issues. www.buddhismtoday.com

Buddhist Publication Society Online Library. BPS publications and some Pāli resources. www.bps.lk/onlinelibrary

Buddhist Studies WWW Virtual Library (T. Matthew Ciolek). www.ciolek.com/WWWVL-Buddhism.html—especially "The Internet Guide to Buddhism and Buddhist Studies".

Budsir Thai Tipiṭaka. Online searchable Mahidol Royal Thai edition of the Tipiṭaka. http://www.budsir.org/budsir-main.html

Chattha Sangayana Tipitaka 3 is a searchable exercise with the Sixth Council edition of the Tipiṭaka. Also *Aṭṭhakathās, Ṭīkās*, and other Pāli works. www.vri.dhamma.org/publications/tpmain.html

Chattha Sangayana Tipitaka 4 is the successor of Chattha Sangayana Tipitaka 3. Version 4 has some advantages when searching (as it immediately shows the context in which a word occurs), but version 4 does not crash unlike version 3. www.tipitaka.org/cst.

Dhammaweb. http://www.dhammaweb.net/index.php Translations of suttas, etc.

Dharma Study. http://dharmastudy.com Includes sutta translations and articles on the Pāli Canon and its teachings.

Gretil Elibrary. www.sub.uni-goettingen.de/ebene_1/fiindolo/gretil.htm#Pali Göttingen University Library Register of Electronic Texts in Indian languages and related Indological materials from Central and Southeast Asia.

H-Buddhism (Charles Muller). The Buddhist Scholars Information Network has been created to serve as a medium for the exchange of information regarding resources, events, projects, publications etc. among the worldwide Buddhist scholarly community. www.h-net.org/~buddhism—especially "Resources: Buddhist Studies Links" > "Resources for the Study of Buddhism" (Ron Epstein) and "Tools for Buddhist Studies" (Marcus Bingenheimer).

Journal of Buddhist Ethics: www.buddhistethics.org. Online journal established to promote the study of Buddhist ethics through the publication of research, book reviews, etc. Includes digital Buddha Jayanthi Tipiṭaka and other resources.

[Links] www.greatwesternvehicle.org/pali/index.htm

Mettā Lanka. Various books and resources including *Dictionary of Pāli Proper Names* and digital Buddha Jayanti Tipiṭaka. www.

mettanet.org/english/index.html (Pāli Canon in Pāli and English) www.mettanet.org/tipitaka/index.html.

Pali Text Society. www.palitext.com.

Resource Gateways, *Individual Web Sites*, *Online Publications* and *Buddhist Publishers*. www.buddhistethics.org/global.html.

Sacred Buddhist Texts. Includes some 19th century translations of Buddhist texts such as the Jātaka edited by Cowell. www.sacred-texts.com/bud/index.htm Various individual sutta, etc., translations and articles are at www.sacred-texts.com/bud/etc/index.htm.

Sādhu: The Theravāda Buddhism Web Directory and Portal. Resources and links related to Theravāda Buddhism. www.dhamma.ru/sadhu.

SuttaCentral: Online Sutta Correspondence Project. www.suttacentral.net Comparing suttas as transmitted in different schools and languages.

Tipitaka, der Palikanon, die Lehre des Theravada Buddhismus. www.palikanon.com/index.html Includes the *Dictionary of Pali Proper Names* and related texts and resources.

Theravada Online Buddhist Directory. www.thisismyanmar.com/triplegemdotnet and www.buddhistethics.org/global.html (under *Resource Gateways*).

Tipitaka, the Pali Canon of Buddhism. http://oaks.nvg.org/tripitaka.html.

Treasures of Pariyatti represents the preservation and dissemination of classical texts related to the teaching of the Buddha. Includes electronic re-publications of issues of the *Light of the Dhamma* and *Light of Buddha*. www.pariyatti.org/treasures.

UK Association for Buddhist Studies. www.seacoast.sunderland.ac.uk.

Web resources for Pali students. www.accesstoinsight.org/outsources/pali.html.

Wikivinaya sites.google.com/site/wikivinaya/Home/goal-and-content-of-wikivinaya Articles and books on Theravāda Vinaya.

Courses, Bulletins and Forums

A Course of the Pali Language www.bodhimonastery.net/bm/programs/pali-class-online/903–audio/55–a-course-in-the-pali-language.html Audio course based on James Gair and W.S. Karunatilleke's, *A New Course in Reading Pali.*

Access to Insight: Theravāda Buddhist website with large sutta translation library and some Pali study resources. www.accesstoinsight.org.

Pāli forum: groups.yahoo.com/group/Pali/

E-sangha, Buddhist Forum and Buddhism Forum www.lioncity.net/buddhism/index.php?showforum=50

Pāli Language Bulletin Board http://emsjuwel.com/palibbs

Kamma and Its Fruit

Selected Essays

by

Leonard A. Bullen, Nina van Gorkom,
Bhikkhu Ñāṇajīvako, Nyanaponika Thera,
Francis Story

Edited by

Nyanaponika Thera

WHEEL PUBLICATION NO. 221/222/223/224

Kamma and Its Fruit

Kamma—or in its Sanskrit form, *karma*—is the Buddhist conception of action as a force which shapes and transforms human destiny. Often misunderstood as an occult power or as an inescapable fate, kamma as taught by the Buddha is in actuality nothing other than our own will or volition coming to expression in concrete action. The Buddhist doctrine of kamma thus places ultimate responsibility for human destiny in our own hands. It reveals to us how our ethical choices and actions can become either a cause of pain and bondage or a means to spiritual freedom.

In this book, five practising Buddhists, all with modern backgrounds, offer their reflections on the significance of kamma and its relations to ethics, spiritual practice, and philosophical understanding.

Action

Francis Story

Kamma is simply action or a 'deed'. Actions are performed in three ways: by body, mind and speech. Every action of importance is performed *because there is desire for a result*; it has an aim, an objective. One wishes for something specific to happen as the result of it. This desire, no matter how mild it may be, is a form of craving. It expresses the thirst (*taṇhā*) for existence and for action. To exist is to act, on one level or another. Organic existence consists of chemical action; psychic existence consists of mental action. So existence and action are inseparable.

But some actions, those in which mind is involved, are bound to have intention. This is expressed by the Pāli word *cetanā*, volition, which is one of the mental properties. There is another word, *chanda,* which stands for wishing, desiring a result. These words all express some kind of desire. And some form of desire is behind practically every activity of life. Therefore 'to live' and 'to desire' are one and the same thing. (There is one ultimate exception to this statement, which we shall come to later. It is that of the *Arahat*.)

An action (*kamma*) is morally unwholesome when it is motivated by the forms of craving that are associated with greed, hatred and delusion (*lobha, dosa, moha*). It is morally wholesome (in ordinary language, good) when it is motivated by the opposite factors, disinterestedness (greedlessness), amity and wisdom. An act so motivated is prompted by 'intention' rather than 'craving'. Yet in every act of craving, intention is included. It is that which gives direction and form to the deed.

Now, each deed performed with intention is a *creative act.* By reason of the will behind it, it constitutes a force. It is a force analogous to the other great unseen, yet physical, forces that move the universe. By our thoughts, words and deeds we create our world from moment to moment in the endless process of change. We also create our 'selves'. That is to say, we mould our changing personality as we go along by the accumulation of such thoughts, words and deeds. It is the accretion of these and the preponderance of one kind over another that determines what we shall become, in this life and in subsequent ones.

In thus creating our personality, we create also the conditions in which it functions. In other words, we create also the kind of world we are to live in. The mind, therefore, is master of the world. As a man's mind is, so is his cosmos.

Kamma, then, as the product of the mind, is the true and only real force in the life-continuum, the flux of coming-to-be. From this we come to understand that it is the residue of mental force which from the point of death kindles a new birth. It is the only actual link between one life ('reincarnation') and another. And since the process is a continuous one, it is the last kammic thought-moment at the point of death that forms the rebirth-linking consciousness—the kamma that reproduces. Other kamma, good or bad, will come into operation at some later stage, when external conditions are favourable for its ripening. The force of weak kamma may be suspended for a long time by the interposition of a stronger kamma. Some kinds of kamma may even be inoperative; but this never happens with very strong or weighty kamma. As a general principle, all kamma bears some kind of fruit sooner or later.

Each individual's kamma is his own personal act, its results his own personal inheritance. He alone has complete command over his actions, no matter to what degree others may try to force him. Yet an unwholesome deed done under strong compulsion does not have quite the same force as one performed voluntarily. Under threat of torture or of death a man may be compelled to torture or kill someone else. In such a case it may be believed that the gravity of his kamma is not as severe as it would be had he deliberately chosen to act in such a way. The heaviest moral responsibility rests with those who have forced him to the action. But in the ultimate sense he still must bear some responsibility, for he could in the most extreme case avoid harming another by choosing to suffer torture or death himself.

This brings us to the question of *collective kamma.* As we have seen, each man's kamma is his own individual experience. No one can interfere with the kamma of another beyond a certain point; therefore no one can intervene to alter the results of personal kamma. Yet it often happens that numbers of people are associated in the same kind of actions, and share the same kind of thoughts; they become closely involved with one another; they influence one another. Mass psychology produces mass kamma. Therefore all such people are likely to form the same pattern of kamma. It may result in their being associated with one another through a number of lives, and in their sharing much the same kind of experiences. "Collective kamma" is simply the aggregate of individual kammas, just as a crowd is an aggregate of individuals.

It is in fact this kind of mass kamma that produces different kinds of worlds—the world we live in, the states of greater suffering and the states of relative happiness. Each being inhabits the kind of cosmic construction for which he has fitted himself. It is his kamma, and the kamma of beings like himself that has created it. This is how it comes about that in multi-dimensional space-time there are many *lokas*—many worlds and modes of being. Each one represents a particular type of consciousness, the result of kamma. The mind is confined only by the boundaries it erects itself.

The results of kamma are called *vipāka*, 'the ripening'. These terms, *kamma* and *vipāka*, and the ideas they stand for, must not be confused. Vipāka is predetermined (by ourselves) by previous kamma. But kamma itself in the ultimate sense (that is, when resisting all external pressures and built-up tendencies) is the product of *choice* and free will: choice between wholesome and unwholesome deeds, good or bad actions. Hence the Buddha said: 'Intention constitutes kamma'. Without intention a deed is sterile; it produces no reaction of moral significance. One reservation, however, is here required; if a deed done in 'culpable negligence' proves harmful to others, the lack of mindfulness, circumspection or consideration shown will constitute unwholesome kamma and will have its vipāka. Though the harm done was not 'intended', i.e. the deed was not motivated by hate, yet there was present another 'unwholesome root', delusion (*moha*), which includes, for instance, irresponsible thoughtlessness.

Kamma is action; *vipāka* is result. Therefore kamma is the active principle; vipāka is the passive mode of coming-to-be. People believe in predeterminism, fatalism, merely because they see results, but do not see causes. In the process of dependent origination (*paṭicca-samuppāda*) both causes and effects are shown in their proper relationship.

A person may be born deaf, dumb and blind. That is the consequence of some unwholesome kamma which manifested or presented itself to his consciousness in the last thought-moment of his previous death. Throughout life he may have to suffer the consequences (*vipāka*) of that deed, whatever it may have been. But that fact does not prevent him from forming fresh kamma of a wholesome type to restore the balance in his next life. Furthermore, by the aid of some good kamma from the past, together with strong effort and favourable circumstances in the present life (which of course includes the compassionate help of others), the full effects of his bad kamma may be mitigated even here and now. Cases of this kind are seen everywhere, where people have overcome to a great extent the most formidable handicaps. The result is that they have turned even the bad vipāka to profit for themselves and others. One outstanding example of this is the famous Dr. Helen Keller. But this calls for almost superhuman courage and willpower. Most people in similar circumstances remain passive sufferers of the effects of their bad deeds until those effects are exhausted. Thus it has to be in the case of those born mentally defective or in the lower states of suffering. Having scarcely any capacity for the exercise of free will, they are subject to predeterminism entirely until the bad vipāka has run its course.

So, by acknowledging some element of predeterminism, yet at the same time maintaining the *ultimate* ascendancy of will, Buddhism resolves a moral problem which otherwise seems insoluble. Part of the personality, and the conditions in which it exists, are predetermined by the deeds and the total personality of the past; but in the final analysis the mind is able to free itself from the bondage of past personality-constructions and launch out in a fresh direction.

Now, we have seen that the three roots of unwholesome actions—greed, hatred and delusion—produce bad results; the three roots of wholesome actions—disinterestedness, amity and wisdom—produce good results. Actions which are performed automatically or unconsciously, or are incidental to some other action having an entirely different objective, do not produce results beyond their immediate mechanical consequences. If one treads on an insect in the dark, one is not morally responsible for its death. One has been merely an unconscious instrument of the insect's own kamma in producing its death.

But while there is a large class of actions of the last type, which cannot be avoided, the more important actions in everyone's life are dominated by one or other of these six psychological roots, wholesome and unwholesome. Even where a life is physically inactive, the thoughts are at work; they are producing kamma. Cultivation of the mind therefore consists in removing (not suppressing) unwholesome mental states and substituting wholesome ones. Modern civilisation develops by suppressing unwholesome (the 'anti-social') instincts. Consequently they break out from time to time in unwholesome eruptions. A war breaks out and the homicidal maniac comes into his own: murder is made praiseworthy. Buddhism, on the other hand, aims at *removing* the unwholesome mental elements. For this, the special techniques of meditation (*bhāvanā*) are necessary.

Good kamma is the product of wholesome states of mind. And to be certain of this, it is essential to gain an understanding of the states of consciousness and one's most secret motives. Unless this is done, it is next to impossible to cultivate exclusively wholesome actions, because in every human consciousness there is a complex of hidden motivations. They are hidden because we do not wish to acknowledge them. In every human being there is a built-in defence mechanism that prevents him from seeing himself too clearly. If he should happen to be confronted with his subconscious mind too suddenly he may receive an unpleasant psychological shock. His carefully constructed image of himself is rudely shattered. He is appalled by the crudity, the unsuspected savagery, of his real motivations. The keen and energetic social worker may find that he is really actuated by a desire to push other people around, to tell them what is best for them and to force them to do his will. The professional humanitarian, always championing the underdog, may find to his distress that his outbursts of high moral indignation at the injustices of society are nothing more than an expression of his real hatred of other humans, made respectable, to himself and others by the guise of concern for the victims of society. Or each may be compensating for hidden defects in his own personality. All these facts are well known to present-day psychologists; but how many people submit themselves to the analyst's probings? Buddhism teaches us to do it for ourselves, and to make ourselves immune to unpleasant or shocking revelations by acknowledging beforehand that there is no immutable personality, no 'self' to be either admired or deplored.

An action (kamma), once it is performed, is finished so far as its actual performance is concerned. It is also irreversible.

The moving finger writes, and having writ
Moves on: nor all your piety nor wit
Can lure it back to cancel half a line—
Nor all your tears wash out one word of it.

(Edward Fitzgerald, The Rubaiyat of Omar Khayyam)

The moving finger is no mystery to one who understands kamma and vipāka. Ask not whose finger writes upon the wall. It is your own.

What remains of the action is its potential, the inevitability of its result. It is a force released into the stream of time, and in time it must have its fruition. And when, for good or ill, it has fructified, like all else its force must pass away—and then the kamma and the vipāka alike are no more. But as the old kammas die, new ones are created—every moment of every waking hour. So the life-process, involved in suffering, is carried on. It is borne along on the current of craving. It is in its essence nothing but that craving, that desire—the desire that takes many forms, is insatiable, is self-renewing. As many-formed as Proteus; as undying as the Phoenix.

But when there comes the will to end desire a change takes place. The mind that craved gratification in the fields of sense now turns away. Another desire, other than that of the senses, gathers power and momentum. It is the desire for cessation, for peace, for the end of pain and sorrow—the desire for Nibbāna.

Now this desire is incompatible with all other desires. Therefore, if it becomes strong enough it kills all other desires. Gradually they fade out; first the grosser cravings springing from the three immoral roots; then the higher desires; then the attachments, all wilt and fade out, extinguished by the one overmastering desire for Nibbāna.

And as they wilt and fade out, and no more result-producing actions take their place, so the current of the life-continuum dries up. Unwholesome actions cannot be performed, because their roots have withered away; there is no more basis for them. The wholesome deeds in their turn become sterile; since they are not motivated by desire they do not project any force into the future. In the end there is no craving force left to produce another birth. Everything has been swallowed up by the desire for the extinction of desire.

And when the object of that desire is gained, can it any longer be a desire? Does a man continue to long for what he has already got? The last desire of all is not self-renewing; it is self-destroying. For in its fulfilment is its own death. Nibbāna is attained.

Therefore the Buddha said, 'For the final cessation of suffering, *all* kamma, wholesome and unwholesome, must be transcended, must be abandoned. Putting aside good and evil, one attains Nibbāna. There is no other way.'

The Arahat lives then only experiencing the residuum of his lifespan. And when that last remaining impetus comes to an end the aggregates of his personality come to an end too, never to be reconstructed, never to be replaced. In their continual renewal there was suffering; now there is release. In their coming together there was illusion—the illusion of self. Now there is Reality.

And Reality is beyond conception.

Kamma and Causality

Francis Story

'Does everything happen in our lives according to kamma?' This question is not one that can be answered by a plain affirmation or denial, since it involves the whole question of free will against determinism, or, in familiar language, 'fatalism'. The nearest that can be given to a simple answer is to say that most of the major circumstances and events of life are conditioned by kamma, but not all.

If everything, down to the minutest detail, were preconditioned either by kamma or by the physical laws of the universe, there would be no room in the pattern of strict causality for the functioning of free will. It would therefore be impossible for us to free ourselves from the mechanism of cause and effect; it would be impossible to attain Nibbāna.

In the sphere of everyday events and the incidents of life such as sickness, accidents and such common experiences, every effect requires more than one cause to bring it about, and kamma is in most cases the predisposing factor which enables the external influences to combine and produce a given result. In the case of situations that involve a moral choice, the situation itself is the product of past kamma, but the individual's reaction to it is a free play of will and intention. For example, a man, as the result of previous unwholesome (*akusala*) kamma either in the present life or some past birth, may find himself in a situation of desperate poverty in which he is sorely tempted to steal, commit a robbery, or in some other way carry into the future the unwholesome actions of the past. This is a situation with a moral content, because it involves the subject in a nexus of ethical potentials. Here his own freedom of choice comes into play; he has the alternative of choosing further hardship rather than succumb to the temptation of crime.

In the *paṭicca-samuppāda*, the cycle of dependent origination, the factors belonging to previous births, that is, ignorance and the actions conditioned by it, are summarised as the kamma-process of the past. This kamma produces consciousness, name-and-form, sense-perception fields, contact and sensation as its resultants, and this is known as the present effect. Thus the physical and mental make-up (*nāma-rūpa*) is the manifestation of past kamma operating in the present, as also are the phenomena cognised and experienced through the channels of sense. But running along with this is another current of action, that which is controlled by the will and this is known as the present volitional activity; it is the counterpart in the present of the kamma-process of the past. It governs the factors of craving, grasping and becoming.

This means, in effect, that the current of 'becoming' which has its source in past kamma, at the point where it manifests as individual reaction—as for example in the degree of craving engendered as the result of pleasurable sensation—comes under the control of the will, so that while the subject has no further control over the situations in which he finds himself, having himself created them in the past, he yet has a subjective control over his response to them, and it is out of this that he creates the conditions of his future. The present volitional activity then takes effect in the form of future resultants, and these future resultants are the counterpart, in the future of the kammic resultants of the present. In an exactly similar way it dominates the future birth-state and conditions, which in the paṭicca-samuppāda are expressed as arising, old age and death etc. The entire cycle implies a dynamic progression in which the state conditioned by past actions is at the same time the womb of present actions and their future results.

Kamma is not only an integral law of the process of becoming; it is itself that process, and the phenomenal personality is but the present manifestation of its activity. The Christian axiom of 'hating the sin but loving the sinner' is meaningless from the Buddhist standpoint. There is action, but no performer of the action; the 'sin' and the 'sinner' cannot be dissociated; we are our actions, and nothing apart from them.

Modes of Conditioning

The conditioned nature of all mental and physical phenomena is analysed under twenty-four heads, called in Pāli *paccaya* (modes of conditioning). Each of the twenty-four paccayas is a contributing factor to the arising of conditioned things. The thirteenth mode is *kamma-paccaya,* and stands for the past actions which form the base, or condition, of something arising later. The six sense organs and fields of sense-cognition—that is, the physical organs of sight, hearing, smell, taste, touch and mental awareness—which, as we have seen, arise at birth in association with name-and-form, provide the condition-base for the arising of subsequent consciousness, and hence for the mental reactions following upon it. But here it should be noted that although kamma as volition is associated with the mental phenomena that have arisen, the phenomena themselves are not kamma-results. The fourteenth mode is kamma-result condition, or *vipāka*, and stands as a condition by way of kamma-result to the mental and physical phenomena by establishing the requisite base in the five fields of sense-consciousness.

That there are events that come about through causes other than kamma is demonstrable by natural laws. If it were not so, to try to avoid or cure sickness would be useless. If there is a predisposition to a certain disease through past kamma, and the physical conditions to produce the disease are also present, the disease will arise. But it may also come about that all the physical conditions are present, but through the absence of the kamma-condition, the disease does not arise; or that, with the presence of the physical causes the disease arises even in the absence of a kamma condition. A philosophical distinction is therefore to be made between those diseases which are the result of kamma and those which are produced solely by physical conditions; but since it is impossible to distinguish between them without knowledge of past births, all diseases must be treated as though they are produced by merely physical causes. When the Buddha was attacked by Devadatta and was wounded in the foot by a stone, he was able to explain that the injury was the result of some violence committed in a previous life plus the action of Devadatta which enabled the kamma to take effect. Similarly, the violent death of Moggallāna Thera was the combined result of his kamma and the murderous intention of the rival ascetics whose action provided the necessary external cause to bring it about.

Causality

The process of causality, of which kamma and vipāka are only one action-result aspect, is a cosmic, universal interplay of forces. Concerning the question of free will in a causally-conditioned universe, the view of reality presented by Henri Bergson, which when it was postulated was new to the West, throws considerable light on the Buddhist concept. Life, says Bergson, is an unceasing becoming, which preserves the past and creates the future. The solid things which seem to be stable and to endure, which seem to resist this flowing, which seem more real than the flowing, are periods, cuts across the flowing, views that our mind takes of the living reality of which it is a part, in which it lives and moves, views of the reality prescribed and limited by the needs of its particular activity.

Here we have a Western interpretation of *avijjā* (ignorance)—'views of the reality prescribed and limited by the needs of its particular activity'—and of *anicca,* the unceasing becoming, the principle of change and impermanence. Bergson also includes in his system *anattā* (no-self), for in this process of unceasing change there is the change only—no 'thing' that changes. So, says Bergson, when we regard our action as a chain of complementary parts linked together, each action so viewed is rigidly conditioned, yet when we regard our whole life-current as one and indivisible, it may be free. So also with the life-current which we may take to be the reality of the universe; when we view it in its detail as the intellect presents it to us, it appears as an order of real conditioning, each separate state having its ground in an antecedent state, yet as a whole, as the living impulse (kamma), it is free and creative. We are free, says Bergson, when our acts spring from our whole personality, when they express that personality. These acts are not unconditioned, but the conditions are not external; they are in our character, which is ourself. In other and Buddhist words, our *saṅkhāra,* or kamma-formation of the past, is the personality, and that is conditioned by nothing but our own volition, or *cetanā.* Bergson details an elaborate philosophy of space and time to give actuality to this dynamic view, which he calls 'Creative Evolution', and his general conclusion is that the question of free will against determinism is wrongly postulated; the problem, like the indeterminate questions of Buddhism, cannot be answered because it is itself a product of that peculiar infirmity, that 'special view of reality prescribed and limited by the needs of a particular activity', which in Buddhism is called avijjā, the primal nescience.

The concept of causality in the world of physics has undergone modifications of a significant order in the light of quantum physics and the increase of our knowledge regarding the atomic structure of matter. Briefly the present position may be stated thus: while it is possible to predict quantitatively the future states of great numbers of atomic units, it is not possible to predetermine the state or position of any one particular atom. There is a margin of latitude for the behaviour of the individual unit which is not given to the mass as a whole. In human terms, it may be possible to predict from the course of events that a certain nation, Gondalia, will be at war by a certain date; but it is not possible to predict of any individual Gondalian that he will be actively participating in the war. He may be a conscientious objector, outside the war by his own decision; or he may be physically disqualified, outside the war because of conditions over which he has no control. We may say, 'Gondalia will be at war', but not 'That Gondalian will be in the war'. On the other hand, if we know that one particular Gondalian is not physically fit we may say confidently that he will not be in the war; the element we cannot predict with any degree of certainty is the free will of the Gondalian individual, which may make of him a chauvinist and national Gondalian hero, or a pacifist and inmate of a concentration camp.

How Kamma Operates

Coming to the details of the ways in which kamma operates, it must be understood that by kamma is meant volitional action only. *Cetanāhaṃ bhikkhave kammaṃ vadāmi*—'Volition, intention, O Bhikkhus, is what I call kamma', is the definition given by the Buddha. Greed, hatred and delusion are the roots of unwholesome kamma; unselfishness, amity and wisdom are the roots of wholesome kamma. As the seed that is sown, so must be the tree and the fruit of the tree; from an impure mind and intention, only impure thoughts, words and deeds can issue; from such impure thoughts, words and deeds only evil consequences can result.

The results themselves may come about in the same lifetime; when this happens it is called *diṭṭhadhamma-vedanīya-kamma,* and the line of causality between action and result is often clearly traceable, as in the case of crime which is followed by punishment. Actions which bear their results in the next birth are called *upapajja-vedanīya-kamma,* and it frequently happens that people who remember their previous life remember also the kamma which has produced their present conditions.

Those actions which ripen in successive births are known as *aparāpariya-vedanīya-kamma*; these are the actions which have, by continual practice, become habitual, and tend to take effect over and over again in successive lives. The repetition condition (*āsevana-paccaya*) is the twelfth of the twenty-four *paccayas*, and relates to that kamma-consciousness in which the preceding impulse-moments (*javana-citta*) are a condition by way of repetition to all the succeeding ones. This is known to modern psychology as a habit-formation, and is a very strong conditioning factor of mind and character. Buddhism urges the continual repetition of good actions, deeds of *mettā* and charity, and the continual dwelling of the mind on good and elevating subjects, such as the qualities of the Buddha, Dhamma and Sangha, in order to establish a strong habit-formation along good and beneficial lines.

The three kinds of kamma described above, however, may be without any resultants if the other conditions necessary for the arising of the kamma-result are lacking. Rebirth among inferior orders of beings, for instance, will prevent or delay the beneficial results of a habitual kamma. There is also *counteractive kamma* which, if it is stronger than they, will inhibit their fruition. Kamma which is thus prevented from taking effect is called *ahosi-kamma.* Just as there are events which occur without kamma as a cause, so there are actions which, as potentials, remain unrealised. These actions, however, are usually the weak and relatively unimportant ones, actions not prompted by any strong impulse and carrying with them little moral significance.

Functionally, the various kinds of kamma operate according to four classifications. The first is *generative kamma* (*janaka-kamma*) which produces the five-aggregate complex of name-and-form at birth and through all the stages of its arising during the life-continuum. The second category is that of *sustaining kamma* (*upatthambhaka-kamma*), which is void of kamma-results and is only capable of sustaining kamma-resultants that have already come into being. In the third category comes *counteractive kamma* (*upapīḷaka-kamma*), which by reason of its moral or immoral force suppresses other kamma-results and delays or prevents their arising. Last in this classification according to functions comes *destructive kamma* (*upacchedaka-kamma*); this is kamma of such potency that it utterly destroys the influence of weaker kamma and substitutes its own kamma-results. It may be strong enough to cut short the lifespan so that it is destructive kamma in the literal sense.

The light and insignificant actions which we perform in the course of our daily lives have their results, but they are not dominant factors unless they become part of a habit-formation. Important actions which become habitual either wholesome or unwholesome, are known as *bahula-kamma*, and their effects take precedence over those of actions which are morally insignificant or rarely performed. Those actions which are rooted in a very strong moral or immoral impulse, and take a drastic form, are known as *garuka-kamma*; they also tend to fall into the diṭṭhadhamma-vedanīya-kamma class and take effect in the same lifetime, or else in the next existence. Such actions are: drawing the blood of a Buddha, the murder of an Arahat, the killing of parents, and attempts to disrupt the Sangha. Although these are the chief demeritorious actions, there are many others of lesser weight which bear results in the next birth in the absence of garuka-kamma. The same applies to good garuka-kamma.[1]

Diṭṭhadhamma-vedanīya-kamma provides us with data for studying the operation of the law of cause and effect objectively. In the usual course of things crime brings its own consequences in the same lifetime, by a clearly traceable sequence of events, but this does not invariably happen. For a crime to receive its due punishment, a complicated machinery of causes has to be brought into operation. First there has to be the act of crime, the kamma. Its punishment then depends upon the existence of criminal laws, of a police force, of the circumstances which enable the criminal to be detected, and many subsidiary factors. It is only when all these combine that the crime receives its due punishment in the same lifetime. If the external factors are missing, the kamma alone will not bring about its consequences immediately, and we say the criminal has gone unpunished. This, however, is not the case; sooner or later either in the same lifetime or a subsequent one, circumstances will link together, albeit indirectly, and give an opportunity for the kamma to produce its results. Hence from the

1. *Niyata micchādiṭṭhi* (chronic scepticism and tenaciously held pernicious views) is also a demeritorious garuka-kamma.

Buddhist standpoint the question of capital punishment rests not on considerations of mercy to the murderer, which must always be a source of contention since mercy to a criminal implies a social injustice to the victim and lack of protection to potential victims; it rests on a consideration of the kamma-resultants to those who are instrumental in punishing him with death, since it is kamma of the worst order to kill or cause another to take life.

It is not possible here to enter into a discussion of the moral difference between the action of one who kills another from greed or anger and one who carries out a sentence of death in the course of his duties to society. That there is a difference cannot be doubted, yet for Buddhist psychology it is clear that no act of killing can be accomplished without the arising of a hate-impulse in the mind. To take life quite disinterestedly, as advocated in the *Bhagavad Gītā*, is a psychological impossibility; there must, in any case, be desire for the accomplishment of the act, or the act itself could never be carried out. This applies to every action except those performed by the *Arahat*. Since there is no 'unchanging Ātman' no distinction can be made between the deed and the doer.

Rebirth

The mode, circumstances and nature of the next birth are conditioned by what is known as the *death-proximate kamma* (*maraṇāsanna-kamma*), which is the volition, wholesome or unwholesome, that is present immediately before death. With this is associated the *paṭisandhi-viññāṇa* or connecting consciousness between one manifestation and another. At the moment just preceding death, the death-proximate kamma may take the form of a reflex of some good or bad deed performed during the dying person's life. This sometimes presents itself to the consciousness as a symbol, like the dream symbols of Freudian psychology. It may bring with it an indication of the future existence, a glimpse of the realm (*loka*) in which rebirth is about to take place. It is due to the arising of some unwholesome consciousness from past kamma that the dying sometimes exhibit fear, while others, experiencing wholesome death-proximate kamma, die with a smile on their lips, seeing themselves welcomed by celestial beings or their friends who have passed away before them. Everyone who has been present at death beds can recall examples of both kinds.

When none of these kamma-manifestations is present, however, as with those who die in a state of complete unconsciousness, the next birth is determined by what is called *reserved kamma* (*kaṭattā-kamma*). This is the automatic result of whatever kamma of the past is strongest, be it good or bad, and has not yet borne fruit or exhausted its force. This may be weighty or habitual kamma.

Heedfulness in Dying and When Living

The importance of keeping the consciousness active and faculties alert up to the moment of death is stressed in Buddhist psychology. Part of the benefit of *maraṇānussati,* the meditation on death, is that it enables one to approach the thought of death undismayed, in full possession of one's faculties and with control of the mental impulses. Instead of charging us to remember our sins and approach death in fear, Buddhism instructs us to call to mind our good actions, put aside terror and meet death with the calm confidence of one whose destiny is under his own control. It is a positive attitude in place of the negative and depressing mental state encouraged by other religions. Modern psychology advises the cultivation of such an optimistic attitude throughout life. Buddhism goes further, and shows it to be a necessary safeguard when we stand on the threshold of a new existence.

It has already been said that those who are able to remember previous lives can trace the course of kamma and vipāka from one birth to another. They are the only people who are in a position to differentiate clearly between the events that occur because of kamma and those that are caused by external agencies. It is certain however, that predominantly good kamma will save us from most of the slings and arrows of outrageous fortune, or help us to rise above whatever obstacles are set in our path. *The need for human endeavour is always present,* for in the very enjoyment of the fruits of good kamma we are generating a new series of actions to bear their own results in the future. It cannot be too often or too emphatically repeated that the true understanding of the law of kamma is the absolute opposite of fatalism. The man who is born to riches on account of his past deeds of charity cannot afford to rest on his laurels. He is like a man with a substantial bank balance; he may either live on his capital until he exhausts it, which is foolish, or he can use it as an investment and increase it. The only investment we can take with us out of this life into the next is good kamma; it therefore behoves every man who is, in the common phrase, 'blessed' with riches, to use those riches wisely in doing good.

If everyone understood the law of kamma there would be an end to the greed of the rich and the envy of the poor. Every man would strive to give away as much as he could in charity—or at least spend his money on projects beneficial to mankind. On the other hand there would be no burning feeling of injustice on the part of the 'have-nots', since they would recognise that their condition is due to their own past kamma, while at the same time its crushing effects would be alleviated by the generosity and social conscience of the rich. The result would be a cooperative scheme of sharing, in which both would prosper.

This is the practical plan of living that Buddhism suggests to us; it is sane, ethical and inspiring, and it is the one answer that a free world can make to the anti-religious materialistic ideologies. To put it into practice would be the greatest step forward in mankind's social as well as spiritual progress, and one that must be made if we are to save our civilisation from the terrible consequences of greed, hatred and delusion. It is not enough to have knowledge of the law of kamma: it must be used as applied science in the ordering of personal and national life for the realization of a happier, more stable and more regulated phase of human history.

Action and Reaction in Buddhist Teachings

Leonard A. Bullen

The whole universe is governed by law, and the unbroken sequence of action and reaction occurs in mental and moral operations just as strictly as in physical processes. In consequence, the Buddha-doctrine emphasizes that morally skilful thought, speech and action bring happiness to the doer at some time or other, while in the same way activities which are morally unskilful give rise to future suffering.

That which determines the moral skill of an activity— whether it be in thought, speech or bodily action—is the volition or mental purpose which motivates it. Where it is based on generosity, on good will, or on selfless motives, it is morally skilful, whereas when the purpose which motivates it springs from greed, hatred or delusion it is regarded as morally unskilful.

Thus the Buddha-doctrine stresses the need for developing a clear comprehension of the purpose behind every activity at every level, at the levels of thought, of speech and of bodily action. Some of these activities build up forces within the mind which eventually lead to an increase in well-being, while others, being aimless or unskilful, result in sorrow or frustration. Thus, if you take on almost any form of mental culture, one of your most important aims should be to comprehend more clearly the ultimate purpose behind all these activities.

In this scientific and technological age, you are familiar with the idea that physical effects have causes, that these effects also become causes in their turn, and that in the ordinary course of events there is no room for chance or luck. But while you accept this invariable sequence of action and reaction in the material realm, you don't always recognize it in the moral sphere. The Buddha-doctrine affirms, however, that the law of cause and effect applies just as invariably and just as exactly in the moral sphere as it does in the physical realm. This doctrine emphasizes the fact that everything in the universe acts according to various laws, and that no being in the universe can set aside or invalidate these laws. It defines five systems of laws (*pañca-niyāma*).

The first of these is the law-system which concerns the rise and fall—that is, the growth and decay—of physical phenomena under the action of heat. Second, there is the group of laws relating to the generation or growth of vegetation and of the bodies of living beings. The third law-system relates to mental action and reaction, that is, to the action of the will and its results in terms of happiness and suffering. Fourth, there are the various laws governing the processes of the mind, the laws which are studied and applied by psychologists. Finally, the fifth law-system groups together the multiplicity of laws which relate to physical and mental phenomena in general which are not embraced by the other systems of laws.

Of these five groups, you'll find that it is the third law-system that interests us in the present context. This, the law-system governing the action of the will and its consequences, is only one of the five groups of laws, but it is the one that is most directly connected with your own happiness and sorrow, your own pains and pleasures.

The original Buddhist terms that are sometimes translated as moral and immoral, or as good and bad, may also be rendered as wholesome and unwholesome. However, the terms skilful and unskilful are often used to convey the meanings of the original terms, for a moral or wholesome action is considered to be skilful because it eventually brings enjoyment as a result; an immoral or unwholesome action, since in time it brings suffering to the doer, is regarded as unskilful.

Any activity—morally good or otherwise—produces, of course, its normal physical result. If you throw a stone through a window it will break the window, whether the motivation behind it be morally skilful or otherwise. The broken window is the normal physical result of the stone-throwing action.

But assuming that the action is motivated by some morally unskilful volition (such as hatred) there will be a mental effect as well. The exercise of hatred will strengthen the hatred which already exists within the mind just as the exercise of a muscle will strengthen its own tissues. In consequence, hatred will become a more dominant factor in your mental make-up.

Now hatred is one of a group of mental factors which lead to suffering. In some way or other, at some time in the near or distant future, this mental factor will bring you suffering of some kind. The basic cause of the suffering is not the action of throwing the stone, but the hatred or ill will present in the volitional act of throwing the stone.

Now it is conceivable that the action of throwing the stone through the window might be motivated, not by hatred, but by some form of good will. You might, for example, use this action as a means of letting air into a smoke-filled room in a burning house in order to rescue someone in the room. In such circumstances, the unselfishness you exercise in your wholesome volitional action would strengthen your existing mental factor of good will, and this strengthened mental factor would eventually bring you into circumstances that would yield happiness.

Thus a morally skilful will-action brings enjoyment at some future time, while an unwholesome volition eventuates in suffering. On the other hand, an action which is not volitional (while of course it gives rise to normal physical effects) does not produce any effects in terms of strengthened mind-factors, and no effects in terms of future happiness and suffering. Where there is no volition there is no moral or immoral element.

The personal will or volition in its primal form is the urge to live, the urge to survive as a self and to assert this selfhood. From this fundamental will to live arise various tendencies, which we know as urges, instincts and desires, and which are accompanied by emotions.

In Buddhist psychology, the instincts and desires are all regarded as manifestations of the fundamental will to live. This will to live, as a rule, is simply called craving: it is the craving or thirst for personal existence, the craving to live and survive as a self for eternity. But the final freedom from unhappiness can be found only by transcending personal existence.

The thirst for personal existence, rooted as it is in ignorance, is said to be a primary condition on which all suffering depends. Thus the ultimate aim of the practising Buddhist is to overcome craving by the attainment of enlightenment.

This means, of course, to overcome desire, but only insofar as desire is personal or self-centred. It has been said:

> "To start from where we are now and unequivocally let go of every desire would be to die, and to die is not to solve the problem of living." (Huston Smith).

The type of desire to be overcome, then, is what may be called ignorant desire or irrational desire. To quote again:

> "The desires for the basic necessities of life can be satisfied, whereas the selfish desires of the ego can never be allayed. These do not spring from the chemistry of the body but are purely mental constructions—to be more and more, to have more and more: money, possessions, power, prestige, love; to outstrip and outshine all others; to be supreme. It is an impossible dream which, if realized, would not bring in its train either peace or happiness.
>
> The greedy, the jealous, the envious can never be satisfied because their dissatisfaction and unhappiness do not spring from any real deprivation of the essentials of life, but from the defects and distortions within their character." (Mettā).

From all this you'll see that in Buddhism the first and last enemy is considered to be ignorance—ignorance, not in the sense of lack of education, but in the sense of lack of the capacity for true discernment.

You'll appreciate, too, that the final victory to be won is the victory of discernment or enlightenment, and that the principal weapon in the battle is the weapon of right mindfulness in its various forms.

The personal will, then, is an aspect of the will to live, the blind thirst for personal existence which, in human life, expresses itself by way of various instinctive and emotional factors. These collectively constitute the dynamic elements in mental life.

Buddhist psychology adopts a system of classifying the dynamic mind-factors which is somewhat different from the classifications you'll meet in Western psychology. It includes not only instinctive elements but also mental habits developed from the instincts, as well as thought-patterns deliberately cultivated in opposition to the instincts.

This classification generally appears in Buddhist literature as a list of fifty active mental factors (in contrast to the receptive mental factors known as feeling and perception), and together these fifty constitute the dynamic components of the mind. Some of them are directly derived from the fundamental urge towards personal survival, while others are cultivated in opposition to the egoistic tendencies, but all of them help to determine behaviour. For this reason they can be conveniently referred to as the fifty determinants.

There is no need to deal here with the determinants in detail. All that we need to mention in the present context are three which are called the roots of unskilful will-activity and their opposites, the three roots of skilful volition.

The three roots of unskilful volition are greed, hatred and delusion, while the opposite three—generosity, good will, and discernment—are the roots of skilful will-activity.

Such activity may take the form of bodily action, it may take the form of speech, or it may take the form of thought; but it is the motive behind the activity, the mental determinant that gives rise to it that is all-important.

Thus, if you think, speak or act from motives of greed, whether in an obvious and intense form or in a subtle and disguised way, you thereby strengthen greed in your mental make-up. On the other hand, when you act from generosity you thereby strengthen this determinant in your own mind.

It is the same with hatred and its opposite factor of good will. One who allows himself to become angry or irritable immediately builds up in his own mind the factor of hatred, whereas when he makes an effort to be tolerant and patient with irritating people or annoying things he increases the mental factor of good will within his mind.

Again, if you think, speak or act in a self-centred way, you are allowing yourself to be motivated by delusion, for delusion in the present context means primarily the delusion of self, together with the self-deceit and feelings of superiority and inferiority that go along with it. As a result you become more and more governed by this delusion, for it becomes a stronger determinant than before.

When, on the other hand, you endeavour to discern the true nature of the illusory self and to break free from self-deceit, you strengthen the opposite factor of discernment. Thus discernment—or non-delusion, as it is often called—becomes a stronger determinant of your subsequent thought-processes.

Now the morally unskilful determinants that exist as parts of your mental make-up, as you can see, retard your progress towards the final liberation; thus we can speak of them as the 'retardants'.

In the same way, you can see that the morally skilful mind-factors help you in your progress towards the final liberation; and therefore we can also call them the 'progressants'.

You'll see from this that from the exercise of a particular determinant there is an immediate effect within the mind. This immediate effect is a strengthening of that determinant, which of course makes it easier to arouse it in the future.

However, there is more to it than that. Each of the determinants that we have been discussing, each of the active or dynamic factors that help to make up the mind as a whole, can be visualized as an accumulation of energy within the mind. You can regard each particular determinant—generosity, for example, on the one hand, or greed on the other—as an accumulation of a specific sort of force within the mind, and each such force will eventually bring about its own kind of experience at some time in the future.

This future experience is the result of the original will-activity—the reaction to the original action. The volitional action in the first place causes an accumulation of a specific mental force, and this force in its turn brings about its reaction in terms of enjoyment or suffering. The accumulated force, therefore, can be termed a 'reaction-force'.

An accumulation of the reaction-force of generosity will at some time give rise to enjoyment of some kind, just as the accumulation of energy within an electrical torch battery may at some time give rise to light. The energy within the battery can give rise to light only when the conditions are favourable: there must be an electric light bulb, and the switch of the torch must be turned on. The current can then flow through the filament, which then glows with light. In the process—unless the current is switched off or unless some replenishment of the battery takes place—the energy will be eventually completely discharged.

In much the same way, the accumulation of the reaction-force of generosity can give rise to enjoyment only when the environment provides suitable conditions; and, until the requisite environmental conditions come about, the reaction-force remains in storage, so to speak. When the suitable conditions do eventually appear, this particular reaction-force will give rise to the enjoyment of happy experiences, and in the process the accumulation will become less and less until completely discharged, unless of course it is replenished by further generosity.

In general, some sort of replenishment may be going on while the discharge is taking place. If, while you're enjoying happy experiences, you continue to exercise your generosity, then the accumulation of this particular reaction-force will be replenished even while it is being discharged. It is then like a water-tank from which you're drawing off water but which is being replenished by rain at the same time.

However, if while enjoying the fruits of previous generous actions you become selfish and greedy, then your mind is like a water-tank during a drought: as the water is all drained off and never replenished, so your accumulation of happiness-producing reaction-force is drained off until finally discharged.

As with the mind-factor we know as generosity, so with its opposite determinant, greed. When one gives way to self-desire in any form, the accumulation of the reaction-force of greed is increased in one's mind. When at some future time the external conditions are suitable, this accumulation will discharge by way of suffering. During suffering, one may give way to further adverse states of mind, such as self-pity, and this will add to the accumulated reaction-force. On the other hand, one may develop patience and other favourable qualities of mind, and thus this particular sorrow-producing accumulation will eventually be fully discharged.

* * *

While each type of mind-factor is a particular reaction-force, in general we can group them into two broad classes—first, reaction-forces that lead to happiness, and second those that lead to suffering. Often these are spoken of respectively as merit and demerit, and thus we say that while one person who has a great stock of merit will enjoy great happiness in the future, another who has stored up much demerit will have to endure great suffering at some later time.

The reaction-forces that exist within the mind are stored, so to speak, below the consciously accessible level of the mind. The subconscious aspect of the mind, in Buddhist terminology, is called the 'life-subcurrent'. It is the current of mental energy which exists below the threshold of consciousness, and it is thus the repository of the resultants of all past actions and past experiences.

This 'life-subcurrent' may for convenience be called the storehouse of the residual reaction-forces from all previous will-actions; but you must not take the idea of a storehouse too literally. The experiences in our lives are not in any real sense stored anywhere in the same way that water is stored in a tank, any more than apples are stored in an apple tree.

You don't believe, of course, that apples are stored in an apple tree. Given the right external conditions of climate, soil and nutrition, the forces within the apple tree will cause apples to grow on its branches; and in the same way, given the right external conditions the forces within the 'life-subcurrent' will project or precipitate experiences in accordance with the nature of these forces.

Wind is not stored somewhere in the air, but under the right conditions of heat or cold, the air will expand or contract and give rise to wind. In the same way, fire is not stored in the head of a match, but under the right conditions of friction the match will give rise to fire.

Again, sound is not stored in a record; but given the necessary conditions—when placed on a turntable of a record-player—the formation of the record gives rise to sound.

Thus the experiences of life, together with their corresponding happiness and suffering, are not stored in a literal sense in the 'life-subcurrent', but under the right conditions these events will develop as the apples develop on the branches of the apple tree.

Thus you can see that no reaction-force can take effect unless suitable conditions for its operation or discharge exist. As the suitable conditions may not arise within your present lifetime, it follows that you may not reap the enjoyment and suffering resulting from these activities within your present lifetime.

You can see, then, that at the end of your present lifetime many undischarged reaction-forces will exist, and for many of your actions the appropriate reactions will not have occurred as yet. In other words, when you die there'll be an unexpended residue of reaction-forces both 'progressant' and retardant which have had no opportunities to discharge during your present lifetime.

What happens to these unexpended or undischarged reaction-forces? When you die, your body will disintegrate, of course; but the Buddha-doctrine teaches that various components of the mind survive in the form of a life-current, a current of mental energy, and that this current of energy consists of undischarged reaction-forces. This is what the life-current actually is, an ever-changing stream of reaction-forces, and at your death this life-current will initiate a new life and thus bring about the birth of a new being.

The new being is you yourself, being an unbroken continuation of the life-current. The new being inherits all the reaction-forces—all the potentialities for happiness, for suffering, and for further volitional activity—from the old being, who is also you yourself. From the point of view of continuity, the new being is the same as the old being (although in another body), for the continuity of the life-current is not broken in any way by the phase of death and rebirth.

You've seen that the moral law of action and reaction, as set out in the Buddha-doctrine, states that we each experience happiness and suffering in exact proportion to the moral and immoral qualities of our past activities. You've seen also that this same doctrine teaches that moral and immoral activities build up forces within the mind, and these forces—reaction-forces, we have called them—eventually precipitate experiences of happiness and suffering.

This is perhaps an oversimplification of the matter, for in more exact terms the Buddha-doctrine says that every cause has a number of effects, while every effect arises from a number of causes. In other words, nothing arises from only one cause, and nothing gives rise to only one effect: everything is interwoven with many other things. However, the main point is that morally skilful activity brings enjoyment of some kind in its train while morally unskilful activity brings suffering.

The concept of the reaction-force enables us to see how the Buddhist idea of rebirth differs from non-Buddhist beliefs in reincarnation, for what is reborn in Buddhist teachings is a life-current, not a soul in the ordinary sense.

This brings us to the matter of the time at which a particular reaction-force (generated by a specific will-activity) operates. If you rob a bank and bungle your escape, you'll be caught immediately and soon punished. If you plan your escape well and make a success of it, but nevertheless leave a few clues, you may not be caught for five years, but when you are eventually punished you'll be able to see the connection between the cause (your immoral action) and the effect in the shape of punishment. However, you may execute the robbery and your escape so well that you will evade suspicion and punishment (a convenient word in the present context but not a very exact one) may not come until several lifetimes afterwards. Then you won't be able to see the connection between cause and effect.

Here again we are over-simplifying the position by talking as if one cause brings about only one effect, but the question at issue is the time at which a particular reaction-force operates.

As we have already seen, a reaction-force cannot discharge its energy until the conditions appropriate to its operation are suitable; and by conditions we mean both the external or environmental conditions as well as conditions within the mind itself. That means that if you carry out a morally unskilful activity—such as a robbery—during a time when you are reaping the benefits of a past series of morally skilful actions, you may not reap the adverse effects of the immoral act until the opposite kind of reaction-force has run its course. You say you're enjoying a run of good luck, and this is true enough so long as you realize that good luck is really the fruition of past good activity.

Similarly, if you carry out some act of generosity you can expect the enjoyment of some sort of happiness as a result, but this may not be in the near future or even in your present lifetime. You may perhaps be in the midst of a long period of frustration and failure, the effect of some past phase of morally unskilful activity whose reaction-force must run its course and exhaust its energy.

Thus the Buddha-doctrine teaches that some actions are immediately effective, since their resulting reaction-forces are discharged soon after their inception; but many will-actions are remotely effective, for the reaction-forces they generate may not produce their reactions in terms of happiness or suffering until many lifetimes afterwards.

The effects of weak volitional actions may be neutralized by stronger reaction-forces of an opposite nature. Thus, if a weak retardant reaction-force is opposed by a stronger one of a 'progressant' nature, then the stronger may render the weaker ineffective, losing some of its own energy in the process.

This does not apply, however, to a strong reaction-force generated by a very definite morally skilful or a very definite morally unskilful activity. The reaction-forces built into the mental structure by such activities can never be neutralized, and even though the suitable conditions for their discharge don't arise until many lifetimes afterwards, they invariably become effective at some time. They are therefore called indefinitely effective reaction-forces, and while dormant they are classed as reserve reaction-forces.

In contrast to indefinitely effective reaction-force, there is a kind called weighty reaction-force, which is generated either by very serious retardant will-activity or else by very exalted states of mind. The operation of weighty reaction-force, the Buddha-doctrine states, takes precedence over all other kinds.

You can see that, however long may be the time lag between the cause and its effect, the end result of volitional activity is inevitable.

At first sight you might take this to imply that the present and the future are completely and inflexibly governed by the past, and that you can experience only what your past actions have determined for you.

This fatalistic view, however, is really not a part of the Buddhist doctrine of cause and effect. It is true that you are largely—very largely—influenced by reaction-forces generated by your past volitional activities, but they are not the only forces in the mind: there is also the possibility of present volition. Volition or will exists as a force within the mind, just as attention and 'one-pointedness' exist as forces within the mind. We're not entering into any discussion on free will, beyond mentioning that everything we do is conditioned by internal and external factors; but we must recognize that volition does exist in the sense that it consists of the force of desire directed towards an objective.

Since volition does exist as desire-force directed towards an objective, we can see that we can use this volition to handle the present results of past activity. By 'handling' the present results of past activity I don't mean that we can cancel these results; I mean that we can utilize our present experiences to help us to make progress, or we can let these same experiences—pleasant as well as unpleasant—retard our progress. But to handle our present experiences—to utilize them as a means of making progress—we must develop the necessary moral skill.

Although the present is conditioned by the past as the future is conditioned by the present, the future is not unalterably fixed by the past, for the future is dependent also on what we do with our present powers of volition. In many circumstances, it is true that there may be little or no scope for a constructive or 'progressant' course of action, for the pressure of reaction-forces from the past may be too great and the present volition too weak. However, in general, even if you have no choice of external action, at least it's possible to regulate your mental and moral responses to a situation, even to a slight extent. Thus, under a difficult set of conditions that you are unable to alter, you can at least exercise patience and tolerance, facing the situation without allowing it completely to overwhelm you.

In this way, while going through a difficult period of painful reaction-force results, you're at least building up within your mental structure new 'progressant' reaction-forces, thus using the situation to its best advantage.

Questions and Answers about Kamma and Its Fruit

Nina van Gorkom

I

A. When people have an unpleasant experience they are inclined to ask: 'Why did this have to happen to me?' One might be very good and kind to other people and yet receive unkind words in return. Could you tell me whether it is true that good deeds will bring a good result? I sometimes doubt it.

B. People ask this question because they do not always understand the reason why they have to suffer in life. It is difficult to know which cause in the past brings about this or that unpleasant experience at the present moment. The Buddha said that everything that happens must have a cause. When we suffer it must have a cause either in the distant past or in the proximate past. If we know how causes and effects in our lives are interrelated, it will help us to develop the right attitude towards unpleasant experiences and sorrow.

A. Are the bad deeds one did in the past the cause of unpleasant experiences at the present moment? The deeds which are already done belong to the past. How can those deeds bring a result later on?

B. In order to have a deeper understanding of how cause and effect are interrelated it is necessary to know first what motivates good and bad deeds; moreover we should know how we accumulate wholesome tendencies in doing wholesome deeds and how we accumulate unwholesome tendencies in doing unwholesome deeds.

A. Why do you use the words 'wholesome' and 'unwholesome' instead of good and bad?

B. The words 'good' and 'bad' generally imply a moral judgement. The Buddha never spoke about sin; he would not judge people as 'good' or 'bad'. He explained about the conditions for their behaviour and about the effects of wholesomeness and unwholesomeness.

An unwholesome deed is a deed which brings harm to oneself or to other people, either at the moment the unwholesome deed is done or later on, whereas a wholesome deed is one which will lead to happiness. Unwholesome is in Pāli *akusala,* and wholesome is *kusala.* With unwholesome mental states or *akusala cittas* one can perform unwholesome deeds or *akusala kamma*; and with wholesome mental states or *kusala cittas* one can perform wholesome deeds or *kusala kamma.*

A. What is a *citta*? Is it a soul or 'self' which directs the deeds? Is it under one's control whether one will have a kusala citta which can perform kusala kamma, or is it beyond control?

B. A citta is not a soul or 'self'. There are many different cittas which succeed one another; there is no citta which lasts. Each citta which arises falls away immediately. We can experience at one moment that we have an akusala citta. However, this does not last, it falls away again. At another moment we might experience that we have a kusala citta; this does not last either, it falls away again. There can only be one citta at a time; we cannot have an akusala citta at the same moment as a kusala citta. Cittas replace one another continuously. How can we take something for self if it does not even last for a second?

Being without the Saint's perfect mindfulness, it is not in our power to have wholesome cittas whenever we want to. People would like to be good the whole day but they cannot have kusala cittas continuously; it is beyond their control.

We cannot help it that we like certain people and certain things, and that we dislike other people and things. We cannot direct all our thoughts; we may be absent-minded although we do not want to. No two people can have the same thoughts, even if they think of the same object, for example, of a country where they both have been. One's thoughts depend on many conditions, for example, on experiences and accumulated tendencies in the past, on the object which presents itself at the present moment, on good or bad friends, or on the food one has eaten.

As it is not in one's power to have a certain citta at a certain moment, we cannot say that there is a 'self' which directs our deeds. Our actions depend on the tendencies that have been accumulated in the past and on many other conditions.

A. I notice that some people always seem to do the wrong thing in life, whereas for other people it is not difficult to be generous and honest. What is the reason that people are so different?

B. People are so different because of different tendencies and inclinations which have been accumulated in the past. People who are very often angry accumulate anger. When the accumulated anger is strong enough they will perform unwholesome actions (akusala kamma) through speech or deeds. Everybody has accumulated both unwholesome and wholesome tendencies.

A. Is it correct that good and bad deeds performed in the past are never lost, that they continue to have an influence at the present moment?

B. That is true.[2] Experiences one had in the past, and good and bad deeds committed in the past, have been accumulated and they condition cittas arising in the present time. If the citta at the present moment is an akusala citta, there is a new accumulation of unwholesomeness, and if the citta at the present moment is kusala citta, there is a new accumulation of wholesomeness.

Therefore cittas which arise are not only conditioned by the object perceived through eyes, ears, nose, tongue, body-sense or mind, but they are conditioned as well by the tendencies and inclinations accumulated in the past and by many other factors.

Cittas are beyond control; they are, as the Buddha said, '*anattā*'. When the Buddha said that everything is anattā, he meant that one cannot have power over anything at all. Everything in our life occurs because there are conditions, and everything falls away again.

Good deeds and bad deeds which we performed will bring their result accordingly. The result will take place when it is the right time, when there are the right conditions for the result to take place. It is not in anyone's power to have the result arise at this or at that moment. Cause and result are beyond control, they are anattā.

---

2. Deeds, however, may also be 'ineffectual' (*ahosi-kamma*) 'if the circumstances required for the taking place of the kamma result are missing, or if, through the preponderance of counteractive karma and their being too weak, they are unable to produce any result" (Ñāṇatiloka, *Buddhist Dictionary*)—Editor.

A. I understand that akusala cittas which perform akusala kamma are cause and that those cannot bring a pleasant result; they will bring an unpleasant result, whereas kusala cittas which perform kusala kamma will bring a good result.

Each cause will bring its result accordingly. Could you explain how the result is brought about? Is it a punishment or a reward for one's deeds?

B. There is no question of punishment or reward because there is no one who punishes or rewards. It is the course of nature that one reaps what one has sown.

Accumulated akusala kamma produces at the right time a citta which experiences an unpleasant object; this citta is the result of a bad deed one did in the past. Accumulated kusala kamma produces at the right time a citta which experiences a pleasant object; this citta is the result of a good deed one did in the past. The citta which is result is called *vipāka-citta*. There will be different results at different moments. For most people it is not possible to find out which deed of the past produces the result one receives at the present moment. However, it is of no use to know in detail what happened in the past; we should only be concerned about the present moment. It is enough to know that akusala kamma produces an unpleasant result and that kusala kamma produces a pleasant result. The result is produced either shortly afterwards or later on.

We cannot blame other people for an unpleasant result we receive. An unpleasant result is the consequence of our own bad deeds.

A. How often during the day is there vipāka? Is there vipāka at this moment?

B. Yes, there is vipāka now, because you are seeing and hearing. Every time you are seeing, hearing, smelling, tasting and experiencing a tangible object through the body-sense there is vipāka. All impressions that we experience through the five senses are vipāka.

A. How can I find out whether there is pleasant or unpleasant vipāka? I am seeing right now but I have no pleasant or unpleasant feeling about it.

B. It is not always possible to find out whether the object is pleasant or unpleasant. Sometimes we are so used to certain pleasant or unpleasant objects that we do not realise whether they are pleasant or unpleasant.[3] When we see or hear we cannot always find out whether there is kusala vipāka or akusala vipāka. When we feel pain or when we are sick we can be sure that there is akusala vipāka.

The moment of vipāka-citta is very short, it falls away immediately.

When we see, we first perceive colour through the eyes. We only see colour. Then we like or dislike it, we recognize it, we think about it. The seeing of colour is vipāka. Like or dislike and thinking about the object are not vipāka. Those functions are performed by other cittas, which are akusala cittas or kusala cittas. The cittas that like or dislike, and the cittas that think about the object, are not results but causes; but they are causes that can motivate deeds which will bring fresh results.

All cittas succeed one another so rapidly that there seems to be only one citta. We are inclined to think that like or dislike and thinking are still vipāka, but that is a delusion.

A. Does everyone receive both akusala vipāka and kusala vipāka?

B. Everyone has accumulated both unwholesome deeds and wholesome deeds; therefore everyone will receive both akusala vipāka and kusala vipāka.

However, we can develop understanding of cause and effect and this helps us to take the right attitude, such as patience, towards the events of our life, even under unpleasant conditions. For instance, when we understand what vipāka is we will be less inclined to feel sorry for ourselves or to blame other people when there is akusala vipāka. If we feel sorry for ourselves or blame other people, there is a new accumulation of unwholesomeness and this will bring us more sorrow in the future.

A. But I cannot help disliking unpleasant vipāka. How can I change my attitude?

---

3. There are also numerous sense-impressions which cause a neutral, or indifferent, feeling (called in Pāli: neither-pleasant-nor-unpleasant). They are of course, likewise, kamma-results (vipāka) but the perception of them is not associated with pleasant or unpleasant feeling, and hence, also not with likes or dislikes. —Editor.

B. You can change your attitude by understanding what vipāka is and what is no longer vipāka. It is very important to know that the moment we feel dislike or regret is not the same as the moment of vipāka. People are inclined to think that the dislike which arises after the vipāka is still vipāka. When they say 'This is just vipāka,' they do not distinguish unpleasant feelings from the moments of vipāka. If they do not really know what is vipāka and what is not vipāka but akusala citta, or akusala kamma, they accumulate unwholesomeness all through their lives. By ignorance, by not knowing when the citta is akusala, one accumulates unwholesomeness.

A. I am inclined to blame people who speak harsh words to me, even when I am so kind to them. Are those people not the cause that I receive unpleasant vipāka?

B. We are inclined to think in this way if we haven't yet understood what vipāka is.

Let us analyse what is really happening when we hear harsh words spoken by someone else. When those words are produced by akusala cittas, it is an unpleasant object we receive through the ear. It is not really we who receive the unpleasant object, but the vipāka-citta receives the unpleasant object through the ear. The vipāka-citta is the result of akusala kamma performed in the past. This was the right moment that the akusala kamma, performed in the past, caused vipāka-cittas to arise at the present moment. The person who speaks harsh words to us is not the cause of akusala vipāka; the cause is within ourselves. Someone who speaks harsh words to us is only one of the many conditions for vipāka-cittas to arise. Our own accumulated akusala kamma is the real cause of akusala vipāka.

A. It seems to me that kamma is a fate which directs our lives.

B. Kamma is not an unchangeable fate outside ourselves but our own accumulated unwholesome and wholesome deeds, and at the right moment it will produce its results in the form of vipāka-cittas.

A. Is it necessary to have aversion every time we hear an unpleasant sound?

B. No, it is not necessary.

A. If a third person would pass and if he would hear harsh words spoken to me, he might have akusala vipāka as well, although the words are not directed to him. Is that right?

B. If it is the right moment for him to have akusala vipāka, he will receive the unpleasant object as well; he might have akusala vipāka through the ear. Whether the words are addressed to him or to someone else does not make any difference.

A. Is it right that the vipāka might not be as unpleasant for him as for the person to whom the harsh words are addressed?

B. Aversion has nothing to do with vipāka. Considering whether the words are addressed to oneself or to another person and the unpleasant feelings about it are no longer vipāka. If we feel aversion there are akusala cittas, conditioned by our accumulations of aversion in the past. There are some short moments of vipāka only at the moment we receive the sound, before the unpleasant feelings arise. Kamma conditioned the vipāka-cittas right at that moment. Kamma is the real cause of vipāka, not this or that person. If we want to have the right understanding of vipāka, we should not think in terms of 'I', 'those people' and 'harsh words'; we should only think of cittas.

If we think of people and if we consider whether harsh words are addressed to ourselves or to someone else, we will not see the truth. If we think in terms of cittas and if we understand conditions for cittas, we will understand truth. When someone speaks harsh words it is conditioned by his accumulated aversion. It is not really important whether he addresses those words to us or to someone else.

If we understand vipāka we will take the unpleasant experiences of life less seriously. It will be of much help to us and to other people if we try to understand ourselves, if we know different cittas arising at different moments. After we have had akusala vipāka we should try not to think much about it. When we think about vipāka it already belongs to the past. It is therefore better to forget about it immediately.

A. I still do not understand why I have to receive harsh words in return for my kindness. How can the result of kusala-kamma be akusala vipāka?

B. This could never happen. Kusala kamma has kusala vipāka as its result; however, the good result might arise later on. It is not possible to tell at which moments akusala-kamma and kusala-kamma produce results. Akusala-vipāka is not the result of one's kindness; it is the result of one's accumulated akusala-kamma. Kindness will certainly bring a good result, but that might take place later on.

A. I cannot help feeling sorry for myself when there is akusala-vipāka. What can I do to prevent the accumulation of more unwholesomeness?

B. When there are conditions for akusala-cittas we cannot prevent their arising. They arise very closely after the vipāka, before we know it. They are 'anattā', they do not belong to a 'self,' they are beyond control. However, we can develop more understanding of the different phenomena that arise. The akusala-cittas that arise after the vipāka are not the same as the vipāka-cittas and they have conditions different from the conditions for the vipāka-cittas.

If we understand that feeling sorry for ourselves and blaming other people is done by akusala-cittas and that in this way we accumulate more unwholesomeness, we will be less inclined to do so. If we understand that at this moment we cannot do anything about the vipāka which has its cause in the past, we will be able to forget about it more easily. At the moment we are aware of akusala vipāka, it has fallen away already and belongs to the past.

Life is too short to waste energy in worrying about things of the past. It is better to accumulate kusala kamma by doing wholesome deeds.

We read in the *Kindred Sayings* (*Saṃyutta Nikāya* I, *Sagāthā Vagga,* Ch. III, Kosala, 111, §5) that King Pasenadi came to see the Buddha at Sāvatthī. The king had been zealously busy with all such matters as occupy kings. The Buddha asked him what he would do if he would hear from loyal men, coming from all four directions, about a great mountain, high as the sky, moving along and crushing every living thing. The Buddha said:

> "And you, sire, seized with mighty dread, the destruction of human life so terrible, rebirth as man so hard to obtain, what is there that you could do?"

"In such a mighty peril, lord, the destruction of human life so terrible, rebirth as man so hard to obtain, what else could I do save to live righteously and justly and work good and meritorious deeds?"

"I tell you, sire, I make known to you sire: old age and death come rolling in upon you, sire! Since old age and death are rolling in upon you, sire, what is there that you can do?"

"Since old age and death, lord, are rolling in upon me, what else can I do save to live righteously and justly, and to work good and meritorious deeds?"

II

A. I understand that the active side of our life consists of unwholesome states of mind or akusala-cittas and wholesome states of mind or kusala-cittas. Akusala-cittas can perform unwholesome deeds and kusala-cittas can perform wholesome deeds. All through one's life one accumulates both unwholesomeness and wholesomeness.

There are other cittas which are the result of one's deeds: those are called vipāka-cittas. The result of unwholesome deeds or akusala-kamma is akusala-vipāka; the result of wholesome deeds or kusala-kamma is kusala-vipāka. Vipāka is the passive side of our life; we undergo vipāka. Seeing, hearing, smelling, tasting and feeling through body contact are vipāka.

I can understand this because sense-impressions are impressions which one undergoes. The cittas which think about those impressions, and which like or dislike them, are no longer result or vipāka; they are cause. They are akusala or kusala-cittas. But I still doubt every time I see there is the result of akusala or kusala-kamma I did in the past. Can you prove this to me?

B. This cannot be proven in theory. One can know the truth only through direct experience.

There are three kinds of wisdom. The first kind stems from thinking about the realities of life such as impermanence, old age, sickness and death. The second kind is understanding developed through the study of the Buddhist teachings. The third kind of wisdom is the direct experience of the truth.

The first and the second kind of wisdom are necessary, but they are still theoretical understanding; they are not yet the realization of the truth. If one accepts the Buddha's teachings because they seem to be reasonable, or if one accepts them on the authority of the Buddha, one will not have the clear understanding that stems from the direct experience of the truth. Only this kind of understanding can eliminate all doubts.

We read in the *Gradual Sayings* (*Aṅguttara Nikāya*, Book of the Threes, Ch. VII, §65, Those of Kesaputta) that when the Buddha was staying in Kesaputta the Kālāmas came to see him. They had heard different views expounded by different people and had doubts as to who was speaking the truth and who falsehood. The Buddha said:

> "Now look you, Kālāmas. Be not misled by report or tradition or hearsay. Be not misled by proficiency in the collections, nor by mere logic or inference, nor after considering reasons, nor after reflection on and approval of some theory, nor because it fits becoming, nor out of respect for a recluse (who holds it). But, Kālāmas, when you know for yourselves: These things are unprofitable, these things are blameworthy, these things are censured by the intelligent; these things, when performed and undertaken, conduce to loss and sorrow—then indeed do you reject them, Kālāmas."

The Buddha then asked the Kālāmas whether greed, malice and delusion, and the evil deeds they inspire, lead to a man's profit or to his loss. The Kālāmas answered that they lead to his loss. The Buddha then repeated that when they know for themselves that these things are unprofitable and lead to sorrow, they should reject them. Thereupon the Buddha spoke about non-greed, non-hate and non-delusion, and the abstinence from evil deeds these inspire. He said that when the Kālāmas know for themselves that these things are profitable and conduce to happiness, they should undertake them.

We have to find out the truth ourselves, by experiencing it in daily life. In being aware of all realities of daily life one develops the third kind of wisdom.

In the practice of *vipassanā* or 'insight', we learn to understand all realities of daily life, in being aware of them at the moment they occur. We learn to be aware of what happens at the present moment. We will know what seeing, hearing, thinking, etc. really are, if we are aware of those realities at the moment they occur.

Only the present moment can give us the truth, not the past or the future. We cannot experience now the cittas we had in the past; we cannot experience the cittas which performed akusala-kamma or kusala-kamma in the past. We can only experience cittas of the present moment. We can experience that some cittas are akusala, some are kusala, and some are neither, that they have different functions. If we learn to experience the cittas of the present moment, we will gradually be able to see realities more clearly. If we realize 'Enlightenment', or the experience of *Nibbāna*, all doubts about realities will be eliminated. Then we will see the truth.

A. I would like to be enlightened in order to know the truth.

B. If you only have wishful thinking about Nibbāna, you will never attain it. The path leading to Nibbāna is knowing the present moment. Only if we know the present moment will we be able to eliminate ignorance about realities and the idea of 'self' to which we are still clinging.

We should not cling to a result which might take place in the future. We should instead try to know the present moment and we must not speculate about the future.

A. Is it not possible for me to know whether seeing and hearing at this moment is akusala-vipāka or kusala-vipāka?

B. Sometimes you can find out. For instance, hearing is kusala-vipāka when the sound is produced by kusala-cittas. Someone who speaks to you with compassion produces the sound with kusala-cittas. When you hear that sound there is kusala-vipāka. Often it is not possible for us to know whether there is akusala-vipāka or kusala-vipāka. Moreover, it is not of great use to know this, because we cannot do anything about our own vipāka.

It is enough to know that akusala-kamma brings about akusala-vipāka, and that kusala-kamma brings about kusala-vipāka. It is important to remember that vipāka is caused by our own kamma, that the cause of vipāka is within ourselves and not outside ourselves.

The *Gradual Sayings* (*Aṅguttara Nikāya*, *Book of the Threes* or *Tika Nipāta*, Ch. IV, §35, The Lord of Death) tells of a man who had been negligent in the doing of good deeds, and was brought before Yama, the lord of death. Yama said to him:

"My good man, it was through negligence that you did not act nobly in deed, word and thought. Verily they shall do unto you in accordance with your negligence. That evil action of yours was not done by mother, father, brother, sister, friends and comrades: not by kinsmen, devas, recluses and brahmins. By yourself alone was it done. It is just you that will experience the fruit thereof."

It is not important to know exactly at which moment there is akusala-vipāka or kusala-vipāka. However, it is most important to know exactly at which moments there is vipāka and at which moments we perform akusala-kamma or kusala-kamma. The moments we perform akusala-kamma and kusala-kamma will condition our future.

A. In order to know how and when one accumulates akusala-kamma and kusala-kamma one should know more about the cittas which perform kamma. I notice that the Buddha spoke about cittas in order to help people to have more understanding about their life and in order to encourage them to perform kusala-kamma. Therefore I think that all through one's life one should develop a clear understanding about cittas. Could you give me a definition of a citta?

B. It is not possible to give a definition that will explain to you what a citta is. You should experience cittas yourself in order to know them. There are so many different types of cittas at different moments that it is impossible to give one definition for all of them. The most general definition is: it knows something. Citta is not like materiality, which does not know anything. The citta which sees knows colour, a citta which hears knows sound, a citta which thinks knows many different objects.

A. Why are seeing and hearing cittas? You explained before that seeing is not thinking, but only the experience of colour through eye-sense and that hearing is the experience of sound through ear-sense. Are those not merely physical processes instead of cittas which know something?

B. Eye-sense and ear-sense in themselves are not cittas; they are physical organs. But eye-sense and ear-sense are conditions for the arising of cittas. There is citta whenever an object, as for example colour or sound, is experienced.

We should try to be aware of the citta of the present moment if we want to know what citta is. We should be aware of the seeing or the hearing that occurs right now.

Many people who are brought up in the West do not understand why it is not possible to give a clear definition of citta, and of everything the Buddha taught. They want to prove things in theory. This is not the way to find the truth. One should experience the truth in order to know it.

A. I still think of citta as a mind which directs seeing, hearing, thinking etc. How can I find out that there is not a 'self' which directs everything?

B. We can only find this out by being aware of different cittas. Thus we will experience that we cannot direct our thoughts. We are absent-minded when we do not want to be so; many odd thoughts arise, in spite of ourselves. Where is the 'self' that can direct our thoughts?

There is one citta at a time; it arises and falls away completely to be followed by the next citta, which is no longer the same. There is no single citta which stays. For example, seeing-consciousness is one citta, but hearing-consciousness is another citta.

A. I don't understand why those functions are performed by different cittas. Why can't there be one citta which stays and performs different functions, and why is it not possible that different functions are performed at the same time? I can see, hear and think at the same time.

B. Seeing occurs if colour contacts the eye-sense. Recognizing it or thinking about it occurs afterwards. Seeing is not performed by the same cittas as thinking about what one saw; seeing has different conditions. Hearing has again different conditions. Thinking about what one heard has conditions that are different from the conditions for hearing-consciousness.

You would not be able to notice that seeing and hearing are different, if those functions were performed by one single citta at the same time. In that case you would only receive one impression instead of several impressions. We experience seeing and hearing as different impressions, even when they seem to occur at the same time. They have different places of origin and different objects, and they occur at different moments, though the moments can be so close that they seem to be one.

Thinking about what one just saw occurs after the seeing-consciousness, thinking about what one just heard occurs after the hearing-consciousness. Seeing-consciousness occurs at a moment different from the moment the hearing-consciousness occurs. Therefore thinking about what one saw cannot arise at the same moment as thinking about what one heard. Thinking is done by many different cittas which succeed one another.

When we have learned to be more keenly aware of the citta which arises at the present moment, we will notice that seeing and hearing arise alternately, at different moments. We will notice that there isn't one long moment of thinking, but different moments of thinking. We will notice that thinking is very often interrupted by moments of seeing and hearing, and these again are conditions for new thoughts. We will find out how much our thoughts depend on different experiences of the past, on unwholesome and wholesome tendencies we have accumulated, on the objects we see and hear and on many other conditions.

A. You said that all cittas are beyond control, that they are 'anattā'. Akusala-cittas and kusala-cittas are conditioned by one's accumulations. It is not in anyone's power that they arise. You said that vipāka-cittas are 'anattā' as well.

Sometimes it seems that I can have power over vipāka, that it is in my power to have kusala-vipāka through the ear. Whenever I wish to hear a pleasant sound, I can put a record of classical music on my record-player.

B. You put the record on because you know the conditions for the pleasant sound. Everything happens when there are the right conditions for it. It is impossible for anything to happen without conditions. When there is fire we use water to extinguish it. We cannot order the fire to be extinguished. We don't have to tell the water to extinguish the fire; the water has the characteristic that it can extinguish the fire. Without the right conditions we would not be able to do anything.

With regard to the beautiful music which you can play, there have to be many different conditions for this pleasant sound. And even when there is this pleasant sound, you have no power over the kusala-vipāka-cittas. If you really could direct them, you could make them arise at any moment, even without the record-player. We should remember that music is not vipāka, only the cittas which experience the pleasant object through the ear are vipāka. Do we really have power over these cittas?

There are many conditions which have to co-operate so that the vipāka can arise. There has to be ear-sense. Did you create your own ear-sense? You received ear-sense before you were born; this also is a result for which you did not ask. Moreover, do you think that you can have kusala-vipāka as long as you wish and whenever you wish? When you have developed a keener awareness you will notice that the kusala-vipāka and the other types of cittas arise alternately.

The vipāka-cittas are followed by cittas which are no longer vipāka; for example, the cittas which arise when you like the music which you hear and when you think about it. Or there might be cittas which think about many different things, perhaps with aversion or with worry. Or there might be thoughts of kindness towards other people.

The kusala-vipāka will not only be interrupted by akusala-cittas and kusala-cittas, but by akusala-vipāka as well. There is akusala-vipāka when there are loud noises outside, when the telephone rings loudly, or when one feels the sting of a mosquito. There cannot be kusala-vipāka at the moment there is an akusala-citta, a kusala-citta or akusala-vipāka.

If you could make kusala vipāka arise at will, you could have it without interruption, whenever you wish. This is not possible. Moreover, if it were not the right time for you to have any kusala-vipāka, you would not be able to receive a pleasant object: the record-player would be broken, or something else would happen so that you could not have kusala-vipāka.

A. Is it not by accident that the record-player would be broken?

B. The Buddha taught that everything happens because of conditions. There are no accidents. You will understand reality more deeply if you think of cittas, and if you do not think of conventional terms like record-player, this person or that person. Vipāka are the cittas, not the record-player or the sound in itself. The record-player is only one of the many conditions for vipāka. The real cause of vipāka is not an accident, or a cause outside ourselves; the real cause is within ourselves.

Can you find another cause for akusala-vipāka but your own akusala-kamma, and for kusala-vipāka but your own kusala-kamma?

A. That is right, I can find no other cause. However, I still do not understand how akusala-cittas which performed akusala-kamma in the past and kusala-cittas which performed kusala-kamma in the past can produce vipāka later on.

B. It is not possible to understand how the events of our life are interrelated without studying cittas in detail and without knowing and experiencing the cittas which arise at the present moment. When one can experience what the cittas of the present moment really are, one will be able to understand more about the past.

When the Buddha became enlightened he saw how everything that happens in life has many conditions and he saw how things that happen depend on one another.

The teaching about the conditional arising of phenomena, the dependent origination (*paṭicca-samuppāda*), is difficult to grasp. We read in the *Kindred Sayings* (Saṃyutta Nikāya I, Sagāthā Vagga, Ch. VI, The Brahmā Suttas, Ch. 1, §1, The Entreaty) that the Buddha, when he was staying at Uruvela after he had just attained enlightenment, was thinking that the Dhamma he had penetrated was deep, difficult to understand:

> "And for a race devoting itself to the things to which it clings, devoted thereto, delighting therein, this were a matter hard to perceive, to wit, that this is conditioned by that—that all that happens is by way of cause."

At first the Buddha had no inclination to teach Dhamma, as he knew that a teaching which is 'against the stream of common thought' would not be accepted by people who delight in clinging. The sutta continues:

> *"This that through many toils I've won:*
> *Enough! Why should I make it known?*
> *By folk with lust and hate consumed*
> *This is not a Dhamma that can be grasped.*
> *Against the stream (of common thought),*
> *Deep, subtle, fine, and hard to see,*
> *Unseen it will be by passion's slaves*
> *Cloaked in the murk of ignorance."*

However, the Buddha decided out of compassion to teach Dhamma, for the sake of those who would be able to understand it. Do you still have doubts about the accumulation of deeds?

A. Is the deed you see a mental phenomenon or a physical phenomenon?

B. You can only see the action of the body, but the action is actually performed by cittas. We can never see the citta, but we can find out what the citta is like when the body moves in doing deeds.

With regard to your question how deeds done in the past can produce a result later on, the answer is that deeds are performed by cittas. They are mentality and thus they can be accumulated. All experiences and deeds of the past are accumulated in each citta, which falls away and conditions the next citta. Whenever there is the right condition, the kamma that is accumulated and carried on from one moment of citta to the next can produce vipāka.

III

A. I would like to know if we only receive vipāka in this life, or is there vipāka in a future life as well?

B. According to the Buddhist teachings one receives the results of one's deeds in future lives as well.

We read in the *Kindred Sayings* (*Saṃyutta Nikāya* I, Ch. III, *Kosala*, 2, §10, *Childless* 2) that when the Buddha was staying at Sāvatthī, King Pasenadi came to see him. A rich man who had lived as a miser had just died. He had performed both good deeds and bad deeds and he therefore had to receive both kusala-vipāka and akusala-vipāka, which he experienced during different life-spans. He had given alms to a 'Silent Buddha' (*Pacceka* Buddha[4]) of a former period, but afterwards he regretted his gift. As a result of his good deed of almsgiving to a 'Silent Buddha' he was reborn seven times in heaven, where he could enjoy pleasant vipāka. After his existences in heaven he was reborn as a human being, which is kusala-vipāka as well. He was born of rich parents, but

4. A Pacceka Buddha is a Buddha who becomes enlightened by himself, but who has not accumulated as many virtues as the '*Sammā Sambuddha*', who could become enlightened by himself and help others as well to become enlightened.

his accumulation of stinginess prevented him from enjoying the pleasant things of life. As a result of regretting his gift to the Silent Buddha, he did not utilize his riches for his benefit or that of others. Although he had the means to buy everything he wanted, he denied himself good food, clothes, etc. because of his stinginess.

After his existence as a human being he was again bound for a different rebirth. He had committed akusala-kamma of a heavy kind and this akusala-kamma would bring akusala-vipāka of a heavy kind. He had killed the only son of his brother because he wanted to get his brother's fortune. This very heavy kamma caused him to be reborn in hell where he would stay for many hundred thousands of years. The Sutta points out how one can receive different results in different existences.

A. Is the existence of heavens and hells not mere mythology?

B. People have different accumulated inclinations which make them perform different kamma. No person acts in the same way as another. Each act brings its own result, either in this life or in the following existences. To be reborn in a heavenly plane or in the human plane is the result of a wholesome deed; to be reborn in a sorrowful plane is the result of an unwholesome deed. Heaven and hell are conventional terms which are used to explain realities. They explain the nature of the vipāka which is caused by kamma. Since both akusala-kamma and kusala-kamma have different degrees, akusala-vipāka and kusala-vipāka must have different degrees as well.

Names are given to different heavenly planes and different sorrowful planes in order to point out the different degrees of akusala-vipāka and kusala-vipāka.

'*Deva*', which means 'radiant being', is a name given to those who are born in heavenly planes. In the *Anuruddha Sutta* (*Middle Length Sayings* or *Majjhima Nikāya III*, *Suññata Vagga* No. 127) Anuruddha spoke about different degrees of skill in meditation which bring their results accordingly. A monk who was not advanced was reborn as a deva 'with tarnished light'. Those who were more advanced in meditation were reborn as devas with a greater radiance. There are different devas with different degrees of brightness.

A. I find it difficult to believe in devas and in different planes of existence.

B. You do not experience devas and different planes of existence right at this moment. But is it right to reject what you cannot experience yet?

If one has right understanding of the cittas of the present moment one will be able to understand more about the past and about the future.

Rebirth-consciousness can arise in any plane of existence. When the right conditions are present a good or a bad deed which has been accumulated can produce a result, it can produce rebirth-consciousness in the appropriate plane.

A. What is the first vipāka in this life?

B. There has to be a citta at the very first moment of life. Without a citta we cannot have life. A dead body has no citta, it is not alive. What type of citta would be the first citta? Would it be an akusala-citta or a kusala-citta, which could bring about a result? Or would it be another type of citta, for example a citta which is not a cause but a result, a vipāka-citta?

A. I think it must be a vipāka-citta. To be born is a result; nobody asks to be born. Why are people born with such different characters and in such different situations? Are the parents the only cause of birth and the only cause of the character of a child?

B. Parents are only one of the conditions for the body of a child, but they are not the only condition.

A. What about the character of a child? Are there not certain tendencies in a child's character he inherits from his parents? Is this not proved by science?

B. The character of a child cannot be explained by the character of the parents. Brothers and sisters and even twins can be very different. One child likes to study, another child is lazy; one child is by nature cheerful, another depressed. Parents may have influence on a child's character after its birth in that education, a cultural pattern, or a family tradition in which a child is brought up will be conditions for cittas to arise. But a child does not inherit its character from its parents. The differentiations in character are caused by accumulations of experiences from previous existences as well.

A. Are parents not the real cause of birth?

B. Parents are only one of the conditions for birth; kamma is the real cause of birth.

A deed, done in the past, brings its result when it is the right time: it can produce the vipāka-citta which is rebirth-consciousness. We read in the *Discourse on the Lesser Analysis of Deeds* (*Middle Length Sayings III*, No. 135) (*Cūla Kamma Vibhaṅga Sutta, Majjhima Nikāya, Vibhaṅga Vagga*) that, when the Buddha was staying near Sāvatthī in the Jeta Grove, Subha came to see him and said:

> "Now, good Gotama, what is the cause, what the reason that lowness and excellence are to be seen among human beings while they are in human form? For, good Gotama, human beings of short lifespan are to be seen and those of long lifespan; those of many and those of few illnesses; those who are ugly, those who are beautiful; those who are of little account, those who are of great account; those who are poor, those who are wealthy; those who are of lowly families, those of high families; those who are weak in wisdom, those who are full of wisdom. Now what, good Gotama, is the cause, what the reason that lowness and excellence are to be seen among human beings while they are in human form?"
>
> "Deeds are one's own, Brahman youth, beings are heirs to deeds, deeds are matrix, deeds are kin, deeds are arbiters. Deed divides beings—that is to say by lowness and excellence."

A. Is rebirth in a human plane the same as reincarnation?

B. If there were reincarnation, a soul or 'self' would continue to exist and it would take on another body in the next life. However, there is no soul or 'self'. There are cittas which succeed one another from birth to death, from this life to the next life. One citta has completely fallen away when the next citta arises. There can be only one citta at a time, and there is no citta which lasts.

Cittas arise and fall away completely, succeeding one another. Death is the conventional word for the end of one's lifespan on a plane of existence, but actually there is birth and death at each moment of one's life, when a citta arises and falls away.

There isn't any citta one can take for a soul or 'self'. Since there is no soul or 'self' in this life, how could there be a soul or 'self' which is reborn in the next life? The last citta of this life is the dying-consciousness. The dying-consciousness arises and falls away, and it is succeeded by the rebirth-consciousness of the next life. The rebirth-consciousness is conditioned by the previous citta, the dying-consciousness; but it is not the same citta.

A. I can see tendencies in people's character which seem to be the same all through their lives. Moreover, there is rebirth in the next life. Therefore there must be continuity in life. However, I do not understand how there can be continuity if each citta completely falls away before the next citta arises.

B. There is continuity because each citta conditions the next citta and thus accumulated tendencies can be carried on from one moment to the next moment. All accumulations of past existences and of the present life condition future existences.

When people asked the Buddha whether it is the same person who is reborn or another person, the Buddha answered that it is neither the same person nor another person. There is nobody who stays the same, not even in this life, because there is no 'self'. On the other hand, it is not another person who is reborn, because there is continuity.

Former existences condition this life, and this life also conditions the following lives.

A. What is the last vipāka in this life?

B. The dying-consciousness (*cuti-citta*) is the last vipāka in this life.

Since there are many deeds which have not yet produced a result, one of the deeds will produce rebirth-consciousness after death. As long as there is kamma there will be vipāka, continuing on and on. There will be future lives, so that the results of one's deeds can be received.

When the dying-consciousness falls away, a deed of the past, or kamma, immediately produces a vipāka-citta: the rebirth-consciousness (*patisandhi-citta*) of the next life. When the dying-consciousness has fallen away, the rebirth-consciousness follows upon it immediately, and thus all that has been accumulated is carried on from the past into the next life.

A. What causes the rebirth-consciousness of the next life?

B. Everyone has performed akusala-kamma and kusala-kamma. Each deed brings its own result. The vipāka-citta which is the rebirth-consciousness can therefore only be the result of one deed, of akusala-kamma or of kusala-kamma.

A. Is birth in the human plane the result of kusala-kamma?

B. Birth in the human plane is always the result of kusala-kamma. Akusala-vipāka which arises afterwards in life is the result of kamma that is different from the good deed that produced the rebirth-consciousness. After birth in the human plane there can be many moments of akusala-vipāka, every time one experiences an unpleasant object through one of the five senses. Those moments are the result of other unwholesome deeds performed in the past.

If the rebirth-consciousness is akusala-vipāka one cannot be born as a human being. The rebirth has to take place in another plane of existence, such as the animal world or one of the woeful planes like the hells or the ghost realm.

A. Can a human being be reborn as an animal?

B. Some people behave like animals; how could they be reborn as human beings? Everyone will receive the result of his deeds accordingly.

A. Is it due to one's kamma that one is born in favourable circumstances, for instance, in a royal family or in a rich family?

B. Yes, this is due to a wholesome deed performed in the past.

A. I notice that even people who are born in the same circumstances, as for example in rich families, are very different. Some rich people are generous, others are stingy. How could this be explained?

B. People are different because they have different accumulated inclinations and tendencies which cause them to behave in different ways. We read in the Sutta that I quoted above about the person who was born of rich parents, but who could not enjoy the pleasant things of life because of his accumulated stinginess. Although he had the opportunity to let other people share in his fortune he did not want to do this.

Other people again who have received pleasant things in life grasp every opportunity to give things away to others. The different inclinations people have accumulated, condition them to do unwholesome deeds which will bring them unpleasant results, or to do wholesome deeds which will bring them pleasant results.

People take different attitudes towards vipāka. The attitude one takes towards vipāka is more important than vipāka itself, because one's attitude conditions one's life in the future.

A. Can kusala-vipāka be a condition for happiness?

B. The things which are pleasant to the five senses cannot guarantee true and lasting happiness. Rich people, who have everything that is pleasant to the five senses, can still be very unhappy.

For instance, when one is sitting in a beautiful garden with sweet-smelling flowers and singing birds, one can still be very depressed. At the moment one is depressed the cittas are akusala-cittas.

One cannot always be happy with pleasant things around. Unhappiness and happiness depend on one's accumulations of unwholesomeness and wholesomeness.

If one feels unhappy it is due to one's own defilements. Unpleasant feeling is conditioned by attachment. If one does not get what one wants one feels unhappy. If one has no attachment at all there would be no unhappiness. One can be perfectly happy if one is purified from defilements.

We read in the *Gradual Sayings* (*Aṅguttara Nikāya*, Book of the Threes, Ch. IV, §34, of Āḷavi) that when the Buddha was staying near Āḷavi, Hatthaka was wandering there and saw the Buddha seated on the ground strewn with leaves. He asked the Buddha:

> "Pray, sir, does the Exalted One live happily?"
>
> "Yes, my lad, I live happily. I am one of those who live happily in the world."
>
> "But, sir, the winter nights are cold, the dark half of the month is the time of snowfall. Hard is the ground trampled by the hoofs of cattle, thin the carpet of fallen leaves, sparse are the leaves of the tree, cold are the saffron robes and cold the gale of wind that blows."
>
> Then said the Exalted One: "Still, my lad, I live happily. Of those who live happily in the world I am one."

The Buddha then pointed out that a man who had a house with a gabled roof, well-fitting doors, 'a long-fleeced woollen rug, a beautiful bed, four beautiful wives', could have lust, malice and delusion. Defilements will cause 'torments of body or of mind'; defilements are the cause of unhappiness. The Buddha had eradicated all defilements completely, and thus it was not important to him whether there was akusala-vipāka or kusala-vipāka. He could live perfectly happy no matter what the circumstance were.

A. How can we purify ourselves so that we take the right attitude towards vipāka?

B. We can purify ourselves only if we know the cause of defilements. The cause of all defilements is ignorance. Out of ignorance we believe in a 'self', we cling to a 'self'. Ignorance conditions attachment and aversion or anger, it causes all unhappiness in the world. Ignorance can only be cured by wisdom (*paññā*). In *vipassanā* or 'insight meditation', the wisdom is developed which can gradually eradicate the belief in a 'self'. Only when this wrong belief has been completely eradicated can all defilements be eradicated stage by stage.

The Arahat, the perfected one who has attained the final stage of enlightenment, has eradicated all defilements. He has no more attachment, ill will or ignorance. As he has no defilements he is perfectly happy. After he has passed away there will be no more vipāka for him in a future life, there will be no more rebirth for him.

In the *Discourse on the Analysis of the Elements* (*Middle Length Sayings III*, No. 140) (*Dhātu Vibhaṅga Sutta* of the *Majjhima* Nikāya) we read that the Buddha taught Dhamma to Pukkusāti when they were staying in the potter's dwelling. The Buddha taught him about physical phenomena and mental phenomena and he taught the mental development which leads to *Arahatship*. The *Arahat* does not cling to life. In order to describe the state of the Arahat the Buddha used the simile of the oil-lamp which burns on account of oil and wick but which goes out if the oil and wick come to an end. It is the same with the conditions for rebirth. So long as there are defilements there will be fuel for rebirth. When defilements have been eradicated completely there is no more fuel left for rebirth. The Sutta goes on to say that the highest wisdom of those who have attained enlightenment is the 'knowledge of the complete destruction of anguish'.

The knowledge or wisdom developed in *vipassanā* leads to Nibbāna, which is the end of all sorrow.

Kamma and Freedom

Francis Story

The problems encountered in relating the Buddhist doctrine of kamma to the issue of causality and freedom, are largely ones of meaning. They particularly revolve around the meaning of such concepts as causation, conditioning and determination. Buddhism does not deny that man is largely conditioned by his circumstances and environment. But the conditioning is not absolute. It may almost amount to determinism, and the margin of free will may be very slight indeed, but it is always present. In Buddhist ethico-psychology great importance is given to the thought-moment of choice—that moment of conscious response to a situation in which we are free to act in a number of different ways. Now it may happen that the predominant propensities of the past impel almost irresistibly towards a particular course of action; but it must be remembered that our past habits of thought and deed are never all of the same kind. Human character is very fluid, and in the critical moment it is never absolutely certain what kind of urge will come uppermost. The whole point of any character development is to systematically cultivate the good urges and eradicate the bad ones.

Then again, some precise definition of the specifically Buddhist terms is necessary, in order to grasp what is meant by kamma. Kamma is simply action, a deed. Its result is called *vipāka*, and the two should not be confused or telescoped into a single concept under the same word, as is done by Theosophists and some popular writers on Hinduism. But the two terms considered together, as *kamma-vipāka*, 'action-and-result', do denote a moral principle in the universal order. Thus a cruel action, because its genesis is mental (*cetanā*), will in course of time ripen as a painful experience of a similar kind for the same person who did the cruel deed—perhaps in this life (the murderer who is hanged) or in a subsequent one.

As to whether it is the *same* person who experiences the result—that can neither be absolutely affirmed nor absolutely denied; its answer lies in the concept of personality and identity held by Buddhism, which can be found in writings dealing with rebirth. The sole identity that can be claimed for a personality, even through the course of one lifetime, is the world-line represented by his kammic continuity. While an individual at any given moment is simply the end result of what his previous actions have made him, he is also projecting himself into the future by his present acts, and it is in these that his freedom of choice lies. He is no more determined absolutely by his own past than he is by his environment or his heredity. Buddhism teaches the principle of multiple causality: that is to say, every phenomenon is the product of more than one cause. And the will, although it is greatly modified by these causes, is itself free to choose between a number of different causes operating upon it from the past. *We are free to select the causes that will determine our action in the moment of choice.* That is why conflicts arise which are sometimes so difficult and painful to resolve. There is always the existential anguish in freedom of choice.

At any time we can see how this works out in concrete instances. A man may have been reared in an atmosphere of squalor, want and anxiety, in which everything pushes towards crime. But in the moment of deciding whether or not he shall commit a crime, other, perhaps latent, causes are at work within him. He may have been taught earlier that crime is morally wrong, or some good influence from a previous life may be stirring within him, or he may have realized, quite simply, that 'crime does not pay'. He may be deterred by some memory of a painful result, imprisonment or flogging, from the present life. Whether these deterrent factors are noble or ignoble, they are always present, and he has to make a choice between the causes that will determine his present action. And very often he will choose not to commit the crime. If this were not so, the moral improvement of individuals and society would not be possible.

We might find it difficult to see that an individual born in an environment of destitution, deprivation, ignorance, want and hunger can be said to be born in such circumstances due to past evil deeds. But in fact what we 'cannot see' is precisely what the Buddha taught. All attempts to reconstruct the Buddha's thought, leaving out rebirth, are doomed to failure. We might be able to have rebirth without the moral order represented by kamma-vipāka—in which case it would only be an infinite extension of the amoral, meaningless life-process envisaged by the epiphenomenalists—but we cannot have a moral order without rebirth.

Why so? Simply because not all murderers get hanged! (And it may be added, neither do they get punished who by their indifference, selfishness and brutality help to make others criminals; at least, not in the same life. Too often they prosper—but the principle of kamma-vipāka is never cheated. At some time they have to pay for it.)

The world is so dominated today by the concepts of materialism that some Buddhist Kierkegaard ought to write another *Concluding Unscientific Postscript* to clear up the muddle. Not anti-scientific, be it understood, but simply *un*-scientific. Not bounded by the dogmas of nineteenth century Darwin-Marx-Huxley materialism, which today is taken for science. We should be ready to accept what is true in this materialism, without fearing to go beyond it.

And what *is* true in that concept of man? That he is conditioned by his environment? Certainly, nobody in their senses would deny it, and the Buddha did not. But no man is *entirely* conditioned by anything, not even by his own accumulated habits of thinking and acting. No character is irrevocably fixed—except that of an *Ariya* (saint), whose destiny is assured. (It is necessary to make this exception, although here it is something of a digression.) The ordinary man is, as I have said, a fluid process; his identity from one moment to another is nothing but the world-line of his continuity as a process in time. Consequently he is always acting 'out of character'. Have not great and noble men arisen from the most sordid environments of want and deprivation? And conversely, have not criminals and degenerates appeared where all the social, economic and even hereditary factors were the most favourable that the world has to offer?

Let it be granted that *in the majority of cases* men are what their circumstances make them. Buddhism teaches that it is they who have created these circumstances by their past kamma. But their present kamma, which moulds their future, is in their own hands. However slight the margin of free will, it is always there. Without it, life would be altogether without meaning, and it would be absurd to try to seek any meaning. In fact, it would be impossible, and we ourselves would not be puzzling over Buddhism! The mere fact that these questions have presented themselves to us shows that we are not automatons, not just cybernetic mechanisms, bound to run like a street car or a train along set lines, but free-swimming organisms—thinking, willing personalities, not plants.

Kamma is not solely responsible for every phenomenon and every experience. The physical aspects of life also have their share in the totality. Still, in the last resort, the mind and will are able to prevail over everything else. Not always by a single act of will, but by repeated acts of the same nature, having the same final goal. Life without suffering is impossible, because of the conditions, physical and psychological, that our desire for personalized life imposes as the condition of our being-in-the-world. But the mind can develop itself—can stop creating and imposing those conditions.

We must distinguish clearly between what we have to submit to—the circumstances of the present which we have made for ourselves by our past actions—and the future we can make for ourselves by our present thinking and doing. That distinction is most important: it represents the whole difference between absolute determinism and free will. The root cause of phenomenal existence is the double one of ignorance conjoined with craving, each being dependent upon the other. When these two joint conditions are removed, all other conditioning comes to an end. That is the whole point of *paṭicca-samuppāda,* the formula of conditioned arising—that it can be reversed by repeated acts of decision. Man can always swim against the current; if he could not, his evolution would be impossible.

It should not be thought that, as a corollary of the above, Buddhism *approves* of poverty, hunger and want. Buddhism approves of nothing in the world except the striving to gain release from it. Its view of the world is realistic. Poverty, hunger and ignorance exist in the world, and they will continue to do so as long as people, by their own infliction of these evils on others in previous lives, cause themselves to be born in such circumstances. We should try to diminish these evils, but it can never be done by purely physical means. The effort is good merely because it represents a good volition which will bear fruit in the future rather than because of any likelihood of its succeeding completely. If the entire world acted according to Buddhist principles of unselfishness, generosity and compassion, there would be no more deprivation, no more slums, no more oppression or exploitation of man by man. Yet still, bad kamma of the past would have to produce its vipāka by some other means. We can be certain that if all the wealth in the world were to be equally distributed one morning, there would be the rich and the poor again by evening. It is a fundamental fact of nature—which hates equality more than it hates a vacuum. There will be equality when all the past and present thoughts and deeds of all men are equal—and when can that be?

The economic structure of society accurately reflects man's muddled, illogical and selfish nature. It will be changed only when that nature is completely transformed. All improvement must come from within, for 'mind creates all phenomena' out of the raw material of the universe. The world-stuff is neither good nor bad; it is man's thinking which makes heaven or hell out of it.

The Buddha said: "In this fathom-long body, equipped with sense organs and faculties, O Bhikkhus, I declare to you is the world, the origin of the world, the cessation of the world and the path leading to the cessation thereof.' Philosophically speaking, these words are the most profound, most comprehensive and most illuminating ever uttered. We create the world literally. The world, in turn, conditions us, but it does not create us. That is the great difference. Since we, each of us individually, are the creators of our world, even the conditioning it imposes is ultimately traceable to ourselves.

Collective Karma

Francis Story

From time to time the question of whether there is 'collective karma', or not, keeps coming up. Is it possible for groups of people—whole nations or generations—to share the same karma? Or is karma a strictly individual and personal thing?

The Buddha treated karma, everywhere and always, as a personal inheritance:

> "Owners of their karma are the beings, heirs of their karma, their karma is the womb from which they are born, their karma is their friend, their refuge. Whatever karma they perform, good or bad, thereof they will be the heirs. (*Majjhima Nikāya*, 135)

None can suffer from the karma of another, nor profit by the karma of another. But it may happen that large groups of people, through being guilty of the same misdeeds—as for instance racial persecutions, mass killings and tortures, etc.—come to make for themselves almost identical karma. Can this be called 'collective karma'?

In a sense it can; yet the term is deceptive. The so-called 'collective karma' is made up of individual karmas, each of which must have its individual fruition. No man necessarily shares the karma of others of his national or other group simply by reason of being one of that group. He is responsible only for his own particular share in its deeds. If he does not share them, his own karma will be quite different.

Most of the confusion of thought arises from the misuse of the phrase 'the law of karma'; and the spelling of the word betrays the source from which the idea of a 'law' of 'collective karma' comes. The Pāli word *is kamma.*

Kamma simply means 'action'—a deed performed by bodily action, speech or thought. Its result is *vipāka.* There is a law of causality, and it is because of this law that kamma, the cause, is invariably followed by vipāka, the result. 'The law of karma' has a mystical sound, and suggests a kind of fatalism. People who say, resignedly, 'It is my karma,' are using the word wrongly. They should say, 'It is my vipāka'. This would remind them that their kamma, the really important thing, is under their control: they are fashioning it from moment to moment. As their kamma is now, so will their vipāka be in the future. We should avoid confusing the cause with the effect.

Kamma is individual because it is *cetanā*—volitional action of an individual mind.

> "Volition, (*cetanā*) O Bhikkhus, is what I call action; for through volition one performs actions of body, speech and mind." *Aṅguttara Nikāya*, 6:63

To what extent can one person dominate and direct the volition of another? Sometimes to a very dangerous extent—but only if there is a surrender of the will to the external influence. That itself involves an act of cetanā, a voluntary submission to another person's will. Such a submission should only be made to a spiritual *guru*; and even then the moral sense should not be suspended. The case of Aṅgulimāla is a warning against a too unquestioning submission to the dictates of an unworthy teacher. Aṅgulimāla was fortunate later in encountering the greatest Teacher of all, who saved him. People of today have to protect themselves against spiritual quacks, and it is not always easy to discriminate.

Apart from this, there is the question of indoctrination, a very great problem in the modern world. We have seen the phenomenon, unknown before in history, of whole nations behaving under a compulsion imposed on them from without. We have seen the development of techniques for manufacturing a mass-mind capable of incredible atrocities. Propaganda, brainwashing, mass-suggestion leading to mass-hysteria—all these are features of the new technique of power. Can these produce 'collective karma'? The answer is that they can certainly produce individual kammas that are practically identical; but they still remain personal kammas, even though they are instigated. No matter to what influences a man is subjected, his reaction to them together with its vipāka remains his own.

But supposing (not, alas, a very far-fetched supposition these days) a man is forced on pain of torture or death to participate in mass atrocities?

To begin with, it must be his past kamma that has placed him in such a terrible position; it is his vipāka from some previous unwholesome kamma. He has two alternatives before him: either he can submit, and for the sake of preserving his life continue to make more bad kamma for himself—or he can refuse and let his enemies do what they like. If he chooses the latter course he will probably exhaust the bad vipāka in suffering, in his current life. His act of self-abnegation, his refusal to participate in deeds of violence and cruelty, will be a positive good. He will have perfected his *sīla,* his moral purity.

In either case his kamma, be it wholesome or unwholesome, will be his own.

But what about the sharing of merits?

This again depends upon cetanā, an act of will. When a good deed is performed and the merit is shared with others, there must be the will to share it on their part. By approving the deed they produce a similar good cetanā in themselves. Their attention must be drawn to the deed, so that they can rejoice in it and generate a good mental impulse connected with *dāna* (liberality), or whatever the meritorious deed may be. Again, the 'sharer' makes his own kamma. We cannot share demerit, because nobody would be willing to share it with us!

The troubles we inherit from our parents' mistakes cannot be said to be sufferings resulting from their kamma. A child that is born in a country devastated by war, if it suffers it is suffering because the situation in which it has been born makes it possible for the child's own bad kamma to fructify. There must always be more than one cause to produce a given result. Another child, in precisely the same situation, and whose parents were even more directly responsible for the mistakes that led to the country's ruin, may be materially in a much better position. Its parents may have made a fortune in the war that brought others to destitution. This child, too, is experiencing the results of its own kamma, not that of the parents. They will have to suffer for theirs.

There are different kinds of causes, and different kinds of effects. Kamma is one kind of cause; vipāka is its corresponding effect. The important thing is to distinguish clearly between the individual cause and effect that carries over from one life to another—the personal kamma and vipāka—and other chains of cause and effect that operate through circumstances in the external world.

Reflections on Kamma and Its Fruit

Nyanaponika Thera

I

Most writings on the doctrine of kamma emphasize the strict lawfulness governing kammic action, ensuring a close correspondence between our deeds and their fruits. While this emphasis is perfectly in place, there is another side to the working of kamma—a side rarely noted, but highly important. This is the modifiability of kamma, the fact that the lawfulness which governs kamma does not operate with mechanical rigidity but allows for a considerably wide range of modifications in the ripening of the fruit. This fact is already implied by those types of kamma called 'supportive', 'counteractive' and 'destructive', and by a classification referring to the different ripening times of the result. But the teaching that kamma-results are modifiable is so important that it deserves to be stressed and discussed as an explicit theme in itself.

If kammic action were always to bear fruits of invariably the same magnitude, and if modification or annulment of kamma-result were excluded, liberation from the *saṃsāra* cycle of suffering would be impossible; for an inexhaustible past would ever throw up new obstructive results of unwholesome kamma.

Hence the Buddha said:

> "If one says that in whatever way a person performs a kammic action, in that very same way he will experience the result—in that case there will be no (possibility for a) religious life[5] and no opportunity would appear for the complete ending of suffering.
>
> "But if one says that a person who performs a kammic action (with a result) that is variably experienceable, will reap its results accordingly—in that case there will be (a possibility for) a religious life and an opportunity for making a complete end of suffering." *Aṅguttara Nikāya*, 3:110

5. Commentary: 'a religious life led for eradication of kamma' (*kammakkhaya-brahmacariya*).

Like any physical event, the mental process constituting a kammic action never exists in isolation but in a field, and thus its efficacy in producing a result depends not only on its own potential, but also upon the variable factors of its field, which can modify it in numerous ways. We see, for example, that a particular kamma, either good or bad, may sometimes have its result strengthened by supportive kamma, weakened by counteractive kamma, or even annulled by destructive kamma. The occurrence of the result can also be delayed if the conjunction of outer circumstances required for its ripening is not complete; and that delay may again give a chance for counteractive or destructive kamma to operate.

It is, however, not only these extraneous conditions which can cause modification. The ripening also reflects the kamma's 'internal field' or internal conditions—that is, the total qualitative structure of the mind from which the action issues. To one rich in moral or spiritual qualities, a single offence may not entail the weighty results the same offence will have for one who is poor in such protective virtues. Also, analogously to human law, a first offender's punishment will be milder than that of a reconvicted criminal.

Of this type of modified reaction the Buddha speaks in the continuation of the discourse quoted above:

> "Now take the case when a minor evil deed has been committed by a certain person and it takes him to hell. But if the same minor offence is committed by another person, its result might be experienced during his lifetime and not even the least (residue of a reaction) will appear (in the future), not to speak about a major (reaction).
>
> "Now what is the kind of person whom a minor offence takes to hell? It is one who has not cultivated (restraint of) the body, not cultivated virtue and thought, nor has he developed any wisdom; he is narrow-minded, of low character and even for trifling things he suffers. It is such a person whom even a minor offence may take to hell.
>
> "And what is the kind of person by whom the result of the same small offence will be experienced in his lifetime, without the least (future residue)? He is one who has cultivated (restraint of) the body, who has cultivated virtue and thought, and who has developed wisdom; he is not limited (by vices), is

a great character and he lives unbounded (by evil).[6] It is such a person who experiences the result of the same small offence during his lifetime, without the least future residue.

"Now suppose a man throws a lump of salt into a small cup of water. 'What do you think, monks: would that small quantity of water in the cup become salty and undrinkable through that lump of salt?'—'It would, Lord.'—'And why so?'—'The water in the cup is so little that a lump of salt can make it salty and undrinkable.'—'But suppose, monks, that lump of salt is thrown into the river Ganges. Would it make the river Ganges salty and undrinkable?'—'Certainly not, Lord.'—'And why not?'—'Great, Lord, is the mass of water in the Ganges. It will not become salty and undrinkable by a lump of salt.'

"Further, O monks, suppose a person has to go to jail for a matter of a half-penny, a penny or a hundred pence, and another man does not have to go to jail on that account.

"Now what is the kind of person that has to go to jail for a matter of a half-penny, a penny or a hundred pence? It is one who is poor, without means or property. But he who is rich, a man of means and property, does not have to go to jail for such a matter." *Aṅguttara Nikāya*, 3:110

Hence we may say that it is an individual's accumulation of good or evil kamma and also his dominating character traits, good or evil, which affect the kammic result. They determine the greater or lesser weight of the result and may even spell the difference between whether or not it occurs at all.

But even this does not exhaust the existing possibilities of modifications in the weight of kammic reaction. A glance into the life-histories of people we know may well show us a person of good and blameless character, living in secure circumstances; yet a single mistake, perhaps even a minor one, suffices to ruin his entire life—his reputation, his career, and his happiness— and it may also lead to a serious deterioration of his character. This seemingly disproportionate crisis might have been due to a chain reaction

6. According to the Commentary, this refers to the taint-free (*khīṇāsava*) Arahat, with regard to offences he may have committed either in this life before attaining sainthood, or in former existences. In his case, he is unbounded by the limiting forces of greed, hatred and delusion.

of aggravating circumstances beyond his control, to be ascribed to a powerful counteractive kamma of his past. But the chain of bad results may have been precipitated by the person's own action—decisively triggered by his initial mistake and reinforced by subsequent carelessness, indecision or wrong decisions, which, of course, are unskilful kamma in themselves, committed either in this life before attaining sainthood, or in former existences. This is a case when even a predominantly good character cannot prevent the ripening of bad kamma or soften the full force of the results. The good qualities and deeds of that person will certainly not remain ineffective; but their future outcome might well be weakened by any presently arisen negative character changes or actions, which might form a bad counteractive kamma.

Consider too the converse situation: A person deserving to be called a thoroughly bad character may, on a rare occasion, act on an impulse of generosity and kindness. This action may turn out to have unexpectedly wide and favourable repercussions on his life. It might bring about a decisive improvement in his external circumstances, soften his character, and even initiate a thorough 'change of heart'.

How complex, indeed, are situations in human life, even when they appear deceptively simple! This is so because the situations and their outcome mirror the still greater complexity of the mind, their inexhaustible source. The Buddha himself has said: "The mind's complexity surpasses even the countless varieties of the animal kingdom" (*Saṃyutta Nikāya*, 22:100).

For any single individual, the mind is a stream of ever-changing mental processes driven by the currents and cross-currents of kamma accumulated in countless past existences. But this complexity, already great, is increased still very much more by the fact that each individual life-stream is interwoven with many other individual life-streams through the interaction of their respective kammas. So intricate is the net of kammic conditioning that the Buddha declared kamma-result to be one of the four 'unthinkables' (*acinteyya*) and warned against treating it as a subject of speculation.

But though the detailed workings of kamma escape our intellection, the practically important message is clear: the fact that kammic results are modifiable frees us from the bane of determinism and its ethical corollary, fatalism, and keeps the road to liberation constantly open before us.

The potential 'openness' of a given situation, however, also has a negative side, the element of risk and danger: a wrong response to the situation might open a downward path. It is our own response which removes the ambiguity of the situation, for better or worse. This reveals the kamma doctrine of the Buddha as a teaching of moral and spiritual responsibility for oneself and others. It is truly a 'human teaching' because it corresponds to and reflects man's wide range of choices, a range much wider than that of an animal. Any individual's moral choice may be severely limited by the varying load of greed, hatred and delusion and their results which he carries around; yet every time he stops to make a decision or a choice, he is potentially free to throw off that load, at least temporarily. At this precarious and precious moment of choice he has the opportunity to rise above all the menacing complexities and pressures of his unfathomable kammic past. Indeed, in one short moment he can transcend aeons of kammic bondage. It is through right mindfulness that man can firmly grasp that fleeting moment, and it is mindfulness again that enables him to use it for making wise choices.

II

Every kammic action, as soon as it is performed, first of all affects the doer of the deed himself. This holds with as much truth for bodily and verbal deeds directed towards others as it does for volitional thoughts that do not find outward expression. To some extent we can control our own response to our actions, but we cannot control the way others respond to them. Their response may turn out to be quite different from what we expect or desire. A good deed of ours might be met with ingratitude, a kind word may find a cold or even hostile reception. But though these good deeds and kind words will then be lost to the recipient, to his own disadvantage, they will not be lost to the doer. The good thoughts that inspired them will ennoble his mind, even more so if he responds to the negative reception with forgiveness and forbearance rather than anger and resentment.

Again, an act or word meant to harm or hurt another may not provoke him to a hostile reaction but only meet with self-possessed calmness. Then this 'unaccepted present will fall back to the giver', as the Buddha once told a Brahmin who had abused him. The bad deed and words, and the thoughts motivating them, may fail to harm the other, but they will not fail to have a damaging effect on the character of the doer; and it will affect him even worse if he reacts to the unexpected response by rage or a feeling of resentful frustration.

Hence the Buddha says that beings are the responsible owners of their kamma which is their inalienable property. They are the only legitimate heirs of their actions, inheriting their legacy of good or bad fruits.

It will be a wholesome practice to remind oneself often of the fact that one's deeds, words and thoughts first of all act upon and alter one's own mind. Reflecting thus will give a strong impetus to true self-respect, which is preserved by protecting oneself against everything mean and evil. To do so will also open a new, practical understanding of a profound saying of the Buddha:

> "In this fathom-long body with its perceptions and thoughts there is the world, the origin of the world, the ending of the world and the path to the ending of the world."
>
> *Aṅguttara Nikāya*, 4:45

III

The 'world' of which the Buddha speaks is comprised in this aggregate of body-and-mind. For it is only by the activity of our physical and mental sense faculties that a world can be experienced and known at all. The sights, sounds, smells, tastes and bodily impressions which we perceive, and our various mental functions, conscious and unconscious—this is the world in which we live. And this world of ours has its origin in that very aggregate of physical and mental processes that produces the kammic act of craving for the six physical and mental sense objects.

> "If, Ānanda, there were no kamma ripening in the sphere of the senses, would there appear any sense-sphere existence?"— "Surely not, Lord." *Aṅguttara Nikāya*, 3:76

Thus kamma is the womb from which we spring (*kamma-yoni*), the true creator of the world and of ourselves as the experiencers of the world. And through our kammic actions in deed, word and thought, we unceasingly engage in building and re-building *this* world and worlds beyond. Even our good actions, as long as they are still under the influence of craving, conceit and ignorance, contribute to the creation and preservation of this world of suffering. The Wheel of Life is like a treadmill set in perpetual motion by kamma, chiefly by its three unwholesome roots—greed, hatred and delusion. The 'end of the world' cannot be reached by walking on a treadmill; this only creates the illusion of progress. It is only by stopping that vain effort that the end can be reached.

It is "through the elimination of greed, hatred and delusion that the concatenation of kamma comes to an end" (*Aṅguttara Nikāya*, 10:174). And this again can happen nowhere else than in the same aggregate of body-and-mind where suffering and its causes originate. It is the hopeful message of the third noble truth that we *can* step out of the weary round of vain effort and misery. If, despite our knowledge of the possibility of release, we keep walking on the treadmill of life, that is because of an age-old addiction hard to break, the deeply rooted habit of clinging to the notions of 'I', 'mine' and 'self'. But here again there is the hopeful message in the fourth noble truth with its Noble Eightfold Path, the therapy that can cure the addiction and gradually lead us to the final cessation of suffering. And all that is required for the therapy is again found in our own body and mind.

The treatment proper starts with correctly understanding the true nature of kamma and thereby our situation in the world. This understanding will provide a strong motivation for ensuring a prevalence of good kamma in one's life. And as it deepens by seeing the human condition still more clearly, this same understanding will become the spur for breaking the chains of kammic bondage. It will impel one to strive diligently along the path, and to dedicate all one's actions and their fruits to the greatest end of action—the final liberation of oneself and all sentient beings.

Karma—The Ripening Fruit[7]

Bhikkhu Ñāṇajīvako

I

With the decline of Newtonian physics and the emergence of quantum theory and relativity, the physical world-picture in the West became centred around a *process-concept*. Natural sciences and nineteenth century scientifically oriented philosophy were in quest of new criteria that could be better adjusted to their specific aims than the crude causal interpretation of the whole world, 'with its men and gods' (as the Buddha would say) in bare analogy to 'dead matter' in its macroscopic common-sense aspect. This was the end of the stiff mechanistic absolutism based on the substance-view, and the corresponding conception of causality as the universal pattern of blind determinism in nature. The dominant role of physics was about to be replaced by a prevalently biological orientation. This at least was the tendency of the new vitalistic philosophy, whose most pre-eminent representative was Henri Bergson.

By this essential turning, modern philosophy seemed to return to pathways that closely, though not explicitly, resembled certain specific features of Buddhism, which have arisen out of different contexts and much earlier in time. The first to advert to this analogy explicitly, in the terms of a new philosophy of culture, was Friedrich Nietzsche. The idea of his 'eternal recurrence' of cosmic and historical cycles, taken over from early Greek philosophy, was not sufficient for his dynamic 'transvaluation of all values'. Yet the way from the early Ionian world-view to the Indian heritage in the dissolving civilizations of the Near East—out of which ultimately the Ionian Renaissance had arisen—was not very long. Thus Nietzsche discovered in the teaching of the Buddha an archetypal model for his own vitalistic attitude in philosophy. His interpretation of Buddhism

7. Reprinted from *Main Currents in Modern Thought*, Vol. 29, No.1 (1972).

became a paradoxical counterpoint accompanying Nietzsche's antithetic position to Christianity.

Despite its rather strange position in the structure of Nietzsche's own thought, his interpretation of Buddhism is neither vague nor unauthentic. Nietzsche found his access to Buddhism through the basic text of *The Dhammapada* (probably Fausböll's masterly Latin translation of 1855, the first in Europe). In Chapter I, 5, the Buddha is quoted as saying: 'Enmities are never appeased by enmity, but they are appeased by non-enmity. This is the eternal law.' In Nietzsche's interpretation, this statement is 'the moving refrain of the whole of Buddhism ... and quite rightly: it is precisely these emotions [of ressentiment] which would be thoroughly *unhealthy* with regard to the main dietetic objective,' since Buddhism "no longer speaks of 'struggle against sin' but quite in accordance with actuality, 'the struggle against *suffering*.'" Suffering is in Nietzsche's existential interpretation 'a state of depression arisen on the basis of *physiological* conditions: against this depression Buddha takes hygienic measures.' The Buddha was a "deep physiologist, whose 'religion' should more properly be called a *hygiene* ... whose effect depends on the victory over ressentiment: to make the soul free from it—this is the first step towards health. 'Enmity is not ended by enmity' ... this is not a moral advice, this is an advice of physiology."[8]

As brutally partial as this interpretation may seem even to Buddhists, it nevertheless singled out an essential point whose deeper implications will remain characteristic for the development of the later philosophical thought on the main subject of the present paper.

On the other hand, at the end of the nineteenth century, and also much later, missionaries of more popular versions of Buddhism, still unaware of the essential purport of the new scientific and philosophical world-view emerging in their own cultural ambience, were praising Buddhism for its eminently rational advantages as a religion founded on the 'solid scientific basis' of the universally valid 'principle of causality', almost in its Newtonian meaning. For at that time the term *paṭicca-samuppāda,* or 'interdependent origination' of

8. Friedrich Nietzsche, *The Anti-Christ*, §20 (Penguin Classics) pp. 129–130, and *Ecce Homo*, §6 (my translation).

all phenomena (*dhammā*), used to be interpreted in analogy to the 'hard facts' of physics and physically oriented 'positive' sciences. This understanding of the principle of causality seemed sufficient to account for the generally Indian teaching on *karma*, the basic principle of moral determinism, and for its peculiarly Buddhist version, distinguished by the Buddha's negation of a permanent soul-principle (*anattā*) in the *process* of becoming, visualized as a 'stream' (*saṃsāra*) of life-experience, and corresponding most closely, as we shall see, to Bergson's *flux du vecu.*

It seems that at that time, and for a long time after, nobody except Nietzsche was interested in taking note of another humble historical fact, namely, that the Buddha's attitude to the world as a whole was emphatically negative: *sabba-loke anabhirati,* disgust with the whole world—not only because the world, whose overlord is Death (*Māro*), is essentially anguish or suffering (*dukkha*), but also because the deeper reason for this existential anguish is the 'nullity' (*suñña*) of our-self-being-in-the-world, or 'nihilation' as we might express it in twentieth century terms:

> "Since in this very life such a being (as the Buddha) cannot be identified by you as existing in truth, in reality, is it proper for you to state that such a being is the superman, the most excellent man who has attained the highest aim, and that such a being, if he has to be designated, should be designated in other than these four terms: 'Such a being exists after death'; or 'he does not exist after death'; or 'he both does and does not exist after death'; or 'he neither does nor does not exist after death'?"
>
> "Surely not, reverend sir."
>
> "Good, Anurādha. Both formerly and now, it is just suffering that I proclaim, and the ceasing of suffering."[9]

II

In the oldest Buddhist texts of *Abhidhamma* (about phenomena), the central conception of phenomenological analysis (*vibhajjavāda*) was concentrated on the idea of a 'stream of existence' (*bhavaṅga-sota*), or, in a free translation, emergence of fluctuating articulation.

9. *Saṃyutta-Nikāya*, XXII, 86 and 85. Quotations from the Pāli Text Society's Translation Series.

Thus, in early Buddhism as in modern philosophy, 'substance-thought' had to be replaced by 'process-thought'. Long before the Buddha, substance-thought was formulated in the Vedāntic conception, contained, among so many other world-views, in the earliest Upanishads as the teaching of an absolute, all-encompassing being, Brahman, conceived as 'changeless, all-pervading, unmoving, immovable, eternal'. In negating all these attributes, the Buddha challenged Vedāntic absolutism by adopting the alternative solution of resolving all 'being' into flux and nullity (*suññatā*), in negating even a permanent or static soul-principle (*anattā,* or the negation of *ātmā,* the Vedāntic Self).

Thus the core of the Abhidhamma conception of the 'stream of existence' consists in its theory of momentariness (*khaṇikavāda*). Its modern analogy has found its first and best formulation in the philosophy of William James, especially in his essay, *Does 'Consciousness' Exist?*, where the 'stream of consciousness' or 'stream of thinking' (which, 'when scrutinized, reveals itself to consist chiefly of the stream of my breathing') is elicited from his basic theory of 'pure experience', defined as 'the instant field of the present ... this succession of an emptiness and fullness that have reference to each other and are of one flesh'—succession 'in small enough pulses', which 'is the essence of the phenomenon.' In the same connection, as 'the result of our criticism of the absolute', the metaphysical and meta-psychical idea of a 'central self' is reduced by James to 'the conscious self of the moment'.[10] Compare this with Whitehead's further elaboration in his metaphysical conception of 'actual occasions' and 'throbbing actualities' understood as 'pulsations of experience', whose 'drops' or 'puffs of existence' guided by an internal teleology of their 'concrescence' (analogous to the Buddhist *saṅkhārā* in kammic formation) join the 'stream of existence'.[11]

10. Quotations from *Classic American Philosophers*, New York, Appleton-Century-Crofts, 1951), pp. 160, 155, 161, 163n.

11. Some analogies between Whitehead and the Buddha by Kenneth K. Inada, *Whitehead's 'Actual Entity' and the Buddha's Anātman*, in *Philosophy East and West*, July 1971. Professor Inada mentions at the beginning that Whitehead 'especially in his later works makes several references to the Buddha', though his knowledge of Buddhism was rather superficial and

All this was summarized by Bergson in a statement which to a Buddhist sounds like a formulation in the simplest and most authentic terms common to all schools and periods of Buddhist thought:

> There are changes, but there are underneath the change no things which change: change has no need of a support ... movement does not imply a mobile.[12]

In his introduction to the French translation of *Pragmatism* by William James, Bergson says that "from the point of view taken by James, which is that of pure experience or of 'radical empiricism,' reality ... flows without our being able to say whether it is in a single direction, or even whether it is always and throughout the same river flowing."[13] And in his own *Introduction to Metaphysics,* he says, 'All reality is, therefore, tendency, if we agree to call tendency a nascent change of direction'.[14]

Bergson's approach to a biologically oriented philosophy of life was entirely different from Nietzsche's intentions. He did not explicitly consider the cultural implications of the biological reorientation of the new philosophy of nature until the last period of his activity (*The Two Sources of Morality and Religion,* 1932). Bergson's most important work, *Creative Evolution,* which appeared in 1907, begins with the question, "What is the precise meaning of the word 'exist'?" The answer, at the end of the first section, is:

---

on certain points basically wrong. Independently of such occasional direct references, Whitehead's philosophy in its original structure 'shows strains of thought remarkably similar to those of the Buddha.' Some of Inada's implicit references could be of much use also for a wider comparison with Bergson from the same Asian standpoint. The article does not deal with the subject of karma.

12. *The Perception of Change* in the *Creative Mind* (N. Y. Philosophical Library, 1946), p. 173.

13. Cf. *The Creative Mind*, p. 250.

14. Ibid., p. 222.

> We are seeking only the precise meaning that our consciousness gives to this word 'exist', and we find that, for a conscious being, to exist is to change, to change is to mature, to mature is to go on creating oneself endlessly.[15]

In such maturing and 'creation of self by self', which 'is the more complete, the more one reasons on what one does',[16] consists the *problem of freedom.* In this process, each individual self-consciousness 'lives and develops itself as an effect of its own hesitations until a free action is detached from it as if it were an overripe fruit'.[17]

The Buddha also speaks of the guidance, or protective care, 'of self by self' in the same process of 'the ripening fruit of action', thus: 'One oneself is the guardian of oneself. What other guardian would there be?' (*Dhammapada,* 160).

> 'If, Ānanda, there were no kamma (*karma*, action) ripening in the sphere of sense existence, would there appear any sensual becoming?'
>
> 'Surely not, Lord'.
>
> '... and wherever the action ripens, there the individual experiences the fruit of that action, be it in this life, or in the next life, or in future lives.
>
> 'The results of kamma are unthinkable, not to be pondered upon.'[18]

Here is Bergson's explanation of the thesis:

> What are we, in fact, what is our *character,* if not the condensation of the history that we have lived from our birth—nay, even before our birth, since we bring with us prenatal dispositions? Doubtless we think with only a small part of our past, but it is with our entire past, including the original bent of our soul,

---

15. H. Bergson, *Creative Evolution*, translated by A. Mitchell (N.Y. Modern Library, 1944), pp. 3, 10 (quoted in the continuation as *C.E.*).

16. Ibid., p. 9.

17. *Essai sur les Donnees Immediates de la Conscience*, 68th edition (Presses Universitaires de France), p. 132.

18. *Aṅguttaranikāya*, III, 76, 33, IV, 77. Cf. translation by Nyanaponika Thera (Kandy, *The Wheel Publication*, No. 155–158), pp. 51, 23, 92.

> that we desire, will and act. Our past, then, as a whole, is made manifest to us in its impulse ... From this *survival of the past* it follows that consciousness cannot go through the same state twice. Our personality, which is being built up each instant with its accumulated experience, changes without ceasing ... This is why our duration is irreversible ... Thus our personality shoots, grows and ripens without ceasing.[19]

Bergson's conception of causality and motivation departs from the classical theories of determinism and freedom of action, and approaches the Indian (not exclusively Buddhist) idea of karma in two essential points: its psychological origin and its creative character. It is based on Bergson's critique of both mechanistic and finalistic theories in biology:

> Evolution will thus prove to be something entirely different from a series of adaptations to circumstances, as mechanism claims; entirely different also from the realization of a plan of the whole, as maintained by the doctrine of finality ... Such a philosophy of life ... claims to transcend both mechanism and finalism, but ... it is nearer the second doctrine than the first.[20]

As for this second doctrine, Bergson maintains that 'the finalistic interpretation, such as we shall propose it, could never be taken for an anticipation of the future ... How could we know beforehand a situation that is unique of its kind, that has never yet occurred and will never occur again? Of the future, only that is foreseen which is like the past or can be made up again with elements like those of the past. Such is the case with astronomical,

19. C.E. p. 8. Sartre has reformulated this problem on a deeper existential level, in his *Being and Nothingness*, translated by H. R. Barnes (N.Y., The Citadel Press, 1966), p. 114f.: "There is no absolute beginning which without ever having past would become past. Since the For-itself, qua For-itself, has to be its past it comes into the world *with* a past. These few remarks may permit us to view in a somewhat different light the problem of birth ... There is a metaphysical problem concerning birth in that I can be anxious to know how I happen to have been born from that *particular* embryo ..." Bergson's emphasis is also always on the concreteness and uniqueness of each creative act even on the lowest biological level.

20. Ibid., pp. 113, 57.

physical and chemical facts, with all facts which form part of a system in which elements supposed to be unchanging are merely put together, in which the only changes are changes of position ... But an original situation, which imparts something of its own originality to its elements ..., how can such a situation be pictured as given before it is actually produced? All that can be said is that, once produced, it will be explained by the elements that analysis will then carve out of it. Now, what is true of the production of a new species is also true of the production of a new individual and more generally, of any moment of any living form.'[21]

Compare the simpler statement of the Buddha, with strict reference to the karmic, i.e. the morally relevant, act:

> If anyone were to say 'this person commits an act and he *will* suffer accordingly'—if that were the case, there would be no (use of leading a) life of holiness, and there would be no opportunity of putting an end to suffering. If anyone were to say 'this person commits an act for which he *deserves* to suffer accordingly'—if that were the case, there would be (a use of leading) a life of holiness, and there would be an opportunity of putting an end to suffering.[22]

The vitalist attempt to re-examine the problems of causality, finality and freedom of will, from Bergson's standpoint of "transformalism"[23] brought us to a wider epistemological problem of establishing adequate relations between science, history and philosophy—a problem extensively discussed by the later philosophies of existence:

> *Science* can work only on what is supposed to repeat itself ... Anything that is irreducible and irreversible in the successive moments of a *history* eludes science. To get a notion of this irreducibility and irreversibility, we must break with scientific habits which are adapted to the fundamental requirements of thought, we must do violence to the mind, *go counter to the*

21. Ibid., pp. 59, 33.

22. Aṅguttara Nikāya, 3:99. Sartre's analysis of "human reality" as "a project of being" brings him to the conclusion: "We can ascertain more exactly what is the being of the self: it is *value*" (*Being and Nothingness*, p. 92).

23. Cf. C. E., pp. 27–35.

> *natural bent* of the intellect. But this is just the function of *philosophy*.[24] Modern science is the daughter of astronomy; it has come down from heaven to earth along the inclined plane of Galileo, for it is through Galileo that Newton and his successors are connected with Kepler ... Each material point became a rudimentary planet ... Modern science must be defined pre-eminently by its aspiration to take time as an independent variable.[25]
>
> But to the artist who creates a picture by drawing it from the depths of his soul, time is no longer an accessory.... The duration of his work is part and parcel of his work. To contract or to dilate it would be to modify both the psychical evolution that fills it and the invention which is its goal. The time taken up by the invention is one with the invention itself. It is the progress of a thought which is changing in the degree and measure that it is taking form. It is a vital process, something like the ripening of an idea.[26]

Compare with this the statement of Buddhaghosa, in *Atthasālinī*: "By time the Sage described the mind, and by mind described the time."[27]

The "scission" of *intellect from* intuition[28] is explained by Bergson (and later existentialists) by the "practical nature of perception and its prolongation in intellect and science"; we could almost say, by the *lack of contemplative interest* in modern, technically oriented science. Thus, in a deduction which reminds us of Heidegger's basic thesis on the scope of metaphysics, Bergson formulates the question:

> But has metaphysics understood its role when it has simply trodden in the steps of physics, in the chimerical hope of going further in the same direction? Should not its own task

24. Ibid., p. 34f. Italicizing in this and following quotations is partly mine.
25. Ibid., p. 364.
26. Ibid., p. 370.
27. Compare the discussion of "The Problem of Time" in Nyanaponika Thera's *Abhidhamma Studies* (Kandy: Buddhist Publication Society, 1965), Chapter V.
28. C. E., p. 380.

> be, on the contrary, to remount the incline that physics descends, to bring back matter to its origins, and to build up progressively a *cosmology,* which would be, so to speak, a *reversed psychology*?[29]
>
> Everything is obscure in the idea of creation, if we think of *things* which are created and of a *thing* which creates, as we habitually do, as the understanding cannot help doing ... It is natural to our intellect, whose function is essentially practical, made to present to us things and states rather than changes and acts. But *things-and-states are only views, taken by our mind, of becoming. There are no things, there are only actions.*[30]

Epoché, refraining from judgments based on such "views" (Greek *doxa*, Sanskrit *dṛṣṭi,* Pāli *diṭṭhi*), the philosophical method brought from India by Pyrrho of Elis at the time of Alexander the Great, has become in the twentieth century the fundamental method of Husserl's "meditating philosopher" in phenomenological analysis. It is a "science of phenomena, which lies far removed from our ordinary thinking, and has not until our own day therefore shown an impulse to develop ... so extraordinarily difficult ... a new way of looking at things, one that contrasts at every point with the natural attitude of experience and thought," whose development is felt, however, as an "urgent need nowadays."[31]

The teaching of the Buddha was, with a still wider purpose, the expression of "the right effort" (*sammā-vāyāmo*) to "swim against the stream" of such world-views, i.e. "the type of views called the thicket of views, the wilderness of views, the contortion of views, the vacillation of views, the fetter of views."[32]

In Bergson's theory of intuition, the act of "swimming against the stream" is interpreted with his basic French term *torsion*:

> Let us try to see, no longer with the eyes of the intellect alone, which grasps only the already made and which looks

29. Ibid., pp. 227f.

30. Ibid., p. 270.

31. E. Husserl, *Ideas: General Introduction to Pure Phenomenology*, translated by W. R. Boyce Gibson (New York: Macmillan, 1931), pp. 41– 43.

32. Majjhima Nikāya 2, Sabbāsava-sutta.

> from the outside, but with the spirit, I mean with that faculty of seeing which is immanent in the faculty of acting and which springs up, somehow, by the *twisting of the will on itself*, when action is turned into knowledge, like heat, so to say, into light.[33]
>
> By intuition I mean instinct that has become disinterested, self-conscious, capable of reflecting upon its object and of enlarging it indefinitely. That an effort of this kind is not impossible is proved by the existence in man of an *aesthetic faculty* along with the normal perception ... This intention is just what the artist tries to regain, in placing himself back within the object by a kind of *sympathy*, in breaking down, by an effort of intuition, the barrier that space puts up between him and his model.[34]

The ultimate metaphysical consequences implied in a theory of causation based on the biological phenomenon of the "ripening fruit" were taken into adequate consideration only in some later philosophies of existence. Yet the preparatory vitalistic stage of modern philosophy remains more important for an Indian reinterpretation of the theory of karma than can be assessed within strictly European limits, where the importance of the missing link between the vitalist and existentialist stages—the link of a new theory of causality—has not yet been fully and explicitly realized. Let us therefore conclude the survey of this cycle of ideas by returning to the lowest level on which Bergson's vitalistic interpretation of cosmic matter had to establish a new starting point:

> Let us merely recall that extension admits of degrees, that all sensation is extensive in a certain measure, and that the idea of unextended sensations, artificially localized in space, is a mere view of the mind, suggested by an unconscious metaphysic much more than by psychological observation. No doubt we make only the first steps in the direction of the extended, even when we let ourselves go as much as we can. But suppose for a moment that matter consists in this

33. C. E., p. 273.
34. Ibid., p. 194.

> very movement pushed further, and that *physics is simply psychics inverted.*[35]

The conception of "a cosmology which would be a reversed psychology," or of physics understood "simply as psychics inverted," was destined to become the fulcrum for a transition from a physical to an historical orientation in other contemporary philosophies. This transition is also clearly marked in Whitehead's later works: "Physical endurance is the process of continuously inheriting a certain identity of character transmitted through a historic route of events."[36]

Bergson expressed this emphasis in terms which brought him still closer to a specific aspect of later existentialist thought: the predominant importance of the future for (karmic) shaping of the present by the past. Though Heidegger's critique of Bergson's idea of the "stream of experience" was concentrated on this point, where in an initial metaphor Bergson compares a "mental state, as it advances on the road of time, continually swelling with the duration which it accumulates" with "a snowball on the snow, rolling upon itself" and thus increasing—we can read a few pages later in the opening chapter of *Creative Evolution* another statement, anticipating Heidegger's objection to some extent: "Duration is the continuous progress of *the past which gnaws into the future* and which swell*s* as it advances."[37]

III

Martin Heidegger, in his basic work, *Being and Time*,[38] seems to take over the meditation on "the ripening fruit" at the critical point reached by Bergson's analysis of its wider biological scope: the karmic predicament of human existence. It can be seen from Heidegger's numerous critical references to Bergson (though in many cases I would not agree with them) that in the meantime it had become obvious that there was more to elicit by the process

35. Ibid., p. 221.

36. *Science and the Modern World*, p. 156.

37. C. E. pp. 4, 7.

38. Martin Heidegger, *Being and Time*, translated by J. Macquarrie and E. Robinson (New York: Harper and Row, 1962), quoted in the following notes as B. T.

philosophy than the biologically oriented thinkers of the vitalist period could realize. The philosophy of existence undertook this work in essentially different dimensions. Heidegger in particular was very careful and explicit in critically adapting new methods of independent historical thinking in the philosophy of culture introduced by Dilthey, and above all the new structure of transcendental logic laid down by his teacher Husserl, for phenomenological analysis independent of natural science. Within the scope of this new framework, similarities with Buddhist thought emerge still more strikingly, especially in the domain of the "suffering/concern" theme and the need for the notion of *karma* in a process-multiple causality structure.

The second part of *Being and Time* deals in particular with problems of human reality and temporality (*Dasein und Zeitlichkeit*). The possibility for human beings to attain to full ripeness in an existence conditioned by man's "being-towards-death" is discussed in the first chapter ("Dasein's authentic potentiality—for-being-a-whole and its being-towards-death"). Chapter Five is dedicated to "temporality and historicality" as essential constituents of the human being[39] involved in this ambiguous process.

> When, for instance, a fruit is unripe, it "goes toward" its ripeness. In this process of ripening, that which the fruit is not yet is by no means pieced on as something not yet present-at-hand. The fruit brings itself to ripeness, and such a bringing of itself is a characteristic of its being as a fruit. Nothing imaginable which one might contribute to it would eliminate the unripeness of the fruit, if this entity did not come to ripeness *of its own accord*. When we speak of the "not-yet" of the unripeness, we do not have in view something else which stands outside, and which—with utter indifference to the fruit—might be present-at-hand in it and with it. What we have in view is the fruit itself in its specific kind of being ... The ripening fruit, however, not only is not indifferent

39. Heidegger's designation of human being as *Dasein* ("being here," i.e. in the world, which is always "one's own") has been interpreted by Sartre, in *Being and Nothingness*, as "human reality," a term which will be occasionally used in the continuation.

to its unripeness as something other than itself, but it is that unripeness as it ripens. *The "not-yet" has already been included in the very being of the fruit,* not as some random characteristic, but as something constitutive. Correspondingly, as long as any Dasein is, it too *is already* its "not-yet."[40]

The implicit emphasis laid on the difference from the "classical" European mechanist theory of causality is obvious enough.

The karmic process, in its Buddhist meaning, can be defined as a vicious circle of "interdependent origination" (*paṭicca-samuppāda*), consisting of a chain of twelve rings (*nidāna*), the first of which is *avijjā*, "ignorance," or better, metaphysical nescience of a human being (defined by Heidegger as a "being-there"— *Dasein*) about his own emergence in the flux of existence. The last ring of the chain is "death." Heidegger's analysis of human reality as a "being there" in the world is not less distinctly determined and delimited by the tension of the same polarity—ignorance and death:

> If the term "understanding" is taken in a way which is primordially existential, it means to be *projecting towards a potentiality-for-being, for the sake of which any Dasein exists.* In understanding, one's own potentiality-for-being is disclosed in such a way that one's Dasein always knows understandingly what it is capable of. It "knows" this, however, not by having discovered some fact, but by maintaining itself in an existential possibility. The kind of *ignorance* which corresponds to this, does not consist in an absence or cessation of understanding, but must be regarded as a deficient mode of the projectedness of one's potentiality-for-being. Existence can be questionable ... When one understands oneself protectively in an existential possibility, *the future underlies this understanding,* and it does so as a coming-towards-oneself out of that current possibility as which one's Dasein exists. Projection is basically futural ... Temporality does not temporalize itself constantly out of the authentic future. This inconstancy, however, does not mean that temporality sometimes lacks a future, but rather that the temporalizing of the future takes various forms.[41]

40. B. T., p. 243. (Marginal German page numbers used here and following.)
41. Ibid., p. 336.

This seems to explain one step further the "hesitation" of the self "until a free action is detached as an overripe fruit," as Bergson expressed the limits of freedom as release (*mokṣa*) within the scope of a karmic determinism.

> With ripeness, the fruit *fulfils* itself. But is the death at which Dasein arrives, a fulfilment in this sense? With its death, Dasein has indeed "fulfilled its course." But in doing so, has it necessarily exhausted its specific possibilities? For the most part, Dasein ends in unfulfilment, or else by having disintegrated and been used up. Ending does not necessarily mean fulfilling oneself. It thus becomes more urgent to ask *in what sense, if any, death must be conceived as the ending of Dasein.*[42]

Arising out of this situation, the problem of karma, implicitly felt as an "anticipatory resoluteness" in "concrete working out of temporality" aiming at an "authentic historizing of Dasein," is further discussed as the existential problem of "Dasein's potentiality-for-being-a-whole."[43]

Since "those possibilities of existence which have been factically disclosed are not to be gathered from death ... we must ask whence, in general, Dasein can draw those possibilities upon which it factically projects itself." The answer is:

> The resoluteness in which Dasein comes back to itself, discloses current factical possibilities of authentic existing, and discloses them *in terms of the heritage* which that resoluteness, *as thrown, takes over.* In one's coming back resolutely to one's thrownness, there is hidden a *handing down to oneself* of the possibilities that have come down to one, but not necessarily as having *thus come down.*[44]

We shall take for granted that the coincidence of the expression (italicized by me) "thus come down" with the literal meaning of the most common attribute of the Buddha— *tathāgata*—is another of many casual cases where a modern philosophy of essentially the same trend as our archaic one will, to some extent, come to

42. Ibid., p. 244.
43. Ibid., p. 309.
44. Ibid., p. 383.

use the same terms in expressing ideas of the same kind. What is meant here by the same trend will be explicated later. Let us first single out the specific meaning of this important term in the specific context.

The word *tathāgatā*, in its widest sense in the early Pāli literature, is used as a designation of "human being" in general. Its logical connection with the Buddha's best known definition of the human being as "heir of his own actions" is obvious, even when it is used as the highest epithet of the Buddha.

What Heidegger wishes to point out is that the "heritage" of a *tathāgato* has not to be understood here as a passive facticity of historically "objectified" social tradition or collective behaviour, which in Heidegger's terms would be designated as "inauthentic heritage." Unlike the social study of external history, Dasein in its intimate ripening "never comes back behind its thrownness" in the "situationality" of its world. In other words, in a personal history there is no possibility of statically objective repetition of one and the same situation. This is the basic law of karmic development that both Bergson and Heidegger try to confirm on different levels of their investigations.

On this point, in Heidegger's philosophy, "thrownness" appears as a critical term whose meaning has to be better determined, in view of the fact that it denotes an obvious Christian "cypher" for a karmically determined situation. This historical implication in basic existentialist terminology could even be interpreted by some critics as revealing an apparent deficiency of our analogy, had not Heidegger, fortunately for us, explained it, in the same context, by an "attribute" synonymous with the basic First Truth of the Buddha, *dukkha*, "anguish" or "worry": "Before we decide too quickly whether Dasein draws its authentic possibilities of existence from thrownness or not, we must assure ourselves that we have a full conception of *thrownness as a basic attribute of care.*"

The translation of the German word *Sorge* by "care" may often diminish the full meaning of "Dasein's character" of this fundamental *"existentiale"* or practical category on which Heidegger's entire ontology is built. From our standpoint, "worry" would often seem a preferable translation. Yet Heidegger himself has left no doubt about the meaning of this term. At the end of the first part of *Being and Time*, whose aim it was to "exhibit Care

(*Sorge*) as the Being of Dasein," i.e. "of that entity which in each case we ourselves are, and which we call 'man,'" the basic "ontical" meaning of *Sorge* is interpreted (and illustrated by an ancient fable) as "worry" and "grief."[45]

The continuation of the inquiry shows how the karmic phenomenon has to be comprised within the scope of this central theme—how the essence of worry and grief is revealed in response to the "call of conscience." First of all Heidegger's philosophy is no longer a philosophy of consciousness, but a philosophy *of conscience.* (The word "consciousness" is never used by Heidegger except in critical disputes, mainly with the Kantians.) Here conscience discloses itself as the awakening call which alone can liberate us from our lost condition (*Verlorenheit*) and thrownness in *avijjā* (ignorance), or metaphysical "nescience." Only in giving heed to the awakening call does "Dasein understand itself with regard to its potentiality-for-being" in man's mindfulness and resoluteness "to take over in his thrownness—right under the eyes of Death—that entity which Dasein is itself, and to take it over wholly," as his karmic load. In Heidegger's words, "Resoluteness is defined as a projecting of oneself upon one's own Being-guilty—a projecting which is reticent and ready for anxiety."[46] This is the ultimate moral aspect of the "hesitation in the ripening fruit" of the Bergsonian "creative activity."

The last metaphysical (or better, eschatological) question to which Heidegger's inquiry into the phenomenon of karma, or "ripening fruit," arrives, concerns the origin of that strange experience, the primeval phenomenon of all religion: being-guilty.

> "The call of conscience" is the call of care. Being guilty constitutes the being to which we give the name of "care." In uncanniness Dasein stands together with itself primordially. Uncanniness brings this entity face to face with its *undisguised nullity,* which belongs to the possibility of its own-most potentiality-for-being.[47]... *The appeal calls back by calling*

45. Ibid., pp. 196–200.

46. Ibid., p. 382.

47. Cf. Nāgārjuna's statement in *Madhyamaka-kārikā* 24:14: "For him who admits nullity all appears to be possible. For him who does not admit nullity nothing appears to be possible."

> *forth*: it calls Dasein *forth* to the possibility of taking over, in existing, even that thrown entity which it is.[48]

The statement italicized by me (*"Der Anruf ist vorrufender Rückruf"*) is the best short definition of karma that I can imagine, even if it had to be formulated by the greatest master of Zen art in Japan (an art not at all unknown to Heidegger). The next one is not less pregnant with deep oriental meaning:

> We have seen that care is the basic state of Dasein.
>
> The ontological signification of the expression "care" has been expressed in the definition: *ahead-of-itself-being-already-in "the world"* as being-alongside entities which we encounter "within-the-world."[49]

Heidegger insists on an implicit consciousness of karma[50] in the experience of care, or worry, as Dasein's "understanding of itself in being-guilty."[51] He equally insists on the fact that even "phenomena with which the vulgar interpretation has any familiarity point back to the primordial meaning of the call of conscience when they are understood in a way that is ontologically appropriate," and that "this interpretation, in spite of all its obviousness, is *by no means accidental.*"[52]

And yet, the call of conscience is "a keeping silent. Only in keeping silent does the conscience call; that is to say, the call comes from the soundlessness of uncanniness, and the Dasein which it summons is called back into the stillness of itself, and called back as something that is to become still."[53] A Japanese student

48. B. T. pp. 286 f.

49. Ibid., p. 249.

50. An we shall see in the continuation, for lack of a better word in European tradition, Heidegger uses the word "destiny" (*Schicksal*) in the meaning which comes closest to karma. Schopenhauer, who was aware of the specific meaning of this category in Indian philosophy (in Vedānta and Buddhism), could not find a better term in European languages, and made efforts to adjust the meaning of "destiny" to the basic Indian idea of karma. An analogous effort is often made by Heidegger.

51. B. T., p. 292.

52. Ibid., p. 294.

53. Ibid., p. 296.

in Heidegger's seminar once interpreted this course of thoughts in terms of a few Zen koans.[54] A follower of Ramana Maharshi in India could do it just as well to Heidegger's full satisfaction.

Having, unfortunately, no better word than "destiny" wherewith to designate the full range of the category of karma (though fully conscious of the wide horizon it encompasses), Heidegger brings us ultimately to the following summary of essential questions on this subject:

> But it remains all the more enigmatic in what way this event as destiny is to constitute the whole "connectedness" of Dasein from its birth to its death. How can recourse to resoluteness bring us an enlightenment? Is not each resolution just *one* more single "experience" in the sequence of the whole connectedness of our experience? ... Why is it that the question of *how the "connectedness of life"* is constituted finds no adequate and satisfactory answer? Is our investigation overhasty? Does it not, in the end, hang too much on the answer, without first having tested the legitimacy of the *question?*[55]

Speaking of the problem of re-emergence or "recurrence" of existential situations in their essential dependence on "destiny" in Dasein's "historizing" course, Heidegger does not even indirectly attempt to formulate any hypothesis analogous to "rebirth" (as, e.g., Nietzsche did in his own way) in Indian religious thought (*punabbhava*), though his sensitivity for the "enigmatic" remainder of the problem, as traced above, permits a still closer approach to this complex issue: "Dasein can be reached by the blows of destiny only because *in the depth of its own being Dasein is destiny* ... a possibility which it has inherited and yet has chosen."[56]

In suggesting the categorial designation of "karma" for the *whole range of problems concerning the organic connectedness of vital processes whose ripening results in creative activity,* my intention

54. Tsujimura Koichi (University of Kyoto), in 1957. I have published the translation of his seminar paper on "The Nothing in Zen" in my Yugoslav book on Oriental Philosophy (cf. C. Veljactc, Filozofija Istocnih Naroda, Vol. II, Zagreb 1958).

55. B. T., p. 387.

56. B. T., p. 384.

remains far from any attempt to propose any overhasty solution or pattern that could be discovered ready-made in the transcendental schematism of some specific type of Asian philosophy or religion, such as Buddhism. Though, for the purpose of the present survey, Buddhism was chosen as the *tertium comparationis*, it was presumed as a well-known fact that the historical origin of the categorial designation of karma in Indian philosophy is considerably older than its specific interpretation by the Buddha.

About the Contributors

Francis Story (1910–1971) was a British Buddhist who lived in Asia for 25 years, deeply absorbing the Buddhist philosophy of life. His collected writings on Buddhism are published in three volumes by the BPS.

Leonard A. Bullen was one of the pioneers of the Buddhist movement in Australia, where he actively propagated the Dhamma until his death in 1984 at the age of 76. He is best known for his book A *Technique of Living* (Wheel No. 226/230).

Nina van Gorkom is a Dutch Buddhist who first encountered Buddhism in Thailand. A keen student of the Abhidhamma, she is the author of *Buddhism in Daily Life* and *Abhidhamma in Daily Life*, both published in Bangkok.

Nyanaponika Thera (1901–1994) was born in Germany and became a Buddhist monk in Sri Lanka in 1936. The founding-president of the BPS, he is the author of numerous works on Buddhism in both English and German.

Bhikkhu Ñāṇajīvako (*Cedomil Veljacic*, 1915–1997) was for many years a lecturer in Asian philosophy at the University of Zagreb in his native Yugoslavia. A prolific writer of scholarly works on Buddhist and Indian thought in his native tongue, he lived in Sri Lanka as a Buddhist monk.

Buddhism and Sex

by

M. O'C. Walshe

WHEEL PUBLICATION NO. 225

Preface

This is the third, further revised version of the original *Sangha Guide on Buddhism and Sex* published by the English Sangha Trust, Dhammapadīpa, London NW3. The greater part of it also appeared in the journal *Sangha*. As one of the older generation, I have felt very conscious of my temerity in trying to write something on this subject which younger people might be willing to read. In this connection, I am very grateful to Alan and Jacqui James for giving me the benefit of their criticism, a task for which they are doubly qualified, being both wise in the Dhamma and at the same time much closer in age to the younger generation who may read this. But the opinions expressed here are, of course, my own.

M. O'C. Walshe
March 1975

Buddhism and Sex

This is an age in which sexual matters are discussed with great openness. There are many who are puzzled to know what the Buddhist attitude towards sex is, and it is therefore to be hoped that the following guidelines may be found helpful towards an understanding. It is of course true to say that Buddhism, in keeping with the principle of the Middle Way, would advocate neither extreme puritanism nor extreme permissiveness, but this, as a guiding principle without further specification, may not seem sufficiently helpful for most people.

In the first place, we must distinguish between the rules undertaken by Buddhist monks for their own conduct, and any guiding principles for lay people.

The Bhikkhu

A bhikkhu, or fully-ordained monk in the *Theravāda* tradition, has taken upon himself a set of 227 rules of conduct. The aim of all of these is to enable him to conduct himself in such a way as is most conducive to the attaining of Enlightenment. The rules are voluntarily undertaken, and if a monk feels unable to live up to them, he is free to leave the Order, which is considered much more honourable than hypocritically remaining in the robe while knowingly infringing the rule. There are four basic rules, the infringement of which, termed *Pārājika* or 'Defeat', involves irrevocable expulsion from the Order. The only one we are concerned with here is the first, which deals with sexual intercourse.

Complete sexual continence is considered an essential feature of the monastic life. Intercourse of a heterosexual or homosexual character is automatically a Pārājika offence. A monk who performs such an act is considered to have expelled himself from the Order, and is no longer in communion with the other monks. Any acts of a sexually unbecoming nature falling short of intercourse result in suspension and require expiation. *Sāmaneras,* or novice monks, who break their training in this respect, are disrobed.

The same principle applies to the *Mahāyāna* schools and, of course, to nuns in those schools where they exist. There is no such thing as a 'married monk', though in certain schools, especially in Japan, a form of 'quasi-monasticism' with married teachers who retain a form of ordination is permitted under certain conditions. But all this has no relevance to the Theravāda Sangha.

Ancient India

Before turning to our main theme, it is as well to have some idea of the sexual *mores* of ancient India in the Buddha's time. Gotama himself, as a prince, was brought up surrounded by concubines and dancing girls as a matter of course. Polygamy was common. Ambapāli, the courtesan from whom the Buddha accepted gifts, was a person of some consequence. It was not expected that young men would lead a life of much restraint, and the Buddha with his profound understanding of human nature knew well what demands to make of people in this respect. Thus we find the following formulation of what a man should avoid:

'He avoids unlawful sexual intercourse, abstains from it. He has no intercourse with girls who are still under the protection of father or mother, brother, sister, or relative; nor with married women, nor female convicts; nor lastly with betrothed girls.'

If a man could observe greater restraint than this, so much the better. The Buddha's outlook on this question was, then, realistic for his age, and we should endeavour to view the subject as realistically as possible in the light of modern conditions.

The Lay Buddhist

The third of the Five Precepts undertaken by lay Buddhists runs: *Kāmesu micchācārā veramaṇī sikkhāpadaṃ samādiyāmi*, 'I undertake the course of training in refraining from wrongdoing in respect of sensuality.' Some lay people who, usually for a specified period, undertake more than the usual five precepts, take this one in the stricter form: *Abrahmacariyā veramaṇī* ..., which commits them, for the duration of the undertaking, to observe the same restraint as the monks. With these, too, we are not further concerned, as their position is now obvious.

For the average lay person, the Third Precept is on exactly the same footing as the other four. There is, in the Buddhist view, nothing uniquely wicked about sexual offences or failings. Those inclined to develop a guilt complex about their sex life should realize that failure in this respect is neither more, nor, on the other hand, less serious than failure to live up to any other precept. In point of fact, the most difficult precept of all for nearly everybody to live up to is the fourth—to refrain from all forms of wrong speech (which often includes uncharitable comments on other people's real or alleged sexual failings!).

What precisely, then, does the Third Precept imply for the ordinary lay Buddhist? Firstly, in common with all the other precepts, it is a rule of training. It is not a 'commandment' from God, the Buddha, or anyone else saying: 'Thou shalt not ...'. There are no such commandments in Buddhism. It is an undertaking by *you* to yourself, to do your best to observe a certain type of restraint, because you understand that it is a good thing to do. This must be clearly understood. If you don't think it is a good thing to do, you should not undertake it. If you do think it is a good thing to do, but doubt your ability to keep it, you should do your best, and probably, you can get some help and instruction to make it easier. If you feel it is a good thing to attempt to tread the Buddhist path, you may undertake this and the other precepts, with sincerity, in this spirit.

Secondly, what is the scope and purpose of this precept? The word *kāma* means in Pāli 'sensual desire', which is not exclusively sexual. It is here used in a plural form which comes close to what is meant by the Biblical expression 'the lusts of the flesh'. Greed for food and other sensual pleasure is also included. Most people who are strongly addicted to sexual indulgence are also much drawn to other sense-pleasures. Though we are here only concerned with the sexual aspect, this point should be noted. For those with any grasp at all of Buddhist principles, the basic reason for such an injunction should be immediately obvious. Our *dukkha*—our feeling of frustration and dissatisfaction with life—is rooted in our desires and cravings. The more these can be brought under control, the less *dukkha* we shall experience. It is as simple as that. But of course, that which is simple is not necessarily easy.

Thus while there is, so to speak, a considerable overlap in the *content* of the Third Precept with the Jewish and Christian commandment, 'Thou shalt not commit adultery', there is a big difference in the spirit and approach. Since most people in the West have some Christian conditioning—even if only indirectly—

it is as well to be clear about this. The traditional Christian view is that sexual intercourse is permissible solely within the marriage-bond. Even then the implication is that, except as a necessary means for the procreation of children, it is really rather a bad thing, and should be restricted as far as possible—hence the debate about 'the pill' and the like. Certain things such as contraception, homosexual activity and so on are often looked on with horror and declared 'unnatural' (which cannot be entirely correct since, after all, they *happen*!). Some of these prohibitions may today be more honoured in the breach than in the observance, but there is no doubt that rigid views of this sort are still widely held and officially propagated. The inevitable reaction, encouraged by some real or alleged psychological experts, is towards an attitude of total permissiveness, in which 'anything goes'. As was said earlier, rigid puritanism and total permissiveness are extreme views, to neither of which the Buddhist teaching subscribes. The one is merely an inadequate reaction against the other. What we have to do—what Buddhism in fact teaches us to do—is to map out a sane course between the two.

Sexual Pleasure and the Concept of 'Sin'

Reduced to essentials, the great debate about sex revolves, for many people, around the concept of sin. To the puritan, indulgence in sexual activity for the sake of pleasure is evil, wicked, or as he tends to say, 'sinful' (i.e. displeasing to God). To the 'permissivist' (to coin an awkward but convenient term), this is nonsense. He probably rejects the term 'sin' as meaningless, and not only sees nothing evil in sexual pleasure but regards it as highly legitimate, perhaps as the highest pleasure there is and certainly as something to which, in principle at least, everybody has a right. Many people, coming from a more or less Christian background with at least some puritanical overtones, find the true Buddhist attitude to this problem rather difficult to see. Perhaps they have never even been given a clear explanation of it, or if they have, it may have seemed too technical for them, and they have not grasped the point. The point, in fact, is of considerable importance, so it is worthwhile attempting to make it clear. It involves a proper elementary grasp of what is meant by *kamma*—something which many people, who may have been 'Buddhists' for years, have never had.

We may, however, perhaps begin more profitably by considering the word 'sin'. 'Sin' to a Christian is primarily thought of as a breach of God's commandments. This explanation is of course not wrong in terms of Christian theology, but is not applicable in Buddhism, where there are no such commandments upon which one can infringe. As already indicated, the so-called precepts are in fact undertakings given to oneself, which is something different. They are more on a par with the instruction, 'Look both ways before you cross the road'. Still there is much agreement between the content of the Five Precepts and some of the Ten Commandments, so it may be wise in many cases to behave accordingly, whichever formulation one follows. However, there is another rendering of the word sin itself which in fact (though less well-known) comes much closer to the Buddhist view of things. In the Bible, 'sin' actually renders Hebrew and Greek words which literally mean 'missing the mark', i.e. behaving inadequately or unskillfully. The sinner, then, is like an unskillful archer who misses his aim (could this be the real meaning of *Zen and the Art of Archery*?). But this comes, surely, very close to the idea of *akusala kamma* or 'unskilled action' in Buddhism.

The Pāli word *kamma* (Sanskrit *karma*) literally means 'action' (i.e. volition: *cetanā*), which can be either skilled (*kusala*) or unskilled (*akusala*). The results of action (*kamma*) accrue to the doer as *vipāka,* which is pleasant when the action was skilled, unpleasant when it was unskilled (if I look before I cross the road, I shall get across safely, which is pleasant; if I don't look I may get run down, which is unpleasant). The feelings we experience are in fact of the nature of vipāka—they are dependent on past kamma. And of course we are continually creating fresh kamma for a good part of our time. It should therefore be noted that the *feeling of pleasure* (sexual or otherwise) is not an *action*, but a *result.* There is, therefore, nothing either 'skillful' or 'unskillful' about experiencing such a feeling. We should therefore not regard it as either 'virtuous' or 'sinful'. So far so good. Such pleasant feelings can be enjoyed with a clear conscience and no guilt feeling. If this were all, there would be no problem. The puritans would be routed and the permissivists justified. Unfortunately, there is another side to the matter. We may recall that a few years ago there was a song 'Money is the Root of all Evil'. Some people pointed out that not money, but the love for money is the root of all evil (well, of a lot of evil, anyway). And here is the snag. *Sexual pleasure* (like money) *is not 'evil'* (or unskilled), but *attachment to sexual pleasure* (like the love of money) is. If we can experience the pleasure *without attachment* we are all right; if we become attached to it, we are not 'hitting the mark'. Now of course it is rather difficult (to put it mildly) to experience pleasure of any sort without feeling attached to it. But *attachment* is kamma, and unskilled kamma at that. And the results of that will inevitably, according to Buddhism, be something unpleasant in the future.

Many people will find this explanation novel. Some will find it puzzling. Some will undoubtedly reject it—with or without investigation—with the excuse that it is overly subtle, or arbitrary or something of the sort. What they mean is, of course, that they find it inconvenient. But it will repay a lot of consideration and mindful investigation. Careful study, in fact, should show that it is the key to the whole problem. The matter can also be considered in terms of the law of Dependent Origination: 'Contact is the basis for the arising of feeling; feeling ... of craving; craving ... of clinging' etc., the ultimate outcome being of course the continued process of becoming, with all the sufferings entailed.

Thus, if we wish to adjudicate between the puritans and the permissivists, we cannot say that either side is entirely right. We might, however, suggest that the puritans are partly right for the wrong reasons. Sexual indulgence is not wicked, but it may be in some degree inadvisable. Most people will not feel able to refrain altogether (nor are they being urged to), but there is merit in moderation.

Marriage

Setting aside all ideas derived from other sources, other religions and philosophies of life, what is the Buddhist attitude towards marriage? For many Buddhists, in the East or the West, there is no great problem. They live a reasonably normal, married life just as do many Christians, humanists, and others. We may say they are lucky, or enjoy the results of favorable kamma in this respect. For others, of all creeds or none, serious problems arise and must be somehow faced.

In the Christian tradition, marriage is usually termed a 'sacrament'. In some branches of Christianity it is treated as an indissoluble bond, though usually there are a few loopholes. Other branches of Christianity permit divorce in certain rather narrowly defined circumstances and of course in most (though by no means all) countries the state permits divorce and the remarriage of divorced persons, with or without the approval of the Church.

In Buddhism, marriage is not a 'sacrament', as such a concept does not exist. And it is not any part of the functions of Buddhist monks to join lay people together in holy wedlock (or deadlock). If it is occasionally done today in Japan, this is just a modern idea in conformity with a general tendency among Japanese Buddhists to imitate (often perhaps unwisely) Christian institutions. In the Buddhist tradition it is often the custom for bhikkhus to give their 'blessing' *after* the civil wedding ceremony has been performed. But even this is really more of a concession to the laity than anything else. And if the marriage does not turn out a success, no bhikkhu has any authority to say that that marriage shall not be dissolved. Divorce, like marriage, is a civil affair. Likewise, if a married couple decides to practise contraception that is entirely their business. The *Sangha* will not feel called upon to interfere or object. It must be admitted that certain bhikkhus have been heard to declare that contraception is wrong and should be banned—but that is their private opinion. It is no part of the Buddhist teaching.

Abortion is of course a different matter. Since this involves the taking of life, it contravenes the First Precept. It can only be condoned in cases of serious health hazards, where it may represent the lesser evil.

In getting married, people obviously take on a responsibility, both towards each other and towards whatever children they have. Any form of irresponsible behaviour is clearly reprehensible by any reasonable standards, whether we call ourselves Buddhists or anything else. If we bear in mind, and try to observe, *all* the five precepts, the chances of a successful marriage are obviously increased. Excessive drinking, for instance (in breach of the Fifth Precept), is a potent source of unhappy marriages.

What, it may be asked, of 'adultery', i.e. extramarital sexual relations? The short answer is that, quite obviously, this is something to be avoided. But the point should be made that Buddhism does not regard this or any other sexual irregularities and deviations, as somehow *uniquely* wicked. In countries nominally Christian the special kind of horror with which such things are, or recently were, regarded can be pushed to grotesque extremes. Not many years ago a certain politician was solemnly declared by some to be unfit to become Prime Minister because he had been the *innocent* partner in a divorce case! More recently still, another politician was hounded from office because of acts of adultery of which his wife forgave him! Yet many politicians in all countries have got away with far worse things of a non-sexual character without a word being said. Buddhists should try to behave themselves sexually, as in other respects, to the best of their ability—but they should learn to exercise the maximum of charity towards the lapses of others. If a marriage has irretrievably broken down, even though it may continue in name, the situation is of course quite different. In such circumstances one may well feel that complete abstinence is a burden greater than one can reasonably be expected to bear.

The things that can go wrong with a marriage are legion. A partner can be impotent, ill, irresponsible, jealous, drunken, a compulsive gambler, deranged, promiscuous, miserly, unemployable or several of these things. Or both partners can be perfectly charming people and yet utterly unsuited to each other. It may be that only the children—poor wretches—hold the 'marriage' together. At the same time, there may be many reasons which make dissolution impossible or impracticable. An extramarital relationship in such circumstances may serve to make the situation tolerable. Those who find themselves in such a situation must make the best job of it they can. It is not for others, more fortunate or more timid, to be excessively censorious.

Sex Outside Marriage

Here again, we should try to look at things calmly and clearly, and above all, responsibly. Nowadays there is pretty frank acceptance of what has always been the case, that a lot of people in fact have sexual intercourse without going through the formality of getting married. No doubt there is more of it now than there used to be because, for one thing, contraception is a lot more effective than it formerly was, and also because religious prejudices are fast breaking down. This is a simple statement of fact, not of what ought or ought not to be the case. In the case of engaged couples, it is probably by now the usual thing, and is not very heavily frowned upon by most people. But it cannot be termed exactly rare among couples who have not the slightest intention of getting engaged.

In the past, it was widely considered (and *almost* openly admitted) that premarital sex was a good thing for young men, but a bad thing for girls. Now sex-equality has caught up on this, as on so many other things. In any case, we may as well accept the fact that whatever we may think about it, preaching by the older generation will, by and large, have precious little effect on the young. This is probably one thing most parents are worried about.

The young people of today are not, usually, notably impressed by the wisdom of their elders. They may quite often be perfectly right in this scepticism, but of course it does not follow that they themselves are really any wiser. It may be that their folly merely takes on a different form. Let us remember that basically, if Buddhism teaches us anything at *all*, it is that almost all human beings are pretty dim-witted, on the whole. That after all is why we are here at all. But still, if those who are parents can succeed in inculcating a sense of responsibility in their young, that in all probability is about all they can do. There are no easy answers.

Queen Victoria reigned for sixty glorious years, and even despite the pioneering efforts of her son and successor Edward VII, it still took England a further sixty years (including two major wars) to cast off the last shreds of Victorian respectability. Now at last the deed has been done, and naked young men can stand on the stage and utter naughty words without a Lord Chamberlain to say them nay. Is this progress, or was Victorian prudery preferable to modern rudery? We are back with the two extremes once again. We must seek the middle way.

Of course, if the young would only listen, there is no doubt we older ones could give them all sorts of quite genuinely good advice. And there is just one chance that they will listen: if we can somehow avoid being patronizing. But the heavy father act is now definitely out, and the establishment line cuts no ice. If we tell the youth of today they stink (even though some of them do), they will simply turn round and tell us our ideas stink.

However, if we *can* succeed in getting across to them at all, we may be able to suggest humbly certain things for their consideration. Sex is something the younger generation of today are intensely aware of. In fact, they would have to be born blind and deaf not to be. It is exploited commercially today in every conceivable way. Our entire commercial civilization is founded on the principle of stimulating bigger and better desires in all of us, all the time. And at a conservative estimate, about 75% of all advertising at the present time includes an element of sexual titillation (sometimes cunningly disguised, at other times blatantly obvious). It has been found, quite clearly, that sex stimulates the sales of anything and everything from typewriters to weed-killers. That it is the mainstay of virtually every conceivable kind of 'entertainment' to which we are voluntarily or involuntarily subjected, goes without saying. In other words, our desires in general, and our sexual desires in particular, are being consistently and grossly overstimulated the whole time on set purpose, and the bland assumption is that if it all suddenly stopped, the country's entire economy would be in ruins. (Parenthetically, it *might* be quite feasible to organize our economy on a different basis—but that is not our concern here.) We all, young and old, have to live with this situation and to put it mildly, it doesn't make self-restraint any easier. So before we start lecturing the young, we should realize this fact. In this game, the dice are loaded against us.

Still, we may manage to get through to them. After all, many young people are themselves against the establishment, and among other things they rebel against the sheer *tawdriness* of our lives. Their ideas may quite frequently be all wrong and badly mixed up, but at least they sincerely yearn for something better, and in fact they are desperately, even if often incoherently, trying to bring about a better state of affairs. They are by no means lacking in idealism, and they have a keen eye for those who seek to exploit their idealism for dubious ends. We can latch on to them if we can only convince them that we are at least *sincere*.

Let us just take a cold, hard look at this question of premarital intercourse among the young. In the first place, it *happens*. And there are just two ways, in principle, by which it can cease to happen. Either young people can exercise self-restraint, or they can get married. A few do the former, and quite a lot do the latter. Now of course, very early marriages can turn out well. But the fact is that they quite often don't for obvious reasons. It is therefore not an entirely self-evident fact that early marriage, as such, is preferable to a little 'experimentation'.

It is, of course, very hard for parents to stand back and silently watch their own children embarking on a course which may seem to them, and indeed may actually be, unwise. Some young people today are only prepared, and able, to learn by trial and error. They are unwilling to ask for advice, or even to accept it if given unasked. They should, however, be aware that there are serious dangers in experimentation, if too rashly undertaken, and the trouble is that while parents may hold back with advice on restraint, there are others who are only too ready (out of misguided 'idealism' or, frequently, because they find it highly profitable) to offer 'permissive' advice without drawing attention to the risks. It is the duty of somebody, whether parents or teachers, to ensure that young people are aware of some of the less comfortable 'facts of life' as well as those they want to know about. Venereal disease is rampant today, and on the increase. And it is by no means always the 'minor inconvenience' it is made out to be in some quarters. It can still cause sterility, serious illness or even death. That 'the pill' is not, and is not meant to be, any protection against VD would seem obvious, but many girls seem unaware of this—till it is too late. Nor is 'the pill' itself as harmless as all that. It can have unpleasant and sometimes quite serious side effects, and one recent (probably conservative) estimate is that 25% of the women who use it ought not to do so, on medical grounds. Even common sense might suggest that prolonged chemical interference with hormone functioning could cause trouble. These are just some of the more obvious *physical* dangers. There are plenty of emotional problems and dangers, too. To take just one example: genuine misunderstandings can arise because teen-age lads want, and expect, to go 'all the way' whereas often the girls only want to flirt. This situation is by no means uncommon: at best it is embarrassing, and at worst it can lead to very ugly incidents.

The way of self-restraint is not necessarily an easy one for all to follow and, under present conditions especially, it is almost more than we can reasonably expect. And it too can be undertaken for the wrong reasons, and in the wrong way. The English public school system was based on the segregation of the sexes and an ideal of sexual restraint, and to a certain extent it worked. It produced the predictable crop of homosexuals as well as quite a few inhibited young men, but it inculcated a genuine respect for women, which was not always quite as ludicrous as some would have us believe. On balance, it may have done more good than harm, from the sexual point of view, to the majority of those who were subjected to it. But it was based on an oversimplified idea. Life is more subtle than Arnold of Rugby allowed for (even if we overlook the 'class' aspect of the whole thing). And yet, the best products of this system of education are in many respects admirable. They have a deep sense of self-discipline and responsibility, qualities in rather short supply today.

Of course, many of the young people of today actually *have* such a sense, quite strongly in some ways. They *do* feel responsible—they feel deeply 'committed'—about *apartheid* or other social questions. And even the hairiest types quite often endure surprising hardships in the way of sleeping rough and the like, with a kind of self-discipline which may appear strangely ill-directed but is nevertheless *there.*

Sex, Religion and Anti-Religion

The present age has been justly called the Post-Christian Age. Traditional Christian teachings are crumbling everywhere. It is not perhaps very difficult to find arguments in support of the view that this is a good thing or that it is a bad thing. It largely depends on what we want to put in place of the dear departed. But in any case, one can scarcely avoid feeling a pang of sympathy for the Christians, especially perhaps the Christian clergy. Most Christian ministers of all denominations are, after all, decent, upright, hard-working and conscientious men who are desperately striving to do a good job and at least save something worthwhile from the wreckage. They are usually desperately underpaid, they preach to their dwindling flock to the best of their ability and they are stuck with an impossible situation. They may often be ignorant and sometimes bigoted, but they find themselves mocked by those who are often enough equally ignorant and bigoted, and whose sole aim is frequently to replace their creed, however inadequate, by something even more negative and destructive. If the Church, even in its present enfeebled state, were to disappear totally from the scene, the loss, despite all doctrinal inadequacies and absurdities, would certainly be greater than any conceivable gain. It is not quite true that *any* religion is better than no religion, for some forms of religion (including some Christian sects) are unbelievably awful. But the best, or even the second-best, of Christianity is assuredly a lot better than most of the purely secular substitutes for it. This, as Buddhists, we should be freely prepared to admit, without thereby in the least falling into the trap of saying, 'Well, it's all the same thing *really*', when it quite obviously isn't. The basic Christian attitude to sex is well enough known, and has been briefly outlined above. It can assume thoroughly unhealthy forms, but in its more moderate aspects it can perhaps still serve as a fairly useful basis for decent behaviour. At least it does provide *some* reasons which a good many people can accept as a basis for morality.

Now of course one *can* have morals without religion. It is not too difficult to produce purely social reasons for a lot of moral conduct, sexual or otherwise, and the best of the anti-religious propagandists today are at pains to do this. But some others do not. Their policy is simply to controvert anything and everything the Churches teach and stand it on its head. Sensuality and aggression, it is argued, are basic drives in man which it is dangerous to dam up and which should, accordingly, be allowed free play. In the case of aggression, the fallacy is so obvious that there are few who would literally subscribe to this, though some societies in practice seem to allow it plenty of scope. But in the case of sex, complete permissiveness really is openly preached in some quarters, and in fact a Swedish doctor has even announced that he wants to organize a corps of volunteers to provide everybody with sexual intercourse. This would apparently make *everybody* happy and the millennium would have arrived ...

What Sex is Really All About

The sexual drive is, in most circumstances, just about the strongest urge there is in man and in the other animals. This is so whether we think (with some) that it was implanted in us by God or (with others) by the devil. It can be denied all direct expression, quite obviously, and whether this is or is not a good thing to do depends very much indeed on how—and why—this is done. When we come to consider sex and religion, we find that in fact this *is* often done, in the Buddhist Sangha and the Roman Catholic Church, to take the two most obvious examples. The ostensible reasons for such a course in these two bodies may be quite different, but it is surely not without significance that they both—and some others—consider it important to even attempt such a seemingly unnatural exercise. But there is no doubt that a good deal of the enormous respect shown to members of both communities stems directly from the knowledge of their celibate way or life. In some parts of the world, indeed, such men are regarded as either supermen or hypocrites, since no normal man could be expected to endure such a life. And of course both communities do include quite a few hypocrites and, probably, a few supermen.

For the vast majority of people, of course, there is no question of their attempting such a thing except perhaps, for relatively short periods. The lady who once asked in a class, 'If everybody became a Bhikkhu, what would happen to the world?' could safely be told not to worry.

The biological function of sex is obvious and requires no discussion here. But the interesting thing for us to note is how sex—like everything else—is a purely impersonal force. We tend to think of it in intensely personal terms, but in actual fact it is a force that just flows through us and uses our most wonderful and inspiring emotions for its own ends, which are totally concerned with the continuance of the race as a whole. The idea that it is just a private and wonderful thing between you and me is merely a part of our general illusion. Altogether, it is a prolific breeder of illusions. It can lead a man to think he has found the most wonderful woman in the whole world while everybody else is thinking, 'What on earth can he possibly see in her?'

To the Buddhist, of course, sex is an expression—perhaps *the* chief expression—of that *taṇhā* or craving which brings *dukkha* in its train. It is therefore quite logical that we should seek to bring it under control. In a sense, that is all there is to the whole question. The aim of the true Buddhist is to bring about the cessation of craving, and from the individual point of view there is no other reason for sexual restraint than this. But from the broader ethical point of view there are, of course, other reasons which are no less important: if we behave recklessly and irresponsibly in sexual matters, we can cause untold harm to others; we can trifle with other people's emotions in a quite devilish way, bring unwanted children into the world, and so on and so forth. But none of these things would, of course, happen if we were able to control 'our own' sexuality: 'our own' in quotes because it is, as we have to remember, an impersonal force working *through* us, which is precisely why it is so difficult to control.

Total sexual control in the sense of perfect abstinence is quite obviously only for the few. It is perhaps one mistake of the Roman Catholic Church that it seeks to impose this discipline on too many people and too absolutely, as some Catholics now recognize. But in fact there will always be more than sufficient people willing and even determined to keep the human race going. Society's problem is rather to prevent the population explosion from getting completely out of hand—hence all the rather dreary arguments about 'the pill'.

Now there are various possible ways of controlling the sex urge, some bad some good. One is through fear: fear of hell fire, fear of venereal diseases, and so on. This is of course not a particularly good way, though it *can* certainly work, and is perhaps not always wholly harmful. After all, there can be various unfortunate consequences of intercourse and we should be aware of them. Even rebirth in some very unpleasant 'hell-state' is not necessarily a complete fantasy. But of course an exaggerated fear of dreadful penalties for minor transgressions is not psychologically very helpful.

Another way is the way of repression. This is of course not a conscious process. It is a form of successful self-deception, as a result of which we are not consciously aware of a thing. Repression, as ought to be better known than in fact seems to be the case, is by no means the same thing as voluntary 'suppression'. Very few people in actual fact have really 'transcended sex'—though quite a lot of people seem to think they have. They never connect their resultant psychological troubles with the root-cause—repressed sex. But it should be firmly stated that, *if we can do it*, suppression with awareness does little or no harm.

A great deal of sexual energy can, of course, be canalized or 'sublimated' into other things: art, music, intense religious faith, and so on. People—especially, but by no means only, women—are well known in all religious groups who have done this with more or less success. And those who have attained the meditative absorptions known as the *jhānas* may find therein an emotional outlet which is superior to that of sex. All this is fine, and very much to the good. But even these things do not in themselves entirely solve the problem, at least in the ultimate sense.

Sex and Rebirth

As long as there remains even a latent craving (including that for sex), according to the Buddhist teaching, rebirth will inevitably continue to take place. For we are reborn, not merely because of the sexual drive which brought about the union of our parents, but also because of that same sexual drive in 'ourselves', i.e. in that stream of consciousness which produces the changing series of patterns of our own particular individuality. And this is in fact the deeper significance of the Oedipus complex and other such matters unearthed by Freud. According to the 'Tibetan Book of the Dead' those whose karmic predispositions destine them for rebirth in human form see couples in sexual union and experience desire for an attractive member of the opposite sex among those couples. By this desire they thereupon find themselves drawn into the womb and reborn—which was not at all what they wanted! The Theravāda scriptures do not specifically describe the process, and it may be rather symbolic than literal, but psychologically at least something like this is what happens.

Quite obviously, the average Buddhist lay person has no present intention of living a celibate life—nor is this being urged here. But some knowledge of the nature of sexuality and of how it can be transcended can help him to solve his sexual problems, if only by helping him to avoid self-deception.

Sex and the Stages on the Path

According to the Buddhist teaching, the path to Full Enlightenment is marked by the successive attainment (and fruition) of four stages. The first of these is that of the stream-winner (*sotāpanna*), who has broken three of the ten fetters and 'glimpsed Nibbāna'. The essential factor here is the clear realization of impersonality (*anattā*). This realization at the same time eliminates sceptical doubt and belief in rites and rituals. In our present connection the important point to note is this: in the moment when anattā is realized—when, that is, the spurious nature of 'self' is clearly seen—there can obviously be no desire of any sort for that 'self" and its gratification.

True, this moment of deep insight passes, but its profound effects remain. Desires return, but their root has been irreparably broken, so that they must eventually die away. In fact at this stage—and this should be realized—sexual desire and aggression may still be quite strong in some types of character. But of course they will never result in the grosser forms of misconduct. However, craving (including the sexual drive) in its more latent form may still be powerful enough to lead to repeated rebirths—up to seven times, it is said.

The second stage, that of the once-returner (*sakadāgāmin*), when 'Nibbāna has been glimpsed' a second time, results in a dramatic reduction of both these urges. Henceforth they have at most only 'nuisance-value', and rebirth in the world of sensuality cannot, it is said, take place more than once. Only at the third stage, that of the non-returner (*Anāgāmin*), are they quite eliminated. Such a person has no more ties with this world, and so will not be reborn here, though he may be reborn in another sphere before attaining Full Enlightenment.

From all this the conclusion may be drawn that, while it is indeed possible to 'transcend sexuality' in this life, it is not by any means as simple as some suppose, and many who think they have done it are deceiving themselves. Nevertheless there are many in the robe and out of it, who without having reached this stage, have in practice gained complete control of the sex impulse.

Gaining Control

How then can control of sexuality be achieved? A large measure of control can certainly be gained by concentrative (*samatha*) meditation practice, which stills the mind and can lead to the jhāna states. In non-Buddhist systems this is probably the best that can be hoped for, and it is not to be despised. Indeed, many people, especially in the West (and probably also e.g. in modern Japan), are so disturbed that some such calming practice is almost essential, perhaps for a very long time. But the other way, and the truly Buddhist way which can lead right to the goal is the way of Insight. The main scriptural basis for this is the *Satipaṭṭhāna Sutta*.

The four foundations of mindfulness as set forth there are: mindfulness as to body, feelings, states of mind, and mind-contents. With reference to 'states of mind', it is said, 'He knows the lustful mind and the mind that is free from lust. He knows how lust arises and how it ceases'. This is not a manual of meditation, and it must suffice here just to indicate how by mindfulness one comes to *discover* how mental and physical phenomena arise and cease, and therefore ultimately how to bring about their cessation.

In this method, there is no forcing. Rigid suppression by an act of will is not required—and will not anyway lead to the goal. When personal problems seemingly quite intractable are fully seen in their true nature, they will dissolve. It may take time and much perseverance, but it is a way of gentleness which does no violence to one's nature. Eventually, if steadfastly pursued, it can lead to the solution of *all* our problems, not only those connected with sex. Slowly and patiently, we can disentangle by mindfulness all the guilt feelings and other complications which may have developed. And we come to realize, probably to our surprise, that the seeing is the cure, when the seeing is deep enough.

Conclusion

Sex is a powerful force in us all. In itself it is neither 'good' nor 'bad'. But it can certainly create problems. And modern Western man is particularly prone to such problems, partly because of the sheer hectic pace and pressure of modern life, which exaggerates *all* our troubles, and more specifically because of his background. A puritanical Church tradition (one extreme) has now been vigorously challenged by a secular spirit of permissiveness (the other extreme). For many people it is not at all easy to find the middle way between these two extremes.

There is nothing 'sinful' about sex. If we make mistakes, we should recognize them and try to avoid repeating them, but we should not develop guilt complexes about them. Sexual lapses are not uniquely wicked, and in fact all but the grosser forms of sexual misconduct are probably on the whole less harmful socially than a lot of other things many people do. But it should be borne in mind that sex does usually involve at least one other person, and potentially the next generation. In this respect it is strictly incumbent on us at all times to act responsibly which means compassionately. Otherwise, the physical and emotional consequences for somebody may be very serious.

The ideal of sex only within monogamous marriage should be just as valid for Buddhists as for Christians. It should, at least, not be lightly departed from.

The Way of Mindfulness has been recommended above. Admittedly, not everybody is prepared to practice intensive mindfulness, whatever benefits may be urged for it. But even a moderate degree of *habitual* mindfulness can produce surprising results. If we learn to watch with detachment our desires at play, it is often quite astonishing how they seem to 'drop away', almost of their own accord. To take as an example a related problem, many people, when they first come to Buddhism, are worried about the Fifth Precept, which deals with intoxication. 'Can't I have a drink occasionally?' they ask, often rather anxiously. The answer is of course, 'It's up to you'. But in this case, too, having tried a little mindfulness, they are frequently surprised to find that they want a drink less and less. As a matter of fact, the same principle applies here too. Having discovered the principle, applied it and found that it works, we can decide for ourselves how far we wish to take it. It will take us as far as we are prepared to go.

Some readers may wonder that there has been no mention of the word 'love' in the foregoing. To have discussed this question would have led too far. So I will merely quote the following two phrases from a newspaper advice-column:

'I am in love' means 'I want me to be happy'; 'I love' means 'I want to make you happy'.

Buddhists might reflect, and even meditate, on these two statements—at various levels.

GOLDEN RULE

Never let Passion override Compassion.

A Technique of Living

Based on Buddhist Psychological Principles

by

Leonard A. Bullen

WHEEL PUBLICATION NO. 226/227/228/229/230

A Technique of Living

Introductory Section

There is one thing that everybody knows by direct experience, and that is that life is a mixture of enjoyment and suffering, happiness and sorrow, pleasure and pain. The intelligent and the stupid, the good and the evil, the rich and the poor, all know some degree of suffering mixed in with their happiness.

There are times, it is true, when we feel free from the heavier burdens of suffering. There are times when our affairs are going well, when we are able to cope adequately with our responsibilities, and when we can meet our obligations without trouble. But there are other times, too, when things do not go so well, when we suffer severe losses and meet with persistent frustrations; and at these times we feel the need for some special mental approach to our problems.

In fact, we need this special approach all of the time, during the good times as well as the bad. We need a special approach to success as well as to failure, to gain as well as to loss, to happiness as well as to sorrow. We need a technique to handle the easy times as well as the difficult periods.

In brief, we need a technique of living. It can be said in general that any technique is better than none at all. Any well considered approach to the problems of life is better than the unthinking drift of life, but perhaps the most efficient technique is one that involves a considerable understanding of life, an increased mindfulness of the mind's own aims and processes, and a certain degree of self-discipline to keep the mind on its chosen path.

In a technique of this kind, then, the three keywords are understanding, mindfulness, and self-discipline.

Understanding life is a matter of gaining an appreciation—either intellectual or intuitive—of the way living beings act and react. Mindfulness of the mind's own aims and processes involves a sort of inner alertness, a form of attentiveness directed inwardly. And self-discipline is the sustained effort to act and think along certain chosen lines, an effort which requires the exercise of the will.

Of these three elements—understanding, mindfulness, and self-discipline—it is mindfulness which, in the Buddhist system of self-training becomes the focal point.

* * *

If you want to take on any system of mental development, either as an aim in itself or as a means of gaining greater value from life, the cultivation of mindfulness in some direction at least must play a major part in it. In other words, any system of mental culture must involve the development of the powers of attention.

As you know from direct observation, your attention may be directed outwardly towards the external world of objects or inwardly towards the internal world of ideas. While the development of mindfulness may bring about greater alertness with regard to external happenings, this is not its main aim, at least from the Buddhist viewpoint; its primary purpose is to bring about an increased awareness of what goes on in that "current of existence" that you call your own self.

Some forms of mindfulness are intended to make you more aware and to give you an increased understanding of your own mental processes in general; for these mental processes are the factors that determine what your life will yield—or fail to yield—in terms of enduring happiness.

Now, the practice of mindfulness is the focal point of a system of mental discipline, a method of mind-training that forms the core of various forms of Buddhism. It is not intended to deal with Buddhist doctrine and practice as a whole, as we are more interested in a specific aspect of them; but in order to fit this specific aspect of Buddhism into its general framework it may be pertinent to set out, very briefly, the main points of the system of mental discipline known as the Noble Eightfold Path. Here are the various aspects of this Path:

1. *Right Understanding*, a knowledge of the true nature of existence;
2. *Right Thought*, free from sensuality, ill will, and cruelty;
3. *Right Speech*, speech which is free from falsity, gossip, harshness, and idle babble;

4. *Right Action*, or the avoidance of killing, stealing, and sexual misconduct;
5. *Right Livelihood*, an occupation that harms no conscious living being;
6. *Right Effort*, or the training of the will;
7. *Right Mindfulness*, the perfection of the faculty of attention; and
8. *Right Concentration*, the cultivation of higher mental states with a view to direct knowledge of the Unconditioned, the ultimate reality beyond the relative universe.

* * *

The particular phase of this Noble Eightfold Path in which we are interested, as you can see, is the seventh step, right mindfulness; but the first step—right understanding, especially in the sense of self-understanding—and the sixth, right effort or the training of the will, are also of special interest in this context.

In some lines of mental development the expansion of the field of attention is the aim, while in other forms the field is narrowed and the awareness is thereby intensified.

The expansion of awareness and the intensification of awareness are opposite but complementary modes of mindfulness, and both involve the development of the normal faculty of attention. It is by training the attention, by directing and controlling it, that awareness can be expanded to cover a broader field, or, on the other hand intensified to confine it to a single idea.

Of the two, perhaps, the concentration of the attention on to a single point is of greater importance, for all mental development requires a sharpened awareness.

Compare the fuzzy, dull awareness of the dream state with the sharpened awareness of the normal waking state. In a dream you experience sensations from the outside world but you misinterpret them. Your feet are cold, perhaps, because the rug across the foot of the bed has slipped off; but instead of correctly interpreting the sensation of coldness, you dream that you are walking on a cold street without your shoes. Or a dog barks nearby and you dream you are being pursued by a pack of hungry wolves. These misinterpretations, we are told, are bound up with your various undischarged emotional accumulations and your various complexes, and the external stimuli—the cold feet and the dog's bark—are used as the means of discharging your emotional accumulations or of giving expression to your complexes, up to a point at least.

In waking life you are not guilty of such gross misinterpretations as you are during sleep. When the rug falls off and your feet become cold, you reach down and pull the rug back into place. When the dog barks, perhaps it brings to mind some childhood story of a boy being pursued by a pack of wolves; but because you are awake and not dreaming you nevertheless realise that the sound you have just heard is nothing more than a dog's bark.

However, while you do not make the gross misinterpretations when in the waking state that you do during sleep, you are nevertheless guilty of some degree of misinterpretation, greater or less according to the extent to which your thought processes are dominated by your emotions and your psychological complexes.

While the concentration of mental energy on a single point is necessary in certain circumstances, a diffuse or widespread distribution of attention is of value in other circumstances, and for an all-round mental development it should be possible to bring the mind into either state with equal facility.

As an example of the restricted scope of awareness, you well know the kind of situation in which you are in the process of writing a letter when the telephone rings in another room. On your way to answer the telephone you put down your pen without giving any special attention to this small act, and afterwards, when you go to take up the pen to continue writing, you have great difficulty in finding it because you are unable to remember where you put it. Unless you make a special effort of mindfulness, the simple task of attending both to the act of putting the pen down and to the act of walking towards the telephone is too much for you, because the scope of your normal awareness is too confined to embrace these two very simple things at the same time. This is an obvious example of the need for an expansion of the scope of consciousness.

In the ordinary course of workaday life, there is little or no time for the practice of exercises in mental development unless these practices are woven into the general fabric of everyday life. If, however, you find the time occasionally to slow down whatever you are doing perhaps for only a few minutes, an hour, or a day, according to circumstances—in order to give to it your fullest possible attention, then this deliberately-increased awareness will help to establish a general all-round mindfulness during the busier periods of your life.

Under ideal conditions, you should be able to become fully aware of whatever you are doing all your normal waking life. Of course, this continual alertness is normally beyond you. To become fully aware of everything you do throughout your waking life is much more than you can ordinarily achieve, and the more you try to develop this enlarged awareness, the more you realise your inadequacies.

However, if your efforts along the lines of right mindfulness do nothing other than make you more aware of your own unawareness they are thereby fulfilling a very important purpose. You come to realise the automatic and mechanical nature of much that you do, and you begin to see that you have hitherto been largely caught up in the unthinking drift of life. Only when you begin to become aware of all this can you start your fight to become free from the unthinking drift.

In your ordinary life, no doubt, you meet a succession of problems. Maybe you are short of money, or your domestic responsibilities are too heavy for you, or the people in the flat upstairs are noisy.

A philosophy of some kind would help you to deal with your problems, of course, but only up to a point, for your problems are mainly practical ones and not philosophical ones. To be of any real use, a philosophy must be developed into a policy and this policy must be organised to become a technique.

Whatever your philosophy and whatever policy and technique you develop from it, it is safe to say that it must embody not only increased mindfulness, but also some form of self-discipline, to be of any real use. Without self-discipline, no form of mental culture can achieve very much.

Self-discipline must be used side by side with the development of mindfulness. You must recognise, of course, that self-discipline alone is of limited value, but coupled with the cultivation of awareness it becomes of much greater value as a part of the technique of living.

Self-discipline is the effort to act and to think along certain predetermined lines and to avoid acting and thinking along contrary lines.

There is a sharp distinction between discipline which is self-imposed and discipline which is imposed from outside.

You will find that a discipline imposed on you from outside sometimes raises a resistance within you, and you will often tend to resent it. This is so when the discipline is harsh and strict, of course, but it may also be so when it is mild and easy-going. The resentment depends not only on the harshness of the actual discipline to which you must submit, but also on your unwillingness to submit to it.

Thus if you are forced to submit to a light discipline with which you disagree, you will feel rebellious and indeed you may actually rebel against it, even though, viewed dispassionately, it is not harsh. On the other hand, if you were willingly and knowingly to undertake a very strict discipline—if, for example, you were to enter a religious order or voluntarily to join the army—you would tend to conform to it without resentment. And you would do so because, taking on the discipline willingly and knowingly, you would up to a point transform it from an external discipline to a self-discipline.

So an external discipline can become either an occasion for resentment and rebellion or else a means of developing your own mental resources, according to your own attitude towards it.

However, discipline of this kind is not really what we are interested in our present consideration, and we mention it only to bring out the difference between an externally-imposed discipline and the type of discipline which is self-imposed.

You might take on a self-imposed discipline for any of a number of reasons. You might start your daily work very early and continue until very late in order to make money. You might undertake a strict and unappetising diet because you want to become slender and more attractive. Or you might take on a rigid routine of training because you want to win a foot race. In each of these the self-imposed discipline is not an end in itself—it is only a way of achieving an end.

However, whether it is meant in that way or not, your self-discipline achieves more than it was intended to do; it does more than make you more money, or slim your figure, or win your race, for it builds up in your mental structure qualities which in themselves will increase your capacity for happiness.

If a discipline is imposed on you by others or by circumstances, this externally-imposed discipline is generally concerned with your outer actions rather than with the mental processes which lead up to them. Self-imposed discipline, on the other hand, may be concerned with your outer actions and their effects, or it may be concerned with the desires and emotions which influence your outer actions; but in either case your inner mental processes and motives are of primary importance, at least in the present context.

At the same time it must be recognised that you can help to control your desires and emotions by controlling their outer manifestations. For example, you may tend to gaze longingly at something you desire but cannot have, and this tends to strengthen the desire as well as the feeling of frustration; but if you refuse to gaze at it—if you turn your vision away from it, even though you cannot turn your interest away—you are doing something, however little, towards controlling the desire and reducing the sense of frustration.

Again, you tend to raise your voice when annoyed, and the louder voice is the effect of the feeling of annoyance; but if by an effort of will you keep your voice at its normal level you are doing a certain amount towards the control of the annoyance itself.

The point of this is that the external manifestations of desires and emotions are integral parts of these desires and emotions, and by inhibiting their outer effects you are helping to weaken their inner causes—provided of course you do so mindfully. While it is true that these things work primarily from the inside outwards, it is true also that to some extent they work from the outside inwards.

Now, let us consider the manner in which you can best apply self-discipline in your daily life. Perhaps the biggest problem in any form of mental culture is not the problem of mastering its principles but that of applying them. One system may be based on psychological theories, another on philosophical or religious concepts; one may be clear-cut and another vague and indefinite; but in most cases the greater difficulty is found not in understanding the principles involved, but in using the practices in the routine of everyday life.

If you lead a too-busy life, with responsibilities and duties bearing down on you, you may feel that your endeavours to develop your own mental potentialities are thwarted by all these external pressures. But if you could miraculously be freed from your problems and frustrations you would also be deprived of the very best opportunities for mindfulness, self-discipline, and other forms of mental culture. Your philosophy and policy of life are worth nothing to you if you cannot weave them into the fabric of your daily living. If, however, they are at all exacting and if they demand from you any degree of self-discipline, it is admittedly not easy to do this.

There is, however, a method whereby you can apply self-discipline in the routine of your everyday life and which involves little if any expenditure of valuable time.

At this point, however, I must make it clear that this method of self-discipline which I am about to place before you is not a traditional Buddhist method; it is a system which I have worked out and applied to my own life. In my early acquaintance with Buddhist ideals and the principles of a similar kind, I found that it was quite easy to talk about them when life was flowing smoothly, but quite as difficult to apply them—or even to call them to mind—when problems arose. For this reason I searched for some way to turn my philosophy into a policy and this policy into a technique. As a result I evolved what I call the self-contract method of self-discipline.

In using this method, you take in hand some adverse tendency which you wish to correct, some habit you wish to break, or some habit you wish to form, and at the same time you select some small pleasure in which you normally indulge.

You then make a sort of pact or contract with yourself to the effect that, soon after each occasion on which you fail to control the adverse tendency or habit, you will deny yourself the small pleasure you have selected.

To take a concrete example, let us assume that you are absent-minded. This, of course, is simply a lack of all-round mindfulness, for although particular forms of mindfulness have certain specialised functions, a general all-round mindfulness is essential for efficient living.

If you lack this all-round mindfulness, you will find yourself mislaying small things such as your keys, or your reading glasses, or your pencil. You will have to search all your pockets or empty out your handbag to find your railway ticket. You will carefully write someone's telephone number on a slip of paper and then just as carelessly lose it.

In this you will have a great deal in common with most other people. Most of us lack all-round mindfulness and therefore most of us would benefit by some self-training in this respect.

Let us assume, then, that you wish to correct this adverse tendency—this lack of all-round mindfulness. Let us assume also that you smoke cigarettes.

You therefore make a contract with yourself along these lines: "I resolve that after each time I neglect to be mindful in small matters I will go without a cigarette for at least two hours."

Now, you will note that this is not merely a resolution to form a new habit; it is something more. If you make a simple resolution without a self-imposed deprivation it is likely to fail, either because you will forget it, or because you will soon decide that absent-mindedness is not such a bad fault after all, or, more likely, because there are too many other matters demanding your attention.

With a self-imposed deprivation, however, the contract which you make with yourself has a great deal more force than a simple resolution, by virtue of the self-imposed deprivation.

At first sight, the deprivation may seem to be a form of self-punishment. This is not its function, however, for it must never be severe enough to be felt as a punishment, and if it were to be felt as a punishment it would tend to defeat its own purpose.

You must regard the deprivation, not as a penalty, but purely as an aid to mindfulness, a help in breaking free from the unthinking drift of life, and a device to give force to your resolution. As such, it must never be allowed to become irksome or unduly restrictive; it must always remain flexible and readily modified, for once you make it too difficult you will tend to throw it aside and forget all about it.

All that you require your self-discipline to do is to exert a gentle and fairly continuous pressure in order to give you greater awareness of your habits, desires, and reactions to circumstances.

To make the self-contract system of discipline work you must begin by forming a new habit. This new habit is that of mentally pausing each time you are about to indulge in the small pleasure—whatever it may be—that you have selected as the basis for your self-contract.

If it happens to be cigarette-smoking, as your hand is about to open the packet your mind must learn to pause to consider whether or not your self-contract allows you a cigarette at this time.

If you have agreed with yourself to take your tea or coffee without sugar after an occasion of lack of mindfulness, then you must train yourself to think back each time before reaching for the sugar basin.

If you like to eat chocolates and have made a pact to deprive yourself of them after being absent-minded, then you must form the habit of pausing to think back before eating them.

It is, in fact, possible to set off one habit against another and so develop greater control over both, but in any case the deprivation must be regarded mainly as an aid to mindfulness and must therefore remain flexible. In another system of self-discipline, perhaps, you might be required to make a more exacting imposition on yourself; but since the method we are discussing is primarily a means of handling small and apparently insignificant failings without interfering with the busy workaday routine, a rigid and severe system of self-discipline would be inappropriate.

If you yourself decide to take on this system of mental culture you would of course have to adapt it to your own requirements and your own mode of life. This would probably apply particularly to the self-imposed deprivations that you would use, and those will depend on your likes and dislikes.

Perhaps you neither smoke cigarettes, nor have sugar in your tea or coffee, nor eat chocolates. But however austere your life may be there must be some small pleasure that you enjoy—or even some small activity that you carry out—with some degree of regularity; and whatever it is you can use it as a basis for the self-contract method of self-discipline.

As opposed to self-deprivation, the idea of self-rewarding is sometimes suggested as a basis for a system of discipline. In general, however, self-appointed rewards do not work as well as self-imposed deprivations.

For example, if you already eat whatever you want whenever you want it, by rewarding yourself with something you like to eat you will find yourself overeating, or if you already smoke whenever you feel like it, by rewarding yourself with an extra cigarette you will find yourself smoking when you do not really want to do so, and so you will be effecting little or nothing. Only if you are already restricting your eating and smoking will a self-rewarding basis in these things be effective.

However, you may sometimes offset a self-imposed deprivation by a self-appointed reward, so that one cancels the other. Everyone's life and circumstances vary from everyone else's, and a system that fails in one person's case may work in another.

What has been written above forms a general introduction to mindfulness combined with self-discipline as a basis for mental culture. With this basis, fortified by an increasing understanding of life—of the ways in which living beings act and react—you can lay the foundation for an efficient technique of living.

In order to help you to build on this foundation, I have compiled a course which is designed to extend over a period of a year. It consists of a series of sections one for each month, on various aspects of mental culture, each with a basic exercise in either mindfulness, self-understanding, or self-discipline. The course is called "A Technique of Living," and this section forms the introduction to it.

In the main, but not entirely, the practices are based on Buddhist psychological principles. The practices do not, however, include exercises which require an appreciable amount of time, nor are the principles involved of a particularly profound nature.

If you wish to take on what is loosely called meditation and to study Buddhist principles in their deeper forms, a good deal of literature is available on the subject; but such practices and study do not lie within the scope of this course. All of the practices in this course are designed to be woven into the fabric of the workaday routine.

Although one month is given to each section of the course, you will almost certainly find that a month is too short to establish it as a well-founded habit, and you will probably need to repeat the series during the following year. In fact, there is no reason why you should not continue with the practices in sequence indefinitely on a yearly cycle.

While each one of the twelve lessons is assigned to one particular month, you may commence the course at any time of the year.

In taking on any system of self-training, the main problem, as already stated, is not the matter of understanding its principles but that of applying its practices; and even then, once you have made a start, there is always the possibility that you will discontinue it.

If you are practising it alone, you may tend to lose interest. If, however, you can form a discussion-group with three or four friends with similar interests, the opportunity to compare notes and to discuss progress and mutual problems will provide a good incentive to continue with the practices.

The First Month

The Practice of Relaxation

It has been said that life is too serious to be taken seriously. We might enlarge on this by saying that life is so serious and so unsatisfactory that by becoming resistant and tense about it we merely make it more serious. In other words, tension increases the seriousness of things.

Not everyone shares this view that life is so serious and unsatisfactory. For some, the continual search for personal gratification is relatively successful, and they feel that they're getting something a little better than the usual fifty-fifty mixture of pleasure and displeasure, a little more rest than effort, a little more happiness than sorrow. This is all they expect and they are reasonably satisfied with it.

There are others who get something worse than the average fifty-fifty mixture of happiness and sorrow; life deals out to them less pleasure than pain, and they must give out more than they receive. They must make great efforts and enjoy little rest, and their sorrow outweighs their happiness. Their unremitting efforts to extract from life more than it can yield create a general state of tension that makes life still more serious.

Those of us who are tense, it seems, outnumber those who are relaxed; but few realise just how tense they are and just how this tension is spoiling things for them.

How does tension arise in the first place? To begin with you must realise that tension is necessary under certain conditions. If you're in a dangerous situation the natural reaction is to tense your muscles; your whole physical mechanism is then geared up for escaping or fighting. This reaction has been instrumental in survival and the processes of tensing the muscles together with the physical changes that take place throughout the body are necessary in special situations.

But this is where the trouble lies. You can't fully turn off the tension; you find that you're always tense, even when there is no occasion for it.

Thus you see that while tension is useful under some conditions, it's not necessary for twenty-four hours a day and seven days a week.

Before we go any further we must ask ourselves this: what do we mean by tension? We know that by muscular tension we mean a state in which some of our muscles are partly contracted and the nerves controlling them are ready to produce a further contraction at an instant's notice.

But what do we mean by mental tension? Our minds control the nerves that lead to our muscles, so that if these nerves are in a continual state of readiness it's because our minds are acting as if they were continually expecting some emergency suddenly to develop.

Your mind is in a state of alertness due to anxiety, resentment, or self-assertion. In some situations the alertness is commendable and useful, but when long sustained it's generally pointless, without an object, and—worst of all—beyond the immediate control of your consciousness. It's controlled from mental levels inaccessible to consciousness rather than by the higher conscious functions of your mind.

The precipitating causes of your inward tension lie in the outer world, it's true; they lie in your need to earn a living, in your family obligations, and in the demands made upon you to compete for prestige; but the real causes lie in yourself. The real causes of tension lie, firstly, in the anxiety you feel when something you value is threatened; secondly, in the resentment you build up towards those that threaten your valued things and your self-importance; and thirdly, in the need you feel constantly to assert yourself.

Let's look at these three basic causes of tension one at a time. The first is anxiety, and this arises when anything you value is threatened. The more things you desire the more vulnerable you make yourself to the onset of anxiety. While anxiety is related to various emotional factors, concern for your own well-being or for the well-being of your near ones and possessions is its main foundation. In Buddhist psychology this concern arises from self-centred desire, which embraces not only the grosser manifestations of desire such as avarice and stinginess but all of its less obvious forms.

The second basic tension-causing mental factor is resentment. Since in the full course of his life the average person meets so many annoyances and frustrations, he builds up an aversion towards the things and people that seemingly cause them.

Because this aversion—in its mild as well as in its intense manifestations—is as a general rule neither fully expressed nor fully resolved, it remains to simmer and smoulder in the form of resentment.

The third of the basic mental causes of tension is the false need you feel constantly to assert yourself, to gain and retain prestige, and to maintain a sense of self-importance even at the expense of self-deceit. You can easily see it in others when it appears in its blatant forms, but as it exists in yourself you're seldom aware of it. In Buddhist psychology it's called delusion, since the self you constantly assert is unreal when understood in ultimate terms; and all your tendencies towards self-assertion (as well as your feelings both of self-importance and of inferiority) are all parts of this deeply rooted delusion.

Thus we see that, according to the Buddha-doctrine, all mental unhappiness springs from self-centred desire, aversion, and delusion. As we're considering them here as tension-causing factors, desire is expressed as anxiety, aversion is expressed as resentment, and delusion is expressed as self-assertion.

Now, until you've developed self-understanding, you're not fully aware of the real causes of your anxiety; you're not completely conscious of your resentment; nor again do you really know the full extent of your self-assertion. Thus you're unable properly to deal with unwanted tension.

Tension manifests in the body as well as in the mind. Thus arises the need to deal with the problem of tension not only at the higher level of the mind but also at the lower level of the body, particularly in the voluntary muscles.

A Buddhist exercise called posture-mindfulness can be readily adapted for the purpose of bodily relaxation. The essence of the adapted practice of posture-mindfulness is to give special attention to the various muscle groups of the body, searching for unwanted tension in the muscles and consciously relaxing them. You can use posture-mindfulness for purposes of relaxation whenever your mind is free from other concerns, but perhaps the best time is before you settle down to sleep each night.

Having assumed a comfortable posture, you let the focus of consciousness move slowly several times from one side to the other across your forehead and eyebrows, keeping in mind the idea that you want the muscles concerned to relax or to become limp instead of tight. You can assist the effect by saying mentally "relax, relax" during the process. You may not at first recognise any tension in the forehead and eyebrows, for it may have become so habitual that it feels quite normal. Even so, the quiet application of consciousness to the muscles will do a great deal towards removing any tension that does exist there.

Then you allow the focus of consciousness to move over and around one eye, across the eyelid, and then behind the eye where so many delicate muscles are located. Then you take the attention across to the other eye and move it around, across, and behind it.

Tension is often more evident in the mouth and jaws than elsewhere. Thus when you move the focus of consciousness to your mouth and jaws you may become definitely aware of tension, manifested by clenched teeth and a firmly set mouth. You slowly apply increased mindfulness to the muscles concerned, and the idea of relaxation which you're all the while keeping in mind will cause the tension to disappear or at least to diminish.

Now, you apply the same degree of attention to your tongue, relaxing it as well as you can and allowing it to become as limp as possible. It may be necessary to spend more time on the mouth, jaw, and tongue than on other parts of the body.

Next you carry the centre of attention down to the neck, spiralling it around and up and down several times. You then do the same to the muscles of the shoulders.

From the shoulders you take the focus of consciousness down one arm, spiralling around and along it and searching for tense muscles. When you reach the hand, it's best to take the back of the hand and then each finger one at a time, trying to become aware of each one separately.

You then let your attention flow on to the thigh of the same side, moving down in a spiral to the knee, the lower part of the leg, and the foot.

From there you can move across to the other foot, spiralling up that leg and thigh to the hand of that side. For many of us it's not necessary to spend a great deal of time on the muscles of the legs and feet, since the tension doesn't usually appear there as much as in other muscle groups.

With the hands, however, it's different, for here there may often be considerable tension. In its extreme form this may show itself in clenched fists.

Therefore, after the focus of attention has travelled down one leg and up the other, when it reaches the hand of the second side it's wise to slow up the movement of consciousness and to give individual attention to each finger as before, to the back of the hand, and to the wrist, and then to spiral the focus of consciousness up the arm to the shoulder.

You've now encircled the body from the head down one arm and one leg to the foot, and back again via the foot, the leg and the arm on the other side. There remain the muscles of the chest and the abdomen. You therefore give attention to the sensations in the upper part of the chest, moving the focus of attention across the chest, around the back, and again across the chest, spiralling downwards until you reach the muscles of the abdomen.

This completes the basic adaptation of posture-mindfulness for the purpose of muscular and nervous relaxation. You may vary it, abbreviate it, or extend it, according to your needs and conditions; but in any form the practice just described is a good foundation for the removal of body tension and, to a certain extent, for the easing of mental tension also.

Apart from Buddhism, you find that both Eastern and Western systems of relaxation employ techniques, which are basically the same as this method.

It is generally considered that in the best form of the practice, you should lie, not in bed, but on the floor, flat on the back and with the arms lying limply by the sides, for the non-yielding floor allows you to detect tense muscles more readily than does the soft bed. The only reason why this muscular relaxation method has been described as being practised whilst in bed rather than when lying on the floor is because, for most of us, the day is so full of other things that it's not until we go to bed that we can find the time to carry out the practice.

Now, while the mindful and systematic application of consciousness to tense muscles is generally effective in relaxing them, they may soon afterwards become just as tense again.

What you must do, then, is to do consciously what for so long you've been doing subconsciously. You must consciously and deliberately tense the muscles so as to make the tension-process accessible to consciousness and to remove it from the realm of subconscious activity.

Therefore you proceed to stiffen or tense the muscles concerned, mindfully feeling the sensations of tension, and then you slowly release the tension, all the while giving attention to the feeling of decreasing tension and increasing relaxation. By this means the conscious aspects of the mind gradually take over functions which were hitherto subconsciously controlled.

Starting with your forehead and eyebrows, you consciously frown and slowly relax. Then you consciously open your eyes widely and stare at nothing, and slowly close them and relax the muscles around them. You grit your teeth and then slowly relax your jaws by attending to the muscles of your face, especially those around your mouth. Similarly you tense your tongue and relax it. When you come to your neck, you stiffen it, move your head rigidly forwards, backwards, and from side to side a little, afterwards slowly letting it become as limp as possible. You then hunch your shoulders forward, draw them stiffly back, and then slowly relax them. And so on throughout other muscle groups.

You may have to carry out this alternation of contracting and relaxing a muscle group many times in the one session before it becomes effective. Sometimes, in the early stages of learning the relaxation technique, it's better occasionally to devote a whole session to only one set of muscles.

In this connection, the device of verbalised thought is very helpful. In using this device, you repeat mentally the name of the part of the body whose muscles you are attending to and also tell yourself mentally when you are tensing them and when you are relaxing them. Thus you say mentally: "Jaws ... tense ... relax. Cheek ... tense ... relax. Mouth ... tense ... relax." This verbalising process helps to keep out unwanted trains of thought.

A system (of non-Buddhist origin) of assisting to relieve mental tension consists of visualising black objects or shapes. Thinking of blackness is the nearest you can ordinarily get to thinking of nothing, and thus to the exclusion of unwanted or disturbing thoughts.

It makes little difference what kind of black image you form; you can imagine a black disc, and you can make this disc grow larger and larger, or you can let it change to an octagon, a square, and a triangle. Or again, you can imagine that you're painting everything in the room black stage by stage.

So long as blackness is the predominant idea, the process will help to relax the mind.

Practical Work

For this period your work consists of establishing the practice of relaxation as a habit. Resolve to undertake the practice on at least four occasions each week; or—particularly if you feel a special need for it—once a day. If you can carry out the practice whilst lying on the floor, all the better, otherwise you can adapt it for use when in bed before settling down to sleep at night. Try to keep ten or twenty minutes free for this purpose.

Use the self-contract method of self-discipline and impose on yourself some small penalty whenever you fail to keep to your resolution.

The Second Month

Basic Principles of Self-Understanding

You'll agree, no doubt, that one of the most important things in your mental life is self-understanding. You'll agree also that most of us have much too little self-understanding and therefore need some sort of training along these lines. And, further, you'll realise that we all possess a natural and inherent tendency towards self-deceit.

It seems that each of us in the ordinary way has a sense of "ego," an unreasoned conviction that he's a distinct ego or self, unique and separate from the rest of life.

In some cases, you find a person whose sense of ego is so strong that he finds it necessary at all costs to feel the rightness of everything he does and the rightness of everything he says, as well as the rightness of everything he possesses. When he can feel this rightness (and too often it's a false rightness), then he feels superior. When he can't feel this rightness he feels inferior and inadequate and thus he develops various complexes and neurotic trends.

Because of this false need to feel a false rightness, he must continually deceive himself in various subtle ways; he must pretend to himself that his motives are better than they are, and he must repress all unwelcome knowledge about himself and about all things that are his.

All this, just to keep his sense of ego intact.

Now, on the other hand there are those who have learnt honestly to recognise their own deficiencies and just as honestly to evaluate their own virtues. These few have made some progress in self-understanding.

Most of us, however, stand somewhere between these two extremes. While we're not entirely free from self-deceit we haven't attained to complete self-understanding; we need, therefore, to develop and to practise some kind of psychological technique directed towards an increase in self-knowledge.

One of the difficulties we find is that we treasure some of our irrational loves and hatreds; we cling to our emotional biases and try not to lose our complexes. Because we've grown up with them we've become attached to them. In some way or other these irrational loves and hatreds, biases, and complexes seem to provide a barrier against something we prefer not to face. This barrier has been called the "dread of enlightenment."

This dread of enlightenment is to be found to a greater or less extent in all of us except the few who have attained a considerable degree of self-honesty. Thus it's probable that, in common with the majority of people, you tend to resist the process of self-analysis because it demands that you let go of these treasured evils. You resist the process of disentangling the web of attachment.

Why is this so? Why do you prefer self-deceit to self-knowledge? Not only do these irrationalities give you a barrier against mental factors that you don't wish to face, but they also give you a kind of individual character, a sort of distinction that helps to build up your sense of being different from others.

Another reason is that you want to retain unaltered all those concepts connected with the things you love. If you subject any of your emotion-laden concepts to the scrutiny of self-analysis you may have to alter it, and in altering it you may need to apply effort. It's much more comfortable to leave things as they are.

It's much the same with the things you hate or dislike; if you subject your concepts of these things to the strong clear light of self-examination you may have to prove yourself wrong, and to relinquish your hates and dislikes requires a great deal of adjustment. Again, it's more comfortable to leave things as they are.

Self-analysis may sometimes turn out to be temporarily very painful. What, then, is the point of it all? If you can be just as happy without self-understanding, why bother?

This, of course, is like saying since you are quite comfortable in your dark cave, why bother to build a house with windows? Once your mind becomes firmly established in its habits, the general trend of awareness becomes less acute and your whole mentality becomes less adaptable. It tends to become more lethargic and to resist change.

Then you think more emotionally—that is to say, more subjectively and less objectively. You become disturbed with less cause, your judgement is more likely to be impaired, you lose your poise more readily, and your self-control crumbles easily. All this, when you prefer self-ignorance to self-understanding.

What is needed, then, in order to break down self-deceit and to increase self-understanding? Buddhism offers the principle of right mindfulness.

You'll find this principle of right mindfulness to be simple enough in its general concept; it's primarily the development or cultivation of the ordinary normal faculty of attention; it's applied to many different fields of experience, but in particular it needs to be directed inwardly. In this sense, mindfulness can be described mainly as self-observation.

While simple enough in its general concept as the cultivation of attention, there are so many fields of experience to which you can apply mindfulness that the whole sphere of mindfulness becomes very comprehensive.

For example, ordinary everyday activities—those of work, family life, and leisure, for example—offer a broad scope for increased self-understanding. With regard to your ordinary actions, the Buddhist system states that you must have a clear comprehension of your own motives and purposes. Without this clear comprehension you may be caught in the unthinking drift.

You know, of course, your own motives behind many of the things you do. But it may be, with some other things you do, that you do them merely because other people do them. If so, on self-examination, you'll find that you do these things largely to gain the approval of the people with whom you associate. The mind feels a need to retain a sense of importance and superiority, and to keep this sense of importance and superiority intact it must employ self-deceit in various forms. And to discover your real motives, you must learn to break through this self-deceit. The clear comprehension of motive, then, is one of the major aspects of self-understanding.

It may be that you have a clear comprehension of your overall motive in life, of your ultimate purpose, or it may be that you have no sense of purpose and perhaps no ultimate purpose at all; yet some sense of purpose is necessary for progress. Mindfulness in the form of self-observation is a forward step in the process of gaining a purpose in life and of becoming aware of what that purpose is.

You, in common with mankind as a whole, have inherited an emotional jungle, a profuse and tangled growth of greeds and hatreds existing side by side with more noble tendencies. It's a natural tendency—even though poor psychology—to try to ignore the vicious elements of the mind, and this is how self-deceit arises.

In its early stages, self-deceit is a refusal to recognise these vicious elements of the mind; but at a more advanced stage it may become a complete inability—much more than a conscious refusal—to recognise them. Sometimes the mind plays tricks on itself in order to keep undamaged its sense of rightness and superiority, and these tricks serve to hide its real motives and desires.

Sometimes the mind twists and distorts the meanings of experiences; it avoids thoughts which offend it and which show it up to itself in an unfavourable light, and it diverts its attention from unwanted thoughts to those which bring out its pleasanter aspects.

Psychology knows these tricks as the mental mechanisms, such as the mechanisms of avoidance, divertance, and fixation. Another aspect of self-observation is concerned with the sensations as they're received through the various sense organs and as they're perceived in the mind with special regard to their pleasure-pain content.

The point about sensation in relation to its pleasure-pain content is that it's at this level that attachment has its origin; and attachment is a major cause of unhappiness. All things in the world change; all things arise and pass away; and the more you become attached to anything at all the more you will suffer when you lose it.

To control attachment, therefore, you must keep watch at the door of sensation. As you become more critically aware of all your experiences at the level of sensation, you learn to prevent the pleasure in one and the pain in another from taking control. That is, instead of being controlled by your pleasures and pains, you learn to pass through them without being swept away by them.

It's when you allow your pleasures and pains at the sensational level to dominate you that you become swept away by your emotions, pleasant and painful; and you're then fully enmeshed in the web of attachment. And then you're incapable of objective reasoning and wise decisions.

You can see, then, that it is desirable to train yourself to keep a critical watch on your experiences at the level of sensation, and just as critically to evaluate the pleasures and pains at this level. You can extend this objective self-observation, then, to the factors that go to make up your mental state.

According to the Buddha-doctrine, there are three basic mental factors that retard the mind's progress. One of these is called selfish desire; it exists in various forms such as greed and possessiveness, and it may be either intense on the one hand or mild and unobtrusive on the other. Then there is aversion, which we find also in the guise of anger, hatred, resentment, and irritability. And the third is called delusion, and this also appears in different forms, principally as self-assertion and self-deceit.

The observation of the mental state, then, is a form of mindfulness whose objective is to shine the full light of consciousness on to these "roots of evil," as they are called, and onto all mental factors derived from them and allied with them. These include not only such factors as envy, conceit, and stinginess, but also rigidity of mind, morbid remorse, and restlessness or agitation.

When, by self-examination, you become aware of these adverse tendencies, you are of course more able to deal with them, and the very realisation that they exist will often act as a controlling factor.

However, it's desirable to discover and uncover not only your adverse and retarding mental elements, but also your good qualities, because these need to be nurtured and developed as instruments of progress.

You can see, then, that the principle of mindfulness can be of value to you in various ways; it can help you to avoid the traps laid for you by your own pleasures and pains. And it can help you to evaluate your progress in breaking down the retarding elements in your own mind and in developing the progressing elements.

While development along such lines is largely a matter of self-observation, and while this is of the utmost importance, it can well be supplemented by observation directed outwardly. That is to say, the observation of other people, together with the understanding that comes from this observation, can be of great value in the task of observing yourself.

In fact, this works both ways; as you observe your own behaviour and learn to know your own motives better, you see this behaviour reflected in other people, and their motives become more transparent to you. In the same way, as you learn to interpret other people's behaviour in terms of their motives (sometimes hidden from them), so your own motives become more transparent to yourself.

So you see that the Buddhist approach to self-understanding is by way of mindfulness, directed primarily internally, and secondarily externally; or in other words by the critical observation of yourself and the penetrating but kindly observation of others.

Practical Work

The Practice of Inwardly-Directed Mindfulness

While the extravert directs his attention mainly to the external world around him, one who is introverted tends to neglect this objective observation of his external world. He is concerned, not so much with what is happening, but with his own emotional reactions as well as his own likes and dislikes of what is happening.

This form of introversion brings with it subjective thinking, and carried to extremes it becomes pathological. Objective thinking, with its clear evaluation of facts and conditions, becomes impossible when emotional thinking of this kind takes over.

Now, in view of this it may appear strange that Buddhism advises a kind of introversion—an "inward turning"—as a part of the technique of right mindfulness; but it is an introversion of a completely different sort. It is a process in which the mind is trained to turn inward on itself, but in an objective manner instead of in the emotional way of the other kind of introversion.

Your practical work for this month, therefore, consists of forming the habit of objective and unemotional self-observation, taking in your mental processes as a whole.

In other exercises in this series you take specific retarding tendencies and watch for their appearance. For example, in the Third Month you look for false valuations, in the Sixth Month for undue anxiety, and in the Seventh Month for irritability and resentment, while in the Eighth Month you watch for self-assertive tendencies.

During this month, however, the work is not so much the observation of specific retarding elements; it is more a matter of watching for that subjective type of thought that is governed by emotional bias and prejudice. It's a process of replacing one type of introversion by another, or replacing emotional thinking by self-analysis.

Assuming that you are working on a self-contract basis, at the end of each day, or at some convenient time, you can think back to see whether your introvert tendencies have taken a constructive and analytical form, or whether you have allowed yourself to become emotionally dominated. You can then enforce your self-contract accordingly.

The Third Month

The Process of Revaluation

If you think back, you'll most likely find that many of the values you now place on things have been established, in part at least, by outside influences; by your parents, for example, and by your teachers, and by the books you were given to read in your earlier years. Added to these are the entertainments you enjoyed then and those you enjoy now, the opinions of your friends, and the vicious and continuous blare of advertisements. Thus very little of your thinking is really your own.

As a result of all this, you are saddled with many false valuations, valuations which are not your own because you haven't arrived at them by a process of independent thinking. They may be good valuations in some sense or other or they may not, but they have been imposed on you from outside and have not been developed within you by your own thought.

To examine your own valuations and, where desirable, to break free from them—assuming, of course, that there's a need to do so—you must exert a sustained effort of mindfulness.

The first work of mindfulness in this connection is to make you aware of your false valuations, in order to help you to realise what is of real value and what is useless mental baggage. As the realisation of false valuations takes hold, new valuations of things tend to take their place as a natural process.

You will agree that what you most highly value will largely determine what you most ardently strive for; and, conversely, what you most ardently strive for is an indication of what you most highly value.

The infantile mind arrives at its beliefs and opinions by imitating others, or else by the impact of authority (and often of spurious authority), but it is only the most mature mind that evaluates things by the process of independent thinking.

In the same way, while the infantile mind formulates its code of values by superficial and immediate considerations, the mature mind takes a long-range view of all things, and penetrates to the ultimate values of things as distinct from their present effects.

The process of revaluation is a slow one, for most of the ideals of the world around us run counter to the true values that we seek.

You will usually find that the opinions of those around you, your obligations to your dependants, and your need to conform—outwardly at least—to other people's standards, all act as obstacles to the inner process of correcting your scale of values. You find that you are forced to spend time in many ways on things that, left to yourself, you would consider insignificant, while you may unwillingly have to give too little time to things of greater ultimate value.

Often you may be led into valueless byways because of economic necessity or social pressure; and this fact you must generally accept, because it's easier to adapt yourself to the world than to adapt the world to yourself. Often, too, there are some futile activities you may take on in the search for excitement or in an endeavour to escape from boredom; and these too, although futile by ultimate standards, are sometimes useful in providing an immediate purpose. But when such activities and interests grow out of proportion they retard your progress simply because of the time and energy they consume.

From the Buddhist viewpoint many such false valuations arise from craving, from that incessant thirst for personal gratification that springs from ignorance. With craving and ignorance at the root of all personal life, false valuations are inevitable, and to break down these false valuations it is necessary to attack them at the deeper levels of the mind.

Now, the basic ignorance, in the Buddhist sense, is the inability to know the true nature of existence, just as blindness is not merely not seeing but the inability to see. This basic ignorance is ultimately found to be the root of all suffering, and the whole of the Buddha-way is a course of self-training directed towards knowing, knowing it in its fullest sense.

Stating this in another way, the final aim of the Buddha-way is enlightenment, the breaking down of ignorance.

* * *

One of the characteristics of existence as emphasised by the Buddha-doctrine is that of impermanence. It needs no profound thought to show that all things arise, last a longer or shorter time, and finally pass out of existence; and to labour the point may seem unnecessary. But do you really accept this fact of impermanence? Does it affect your valuations of things? Or does it pass over your head? Perhaps you do accept it up to a point, but generally it needs a tremendous emotional jolt to bring it right home.

To the extent that you accept the fact of impermanence you relinquish some of your futile valuations because you realise their futility. It has been pointed out that the harder you grasp a handful of water the more of it slips through your fingers, for the best way to hold water in the hand is to hold it loosely. And in the same way, the best way to hold anything in the mind is to hold it loosely. Thus, slowly, you learn to grasp things a little less tightly; but for a long time you continue to grasp, and thus continue to lose.

If only you could stop grasping, if only you could relinquish the wish that the transient would become permanent, then you could enjoy the pleasure while it lasts and be ready for the next experience when it comes, whether it be one of happiness or of sorrow. By one approach to life you increase its unsatisfactoriness by seeking to prolong your pleasures, while by the other way you leave yourself free to gain the fullest value from every experience.

Whatever experience life brings to you, whether bitter or sweet, it has some value if you use it skilfully, and you can use it skilfully only if you take it when it comes and accept its imperfections.

The Buddha-doctrine points out that, within personal life, everything is imperfect, everything is ultimately unsatisfactory. Nowhere within the sphere of personal life is permanent happiness to be found, and only by attaining to the "existence beyond existence," only by breaking free from the bondage of selfhood, can permanent freedom from suffering be found.

The more comfortable are your external conditions, the less incentive is there to make an effort towards the final enlightenment. The more comfortably you pad out the walls of the cell of your own personal life, the less you will feel its shocks and jolts. But is this comfortable upholstery of any ultimate value? A padded cell is still a cell, and all the padding can never give you freedom.

Not only so, but the padding eventually wears thin, and the question arises: which requires less effort—to keep on re-padding the cell, or to fight your way to freedom? It has been said:

"The wise man obtains liberation by a hundredth part of the suffering that a foolish man endures in the pursuit of riches."

The Buddha-doctrine affirms that there is no permanent freedom from suffering and unsatisfactoriness within the bondage of personal life, and that while you are perpetuating the delusion of selfhood you are perpetuating suffering.

Further, the Buddha-doctrine emphasises that the self is a delusion, and that life is one indivisible whole. Thus everything you gain at the expense of another's loss is of no ultimate value; the gain is transitory and eventually becomes a burden to carry. If you gain by knowingly depriving another of something, you eventually become the real loser. Every self-centred valuation carries within itself the seeds of sorrow.

It is, of course, often very difficult to detect the self-centred valuation behind your desires and actions. If you're influenced by a possessive valuation, in which your aim is to possess more and more property or material objects, the element of self is quite obvious in the motive; but the same possessive valuation might apply just as definitely but much less obviously in your attachment to your own children in the guise of love. In this guise it can cause more unhappiness than when it applies to material things.

This same possessive valuation is often at the back of love problems, for many love problems are not so much concerned with love in its higher meaning as with possessiveness, at least in part.

Then there is what we can call the aesthetic valuation. Here, when applying a penetrating self-analysing mindfulness, you might find that your high appreciation of art, music, or one of these finer and less mundane things, is really a means of bolstering up your own self-esteem. No doubt this appreciation of finer things really exists, but its virtues are often vitiated when it is used as a means of asserting your own superiority.

The same may be said of the intellectual valuation, in which scientific knowledge, an intellectual grasp of a subject, or a love of hair-splitting argument provides a means of self-assertion.

It may be just the same with a religious valuation or a highly moral valuation—there may be a good deal of self present in the form of self-righteousness.

Even when there's a predominance of altruism in the major valuation, it may be possible to find an element of self-interest in the shape of a desire for admiration or thanks, or perhaps a feeling of self-approval.

In the process of revaluation, then, from the Buddhist viewpoint, you must first adopt a philosophy which emphasises fundamentals rather than superficialities and places ultimate effects higher than immediate ones; then you must recognise and assess your own dominant valuation; and finally you must progressively move the point of interest away from self-interest and towards the interest of life as a whole.

In order to work from the inside outwards, you must gradually work on your valuations of things in general. This means that you must become increasingly aware of your false values, and, with this increased awareness you must progressively discard these false values.

In time, then, you'll find that many things which previously aroused your anger, resentment, possessiveness and other adverse emotions will then fail to do so. You will then move your focus of interest away from the things that arouse these retarding emotions, away from the emotions that retard your progress.

This, of course, will in general be a long and continuous process, and one that involves many readjustments of the values you now place on all sorts of things.

Practical Work

The Practice of All-Round Mindfulness

We can use various synonyms for mindfulness. We can speak of it as expanded awareness and intensified awareness, as increased attentiveness, and in a certain sense as presence of mind. Lack of mindfulness, similarly, can be referred to as unawareness, inattentiveness, and absence of mind.

In this last-mentioned expression—absence of mind—we can each recognise lack of mindfulness both in ourselves and in others. Putting aside for the present the more profound aspects of mindfulness, let us consider its application to the more mundane and superficial matters of the workaday life.

You are familiar with a situation in which you are writing a letter when the telephone rings in the next room. On your way to answer the telephone you put your pen down somewhere—but where? When you return to your letter writing you're unable to remember where you put your pen, and you have to waste time in searching for it. You may feel that this kind of absentmindedness is unimportant except for the exasperation and inconvenience it causes; but the point is that if you have too little mindfulness to observe where you put your pen, you must also have too little to make much progress on the path of self-development.

You may consider that the example just given doesn't apply to you. However, you would probably find a number of minor situations in your own life in which you could profitably employ greater presence of mind. This increased mindfulness will give you greater efficiency, but this is only its secondary objective; its primary aim is to increase your inner alertness.

For a period of a month or longer, then, set out to develop a greater degree of all-round mindfulness in the small routine activities of your life. To do this it will be helpful if you slow down these activities whenever you can and do them more deliberately and attentively. This slowing-down will help to establish more mindful patterns of thought and action which—if continued over a long enough period—will extend or infiltrate into other activities, activities which must of necessity be carried out more hurriedly.

It is helpful if you increase your awareness of your actions by verbalisation. For example, as you put your pen down, say to yourself "I put my pen on top of the bookcase." Or having bought a bus ticket and put it in your pocket, say, "The ticket is in my left-hand side pocket." This form of verbalisation assists in the general development of all-round mindfulness. It would be pointless to try to apply it to too many things, but it's especially useful in relation to the few small activities in which you happen to be absentminded.

One way in which you can apply the self-contract method to this discipline is to make a mental note of each time you act absent-mindedly. For each occasion of absent-mindedness mentally note one point; and, when you reach a total of, say, ten points, make the next twenty-four hours a discipline day.

You will need to define just what you yourself mean by a discipline day. It may mean that you'll smoke only half your usual number of cigarettes, or that you'll go without sugar in your tea, or that you'll eat no sweet biscuits during the twenty-four hours.

The exact nature of the pact you make with yourself is unimportant, so long as you use it to increase your general level of awareness.

The Fourth Month

The Path of Increasing Awareness

From certain viewpoints it can be said that the evolution of the mind consists largely in the intensification of awareness on the one hand, and, on the other, the expansion of awareness.

Let's consider it in this way. In some situations awareness needs to be intensified but not expanded. If you're carrying out a difficult repair on a delicate piece of mechanism, such as a watch, your consciousness needs to be concentrated and you need to be aware of only a limited range of sense-impressions, covering only those relevant to the work in hand and excluding all others. That is to say, your awareness must be intensified but not expanded.

In other circumstances your consciousness needs to take in a very broad field of sense-impressions. If you're driving a car in heavy traffic, for example, it is very necessary to be conscious of a large range of sense-impressions without generally concentrating on any one of them. You need to be aware of the car ahead, of pedestrians crossing the road, of vehicles coming towards you or darting out of side streets, and of anything and everything that could conceivably constitute a hazard. You may have a chattering passenger or a back-seat driver, or perhaps a restless child in the car.

All these factors and sometimes others as well demand that you spread your attention over a broad sphere of awareness; your awareness needs to be expanded, not concentrated. It must be intensified in a certain sense as well as expanded, also, in that you must keep at a high pitch of alertness, but it is not intensified with regard to any one object or at any one point to the exclusion of others.

Now, while some things that you do demand some degree of alertness or awareness, either in a concentrated form or in an expanded or diffuse form, there are many other activities that you carry out with little or no awareness. These activities are largely the things that you do by habit.

In any habit, your awareness tends to sink to a lower level, and because of this you give little or no thought to the purpose of the activity or the exact manner in which you carry it out. It takes on a mechanical character.

In many cases this mechanical nature of a habitual activity is a good thing, for it leaves you free to devote your awareness to more important activities. It is true also that if too many of your general activities are based on habits, both of thought and of action, your whole life tends to sink into the unthinking drift; but in its sphere habit has a real function. That function is to set the consciousness or awareness free for more important things.

When you set out to work on the problem of breaking a bad habit—a habit that gives rise to adverse consequences—you must first realise that you probably retain some of your habits, good and bad, largely because they yield some form of satisfaction; and this is true, very often, even if they also cause dissatisfaction of another sort.

Before you begin to use self-discipline on a habit, then, it may be as well to make some attempt to analyse it in order to find out whether or not it yields any satisfaction, and then to find the nature of the satisfaction it yields, a satisfaction that in some cases may not be apparent on the surface. And if you are successful in doing so, it may then be necessary to find a way to gain the same satisfaction in another way.

In this matter it is not possible to do much more than generalise. The main point is that you may find that self-discipline alone is not always adequate in attempting to break a bad habit, and in many cases it is necessary to develop an increasing mindfulness of your own mind—its hidden motives, its half-recognised greeds, hatreds, and delusions—in order to clear a field in which self-discipline can work more effectively.

In any form of mental culture it is generally better to work for an all-round improvement in the mental operations as a whole than to devote too large an effort to one isolated characteristic. There are exceptions, of course, as for example when that characteristic is so bad that it justifies concentrated effort.

In any case, no single trait can rightly be considered on its own; it must be considered in relation to or as a part of the whole mental structure considered as a totality.

Many of your habitual activities have no special moral significance and play little part in strengthening or weakening the mental functions.

In driving a car, for example, your habitual response to situations encountered on the road—traffic signals, a dog darting across the street, and so on—have no moral significance. But sometimes, perhaps, you habitually respond to traffic jams by impatience, or you thoughtlessly become angry with pedestrians who foolishly wander into the road without looking. Impatience and anger are habitual responses which need to be dealt with, not only because they are of an adverse or retarding nature in themselves, but also simply because they are habitual.

There are other examples of unmindful or habitual responses which may need to be handled, largely because they are habitual. There is the habit of complaining about the weather, about the rising cost of living, and about what other people do or fail to do. The point is that when you complain about these things it may be that you do so as an automatic or mechanical release for your adverse emotions. In the present context, it is in the mechanical or habitual nature of these complaints that the fault lies; your complaining may be justified, or it may not, but that's another matter of secondary importance from the present viewpoint.

You need some sort of release for these emotions of course; but habitual and unthinking releases are retarding because they come about without mindfulness, and because your mind is then in a rut.

The thing to do is to try to develop an awareness, a watchful attitude towards your own responses, and to try, whenever the situation allows it, to act in a manner directly opposite to the old mechanical way. If you want to raise your voice in anger, try to speak quietly. If you feel a tendency to turn away without speaking, try to make a courteous reply. If you feel a desire to strike out, verbally or otherwise, try to react in a kindly way.

In all such situations, the thing to do is to react in a manner directly contrary to the automatic, mechanical, or habitual response. This will help to weaken and break down the adverse mental factors involved and also make the mind keener.

Building up new habits involves the use of increased awareness or attentiveness. One habit worth cultivating in most cases is the habit of observation, and this forms the subject of the practical work for this period.

Practical Work

Outward Observation

Mindfulness has many aspects. That is to say, there are many things towards which you may direct increased attention and many directions in which you may cultivate greater awareness. From the Buddhist viewpoint, the chief value of mindfulness lies in directing the attention inwardly and in cultivating a penetrating awareness of the physical and mental phenomena that together constitute your own "current of existence," your own self.

However, from the viewpoint of greater efficiency in the workaday routine, there is generally some scope for increased mindfulness with regard to external things as well as for inwardly-directed attention. Some of us need to cultivate a penetrating awareness not only of our own mental state but also of the things around us.

This applies more to the introvert than to the extraverted type of man or woman. If you are naturally an extravert, you will tend to have an inherent tendency to take notice of things around you and of events going on in the external world; you will have an acute power of observation together with a retentive memory for all such things.

You may then conclude that you have no need for increased outwardly-directed mindfulness. But this practice, although primarily one in which the attention is directed to things and happenings outside you, doesn't stop there; it is meant to be linked up with self-observation as well. In other words, you can use your observational powers to take notice of your own emotional reactions to things and happenings around you as well as of the things and happenings themselves.

If, on the other hand, you tend to be a little too introverted, and if you feel that your powers of external observation need to be developed, you may feel that the cultivation of attention towards external things would help you, not only towards greater efficiency in your workaday life, but towards a better standard of general mindfulness. It is quite possible that an increased attentiveness towards your outer environment would reflect itself in a greater awareness—and thus in a greater control—of your emotional biases and faulty perceptions.

To undertake this practice, then, you make up your mind to observe the various objects in your immediate environment in greater detail and with greater care. If your powers of observation are already good, your primary objective would be to pay special attention to your own emotional reactions to the things, people, and events that affect you.

Some things will stimulate your desires and start trains of thought in your mind. Some people will irritate you and arouse resentment and other forms of aversion. And some events will bring out your self-assertive tendencies.

The three basic mental factors that most retard progress, according to Buddhist psychology, are selfish desire, aversion, and self-assertion; and to deal with them the essential step is to become aware of them.

If your powers of observation are already well developed, you can give primary attention to your own reactions. If, on the other hand, your powers of observation are not as good as you would like them to be, you should use this practice to improve them. In that case you can make the detailed observation of external matters your primary aim in this practice.

In any case, it will help considerably if, whenever you can, you slow down your own activities in order to observe or to perceive things more carefully. For most of the time you will probably be unable to do this, but if you set out to slow down when you can, you will establish better habits of observation which will carry over into the more hurried periods.

At first, perhaps, you would do well to restrict your increased observation to one small sphere; for example, to the people you meet in the course of the day's work and other activities. At some convenient time recall several people and jot down the colours of their hair and eyes, their facial characteristics, and some details of the clothing they wear. Or if you prefer it, take the houses you pass on your way to the railway station and set out to observe them in greater detail; then, later on, see if you can describe them to yourself in detail.

It is worthwhile to take an occasional walk with the specific objective of observing the details which you normally miss.

The essence of this practice is pure observation; it is not meant to be a form of memory training, although, of course, the memory will benefit. There are systems which employ various tricks of mental association, the rhyming and alliteration of words, and the building up of vivid and sometimes ludicrous mental images as aids in memory training; but these tricks—useful and beneficial as they are—should play no part in the present practice. You are, in this connection, interested in pure observation as an aim in itself and not as a memory aid.

Apply the self-contract method of self-discipline to the practice, and when you find you have neglected to use an opportunity for pure observation impose on yourself some small penalty.

The Fifth Month

The Principle of Acceptance

What we know as the conscious level of the human mind is only a very small part of the mind in its entirety. General usage of the concept of two levels of the mind, distinguished as the conscious and the subconscious, suggests that the mind has two separate and well-defined compartments; but this concept is by no means an accurate one. It would be far better to compare the mind as a whole to a blackboard in a very dark room, with many words and phrases chalked over the whole surface. Because of the darkness of the room you can't see any of the words or phrases. However, if you shine the beam of an electric torch onto the centre of the blackboard, you'll be able to read the word that the centre of the beam illuminates, and you will be able also to see the words around the outside of the torch beam where the light is less bright.

The centre of the torch beam where the light is brightest can be compared with full consciousness, the chalked word that the beam fully illuminates being like the focus of consciousness. The words within the less bright area on the outside of the lighted area are like the ideas in the fringe of consciousness, while those on the rest of the blackboard represent the multitudinous ideas in the subconscious mind.

As you move the torch beam on to different areas of the blackboard different words and phrases come momentarily into the centre of the beam, with others, less brightly lit, towards the outer edges of the beam. The rest of the blackboard remains in darkness.

In just the same way, the focus of consciousness moves and brings into full consciousness one idea after another, with generally a few associated ideas in the fringe of consciousness. At all times, the rest of the ideas remain in the subconscious mind.

If the blackboard were to be completely clear of obstructions you could shine the torch on to any and every word or phrase and bring it into the focus of the beam. But let's imagine, for the purpose of illustration, that some parts of the blackboard are concealed. A tall filing cabinet stands in front of one corner with a poster pinned over another corner, while on odd parts of the board numerous pieces of sticking plaster obscure various words and phrases. You can't illuminate the hidden words with the torch beam unless you can remove the filing cabinet and the poster as well as the pieces of sticking plaster.

In a similar way, the mind of the average person has many regions which are inaccessible to the torch beam of full consciousness. These are the regions which, over the years, have been blocked off by pain and fear, by horror, guilt, and inferiority feelings. To clear these away and make the concealed ideas accessible to consciousness is generally a much greater task than can be accomplished by the average person during his lifetime.

However, even though you cannot discover and remove all the fear, guilt, and inferiority feelings that both in childhood and in later years have blocked off some regions of your mind, you can at least endeavour to accept yourself as you are, with your inheritance of primitive urges and your acquired hatreds, fears, and greeds.

This acceptance demands continuous mindfulness, for this is the key to self-improvement. Mindfulness in Buddhism has many forms, and that form which has a special value in this connection is called mindfulness of the mind. This is a matter of training yourself to be aware of your own emotional state at all times and to recognise it for what it is. If at a particular time the emotional state is one of annoyance and resentment, or of envy, ill will, or some other retarding mental factor, then the honest recognition of this factor, freed as far as possible from feelings of guilt and attempts at repression, is in effect the acceptance of yourself as you are.

It is necessary also to develop an awareness of your own progressive mental qualities, such as those of generosity, good will, and the discernment of the illusory nature of your own ego, without any element of personal pride or smugness.

Thus the simple recognition of both the retarding and the progressive mental factors, as and when they arise in your daily contacts and activities, is seen to be the first application of the principle of acceptance.

The acceptance of yourself as you are must be balanced by the acceptance of other people as they are. As your self-knowledge increases so also your knowledge of other people increases. While people vary tremendously in their levels of self-development as well as in their reactions to circumstances, their most basic instinctive and emotional structures are very similar to your own.

* * *

They too, deep below the consciously accessible regions at their minds, have their own heritages of primitive urges, carried over from their prehuman and caveman ancestors. They too were subjected in childhood to varying degrees of parental mishandling and repressive control, and they too need some degree of deep understanding.

By way of this deep understanding of others, you learn to accept them as they are, so that, to the degree that you understand and accept them (but only to that degree) you will be likely to react to them without annoyance and resentment.

You may not be able to eliminate annoyance and resentment entirely from your dealings with others, of course, but you can use such occasions for the recognition and acceptance of both your own and others' failings. With this acceptance must come greater harmony, both internally and externally.

* * *

So here are two spheres of life in which to practise the principle of acceptance—one's own emotional and mental structure and the emotion-laden reactions of other people. There's a third sphere in which to apply the same principle, and this is the world as a whole with its mixture of pleasure and pain.

If you were to become a prisoner you could adopt any of three attitudes towards your prison. Firstly, you could kick the walls, thump the bars, shout abuse at the guards, and reject it at every point with bitterness and resentment. The effect would be to make your imprisonment more severe and traumatic in every way, and to increase the very things you reject.

At the other extreme you could sit in passive resignation and brood in an inert manner, making no effort to find a means of escape. Your apathy would serve only to magnify your misery and resentment.

Both of these extreme attitudes would tend to paralyse your powers. However, there's a third kind of attitude you could adopt: you could accept your prison as a problem to be solved, assessing it realistically and in great detail, searching for its flaws, and remaining always alert and ready to take the first real opportunity to escape. This attitude, ideally, should have no resentment in it, for resentment and its kindred mental states cause emotional biases, which in turn impair your judgement; and impaired judgement brings unrealistic action.

The acceptance of the world as it really is must embrace the acceptance of yourself, of all the other people in your environment, and of everything that in any way impinges on you. Positive acceptance doesn't mean inert resignation. It means acceptance of things as they are as the starting point in the long trek towards freedom.

This mental attitude of acceptance makes it easier to deal with life and effectively to resist all the difficult things in the environment, as well as all the difficult things in the mind itself.

This non-resentful acceptance of things as they are is a matter of squarely meeting all things, a matter of learning to control anxiety, to conquer resentment, and to keep self-assertion in check.

With this attitude of non-resentment and positive acceptance you learn not to tense up more than necessary against adversity. This is not passive resignation; it is the positive acceptance of every problem as the raw material out of which you can build achievement. If all your problems were miraculously taken away, you would find yourself without any raw material and thus without any possibility of achievement. This principle of non-resentful acceptance must seep through the whole of life; it cannot be made into a specific practice or a concisely-formulated exercise. The practical work for this period, then, is only the first step. It is meant to help you to acquire an insight into the degree to which you resent the problems and difficult things in your life, and from this insight the rest will follow.

Practical Work

A Self-Questionnaire on Non-Resentful Acceptance

In answering the following questionnaire, you could probably go through the whole series of questions and give an immediate answer to each question. In many cases an immediate answer will readily come to mind, but it will not necessarily be a true one, nor will it be of real value to you.

The aim of each question is not so much to arrive at an answer as to start a train of thought, and the aim of this in turn is to give you some degree of self-understanding.

Take one question at a time, then, and think about it at odd times during the day; the resulting train of thought will be of greater value than a clear-cut snap answer to the question.

As a result, it may be that other questions and other ideas, related in some way to the original question, will come into your mind. These, too, will help in the process of self-understanding.

To start these trains of thought, then, ask yourself the following questions:

1. Do I resent my problems and the difficult things in my life?
2. Or do I accept these problems and difficult things as the raw material for achievement?
3. Do I resent being dominated or controlled by others?
4. Do I deeply envy the good fortunes of others?
5. Do I resent being ignored by others?
6. Do I accept these problems and difficult things in an inert, defeated way?
7. If so, has this brought about a half-repressed bitterness and a smouldering resentment towards them?
8. Do I tend to resent any particular religious group?
9. Or any particular racial group?
10. Have I a defensive attitude towards life or people as a whole?
11. Or an aggressive attitude?
12. Or a suspicious attitude?
13. Do I harbour any grudges or desires for revenge?

14. Do I have any strong motivations which are based on resentment?
15. Do I react to criticism with hostility or resentment?

* * *

Assuming that you are employing the self-contract method of self-discipline, look back every few days to see if you have used the questionnaire consistently and in a sufficiently penetrating manner; and, if you feel you have not done so, deprive yourself of some small pleasure.

The Sixth Month

The Awareness of Emotion

If you want to control something—whatever it is—the more you know about it the better you will be able to control it. If you want to drive a car, you can manage with a minimum of knowledge of its workings while conditions are good; but when it breaks down, miles from help, the greater your knowledge of its mechanism the greater will be your chance of getting it on the move again.

It is the same with your own emotional problems. You can go only a small distance in life without emotional problems, and while you need no special understanding of them when the going is smooth you do need all the self-knowledge possible when you enter a rough phase.

Can you imagine a motor mechanic who has no clear understanding of what goes on under the bonnet of a car? Yet many of us have no clear understanding of what goes on under our own bonnets.

The greater the self-knowledge you possess the better, and this is true both of knowledge gained by your own self-observation and of knowledge gained by book-learning. One supplements the other, and this applies particularly to the knowledge of emotion. Let us therefore consider emotion at the theoretical level.

Emotions are accompanied by certain bodily changes, or perhaps we should say that emotions consist of the awareness of the bodily changes that take place under certain conditions.

In order to illustrate this point, let us take the condition of fear. When you become frightened it begins with some frightening idea in your mind. This frightening idea is the cause of your emotion of fear, and is accompanied by a nervous current in certain parts of your brain.

From the brain, this nervous current travels to your adrenal glands, and this causes these glands to discharge into your blood stream a substance known as adrenalin. Your blood stream conveys this adrenalin to various organs of your body.

The adrenalin has a definite effect on many of these organs; for example, when it reaches your liver it causes it to discharge into your blood stream an extra supply of sugar, this sugar giving to every muscle that it reaches an additional energy supply.

As further results of the adrenalin in your blood, your heart beats more rapidly, your eyes open wider, and your blood itself clots more readily should you be wounded.

You can see that all these bodily changes would have a very definite value during actual physical combat or any rapid muscular activity; these are the extra supply of fuel to your muscles, for example, and the quicker heartbeat and circulation which replenish this fuel supply and remove the ash from your cells; these are all valuable to you if you are fleeing or fighting, running or climbing.

There are some side-effects, too. For example, your hair tends to stand on end. This does not help you, of course, but it does help some of your subhuman relations when it happens to them. It helps a cat to appear bigger and more formidable and thus more frightening to an enemy, and it helps a porcupine because its quills are an actual defensive weapon.

When your hair stands on end, then, you are automatically responding in the same way as did some of your prehuman relations. But in you it is an obsolete mechanism.

The bodily changes are of no real use unless the need for action arises; but that is not the whole story. Man of the civilised world does not generally solve his problems in the same way as did his cave-dwelling ancestors or his primitive brothers, because his problems and his outside conditions are different. Nevertheless his involuntary reactions are much the same.

In most cases when a man becomes frightened, fighting or fleeing will not solve the problem, as there is often no tangible aggressor to fight and no place to which to flee. Yet the bodily changes occur just the same.

Your bodily changes during fear, therefore, are often inappropriate; not only so, they are also frequently an embarrassment because too much fuel is released into your blood-stream without any purpose to fulfil. In this way you may have various physical and nervous disorders as a result of repeated emotional disorders, disorders arising not only from fear but also from anxiety, jealousy, resentment, anger, and inferiority feelings.

But the story is not yet complete. During an emotional disturbance, in order to allow full activity to various muscles—

those of the legs for running, the arms for fighting, and so on— the arteries that serve the digestive system are contracted so that they receive a diminished blood supply. To divert their fuel to the other muscles, the muscles of the digestive system are deprived of it and in consequence the digestive activities are held up for the time.

Such disturbances may last for hours, and you can see how easy it is for digestive troubles to arise as a result of fear, anxiety, jealousy, resentment, anger, and inferiority feelings.

It has been shown by experiment that adverse emotions generate poisons within the bodily system, and that under extreme conditions some of the brain cells may be temporarily or permanently injured by intense emotion.

So from all this you can see that some sort of emotional discipline is desirable. Of what possible use are the bodily changes of fear or anger when a man insults you over the telephone? Certainly they give you extra strength to throw the telephone out of the window, but this solves no problems. If a man falls in love with a screen actress his heart will beat more rapidly to enable him to begin a primitive love-chase; but in the circumstances of modern civilisation where would this chase end—or begin?

* * *

Now, there are three aspects to the matter of disciplining the emotions. The first aspect of emotional discipline is the development of a habit of self-observation with regard to your own emotional conditions. In Buddhist terminology, this is called the detailed observation of the mental state. The second aspect involves the control of emotional manifestations as these arise. The third aspect is a matter of developing a new set of values of such a kind that many of the circumstances that previously called out the responses of fear, anger, self-assertion, and so on, then fail to do so, or at least do so to a reduced extent.

Little need be said about the need for controlling the powerful emotions that lead to both external discord and internal conflict; their effects are in most cases distressingly obvious. Racial hatreds, religious prejudices, and political biases—these lie at the root of many quarrels between individuals and between nations.

Ambivalent feelings of love and hate towards others within the family, as well as irrational fears and guilt complexes, give rise to neuroses and other mental aberrations.

To wait until an emotional problem reaches major proportions before dealing with it is like waiting until a trickle becomes a flood. The Buddhist method is to keep constant watch—to apply constant mindfulness—while an adverse emotion exists as a trickle, and to deal with it at this stage; for when it reaches the proportions of a flood much of the damage inwardly and outwardly is already done.

To try to deal with major emotional problems by any sort of repressive emotional control either drives the real causes into other channels or else intensifies the outer effects, so that emotional control requires something better than any possible form of surface treatment can offer.

Emotional control must begin with what in Buddhism is called the detailed observation of the mental state. This is a matter of continual self-observation with a view to detecting the presence of any emotion which might retard the mind's progress towards enlightenment.

The recognition of such retarding emotions in their mildest and most unobtrusive forms is regarded in Buddhist practice as highly important, for it is necessary to see them for what they are before they reach greater proportion. Recognition is the first essential to control.

In order to control your emotions you must know what you are controlling, and this knowledge (apart from its theoretical aspect) is the work of mindfulness. Without it attempts at control by will-power alone might degenerate into harmful repression.

Repression is a matter of pressing unwelcome mental states below the level at which they are accessible to consciousness. The work of mindfulness, on the other hand, is the work of bringing the full light of sharpened awareness to bear on all mental states, unwelcome and otherwise, and this is the very opposite of repression.

There are, of course, occasions in your everyday life when you must exercise a great deal of effort of will to prevent an emotional outburst. You must bottle up your emotions even though you know that this bottling-up is building up harmful tension, tension of mind and body.

At other times you feel that it is absolutely imperative to give vent to your adverse emotions, hateful and petty and spiteful as you know them to be. You feel you must have your emotional splurge whatever the consequences.

Which is right and which is wrong? Right and wrong are conventional words which sometimes obscure the real point. The real question is, which does the less harm in the long run? You must either keep control at all costs—and this, according to some standards, is the right thing to do—or you must let go and give your wrong emotions an outlet.

The answer, in part at least, is that whatever you do, you must do it as mindfully as possible in the circumstances. If you must let go and have your emotional splurge, if you must give way to your annoyance, self-pity, envy, or whatever it is, you should be as fully aware of it as you can and realise its nature. In this way you will keep some control over it; but once you seek to justify yourself or deceive yourself as to what you are doing you begin to lose this control.

You must, of course, consider its effects on others, and from this viewpoint an emotional outburst is often quite wrong. From one viewpoint—from the viewpoint of your own development—it is better to do wrong mindfully than to do right mindlessly; it is better to be fully aware of what you are doing and why you are doing it—however conventionally wrong it is—than to do the conventionally right thing without knowing why.

When your emotions are too strong and you give way to an emotional outburst, this outburst can be considered a failure; but because you are an ordinary human being and not a superhuman these failures will occur from time to time. If you train yourself in mindfulness—especially in the detailed observation of the mental state—such failures will occur less and less frequently. The important thing is that progress is taking place.

Practical Work

The Control of Anxiety

To become tense in circumstances of stress is easy; to remain calm and free from agitation is difficult. Being difficult, it requires self-training, self-training not only at the level of muscular relaxation but also at the mental level. Methods of muscular relaxation are of great value in bringing about a generally relaxed condition of both mind and body, for mind and body interact; but muscular relaxation needs to be supplemented by mental relaxation.

Let us consider, therefore, how best you can approach the problem of tension at the mental level. To do this, of course, you must go further back than the tension itself; you must go back to the tension-causing factors in the mind; and these can he defined in broad terms as anxiety, resentment, and self-assertion.

These three factors arise from what in Buddhism are called the three roots of mental evil—selfish desire, aversion, and delusion. From selfish desire arises anxiety; from aversion arises resentment; and from delusion arises self-assertion. Of these three tension-causing factors—anxiety, resentment, and self-assertion—let us take just one as the basis for an exercise in mindfulness.

Therefore, during a period of a month or more, take in hand the problem of anxiety. Make a contract with yourself to the effect that after each time you allow yourself to become unduly anxious about anything at all you will apply some small self-imposed penalty on yourself.

Just what penalty you use is for you to decide, but it should be an easy one, one that you can impose on yourself without tending to throw it aside. If you find it too irksome you will need to break it down a little; on the other hand if it becomes too easy and ineffective you will need to stiffen it up to some extent.

You must recognise that anxiety is related to desires of various kinds (selfish and otherwise), to attachment, and to possessiveness. In tackling the problem of anxiety, then, you are working on these other factors as well to some extent.

The Seventh Month

The Mechanisms of Self-Deceit

There exists within the mind of every normal person a heritage of primitive urges, brought over from mankind's early human and prehuman ancestors in their battle for survival. To recognise that these primitive urges exist in you is one of the first steps you must make in your progress along the path of self-understanding; to refuse to recognise them, to refuse to see them as parts of your mental make-up, is to build up a wall of self-deceit within your own mind.

In your early life, because other people disapproved of these primitive urges, you learnt to disguise them and in some cases to be ashamed of them. At first you learnt to refuse to admit them to other people, while at a later stage you refused—at least, you tried to refuse—to admit them to yourself.

One reason for this refusal was that you wanted to think highly of yourself, to keep your sense of ego intact at all costs. It is, incidentally, this sense of ego which is the focal point of self-deceit, and it is also the same sense of ego which is the focus on which the Buddha-doctrine centres its attack.

* * *

As to the mechanisms which the mind uses in its efforts to deceive itself, it will be helpful if we consider them in terms of brain structure and function.

In a certain sense you may regard the brain as a highly complicated system of pathways or circuits along which the nervous energy travels. Each such pathway is called a neurogram. When the nervous energy travels along one particular pathway or neurogram, a corresponding idea tends to arise in consciousness, and when the nervous energy moves into another pathway or neurogram the first idea fades and another one arises in consciousness.

Now, if one of these nervous pathways becomes impaired or damaged in some way it will be able to carry the nervous energy only with difficulty, if at all. You can compare this situation with a road which develops potholes, so that a car travelling along it does so in a series of bumps and lurches. The driver whenever possible avoids this bumpy, difficult, and painful road.

This simile will help you to understand the "avoidant mechanisms" of the mind, for in a similar manner the nervous energy will avoid travelling along or through a neurogram which has been made difficult and painful.

It needs no technical jargon or psychological training to say that we all tend to avoid the painful and unpleasant. That, of course, is what defines the painful and unpleasant; we tend to avoid it.

Let us consider an example. A child undergoes a frightening experience; it does not matter much what sort of experience, but he is very frightened by it. When it has been over for some time he tries not to think about it, because when he thinks about it he becomes afraid again. This is reasonable and easy to understand, and it all takes place at a conscious level. Later, it becomes subconscious.

But this does not mean that the child immediately blots out all memory of the frightening experience; the process as a rule is a gradual one, and the child's refusal to think about it is at first ineffective. Later, however, it gradually becomes successful, and at the same time it becomes habitual. When an activity, mental or bodily, becomes habitual, it also becomes less conscious.

Thus the mechanism of avoidance, at first conscious, gradually sinks to the subconscious level.

There are other types of experience besides fear that set in motion the mechanism of avoidance; those of horror, nausea, and physical pain, for example. The feeling of inferiority is another of these, and so are the feelings of guilt and unworthiness. No one likes to feel inferior, guilty, or unworthy, and the mind at both conscious and subconscious levels tends to avoid these feelings.

But back to the car driver; having found the road full of potholes, difficult, and even painful, he avoids it; but he nevertheless wishes to reach his destination somehow, and he does not abandon his journey just because the road is in poor condition. He finds an alternative road, even if it means a lengthy detour and a longer route.

In the same way the nervous energy refuses to cease its activity because one neurogram is pain-blocked, and it finds another neurogram which offers it a pleasant pathway. When this happens in the brain there arises in the mind a substitute-idea, for while the mind refuses to allow the pain-blocked idea to arise in consciousness it diverts its energy to a more acceptable idea. This is the mechanism of "divertence." Because of the mechanism of divertence, there are times when you experience emotion but deceive yourself as to its true object. For some reason or other you do not wish to attach that particular emotion to that particular object.

For example, a child both loves and hates his mother. It must be realised that practically every child has ambivalent emotions towards his parents. In fact, he has ambivalent attitudes towards many significant things in his life, which means that he both loves and hates them. He loves his parents at one time because they look after him and he hates them at another when they scold and punish him; but both opposites exist potentially in his mental structure all the time.

But while his expressions of love are well received by his parents, his expressions of hate bring him disapproval, scolding, and spankings, and perhaps lectures on the wickedness of not loving one's parents.

In the case of the sensitive child all this disapproval and lecturing produce a sense of guilt and unworthiness, and when—later on—he becomes aware of his hate he tries to suppress it. But, without any real understanding of the way his mind functions, his attempts to control his instinctive upsurges lead only to their repression.

But any mental factor which is repressed is not thereby destroyed, and the repressed emotion of hate must find its outlet. As the child's hate cannot attach itself to his mother it must attach itself to something else, something less likely to arouse the disapproval of his elders. This substitute object may be his school teacher, for example.

Thus the disapproved emotion is displaced from its true object, his mother, to a substitute object, the teacher.

You can see, easily enough, that the avoidant mechanism and the divertant mechanism work hand in hand. The nervous energy avoids travelling along a brain pathway or neurogram that arouses ideas and emotions of guilt, inferiority, unworthiness, and pain, and it is diverted into neurograms that avoid these unpleasant feelings. And if these neurograms arouse ideas of self-righteousness, superiority, or self-importance, so much the better; or at least so it seems in a superficial sense.

* * *

Now, just as pain and unpleasant emotions can damage a neurogram, so pleasure, physical or emotional, can smooth and improve another neurogram and thus facilitate the passage of the nervous energy through it.

To revert once again to our car driver, he will avoid a narrow road whose surface is full of potholes, and he will divert his course to a road which is in good condition. But if there is yet a third road which has been broadened and well-surfaced, and which gives beautiful views and interesting vistas throughout its whole length, then he will travel on this road whenever he can. And he will do this not always because it leads to any special destination but for the sheer pleasure of travelling along that road, with its views and vistas. He may even do this when he should be travelling to his work or attending to other responsibilities.

In the same way the mental energy will flow along a neurogram that yields pleasure, even though there is no other purpose to it than the pleasure it yields, and even though it solves no other problem or brings about no particular decision. This describes the mechanism of "fixation."

As an example, if a child is spoilt, if his mother fusses over his comforts and pleasures, if she overprotects him and gives him excessive praise, all at the expense of his character development, then his mental energy will become fixated on the mental image of his mother.

* * *

So here you have three basic mental mechanisms—avoidance, caused by a pain-blocked neurogram; divertence, dependent on an alternative neurogram; and fixation, arising from an over-facilitated neurogram.

If you accept the idea that—in common with humanity at large—your mind employs various modes of self-deceit, you can see that these mechanisms are at the root of much of this self-deceit, and it is the pain-blocked neurograms that account for the very natural resistance that sometimes comes to the surface when you are required, in the process of self-understanding, to face the less savoury aspects of your own mind.

This resistance arises when someone questions the rightness or value of some self-deceit you have been treasuring. Such a resistance comes to the surface as annoyance, fear, or maybe some kind of irrational mental attitude. Its function—if you can call it a function—is to keep the self-deceit intact.

Until you can overcome this resistance and face all your self-deceits you are helpless against them; they dominate your thinking, and this is one of the greatest difficulties in the task of self-understanding.

Practical Work

The Control of Irritability and Resentment

Few of us have entirely overcome the tendency to speak or respond irritably in difficult circumstances, nor are many of us free from a tendency to harbour some degree of resentment. This resentment generally concerns petty injustices and hurts, inflicted—in reality or sometimes in imagination—by others.

For present purposes we shall assume that you are amongst the majority in this respect. For a month or longer, then, take in hand your own tendencies towards irritability and resentment, however slight they happen to be, and use them as the basis for an exercise in mindfulness.

In the ordinary but unnatural tempo of life it is difficult to maintain a condition of tranquillity in all circumstances, for there are often too many petty annoyances in the daily routine and in consequence the mind is too often aroused to a state of anger. Now, this anger does not have to take the form of rage or fury to be anger; very often you are merely mildly angry, and you fail to realise just how often in the ordinary course of the day your anger is aroused in a mild way.

This practice, then, is a matter of watching yourself critically and dispassionately, with a view to realising just how often and under what conditions your anger is slightly aroused. In this practice you are not interested in the major displays of anger that sometimes occur, for you are fully aware of them. It is the occasional small annoyances, the petty irritations, that should be the object of increased awareness in the daily routine, for, once the minor forms of anger become well-controlled as a matter of habit, the major displays of anger are easier to control.

It is essential at this point to note that control does not mean repression, for the repression of an emotion-laden thought means that it is pressed down below the level at which it is accessible to consciousness. Such a process is the very opposite of the process of mindfulness, which in one sense is the process of extending the range of consciousness.

If you can develop the habit of dispassionate observation with respect to your mental state at all times, you can progressively increase your control over your reactions to the outside world and gradually find a greater degree of inward balance and tranquillity.

In acquiring a more detailed awareness of the functions and contents of your own mind, an essential part of the process is the work of making the acquaintance of its more unsavoury elements, the retarding factors of the mind. If you become more familiar with your hidden hatreds, fears, and jealousies, you then know better how to deal with them.

Make a contract with yourself, a pact-resolution, to the effect that you will impose on yourself some small penalty soon after any occasion on which you respond irritably or harbour resentful thoughts.

The Eighth Month

The Buddhist Doctrine of Egolessness

Self-assertion, the assertion of one's own rights and privileges, of one's importance, and of one's individual and distinctive existence; this is one of the major modes of instinctive response to many of the circumstances of life. It is one of the prime elements in the search for personal gratification.

It is a never-ending search, this search for personal gratification; for each satisfaction that is achieved is only a temporary one, and sooner or later the search must be resumed. To seek happiness by way of self-assertion, according to the teachings of Buddhism, is the surest way to perpetuate the sorrows and unsatisfactory factors in personal life, for enduring happiness can be found only by breaking free from the false belief in a self separate from life as a whole.

The most distinctive feature of Buddhism is the teaching that the innermost core of individual existence is not a fixed unchanging ego or self but a momentary and ever-changing current of forces. This, if followed through, leads to a policy of non-assertion instead of self-assertion; and therefore non-assertion must be cultivated in the quest for ultimate happiness.

One of the basic characteristics of the world around us is the complete absence of permanence. Some things last a long while, it's true, and seem to change very little over the years; but nothing is permanent in any true sense.

You will find that the fact of impermanence is easy to acknowledge in a superficial way; but you will also find that it's very difficult to accept it with all its implications.

We live in a world of impermanence, yet at the same time we try to stave off this impermanence by making our desired things last as long as we can. Growing old, we try to keep up some semblance of youth. While recognising the fact of impermanence, we find it unpalatable and therefore refuse to accept it. Up to a point, we succeed in rejecting it; and to this extent we delude ourselves.

We know, of course, that we must accept some suffering, some pain and sorrow, mixed in with our happiness in this round of birth and death; but knowing of no other existence, we have no option but to keep on seeking for happiness by gratifying our desires. We think that this is the only way in which we can gain happiness; and here again we delude ourselves.

In our efforts to stave off the impermanence always closing in around us, and in our struggle for happiness in a universe of mixed pleasure and pain, we are impelled, much of the time, to assert ourselves and to act from self-interest, not knowing that, in the ultimate, self-assertion is the arch-enemy of happiness. Here, once again, we delude ourselves.

So we are deluding ourselves in three main ways. In seeking for permanence in a world essentially impermanent, we are reducing rather than increasing our happiness. In looking for happiness within the round of birth and death we are looking in the wrong direction. And in asserting ourselves we are doing the very thing that makes complete happiness impossible.

So the Buddha-doctrine states, in effect, that we must understand and fully accept three salient characteristics of existence, namely:

1: the fact that everything in the relative universe is impermanent;
2: the fact that everything in the relative universe is in a constant state of agitation, a state which in conscious, living beings may become suffering; and
3: the fact that no being possesses a fixed, unchanging, eternal self, soul, or ego.

You will find that these three characteristics of the relative universe—impermanence, suffering, and egolessness—are of fundamental importance in Buddhism.

The first of them, the characteristic of impermanence, is emphasised again and again, as our attachment to the impermanent keeps us imprisoned within the wheel of birth and death.

The second characteristic, suffering, is the starting point in Buddhism, for the Buddha-way is concerned primarily with suffering and the cure of suffering. In terms of fundamentals, every particle of the universe is in a state of agitation, and in conscious living beings the higher degrees of this agitation become different degrees of suffering. Some of the lower degrees of this agitation are known as pleasure, and the differences between pleasure and suffering lies in the intensity of the agitation.

The third characteristic, egolessness, is the focal point of the whole of the Buddha-doctrine, the central element in the whole teaching. You can't understand the Buddha-doctrine unless you understand the meaning of egolessness from the beginning. It doesn't matter a great deal if you miss the technicalities of the law of action and reaction, or the subtleties of Buddhist metaphysics; but it does matter if you fail to grasp the meaning of egolessness. Everything is focused on this point, and without an understanding of it many things in Buddhism may fail to make sense.

In the practice of the Buddha-way the emphasis on the doctrine of egolessness is even more important and vital. If you want to practise Buddhism, as distinct from making it a parlour-game like chess, you must focus your attention on the problem of subduing your ego-concept and of realising its falsity.

Following the outer forms of morality is just the first stage of the work. The traditional customs of Buddhism as carried out in the East are conventionally right in their own place, but those customs imported into the West may merely provide side-interests which weaken the attack on the self-concept. Talking about Buddhism until the jaws ache may enlighten others, but too often it mainly functions as a means of self-assertion. None of these things—superficial morality, the observance of customs, and talking about Buddhism—has any ultimate value unless it leads up to the effort to eradicate the self-delusion.

The reason for the supreme importance given to the teaching of egolessness is that the belief in a separate permanent self is the salient point in that basic ignorance which, in Buddhism, is regarded as the source of all suffering; for when the delusion of selfhood is finally broken down the basic ignorance also is destroyed.

This matter of egolessness is really a particular case of impermanence; for it means that a being does not possess a permanent or unchanging soul at the centre of his existence, but consists of an impermanent and ever-changing life-current, which is never the same for two consecutive moments. There is, according to this, no hard core at the centre of a being's existence, no eternal soul, no fixed or unalterable ego. In this sense, the self doesn't exist.

However, to say that the self doesn't exist, flatly and boldly like that, doesn't give a true picture. It is much better to say that the self doesn't exist in the way in which we think it exists. The self doesn't exist as an unchanging entity, but it does exist as a fluid or fluctuating life-current, an ever-changing stream of existence.

A living being has been described, according to the Buddhist concept of things, as "a flame-like process which burns by virtue of a force peculiar to itself." Note particularly the term "a flame-like process". This expresses the idea very concisely, for you will find that, over and over again, the Buddha-doctrine insists on the dynamic nature of existence, with no static entity to be found anywhere.

This flame-like process (which is the nearest approach to a self or soul you will ever find in Buddhism) is the life-current. In the human being it manifests in a fivefold way. First, it builds around itself a material body. Secondly, by way of this material body it experiences existence in terms of pleasurable feelings, neutral feelings, and unpleasurable feelings. Thirdly, it experiences existence in terms of perceptions. Fourthly, it reacts to these experiences by way of volitional tendencies, or determinants, whereby it sorts out the feelings and perceptions and determines lines of activity. And fifthly, there is the basic cognitive faculty functioning as consciousness and also operating on that subconscious level.

In other words, the flame-like process we call the life-current consists of a multitude of components, some material and some mental; these components, for the purpose of analysing the individual human being, are classified into five groups. These five component-groups, which we have just touched on briefly, can be described more fully in the following way.

Component-group 1—the body. You as an individual human being consist of a mind and a body; and your body, broadly speaking, can be spoken of as the group of material components that help to make up your life-current, your so-called self.

Component-group 2—the feelings. You are aware of the world around you by way of your five physical senses and also by way of ideas that you build up out of your sense-impressions. In thus becoming aware of a stimulus—that is, either of a sense-object or of an idea—you experience either a pleasant awareness of it, unpleasant awareness of it, or a neutral awareness of it with neither pleasure nor displeasure. This quality of awareness is called feeling, and all pleasant, neutral, and unpleasant feelings are included in this second group of components.

Component-group 3—the perceptions. In Buddhist psychology there are six different kinds of perception. These are (1) vision, (2) hearing, (3) smell, (4) taste, (5) body-sense-perception (or, to use the neurological term, somaesthetic perception, including the perceptions of temperature and contact), and (6) mental perception. The word translated as perception embraces also awareness and the faculty that recognises, identifies, and compares the differences and similarities between stimuli.

Component-group 4—the determinants. The previous two groups of components (the feelings and the perceptions) consist of somewhat passive mental factors. That is to say, the feelings and the perceptions are forms of awareness that occur in relation to the reception of incoming stimuli. In contrast, the fourth group comprises components of an active or dynamic nature. These centre around the volition or will, and determine the person's activities; and for this reason we can call them the determinants.

There are fifty of these determinants as usually listed, and I do not intend to bore you by discussing the whole lot of them. However, I will mention a few.

The first is contact-awareness, the initial impingement or meeting of a sense-object or a mind-object with a sense-organ and consciousness.

The next to be mentioned is the volition or will. This dominates all the other determinants and to some extent controls their activities, thus influencing the tendencies of thought, speech, and bodily action.

Then there is one-pointedness, whereby the mind is centred on one sense-object or idea at a time. Mental vitality is next, and is roughly parallel though not identical with the nervous energy. The next is attention, the mental faculty which brings a sense-object or idea into the focus of consciousness.

These five that I have just mentioned are present in all forms of consciousness, together with feeling and perception, which make, in all seven, universal mental factors.

Others in the group of determinants are application (the initial application of consciousness when a new impression enters the mind); discursiveness, which is the faculty of searching within the mind for the identification and associations of a newly-entered impression; mental effort; interest; intention; and decisiveness, or the faculty of deciding between two courses of action.

None of the determinants so far mentioned has either a moral or an immoral character. The remaining members of this component-group, however, do have such a relationship, and they are classified into twenty-five morally-skilful determinants and fourteen morally-unskilful determinants.

Included in the morally-skilful determinants are generosity, good will, and non-delusion; while the morally-unskilful impulses include greed, ill will, delusion, dogmatism, envy, and anxiety. Another, generally called conceit, is practically the same as the Western concept of the inferiority complex.

You will no doubt see that some of the determinants can be roughly equated with the instincts of Western psychology, the desires and emotions that arise with the operation of these instincts, and the thought-habits that are built up by the frequent repetition of thoughts.

Component-group 5—the basic cognitive faculty. In Buddhist psychology the mind—both in the form of full consciousness and in its subconscious functions—is a form of energy, in the same sense in which light and electricity are forms of energy; and, without the presence of this special form of energy, the other mental component-groups could not arise.

The basic cognitive faculty operates in a sixfold way through the various sense-organs. First, it operates as visual consciousness when it functions by way of the eye and the total visual sense; secondly, as auditory consciousness through the ear and the auditory sense; thirdly, as olfactory consciousness by way of the sense of smell; fourthly, as gustatory consciousness by way of the taste buds of the tongue and elsewhere; fifthly, as body consciousness through innumerable sensory end-organs of contact, temperature, and other somaesthetic senses; and sixthly, as mind-consciousness—the perception of ideas—through the organs of mind.

All mental states are regarded as having a degree of consciousness, even those states which appear to be unconscious; but in so-called unconscious and subconscious states the consciousness is too low in intensity to register in the memory, and therefore cannot afterwards be recollected.

Now, this analysis of the individual being into five groups of components may appear to you to be dry and somewhat overburdened with technicalities, and perhaps rather pointless. But it has a point, and a point that bears directly on the doctrine of egolessness. The point is that each of the component-groups is impermanent, fluctuating, and ever-changing; and in the multitudinous components of individual existence nothing whatever of a fixed or permanent nature can be found.

The first component-group, the body, is changing all of the time, slowly or quickly, growing larger or smaller, wearing out, or repairing itself, getting warmer or cooler, or changing in some way.

The four mental component-groups are equally transient, or more so. The feelings arise and fall away from minute to minute, and the perceptions behave in a similar manner; while the determinants, conditioned by or dependent on the feelings and the perceptions, change accordingly. The basic cognitive faculty, functioning as consciousness, continually changing from instant to instant, is just as impermanent as all the rest.

You can see, then, that the purpose of this analysis of individual existence is to show that nowhere is there any possibility of a permanent self, soul, or ego. A wave arises on the ocean of becoming, and you are that wave; another wave arises nearby, and I am that wave; while all around us are other waves, other beings, people, ants, elephants, cats, and dogs.

In time, each wave sinks back into the ocean of becoming; but the forces that comprise it cause a new wave to arise somewhere else. The new wave is not identical with the old one, but it is not altogether different; there is continuity, but there is no fixed unchanging identity. In the same way, when a being dies, certain of the forces of which the life-current consists cause a new being to come into existence. The new being is not identical with the old one, but the new being is not altogether different from the old one; there is continuity, but no fixed entity.

Since the focal point in Buddhism is the realisation that the self is a delusion, the final goal is naturally the annihilation of the delusion. This final goal is the Unconditioned, the ultimate bliss which lies beyond the ordinary happiness of personal life. In a sense it is annihilation, but only the annihilation of the unreal. The Unconditioned is the state beyond words and beyond thought that supervenes when the delusion of selfhood is destroyed; for it is the world of impermanence and suffering that is found to be unreal when measured in ultimate terms.

Now, what is the significance of egolessness as far as your daily life is concerned? Its significance is that the self you so lovingly nurture, the ego you love to expand and hate to withdraw, is a delusion and the ultimate cause of your suffering. Every act you carry out on behalf of the self-delusion is just so much energy tipped down the drain. Once you realise this fact of egolessness, once you learn to become constantly aware of it and to discipline your behaviour accordingly, it must of necessity modify your lifestyle and enable you to stand up to the rebuffs, neglects, and denials that the world heaps on you from time to time.

The doctrine of egolessness can be concisely summed up in this way:

> "You who are slaves of the self, who toil from morning until night in the service of self, who live in constant fear of birth, old age, sickness, and death, receive the good news that your cruel master does not exist."

The Inferiority Complex

You may find it interesting to consider the Western concept of the inferiority complex in the light of the Buddhist doctrine of egolessness. You will recall that, in discussing those components of personal existence that we referred to as the determinants—the active or dynamic mental factors—we mentioned one which is generally called conceit. This determinant, according to the Buddha-doctrine, is of three kinds.

First, there is the conceit which makes one think "I am inferior to another"; then a second form of conceit gives rise to the idea "I am equal to the other person"; and thirdly there is the kind which causes one to think "I am superior to the other."

From this, it is apparent that conceit in this sense means a factor of the mind which not merely makes one feel superior to another (the meaning which is ordinarily attached to the word) but which prompts one to be concerned with one's own inferiority, equality, or superiority by comparison with another person.

You can see, then, that the meaning of conceit is closely paralleled by the Western idea of the inferiority complex, which arises from one's own self-centred and pathological concern with one's inferiority, equality, and superiority as compared with others.

Let's consider this matter of the inferiority complex as seen from the standpoint of Western thought.

We all know how it feels to be left out of a conversation. We all know what it feels like when others in a group are talking about things of which we know nothing, and, what is worse, talking about them almost as if we were not there at all. No one—neither you nor I nor any other normal person—likes to be ignored.

To be ignored when we want to be recognised means to feel inferior.

We all know, too, what it feels like to be painfully self-conscious. You, no doubt, can recall a situation in which you were expected to say something or to do something when attention was focused on you. You halted and you faltered without quite knowing what to say or what to do.

To be given too much attention when you feel unequal to the occasion, then, means to feel inferior.

This means, then, that there are situations in which you welcome attention, because you know that you can deal adequately with the matter in hand. You then feel perhaps a little superior. And there are times when you prefer not to be brought into focus but to remain on the outskirts of things, so to speak.

Sometimes attention shows up your inadequacies and you resent it because it gives you a sense of inferiority; at other times attention shows up your good points, so that you welcome it; it makes you feel superior and important.

Your feelings of superiority and inferiority depend largely on whether or not others applaud you, or at least approve of what you say and do.

Throughout the course of your life, no doubt, you have had experiences in which you have felt inferior, and all these experiences have been built up into a complicated mental structure that is generally known as the inferiority complex.

All of us, as normal people, have some sort of inferiority complex. Your own may be a powerful one or it may be only a mild one; it may be so strong that it dominates you, or you may have learnt to understand and control it; but unless you happen to be superhuman you must have an inferiority complex of some kind. It is a piece of standard equipment in the human mind and it has had its own special evolutionary value in the past.

You seldom hear the superiority complex mentioned. Why? The fact is that the superiority complex—apparently the direct opposite—is the same as the inferiority complex. To want to feel superior is largely the same as the dislike of feeling inferior, and the mental mechanism of the one is the same as the mental mechanism of the other.

Let us consider the meaning of the term, the inferiority complex. Apart from its psychological implications, a complex is a number of things all held together in some way so that they all function as one unit. In this sense you could call a sewing machine a complex, because it consists of a number of parts all held together so that they function as one unit; you could not, of course, call these same parts a complex if they were all piled in a heap.

In its psychological meaning you can take a complex to mean a number of ideas all held together so that they all function as one unit.

One such complex may be related to the aggressive instinct and arouse the feeling of anger. Another complex—or any idea that forms part of it—may set to work the instinct of escape and thus generate some form of fear; such a complex is called a phobia.

Yet another complex may stimulate the instinct of self-assertion and bring with it a feeling of superiority and self-importance, or, if it is thwarted, a feeling of inferiority.

The particular instinct to which a complex is related—aggression, escape, or self-assertion, for example—is the binding and co-ordinating element in the complex.

Now, when you assert yourself in some way and are thwarted, or when you attempt to display your superiority and fail, you naturally feel inferior, and every such defeat you suffer leaves its vestige in your memory-store. The sum total of all the vestiges of these thwarted attempts at self-assertion constitutes your inferiority complex. The inferiority complex is not the same as the inferiority feeling, for this is the feeling that arises when the complex is stimulated and then thwarted.

On the other hand, when your inferiority complex is stimulated into activity and this activity is successful, you have a feeling of superiority.

Why should the inferiority complex be as important as it is? In the evolution of man from his prehuman ancestors, we can see that the individual with the strongest instincts of aggression and self-assertion would be the most likely to survive under difficulties. In a fight, the one who is less aggressive is likely to perish. In a scramble for food, those lacking in self-assertion are likely to go hungry, to weaken, and to die.

Aggression and self-assertion are closely related instincts. The main function of aggression is to defeat an enemy or a rival, while that of self-assertion (in part) is to intimidate the enemy or the rival. Self-assertion also has another aspect, for we see it at work in the form of self-display in courtship.

You can see, then, that self-assertion has a survival value not only in the sphere of individual survival, but also in the sphere of race-survival.

Because your self-assertive instinct is so important, then, your inferiority complex also is important; and because of this, in turn, it has deep-reaching effects on your life as a whole.

The Practice of Non-Assertion

If you find your inferiority complex has adverse effects on your life, and if you decide to deal with it by some form of mental culture, there is an ancient Buddhist technique which has a direct application to this matter.

A major working principle in Buddhist psychology is to strive always to see things as they really are, to work always for clear discernment as opposed to self-deceit or delusion. The technique used for this clear discernment we know as right mindfulness, and one aspect of right mindfulness is called the detailed awareness of the mental state.

The detailed awareness of the mental state is designed to give increased self-understanding, with specific regard to the emotional quality of various mental states.

This does not mean a theoretical knowledge of what goes on in people's minds in general. Although this theoretical knowledge is sometimes very helpful, it means a detailed and direct awareness of what goes on in your own mind.

It is a sharpened awareness of the emotional quality of each mental state as and when it arises, and also to a certain extent in retrospect. It is a form of self-observation designed to break down self-deceit and to keep the stream of consciousness free from delusion.

The technique consists of the formation of a new habit, the habit of bare attention. Note this term, bare attention; it means attention which is stripped bare of all emotional overtones and undercurrents, attention free from bias, free from prejudice, and free from self-deceit.

It is only by bare attention that you can see things as they really are, for emotion clouds and colours your perceptions.

To form this new habit is not easy. Your mind, as you know, likes to run in its old deep ruts, and it needs persistent self-observation and self-honesty to break out of these ruts.

There is no easy way and there is no quick way to form the habit of bare attention, but there is a valuable guide in relation to the matter of the inferiority complex. It is this: every time you feel self-important or superior, you should try to realise that it's merely a primitive instinct dominating your intellect. When your intellect can dominate your primitive instincts, you will be well on the way—not to a better feeling of superiority—but to true superiority.

As you learn to apply the detailed awareness of the mental state, you will see the part that the self-assertion instinct plays in your own life. You will see that while your inherent tendency to assert yourself in primitive circumstances had a survival value, under the conditions of modern civilisation this tendency can sometimes do more harm than good.

You have seen that when your self-assertion instinct is stimulated it brings about certain activity on your part, and if this activity is successful you tend to feel superior or self-important. But when, on the other hand, this self-assertive activity is thwarted or does not meet with success, you feel inferior.

Time after time in the course of life your strivings towards self-assertion are defeated; time after time your self-importance is challenged, and in consequence you feel inferior and inadequate to meet the challenge.

Now, with so many attacks on your self-importance, your strivings are largely motivated by your self-assertive tendencies, but this motivation is largely subconscious.

Many of your strivings against the great outside world are attempts—conscious as well as subconscious—to adapt your environment to your own wishes; but the people in this great outside world have their own self-assertiveness, just as self-centred as yours, and, in the mass, vastly more powerful.

The result is conflict, and very often defeat. Another element is added to your inferiority complex; another vestige in the memory-store, being painful, must be pressed down to a level at which consciousness can not reach it.

As a result, either you become more timid or retiring on the one hand, or on the other you develop along more bombastic and self-assertive lines. There will be effects of some sort in your general lifestyle, tending frequently towards either one extreme or the other, unless very early in life you have learnt how to handle the whole situation.

Undoubtedly there are some occasions on which your self-assertion centres around someone else's success or defeat. Maybe your young son becomes the best of his school, or perhaps he loses his first job through inefficiency, and so you share his success or failure; but in such cases your feelings of superiority or inferiority arise because something that belongs to you is involved and is an extension of your own ego.

It is your own self that feels superior and enjoys it, and it's your own self that feels inferior and seeks some way or other to feel superior.

Now, it is precisely the importance of the self to the self that you must break down if you want to deal adequately with the inferiority complex, and for this reason you must realise that in order to get rid of the inferiority feeling you must get rid also of the superiority feeling. To be free of this feeling of inferiority you must be free of the feeling of superiority.

You will see, then, that the ancient Buddhist teaching of egolessness is very up-to-date; for hand-in-hand with the deep-rooted belief in the importance of one's own self goes the equally deep-rooted assertion of superiority.

As I have already said, it is important to understand the teaching of egolessness if you want to understand Buddhism. On the other hand, whether you believe in this doctrine, merely because it is a part of the teaching as a whole, is somewhat less important. It's quite unnecessary to believe anything uncritically or to accept anything without thoroughly examining it. What is really important is to realise that you can never achieve any enduring happiness by way of self-assertion.

At the very least, it is necessary to understand and accept the fact that excessive self-assertion causes conflict with others and conflict within your own mind.

On this basis, then, your self-training in this connection is a matter of endeavouring to keep all your actions free—as far as possible—from self-assertion.

You begin by self-observation, for self-observation is the key to self-training. You begin by critically observing your reactions to external events and situations with a view to finding out when and how you assert yourself, and this self-observation must become habitual and continual. You must learn to turn the searchlight of mindfulness onto every one of your actions and reactions.

This increasing mindfulness, this inwardly-directed attentiveness, helps you discover your own mental mechanisms, those of rationalisation and repression, for example, which are motivated by your own reluctance to confront the things in your own mind.

Then, as you gain increased self-understanding, you will begin to see your own self-assertive tendencies as they really are. You will begin to see yourself pushing to the fore in circumstances which give you an opportunity for self-importance, and hanging back from a duty when that duty arouses feelings inferiority.

The increased awareness and self-understanding will act as a brake when you would otherwise seek a superiority feeling, and will spur you on to action when you'd otherwise hang back for fear of an inferiority feeling. Superiority and inferiority in the subjective sense—that is the feelings of superiority and of inferiority—will gradually disappear and just as gradually be replaced with a true superiority. And this true superiority will be quite distinct from the spurious superiority of the emotions.

As the work of self-observation goes on, you may find it helpful to exert some disciplinary pressure on yourself; and this self-disciplinary pressure will work in three main directions.

First, in thought. You may be offended, for example, by something said to you, or because you have been left out of a conversation, or because your good qualities have not been recognised. You may tend to brood, to reflect unwisely on whatever it is that has hurt you, to dwell on the incident. Thus you magnify its importance, you magnify your own sense of inferiority, and you magnify your own wish to find a feeling of superiority to displace it.

Secondly, in speech. You may be such a good talker that you are a poor listener, and you may interrupt other people's conversations in order to have your say. Your speech may be full of self-references. When, for example, if the conversation turns to gardens, you boast about your own garden; or if someone mentions having had lumbago, you set out to show that your own lumbago was far more painful and crippling than was the other person's. Thus you tend to blow up your own ego with hot air like a balloon.

And thirdly, in action. You may, perhaps, find yourself elbowing to the front because you like the limelight, or else hanging back because of stage fright, both extremes being due to an over-valued ego.

Whether your self-assertion shows itself in thought, in speech, or in action, it's a potential source of unhappiness in some way or other. It lays you open to hurt feelings or deflation. If you work always towards a progressively increasing mindfulness of all of the forms that your self-assertive tendency takes, coupled with a continued effort to control it as and when it arises, you will attain a calm and balanced state of mind in which feelings of superiority and inferiority have no place.

And as these disappear, so also the consequent outward and inward conflicts disappear.

Practical Work

If you want to place the various things that have been said on a practical basis, I suggest that you set yourself a period of at least a month—or, better still, a period of three months or longer—and during that period set out to discover and to become more aware of the various ways in which your self-assertive tendencies find their expression—expression sometimes in terms only of thought, sometimes in the form of speech, or at other times by way of bodily action.

It is in the daily round of your work, your domestic life, and your social contacts with other people that the delusion of selfhood does its damage and it is therefore right in the middle of this daily round that you must take the first corrective steps.

When your self-assertive tendencies are curbed by your own understanding and your own will, it's good; when they are curbed by fear or by intimidation by others, it's not so good. You are then not following the principle of non-assertion at all.

However, the essence of the exercise is mindfulness. If you can observe your self-assertive tendencies as and when they arise, so much the better, but, failing that, you can recognise them in retrospect; but the main point is to become aware of them in some way or other.

Place the exercise on a self-disciplinary basis, make a contract with yourself to impose on yourself a small penalty whenever you unreasonably assert yourself, not only in bodily action and in speech, but also in thought.

This element of self-discipline is an important one. You will find that if you merely resolve to correct your self-assertive habits, you will be likely to forget your resolution after a while. However, if you make a self-contract and, whenever you find yourself unduly asserting your own importance, you go without cigarettes for a few hours or have less sugar in your coffee, you will be more likely to keep to your resolution.

In this way, you will be using the principle of self-discipline side-by-side with the principle of mindfulness.

The Ninth Month

The Practice of Thought Control

In most communities the thoughts of the average person are governed by the thoughts of the majority of other average people, and this holds good from early childhood right through to old age. Only to a limited extent does the average person think for himself.

During early childhood you learnt largely by exercising your senses; you looked at things, you listened to sounds, you smelt and tasted things, you touched and handled them, and you experienced physical pain and physical pleasure from them. Thus by direct first-hand sensory contact you became acquainted with the fundamental elements of experience.

When by exploring the world with your senses you found something that yielded pleasure or satisfaction, you regarded that thing as good, and similarly when you encountered something that gave rise to pain you regarded it as evil. Good and evil at this stage were identical with pleasure and pain.

But your elders soon complicated matters for you by scolding you for enjoying your pleasures and by forcing you to do things which, although unpleasant, were called good. As you learnt the language of your elders your concrete concepts of good and evil became further confused with the abstract concepts of right and wrong, while the rightness and wrongness of things were measured by the approval and disapproval of others.

From the beginning, then, your thoughts were governed largely by the thoughts of those about you, conveyed to you by their approval and disapproval.

There were other external influences to shape your thoughts as you grew older, but to a large extent the effects of these later influences—although less definite—followed the patterns laid down in earliest childhood. You tended to approve of those things that were approved by the people you liked and admired, and to disapprove of the things associated with people you disliked.

In your present phase of life, whatever it happens to be, you still largely follow the childhood patterns. Sometimes, perhaps, it may be that you believe a thing because it pleases you to believe it, and not because your reason supports it. Or you believe it because everybody around you believes it, or because, years ago, your parents taught you to believe it.

For the childlike mind, authority forms the only basis for belief; but even if your mind is more mature it probably still retains old beliefs and builds new ones on inadequate foundations, mainly because you are never called upon to apply the critical function of your reasoning powers to the matters concerned. You take them for granted.

There is a very powerful factor in modern life that continually conditions your thinking, or perhaps your lack of thinking. The patterns and channels of your thoughts are conditioned to a large extent by the continual blare of advertising. This uses both blatant and subtle means to keep at the highest pitch both your desires for sensory enjoyment and your sense of self-importance.

You can realise that it is of vital importance to develop a technique of thought control. In this connection, Buddhist psychology offers a method called bare attention.

This is one of the most important forms of mindfulness. In bare attention, the attention is stripped bare of all emotional biases, prejudices, self-references, and associated thoughts. This emotion-free attention is essential for seeing things as they really are, because emotional biases, prejudices, and uncontrolled associations bring about falsifications or distortions of perceptions.

Bare attention thus means the bare uncluttered awareness of a perception, without any reaction to it in the form of deed, speech, or mental comment.

If you were to examine your normal everyday perceptions, you might find that they are often muddled, cluttered up with mental material that belongs elsewhere, and obscure or distorted.

Sometimes these falsifications cause misunderstandings, conflict, and discord. You can see that if you apply the principle of bare attention to your everyday thinking, you can reduce the misunderstandings that sometimes occur, together with their consequent conflict and discord.

It is not until you become aware of your own mental functioning that you realise just how widespread and deep-seated your strong emotional biases really are. They are, in fact, so widespread and so deep-seated that without special self-training it is impossible to perceive a sense object, to form a clear idea of a situation, or to recollect an event without some distortion or other.

In the jungle of emotionally-distorted ideas that constitutes a large part of the average mind there are danger zones, and when these are stimulated they give rise to irrational thinking, bad temper, and misjudgements. Any of these can cause quarrels and heartaches when they intrude into your associations with other people.

And it is important to recognise the fact that you cannot as a rule see the danger zones in your mind, because the tangled masses of emotional undergrowth make them inaccessible to consciousness. Until the light of full consciousness can be brought to bear on them, to identify them, and to clear them away, they will remain as danger zones.

Much of this undergrowth was planted during childhood and before, and if you really want to arrive at the detailed awareness of your own mind in its fullest sense you must learn to break the false emotional connections formed in your early life. It's probable that many buried complexes exist in your mind and are at the root of your irrational behaviour, of your unaccountable likes and dislikes, and of your fears and resentments.

Now, it is not my intention to discuss methods of self-analysis or systems of reaching buried complexes. This is specialist's territory and any endeavours to enter the danger zones of the mind by a frontal attack could raise more problems than it solves.

The practice of bare attention, at least in the sense in which we are considering it here, does not make a direct or frontal attack on such problems; it works by establishing a foothold in the observations and perceptions of the present and cleansing these of their biases and prejudices; and then, as these current experiences are purified, the cleaning-up process extends backwards, so to speak, into the past. In other words, as your current experiences are progressively stripped bare of their retarding emotional clutter, the increased awareness extends to the memory patterns of earlier emotional experiences.

Whereas a direct frontal attack in approaching a touchy complex is practically certain to fail, the gradual and subtle influence of bare attention seeps through into lower layers of the mind—layers normally inaccessible to consciousness—and cleanses them at their own level. However, it must be realised that this is not the work of weeks, or months, or years; it must be considered as a process of decades at least; in fact, it is a lifetime task.

There is another point of interest in applying bare attention to that jungle of emotional undergrowth called the human mind. As you employ the technique of bare attention to your current experiences—as you endeavour to keep your present observations and perceptions clear of bias, prejudice, and irrelevant emotion—so your mind itself changes. It is like cleaning a mirror which has accumulated spots and splashes. As you proceed with the cleaning process, so you find the reflection becoming truer and clearer. In the same way, as you gradually clean up the perceptive faculties of your mind, so you enable it to see into itself with greater clarity and so to reach to greater depths.

* * *

This matter of bare attention forms an extremely important factor in the Noble Eightfold Path, which is the core of Buddhism. To make this point clear, let's run through the eight steps.

Right understanding is the first step. In one sense, this is intellectual understanding of the Buddha-doctrine; in another sense it is the understanding of the true nature of existence; while in yet another sense it becomes a direct insight into the ultimate reality beyond all things.

The second step, right thought, is one of the specifically psychological aspects of the Path, since it involves the control of mental processes. Next in order come right speech, right action, and right livelihood, which three together summarise the moral aspects of Buddhism.

Then comes the sixth step, right effort, which, being the training of the will, is an essential part of Buddhist psychology. The seventh step, right mindfulness, is also psychological, since it comprises the process of perfecting the normal faculty of attention; while the last of the eight steps, right concentration, takes us beyond the realm of normal psychology into the cultivation of supernormal faculties of the mind.

Now, it is the second step of the Eightfold Path, the step called right thought, that we're primarily concerned with at present. Right thought is usually described as thought which is free from uncontrolled sensory desires, from ill will, and from cruelty.

To a large extent, mental processes involve the use of words, not only for expressing thoughts but also for formulating them; and therefore the control of these mental processes can be assisted by the use of the verbalised function of the mind.

Before we deal with verbalised thought, however, it will be of interest to consider what Buddhist psychology has to say about the nature of thought in a broad sense, and later on we can discuss the type of thought which uses words as its instruments.

The Buddha-doctrine describes thought (in the sense of the general process of cognition) as a conscious process, as a process whereby various stimuli affect consciousness.

Thought, of course, must always be conscious. There can be no such thing as unconscious thought; and, although we may speak of subconscious mental processes, these processes cannot properly be called thought.

Just as thought must be conscious, so any kind of consciousness must have a stimulus or object. This stimulus may come from outside by way of one of the five physical senses (vision, hearing, smell, taste, and body-sensibility), or it may come from within the mind itself in the form of an idea or a mental image.

Thus, if there be no stimulus (no sound, no odour, no recollection, nor any other sense-object or mind-object), then there can be no consciousness.

Under such conditions, the state of mind that prevails is, in Buddhist psychology, called the mental sub-current; it is that form of mental energy which gives to the body its life, and without this mental energy the body could not live.

It can be visualised as an undercurrent of mental life from which full consciousness arises. In English writings on Buddhism it is often called the subconscious mind, but to avoid confusion with Western concepts it is better to use the term mental sub-current.

The mental sub-current may be illustrated by a stream of water flowing placidly and evenly; and, when this flow of water is disturbed, waves arise on the surface. Similarly, when the sub-current is disturbed by stimuli (either external sense-objects or internal mind-objects) then consciousness arises, as waves arise on the surface of the water.

The mental sub-current is the essential foundation of individual life, and without the mental sub-current individual physical life cannot exist. In it are stored the resultant impressions of all previous experiences; and these sometimes enter consciousness in the form of memories.

The sub-current possesses no volition of its own, since volition belongs only to consciousness; but the subconscious mental processes that go on within it are directed by habits which have been formed by conscious will-activity in the past.

During ordinary waking life consciousness seems to be completely continuous, but the Buddha-doctrine teaches that this is not as it seems, since ordinary waking life consists of conscious phases rapidly alternating with subconscious phases.

If we were to look at an electric light being switched on and off many times each second, it would appear to be a completely continuous light, whereas there would actually be a rapid alternation of light and darkness. In the same way, what appears to be continuous consciousness is really a rapid alternation of conscious and subconscious states.

Each mind-state lasts for an inconceivably small fraction of a second and then passes away, to be followed immediately by the next mind-state. In passing away, each mind-state transmits its energy to the following state, which is thus in some degree similar to its predecessor. But this new mind-state is not necessarily similar in all respects to that which preceded it, for new external stimuli may have arisen.

Thus any mind-state consists of the energy of its predecessor, plus sometimes some degree of modification.

In waking life, consciousness arises from the mental sub-current and sinks back to the subconscious condition millions of times a second, and the rapid succession of these alternating states gives the illusion of continuous consciousness. The unit of time used in describing the processes of cognition is called a thought-moment; millions of thought-moments go to make up a second.

When the mind is in a subconscious state and a strong stimulus occurs, full consciousness may arise, and the process of its arising will occupy a period of seventeen thought-moments.

The following description of the process describes these thought-moments one by one:

Moment 1: The mental sub-current is evenly flowing below the level of consciousness and the sudden strong stimulus occurs.

Moment 2: The mental sub-current is irritated or disturbed.

Moment 3: The mind turns towards the stimulus or object. (This stage is called advertance, but it must not be interpreted as attention since as yet there is no mind-consciousness.)

Moment 4: Consciousness of the sense-object now commences, but this is sensation and nothing more, for it occurs as yet only in the physical sense-organ; it has not as yet been received by mind-consciousness.

Moment 5: The stimulation is now conveyed via the nerve-fibres to the central nervous system and is received into mind-consciousness. This function, called reception, is more or less under the control of the will, and unless it takes place no further perception of the object can occur. In the case of a weak stimulus, it may be possible volitionally to cut it off; but in the case of a strong stimulus it is not normally possible to keep it out of mind-consciousness.

Moment 6: In the next phase, the function called investigation takes place. Now, investigation as ordinarily understood is a process spread over a period of time, so we are not to suppose that in one thought-moment the whole process of investigation of the nature of the sense-object takes place. What is meant is that in any conscious period of this kind, the mental energy seeks to connect up the new sense-object with the existing impressions left by earlier sense-stimulations. In each succeeding phase of cognition this momentary process is repeated.

Moment 7: Following on the previous thought-moment's activity (the investigation phase) some degree of connection with the impressions of earlier similar sense-stimulation is effected, and by virtue of this connection the mind is able to begin to classify the particular sense-object. Here again, the process is repeated in each cognitive process until the classification is complete.

Moments 8 to 14: During the next seven thought-moments, the mind determines an attitude of liking or dislike towards the object, an attitude of either good-will or ill will. This phase in the conscious period is called impulsion; it is mentally the most active part of the process, and to an extent it is under volitional control. During these seven impulsion-moments, reaction-forces are generated within the mental structure, and each separate thought-moment brings into being its own particular kind of reaction force.

Moments 15 and 16: During a period of two thought-moments, the process is finally impressed or registered on the mind, or in other words it is passed into the memory-store.

Moment 17: In the final thought-moment, full consciousness ceases for this period, after which the whole process of cognition may be repeated over and over again while the stimulus lasts.

The above description applies to a strong sensory stimulus, but if the stimulus is very weak there is no more than a slight disturbance of the mental sub-current.

When the stimulus is not a sense-object but a mind-object in the form of an idea or a recollection, the process is slightly different; but the effects of the impulsion-moments are in general the same. Conscious and unconscious periods alternate with so great a frequency that there is an illusion of continuous consciousness.

Now, as the word *thought* is used in the second step of the Noble Eightfold Path—the step called right thought—its meaning is to a large extent restricted to what is called the verbalising function of the mind. We carry out a great part of our thinking by means of words, for words are symbols for ideas, while ideas in their turn are the mental representatives for things, ideas, processes, and abstractions.

Whereas an idea of a complicated thing is necessarily complicated, it can generally be condensed into a simple word; thus while thinking with ideas (in the absence of words) would be clumsy and laborious, thinking with words is much quicker and easier.

Thus thought-control largely means the control of the verbalising function of the mind, of the "inner speech" whereby we silently use words to consider a problem, to reason about it, to reach a decision, and to plan out a line of action.

We can see, then, that we use words not only to express our thoughts but also to formulate our thoughts. While it can't be said that all our thinking takes the form of silent speech, or thinking in verbalised form, we must realise that a large part of our thinking does take this form.

Obviously, then, if the words we choose to formulate our thoughts do not accurately represent the ideas they are intended to represent, our thinking will be loose and inaccurate, so that any tendency towards self-deception we possess will be accentuated.

Few of us are free from some tendency, however slight towards self-deception. While we are generally aware of the extreme forms of sensory desire, ill will, and cruelty as they appear in our own make-up, we are not always aware of these adverse qualities when they appear in their mild and unobtrusive forms.

Thus when we allow one of these adverse qualities to operate in our mind in a small way, we may tend to gloss it over, to excuse it, and to make no effort to deal with it. We feel it is too unimportant to worry about it.

Yet the small everyday operations of an adverse mind-factor in its minor manifestations strengthen it little by little, and thus lay the foundations for its major appearance at some later time when, perhaps, a crisis arises.

In cultivating the second step of the Noble Eightfold Path, then, it is essential to watch the small everyday outcroppings of sensory desire, ill will, and cruelty, and recognise them in their many mild and unobtrusive forms. It is almost useless to wait until they appear in their extreme forms, for then they are too powerful to he handled effectively.

As long as we allow our thinking to remain vague and fuzzy, we are unlikely to recognise the lesser forms of adverse qualities. If, on the other hand, we verbalise our thoughts in the form of precise words, we are likely to discover these qualities and can then more easily deal with them.

This brings us to the use of the verbal formula as an instrument in thought control. A carefully worded or well-selected phrase, silently repeated, can act as a kind of mechanical aid to direct the thoughts along a particular channel, or alternatively to divert the thoughts from unsuitable or unwanted mind-objects.

Thus if we are suffering from an acute sense of loss—as for example after a bereavement—it may be helpful to use a phrase like this: It is in the very nature of things that at some time or other we must part from all that is dear to us; and by yearning for a return of that which is past we merely prolong our sorrow.

Of course, the main problem here is to remember to use the formula at the times when it is most needed, for at these times we are generally overwhelmed with our sense of loss; but this is a matter of developing the habit of mindfulness, which in itself is a major part of Buddhist mind-training.

Ideally, we should not wait until a severe loss occurs to begin to train ourselves in detachment. One aspect of right thought is that it is characterised by mental detachment from objects, people, experiences, memories, and anticipations that give pleasure.

Since ordinary life largely revolves around such things, we generally become enmeshed in the web of attachment, and to break free from this web is normally beyond us.

Thus when a severe loss does occur, it becomes very important to use every aid—such as that afforded by the mental repetition of a formula—to make an adjustment to the new circumstances.

* * *

Now, we must admit that thought free from all sensory desire is a good deal to expect from average people, like ourselves, who must live ordinary lives in equally ordinary environments. Perhaps it will help us to understand the problem if we consider what is meant by sensory desire.

Briefly, sensory desire is thought loaded up with the desire for enjoyment by the six senses, namely by impressions of visual objects, by sounds, by odours, by tastes, by body sense-impressions, and by mental reflections on any of these.

Sensory desires include the wish to see a sunset, the lights of a town seen across a valley, a beautifully patterned wallpaper, or a glimpse of a loved one's face; these are all visual things. Many desires are auditory: the desire to hear a piece of music or even a single chord, the trickling of a mountain brook, or the sound of a loved one's voice. There are desires to experience pleasant perfumes, tastes, and body-impressions, such as of comfortable warmth, and there is the desire to look back on any of these physical sense-enjoyments or to look forward to them.

Now, freedom from all these forms of sense-desire would seem to be freedom from all ordinary forms of motivation; and up to a point this is true. Ordinary motivation is based on the desire for sensory or mental enjoyment of some kind; and without the prospect of enjoyment many of our activities would come to a stop.

All this is so, of course; but the Eightfold Path is not the path to ordinary life with its ordinary enjoyments, but to the Transcendental, the realm which lies outside and beyond the relative world that we ordinarily know; and attachment to sensory and mental enjoyment becomes an obstruction to one who is aiming to transcend the relative world.

Nevertheless, for those of us who do not feel yet ready to follow this high aim, some degree of control over the desire for sensory enjoyment is necessary if we are to gain the fullest value from life. While this limited application of sense-control may not involve a complete renunciation of sense-pleasures, it must bring about some degree of detachment to be of any value; and this detachment, instead of reducing the pleasures of living, increases them by cutting away the grasping tendencies which often tend to vitiate these pleasures.

Sometimes we are advised to be aware of the present and not to live in the past. At first glance this appears to be good practical advice; but when we try to put it into practice, how often do we succeed?

We are told: "Kill in yourself all memory of past experience. Do not look behind you or you are lost." But if we were to follow this literally—assuming it to be possible—the ordinary processes of thinking would cease.

We are told also that: "the past must not control the future, where each minute is a new birth." But if we were to follow this to the letter, we'd be unable to add up next week's grocery bill because we refused to allow our past (during which we learned arithmetic) to influence our future household shopping.

Does this mean that the advice is useless? No. It means we have misunderstood it. What it really means is that we should accept the past with its losses and mistakes, its sorrows and heartbreaks, its joys and pleasures. We must accept the fact that the joys and pleasures of the past had to come to an end at some time or other—this is inherent in the very nature of this universe—and if we look back on them and yearn for them to return, then all we are doing is to vitiate this present moment.

If we look back on a happy event of the past and gain from it the pleasure inherent in a happy recollection or memory, without yearning for its return, memory—as then we are living in the present, for that happy memory as a memory but not as an event—is a part of this very present. As an event, it is part of the past, but as a memory that comes into our consciousness at the present moment then it is in fact our present experience.

As a memory, we may enjoy it without vitiating the present; but if we yearn for its return or its repetition we are divorcing ourselves from the present and trying to throw ourselves back into the past, which at this moment is non-existent.

* * *

So much for the matter of that type of right thought which is called freedom from sensory desires.

Another aspect of right thought is freedom from ill will, or, expressed positively, thought that is characterised by good-will. Sometimes even the most even-tempered of us become annoyed with our fellow men; and although often this annoyance evaporates when the occasion for it has passed, it sometimes leaves a residue of resentment or ill will which needs special handling.

It is easy to see that no progress is possible to a mind that is poisoned by ill will or hate, or by any of its associated mind-factors such as revengefulness, annoyance, or anger.

* * *

Again, right thought is thought that is free from cruelty. While cruelty often springs from hate or anger, much cruelty also arises through an indifference to the suffering of others or to thoughtlessness. Right thought, then, involves not only the absence of active and positive hate, but also the absence of its more negative and passive indifference to the sufferings of others.

* * *

The second step of the Eightfold Path—right thought—must be based on the first step, right understanding; for it is necessary to recognise right thought as right thought, and wrong thought as wrong thought. Without the attentive mind developed by right mindfulness, right thought is not possible in the fullest sense. Thus you can see that the second step of the Noble Eightfold Path must be carried along parallel with various other steps, and each one is inseparable from the others.

In particular, the practice of right thought must be carried along parallel with that of bare attention, for without the practice of bare attention—an aspect of right mindfulness—all thought processes tend to become cluttered with emotion.

Practical Work

Bare Attention

In ideal circumstances, if you wished to establish the mental patterns of bare attention in a complete form, you would put aside all responsibilities and all other interests for a period of some weeks and devote yourself to a strict course of self-training. Under such conditions, you would avoid all but the barest essentials in the way of physical work, and you would put aside writing and reading, and even talking as far as possible.

But these ideal circumstances are beyond the reach of most of us. Unless you are fortunately situated, it is probable that you can't find sufficient time and freedom from responsibilities to carry out the strict practices of mindfulness to the exclusion of other activities for a long period. How, then, are you to establish the practice of bare attention?

What you can't do in its entirety, then, you must do in part. Since you are unable to place yourself in ideal conditions, you must use your daily activities as the basis for your inner development; and it may be, in fact, that these daily activities are really more ideal for the purpose than a life of seclusion would be.

In order to establish the mental patterns of bare attention you must slow down some activities. As a starting point you can select one definite activity so that, without detriment to anything else, you can carry out this one activity more slowly than usual. If you have to catch the 8.17 train every morning, you obviously cannot slow down in that particular activity. If you are a housewife with children to look after you can hardly slow down the chores involved in getting them off to school. Again, if you are a bus conductor you cannot use the peak travelling periods to inaugurate the practice of bare attention.

However, there must be some daily activity that you can use as a basis for the establishment of the practice. There must be some short periods when the pressing urgency of duty subsides for a time.

Maybe the office worker can relax in a cafe at lunchtime, or the housewife can pause for a few minutes once the children have been bundled off to school, while the bus conductor has a few minutes at the depot during which he can smoke a cigarette.

In each of these cases there is an opportunity to make a start on the development of bare attention, even in a small way. The office worker can usually slow down during his lunchtime and mindfully observe the weight of the knife and fork in his hands, he can chew more slowly and observe the taste of food, and he can observe the colour and shape of his cup and saucer. And, more important, he can at this time observe his own general muscular state, feeling whether his muscles are taut or relaxed.

In the same way the housewife, when she pauses, can intentionally slow down the process of making a cup of tea for herself, in order to give her full attention to it. She can then become more conscious of the steam rising from the kettle, of the sequence of her own muscular actions as she makes the tea, lifts the cup to her lips, sips and swallows the tea, and so on. In this exercise in attentiveness she can become more aware of the details she normally misses. These details are unimportant in themselves; the point is that they can supply an opportunity for an increase in mindfulness.

Again, when the bus conductor smokes his cigarette during a few minutes' rest at the depot, he can apply increased attention to the sensation of the cigarette between his lips, to the taste, and to the appearance of the wisp of smoke rising from the glowing tip.

Obviously these small attempts at bare attention will be of little value if they end where they begin. The value of taking one small, frequent or regular occasion for mindfulness and consistently applying bare attention to it lies in the fact that it helps to establish a foothold. Once this foothold exists it is relatively easy to extend the practice to other small things throughout the day. However, to change the simile, it is only the thin end of the wedge, and unless the wedge is driven right home it effects very little.

Your approach to the practice of bare attention, then, should be to select one small thing that you do with some degree of regularity and which you can do more slowly and mindfully than usual. You should resolve to give this one small activity increased attention for a period; and to do this without looking for results, but purely as an exercise in mindfulness.

You will find, of course, that to make a vague resolution that when an opportunity occurs you will slow down and apply increased mindfulness will be of little use. You will need to be more specific, and you will need to enforce your resolution by a self-imposed penalty.

To be specific, therefore, resolve that during a period of at least a month you will take twice as long as usual over some small task, such as the task of taking off your shoes each night before going to bed. Should you neglect or forget to slow down this one action and to give increased mindfulness to it, you can impose some small penalty on yourself the next day.

Then, later on, you should search for another activity and use it also for the same purpose, slowing it down and giving it increased and sharpened awareness. Once the initial phase is established it will be somewhat easier to give increased attentiveness to other activities without the need for greatly slowing them down.

While this exercise relates mainly to your physical actions rather than to your mental functioning, you will find that it will help in your general overall plan of self-observation, and in this way will reinforce the effects of other practices.

The Tenth Month

The Cultivation of Detachment

On looking at life as a whole, you will agree that it is a mixture of pain and pleasure, effort and rest, dissatisfaction and contentment. You would like this mixture to be proportioned differently, of course; you would like to have less pain and more pleasure; you would like a little less effort with a little more rest, and then you would be less dissatisfied and more contented.

But you must realise that without some pain and some sorrow in life there would be no incentive for effort; and without effort you cannot make progress. Without dissatisfaction your life would become too static to be of any ultimate value. It has been said:

The bread of bitterness is the food on which men grow to their fullest stature.

From the Buddhist viewpoint, liberation from suffering can be achieved only by transcending personal existence and by attaining to a state beyond words and beyond thought, a state which is sometimes called the Unconditioned or the Transcendental. This "existence-beyond-existence" is a state in which all traces of craving, aversion and ignorance have been destroyed, and in this state there is said to be no suffering. The attainment of this "existence-beyond-existence" is the ultimate goal of Buddhism.

However, while the separate self remains—while personal consciousness with its separation from life as a whole still exists—some degree of suffering is inescapable. Nevertheless it is possible to lessen its impact by the cultivation of detachment, or, stated differently, by the progressive reduction of attachment to the pleasures of life.

There is a Buddhist practice which consists of becoming aware, as fully as possible, of the feelings of pleasure and displeasure as and when they arise and at the same time observing them as dispassionately as possible. The aim, of course, of this increased attention is to evaluate more clearly the pleasures and displeasures of life and thus to avoid becoming overwhelmed by them.

Without this dispassionate or detached mental attitude you sometimes tend to become too immersed in your pleasures, and, at other times, to swing to the opposite extreme and become immersed in your sorrows and pains. There are times, perhaps, when you wallow in your emotions and let yourself be completely governed by them.

The objective, then, is to learn to stand off from your experiences both of happiness and of sorrow and to observe them dispassionately, without being swamped by them. You need to learn to do this in retrospect with regard to experiences of the past, and to try to do so also with experiences of the present just as they come to you; while in the same way you must learn to anticipate the experiences of the future without undue emotion. As you learn the futility of grasping at things of the present and yearning for things of the past and future, so your mind develops greater flexibility.

Whatever you depend on for your happiness is an object of attachment, a prop on which to lean; and whenever you lean on any prop at all you lay yourself open to sorrow. At any time there is the possibility that some of your props will be knocked away, for life has an unpleasant tendency to knock your props from under you.

Your youth disappears in the passage of time; you lose a loved one, perhaps, and the old familiar externals in your own individual world give place to new and strange externals. If your mind is not flexible enough to keep pace with the losses and changes as your props are knocked away, you suffer all the more in consequence.

Generally, however, on looking back, you may find that you manage to keep pace with the changes and the impermanence of life by exchanging one prop for another, so that in the long run you are little better off; you are still dependent on props of some kind.

And this applies not only to the outer world of sense-objects but also to the inner world of mind-objects, for attachment to memories of the past and anticipations of the future is just as strong a bondage as is attachment to external things of the present.

There is a Buddhist statement that goes like this:

From attachment comes grief, from attachment comes fear. He who is free from attachment knows neither grief nor fear.

The stronger is your attachment to something you love, the greater is the happiness you experience when circumstances allow you to enjoy it; but, when it is wrenched away from you, your suffering then is just as great as your happiness previously was.

If you strongly desire something, this thing becomes an attachment-object. You naturally cling to your attachment-objects, you grasp at them and clutch them tightly when they are away from you, you long for their return. But all that this clinging, grasping, clutching, or longing does for you, in the long run, is to make the sorrow of loss so much greater.

It is axiomatic in the Buddhist philosophy that at some time or other you must part with everything that is nearest and dearest to you, and that the stronger is your attachment to these near and dear things, the harder will be the wrench when it comes.

Once the vice-like grip of attachment is established, it is impossible to break it by philosophising, and the strength of attachment depends on the strength of the craving for that which has been lost. Once the craving for the lost thing has gained a foothold it cannot be dislodged by theorising, and this craving can arise only when you allow yourself to be dominated by your feelings of pleasure and displeasure.

This is the Buddhist view of attachment and its related factors, a view that can be expressed in a simplified form in this way:

Attachment depends on craving; craving depends on the feelings of pleasure and displeasure; and the feelings of pleasure and displeasure depend on the contact of the senses with the external world.

In ordinary life, it is impossible to solve the problem of attachment by cutting off the contact of the senses with the outer world of sense-objects, and it is equally impossible to prevent pleasure and displeasure from arising once this contact is made. This means that if this chain of "dependent arising" (or, less accurately, this chain of cause and effect) is to be broken at all, it must be broken at the link of pleasure or displeasure. The chain of sorrow must he attacked at the phase of liking-and-disliking, desire-and-aversion, attraction-and-repulsion.

Now, all this, at first glance, seems to mean that you must give up everything that gives happiness or pleasure; but this is not the idea at all. What it really means is that you must learn to be independent of your feelings of pleasure and displeasure, as far as possible, and not to be controlled by them. It means that your intellect must control your life, not your emotional complexes or your irrational likes and dislikes; and thus it is essential (in the Buddhist technique at least) to become as fully aware as possible of all that goes on in your own mind.

In this technique, an ever-increasing mindfulness of all feelings of pleasure and displeasure as they arise is of great importance. Thus, in the first place, it is essential to be fully aware of the true value of your feelings of pleasure and of their real significance in order to prevent them from causing emotional biases and prejudices.

The same applies, of course, to your feelings of displeasure, for they also tend to give rise to emotional biases and prejudices if not well-controlled. Aversion gives rise to craving and attachment just as does desire, and you are just as much in bondage to the things you hate as you are to the things you desire.

If you can reach even a partial degree of detachment, if you can even partially lessen your grasp on the things that hold you in bondage, you are then more free to enjoy them without attachment, and for the same reason your sense of loss will be less when they have gone.

The fully-alert mind can make an objective assessment of each experience as and when it arises; but for many of us this dispassionate self-observation cannot be made at the time and can be made only in retrospect. But whether you make it at the actual time of the experience or afterwards, the main thing is to prevent your pleasures and your displeasures from controlling you.

Once a strong emotional charge of a pleasant or unpleasant nature becomes attached to an idea, this emotional charge can easily get out of hand and cause all sorts of inner disturbance and outer conflict. Only by increased mindfulness can you free the mind from the false emotional associations and the consequent disturbance and conflict.

The cultivation of detachment, then, aims at freedom from emotional domination and from the domination of pleasure and displeasure; it aims at freedom from attachment to external things, from memories and anticipations, from desires and aversions, and even from the desire for detachment itself.

Practical Work

The Cultivation of Emotional Detachment

In the human mind there are many blind spots—blind spots which are sometimes the causes and sometimes the effects of prejudices and emotional biases—and because of these the mind is unable to see itself as it really is. Such blind spots prevent us from realising the extent and ramifications of our false attachments, and any device that we can use to reduce them is an aid in the work of inwardly-directed mindfulness.

The following questionnaire is meant to be such a device and to aid you in the process of discovering and evaluating your own attachments.

In answering the questions, you may find that the first answer that comes to mind may be the correct answer or it may not. Therefore it is desirable that you go through the full questionnaire about six times during the month; allow it to start trains of thought rather than trying to arrive immediately at clear-cut answers.

A question that is difficult to answer will as a rule be of much greater value to you than one which is easy to answer. The real value of the answer lies, not in itself, but in the amount of self-observation or mindfulness employed in arriving at it.

There is no need to try to make your answers consistent in any respect. You must realise that normally you have ambivalent attitudes towards many of the important things in life; for example, you could both love and hate the same person at different times, or you could feel attracted to one aspect of something and repelled by another aspect of it.

With ambivalent attitudes of this kind, it may be that one of the two contrary emotions has been repressed, but from some consciously-inaccessible region of your mind it continues to influence your mental life.

It is impossible to isolate your objects of attachment from your sense of possessiveness, your valuations, your self-assertiveness, or various other aspects of your mental life. The questions which follow, therefore, are intended not to pinpoint specific objects of attachment, but to help you to develop a greater awareness of your own mental contents; and in the process, specific objects of attachment—and perhaps of misplaced attachment—may emerge.

Here, then, are the questions:

1. Do I agree with the following statement? "From attachment comes grief, from attachment comes fear. He who is free from attachment knows neither grief nor fear."
2. Am I unduly attached to material possessions, as a whole, or in other words do I have a possessive attitude to them?
3. Am I possessive with regard to other people—my family, my children, my friends, for example?
4. Do I desire power of some kind, not for what I could accomplish with such power, but purely for the sake of having power?
5. Do I have any attachment that interferes with my mental and emotional tranquillity?
6. Am I selfish or self-centred in any particular sphere of life?
7. Am I more dominated by emotional bias and prejudice than is the average person?
8. Do I like to dominate my friends, children, and other people?
9. Do I resent being dominated by others?
10. Am I too attached—rigidly or inflexibly so—to my beliefs and opinions in any sphere of thought?
11. Am I held back in any way by an excessive or misplaced attachment to anything or anyone?
12. Do I like people to admire certain of my possessions to which I am attached?

Any form of dispassionate observation—whether directed inwardly towards the mind itself or outwardly towards the world of events—is an aid in the cultivation of detachment. As a specific exercise in mindfulness, you can endeavour to apply the principle of dispassionate observation to your relationships with other people.

Sometimes you misunderstand something that another person says or does, perhaps because you happen to be upset or annoyed about something quite different. In such a case you give to the other person's meaning completely false colouring. Or perhaps you misinterpret a question, and give an answer which more properly applies to an altogether different question.

In this practice, then, and in your daily contacts with other people, you set out to pay unbiased, dispassionate observation to the other person's meaning, uncoloured by your own emotions or prejudices. You will often find that the true meaning is quite different from your own first interpretation of it.

You may find it necessary to train yourself not to interrupt others without good reason. Few people are good listeners, and you may be one of the few. If you are not—if you hear only half of what another is saying, and if you tend to interrupt with irrelevant side issues—then you need to teach yourself to listen, as far as possible, without allowing your own emotional associations to interfere.

Good listening demands effort, for good listening means listening to all of what is said and interpreting it as correctly as possible. In the process of good listening you will learn to pinpoint any emotionally-charged words and ideas that arise, words and ideas that bring into play your own biases and prejudices. Thus, by pinpointing such words and ideas, they will no longer be able to work from the subconscious levels of your mind, and thus you will gain greater knowledge and control of your own mental processes.

The practice of dispassionate listening, then, consists largely of careful and attentive listening, coupled with an endeavour to keep free from emotional reactions.

Assuming that you are employing the self-contract method of self-discipline, look back every few days to see if you have used the questionnaire consistently and in a sufficiently penetrating manner, and if you have carried out the practice of dispassionate listening to a sufficient extent. If you feel that you have not done so, deprive yourself of some small pleasure.

The Eleventh Month

The Attainment of Tranquillity

In his evolutionary history man has attained to the dominant position in his world by virtue of his intellect; but nevertheless he's been governed largely by his instincts and emotions. Man's primary motivation has come from his self-preserving and race-preserving urges towards fighting, escaping, mating, and so on. His intellect has functioned, in part at least, by steering him where his instincts have urged him to go. However, without his instincts and emotions, man would never have survived. It has been said:

> Were it fully understood that the emotions are the masters and the intellect the servant, it would seem that little could be done by improving the servant while the masters remained unimproved. Improving the servant does but give the masters more power of achieving their end. (Herbert Spencer)

These primitive urges, then, have served a purpose in man's evolution, but in general they are appropriate to primitive conditions; they were evolved under primitive conditions, and in many ways they fail to fit into the circumstances of civilised life. Thus for further human progress and for the fulfilment of man's potentialities, it now seems that his motivations must be transformed and refined.

Progress so far has been racial rather than individual; that is to say, it is mankind as a whole that has progressed or evolved, and the individual in most cases has been simply a unit in the evolving race. Now, however, it appears that many individual human beings have reached a point at which their progress along the evolutionary path is largely in their own hands.

Thus it seems that some of us have reached a point at which our further evolution can be consciously motivated and individual, rather than unconsciously motivated and racial.

Nevertheless the primitive urges are still with us, still integral parts of our mental make-up; and in one way or another they are responsible for a great deal of our emotionally-biased thought processes and for many of our falsely-coloured mental attitudes. They are at the root of many of our inner disturbances and of many of our conflicts with others. In this way, these primitive urges—once the essential factors in our earlier evolution—are now (to some extent) retarding factors. They can become obstacles to the attainment of tranquillity.

The Buddha-doctrine stresses a number of mental fetters and various inner hindrances which prevent the mind's proper functioning, and therefore stand in the way of tranquillity. Among the retarding factors are scepticism, the feeling of separate selfhood, and ill will; these, and others, are spoken of as the paralysing defilements of the mind.

Let's consider these obstacles or retarding factors one at a time, beginning with scepticism. From the Buddhist standpoint, scepticism is a state of mental rigidity, and this condition is no better than the opposite one of gullibility. The middle way between the extremes of scepticism and gullibility is a state of mental flexibility, a state of readiness to examine new or strange ideas and to evaluate them without prejudging them.

Scepticism or rigidity of mind is an obstacle to tranquillity because it is a refusal to examine and evaluate new ideas without emotional prejudgement. The dominating emotion in many cases may be a feeling of superiority, or there may be some kind of fear or an element of resentment towards the source of the new ideas; but, except where the intellect is incapable of grasping the new ideas, the rigidity is due to the domination of emotion of some kind or other.

The conception and conceit of selfhood is another obstacle to tranquillity. According to the Buddha-doctrine, the self is an illusion. It has been said: "The self is a label with nothing attached to it."

You may agree with the theoretical considerations of this "doctrine of egolessness," as it is called, or you may not; this is unimportant at this stage. The important thing is your own inner attitude, your own feelings about it. As you feel for the sufferings of others (and for their enjoyments too), so to that extent you have broken down this obstacle, the illusion of selfhood.

As further progress takes place, the focus is slowly and gradually removed from self-centred interests and transferred to the welfare of life as a whole; and, as the steel grip of self-centredness loosens, so an inner tranquillity begins to take the place of anxiety, resentment, and self-assertion.

This inner tranquillity may not yet show itself outwardly in the form of completely calm and unruffled behaviour. It is felt at first as a still centre, even though there is yet a great deal of turmoil around it, and to establish this still centre is the first stage in the attainment of tranquillity. It can be expressed in this way:

Enlightenment is the one still point in the centre of the turmoil, just as the axle is the one still point in the centre of the moving wheel.

Now, another obstacle to tranquillity is ill will, and this includes all grades of ill will, from the mildest and almost unnoticeable resentment up to the most raging fury. While you probably think of it as ill will directed towards the people you dislike, you must recognise that ill will towards your problems and your circumstances can be just as great an obstacle to tranquillity as is ill will towards people.

It is essential, then, to approach all your problems with an attitude of good will, and to break down all resentment towards them. This applies to the bills you have to pay and the unpleasant chores you have to do, just as much as to the people who have harmed or hindered you in some way, and equally to the impersonal things that have caused you delays and worries.

A mental attitude of non-resistance towards the difficult things in your life will help in this respect; but this does not mean that you must cease to resist them physically if you feel they are wrong. A mental attitude of non-resistance does not mean a cessation of effort towards improvement; what it does mean is breaking down of anxiety, resentment, and self-assertion, which are the primary causes of mental tension.

As a mental attitude, non-resistance must be applied to anything and everything that comes into your life—to the people you meet, to the jobs you must do, and to the problems you have to solve. If you resist your daily work, if you find it too boring, too unskilled for your talents, too much like drudgery, then this resistance will bring about greater fatigue; and so it will form a vicious circle.

Life presents you with many opportunities to learn, but these opportunities are often disguised as drudgery. It has been said:

Drudgery is as necessary to call out the treasures of the mind as harrowing and planting those of the earth. (Margaret Fuller)

If then, in doing something irksome, you can realise that it may enable you to call out the treasures of your mind, then the attitude of non-resistance will follow. If, in dealing with someone you dislike, you can use the occasion to develop good will, you will thereby take a step towards tranquillity. And if you are in a difficult situation, or even a painful one, and you are determined to learn from it everything it has to teach you, then you will have learned the secret of the great attainment. This secret of the great attainment is to love whatever you hate.

So, with greater flexibility of mind instead of rigid scepticism, with the understanding of the illusionary nature of the self, and with the growing ability to love whatever you hate, then you have made a good start. You have begun—in theory at least—to break down some of the main obstacles to tranquillity.

There are other obstacles, of course. There is conceit, which is just an over-valuation of the separate self—an over-valuation of a delusion, according to the Buddha-doctrine. There are envy and stinginess, which again spring largely from the self-delusion; and there is agitation, the churned-up state that comes from anxiety, resentment and self-assertion.

Now, you can deal with all these obstacles to tranquillity, in the Buddhist technique, by mindfulness and self-discipline combined. Mindfulness in this connection means dispassionate self-observation; it means an honest recognition of the retarding mental factors in whatever guise they appear. Self-discipline involves a gentle yet persistent effort to keep them in hand without harmfully repressing them.

All this reduces itself to a matter of forming new habits and thought-patterns and breaking old ones.

The task may become easier and more specific if you take one of your own mental factors at a time and subject it to observation for a period, to the exclusion of other factors.

For example, it is possible that in the course of your daily life various occasions arise which cause you to become agitated or flustered; minor critical situations arise from time to time. If you train yourself not to be easily agitated—to refuse to panic—then your judgements will be more accurate, your decisions more wise, and your life more harmonious.

To begin, you must at first form the habit of observing yourself closely to discover when and under what conditions you tend to become agitated. You may be serving behind the counter in a shop during a rush period, with an impatient customer making things difficult; you may be driving a car when the engine stalls at a busy intersection; or you may be looking after some troublesome children. In such circumstances, you tend to become more agitated than you realise.

You need first of all to become aware of this fact, and with this increased awareness a gradual improvement will come about. This natural improvement can then be assisted, as necessary, by a definite effort of self-discipline.

The attainment of tranquillity, then, is not a matter of finding ideal circumstances or of finding freedom from outer disturbances. It is a matter of discovering the inner mental obstacles to tranquillity (one by one) by dispassionate self-observation, and of removing them (one by one) by a gentle yet persistent effort of self-discipline.

Practical Work

The Dispassionate Observation of Emotion

To become a little flustered during a minor crisis seems—and generally is—only a small failing. So also are slight anger against frustrating circumstances, mild anxiety, and a limited degree of conceit. These are all normal and small failings, even if they are not ideal states of mind.

If any one of these minor mental factors is allowed to become excessive, it becomes pathological. It is one of the main tasks of mindfulness to bring about a precise and clear-cut awareness of emotional states when they are mild and ill-defined, for at this stage they are far easier to control than when they reach a pathological degree.

At any stage, not only in their extreme forms, these mental factors are obstacles to the attainment of tranquillity. At any stage they need to be kept under close observation.

For a period of at least a month, then, observe yourself closely with a view to discovering the emotional factors within yourself that prevent you from attaining tranquillity. This self-observation will help you to understand and thus to control those emotional factors that work against tranquillity.

Several times during the month you should decide that, for a period of two or three days, or even a single day, you will make a mental note of all the emotions you experience during that period. You can regard these as experimental periods in which you try to hold a mental attitude of pure observation, at least as far as conditions allow.

As an aid to dispassionate observation, it is helpful to identify and name each emotional state as it arises, if possible, or if this is not possible, to do so in retrospect. It will help to keep it in check if you can pause, observe yourself critically, and say to yourself "I am becoming envious," or "I am becoming agitated." The idea is to register the fact clearly in your mind without becoming further disturbed by it and without either feeling guilty about it or excusing yourself for it. The simple process of clearly naming the mental condition will sometimes help you to deal with it.

This may not necessarily be so of course, in the case of strong emotions, but its greatest value is in the recognition of mild ones whose significance may be much greater than at first appears.

In your home life, in your work, and in your social contacts with other people, you must of necessity react by word and action of some kind, but during the experimental period you must try to make these reactions as free as possible from emotional biases.

But more important than the outer reactions of word and deed are the inner reactions of thought. You must observe your currents of thought to see how much misplaced, inappropriate, and excess emotion they contain, how much they are biased by prejudices, and how much inner conflict they express.

This self-observation, growing more and more dispassionate, will bring you greater harmony within your own mind. You will tend to react to things with less misplaced or excess emotion, and thus with less inner conflict and less misunderstanding. The greater harmony in your relationships with other people will in itself repay the effort of mindfulness involved.

Assuming you are working on the self-contract method of self-discipline, you can impose on yourself a small penalty whenever you become lax in this form of self-observation.

The Twelfth Month

The Practice of Clear Comprehension

In developing an efficient approach to the problems of life, one of the first essentials is to reach a clear comprehension of what you really want from life. You could simplify—or over-simplify—the answer to this question by saying that all you want from life is happiness. On the other hand, you could enumerate a multitude of hopes and ambitions which might become so complicated and so mutually contradictory that you would need to undertake a lengthy process of self-analysis before you could sort it all out.

Some sort of answer halfway between the too-simple and the too-complex is what is really wanted. Without a well-defined understanding of what your central aim in life is, that is to say, without a clear comprehension of motive, as it is called in Buddhist psychology—there is a tendency to sink into the unthinking drift of life; and once caught up in the unthinking drift your whole life lacks focus.

To know what you want is very important. To know why you want it is also very important, and it will help you to do this if you understand in theory the nature of your desires, their origins in the instincts, and the emotions associated with them.

To understand your emotions and desires, you must first understand your instincts. These instincts are inherent tendencies to act in specific ways in specific circumstances. The instincts themselves exist below the level of the intellect—that is to say, below the level of your conscious reasoning processes— and being so much older than the intellect (in an evolutionary sense) they are so much stronger.

While your instincts are subconscious, your emotions and desires are conscious—sometimes too much so. In fact your emotions and desires are upthrusts into consciousness from your instincts. An instinct is like a volcano; it exists largely below ground level, but when it becomes active it throws lava and smoke upwards. In the same way, an instinct exists below consciousness, but when it becomes active it throws emotions and desires upwards into consciousness.

You can see, then, that the emotions and desires are upthrusts into consciousness from the instincts; but an emotion is not the same as a desire. An emotion is a comparatively vague and diffuse form of awareness at the level of bodily sensation, while a desire is a form of awareness at a higher level, at the level of ideas.

Your desires are, in fact, ideas of a sort; they are ideas of activities you want to carry out or else ideas of sensations you want to experience.

Thus if you are angry you have the idea of striking out at something; this can be called a motor idea, an idea of muscular activity, and it is aroused by the instinct of aggressiveness.

Again, if you are hungry, the sensory idea of food arises in your mind, energised or aroused by the inherent tendency to eat when the body requires food.

Perhaps the classification into motor desires and sensory desires—into desires to act and desires to experience—is an over-simplification; perhaps all desires include both motor ideas and sensory ideas; but the main point in the present context is that a desire exists at the ideational level of the mind while an emotion exists at the level of diffuse bodily awareness.

Let's look at it in this way; when one of your instincts becomes active your body automatically prepares itself for the appropriate activity by various changes. You become aware of the bodily changes, and the diffuse awareness of them constitutes an emotion.

At the same time, some specific idea of undertaking some action or undergoing an experience may arise in your mind; this also is a result of the instinct which has been aroused. This idea is emotionally charged—that is to say, it is exercised by the energy of the instinct—and thus it becomes a desire.

In subhuman life all activity is primarily instinctive, and whatever intellect does exist is directed towards finding ways to satisfy the instinctive promptings.

In human life the situation is not basically different from the situation in subhuman life, but it is vastly more complex. Most activity is primarily motivated in the first place by the instincts, represented in consciousness by the emotions and desires. The intellect functions mainly by seeking ways—most often very devious ways—to gratify the desires and to produce pleasant emotions. This means that the intellect functions mainly by seeking ways to satisfy the instincts. The instincts are like the engines of a ship while the intellect is like the rudder.

Very little activity, if any, is motivated primarily by the intellect, and intellectual motivation is secondary to instinctive motivation.

Thus your thoughts, your beliefs, your opinions, and your plans—these are all largely conditioned by the way you feel, by what you like and dislike, by what you want to do, and by what you want to avoid.

So you see that most of your thinking is emotional thinking, and very little of it is objective or dispassionate thinking.

In emotional thinking, facts and observations are falsified or wrongly coloured by desires and biases and prejudices. On the other hand, in dispassionate thinking—what little of it there is—the same facts are seen clearly and the same observations are unbiased and free from desires and prejudices, with no false colouring.

In emotional thinking, you tend to believe a thing because it pleases you to believe it or to reject an idea because it displeases you. In objective thinking you accept an idea if it is reasonable, whether it pleases you or repels you, and you reject an idea, however much you like it, if it fails to measure up to reason; or at least you accept it only tentatively and in an experimental spirit.

It is true that one of the main factors that gave primitive man his supremacy over his subhuman rivals and enemies was his intellect, his ability to use ideas as tools with which to reason, and to use simple words as shorthand symbols, so to speak, for complex ideas.

At the same time it is important to realise that, when opposed to emotions and desires, the intellect shows up as a relatively feeble and sometimes ineffective force. Emotions and desires are upthrusts into consciousness from the tremendous instinctive forces, and even the most powerful intellect may find itself powerless in the face of such opposition.

To control a desire by simple will-effort, then, is often very difficult, sometimes impossible, and at times perhaps harmful.

It is difficult when the desire is anything more than a superficial one. It is impossible when the desire serves as an outlet for a powerful instinct. And it may be harmful when the desire serves as an outlet for an instinct which has been denied other outlets. This is especially so when there is a guilt sense or a feeling of shame acting as a repressing force.

It is then that extensive and deep-reaching self-understanding becomes necessary in order to understand and control your desires; but you cannot deal adequately with strong desires unless you train yourself to handle the small desires that crop up from time to time in your everyday life.

While some forms of Buddhist mind-training can be best undertaken in a quiet and secluded environment, others can be woven into the fabric of everyday concerns and thus can be made an integral part of these concerns.

The practice of clear comprehension is one of the latter kind, for it has considerable scope for application in the busy workday routine.

While the term clear comprehension is fairly self-explanatory, it would be well to discuss, for a short time, what it means in terms of Buddhist mental culture. In the first application of the term, clear comprehension means the clear comprehension of the motive or purpose of an activity.

In other words, whatever you are doing, you should clearly comprehend why you are doing it. Instead of having a vague or fuzzy idea of what you expect to achieve by it you should try to get a clear-cut idea of its purpose, which is to say a clear-cut idea of the desires that prompt you to carry out the activity.

Secondly, having clarified your mind as to the motive of an activity, you should get an equally clear-cut idea of whether or not it is really suitable for its purpose. Thus the Buddha-doctrine shows the need not only for a clear comprehension of the motive of an action but also for a clear comprehension of the suitability of the action for its purpose.

Thirdly, there is the need for absorbing the element of clear comprehension into every activity. In other words, the whole of one's life, embracing every activity and every experience, is the domain of mindfulness, and thus, by extending the domain of mindfulness into every activity and every experience, the whole of life becomes the basis for mental culture.

Finally there is a form of mindfulness called the clear comprehension of non-delusion. The full implication of this clear comprehension of non-delusion involves the fundamental Buddhist teaching that the separate self is a delusion; thus the clear comprehension of non-delusion is a sharpened awareness that breaks through self-deceit and penetrates right through the illusion of selfhood to the reality of one's own being.

* * *

Let us now return to the first kind of clear comprehension, the clear comprehension of motive. When you apply this to the whole of your life, to your hopes and desires, and to all your planning and striving, it presupposes that you have some fundamental purpose in life. You may not have an overall motive in your life, however; you may be caught in the unthinking drift, and if this is so the first thing to do is to become aware of this fact, and if possible to define some kind of overall motive.

Assuming however, that you have such a motive or purpose in life, it's desirable, in the interest of efficient living, that you give thought to your activities as a whole to see if they line up with the focus of your life or whether they take you into all sorts of unprofitable side issues.

This is not to say, of course, that you cannot have side issues; these are unavoidable in ordinary life. There are many things you have to do, quite contrary to your central purpose, which left to yourself you would never even think of doing; yet because of your need to earn a living or your responsibilities and duties towards others, you must do those things.

Now, if you allow the need to do these things to build up resentment and annoyance, they certainly will take you aside from your central purpose, whereas if you use them as opportunities to develop patience and tolerance you then bring them into line with your central purpose.

Thus by the clear comprehension that every experience is the domain of mindfulness you can make the best use of activities that otherwise would be unprofitable.

While it may not be easy to define your ultimate objective in life, you can generally define the immediate purposes of your everyday activities. You know why you always catch a certain train every working morning; you know why you go to work;

and you know why you must earn money. You know also why you buy the necessities of life, and perhaps you know why you also buy some of the luxuries of life.

Do your luxuries really make life more enjoyable? Some of them do; others make life more difficult. These are the luxuries you must buy for their prestige value, because your neighbours have them, perhaps, or because in your social set you are expected to have them. But these luxuries may become burdensome necessities, and because they must be paid for and maintained, they cost more than they yield.

This is where the clear comprehension of non-delusion comes into the picture. To what extent are you motivated by self-assertion, for the desire for prestige and approval?

Perhaps having found the answers to these questions, and having found them to be not very flattering, you find you must continue to do things of no ultimate value. Because of family obligations, or responsibilities to others, or business necessities, you must continue to do things that cut across your fundamental purpose in life. You have applied the principle of clear comprehension of suitability and found certain activities quite unsuitable for their ultimate purpose; but such situations are often unavoidable.

But at least you are not deceiving yourself. It is when you unmindfully take on unnecessary activities—activities that cut across your central purpose—that you sink into the unthinking drift. The important thing, then, is freedom from the unthinking drift, and the key to this freedom is clear comprehension—the clear comprehension of the purpose of an activity and of its suitability, the clear comprehension that every activity is the domain of mindfulness, and the clear comprehension of that non-delusion.

This is the Buddhist practice of clear comprehension in its various forms.

Practical Work

Recognition of Motive

In the path to self-understanding you will find that it is of great importance to gain a clear comprehension of the true motives of your various activities. It is in the sphere of motivation that the human mind finds perhaps the greatest scope for self-deceit, and in consequence self-centred anxiety, resentment, and self-assertion are often at the base of activities which on the surface seem to have nobler and less self-centred motives.

Your practical work for this period then, consists of constant endeavour to become critically aware of the fundamental motives behind your everyday activities. An activity which appears to you yourself and to others to be generous, full of good will, and devoid of self-interest, may on self-examination prove to be motivated by self-centred anxiety, resentment, or self-assertion in some form; and the recognition of your true motives is an essential part of self-understanding.

The exercise of a constant endeavour to become critically aware of these motives is, as you can see, essential; but this constant endeavour may tend to become swamped by the pressure of everyday concerns. This is where the self-contract method of self-discipline will prove most useful. To apply it, every day throughout the period of a month you will look back at the day's main activities and critically examine your various motives. When you fail to do this, impose on yourself some small penalty.

ABOUT PARIYATTI

Pariyatti is dedicated to providing affordable access to authentic teachings of the Buddha about the Dhamma theory (*pariyatti*) and practice (*paṭipatti*) of Vipassana meditation. A 501(c)(3) nonprofit charitable organization since 2002, Pariyatti is sustained by contributions from individuals who appreciate and want to share the incalculable value of the Dhamma teachings. We invite you to visit www.pariyatti.org to learn about our programs, services, and ways to support publishing and other undertakings.

Pariyatti Publishing Imprints

Vipassana Research Publications (focus on Vipassana as taught by S.N. Goenka in the tradition of Sayagyi U Ba Khin)

BPS Pariyatti Editions (selected titles from the Buddhist Publication Society, copublished by Pariyatti)

MPA Pariyatti Editions (selected titles from the Myanmar Pitaka Association, copublished by Pariyatti)

Pariyatti Digital Editions (audio and video titles, including discourses)

Pariyatti Press (classic titles returned to print and inspirational writing by contemporary authors)

Pariyatti enriches the world by

- disseminating the words of the Buddha,
- providing sustenance for the seeker's journey,
- illuminating the meditator's path.

www.ingramcontent.com/pod-product-compliance
Lightning Source LLC
Chambersburg PA
CBHW020347170426
43200CB00005B/76
* 9 7 8 1 6 8 1 7 2 1 8 0 4 *

MANUEL

DU

CONDUCTEUR

TYPOGRAPHE

CET OUVRAGE

EST COMPOSÉ AVEC LES CARACTÈRES

DE LA FONDERIE TURLOT

ET IMPRIMÉ

SUR LE PAPIER DE LA MAISON LANOS

BESSÉ-SUR-BRAYE (SARTHE).

A DIXMUDE (Flandre)

Reproduction d'une aquarelle de Louis Titz

Photochromogravure 4 couleurs
des Etabl^ts Jean Malvaux
Bruxelles-Ouest

GRAVURE EN QUATRE COULEURS

(*Malvaux*, Bruxelles).

MANUEL

DU

CONDUCTEUR

TYPOGRAPHE

PAR

AUGUSTE RIETSCH

OFFICIER D'ACADÉMIE

PROTE DES MACHINES DE LA MAISON A. MAME ET FILS

4ᵉ ÉDITION, ENTIÈREMENT REFONDUE

AVEC UNE PRÉFACE DE M. ALEXANDRE REY

Vice-Président de l'Union des Maîtres Imprimeurs de France.

TOURS

MAISON ALFRED MAME ET FILS

PRÉFACE

Vous me demandez, mon cher Rietsch, de vous envoyer quelques lignes à mettre en tête de la quatrième édition de votre Manuel du Conducteur typographe. *Je suis vivement heureux de l'occasion qui s'offre à moi de dire tout le bien que je pense du livre et de l'auteur.*

J'ai pu apprécier déjà l'un et l'autre quand, succédant au vénéré maître Pitrat, je vous voyais à l'œuvre dans notre atelier de machines, mettant dans vos courts moments de loisir la dernière main à votre première édition. Le livre que vous offrez aujourd'hui au monde de l'imprimerie, et dont je viens de parcourir avec tant de plaisir les bonnes feuilles, a profité de toute l'expérience que vous avez acquise dans la direction qui vous a été confiée dans l'une des premières imprimeries de France.

Notre belle profession n'a plus de secrets pour vous, et vous rendez à vos confrères, plus jeunes et désireux de se perfectionner, un réel service en les initiant aux tours de main que d'autres gardent jalousement, et en les faisant profiter des connaissances qu'une longue pratique permet seule d'acquérir.

Votre livre a toute la saveur d'une leçon parlée, je le considère comme un véritable cours d'impression à la portée de tous.

Il faut avouer en toute sincérité que le besoin d'un tel manuel se faisait sentir dans notre pays, où l'on devient conducteur sans apprentissage préalable et, pour ainsi dire, au hasard des circonstances. Nous ignorons en France l'institution des élèves-conducteurs, *dont se trouvent bien nos voisins, et c'est à de véritables* attrape-science, *comme disent familièrement les compositeurs, que nous confions bien souvent des outils de plus en plus délicats et d'un prix élevé.*

Vous le dites, et nous ne saurions trop le répéter avec vous : La presse à bras est celle sur laquelle tout conducteur devrait commencer son apprentissage; le mécanisme en étant simple, il lui serait bien plus facile que sur la presse mécanique de se rendre compte de l'effet produit par telle ou telle cause. N'est-ce pas, du reste, ce qui existe en lithographie? ne serait-ce pas la logique même? La vérité, c'est que l'imprimeur a presque totalement disparu des ateliers de typographie, et que nous en sommes réduits généralement à confier la presse à bras, qui n'est plus qu'une presse à épreuves, à un compositeur de bonne volonté, quand ce n'est pas à un simple manœuvre.

Contre cela il faudra réagir tôt ou tard, et le plus tôt sera le mieux, en créant, comme pour toutes les autres professions, un apprentissage sérieux pour les conducteurs. Dans cet ordre d'idées, votre livre est venu à point, car il est précisément conçu en vue de cette instruction technique toute professionnelle devenue indispensable.

Vous débutez par des notions générales sur l'entretien des machines, laissant le mécanisme même, qui vous eût entraîné trop loin, aux ouvrages spéciaux, et souhaitant que tout conducteur soit doublé d'un mécanicien; cela encore devra faire partie de l'apprentissage que nous souhaitons. Mais vous n'avez garde de laisser dans l'ombre le moindre détail de la mise sous presse : calage des formes, taquage, serrage et lavage. Ces diverses opérations sont, il est vrai, le b a ba *du métier; mais combien peu les pratiquent avec le soin nécessaire !*

L'entretien des rouleaux et la préparation du papier vous fournissent deux autres chapitres, qui seront lus avec fruit par tous les conducteurs qui tiennent à faire bien.

L'habillage des presses suivant la nature du travail, la mise en train, le registre, le réglage des encriers, vous étudiez tous ces points si importants avec le souci de l'homme de métier qui ne laisse rien à l'imprévu, et qui a tout autant le souci de ménager le matériel qui lui est confié, que de tirer de son outil le meilleur parti possible. Après avoir passé en revue les diverses précautions à prendre pour les travaux courants sur mobile ou sur clichés, vous arrivez à l'impression des gravures.

C'est une des parties les plus importantes et non des moins intéressantes de votre ouvrage : j'ai lu avec le plus grand intérêt vos conseils sur les découpages des gravures sur bois et des similis en particulier, ce procédé si répandu maintenant et dont peu de conducteurs de province se tirent honorablement. Qu'ils méditent vos conseils, et ils auront bien vite raison des réelles difficultés qu'il présente, pour ceux surtout qui ne disposent pas de machines à encrage cylindrique.

Vous avez consacré à l'impression des couleurs toute la seconde partie de votre ouvrage, et vous avez eu grandement raison. Le goût du public, en effet, devient plus exigeant à mesure que les procédés d'exécution se perfectionnent, et l'on peut dire que depuis moins de vingt ans toute une rénovation s'est faite sur ce point dans notre profession.

Après une étude détaillée sur l'impression des couleurs en général, sur les soins qu'elle exige dans ses moindres détails, vous avez traité magistralement de la nature même et de l'emploi des couleurs, et vous nous donnez sur leur contraste un chapitre particulièrement intéressant au point de vue artistique. Cette dernière partie s'adresse autant et plus au maître imprimeur qu'au conducteur : l'un et l'autre y trouveront, en tout cas, de précieux enseignements.

Le caractère de votre livre, mon cher Rietsch, est d'être à la fois simple et pratique : ce sont ces deux qualités qui le feront surtout apprécier. Je vous félicite, pour ma part, d'avoir produit une œuvre aussi éminemment utile, et je souhaite vivement qu'elle obtienne tout le succès qu'elle mérite.

A. REY.

FIG. 1. — Moderne.
Machine en blanc à grande vitesse (Marinoni).

AVANT-PROPOS

Il ne manque certes pas en France d'ouvrages, et d'ouvrages excellents, concernant l'art typographique; et le lecteur curieux de s'instruire peut trouver là, en plus des éléments mêmes du métier, mille renseignements précieux concernant l'invention et les inventeurs de l'imprimerie, les perfectionnements dans la suite des temps, les méthodes anciennes et modernes, des notions de mécanique, de physique, de chimie, des critiques, des considérations économiques, voire même philosophiques, en somme beaucoup de choses intéressantes et instructives parmi quelques-unes vraiment utiles aux gens du métier. Aussi semble-t-il que le nom de Manuel qu'on lit parfois à la première page de ces ouvrages ne s'y applique peut-être pas très régulièrement.

Un manuel doit avant tout être clair, court et pratique. Autrement, le jeune conducteur typographe désireux de se perfectionner, en quête d'un bon guide, risque fort de se perdre au milieu de ces mille considérations dont il n'a que faire et qui finissent par le rebuter. Ajoutez à cela que le prix de ces ouvrages, naturellement en rapport avec leur importance, doit effrayer souvent des bourses trop modestes, et avouez que notre jeune conducteur se trouvera bien embarrassé. Ce sont ces réflexions, longuement mûries, qui me déterminèrent, en 1891, à publier la première édition de mon « Manuel du Conducteur typographe ». C'était un essai sans prétention. De simples notes recueillies au jour le jour, fruits d'une observation personnelle; des réflexions faites par des confrères ou puisées dans des études de revues techniques : tels furent les matériaux de mon modeste ouvrage.

Cependant le succès, et un succès inespéré, vint couronner mes efforts et me prouver que j'avais été compris, m'encourageant à continuer. Successivement deux autres éditions, augmentées et mises à jour, parurent et reçurent le même bienveillant accueil. Aujourd'hui c'est la quatrième édition que je présente à mes lecteurs.

Je me suis efforcé de suivre l'art typographique dans ses transformations et ses progrès de tous les instants, afin d'en donner une idée aussi exacte que possible. Les méthodes anciennes sont brièvement indiquées, les nouvelles plus longuement exposées, faisant ressortir les avantages, parfois les inconvénients. Chaque genre de travail exige une manière différente pour faire plus vite, ou mieux, ou plus économiquement, souvent le tout à la fois. Les divers perfectionnements, les inventions nouvelles, tout ce qui a déjà véritablement fait ses preuves trouve sa place, plus ou moins longuement exposé, afin que le conducteur n'ignore rien de ce qu'il doit savoir, rien de ce qui puisse lui servir.

J'ai tenu néanmoins à ne pas augmenter sensiblement le volume de mon ouvrage, afin qu'il restât bien un véritable Manuel, le *vade mecum* de tout jeune conducteur sérieux, désireux de se perfectionner.

En terminant, cher lecteur, je vous redirai comme lors de la première édition :

Mon « Manuel du Conducteur typographe » n'a pas la prétention d'être un ouvrage complet de l'art d'imprimer : c'est un essai d'enseignement sommaire dans lequel je m'efforcerai d'introduire, le plus clairement possible, et en peu de mots, les notions principales d'impression typographique, ce que tout conducteur doit connaître. En cherchant à pouvoir être compris aussi bien de l'ouvrier que de l'apprenti, je crois que j'aurai mené à bien ma tâche et que je recevrai l'approbation d'un grand nombre de mes collègues.

A. Rietsch.

TABLE DES MATIÈRES

Préface v
Avant-propos ix

PREMIÈRE PARTIE

DE L'IMPRESSION EN GÉNÉRAL

I

PRÉLIMINAIRES

I. — Étude du mécanisme 2
II. — Entretien des machines 3
III. — Calage des formes 3
IV. — Taquage 4
V. — Serrage 5
VI. — Lavage des formes 10

II

ROULEAUX

I. — Composition des rouleaux 15
II. — Fabrication des rouleaux 17
Fonte neuve de matière préparée 17
Refonte de vieux rouleaux 17
Fabrication de la pâte 18
Coulage des rouleaux 18
Démoulage 19
III. — Qualités des rouleaux 20
IV. — Lavage des rouleaux 23
Lavage à la potasse 23
Lavage à l'essence 24
Machine à laver les rouleaux. *La Kérosine* 25

III

ENCRES

I. — Fabrication 26
II. — Conservation 28
III. — Emploi 29

IV

PRÉPARATION DU PAPIER

I. — Trempage. 31
Trempage à la main. 31
— au balai. 33
— mécanique 33
II. — Glaçage 37

V

PRESSE A BRAS

I. — Mise sous presse. — Supports. — La première opération. 42
II. — Étoffage du tympan. 44
III. — Frisquette 46
IV. — Rouleaux. 47
V. — Pointures 48
VI. — Mise en train 50
Clichés 53
Reports. 53

VI

PRESSES MÉCANIQUES A CYLINDRES

I. — Habillage des cylindres. 55
Travaux courants. Labeurs 56
Clichés blancs. 58
Galvanos 58
— gravures. 59
Photogravures. 59
Lavage et entretien des blanchets. 59
Mérinos et cuir-laine 60
Paraffine 60
II. — Supports. 61
III. — Registre. 63
IV. — Pointures. 64
V. — Mise en train. 65
VI. — Réglage des encriers 66
Margeur automatique 67

VII

MACHINES A PÉDALE

I. — Minerves. 69
Habillage. 70
Marge. 70
Nouveaux systèmes. 73
Vitesse 73
II. — Nouvelles machines dites à platine 73
III. — L'estampage. 75
IV. — Le numérotage 76

VIII

IMPRESSION DES GRAVURES

I. — Vérification des clichés 82
II. — Découpages 85
Découpage au couteau. 85
Gravure sur bois et galvano de gravure sur bois. . 87
Gravure au trait ou dessin à la plume. 94
Photogravure et similigravure. 94
Découpage au pinceau. 97
Mise en train mécanique S. A. D. A. G. 99
Mise en train « Korekta ». 99
II. — Tirage. 99
Habillage. 99
Papier. 100
Rouleaux 100
Encrage. 100

DEUXIÈME PARTIE

DE L'IMPRESSION EN COULEURS

I

PRÉLIMINAIRES

CONDITIONS SPÉCIALES A L'IMPRESSION EN COULEURS

I. — Local. 104
II. — Machines. 105
III. — Rouleaux. 106
IV. — Formes. 107
V. — Pointures. 108
Pointures fines. 109
Grosses pointures. 110
Pointure automatique Taesch 111
VI. — Encres 112
VII. — Papier 113

II

ÉTUDE DES COULEURS

I. — Notions sur la lumière 115
II. — Couleurs complémentaires 117
III. — Contraste des couleurs 118
Contraste successif des couleurs. 118
Contraste simultané des couleurs 118
IV. — Applications. 119

III

LES ENCRES DE COULEUR

I. — Encres simples. 125
II. — Encres composées. 128

IV

ENCRES COMMUNICATIVES. — ENCRES A DOUBLE TEINTE

I. — Encres communicatives 131
II. — Encres à double teinte. 133

V

CONSEILS PRATIQUES POUR LES TIRAGES EN COULEURS

VI

DU BRONZAGE

I. Bronzage aux poudres. 136
II. — Bronze direct. 138

VII

DES FONDS

I. — Diverses espèces de fonds. 140
II. — Tirage des fonds. 144

VIII

CONSEILS PRATIQUES POUR L'EMPLOI DES ENCRES DE COULEUR

I. — Le portrait. 146
II. — Zoologie. 149
III. — Botanique. 151
IV. — Paysages 158

IX

SÉCHAGE, SATINAGE DU PAPIER

X

PROCÉDÉ « DES TROIS COULEURS »

MANUEL

DU

CONDUCTEUR TYPOGRAPHE

PREMIÈRE PARTIE

DE L'IMPRESSION EN GÉNÉRAL

I

PRÉLIMINAIRES

Nous ne saurions débuter dans cette étude sur l'impression sans dire quelques mots touchant les machines typographiques. Sans entrer dans tous les détails de construction et de fonctionnement, qui trouveraient leur place dans un ouvrage plus complet et plus savant, nous nous bornerons à quelques considérations en rapport avec l'allure modeste de notre Manuel et dont la connaissance est indispensable à tout conducteur sérieux.

I. — ÉTUDE DU MÉCANISME

L'ouvrier imprimeur, désireux de tirer un bon parti de la machine à lui confiée, devra s'efforcer d'acquérir quelques notions sommaires de mécanique pour se bien rendre compte du fonctionnement général, du mouvement des engrenages, excentriques, ressorts, etc.

Cette connaissance lui sera fort utile dans les cas si fréquents de dérangements ou d'usure de pièces. Souvent il pourra se rendre compte d'un accident léger et y remédier lui-même. Dans les cas plus graves il sera parfois plus à même d'indiquer les réparations qu'un mécanicien non spécialiste.

Le conducteur doit vérifier de temps en temps l'assemblage de la machine, pour s'assurer qu'aucune pièce ne s'est déplacée ou n'a pris du jeu. Il arrive en effet, à la longue, résultat du simple fonctionnement, que les boulons se desserrent ou que les coussinets s'échauffent faute d'huile ou par suite d'un serrage excessif : autant de causes d'accidents qu'on peut éviter en y apportant aussitôt remède. Lorsqu'on entend rouler une machine avec un bruit anormal, il faut l'arrêter aussitôt et chercher la cause.

C'est surtout pour les imprimeries installées dans les étages que cette vérification est importante. Les trépidations des planchers sont une cause permanente de dislocation des machines et, par suite, de mauvais fonctionnement.

II. — ENTRETIEN DES MACHINES

L'entretien des machines comprend deux choses : le nettoyage et le graissage, conditions également indispensables à leur bon fonctionnement.

Généralement on profite, pour nettoyer les machines, d'un arrêt entre deux tirages. Toutes les pièces sont débarrassées de l'encrassement produit par la poussière, le papier, l'huile, etc. S'il en est besoin, on emploie du pétrole. Le marbre surtout doit être attentivement essuyé après chaque tirage.

Les machines doivent être soigneusement graissées tous les jours, et même deux fois par jour. Avant la mise en marche, tous les frottements sont huilés amplement, sans excès cependant, avec de l'huile spéciale de bonne qualité.

Faute de ces soins, une machine ne tarde pas à s'user rapidement et à prendre du jeu. Parfois il s'ensuit même des accidents plus graves, comme la rupture de certaines pièces. Dans tous les cas, c'est une cause de perte de force motrice et de mauvais fonctionnement.

III. — CALAGE DES FORMES

La forme est montée sur le marbre et placée avec précaution, pour éviter de mettre en pâte et de fausser les châssis.

Avant de caler, l'imprimeur relève la forme pour s'assurer qu'il n'est pas tombé de caractère et qu'il ne se trouve au dos ni lettre, ni poussière, ni débris de papier. Au besoin, il donne un coup de brosse.

Cette précaution prise, il pourra caler, en ayant soin de le faire modérément, pour ne pas faire lever le châssis.

Il faut, autant que possible, caler les formes au milieu du marbre, au centre de pression, à moins d'en être empêché par la marge du papier.

Dans les presses mécaniques, la prise des pinces sera observée avec soin, surtout s'il y a des pages ou des gravures débordantes, afin d'éviter l'écrasement; cela est chose facile, des lignes de repère étant généralement tracées sur les marbres.

IV. — TAQUAGE

On desserre la forme, qui, pour la sûreté de sa manipulation, a été serrée à l'excès. Il semble inutile de recommander, pour le serrage aux coins, de toujours se servir d'un décognoir en bois ou en fer; on risquerait autrement de détériorer le marbre et les châssis par des coups de marteau.

Pour taquer, on promène le taquoir sur les pages en évitant de le soulever après chaque coup de marteau. De cette façon, si, par hasard, il se trouve une lettre, un filet, qui piquent, maintenus en l'air par quelque défaut de composition, le taquoir est accroché; l'attention de l'imprimeur étant éveillée, il peut remédier au défaut avant qu'il y ait eu écrasement. Si la forme sonne le creux, c'est que les pages sont en l'air; il faut desserrer pour en chercher la cause : serrage trop fort ou garniture faussée.

Beaucoup de conducteurs ont l'habitude, pour le petit caractère, les légendes de gravure, les notes des bas de pages, de se servir d'un taquoir minuscule, très souvent en bois dur, par exemple un coin de serrage. Nous ne saurions trop recommander l'attention qu'il faut avoir en se servant de cet instrument; il suffit d'un coup de marteau porté trop fort ou à faux pour détériorer l'œil de ces petits caractères; il serait bien préférable de ne pas s'en servir du tout, ou tout au moins de se servir de bois tendre.

Même pour le grand taquoir, le bois dur ne devrait pas être employé. Sur un texte compact son effet est peu sensible; mais sur les lignes isolées, les filets de plomb maigres, il est bien apparent et se traduit par des dégâts tels que : filets écrasés, lettres éraflées, accents brisés, etc. Le taquoir ordinaire, en bois blanc doublé de bois dur du côté frappé par le marteau, doit être préféré. On peut aussi garnir le dessus du taquoir d'un vieux morceau de cuir pour amortir les coups de marteau et préserver le bois de l'écaillement.

V. — SERRAGE

Le serrage d'une forme demande beaucoup d'attention. En effet, sans parler des lignes couchées, cintrées, etc., si le serrage est mauvais, l'imprimeur s'expose à ne plus voir tomber son registre et sa mise en train, après avoir serré et desserré deux ou trois fois.

Voici la meilleure façon de procéder pour un serrage aux coins de bois. Après s'être assuré qu'il n'y a pas de lettres tombées sur le bord des pages, de lettres qui chevauchent, ni de garnitures qui butent, on fait avec le marteau une légère pression sur les biseaux du bas, puis sur ceux des côtés, de façon à remettre d'aplomb la composition. Si l'on s'aperçoit que les pages se soulèvent, *font ventre,* c'est qu'elles sont couchées; il faudra les redresser parfaitement avant de procéder au serrage.

On commence alors à mettre le premier coin du biseau du pied des pages, puis le premier de côté, le deuxième du bas, le deuxième de côté, et ainsi de suite alternativement; puis on chasse légèrement les coins au marteau en commençant toujours par le pied, dont le serrage doit être fait plus fortement; on baisse les coins, on taque et on finit de serrer de la même façon, en chassant les coins avec le décognoir. Un dernier et léger coup de taquoir sert à vérifier si le serrage n'est pas trop fort, et si le texte ou les gravures ne sont pas soulevés.

Nous recommandons de serrer toujours un peu plus fortement en pied que sur les côtés, parce que sur ces derniers il se produit très peu d'élasticité, le serrage portant de suite sur les interlignes et les lingots dans le sens de leur longueur. Si, au contraire, on serrait trop fortement sur les côtés sans serrer en pied, on ferait cintrer les interlignes et le serrage serait défectueux.

Lorsqu'une page renfermant une gravure fait ventre au serrage, c'est généralement que le bois de montage de cette dernière n'est pas d'équerre. Si l'on a un rabot à dresser sous la main, on met la face défectueuse d'aplomb, en ayant soin naturellement de remplacer dans le parangonnage de la gravure l'épaisseur de bois enlevée. A défaut de rabot, on colle sur la partie faible, qui est dans ce cas le pied du bois, une bande de papier qui rétablit l'équerrage.

Avec les serrages mécaniques : biseaux et coins en fer, coins à noix, doubles coins à clefs, etc., on doit procéder dans le même ordre, progressivement et avec encore plus d'attention ; un mauvais serrage par ces systèmes, plus durs que celui en bois, fausserait les garnitures. C'est pour cette raison que, lorsqu'on emploie des serrages de petite dimension, il faut toujours interposer, entre le biseau ou coin métallique et la garniture, une réglette de bois de douze à dix-huit points, si c'est possible ; de cette manière, si le serrage est fait un peu fortement, c'est le bois qui cède et non la garniture.

Le serrage aux noix est très défectueux lorsqu'on fait usage d'un châssis dont les montants ne sont pas d'équerre : si le fer se trouve plus fort en pied qu'en tête, en serrant la noix, on fait lever la matière. Dans ce cas, il faut envoyer le châssis au serrurier ou serrer aux coins de bois, avec lesquels ce défaut n'a pas d'inconvénients. C'est du reste le système de serrage que nous préférons à tout autre.

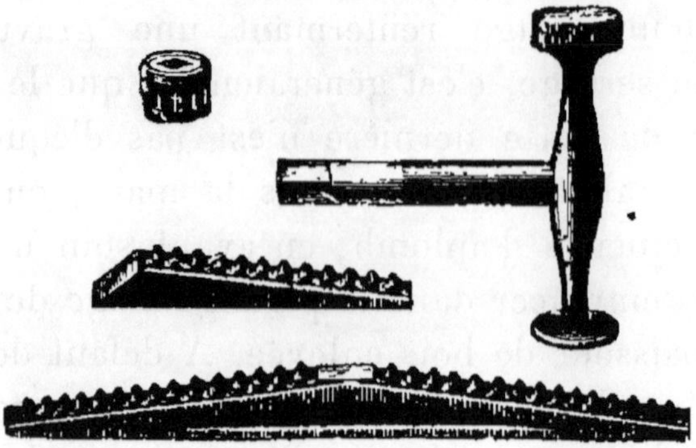

Fig. 2. — Serrage Marinoni à noix.

Avant de rouler, il faut vérifier si les coins ou noix tiennent bien : un coin ou une noix sortant de

Fig. 3. — Serrage Caslon.

la forme pourrait faire des dégâts, soit à la forme, soit à la machine. Cet accident n'arrive que trop

Fig. 4. Serrage Hempels (*Caslon*).

fréquemment, surtout avec les coins ou noix en fer.

Nous indiquerons pour mémoire les serrages Mari-

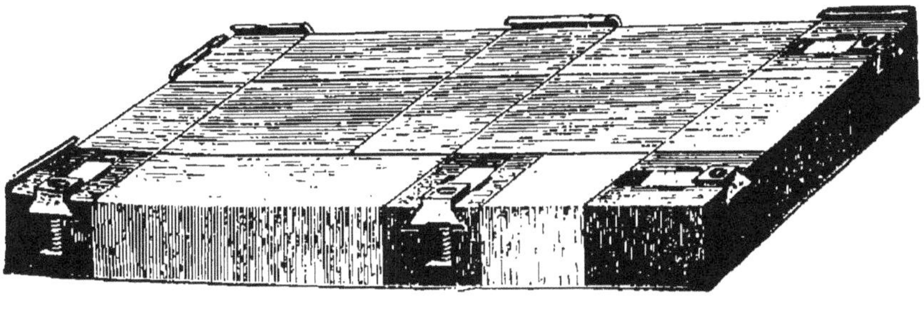

Fig. 5. — Bloc à griffes mobiles (*Caslon*).

noni (fig. 2), Caslon (fig. 3), Hempels (fig. 4), le serrage à expansion, le « Nouveau serrage américain » pour le serrage des formes sur les marbres des presses, et le marbre-bloc en fonte pour le tirage des galvanos stéréotypes et stéréo-nickel (fig. 5).

VI. — LAVAGE DES FORMES

Pour le lavage de la forme sous presse, on emploie ordinairement l'essence de pétrole ou celle de térébenthine, qui dissolvent bien l'encre et s'évaporent rapidement. Lorsque la forme peut être lavée quelque temps avant la mise sous presse, on peut aussi employer une dissolution de potasse, ce qui est plus économique. L'imprimeur ne devra mettre sur la brosse que peu de liquide à la fois et brosser en rond sur chaque page ; en opérant dans le sens des lignes, les lettres minces des bords et les ponctuations seraient brisées par le frottement. Il est complètement inutile d'inonder la forme d'essence ; ce n'est qu'un gaspillage, ce liquide coûtant assez cher, et une perte de temps, le séchage étant plus long. En effet, si l'essence coule entre les lettres, on aura beau sécher l'œil, l'impression fera remonter le liquide, qui tachera le papier et, de plus, empêchera l'encre de se fixer sur le caractère.

On ne doit se servir de la petite brosse à poils courts, appelée *chien* ou brosse de *verre*, que lorsque le caractère est très encrassé et ne peut se nettoyer avec la brosse à soies longues.

Pour sécher la forme après le lavage, on se sert d'une éponge, d'un chiffon ou d'étoupe que l'on roule dessus ; il faut éviter de frapper ou de frotter, surtout les formes qui renferment du petit caractère : on pourrait accrocher ou briser les lettres isolées. Il faut aussi prendre garde que le chiffon

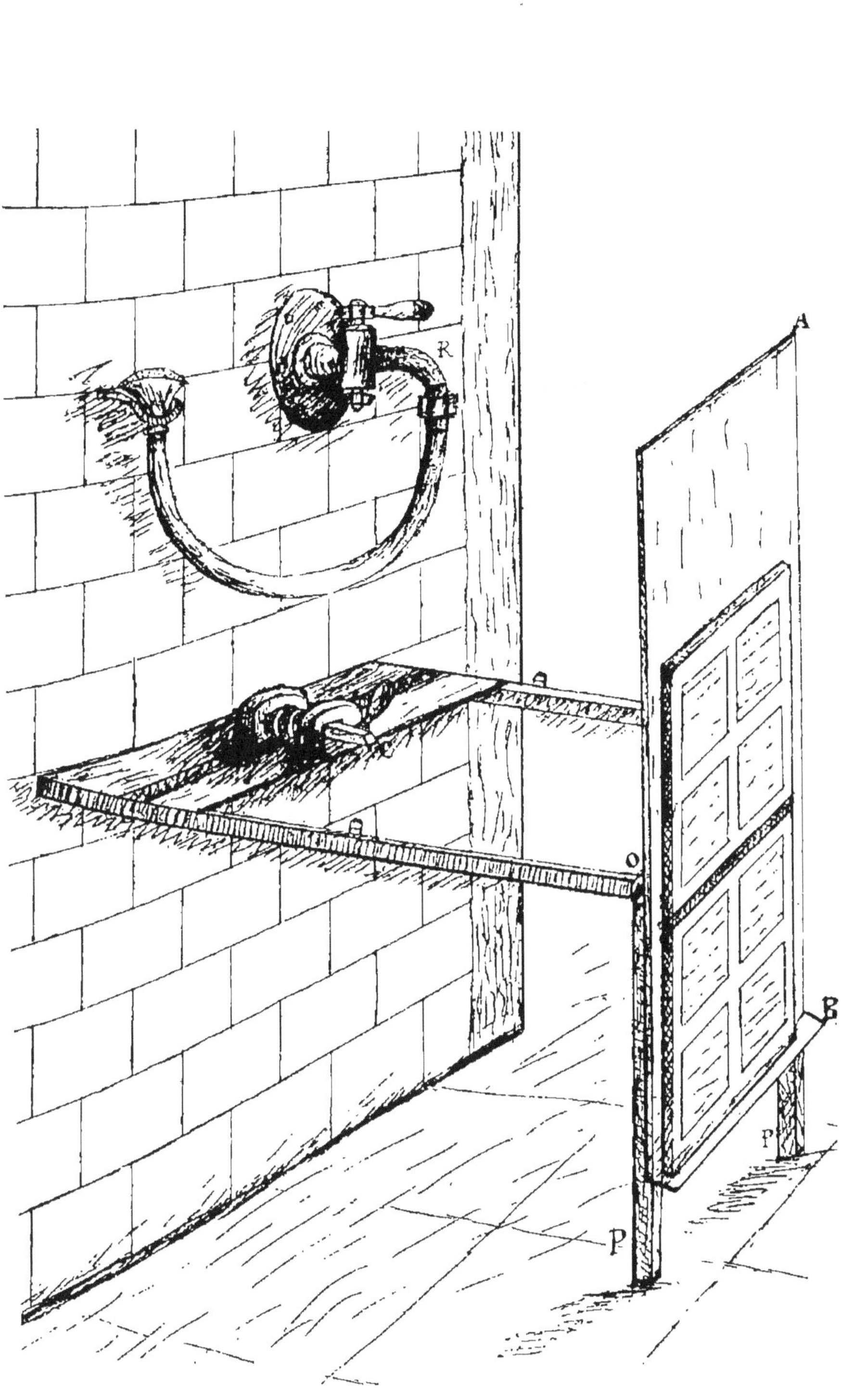

Fig. 6. — Position verticale de l'évier contenant une forme.
(Avant le lavage.)

employé ne renferme aucun bouton ou crochet qui érailleraient l'œil du caractère.

On lave les formes toutes les fois qu'il y a dans le tirage une interruption assez longue qui permettrait à l'encre de sécher sur le caractère ; elle devient alors très difficile à enlever et réclame un brossage énergique, au détriment du caractère et des gravures.

Quant le tirage est terminé, on enlève les formes de la presse et on procède à un lavage plus sérieux. On se sert généralement d'une dissolution de potasse ; la *lessive-typo* de la maison Lorilleux (1 kilog. dans 30 litres d'eau), bien que d'un prix peu élevé, donne de bons résultats. Pour obtenir un bon lavage, la forme est placée sur un évier en pierre ou en fonte, et on brosse avec la dissolution de potasse chaude, qui nettoie mieux et plus économiquement que froide. On rince ensuite, toujours à l'eau chaude si c'est possible.

Cette opération doit être faite avec grand soin, surtout si la forme a été tirée avec de la couleur ou s'il a été fait de nombreux lavages à l'essence. Le conducteur s'attirera ainsi la reconnaissance de son confrère le compositeur, qui pourra faire sa distribution sans se voir obligé de prendre des tenailles pour décoller les lettres.

Voici, pour le lavage des formes, une disposition (fig. 6) très commode, en même temps que peu encombrante.

Elle consiste en un plateau métallique AB formant évier ; c'est un cadre de fer avec fond en tôle pouvant contenir les plus grands châssis et pivotant en son milieu O sur un pied P. Ce plateau peut s'abattre horizontalement sur les supports D, où il est maintenu par un loqueteau C.

La forme, apportée près du porte-forme, est posée

FIG. 7. — Position horizontale de l'évier pour le lavage et le rinçage.

sur le rebord de l'évier ; on fait basculer, le loqueteau s'ouvre par la pression de l'évier, puis, se refermant après le passage de la forme, la maintient pendant le lavage. Après avoir brossé à la potasse, on procède au rinçage (fig. 7), à l'aide d'un tuyau de caoutchouc muni d'une pomme d'arrosoir et relié à une prise d'eau. Le lavage terminé, on repousse le loqueteau et on replace l'évier verticalement pour enlever la forme.

L'ouvrier préposé au lavage doit faire grande attention aux gravures que peut contenir la forme. Les gravures sur zinc seront soigneusement essuyées, puis graissées, afin d'empêcher l'oxydation. Les gravures sur bois ne doivent pas être lavées à l'eau chaude, qui les ferait disjoindre en plusieurs pièces et détériorerait les tringles. On les retire avant le lavage.

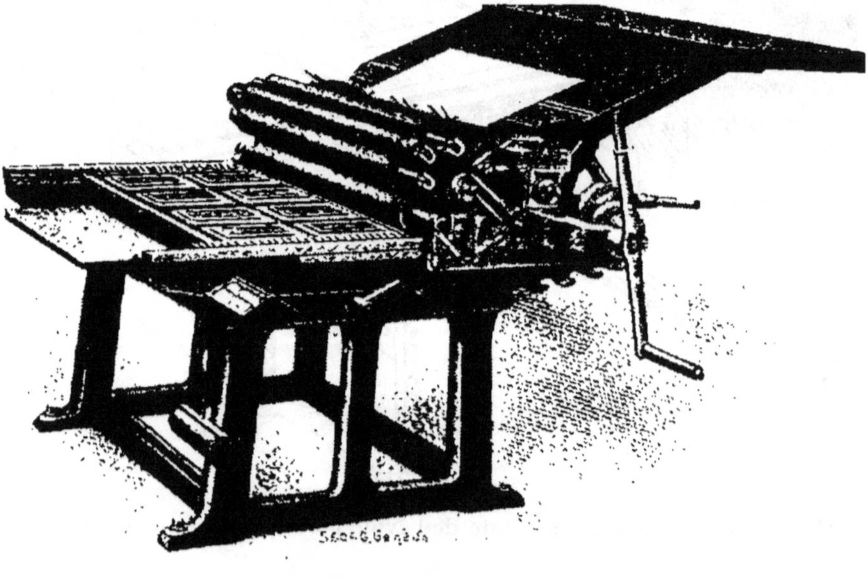

FIG. 8. — Presse à épreuves " Éclair " (*Caston*).

II

ROULEAUX

Le choix des rouleaux est d'une très grande importance en imprimerie : c'est l'une des principales conditions d'une bonne impression. Aussi n'est-ce pas sans raison que les fabricants rivalisent d'efforts dans le but d'améliorer leurs produits. La pâte idéale serait d'une consistance bien élastique, d'un entretien facile, ne diminuant pas de diamètre à l'usage et subissant le moins possible les variations de température.

I. — COMPOSITION DES ROULEAUX

Toutes les pâtes à rouleaux sont à base de gélatine blonde (colle de nerf) dissoute dans l'eau ; comme la gélatine seule abandonnerait trop vite son eau de fusion, et par conséquent durcirait, on l'additionne d'une certaine quantité de mélasse ou de glycérine, qui lui conserve plus longtemps son élasticité et son volume.

L'emploi de la mélasse commence à être abandonné; on lui préfère la glycérine et la glucose, comme donnant de meilleurs résultats.

Voici une formule qui permettra de se faire une idée de la quantité proportionnelle des éléments qui peuvent entrer dans la composition de la pâte à rouleaux :

Colle forte	2k,800
Glycérine.	1 ,300
Glucose	0 ,300
Colle de poisson	0 ,600

On divise ordinairement les pâtes à rouleaux en trois qualités principales : la pâte forte, la moyenne et la faible. On se sert des unes ou des autres suivant les travaux et les circonstances.

Parmi les différents fournisseurs de pâtes à rouleaux, citons : Lorilleux, Lefranc, Laflèche et fils, Heuer; nous n'en préconiserons aucun aux dépens des autres : leurs produits sont de première qualité. Nous ferons remarquer à ce sujet que ce n'est pas seulement la composition de la pâte qui fait les bons rouleaux, il faut tenir compte aussi du soin apporté à la fusion de la matière et à la conservation des rouleaux dans un local convenable.

II. — FABRICATION DES ROULEAUX

En général, les imprimeurs aiment mieux faire fondre leurs rouleaux chez les fournisseurs que s'exposer aux ennuis d'une fabrication souvent plus onéreuse dans leurs ateliers. Il s'agit, bien entendu, des imprimeurs de villes importantes, qui ont des industriels sous la main. Vu la pratique constante qu'ils en ont, ces spécialistes arrivent à une fabrication très soignée. La fonte se fait d'habitude à l'abonnement. A mesure que les rouleaux sont hors d'usage, l'imprimeur les envoie au fondeur. De cette manière, celui-ci a tout intérêt à ce que les rouleaux soient bien confectionnés et par là même d'un long usage.

Dans les petites localités, les imprimeurs ont tout au moins la ressource de faire venir leur pâte en pains et toute préparée.

Fonte neuve de matière préparée. — On commence par déchiqueter les pains en morceaux de la grosseur d'une noix. Ces morceaux sont mis au bain-marie sans addition d'eau ; pendant la fusion, il faut, de temps en temps, remuer la pâte avec une spatule jusqu'à ce qu'elle soit complètement fluide.

Refonte de vieux rouleaux. — Il faut d'abord les bien laver, puis, à l'aide d'un racloir, enlever toute la partie desséchée, la peau, qui ne se liquéfierait pas. On dépouille ensuite les rouleaux de leur matière, que l'on réduit en petits morceaux. Si elle est trop desséchée, on peut la faire tremper quelque temps dans l'eau froide. Il est bon d'ajouter de la pâte neuve, à raison de quinze à vingt pour cent.

Quand, après une ou deux heures de fusion, il reste des parties insolubles, il faut, avant la coulée, passer au tamis pour enlever les grumeaux.

Fabrication de la pâte. — Pour fabriquer la pâte de toutes pièces, on fait d'abord gonfler la gélatine dans l'eau froide pendant quelques heures, après quoi on la fait fondre. On ajoute alors les autres substances qui doivent entrer dans sa composition.

Coulage des rouleaux. — Quel que soit le genre de pâte employé, la coulée des rouleaux demande le plus grand soin. Les moules sont tantôt d'une seule pièce, tantôt de deux. Avec les premiers, on évite les bavures longitudinales, mais le démoulage est plus difficile. Les mandrins sont en fer, ou recouverts d'un manchon de bois. Pour augmenter l'adhérence de la matière, les premiers sont entourés d'une ficelle, les autres sont creusés d'une rainure hélicoïdale.

La maison Ch. Lorilleux possède une peinture très adhésive, l'*Adhérente*, qui supprime l'emploi de la ficelle autour des mandrins et bouche les trous imperceptibles qui peuvent se rencontrer et qui occasionnent des soufflures. Il n'est cependant pas inutile de faire une bague en ficelle à l'extrémité des grands mandrins, pour empêcher le glissement de la matière lors d'un démoulage trop hâtif.

La fonte étant prête pour le coulage, on nettoie les moules très soigneusement, puis on les graisse à l'aide d'un chiffon ou d'une étoupe, en ayant soin de ne laisser sur les parois aucun débris de chiffon ou amas d'huile de pied de mouton. C'est surtout dans le graissage des moules d'une seule pièce qu'il faut apporter tous ses soins. Si la pâte se fixait au moule, la fonte serait à refaire, le rouleau ne pouvant sortir sans se déchirer ou se décoller de son mandrin.

Pour faciliter la coulée et obtenir de meilleurs résultats, on chauffe légèrement le moule, soit au moyen d'un bec de gaz, soit de toute autre manière.

Alors, le mandrin étant bien symétriquement placé dans le moule et muni de l'étoile, on procède au coulage en versant sans arrêt et sans secousse la matière au sommet de la fusée.

Démoulage. — Le démoulage du rouleau peut se faire un jour ou deux après la coulée. Si la surface présente quelques défectuosités : crevasses, soufflures ou grumeaux, il ne faut pas hésiter à remettre à la fonte.

Le rouleau est ensuite débarrassé de ses extrémités excédentes et placé dans un endroit sec pendant deux ou trois jours. On peut ensuite le dégraisser avec une éponge imbibée d'eau et le mettre en service. On conservera les rouleaux en les enduisant très légèrement de suif dissous dans l'essence de pétrole.

L'emploi pour la fonte des rouleaux de nouveaux appareils d'origine américaine appelés *mitrailleuses* permet, par la précision du fonctionnement, d'assurer la qualité irréprochable des rouleaux. Le centrage est automatique, d'où parfait.

La coulée se fait par le bas, ce qui supprime toute soufflure, et le démoulage se produit de lui-même par le seul poids de la matière refroidie, étant donnée la perfection de l'alésage des moules. Ceux-ci sont tour à tour chauffés et refroidis par des courants d'eau à la température convenable.

III. — QUALITÉS DES ROULEAUX

Un rouleau, pour faire un bon usage, doit être parfaitement rond, sans soufflures ni piqûres, et bien élastique ; les bavures provenant des jointures du moule seront donc enlevées avec grand soin. En effet, au tirage, et surtout dans la similigravure, cette sorte de couture apparaîtrait sous forme de taches d'un aspect très désagréable.

C'est pour éviter cet inconvénient qu'on se sert quelquefois des moules d'une seule pièce dont nous avons parlé plus haut : la fabrication est plus difficile, mais les résultats sont bien meilleurs.

C'est au toucher que le conducteur reconnaît la qualité de ses rouleaux : l'élasticité et le degré de mordant, ou *amour*, qu'ils possèdent.

Pour qu'un rouleau touche bien toutes les parties d'une forme de composition ou de gravures, il faut qu'il soit suffisamment élastique. Pour que l'encrage donne une impression bien nette et brillante, le rouleau doit posséder un certain degré d'amour.

On reconnaît l'amour, ou mordant d'un rouleau, à la propriété qu'il a d'adhérer légèrement aux doigts.

Pour les tirages en noir, le rouleau doit avoir peu de mordant. On reconnaît qu'il possède la consistance voulue, si la matière, après une pression de l'ongle, reprend sa forme première.

Pour le tirage des gravures, on le tiendra un peu plus frais et avec beaucoup de mordant.

L'impression à l'encre rouge, au contraire, demande des rouleaux secs et presque sans mordant; si le rouleau est trop frais, l'encre ne prend que par plaques et ne se distribue pas bien.

Pour les teintes légères de fonds, qui sont faites d'un peu d'encre avec beaucoup de vernis, il faut des rouleaux très frais; pour les couleurs foncées, on se sert des mêmes que pour le noir.

L'encre communicative demande des rouleaux secs; si l'encre ne se distribue pas bien, on peut passer une légère couche de glycérine.

En règle générale, lorsque la forme prend mal l'encre, c'est que les rouleaux sont trop frais; il faut les remplacer. Si ce défaut est léger, un séjour dans un lieu sec et aéré peut les remettre en état; s'il est trop accentué, il n'y a qu'à les refondre.

Si l'impression est baveuse, sans netteté, c'est que les rouleaux sont trop secs, trop durs. On peut essayer de remédier à ce défaut en les humectant avec une éponge. Si cela ne suffit pas, il faut les remplacer et les laisser séjourner quelque temps dans un lieu humide, ou bien encore passer une ou deux fois un chiffon imbibé de glycérine et les laisser reposer quelque temps. Si le défaut est par trop prononcé, il vaut mieux refondre les rouleaux.

En été, lorsque l'air est très sec, on est souvent obligé de fermer les fenêtres des ateliers pour supprimer les courants d'air qui dessèchent très vite les rouleaux.

Il ne faut pas, en hiver, placer les poêles ou calorifères trop près des machines : la chaleur produite par rayonnement ramollit les rouleaux, qui s'arrachent alors facilement en roulant.

Si les papiers employés pour l'impression donnent beaucoup de poussière, ce qui est le cas des papiers tirés à sec, on est obligé, pour de longs tirages, de changer de temps en temps, et successivement, un ou deux rouleaux, que l'on remplace par de plus propres; si l'on n'a pas de rouleaux de rechange, on peut passer une éponge humide, qui enlève une partie de la poussière et redonne un peu de fraîcheur.

On ne peut guère fixer la durée du service que peut faire un rouleau; cela dépend de la pâte employée, du local et de la qualité de l'encre en usage. C'est au *conducteur* à s'assurer, par les feuilles de son tirage, que la touche se fait toujours bien normalement, et à s'arrêter lorsque ses rouleaux sont trop secs ou malpropres.

L' " Universelle ". — Encrage cylindrique. Modèle 1908 (*Marinoni*).

" L'UNIVERSELLE "

Avec encrage cylindrique et receveur mécanique

SYSTÈME PERFECTIONNÉ

La Presse " Universelle " peut être placée à tous les étages.

Très grande facilité pour la mise en place et l'enlèvement des rouleaux. Les rouleaux peuvent être enlevés sans démonter les peignes qui les supportent.

Les rouleaux peuvent être mis au repos sans les enlever et sans les dérégler. Le réglage de la touche sur la table cylindrique et sur la forme est très simple. Le mouvement de va-et-vient de la table à encrer circulaire et des rouleaux distributeurs se fait avec une grande douceur et une régularité absolue ; il assure une très bonne distribution.

Disposition spéciale pour pouvoir glisser les formes sur le marbre ; le serrage de la forme peut alors se terminer sur le marbre même.

Avec cette presse sont livrés, outre les accessoires d'usage, un marbre de composition en fonte, un ais en bois garni de zinc, pour pouvoir glisser les formes sur le marbre, et deux châssis spéciaux, un pour le plus grand format que peut imprimer la presse.

IV. LAVAGE DES ROULEAUX

Pour faire un bon usage, il faut qu'un rouleau soit propre. La poussière de l'atelier, celle du papier, se mélangent à l'encre et viennent se fixer sur le rouleau, auquel ils font perdre en partie ses qualités de touche ; il est donc nécessaire de le nettoyer de temps en temps, par exemple tous les soirs. Il faut éviter aussi de laisser les rouleaux trop longtemps au repos recouverts d'encre, car celle-ci sèche et forme une enveloppe nuisible à un bon encrage.

Voici quelques conseils pour le lavage des rouleaux.

En principe, il faut les mouiller le moins possible ; car la glycérine, la mélasse ou la glucose qui entrent dans leur composition sont très solubles dans l'eau, et, à la suite de lavages trop abondants, leur surface finirait par ne plus renfermer que de la gélatine, se durcirait, perdrait son *amour*, et les rouleaux ne seraient plus bons à rien.

Voici deux procédés de lavage qui peuvent être employés :

Lavage à la potasse. — C'est, de tous les modes de lavage, le plus économique. Les produits les plus généralement employés sont : les carbonates de soude et de potasse, connus sous les noms de potasse d'Amérique, de Dantzig, de Russie, etc., ou encore la potasse et la soude caustique, appelées potassium, potasse-lessive.

Suivant leur force, il faut dissoudre ces produits dans plus ou moins d'eau; la potasse caustique doit être employée en dissolution très étendue, pour éviter de brûler les rouleaux.

D'ailleurs, en général, vu son action nocive sur la matière des rouleaux, il faut se servir de la potasse en solutions plutôt faibles, quoique néanmoins suffisantes pour décomposer l'encre; aussi le conducteur devra surveiller attentivement cette opération, surtout si elle est confiée à des jeunes gens qui ne cherchent, la plupart du temps, qu'à se débarrasser au plus vite d'une besogne ennuyeuse.

Le lavage à la potasse se fait au moyen d'une brosse à poils souples, ou d'un morceau de vieux blanchet ou de chiffon. L'encre enlevée, on rince le rouleau à l'eau propre et on passe une éponge pour enlever les gouttes d'eau qui pourraient rester à la surface et produire des gonflements partiels.

Au lieu d'employer la brosse, *on peut se servir de sciure de bois* tamisée. On la mélange d'un peu d'eau, de manière à en faire une sorte de bouillie épaisse, et l'on en frotte le rouleau à la main; on passe ensuite une éponge humide. Cette manière de faire a l'avantage de donner un nettoyage parfait et économique.

Lavage à l'essence. — Dans certains cas, où l'on a besoin de suite des rouleaux, ou bien encore pour enlever les encres de couleur, on se sert d'essences volatiles. La plus économique serait l'essence de pétrole, mais elle a le désavantage, après un usage trop répété, de faire perdre aux rouleaux leur *amour*; il faut donc en user modérément. L'essence de térébenthine est moins nuisible, mais coûte plus cher. Après le lavage à l'essence, il faut passer une éponge humide.

La maison Lorilleux possède, pour le lavage des rouleaux, un produit donnant d'excellents résultats.

Machine à laver les rouleaux typographiques. La Kérosine. — Cette machine américaine supprime l'emploi des chiffons, donne un lavage régulier, rapide, propre et économique. Elle emploie la *Kérosine* ou toute autre essence peu volatile. La dépense est d'environ neuf litres par mois pour une imprimerie moyenne. Le rouleau le plus grand est lavé en une demi-minute.

Fig. 9. — Rotative à quatre couleurs (*Marinoni*).

III

ENCRES

L'encre d'imprimerie est formée d'une matière appropriée, minérale, végétale ou animale divisée en parties infinitésimales, mélangée intimement avec du vernis à l'huile. La matière colorante de l'encre noire est le noir de fumée.

I. FABRICATION

Autrefois, un grand nombre d'imprimeurs fabriquaient eux-mêmes les encres dont ils avaient besoin. Mais cette fabrication étant souvent longue et minutieuse, ils aiment mieux aujourd'hui s'adresser aux fournisseurs, qui leur expédient les encres toutes préparées et prêtes à servir. Il ne s'agit donc que d'y mettre le prix pour avoir la qualité.

Néanmoins, on peut se trouver parfois dans la

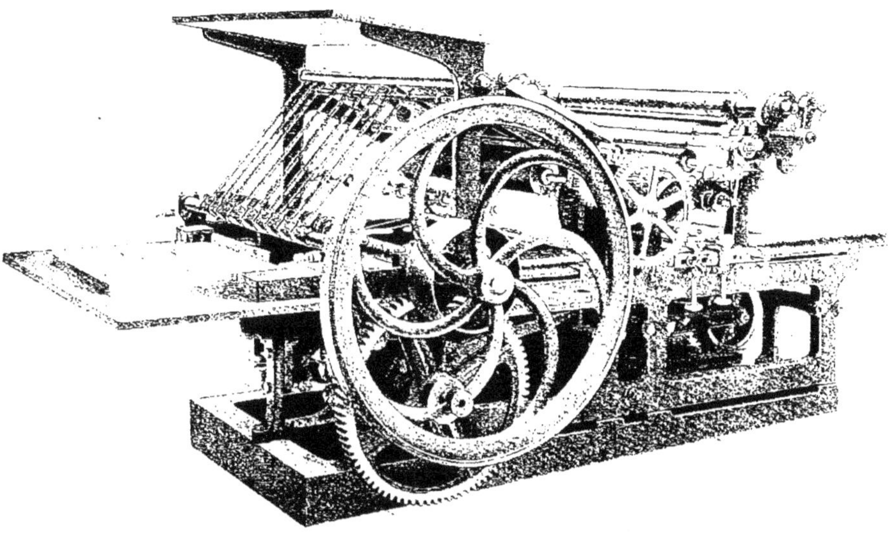

La " Moderne ", modèle A. — Machine en blanc à grande vitesse, encrage cylindrique (*Marinoni*).

" LA MODERNE "

C'est une presse en blanc à encrage cylindrique, de dimensions réduites, de construction robuste, dans laquelle toutes les dispositions ont été prises pour obtenir le maximum de vitesse, la frappe la meilleure pour permettre l'impression des similigravures les plus fines avec le roulement le plus silencieux.

Pour arriver à ce résultat, voici quelques-unes des dispositions particulières qui s'y trouvent résumées :

Socle et bâtis robustes ;

Bielle de commande travaillant en traction pendant l'impression ;

Bielle d'arrêt du cylindre de longueur calculée pour éviter les vibrations au départ et à l'arrêt du cylindre ;

Grandes cames du temps d'arrêt du cylindre ;

Marbre supporté par six galets de train de grand diamètre pourvus chacun d'une roue d'engrenage ;

Tous les engrenages taillés ;

Encrage cylindrique avec grande distribution ;

Marge facile ;

Réception mécanique.

Grâce à la combinaison de tous ces organes, la vitesse atteint sans effort et sans fatiguer la machine 2 500 exemplaires à l'heure pour le format spécial (85 × 56), le plus grand dans lequel elle se construit.

En somme, la vitesse de cette machine n'est limitée que par l'habileté du margeur à la main ; elle dépasse celle à laquelle jusqu'à présent les margeurs automatiques ont pu fonctionner.

nécessité de fabriquer soi-même une certaine quantité d'encre; aussi est-il bon de connaître d'une façon au moins sommaire la manière d'opérer.

Dans les fabriques, les encres sont broyées au laminoir; dans les imprimeries, l'opération se fait à la main.

On se sert d'une table de marbre, ou plus généralement d'une pierre lithographique bien poncée. On doit éviter de se servir d'une table de zinc, ce métal altérant les couleurs.

Les couleurs sont écrasées au moyen d'un instrument appelé broyeur. Les broyeurs sont en pierre ou en verre. Ces derniers ont l'inconvénient de s'écailler, soit en tombant, soit par le simple broyage. Avant de commencer l'opération, il faut vérifier la propreté de la pierre et du broyeur; au besoin même, la pierre sera poncée.

A l'aide d'une palette on commence par mélanger une petite quantité de couleur avec une dose suffisante de vernis; on l'étend uniformément sur la table, et au moyen du broyeur, que l'on passe et repasse en appuyant fortement, on achève le mélange intime des substances.

Après un broyage jugé suffisant, on met de côté la quantité d'encre préparée, et on continue l'opération sur une autre.

On reconnaît une encre bonne pour l'impression à son aspect lisse et brillant, exempt de grain.

II. — CONSERVATION

Que l'encre vienne de chez le fournisseur ou qu'elle ait été préparée par l'imprimeur lui-même, il y a certaines précautions à prendre pour lui conserver ses qualités et éviter les pertes.

Les encres sont généralement livrées dans des boîtes de fer-blanc hermétiquement fermées. Une fois ouvertes, et sous l'action de l'air, elles ne tardent pas à se dessécher et à se recouvrir d'une pellicule d'abord mince, mais qui s'épaissit de plus en plus et qu'il est impossible d'utiliser.

On peut obvier un peu à cet inconvénient en étalant sur le papier qui recouvre l'encre une couche de vernis moyen, qui empêche l'action de l'air.

On peut aussi remplir d'eau la boîte ou le récipient qui contient l'encre. Pour prendre celle-ci, on commencera par vider l'eau ; on en remettra ensuite de la propre.

Certains fabricants ont eu l'ingénieuse idée de renfermer les encres dans des tubes de métal analogues à ceux qui servent pour les couleurs à l'huile et d'aquarelle ; ces tubes, formés d'un alliage de plomb et d'étain, sont fermés au moyen d'un bouchon à vis. Pour prendre l'encre, il suffit d'enlever le bouchon et de comprimer le tube. De cette façon, l'encre ne se trouve jamais au contact de l'air, et le séchage est presque nul ; mais ce système n'est guère pratique que pour les encres de prix, d'un usage moins fréquent.

III. EMPLOI

Si l'on a eu bien soin d'indiquer exactement au fabricant l'usage qu'on en veut faire, l'encre qu'il enverra se trouvera ordinairement toute prête à servir. Cependant si, à défaut de cette précaution ou pour toute autre cause, une encre se trouve être trop dense, c'est-à-dire n'a pas la fluidité voulue, on y ajoute un peu de vernis, et pour bien faire le mélange, on rebroie, au moins partiellement, l'encre avec le vernis.

Quand on se sert d'encre à vernis très siccatif, il faut éviter les courants d'air, qui dessécheraient l'encre et nuiraient à sa bonne distribution.

FIG. 10. Rotative à illustrations (*Marinoni*).

IV

PRÉPARATION DU PAPIER

On pourrait presque dire du papier ce que nous venons de dire de l'encre en commençant. Autrefois, en effet, il subissait avant le tirage une certaine préparation. Aujourd'hui elle est en grande partie supprimée ou faite en fabrique. Ce n'est donc guère que pour mémoire que nous allons parler successivement du trempage et du glaçage, qui constituaient ce qu'on appelait la préparation du papier.

Le trempage consiste à humecter plus ou moins le papier, suivant sa qualité ou sa dureté.

Le glaçage écrase le grain du papier et le rend lisse, dans le but d'obtenir à l'impression toute la netteté et le fini désirables.

Mais le grand reproche qu'on a fait à cette préparation, c'est d'exiger beaucoup de temps. Aussi l'a-t-on supprimée peu à peu, et d'abord pour les ouvrages communs ; aujourd'hui on l'a pour ainsi dire complètement abandonnée.

I. — TREMPAGE

Le trempage, avons-nous dit, est une opération qui a pour but de faire pénétrer dans les pores du papier une certaine quantité d'eau.

Ses avantages sont de donner au papier plus de souplesse, de moelleux à l'impression et plus d'affinité pour l'encre, ainsi que de supprimer, au moins en partie, les poussières qui encrassent les rouleaux et nuisent au tirage.

Pour les papiers communs, et même pour les bons papiers de pâte douce et bien glacés, le trempage peut être supprimé sans grand inconvénient. Il n'en est pas de même quand il s'agit de papiers durs, duveteux, vergés.

De ce côté-là, en regard d'une économie de temps insignifiante, la suppression du trempage se traduit par un résultat inférieur et une usure considérable du matériel.

On peut faire le trempage de trois manières principales : à la main, au balai, à la mécanique.

1° Trempage à la main. — On se sert d'une cuve pouvant contenir les plus grands formats que l'on ait à préparer ; l'eau employée doit être de la plus grande propreté. Des plateaux sont disposés à gauche et à droite de la cuve ; sur l'un est placé le papier sec, sur l'autre on déposera le papier mouillé. On prend à deux mains, et par les deux extrémités, une pincée de quinze, vingt ou trente feuilles, sui-

FIG. 11. — Trempage au balai.

vant le degré d'humidité que l'on veut obtenir, et on la fait glisser dans l'eau; c'est-à-dire que, faisant pénétrer l'extrémité droite du papier dans la cuve, on la ressort aussitôt en lui faisant décrire une courbe, de telle façon qu'une certaine masse d'eau se trouve constamment dessus. Il faut éviter que l'eau pénètre entre les feuilles du papier par les bords.

Cette première pincée placée sur le second plateau, on en pose par-dessus une deuxième, mais sans la passer dans l'eau, puis une troisième mouillée, une autre sèche, et ainsi de suite.

Pour éviter que l'eau ne pénètre entre les feuilles lors de leur passage dans la cuve, certains trempeurs se servent de deux planchettes avec lesquelles ils pincent les bords antérieurs des feuilles.

Ce mode de trempage, qui est assez rapide, ne peut convenir aux papiers sans colle, car ils absorbent trop d'eau et sont d'un maniement difficile. On leur applique le trempage au balai.

2° Trempage au balai. — Le papier est posé comme précédemment, par petites pincées sur un plateau, et à l'aide d'un balai fait de fines brindilles, on asperge successivement la feuille supérieure de chaque pincée (fig. 11). L'eau doit être projetée le plus régulièrement possible.

3° Trempage mécanique. — C'est le procédé le plus moderne et le plus parfait. L'instrument se compose généralement d'un tube vertical en cuivre, à la base duquel est fixé horizontalement en T un autre tube plus petit, fermé à ses deux extrémités et percé en dessous de trous de faible diamètre.

L'extrémité supérieure du tube vertical est fermée par un robinet relié par un tuyau de caoutchouc à une prise d'eau. La clef du robinet sert de support pivotant à l'appareil, de telle façon qu'il est ouvert lorsque le tube d'arrosage passe au-dessus du papier, et fermé lorsqu'il est sur les côtés ; l'eau se répand ainsi sur le papier en pluie fine. On fait aller et venir le trempeur une ou plusieurs fois sur le papier,

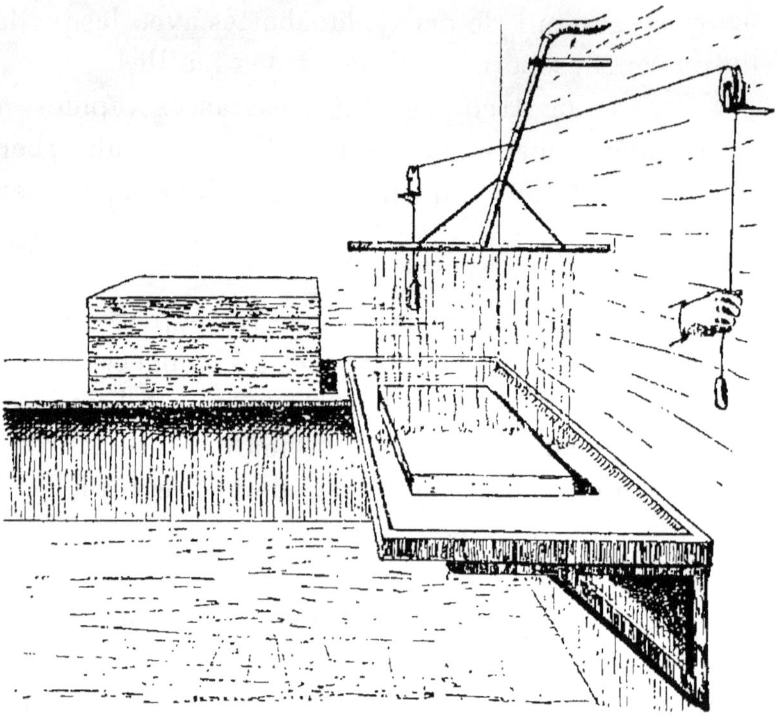

FIG. 12. — Trempage mécanique.

suivant la quantité d'eau qu'on veut lui donner (fig. 12).

Il faut avoir soin de ne pas laisser boucher les orifices, pour que le trempage se fasse bien régulièrement.

Dans d'autres appareils de même nature, le robinet qui se trouve à la base du tube de support est ouvert ou fermé à la main, en donnant le mouvement de va-et-vient au trempeur.

Le trempage des bobines de machines rotatives se fait aussi mécaniquement, mais à l'aide d'un appareil spécial.

Le papier doit être plus ou moins trempé, suivant sa qualité ; car plus il est dur, plus il a besoin d'eau. Les papiers nerveux doivent, après le trempage, rester en piles sans être chargés, de façon que l'eau pénètre bien dans les pores, tandis que les papiers tendres, et surtout les sans colle, doivent être pressés assez fortement pour chasser l'excès d'eau.

Pour obtenir un trempage bien régulier, il faut remanier le papier au bout d'une heure ou deux ; on l'empile de nouveau par petits paquets, de telle sorte que les supérieurs deviennent inférieurs ; on peut même, tous les deux paquets, en retourner un en aile de moulin.

Plus un papier est remanié, plus sa trempe est uniforme ; autrement on aurait à l'impression, dans une même feuille, des parties noires et d'autres grises.

Lorsqu'on a du papier trempé à l'avance pour plusieurs jours, il faut avoir soin chaque jour de tamponner légèrement les quatre faces des piles à l'aide d'une éponge imbibée d'eau, afin d'entretenir l'humidité sur les bords et empêcherle plissage.

La coloration jaunâtre que prennent quelquefois les papiers après leur trempage est due la plupart du temps à l'emploi d'une eau malpropre.

Voici quelques indications sur la façon de tremper différents papiers d'usage peu courant.

Le *papier de Hollande*, qui est dur et vergé, a besoin, pour bien recevoir l'impression, d'être fortement trempé. Il le sera donc par petites pincées, et on ne le chargera pas en pile. Remanier deux ou trois fois en aile de moulin.

Le *papier anglais*, qui est vergé et filigrané, s'imprimerait mieux trempé; mais, comme il n'est utilisé que pour les travaux commerciaux, il est généralement tiré à sec. Cependant, pour les qualités inférieures, et lorsqu'on en aura le temps, il sera toujours préférable de le tremper.

Le *papier de Chine* peut s'imprimer sans être trempé; si, pour des travaux demandant de grandes finesses ou pour des épreuves pour reports lithographiques, il est nécessaire de le faire, ce ne sera pas directement, à cause de son peu de consistance. On l'intercalera par pincées sèches avec des pincées trempées d'un papier ordinaire, non collé de préférence. Comme, en général, les tirages sur ce papier ne sont pas en grand nombre, la chose peut être faite facilement. Il ne faut donner à ce papier qu'une très légère humidité.

Le *papier du Japon* ne se trempe pas ordinairement, à moins d'être très fort; on le traite, dans ce cas, comme le chine.

Le *parchemin* véritable de belle qualité se trempe encarté feuille par feuille dans du papier sans colle fortement trempé; charger légèrement et bien remanier. Aussitôt après le tirage, on l'intercale avec du papier sec et l'on charge fortement pour l'empêcher de se recroqueviller en séchant. Le par-

La " Moderne ", modèle B. — Nouvelle presse typographique en blanc, encrage cylindrique et quatre toucheurs (*Marinoni*).

NOUVELLE PRESSE TYPOGRAPHIQUE EN BLANC

Encrage cylindrique et quatre toucheurs

(MARINONI)

Cette machine *avec encrage cylindrique* est construite spécialement pour les travaux de grand luxe ; la distribution et la touche ont été l'objet d'importants perfectionnements. La touche est donnée *par quatre rouleaux,* dont le réglage très simple peut se faire pendant la marche. La distribution est faite au moyen de trois tables à encrer cylindriques en métal ; deux de ces tables ont en même temps un mouvement de rotation et un mouvement de va-et-vient dont l'amplitude peut varier suivant les travaux à exécuter. Le guidage parfait du marbre empêche tout jeu de se produire. La machine est munie d'un abat-feuilles donnant avec les pointures une grande précision au repérage ; nouvelle pointure perfectionnée à mouvement rectiligne, ne déplaçant pas la feuille et évitant ainsi le déchirement ou l'agrandissement des trous de pointures. Débrayage actionnant le frein et arrêtant instantanément la machine ; on peut agir sur le débrayage des deux côtés de la presse.

chemin grossier pour étiquettes peut être trempé directement : le charger fortement.

Le *faux parchemin*, ou *peau d'âne*, se trempe directement et fortement, car il est très dur et peu poreux ; il faut le remanier plusieurs fois. Comme le parchemin vrai, il se voile, se plisse en séchant; après l'impression, il faudra donc l'encarter dans du papier sec et le charger.

Les papiers *couchés* et *frictionnés* ne se trempent jamais, et de même tous les papiers de fantaisie : *ivoire*, *gaufrés*, *moirés*, etc. ; l'enduit qui les recouvre serait enlevé par le trempage.

Pour les tirages en couleurs, on ne doit pas tremper le papier : la propriété qu'il a de s'allonger sous l'influence de l'eau et de se resserrer en séchant empêcherait tout repérage. Cependant, s'il ne doit subir que deux ou trois tirages peu longs ou peu délicats, on pourra le tremper légèrement; mais alors il faut avoir soin de le tenir constamment couvert et légèrement chargé après chaque impression, pour que l'eau qu'il renferme ne s'évapore pas, ce qui ferait varier les dimensions du papier.

II. GLAÇAGE

Pour donner toute la netteté et le fini désirables, l'impression des caractères et surtout des vignettes exige le papier le plus uni possible. On obtient ce résultat au moyen du glaçage.

Autrefois, quand le papier était trempé avant

l'impression, l'imprimeur devait nécessairement recourir au glaçage pour abattre le grain. Aujourd'hui, ni l'une ni l'autre de ces opérations ne se pratique plus guère qu'exceptionnellement.

Il a paru plus simple et plus économique aux imprimeurs de faire venir leur papier de la fabrique tout glacé et prêt à servir.

Nous donnerons néanmoins, à titre de renseignements, quelques notions sur le glaçage avant le tirage.

Comme nous le disions plus haut, c'est ordinairement après le trempage qu'a lieu cette opération. On doit prendre garde que le papier ne soit pas trop mouillé, car dans cet état il se collerait après les plaques de zinc, et il serait très difficile de l'en arracher. De plus il oxyderait les plaques, qui deviendraient inutilisables.

Parmi les divers appareils en usage pour cette opération, le plus ancien est le laminoir simple. Il consiste en deux tables de fonte supportées par un bâti et en deux cylindres à surface très lisse doués d'un mouvement rotatif. Ces deux cylindres peuvent se rapprocher plus ou moins à l'aide de vis de pression.

Le papier est intercalé feuille par feuille entre de minces plaques de zinc, par mains, c'est-à-dire par jeux de vingt-cinq. Le jeu est posé sur la table du laminoir et engagé entre les deux cylindres; il est entraîné par la rotation du cylindre inférieur et subit une pression d'autant plus forte que les cylindres ont été rapprochés davantage.

Les cylindres du laminoir ne devront pas patiner sur les plaques, car il se produirait dans le papier des marbrures qui le détérioreraient complètement. On évite cet inconvénient en donnant au laminoir une force motrice suffisante.

Lorsque cette dernière est insuffisante et que le papier a besoin d'être fortement glacé, il vaut mieux le passer deux ou trois fois sous les cylindres.

Le glaçage poussé à l'excès a pour résultat de brûler le papier; il devient dur et cassant, prend une teinte brune et reçoit mal l'impression.

Il est bon d'avoir un jeu de plaques de zinc pour chaque format de papier. On comprendra que si dans des plaques jésus on glace une assez grande quantité de papier raisin ou carré, il se produit un amincissement du zinc à la dimension du format glacé, tandis que les bords conservent leur épaisseur primitive; si alors on glace de nouveau du jésus, il sera brûlé sur les bords, où les lames de zinc sont plus épaisses, tandis que le milieu sera à peine touché.

Il est bon de procéder de temps en temps au nettoyage des plaques avec des étoupes bien propres, ou tout simplement des bourrons de papier; on les talque ensuite légèrement.

Il existe d'autres espèces de laminoirs munis de quatre cylindres, ainsi que des appareils de grande production appelés calandres; nous n'entrerons pas dans le détail de leur fonctionnement.

Comme nous l'avons dit, on trouve aujourd'hui

chez les fabricants des papiers préparés ayant à la fois tout le moelleux et le glaçage nécessaires aux impressions les plus soignées. On y trouve aussi les espèces de papiers dits couchés, frictionnés : *miroir*, *idéal*, etc., si appréciés pour l'impression de la photogravure.

FIG. 13. — Rotative à plieuses
pour journaux de 4, 6 et 8 pages (*Marinoni*).

V

PRESSE A BRAS

La presse à bras, la plus simple des presses typographiques et la plus ancienne, ne sert plus guère aujourd'hui qu'à des travaux sans grande importance, ainsi qu'à l'impression des épreuves. Il s'ensuit de là que le nombre en diminue chaque jour et que l'on ne se met plus en peine d'en tirer bon parti. Erreur regrettable : c'est à la presse à bras que tout conducteur devrait commencer son apprentissage. Vu la simplicité de son mécanisme, il est bien plus facile que sur la presse mécanique de suivre le résultat de son travail, d'en voir chaque défaut et d'y remédier. Nous l'étudierons donc d'une façon sérieuse, étant intimement persuadé qu'un ouvrier connaissant parfaitement la presse à bras est appelé à devenir un bon conducteur de toute autre presse mécanique.

Nous n'entreprendrons pas néanmoins la description ni de cette presse ni d'aucune autre, le format que nous nous sommes imposé pour cet ouvrage s'opposant à des développements par trop considérables. La description la plus exacte et la plus claire ne saurait d'ailleurs remplacer le travail d'une journée pour donner au débutant la connaissance de sa machine.

I. — MISE SOUS PRESSE. SUPPORTS LA PREMIÈRE OPÉRATION

Après avoir calé la forme de façon à ce qu'elle soit le plus possible au milieu du marbre, et que, placée sous la platine, elle se trouve au centre de pression, le pressier vérifiera si le tympan ne renferme pas d'épingles, de pointures ou de mise en train d'une impression précédente qui pourraient écraser la forme. Puis il s'occupera de régler le foulage.

Si la forme est de grandes dimensions et pleine, huit pages de texte par exemple, la presse étant en bon état, le foulage doit se faire régulièrement. Si, au contraire, elle est petite ou renferme de grands blancs d'un côté, la pression a besoin d'être soutenue à l'aide de *supports*.

Les supports sont de petits blocs, soit en fer, soit en plomb ou même en bois, exactement de la hauteur de la lettre, et ayant de vingt à vingt-cinq cicéros de longueur sur trois ou quatre de largeur. Les arêtes supérieures doivent être arrondies pour éviter de couper le tympan. Ces supports se fixent soit dans le calage du châssis, soit dans le serrage de la forme.

Si la forme à imprimer offre peu de surface de foulage, on met des supports aux quatre coins du marbre ; si elle est de grandes dimensions, mais renferme d'un côté seulement de grands blancs ou de la composition demandant très peu de foulage, on place un support vers ce côté pour soutenir la pression de la platine. Il faut éviter, quand on a de grands foulages à obtenir, de placer les supports de façon à ce qu'ils portent sur les bords extrêmes de la platine ; on risquerait ainsi de la fausser.

La forme desserrée, taquée et resserrée, on passe sans encrer une première feuille pour vérifier le foulage. Il vaut mieux commencer avec une pression plutôt faible ; au coup de barreau, le pressier expérimenté voit ce qu'il doit ajouter et procède ainsi par tâtonnements. Le foulage normal doit produire un léger gaufrage du papier.

Si le foulage se fait trop sentir d'un côté, on exhausse le support correspondant d'une bande de papier ou de carton mince collée dessus. Lorsqu'il se produit un foulage anormal, il est bon de vérifier s'il ne provient pas de ce que les boulons réunissant la platine à la contre-platine sont dévissés ; en les resserrant, on corrige facilement ce défaut, tandis qu'en cherchant à y remédier par les supports, on risque de trop forcer la platine et de la fausser.

Ces préliminaires terminés, on tire une bonne

épreuve pour la vérification des blancs et la lecture de la tierce.

Lorsqu'on lave la forme à la potasse avant la mise sous presse, il arrive qu'elle n'est pas suffisamment sèche au moment de l'impression et que le caractère refuse de prendre l'encre. Dans ce cas, on dresse la forme et on promène sur toute la surface un chiffon de papier enflammé; on brosse ensuite à sec pour enlever les débris de papier qui auraient pu rester sur la forme.

On obtient le même résultat en frottant légèrement d'huile la surface de la forme avec la paume de la main. L'encrage se fait alors très bien, l'huile empêchant l'eau de remonter à la surface du caractère.

II. — ÉTOFFAGE OU TYMPAN

L'étoffage du tympan varie un peu suivant le tirage à effectuer.

En règle générale, pour obtenir un foulage sec, il faut le moins d'étoffage possible, surtout peu de feuilles de papier.

Pour les impressions courantes, texte ou gravures ordinaires, la garniture fixe du tympan sera faite d'un calicot fin ou lustrine à tissu serré, sans défaut de tissage et très tendu sur la monture. Sur ce calicot ou lustrine on épinglera aux quatre coins un blanchet de mérinos fin. Pour fixer la mise en train, on mettra sur ce blanchet une feuille de papier mince, épinglée à sa partie supérieure. La couverture, ou faux tympan, sera faite en calicot, et toujours bien tendue.

Pour le tirage de gravures délicates de grand

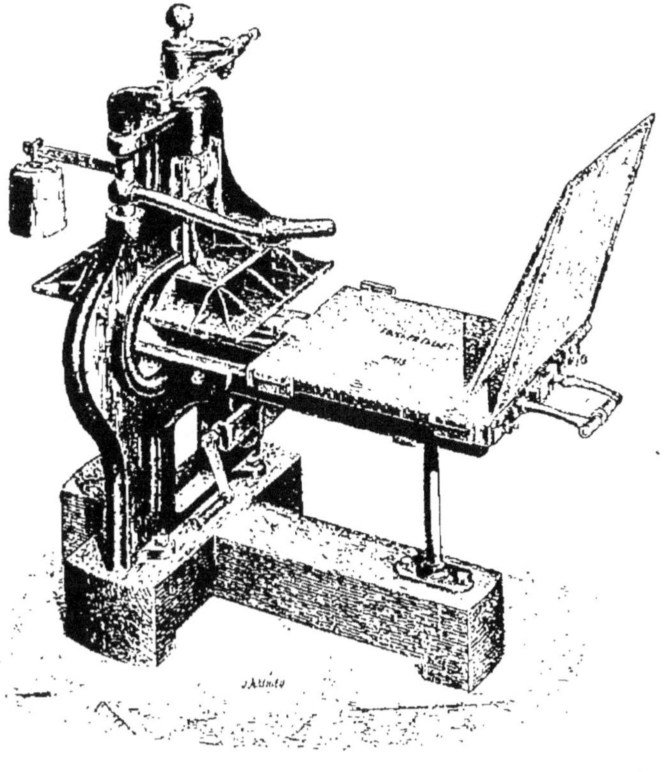

FIG. 14. — Presse à bras, système Stanhope (maison *Foucher*).

luxe, on remplacera le blanchet de mérinos par du satin, et la garniture du tympan par un tissu léger de soie. Pour les fonds qui ont besoin d'un foulage sec, on pourra supprimer le blanchet, auquel on substituera deux ou trois feuilles de papier fort et légèrement glacé; cependant le satin est préférable.

Si l'on a une impression à faire sur du caractère usé ou d'affiches, l'habillage devra être plus élastique; on mettra un blanchet plus épais.

III. — FRISQUETTE

La frisquette est un appendice du tympan qui empêche la feuille de se tacher au tirage en plongeant dans les grands blancs de la forme; elle sert aussi à éviter le papillotage. Elle varie donc suivant chaque forme et chaque composition.

La frisquette doit être garnie avec un papier un peu fort bien tendu sur la ferrure. Pour la découper, on encre la forme, on abaisse la frisquette sur le tympan et le tympan sur la forme, et à l'aide de la main, en frappant à petits coups, on imprime légèrement la composition sur le papier de la frisquette. On n'a plus qu'à découper toutes les parties imprimées.

Il ne faut jamais imprimer la frisquette avec un coup de barreau, car le papier dont elle est faite renferme des impuretés qui écraseraient le caractère ou les gravures de la forme.

Il est inutile de refaire complètement la frisquette lorsqu'il n'y a que le milieu qui a été utilisé; on colle tout simplement une feuille de papier sur l'ouverture.

Lorsqu'on abat le tympan sur la forme, il se produit un frisottement auquel on remédie en garnissant la frisquette de supports, qui soutiennent la

feuille de tirage tant que la platine n'exerce pas sa pression sur la forme.

Les supports sont formés de petits cylindres creux que l'on fait en enroulant sur elle-même une feuille de papier, et que l'on aplatit légèrement afin qu'ils fassent ressort.

Lorsqu'il n'est pas possible de placer des supports sur la frisquette, comme pour un cadre, par exemple, on est obligé de placer à la main le support sur la forme, après avoir encré ; on lui ménage une petite patte en entaillant le papier que l'on relève, ce qui donne plus de facilité pour le prendre.

IV. ROULEAUX

Une presse à bras doit avoir pour son service deux ou trois rouleaux de grandeurs différentes et appropriés à la dimension des formes à tirer. Il est en effet impossible de bien encrer une petite forme avec un rouleau trop grand, qui ne pourrait pas toucher bien d'aplomb.

Lorsque la forme n'est pas de texte plein, ou qu'elle est très petite, on place de chaque côté des *chemins*.

Les chemins sont des supports en bois de la hauteur du caractère, ou un peu plus bas, qui servent à soutenir le rouleau dans sa course. Si de trop grands blancs se trouvent dans la forme, on peut aussi y mettre des supports, mais alors ils devront porter sur la frisquette pour ne pas maculer la feuille d'impression.

On se sert quelquefois, au lieu de supports en bois, de bouchons de liège fixés dans les blancs.

V. — POINTURES

A la presse manuelle, la feuille se marge ordinairement au moyen d'épingles fixées au tympan.

Mais s'il doit y avoir une ou plusieurs retirations, on est le plus souvent obligé, pour obtenir un bon registre, de se servir également de pointures. Ce n'est que pour des tirages sur papier fort ou sur carte, que la marge aux épingles peut suffire dans le cas de plusieurs retirations.

Il faut distinguer les pointures suivant que le tirage a lieu en blanc, ou en retiration.

Dans le premier cas, elles ont pour but de percer la feuille d'un certain nombre de trous qui serviront de points de repère pour les tirages supplémentaires.

Ordinairement, ce nombre de trous doit être double de celui des tirages subséquents. Cependant, si le papier est assez fort ou le repérage de peu d'importance, on peut en réduire le nombre et utiliser plusieurs fois le même trou.

Parmi les pointures en blanc, les unes sont fixées au tympan, les autres placées dans la forme.

Les premières sont de petites baguettes d'acier terminées d'un côté par une patte à deux branches qui sert à les fixer au tympan à l'aide d'un écrou à ailettes ; à l'autre extrémité est rivée perpendiculairement une petite pointe ou piquot.

On emploie ces pointures dans les cas où l'on n'a besoin que d'un double trou de pointure.

Dans les autres cas, on doit recourir à des pointures placées dans la forme.

Ces pointures sont de petites pointes fixées sur des cadrats, et un peu plus hautes que le caractère.

Elles se placent dans les blancs. Dans les formes de plusieurs pages, quand la barre du châssis se trouve au milieu d'un grand blanc, on se sert de piquots fixés sur de petites bandes de fer courbées à angle droit; la patte qui porte le piquot repose sur la barre, tandis que l'autre est serrée entre les garnitures.

Les pointures doivent être disposées de telle manière que les trous viennent tomber soit sur les bords de la feuille, soit dans les grands blancs, où on pourra les faire disparaître au façonnage.

Il faut veiller aussi, s'il doit y en avoir un certain nombre, à ne pas trop les rapprocher, de crainte que la feuille ne se déchire.

Avant de commencer un tirage, on aura toujours grand soin de s'assurer que les pointures sont bien fixées et ne courent pas le risque de se déplacer pendant le tirage; l'exactitude du repérage en dépend.

La feuille étant margée et le tympan abaissé, les piquots percent la feuille par la simple pression de la platine. Pour obtenir plus de netteté quand les pointures sont placées dans la forme, on les fait porter entre deux petits supports que l'on place dans la frisquette.

Le premier tirage terminé, on procède aux retirations successives en se servant des pointures de retiration et, comme point de repère, des trous de pointures obtenus.

Les pointures de retiration pour la presse manuelle sont ordinairement celles à baguette dont nous avons parlé plus haut, et qui se fixent de la même manière de chaque côté du tympan.

A défaut de ces pointures, ou si la forme est trop petite, on se sert de simples pointes soudées sur un petit carré de zinc ou de fer blanc et collées sur le tympan.

Après avoir convenablement réglé la position des pointures et celle de la forme, on marge chaque feuille en introduisant les piquots dans les trous de pointure.

On fait de même pour les autres tirages subséquents, en se servant successivement des différents trous de pointures.

VI. MISE EN TRAIN

Pour corriger les petites différences de foulage provenant du caractère ou de l'étoffage du tympan, on a recours à une opération assez délicate, appelée *mise en train*.

Voici la façon de procéder :

Après avoir régularisé le foulage général de la forme, on encre légèrement et on tire une épreuve sur papier de force moyenne. Mais avant de relever le tympan, on le pique, en deux ou trois points espacés les uns des autres, à l'aide d'une épingle,

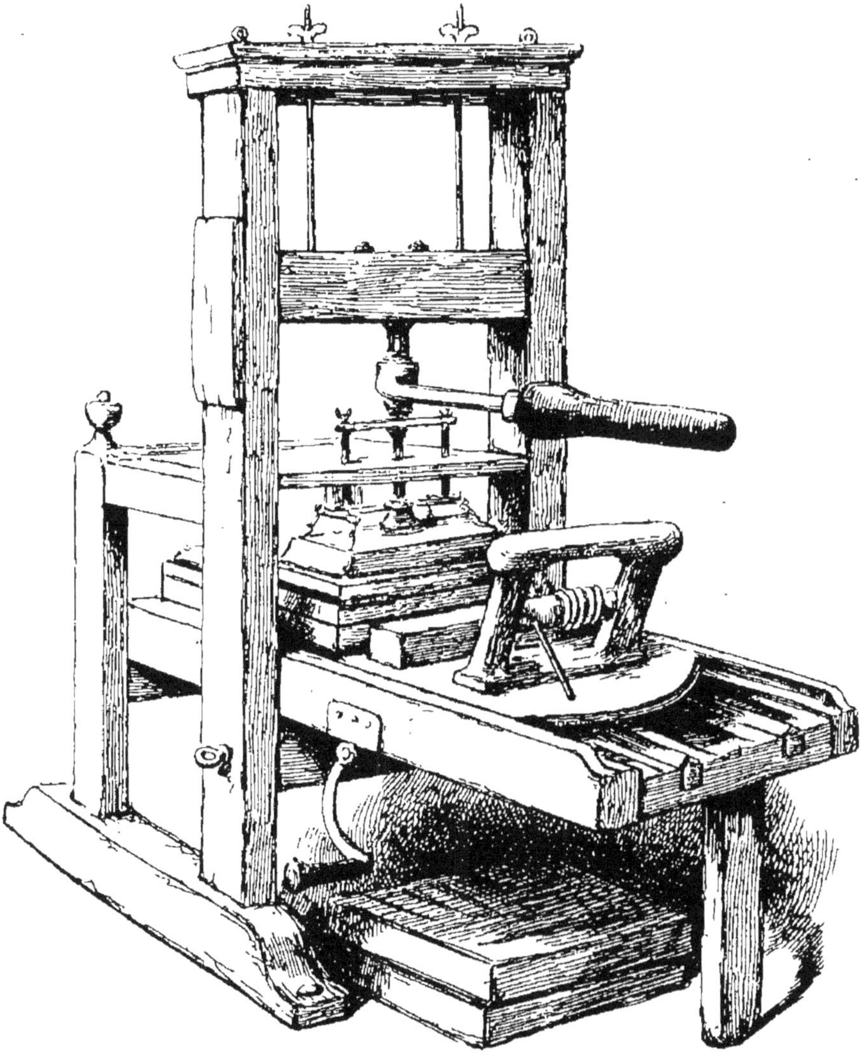

FIG. 15. — Presse typographique du commencement du XVIe siècle.

de façon que l'épreuve soit perforée, ainsi que la feuille qui se trouve dans l'habillage du tympan. Il faut avoir soin de mettre la frisquette, ou tout au moins des supports, pour que l'épreuve ne plonge pas dans la forme, ce qui empêcherait le repérage.

C'est avec cette première feuille imprimée que l'on commence la mise en train. On découpe les parties qui piquent, et on colle des feuilles plus ou moins épaisses aux endroits faibles, suivant leur forme et leur profondeur. Il ne faut jamais égaliser le foulage à l'aide de grandes bandes de papier garnies de colle; c'est plus vite fait, mais tout à fait mauvais. Sans parler du papier presque toujours en excès, la mise en train sèche irrégulièrement, et la colle en durcissant forme des croûtes rugueuses qui nuisent à l'impression.

Au contraire, pour fixer un morceau de papier, il ne faut mettre qu'un peu de colle en deux ou trois points, juste assez pour le maintenir. Le papier dont on se sert pour les mises en train doit de préférence être déchiré et non coupé aux ciseaux; les bords déchirés forment une légère pente, et la différence de foulage se fait moins sentir qu'avec le papier dont les bords ont été coupés franchement.

La première feuille de mise en train finie, on la repère sur la feuille du tympan à l'aide des trous d'épingle, et on la colle en deux ou trois points.

On tire ensuite, sur un papier un peu plus mince, une seconde épreuve qui est piquée également avec la feuille du tympan. C'est la deuxième feuille de mise en train, qui doit être traitée avec un très grand soin. On découpe aux ciseaux toutes les lettres qui piquent, et on colle de petits béquets de papier mince sur toutes les lettres faibles. Cette seconde

feuille est placée et fixée comme la précédente, et la mise en train est terminée.

Cependant si, après avoir roulé quelques feuilles d'essai, on aperçoit encore des parties trop faibles ou trop fortes, on corrige sur le tympan même.

Clichés. — La mise en train des formes de clichés ne se fait pas tout à fait de la même manière. Nous parlons ici des clichés mobiles, griffés sur blocs.

Si les clichés sont montés sur bois, on procède comme si on avait à mettre des gravures de hauteur, ce que nous verrons plus loin.

Après avoir passé une première feuille pour égaliser le foulage des pages et corriger les défauts les plus apparents, on enlève les bords des pages, qui piquent toujours un peu, ainsi que les parties renfermant des lignes de points, des vignettes isolées etc.; on colle aussi des épaisseurs sur les parties faibles. Cette mise en train se fait page par page et se place entre le cliché et sa monture. On passe ensuite une autre feuille, deux au besoin, détaillées alors lettre par lettre; ces feuilles se placent dans le tympan, comme la mise en train ordinaire.

Reports. — Pour faire les reports, on se sert de papier de Chine ou similaires.

L'impression doit être légère et sans foulage; on se servira d'encre lithographique et on encrera légèrement, car trop d'encre donnerait une impression pâteuse qui s'écarterait sur la pierre. Pour faciliter la distribution et l'encrage, on peut ajouter une pointe d'encre typographique.

On imprime du côté où la feuille de chine se trouve encollée, ce qui est facile à reconnaître par les traces du pinceau.

On trouve dans le commerce différent papiers de Chine spéciaux pour le report, notamment le papier *Hydro-Chine*, et surtout le *Chine moderne*, de la maison Gentil, que nous recommandons tout particulièrement.

FIG. 16. — Réaction (*Marinoni*).

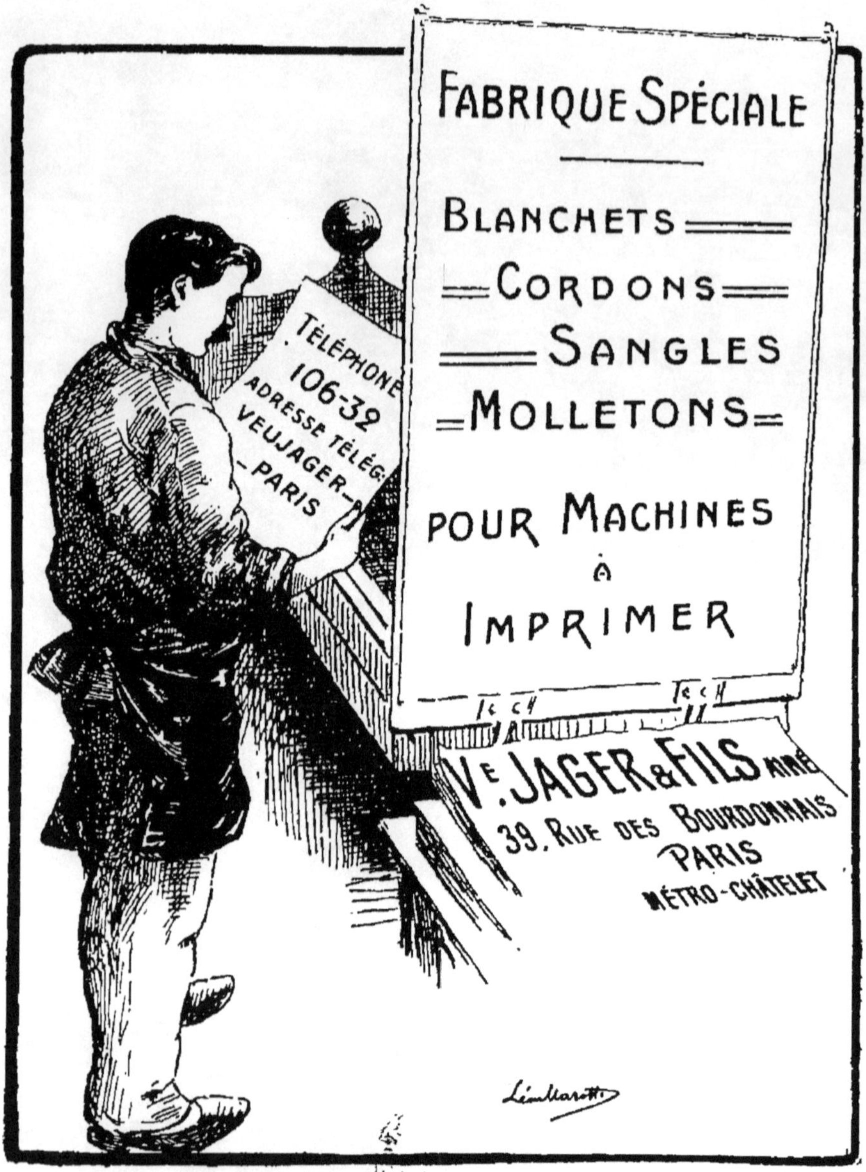

DIPLOMES D'HONNEUR
MÉDAILLES D'ARGENT, VERMEIL ET OR
AUX EXPOSITIONS INTERNATIONALES

VI

PRESSES MÉCANIQUES A CYLINDRES

Comme nous l'avons déjà dit, nous laissons de côté la partie mécanique pour nous occuper exclusivement du travail du conducteur.

Nous étudierons successivement tout ce qui a trait à l'impression sur les machines à cylindres, quel que soit le système employé.

I. — HABILLAGE DES CYLINDRES

L'habillage des cylindres varie non seulement suivant le genre d'impression, mais encore suivant les pays. Ainsi les machines allemandes, sur lesquelles les sangles sont supprimées et dont les cylindres roulent fonte sur fonte, sont habillées à sec avec du papier seul; les anglaises et les américaines emploient le papier et une satinette.

Nous donnerons ici les différents habillages en rapport avec les travaux à exécuter.

Travaux courants. Labeurs. — On recouvre le cylindre d'une forte toile de tissu serré, très régulier et sans aucun défaut, et on la tend fortement à l'aide de la tringle à cliquet; on prend ensuite une feuille de papier fort, légèrement glacé, que l'on colle par un côté dans la gorge du cylindre. Cette feuille servira à fixer la mise en train.

Si la mise en train doit avoir des découpages de gravures, il faut avoir soin de coller la feuille des deux côtés, après l'avoir humectée pour qu'elle se tende bien en séchant.

On met alors le blanchet ou molleton, qui sera plus ou moins épais suivant que l'on veut un foulage plus ou moins sec; on l'étire bien et on fixe l'extrémité libre sur la toile à l'aide de quelques épingles. La mise en train doit toujours se coller sous le blanchet, sur la feuille de papier. On obtient ainsi une impression très douce et qui ne fatigue pas l'œil des caractères.

Nous n'approuvons pas la manière de faire qui consiste à n'habiller les cylindres qu'avec des feuilles de papier glacé, ou bien avec du papier-affiche, pour obtenir un foulage plus sec, moins apparent. En plus de l'usure rapide du caractère, on court de grands risques par suite du mauvais réglage de la pression, du bris d'un cordon, etc.; le papier seul étant peu élastique, les accidents seraient très préjudiciables au matériel.

Machine à retiration à grande vitesse, système Chapot. Modèle K (*Marinoni*).

MACHINE A RETIRATION A GRANDE VITESSE

Système Chapot

(MARINONI)

Cette nouvelle machine est conçue d'après des *principes entièrement nouveaux*. Elle réunit les avantages de la vitesse des machines à double révolution et de l'impression en retiration.

La *suppression du mouvement ancien*, avec le pignon et le joint de cardan, permet de garantir l'*absence absolue de papillotage*.

La vitesse est augmentée sans inconvénients pour la *régularité et la finesse de l'impression*. Suivant le format, elle varie entre 1400 et 2200 à l'heure sans aucun danger.

La *liaison du marbre avec les cylindres*, au moment de l'impression, donne à cette machine les avantages des machines en blanc pour la *beauté et la précision de la frappe*.

Receveur à pinces. — Receveur à raquettes. — Encrage mixte. — Graissage entièrement automatique.

Le système du mouvement du marbre a été étudié pour être appliqué aux machines ancien modèle.

La *transformation* peut se faire avec la plus grande facilité, *sans changer le format* ancien et en *augmentant le rendement* dans la proportion de 30 à 40 %.

L'appareil à papier continu peut être adapté à tous les genres de machines : machines en blanc, machines doubles, machines à réaction.

Appareil paraffineur. — Molette coupeuse. — Encrage cylindrique.

Sur les machines à retiration munies de rouleaux paraffineurs, il faut prendre certaines précautions au sujet de la feuille collée sur le deuxième cylindre.

Cette feuille ne devra pas être trop mince, car les paraffineurs, en essuyant le blanchet, finiraient par la couper à la gorge et feraient déplacer la mise en train.

Il peut arriver que les épingles qui fixent le blanchet soient arrachées par les paraffineurs. Pour éviter cet accident, capable de détériorer la forme, il suffit de prendre une bande de flanelle et de l'épingler de telle façon que les têtes des épingles soient placées du côté de l'attaque des rouleaux paraffineurs.

Dans les imprimeries où l'on fait des tirages très soignés, on a, pour l'habillage des cylindres, un blanchet pour chaque format. En effet, le tissu se modifie, se resserre sous l'influence de la pression, et le lavage n'enlevant jamais complètement cette dureté, il en résulte que, si après avoir tiré du *carré* on tire du *jésus*, les pages, tombant partie sur tissu foulé et partie sur tissu non foulé, reçoivent un foulage inégal, que l'on ne peut corriger qu'imparfaitement par la mise en train.

C'est pour cette même raison de resserrement du tissu qu'il faut laver de temps en temps les blanchets pour leur redonner leur élasticité première. Lorsqu'ils ne sont pas maculés d'encre, un simple lavage à l'eau suffit; dans le cas contraire, un lavage au savon noir est nécessaire

Clichés blancs. — Pour l'impression des clichés blancs, on peut se servir de l'habillage que nous venons de décrire avec blanchet mince.

Galvanos. — Pour le tirage des galvanos, l'habillage doit être plus sec. Voici un habillage qui, expérimenté sur des tirages à deux cent cinquante mille exemplaires, a donné de très bons résultats.

On supprime la toile du cylindre et l'on met seulement le blanchet bien tendu (comme presque toujours le blanchet ne peut faire le tour du cylindre, on ajoute une bande de calicot), sur lequel on applique une feuille de papier fort, mouillée et collée par ses deux extrémités ; c'est sur cette feuille que l'on place la mise en train recouverte par une autre feuille volante, le tout protégé par un calicot très fin.

Pour rouler, il faut commencer par un léger foulage, que l'on augmente progressivement, car les clichés prêtent toujours un peu et s'affaissent sous la pression du cylindre. On obtient ainsi une bonne impression qui fatigue peu le cliché.

A propos de l'usure des clichés, nous ferons remarquer qu'elle est bien moins rapide avec les machines à grande vitesse pour le même nombre d'exemplaires. Cela se comprend facilement : si une machine roule deux fois plus vite qu'une autre, le cliché reste en pression deux fois moins de temps que sur cette dernière, d'où un écrasement beaucoup moindre pour le même nombre de feuilles imprimées.

Galvanos gravures. — Lorsque le texte à imprimer renferme des gravures, il faut se servir d'un habillage très soigné : un blanchet fin, sans maculature d'encre et sans racommodages.

Photogravure. — Pour la photogravure, on obtient un bon résultat en remplaçant le molleton par du satin ou même du calicot, qui donne un foulage moins plongeant quoique assez doux. On tire même quelquefois à sec, en remplaçant le blanchet par du papier glacé.

Comme ces gravures sont imprimées avec beaucoup de foulage, elles ne peuvent résister à un long tirage, et parfois même se fendent sous la pression. C'est surtout à l'attaque et à la sortie du cylindre que le foulage se fait le plus sentir. Les deux extrémités des gravures se trouvent en quelque sorte laminées.

Nota. — Dans les machines à retiration, un cylindre ne doit jamais être habillé plus que l'autre ; pour obtenir le même foulage aux deux cylindres, on serait en effet obligé de les descendre inégalement, ce qui nuirait au bon fonctionnement de la machine.

Lavage et entretien des blanchets. — Il faut éviter de faire rendre de multiples services aux blanchets sans les laver. Pour le lavage et le rinçage, ne pas employer d'eau trop chaude, qui occasionnerait un rétrécissement de l'étoffe.

Il est avantageux de se servir de lessive de cendres de bois ou d'eau légèrement additionnée de cristaux et de bon savon blanc de Marseille. Les potasses trop fortes pour ce lavage dessèchent le lainage et le rendent dur et cassant. Choisir des brosses douces et sécher à l'air libre est préférable.

Mérinos et cuir-laine. — On les fait tremper environ vingt-quatre heures dans de la lessive de cendres de bois si possible, ou, à défaut, de cristaux légère.

Les enduire de bon savon de Marseille pour les débarrasser de l'encre et frotter l'une contre l'autre les parties de l'étoffe.

Les rincer dans l'eau savonneuse et tiède.

Ces opérations terminées, faire le séchage à l'air libre ou à une température de 20 à 25 degrés environ.

Paraffine. — La paraffine est un produit destiné à empêcher le maculage des feuilles de tirage par le blanchet du deuxième cylindre dans les machines à retiration. On humecte légèrement de ce produit des rouleaux dits paraffineurs, qui viennent frotter contre le deuxième cylindre et essuient le blanchet.

Parmi les espèces de paraffine les plus employées, citons : la Paraffine Nelson, l'Antimaculine et la Nouvelle Paraffine de Rietsch. Ces deux dernières sont d'un bon usage et plus économiques que celle de Nelson, qui nécessite l'emploi d'un appareil dit Nelson.

Voici la formule de ce dernier produit :

Essence de paraffine à 110°.	5 litres
Paraffine en pain.	1 kilo.
Cire jaune.	385 gr.
Savon noir.	250 gr.
Citroline.	Petite quantité.

Ces diverses matières sont fondues au bain-marie. On peut remplacer l'essence de paraffine par du pétrole et faire dissoudre à froid.

Il existe aussi des siccatifs qui, mélangés à l'encre dans les encriers, opèrent un séchage très prompt, permettant un façonnage immédiat. Parmi ces produits, nous indiquerons le siccatif *Supra* de la maison Lorilleux, qui se vend en tube de 250 grammes, et le *Perfecteur d'encre* de Blot et Cie.

On emploie aussi des papiers à décharge d'une préparation spéciale qui assurent une grande propreté au tirage, suppriment les feuilles huilées ou pétrolées et le margeur en décharge. Nous citerons tout particulièrement la *décharge imperméable* de la Maison Failliot et Fils, 145, rue de la Chapelle, Paris.

II. — SUPPORTS

L'habillage doit être fait juste au niveau des nervures des supports qui se trouvent de chaque côté du cylindre, en tenant compte de l'épaisseur que doit avoir la mise en train.

Le conducteur devra user modérément des supports : seulement quelques bandes de papier mince sous la sangle, vis-à-vis des grands blancs de la forme, afin de soutenir le cylindre à son entrée et à sa sortie de pression sur les pages.

Pour s'assurer que le cylindre ne porte pas trop

Fig. 17. — Cales pour le serrage des formes sur les marbres (*Marinoni*).

sur les supports, on place sur les sangles une bande de papier qui ne doit être que légèrement comprimée par le cylindre.

Lorsque le cylindre est trop supporté par les chemins, il en résulte du papillotage dans l'impression. Il arrive même à la longue que les marbres viennent à fléchir et à se fausser.

Une cause assez fréquente d'ennuis pour les conducteurs, c'est le retard du soulèvement des cylindres dans les machines à retiration.

Ce retard provient de l'usure des plaques de la cage d'excentrique. Il a pour effet soit le rabotage de la forme par les pinces, le blanchet ou les épingles, soit le coupage des sangles, ou le papillotage.

Pour remédier à cet inconvénient, le mécanicien devra redresser les plaques de la cage et ajouter des épaisseurs par derrière. On peut aussi déclaveter la roue de cent dents, la dégrener et faire avancer son pignon de commande d'une dent ou deux, suivant le cas, par rapport à la roue. Mais ce demi-remède ne dispense pas d'une réparation plus sérieuse par le mécanicien.

III. — REGISTRE

Ce n'est qu'après avoir vérifié le bon état et la position des cordons que l'on devra s'occuper du registre. Il arrive souvent qu'après avoir fait son registre exactement, on s'aperçoit en roulant que les feuilles ne tombent pas en retiration. Pour éviter cet inconvénient, il faut passer ses feuilles de registre en faisant rouler la machine à sa marche normale, et, si c'est une machine à retiration, en passant les feuilles de décharge s'il y en a.

Un mauvais registre provient aussi quelquefois de l'usure des dents de l'engrenage de commande ou de la crémaillère; c'est alors au mécanicien qu'il faut avoir recours.

La prise des pinces ne doit pas excéder dix-huit points ; autrement elles repoussent la feuille, d'où mauvaise marge et registre irrégulier.

Les cordons devront aussi être tendus par leur contre-poids et ne pas mordre sur les pinces.

Il arrive souvent que l'on ne peut mettre le cordon de dessous avec le cordon de sortie de feuilles, à cause des blancs trop étroits. Il faut, dans ce cas, ne laisser que le cordon de sortie et mettre les cordons du bas en faux cordons, c'est-à-dire passer à la première tringle et au rouleau de sortie de feuilles, afin qu'ils ne passent pas sur la forme.

Il faut aussi se rendre bien compte que toutes les fois que l'on augmente ou que l'on diminue le foulage, l'impression ne se fait plus aux mêmes points du cylindre; on devra donc faire varier la prise des formes de un ou deux points chaque fois que l'on aura une différence sensible de foulage.

IV. — POINTURES

Dans les presses en blanc, on se sert de pointures pour la régularité du registre : la marge seule ne suffirait pas le plus souvent, en raison des petites différences de grandeur que l'on trouve toujours dans le papier du même format.

Ces pointures, pour le tirage en blanc, sont généralement deux piquots qui se vissent ou s'enfoncent dans des trous situés au milieu ou sur les côtés du cylindre. Le premier piquot se place près de la gorge : si le second ne correspond pas à un trou du cylindre, on le colle sur le cylindre, et il se trouve maintenu par l'habillage et la mise en train.

Pour la retiration, on conserve la pointure placée près de la gorge; la seconde, dite mobile, est fixée dans la marge, à une tige, qui, au moyen d'une tringle, fait alternativement lever et baisser la pointure; ce qui permet la pointure, puis le départ de la feuille.

Pour faciliter l'établissement du registre à la retiration, on fait parfois usage sur le cylindre de la pointure dite à coulisse. Le piquot est fixé à l'extrémité d'une lame métallique très flexible, munie d'une fente longitudinale. Cette pointure se fixe au moyen d'une vis dans l'un des trous disposés à cet effet. Grâce à la fente dont elle est munie, on peut très facilement faire varier sa position.

V. — MISE EN TRAIN

Pour faire la mise en train, on commence par régler le foulage en le tenant d'abord un peu fort; puis on passe la première feuille en roulant à la vitesse normale de la machine.

Pour pouvoir remettre cette première feuille de mise en train à sa place sous le blanchet lorsqu'elle sera terminée, on la pique en quelques points sur la feuille du cylindre avec un petit poinçon d'acier; il faut éviter de frapper trop fort, pour ne pas détériorer le cylindre.

On peut aussi enlever le blanchet et passer sur la

feuille du cylindre en ajoutant un peu de foulage; seulement, comme nous l'avons déjà dit, il faut faire varier la forme, c'est-à-dire ajouter un ou deux points à la prise; on les enlèvera en replaçant le blanchet.

On fait ensuite la mise en train de la même manière que pour la presse à bras.

VI. — RÉGLAGE DES ENCRIERS

On doit régler un encrier avec précaution, en observant qu'une lame de fonte de l'épaisseur du couteau ne peut fléchir que graduellement; il est donc inutile de chercher à donner de l'encre en un point en la supprimant complètement à côté : on n'arriverait qu'à fausser le couteau.

S'il est une partie qui ne doit donner que très peu d'encre, après avoir réglé l'encrier d'une façon générale, on glisse entre le cylindre et l'encre une bande de papier que l'on fixe par l'autre extrémité au couvercle de l'encrier à l'aide d'un peu de colle.

Dans la plupart des cas, les formes à tirer sont de dimensions moindres que la longueur de l'encrier, et l'on réduit la surface encrée du rouleau à l'aide de *plombs*. A défaut de ces derniers, on peut employer des morceaux de savon très dur. Les plombs sont fondus dans l'encrier même, de façon à occuper exactement l'espace compris entre la boîte de l'encrier et le cylindre. Ils ne doivent pas avoir plus de trois à quatre centimètres d'épaisseur, sinon ils exerceraient une trop forte pression sur le cylindre de l'encrier.

Historique de la Maison

ARTHUR MULLER

PARIS

MACHINES KRAUSE

La vente de ses machines en France prenant une extension de plus en plus grande, la maison KARL KRAUSE, Leipzig, créa en janvier 1900, à Paris, 21 bis, rue de Paradis, une succursale chargée de s'occuper de toutes les affaires se traitant avec la France. Au début, le personnel de la succursale se composait d'un directeur, d'un employé, d'un monteur et d'une dactylographe.

La succursale fondée, les affaires devinrent encore bien plus nombreuses, et en juillet 1901, la Maison KARL KRAUSE confiait à M. ARTHUR MULLER la direction de la succursale parisienne.

A partir de ce moment, le chiffre d'affaires doubla pour ainsi dire, et tandis que, jusqu'à cette époque, la maison KARL KRAUSE était surtout connue à Paris, son activité, avec l'entrée de M. MULLER, a commencé à se répandre dans toute la France. De plus, depuis l'arrivée de M. MULLER, la succursale s'est vu adjoindre la représentation de machines à imprimer, à perforer, à coudre au fil métallique, que la maison KARL KRAUSSE ne construit pas elle-même.

Afin d'être encore davantage en rapport avec sa nombreuse clientèle, M. MULLER, à partir de 1902, a envoyé dans les différents centres industriels des représentants très compétents, choisis parmi ses employés.

Le 1er avril 1904, M. MULLER a acheté la maison KARL KRAUSE, Paris. Depuis ce moment, les affaires ont pris un développement tel, que M. MULLER a été obligé de transférer sa maison, le 1er octobre 1904, au 44, rue des Vinaigriers, où il a installé en outre un atelier de réparations et un atelier mécanique d'affûtage de lames.

Le 31 octobre, M. A. MULLER s'est rendu acquéreur, pour la partie mécanique et les fournitures d'imprimerie, du Comptoir des Fonderies Nouvelles (anciens Établissements HOUPIED, 16, rue Royer-Collard), et il s'est adjoint, comme fondé de pouvoir, M. G. LEVESQUE, qui occupait ces mêmes fonctions, depuis de longues années, aux Établissements HOUPIED.

L'installation dans ces locaux comprend un moteur de 10 chevaux servant à la production de la force motrice et de la lumière électrique.

L'atelier de réparations, depuis sa création en 1904, a pris une très grande extension et va toujours en se développant, vu les très grands services qu'il rend à la clientèle par une exécution excellente, rapide et bon marché des différents travaux de la mécanique, pour lesquels auparavant les clients devaient s'adresser aux constructeurs se trouvant souvent à l'étranger, d'où résultaient perte de temps et frais considérables. Le service de réparations, qui comprenait au début deux tours, une raboteuse, une perceuse et quelques étaux, possède aujourd'hui quatre tours, une raboteuse, deux perceuses, une fraiseuse et douze étaux. L'atelier d'affûtage, qui est également très prospère, possède une machine à affûter automatique, ainsi que deux meules supplémentaires.

Dans les autres services de la maison, les perfectionnements modernes ont été également appliqués ; dans le service d'emballage, une scie circulaire, actionnée par la force motrice, sert à la confection des caisses ; un palan et un monte-charge mécanique facilitent le déchargement ; dans les magasins, toutes les machines, même celles fonctionnant au moteur, peuvent être mises en marche à tout moment, grâce à un service de moteurs ingénieusement établi.

Quatre machines à écrire servent à la correspondance.

La maison possède un dépôt de plus de deux cents machines, dont une partie tout emballées, afin de pouvoir être expédiées au reçu de la commande.

Citons, pour terminer, quelques chiffres concernant le nombre d'employés :

Au début : 4 employés.

Fin de l'année	1900,	7 employés.		Fin de l'année	1904,	17 employés.
»	» 1901,	9	»	»	» 1905,	30	»
»	» 1902,	11	»	»	» 1906,	39	»
»	» 1903,	14	»	»	» 1907,	55	»

On rapproche plus ou moins les plombs suivant la forme que l'on tire, et les côtés de l'encrier dépourvus d'encre sont garnis d'un peu d'étoupe légèrement huilée ou suiffée, pour empêcher que l'encre qui pourrait passer sous les plombs ne se répande et n'encrasse les extrémités de l'encrier.

Il faut éviter de laisser sécher l'encre dans les encriers, car le cylindre encrassé, forçant pour tourner, pourrait faire briser les engrenages de commande, et même le cylindre encreur.

Margeur automatique. — Après un certain nombre d'essais infructueux, il existe enfin aujourd'hui des margeurs automatiques donnant toute satisfaction. L'Amérique fut la première qui chercha à doter ses machines rapides de margeurs automatiques. Dans un premier système, la feuille était aspirée par des ventouses; mais, outre le défaut de régularité, il fallait l'emploi d'une pompe pneumatique et l'encombrement d'un tuyautage compliqué. Un autre système utilisait l'électricité statique : au moyen de petits plateaux, elle attirait la feuille vers la prise des pinces. Mais ce n'était encore qu'un essai.

Le premier margeur pratique fut celui adopté par le « Cross Sheet paper Feeder », système purement mécanique. La feuille est séparée des autres au moyen de petites molettes en forme de peignes, qui la poussent et l'amènent en contact avec les taquets de marge. Ce système fonctionne avec toute la régularité et la précision désirables, dépassant de 25 % la production d'un margeur ouvrier.

Un autre système français a repris l'emploi des ventouses, mais avec une installation moins encombrante et un fonctionnement plus régulier et plus précis.

Les margeurs automatiques les plus répandus à ce jour sont : l'Universel, le Kœnig, le Dexter, l'Auto, le Cross-Feeder et l'Auto-Falion. Tous peuvent s'adapter aux machines en blanc et à retiration, ainsi qu'aux presses à deux tours.

FIG. 18. — Rotative à retournement pour journaux de 4 pages 40 × 24 (*Marinoni*).

LA MINERVE

SÉRIE B

Encrage Spécial

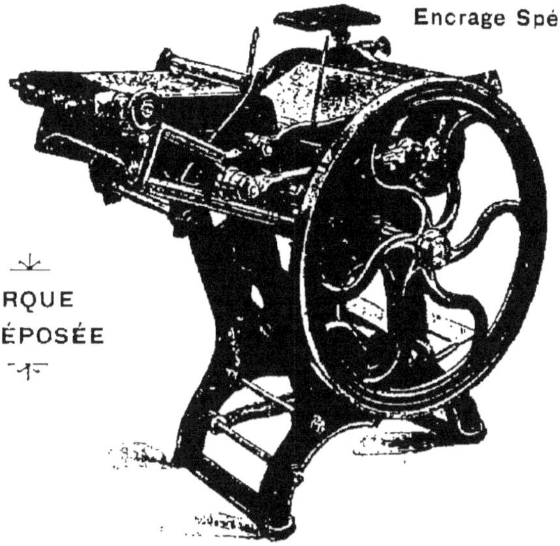

MARQUE
DÉPOSÉE

Prix de la Machine . . . . 1075 fr.
Avec réglage de la touche des rouleaux (en plus) 30 »

Cette machine possède les mêmes avantages que la "MINERVE" de notre série courante : grande solidité, bâtis fondus d'une seule pièce assurant une stabilité parfaite, position de la platine presque horizontale permettant une mise en train aisée et une marge facile, réglage instantané de la pression par la barre de foulage avec possibilité de passage en blanc, une seule table tournant dans une table fixe, un rouleau preneur et trois toucheurs.

Un outillage tout à fait perfectionné nous permet de construire en série ce seul format de 23×33 d'intérieur de châssis, d'une façon très économique sans nuire en quoi que ce soit au parfait ajustage des pièces. Nous garantissons d'ailleurs le parfait fonctionnement et la bonne construction de cette machine.

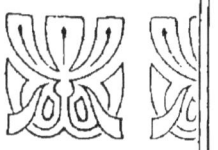

FONDERIE TYPOGRAPHIQUE
S. BERTHIER & DUREY
19 21, RUE BOISSONADE, PARIS
« MACHINES A IMPRIMER »

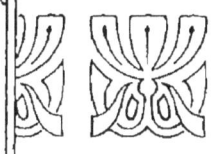

VII

MACHINES A PÉDALE

I. — MINERVES

Les machines à pédale, appelées aussi minerves (nom donné au premier type créé dans ce genre), se sont propagées depuis quelques années dans de très grandes proportions. Il est peu d'imprimeurs faisant des bibelots qui n'aient au moins une pédale; la plupart des petites imprimeries, si nombreuses dans toutes les villes, ne possèdent même que ce genre de machines. On doit en effet reconnaître que, d'un prix relativement restreint, elles rendent de grands services pour l'impression de tous les petits travaux de ville, tels que programmes, prospectus, lettres de mariage, de décès, cartes d'adresse, de visite, etc.

On est même arrivé aujourd'hui à une telle précision dans la construction de ces machines, qu'il peut y être fait des tirages en plusieurs couleurs avec le registre le plus impeccable.

Le maniement en est d'ailleurs facile et n'exige qu'une seule personne, qui tout à la fois pédale, marge et tire la feuille.

Malheureusement ces machines sont, le plus souvent, confiées à des jeunes gens qui n'apportent pour la plupart ni le soin ni le talent voulus; aussi ne donnent-elles pas tous les résultats qu'on pourrait en attendre.

On les a même surnommées « machines à écraser le caractère », vu le reproche qu'on leur fait de mettre rapidement la lettre hors d'usage. En réalité, ce reproche serait plus justement adressé à l'ouvrier qu'à la machine.

Il n'est pas rare, en effet, de voir des pédalistes habiller leur machine d'un carton bristol mince et de quatre ou cinq feuilles de papier glacé, sans aucune toile ni blanchet. Cet habillage qui, sans doute, donne de très belles impressions sans foulage et presque sans mise en train quand le caractère est neuf, est tout à fait préjudiciable à ce dernier.

Habillage. — Pour avoir un bon habillage, on peut se servir d'un blanchet de mérinos mince, recouvert d'une ou deux feuilles de papier. Cet habillage devra être refait de temps en temps en lavant le blanchet et en changeant les feuilles.

Marge. — La marge, sur les pédales, se fait soit aux taquets de carton collés sur la platine, soit aux

Fig. 19. — Pédale Marinoni.

épingles courbées piquées dans l'habillage, ou bien encore au moyen de cadrats collés et maintenus sur la platine par des bandelettes de papier.

Nouveaux systèmes. — La plupart des anciennes pédales ont cependant un grand défaut : on ne peut pas corriger dans la forme sans la sortir de la machine. Cet inconvénient n'existe plus dans les pédales à marbre renversable, construites depuis peu par Marinoni, Alauzet, Voirin, Berthier et Durey, Nebiolo. En basculant, le marbre prend une position horizontale, d'où faculté de desserrer et de resserrer sans décaler.

Vitesse. — La vitesse de ces machines est de douze à quinze cents à l'heure; mais, pour des tirages un peu soignés, il ne faut marcher qu'à mille au plus, si l'on veut éviter la trépidation, qui nuirait à la marge. D'ailleurs, une trop grande vitesse détériore rapidement ces machines, surtout lorsqu'elles sont fixées sur un plancher d'étage et non au rez-de-chaussée : elles prennent du jeu dans leurs pièces.

II. — NOUVELLES MACHINES DITES A PLATINE

Ces machines présentent d'importantes améliorations sur les anciens systèmes : réglage des chemins de rouleaux, chemins de rouleaux garnis de cuir, distribution par grande table cylindrique avec mouvement latéral facultatif, chargeurs des distributeurs avec mouvement latéral, touche parfaite avec trois ou quatre rouleaux suivant le format (deux rouleaux touchant la forme à la descente et les

FIG. 20. — Pédale Alauzet.

autres à la montée), suppression instantanée de la pression, marge au moyen de taquets, embrayage par friction avec frein, lubrification automatique des organes. Ces machines peuvent aussi faire l'estampage.

Enfin, dernier et grand avantage qui leur est propre, la forme reste fixée sur le marbre, la platine seule étant douée d'un mouvement de va-et-vient qui donne la pression.

Sur demande, les presses à platine sont fournies pour être chauffées, ce qui facilite beaucoup le bronzage.

Remarque très importante, dans ces pédales, il faut avoir soin de placer la forme en bas de la platine afin d'obtenir une pression bien régulière et éviter le papillottage qui se produit parfois au cours du tirage, surtout si l'on a besoin d'une forte pression.

III. — L'ESTAMPAGE

Toutes les presses à platine, soit manuelles, soit à pédale, peuvent servir à l'estampage pourvu qu'elles soient suffisamment solides ; c'est pourquoi nous allons donner sur ce genre de travail quelques notions sommaires.

Il faut, pour estamper : 1° une planche d'impression ; 2° une matrice en creux de cette planche ; 3° une contre-matrice en relief.

La planche d'impression peut être une gravure quelconque, ou du texte.

La matrice. On peut se la procurer facilement. Pour cela on tire une épreuve, sur papier très blanc et en bleu très clair, de la planche d'impression ; on noircit ensuite à l'encre tout le reste de la feuille non imprimée et on l'envoie au photograveur. Le zinc qu'il fournira sera la matrice en creux de la planche.

La contre-matrice. On peut fabriquer soi-même cette dernière. On prend quatre ou cinq feuilles de fort papier buvard, que l'on réunit ensemble au moyen d'une épaisse couche de colle de poisson. Ces feuilles encore humides sont posées sur la matrice et le tout est mis sous presse. La pression de la machine est suffisante pour produire le relief nécessaire. Une fois sèche, la contre-matrice est prête à servir.

Lorsqu'on veut procéder à l'estampage, pour repérer exactement la contre-matrice sur la matrice, on les place l'une sur l'autre de façon que les creux correspondent bien aux reliefs, et on enduit de colle le dos de la contre-matrice. La simple pression de la machine colle cette dernière à sa place sur la platine.

IV. — LE NUMÉROTAGE

Il existe aujourd'hui un très grand nombre de travaux qui exigent le numérotage, tels que : actions et obligations, carnets à souche, registres, billets de tombola, etc.

On peut diviser en trois les différents systèmes de numérotage : le foliotage à la main, le numérotage à pression, et le numérotage par châssis spéciaux.

1° Foliotage à la main. — Ce système, le plus ancien, le seul même en usage jusqu'à ces derniers temps, sert encore pour les travaux de peu d'importance. Tout le monde connaît le folioteur à main.

Nouvelle pédale " HÉRAKLÈS " (*Voirin*).

NOUVELLE PÉDALE

" HÉRAKLÈS "

(J. VOIRIN)

Les machines à platine à encrage cylindrique, qui conviennent si bien à l'impression des travaux de grand luxe en petits formats, se répandent de plus en plus, et nombreuses sont les imprimeries qui en possèdent plusieurs de différentes grandeurs.

Les établissements J. Voirin, si bien organisés et outillés, n'ont pas voulu laisser aux maisons étrangères le monopole de la fabrication de cette machine qui nous est venue d'Amérique, bien qu'elle fût à son origine de création française. Ils construisent depuis plusieurs années un modèle qu'ils ont dénommé « Héraklès » et qui répond bien à l'idée de puissance et de force qu'implique cette appellation.

Établie sur les mêmes principes que toutes les machines similaires, l'Héraklès se particularise par sa solidité incomparable et le soin extrême qui est apporté aux moindres détails de sa construction.

Nous nous contenterons donc d'en indiquer les caractéristiques essentielles :

Bâti d'une seule pièce. Platine très massive, d'une seule pièce également, se déplaçant parallèlement à elle-même et parfaitement guidée.

Bielles à forte section, en acier forgé.

Réglage précis et rapide de la pression.

Suppression instantanée de la pression.

Rectificateur automatique de marge.

Encrage puissant :

Rotation continue de l'encrier et faculté de le tourner à la main.

Encrier à lames.

Quatre toucheurs à tous les formats, deux encrant à la descente, les deux autres à la montée.

Arrêt facultatif des rouleaux en haut de course.

Chemin des galets réglables de hauteur.

Tous ces avantages font de l'Héraklès une excellente machine pour l'exécution des travaux de similigravure de trois couleurs, de découpage et d'estampage.

Il doit présenter trois qualités principales : la solidité, la régularité de l'encrage et la douceur.

2° Numérotage à pression. — Le folioteur à main ne pouvant suffire pour des travaux importants, on a dû chercher et on a trouvé un procédé plus expéditif. Le numéroteur à pression, d'un volume

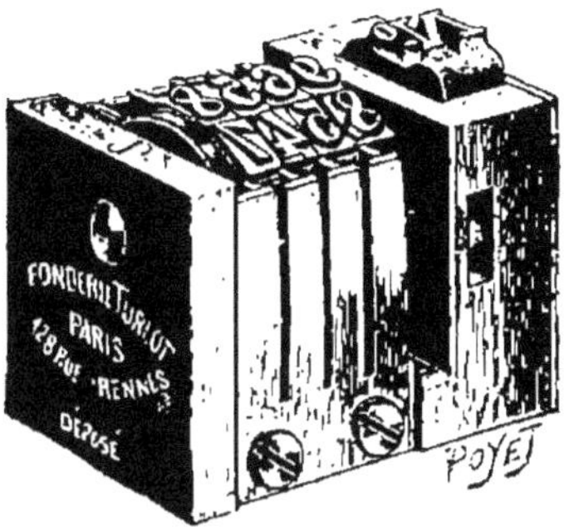

Fig. 21. — Le " Parfait ", numéroteur à pression.
(Fonderie Turlot; Henri Chaix, gendre et successeur.)

très restreint et de la hauteur du caractère, prend place dans la forme et fonctionne par la simple pression du cylindre. Le signe (N°), un peu plus élevé que le reste du système, sous la pression qu'il reçoit, commande un mécanisme qui change successivement les mollettes qui portent les chiffres.

Le numéroteur à pression le « Parfait » (fig. 21), de la fonderie Turlot, est bien l'appareil idéal pour numéroter vite et bien. D'un petit volume, se plaçant dans une forme quelconque, à l'endroit que l'on désire, sans dispositif spécial, il numérote en même temps que se fait le tirage des caractères.

Le « Parfait » a vaincu la grande difficulté qui résidait dans le mouvement du signe (N°) qui actionne la griffe. Ce signe est forcément plus haut que la hauteur du caractère, puisqu'il doit subir la pression de la platine ou du cylindre; mais, s'il dépasse trop la hauteur typographique, il détériore les rouleaux encreurs et empêche ces derniers de toucher l'œil des molettes. Au contraire, s'il est trop bas, la course étant moindre, la force est diminuée, et l'on risque d'avoir des ratés, surtout au moment où le passage du mille doit entraîner quatre molettes.

La solidité du « Parfait » lui permet de tirer plusieurs millions d'exemplaires sans aucune usure, étant fabriqué avec des matières de première qualité. Les rochets sont en acier trempé et les molettes sont fondues en bronze blanc, ce qui a permis de donner aux chiffres la régularité et la beauté d'œil des caractères typographiques, chose impossible avec les molettes gravées. Sa simplicité permet très facilement le démontage et le nettoyage de toutes les pièces.

D'une exactitude certaine, le « Parfait » se prête à toutes les combinaisons de numérotages possibles : *en décomptant*, c'est-à-dire en commençant par le chiffre le plus élevé et revenant à 0, les feuilles qui sortent de la machine étant classées dans l'ordre normal, la première en dessus; *en numérotant pair ou impair* pour le foliotage; *en numérotant par séries* pour les billets ou tickets devant être brochés par séries. On peut aussi *revenir à 0* par un jeu de combinaisons et *numéroter en double*, le nombre ne changeant que toutes les deux feuilles.

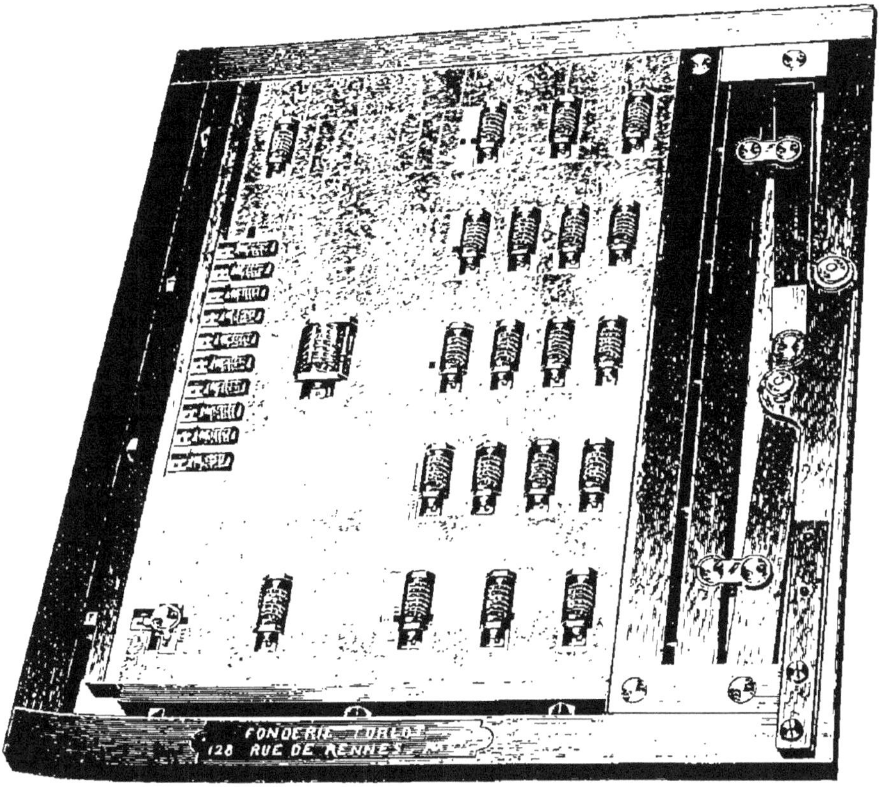

FIG. 22. — Châssis Derriey.
(Fonderie Turlot; Henri Chaix, gendre et successeur.)

Qualité appréciable, son prix est très peu élevé et varie suivant la grosseur des chiffres et le nombre des molettes.

3° Châssis numéroteur. — Les châssis numéroteurs sont employés pour des tirages très importants, actions, obligations, etc., où les numéros se trouvent parfois très rapprochés. Ces numéroteurs sont de deux sortes : le *châssis Derriey* et le *châssis universel.*

Fig. 23. — Numéroteur à griffe.
(Fonderie Turlot : Henri Chaix, gendre et successeur.)

A. Châssis Derriey (fig. 22). Dans ce châssis, appelé aussi *châssis à blancs typographiques,* les numéroteurs sont placés dans la forme comme des caractères et maintenus par des blancs spéciaux dits *blancs à pont,* évidés à leur partie inférieure pour le passage des tringles. Le changement des numéros est automatique. Chaque numéroteur est relié, au moyen de deux fourchettes, à des tringles qui viennent aboutir à un mouvement de commande situé sur un des côtés du châssis. Au moyen d'une butée, à chaque fin de course du marbre, le mouvement de commande fonctionne automatiquement.

Les avantages du châssis Derriey sont la simplicité du réglage et la faculté de rapprocher les numéroteurs.

B. Châssis universel ou à glissières. — Comme son nom l'indique, dans ce système, les numéroteurs glissent sur un système de glissières. Il présente comme avantage sur le précédent plus de légèreté et un maniement plus facile ; par contre, le rapprochement des numéroteurs n'est pas possible au delà d'une certaine limite.

Ces deux systèmes peuvent indifféremment servir aux divers genres de numérotages : numérotage par séries et numérotage par identique. Il suffit, suivant les cas, de combiner différemment les molettes portant les chiffres.

Le numéroteur employé dans le *châssis Derriey* et dans le *châssis universel* est le *numéroteur à griffe*, représenté ci-contre fig. 23.

VIII

IMPRESSION DES GRAVURES

L'impression des gravures demande plus de précautions encore et une mise en train plus soignée que celle des caractères. Dans une page de texte, à moins de lignes de titres un peu noires, le foulage se répartit également sur toutes les parties, la surface de l'œil de chaque lettre étant à peu près équivalente. Dans une gravure, la chose est bien différente : on a des parties chargées, noires, qui réclament plus de foulage ; d'autres légères, du trait, des demi-teintes, qui en demandent très peu. Pour obtenir cette impression à foulage inégal, il faut, pour chaque gravure, faire une opération, sorte de mise en train spéciale, qui s'appelle *découpage*.

I. — VÉRIFICATION DES CLICHÉS

Avant toute autre chose, le conducteur doit vérifier la hauteur des clichés. Les gravures peuvent être tenues plus ou moins hautes, suivant leur nature et les effets que l'on veut obtenir. Pour ce travail, on se sert d'un instrument appelé *pont de calibre* (fig. 24). Si le cliché est trop fort ou trop faible, on diminue le bois au moyen d'une râpe, ou on le surélève au moyen de hausses collées au pied.

On passe ensuite une première épreuve pour

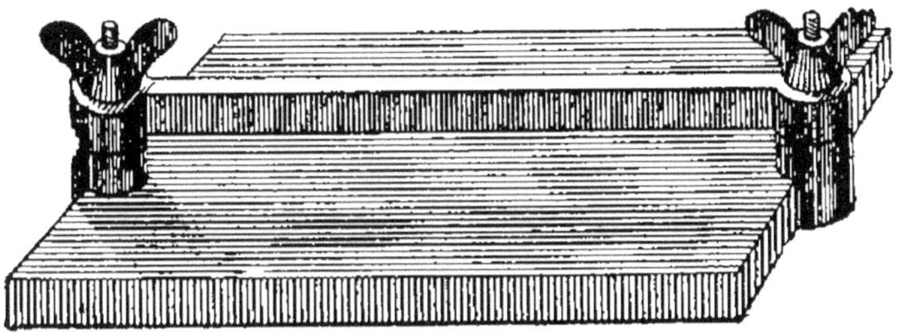

Fig. 24. — Pont de calibre (*Maison Foucher*).

voir si le cliché est d'aplomb et s'il reçoit un foulage bien égal. Lorsqu'une gravure se trouve creuse en un point, il faut la démonter et coller en dessous deux, trois ou quatre feuilles de papier très mince, que l'on déchire de plus en plus petites, suivant la forme de la faiblesse; on recloue la gravure, et la pression de la machine fait le reste.

Si la faiblesse est produite par une soufflure de la matière, on repousse délicatement le métal avec un chasse-pointe; au besoin on coule un peu de résine dans le trou ainsi produit.

Pour déclouer un cliché sans le fausser, on donne deux ou trois coups de marteau sur un des côtés du bois; le cliché se soulève facilement de lui-même et on peut le séparer à l'aide d'un ciseau quelconque.

Il est préférable, en reclouant un cliché, de faire de nouveaux trous pour les pointes, si l'on veut qu'il soit solidement fixé.

Si le bois de montage d'un cliché est voilé, on corrige ce défaut au moyen d'un ou de plusieurs traits de scie dirigés dans le sens de la hauteur jusqu'à deux ou trois millimètres de la surface du bois. La pression du cylindre le redresse.

Cette correction des clichés devra de préférence être faite avant la mise en pages; on évite ainsi des pertes de temps sous presse. C'est pourquoi, lorsque le metteur en pages recevra ses gravures, il les remettra sans tarder au conducteur, qui pourra les préparer entre deux mises en train.

Cette précaution est surtout utile lorsque la gravure doit être encastrée dans le texte d'une façon compliquée; l'extraction en est souvent assez difficile et non sans danger pour la composition.

La gravure sur bois doit se mouiller le moins possible. Pour le lavage sous presse, on frottera le cliché avec une flanelle humectée légèrement d'essence. Le bois imbibé d'eau ou d'essence est sujet à se voiler et supporte moins bien le tirage.

Un nouveau procédé de mise de hauteur des clichés consiste dans l'emploi d'une pâte appelée « Métal plastique ». On enduit le pied du cliché trop faible d'une forte couche de cette composition et, après l'avoir recouverte d'un buvard mince, on le soumet à la pression de la presse jusqu'à obtention de la hauteur voulue. Une fois sec, on coupe le papier tout autour et on polit à la toile émeri les quatre côtés.

II. — DÉCOUPAGES

Quel que soit le procédé employé, un bon découpage doit reproduire exactement le relief de la gravure : les parties fortes en représentent les noirs, et les creux les blancs. Le découpage a pour but de mettre en couleur la gravure, de lui donner de la vigueur, du relief : ce qu'on ne pourrait obtenir autrement.

Pour arriver à ce résultat, il faut d'abord se bien rendre compte de la gravure à traiter, des différentes nuances à obtenir. Nous ferons donc une épreuve très nette, de façon à bien remarquer tous les détails avant de procéder au découpage.

On connaît surtout trois sortes de découpages : au *couteau*, aux *ciseaux* et au *pinceau*.

Il existe aussi une nouvelle méthode de MM. Albert Bierstardt et Théodore de Vienne, de New-York, une sorte de découpage chimique ; mais cette manière est peu pratique.

Découpage au couteau. — Parmi ces divers genres de découpages, c'est au premier que nous donnons la préférence, le couteau étant plus facile à manier et donnant un résultat plus exact, plus délicat.

Un bon couteau à découpage doit être bien pointu.

flexible sans excès et bien tranchant. On peut décou-

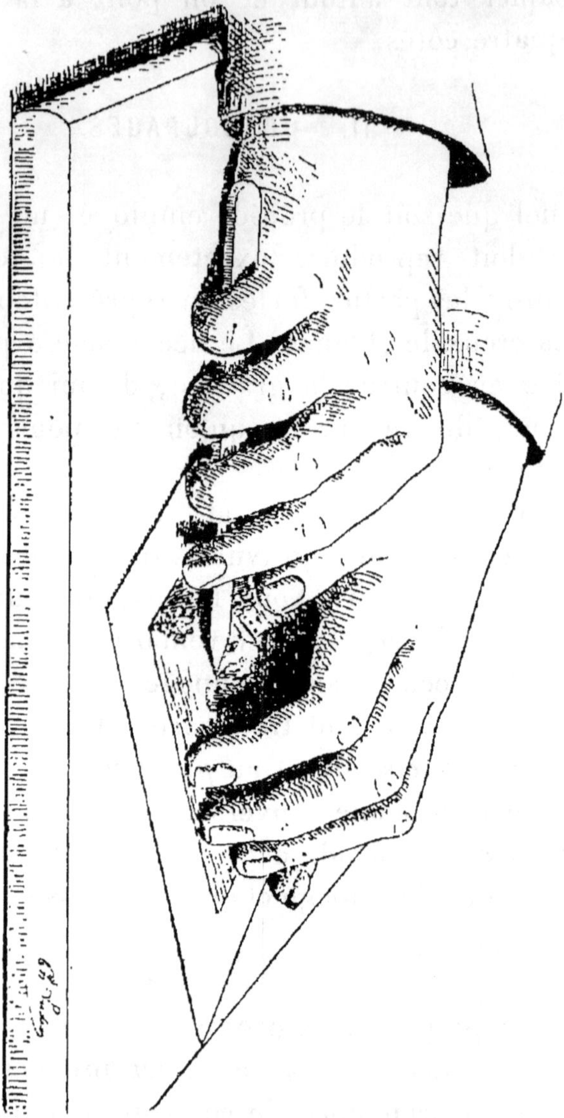

FIG. 25. — Position du couteau pour le découpage d'une gravure.

per sur un petit marbre ou tout simplement sur une glace un peu forte, en ayant soin d'interposer sous la gravure à découper un carton mince, pas trop dur, sans gravier et un peu plus grand que celle-ci.

Le couteau se tient comme un grattoir, la main en dessus (fig. 25), et la tranchée se fait en biseau, afin d'atténuer le plus possible les différences de relief. On présente successivement chaque partie de la gravure au couteau en faisant tourner le carton sur lequel elle repose.

La colle employée doit être de bonne qualité, pas trop liquide, et ne renfermer aucune matière étrangère susceptible de produire des aspérités en séchant.

Le découpage varie un peu, suivant le genre de gravure et le mode d'impression.

Nous parlerons, en premier lieu, des découpages pour gravure sur bois ou galvano de gravure sur bois.

Gravure sur bois et galvano de gravure sur bois. — On tire sur papier de huit kilos environ (carré) trois épreuves de la gravure, et on les laisse bien sécher avant de s'en servir, afin d'éviter le maculage.

Pour gagner du temps, on peut passer un peu de colle de pâte liquide sur les épreuves. Deux ou trois minutes après, les épreuves sont sèches, et l'on peut procéder au découpage sans craindre le maculage.

Dans la première de ces trois épreuves, on enlève au couteau tous les blancs et les extrémités des traits qui pourraient piquer.

Dans la deuxième, les parties bien accusées de la gravure sont prises et collées sur la première feuille exactement à leurs places respectives. Il faut employer dans cette opération le moins de colle possible pour éviter que les découpages ne varient en séchant, ce qui rendrait le repérage impossible, surtout dans les gravures de grandes dimensions. Lorsqu'on a de grands morceaux à coller, il vaut mieux, s'ils se sont allongés sous l'influence de la colle, les couper en deux et en supprimer un petit morceau.

Le deuxième plan fixé en place, on met le découpage entre deux petites plaques de zinc ou de carton, et l'on charge légèrement pour l'empêcher de se voiler; on passe ensuite à la troisième épreuve.

Ici, l'on ne prend que les parties fortement ombrées, les noirs du dessin : on procède de la même manière et avec les mêmes précautions que précédemment, et on met de nouveau un peu sous presse.

Il ne reste plus maintenant qu'à finir le découpage, en le suivant dans tous les détails de la gravure. Dans les parties que nous avons mises en relief, il y a de nombreux petits blancs qu'il eût été difficile d'enlever dans notre premier travail : ce sont de petites lignes, des éclairages à ménager dans certaines parties du dessin. Dans un portrait nous aurons, par exemple, des cheveux, de la barbe, certains traits de la figure à mettre en lumière; dans un paysage, des reflets d'eau, des feuilles d'arbres, etc. Tout cela doit être enlevé à demi, et même à

Fig. 26. — Gravure au trait tirée sans découpage.

Fig. 27. — Gravure au trait tirée avec découpage.

ATELIERS ARTISTIQUES DE LA FONDERIE CASLON

Cliché obtenu d'après une photographie bonne, mais sans aucune retouche.

Cliché obtenu d'après la même photographie retouchée à l'*Aérograph*.

pleine épaisseur de papier, suivant l'éclairage à obtenir, mais toujours en ayant soin de biseauter le coup de couteau. Enfin, on enlève au couteau les marges du découpage, et on peut le repérer sur le cylindre de la machine ou sur le tympan de la presse à bras.

Lorsqu'une gravure est tirée avec un découpage bien fait, on ne doit apercevoir aucune trace de foulage au dos de l'impression, si toutefois l'habillage du cylindre a été fait avec soin.

Si les gravures doivent être tirées avec du caractère, on mettra en place les découpages dans la première feuille de mise en train; on pourra ensuite corriger avec du papier mince les petites faiblesses qui proviendraient de l'habillage du cylindre. Puis on aura soin, dans la seconde feuille de mise en train, de découper la place de la gravure, pour ne pas trop supporter le texte environnant qui ne viendrait plus.

Pour certains galvanos de gravures sur bois dont les tailles sont très faibles, il faut tenir le découpage très léger, bien exact, et tirer avec peu d'encre et un foulage bien sec.

Pour les gravures sur bois, les découpages devront toujours être plus faibles que pour les galvanos de ces gravures, afin de ne pas déterminer un foulage trop fort, qui les détériorerait rapidement. Les découpages doivent aussi être plus légers pour un tirage à la presse à bras, et les bords en seront coupés droit, le foulage étant plus sec et se faisant verticalement.

Gravure au trait ou dessin à la plume. — On peut traiter la gravure au trait, ou dessin à la plume, comme la gravure sur bois, en ayant soin de découper l'extrémité de tous les traits isolés, qui, autrement, piqueraient.

Photogravure et similigravure. — La photogravure, étant plus délicate comme finesse de traits et d'une profondeur de taille moins grande que la gravure sur bois, exige plus de précision et de délicatesse dans le découpage.

Voici de quelle façon on peut procéder pour le découpage des photogravures ou similigravures, obtenues d'après photographie ou d'après dessin sur papier Gillot, dessin à la plume ou gravure sur bois.

Nous faisons d'abord quatre bonnes épreuves de la gravure sur du papier glacé de six kilos environ (carré); le papier choisi doit être bien régulier, et surtout sans impureté. On emploie de la colle pas trop épaisse et sans grumeaux; les morceaux découpés n'en doivent pas être enduits complètement, mais seulement de place en place.

Une des épreuves est laissée intacte, pour servir de support aux autres. Dans la seconde, on enlève au couteau toutes les teintes légères du dessin et les pointillés les plus fins, qui doivent à peine paraître. Ici, encore plus que pour la gravure sur bois, il ne faut employer que la coupe biseautée; sinon, dans une photogravure un peu délicate, on pourra suivre sur l'épreuve avec découpage tous les reliefs de

FIG. 28. — D'après un dessin au crayon.
Gravure extraite de *Madame Corentine* (Maison Mame, Tours).

celui-ci. C'est pour cette même raison que l'on prend du papier plus mince que pour les découpages de gravures sur bois.

De la troisième épreuve, on ne prend plus que les teintes accentuées du dessin, et dans la quatrième, seulement les ombres les plus fortes.

Le tout est ensuite fixé et superposé exactement sur la première épreuve, et nous avons ainsi un découpage à quatre plans, qui donnera au tirage quatre foulages différents.

On charge légèrement ce découpage pour en faire sécher la colle et l'empêcher de se voiler, puis on le finit dans ses détails ; il est prêt alors à être mis en place.

Lorsque, par suite de gravures défectueuses, on a des ciels tachés à imprimer, il faut les rendre le plus légers possible pour atténuer ce défaut. On décloue les gravures et l'on fixe entre elles et le bois une feuille de papier raisin de vingt kilos, dans laquelle on a découpé la partie correspondante au ciel. La gravure est reclouée ensuite ; la partie non soutenue par la feuille intercalée cède sous la pression, et le foulage se fait forcément moins sentir en cet endroit. Pour certains travaux, cette sorte de découpage sous le cliché peut remplacer avantageusement celui que l'on colle sur le cylindre.

On peut aussi recourir à un moyen plus rapide pour faire un découpage de photogravure. Si le dessin n'est pas trop délicat, au lieu d'employer quatre feuilles superposées, on n'en prend que deux de papier fort, collées l'une sur l'autre, ou même une seule, et on fait son découpage en enlevant au couteau plus ou moins d'épaisseur de papier, suivant les différents plans du dessin.

On comprend facilement que l'on n'obtiendra ainsi qu'un résultat approximatif, bon tout au plus pour des clichés grossiers.

Il arrive qu'un fabricant a livré un cliché de photogravure accompagné d'une épreuve impeccable, et que l'imprimeur, au contraire, ne peut en tirer aucun bon résultat; au lieu de la teinte fondue qui encadre le sujet sur l'épreuve du graveur, il obtient une bande sale et empâtée du plus mauvais effet. Il serait injuste d'incriminer l'imprimeur, qui n'y peut mais : la faute est au graveur. Ce dernier, après l'encrage de sa gravure, en a tout simplement essuyé les bords, et il a pu ainsi livrer une bonne épreuve d'un mauvais cliché. Mais comme l'imprimeur ne saurait en faire autant pour chaque feuille du tirage, c'est à lui de veiller et de renvoyer au fabricant le cliché défectueux.

Découpage au pinceau. — Le découpage des photogravures peut également se faire au pinceau et donner de bons résultats; mais c'est plutôt là un travail d'amateur, qui ne peut lutter pour la facilité et la rapidité avec le découpage au couteau. Voici, néanmoins, la façon de procéder.

La matière employée est un mélange de gélatine blonde et de rouge d'Angleterre. On fait dissoudre au bain-marie la gélatine dans une petite quantité d'eau, et on mélange la couleur de manière à obtenir une pâte très fluide. Il faut avoir soin d'enlever tous les grains et grumeaux qui pourraient s'y trouver.

Avec un pinceau dont la finesse est en rapport avec l'étendue de la partie de dessin à couvrir, on applique cette composition sur une épreuve de la gravure en évitant de laisser paraître les coups de pinceau. On passe ensuite deux ou trois couches successives, dont l'épaisseur varie suivant les parties plus ou moins accentuées de la gravure et le degré de foulage que l'on veut obtenir, et l'on a ainsi une sorte de peinture en relief qui remplit le même office que le découpage au couteau.

Ce procédé, assez simple en théorie, présente en pratique plusieurs inconvénients : en premier lieu, il faut constamment tenir la gélatine chaude, ce qui nécessite l'emploi d'un petit réchaud ou veilleuse à bain-marie; il faut aussi passer son pinceau rapidement, sans hésitation, car autrement, la gélatine se refroidissant très vite, il serait complètement impossible de l'étendre sans former des aspérités qui nuiraient au résultat.

De plus, l'humidité fait gonfler et déformer l'enduit; de sorte qu'il faut éviter de mettre de la colle ou du papier humide sur la mise en train si l'on ne veut pas avoir son travail à refaire. Si l'on remarque enfin que les corrections sur le cylindre ne sont pas des plus commodes, attendu qu'il faut transporter le bain-marie sur la machine, on en conclura que ce genre de découpage est très peu pratique.

Mise en train mécanique S. A. D. A. G. — La Société anonyme des arts graphiques de Genève a acquis la propriété d'un procédé dit : « mise en train mécanique S. A. D. A. G. » Cette mise en train a pour but de remplacer le découpage des photogravures. Elle est livrée, prête à servir, en même temps que le cliché. Avec ce procédé, l'impresion de la photogravure est garantie parfaite, et cette sorte de découpage résiste aux plus forts tirages, tout en conservant aux illustrations leur netteté et leur finesse.

Mise en train " Korekta ". — Citons pour mémoire un procédé très expéditif, la « mise en train *Korekta* », au moyen de colophane en poudre dont on recouvre les épreuves très nettes des similigravures et que l'on fixe en passant au-dessus un fer chaud.

III. — TIRAGE

Habillage. — L'habillage des cylindres pour le tirage des gravures doit être très soigné, et l'étoffage léger ne devra pas plonger. Les blanchets seront tenus en bon état, et on aura soin de les laver de temps en temps pour rendre l'élasticité au tissu.

Si, le découpage en place, une gravure présente encore des parties faibles, on fait la correction sur le cylindre avec de la coquille mince. Pour une photogravure, on n'emploiera que du papier pelure, surtout dans les ciels, les fonds légers ; si l'on veut éviter de produire des taches, nous recommandons encore une fois de déchirer le papier au lieu de le couper au couteau ou aux ciseaux.

Papier. — Pour l'impression des gravures, il faut choisir un papier bien glacé, d'une pâte régulière et homogène.

Rouleaux. — Pour l'impression des gravures, il faut de bons rouleaux parfaitement ronds, élastiques, un peu plus frais que pour le caractère et peu chargés d'encre. On aura soin d'enlever aux rouleaux toutes les aspérités résultant de la fonte, qui produiraient des taches dans le tirage des gravures.

Lorsqu'on tire des photogravures intercalées dans le texte, il faut augmenter la touche ; à défaut d'un rouleau, on met un chargeur.

Si les gravures présentent un fond noir ou un ciel très clair, il est nécessaire que les rouleaux soient réglés de façon à affleurer, suivant le cas, soit les vignettes, soit le texte. De cette façon, les rouleaux ne plongeant pas dans les tailles du dessin, celui-ci reste toujours très net et l'encrage brillant.

Encrage. — Nous dirons en passant que l'encrage cylindrique est supérieur à tout autre pour la régularité de la distribution.

Grâce à ces quelques notions, le conducteur intelligent arrivera rapidement à de bons résultats, même dans le tirage des photogravures, sans être obligé de recourir à des tâtonnements sans fin.

FIG. 29. — Gravure d'après aquarelle rehaussée de gouache.
Extraite de *Les Noellet*, par René Bazin, de l'Académie française (Maison Mame, Tours).

DEUXIÈME PARTIE

DE L'IMPRESSION EN COULEURS

I

PRÉLIMINAIRES

Tous les conducteurs typographes ne sont pas appelés à faire habituellement des tirages en couleurs ; quelques-uns n'en font même jamais, ou de si simples, que les notions qu'ils ont du tirage en noir leur sont à peu près suffisantes pour obtenir des résultats satisfaisants.

C'est là le prétexte allégué par certains auteurs de manuels pour passer sous silence l'étude de l'impression en couleurs.

Sans doute, ces auteurs n'ont-ils pas tout à fait tort en théorie ; mais en pratique, ils sont loin d'avoir raison.

Il vaut mieux savoir un peu plus qu'il n'est rigoureusement nécessaire, que risquer de se voir arrêté, faute de connaissances, par un travail quelquefois sans grande difficulté.

C'est pourquoi j'ai cru bien faire en consacrant la seconde partie de mon manuel à une étude relativement développée de l'impression en couleurs.

Plus nous allons, plus ce genre devient à la mode, grâce au perfectionnement incessant de l'outillage, des clichés, de l'encre, du papier, des rouleaux, etc. ; et l'imprimeur sérieux ne doit rien négliger pour mettre son habileté au niveau de la perfection de tout le reste.

Après une étude sommaire des conditions spéciales à l'impression en couleurs concernant le local, les machines, les rouleaux, etc., nous étudierons les couleurs, les encres, le bronzage, etc. etc.

Conditions spéciales à l'impression en couleurs.

I. — LOCAL

La plupart des notions concernant l'impression en noir, comme nous l'avons dit plus haut, s'appliquent naturellement à celle en couleurs. Néanmoins, cette dernière comportant plus de précision, et par suite plus de difficultés, il s'ensuit certaines modifications dans l'outillage et les divers éléments de ce genre d'impression.

Le choix du local a une très grande importance dans l'impression des travaux en couleurs. Les rez-de-chaussée sont, en général, préférables aux étages,

Nouvelle machine en blanc à deux tours du cylindre (*Maison Alauzet*).

NOUVELLE MACHINE EN BLANC

à deux tours du cylindre

(Maison ALAUZET)

La machine en blanc à deux tours de cylindre est construite sur le principe de la machine à retiration, c'est-à-dire que le cylindre continue sa rotation, mais qu'au retour de la forme il se soulève au lieu de s'arrêter comme dans les machines en blanc ordinaires, ce qui évite les chocs d'arrêt et permet d'obtenir une vitesse beaucoup plus considérable.

Encrage mixte; quatre rouleaux toucheurs commandés par crémaillère; distributeurs munis de rouleaux chargeurs lisses en acier; table à encre en fonte.

Le receveur mécanique est placé sur le devant du cylindre, il est avec pinces qui viennent prendre la feuille prise déjà dans les pinces du cylindre de pression.

Réglage du mouvement du marbre à fin de course au moyen de quatre pompes à air.

Construction très robuste.

Rendement en double jésus : 2000 exemplaires à l'heure.

Convient pour impressions de catalogues en similis.

Pour les tirages en couleurs, ne pas dépasser 1200 à l'heure.

où la trépidation rend le repérage plus difficile et l'usure des machines plus rapide.

Le local doit être aussi bien éclairé et très sec, conditions qu'il est difficile de rencontrer unies à la précédente. Néanmoins, pour tout concilier, on pourrait choisir un rez-de-chaussée bien aéré, éclairé par en haut au moyen d'un vitrage formant couverture. En disposant ce vitrage en plusieurs petits toits obliques, on aurait une lumière plus diffuse donnant un éclairage excellent.

Il faut aussi que le local soit à l'abri de la poussière, celle-ci pouvant, surtout dans les teintes légères, dénaturer la couleur en la salissant.

II. — MACHINES

Plus encore que pour l'impression en noir, les machines devront être tenues dans le plus grand état de propreté, en vue d'un fonctionnement irréprochable et de la plus grande netteté des teintes.

La table à encre et l'encrier seront nettoyés à fond, surtout ce dernier qui est sujet à garder des traces d'encre dans les encoignures. Au besoin, on démontera les différentes pièces de la machine.

Si le tirage n'est que de deux à trois cents exemplaires, on peut se dispenser de se servir de l'encrier. On supprime le preneur et l'on étend l'encre directement, soit sur la table, soit sur les gros rouleaux d'encrage, si l'encrage est cylindrique.

Dans les machines de construction un peu ancienne,

la table à encre est ordinairement en bois, et s'imprègne fortement d'encre, ce qui la rend très difficile à nettoyer. Pour obvier à cet inconvénient, il suffit de la recouvrir d'une feuille de zinc. On fixe celle-ci d'un côté sous la tringle de fer contre laquelle s'appuie le serrage des formes, et l'on recourbe l'autre côté sous la table, pour empêcher les rouleaux de l'arracher. De cette façon, le nettoyage est plus facile.

Les machines nouvelles, avec leur table en fonte, ne présentent pas cet inconvénient. Elles ont, par contre, en hiver, celui d'être trop froides. Les encres de couleur, les rouges surtout, se distribuent très mal, et l'on est obligé de chauffer la table en commençant. Le fonctionnement de la machine entretient ensuite une chaleur suffisante pendant le cours du tirage.

III. — ROULEAUX

On n'emploiera pas, surtout pour les couleurs vives et les teintes claires, des rouleaux ayant servi pour le noir ; cette encre, même dans des rouleaux ni piqués ni crevassés, pénétrant profondément dans la matière.

C'est pourquoi il est bon, dans les imprimeries faisant couramment de la couleur, d'avoir un jeu spécial de rouleaux à cet usage : c'est là une grande économie de temps et la condition indispensable d'un bon travail.

Si l'on est dans la nécessité d'employer des rouleaux ayant déjà servi pour une autre couleur, on

les lavera très soigneusement. Une fois secs, ils seront fortement encrés, puis lavés à l'essence de térébenthine. Après les avoir bien rincés, on les laissera sécher, le temps d'acquérir le degré d'amour voulu.

Pour obtenir un séchage rapide, il faut placer les rouleaux dans un courant d'air légèrement chaud. On peut, dans les cas urgents, passer une dissolution d'alun ou de tannin, qui a pour but de durcir la gélatine et de former une peau mince à la surface du rouleau. Mais ce procédé détériore rapidement la matière, et il faut éviter d'en abuser.

IV. — FORMES

La forme à tirer doit être soigneusement lavée avant le tirage, et aussi durant le tirage, dès que l'on s'apercevra que le caractère ou la vignette commencent à s'encrasser, ce qui arrive fréquemment lorsqu'on tire du rouge, et surtout les bruns, ocres, terre de Sienne, etc. Il faut mettre sur la brosse très peu d'essence quand la forme contient du texte. La couleur délayée, une fois sèche, rendrait la distribution à peu près impossible.

Le tirage terminé, on brossera la forme à la potasse et on la rincera à grande eau.

V. — POINTURES

Une des conditions les plus importantes d'une bonne impression en couleurs, c'est un repérage parfait, c'est-à-dire la superposition exacte des différentes teintes.

Dans certains cas, on peut, au moyen de la marge

Fig. 30. — Pointures. — Vis de pointure.

seule, arriver à ce résultat et obtenir de bons tirages en couleurs. Mais il faut pour cela que la pédale ou la machine en blanc soit en parfait état; qu'elle n'ait à subir aucun ébranlement qui pourrait déplacer la feuille; que le papier soit d'une force suffisante pour n'être pas sujet à se voiler à la marge; il faut aussi que le margeur ait soin de marger la feuille toujours du même côté et de la retenir jusqu'à ce que l'abat-feuille ou les pinces l'aient prise.

Le plus généralement, l'impression en couleurs exige l'emploi des pointures.

Ces pointures se placent dans la forme au premier tirage.

Il y en a un grand nombre d'espèces différentes, divisées en deux classes principales : les fines et les grosses. On les trouve chez les fournisseurs, ou bien on les fabrique soi-même.

Pointures fines. — Les unes sont simplement formées d'un petit bloc de métal où vient se visser ou s'enfoncer un piquot analogue à ceux du cylindre. Ces sortes de pointures se justifient dans la forme.

D'autres sont formées d'une petite lame métal-

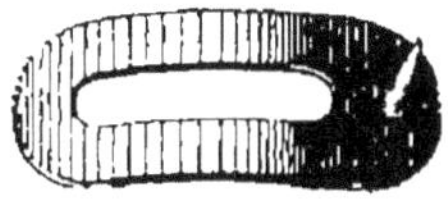

Fig. 31. — Pointure à coulisse.

lique coudée vers le milieu à angle droit et portant un piquot à l'extrémité d'une de ses branches. Cette branche est placée de façon à reposer sur la barre du châssis ; l'autre branche est serrée entre les garnitures et le châssis, et maintient le système.

On se sert aussi comme pointures de simples piquots fixés, au moyen d'un pas de vis, dans des trous ménagés à cette intention dans la barre du châssis.

Enfin les pointures à coulisse se fixent également au moyen d'une vis sur la barre du châssis. Elles sont formées d'un piquot fixé à l'extrémité d'une mince lame d'acier munie d'une fente longitudinale.

Cette disposition permet de varier facilement

la position de la pointure, tout en conservant sa stabilité.

On peut aussi fabriquer soi-même les pointures dont on a besoin.

Parfois, on fixe dans une réglette de bois autant de pointes qu'il est nécessaire, de façon à ce qu'elles soient de hauteur avec le caractère. On façonne la tête en pointe au moyen de la lime.

On se sert aussi de filets de cuivre de trois ou six points. Le filet est entaillé du côté de l'œil sur douze ou quinze points de hauteur, de façon à former une série de pointes.

En règle générale, l'extrémité des pointures fines ne doit pas être trop aiguë, il vaut mieux les émousser légèrement : de cette façon, elles font l'effet d'un emporte-pièce et donnent un perforage régulier, au lieu de déchirer le papier.

Le piquot doit être tenu un peu plus bas que l'œil de la lettre, risque à charger avec un petit carton sous la mise en train.

Pour les retirations successives des impressions en couleurs, on se sert, comme pour une retiration ordinaire, de la pointure d'avant du cylindre et de celle de la marge.

Grosses pointures. — On emploie, surtout pour les tirages en trois couleurs, qui demandent une grande précision de repérage, de grosses pointures de 5 à 6 millimètres environ.

Comme on ne saurait percer des trous de cette dimension de la façon qu'on le fait pour les petites pointures, on doit recourir à une opération préalable.

Le papier est margé sur une table spéciale, dite table à perforer, par paquets de dix à vingt feuilles, suivant l'épaisseur, et percé des trous de pointures au moyen de deux emporte-pièce, placés de chaque côté et mis en mouvement par une pédale.

Pour les retirations, on se sert de pointures de même diamètre. Vu leur dimension, ces trous de pointure sont moins sujets à s'agrandir et peuvent servir pour huit et même dix repérages.

Pointure automatique Taesch. — La pointure automatique Taesch est un genre de grosse pointure perfectionnée. Le perforage se fait automatiquement au premier tirage et n'exige pas d'opération préalable.

Les pointures, au nombre de deux, avec, entre elles, un même nombre de taquets, sont fixées par un dispositif spécial dans la gorge du cylindre. La feuille est margée, puis perforée automatiquement, après quoi elle est entraînée par les pinces. La feuille se trouve percée de deux gros trous de pointure et munie de deux échancrures en forme de V.

Pour la retiration, les pointures et les taquets ne changent pas de place. Il suffit de placer la feuille de façon à faire coïncider ensemble les échancrures et les taquets. Les pointures se lèvent, et la feuille est pointée automatiquement.

Quand on veut se servir de grosses pointures, il

faut calculer le format du papier de façon à pouvoir faire disparaître les trous de pointure et les échancrures au façonnage.

VI. — ENCRES

Comme nous l'avons déjà dit dans notre première partie en parlant de l'encre noire, il est plus simple pour l'imprimeur de commander au fabricant les encres de couleurs toutes préparées. S'il a eu soin de bien désigner la teinte et l'emploi qu'il en veut faire, il recevra exactement l'encre appropriée, toute prête à servir.

Si l'on se trouve parfois dans la nécessité de préparer soi-même une petite quantité d'encre, on veillera à ce que le broyage soit fait avec beaucoup de soin, certaines couleurs, comme le vermillon et le bleu de Prusse, étant très difficiles à bien mélanger. Pour cela on aura soin d'opérer à la fois sur de très petites quantités d'encre et de vernis.

Les encres en boîtes se conservent, comme nous l'avons indiqué dans notre première partie, au moyen d'eau. C'est surtout pour les encres de couleurs que sont employés les tubes avec bouchon à vis. De cette manière, un imprimeur peut se munir des principales teintes en usage, sans risquer trop de perte.

Après une interruption de tirage de quelques heures, il faut laver la table à encre, les encres de couleurs perdant généralement de leurs qualités en séchant.

On pourra laisser les rouleaux encrés, mais en ayant soin de les recouvrir de feuilles de papier pour les garantir de la poussière et empêcher l'encre de sécher.

Quand on se sert d'encre à vernis très siccatif, il faut éviter les courants d'air, qui accélèrent fortement le séchage de l'encre.

Pour les tirages à grande vitesse, principalement sur les machines rotatives à plusieurs couleurs, on emploie des encres spéciales, qui sèchent pour ainsi dire instantanément sur le papier. Dans ce cas, il est nécessaire de brasser de temps en temps avec la palette l'encre contenue dans les encriers. En effet, celle-ci, par suite du mouvement de rotation du cylindre de l'encrier, se prend en masse et ne passerait plus entre le cylindre et le couteau, ou bien le vernis passerait seul tandis que la matière colorante resterait dans l'encrier.

VII. — PAPIER

En règle générale, le papier de tirage en couleurs devra être glacé le plus possible, et ne pas produire de poussières qui pourraient altérer la couleur et nuire à la netteté de l'impression.

On aura bien soin d'observer que seul un papier bien blanc et bien opaque conservera fidèlement la teinte employée, et que la plus légère coloration ou transparence aurait pour but de la modifier plus ou moins.

Le glaçage a pour but de rendre le papier

plus insensible à l'humidité et à la pression répétée du cylindre, et d'obtenir un repérage parfait au cours des divers tirages.

Pour obtenir un très bon glaçage, on opère à deux ou trois reprises consécutives, après quelques heures d'intervalle chaque fois, en ayant soin de faire passer les feuilles en long et en large, afin que le glaçage se produise bien dans les deux sens.

On évitera, dans le tirage des couleurs, de tremper le papier, surtout dans les repérages délicats.

II

ÉTUDE DES COULEURS

I. — NOTIONS SUR LA LUMIERE

Il n'est pas inutile pour l'imprimeur sérieux d'avoir quelques notions sommaires sur la lumière et sur les couleurs. Il pourra se rendre compte plus facilement des moyens à employer pour obtenir certains effets voulus et éviter ainsi de longs et fastidieux tâtonnements.

La lumière solaire, que nous voyons blanche, est formée en réalité de la combinaison de rayons diversement colorés. On s'en rend compte en faisant passer un rayon lumineux à travers un prisme de cristal : la lumière, reçue sur un écran disposé à cet effet, se trouve décomposée en sept couleurs placées dans l'ordre suivant : rouge, orangé, jaune, vert, bleu, indigo, violet; c'est ce qu'on appelle le spectre solaire. C'est un phénomène analogue, dans des proportions autrement grandes, qui produit ce que nous appelons l'arc-en-ciel.

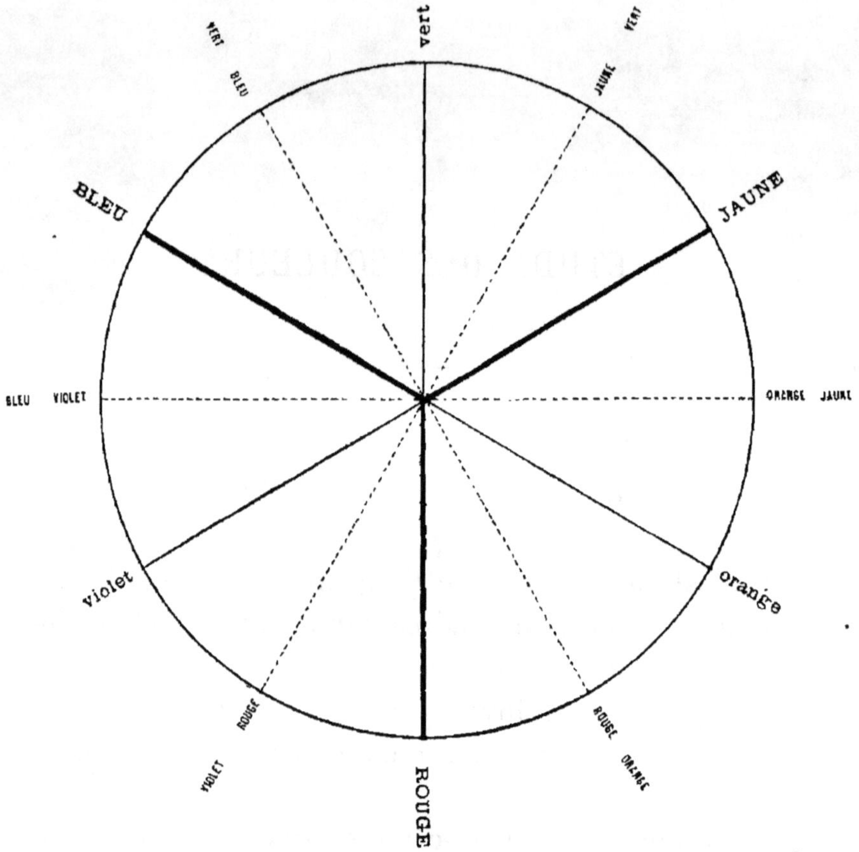

Fig. 32. — Couleurs fondamentales et leurs complémentaires.

Parmi les sept couleurs du spectre, le jaune, le rouge et le bleu, qui sont des couleurs simples, sont appelées fondamentales, parce que leurs différents mélanges peuvent produire toutes les autres teintes. Les quatre autres couleurs du spectre : l'orangé, le vert, l'indigo et le violet, sont déjà le produit de diverses combinaisons des trois couleurs fondamentales. Le noir, en tant que couleur, est l'absence de la lumière; et le blanc est la lumière elle-même, résultant de la combinaison des trois couleurs fondamentales.

II. — COULEURS COMPLÉMENTAIRES

Deux couleurs dont la combinaison produit la lumière blanche sont appelées complémentaires l'une de l'autre. Ainsi, le vert est complémentaire du rouge, l'orangé du bleu, le violet du jaune, et *vice versa*.

Voici le moyen de trouver la complémentaire d'une couleur donnée. On trace une circonférence (fig. 32), et on la divise en trois parties égales au moyen de trois rayons. A l'extrémité de ces rayons, on inscrit le nom des trois couleurs fondamentales : rouge, jaune, bleu. On prolonge ensuite chacun des rayons du centre à la circonférence, et à l'extrémité des nouveaux rayons obtenus on inscrit le nom des couleurs résultant de la combinaison des deux avoisinantes; ainsi le prolongement du jaune se trouvant entre le bleu et le rouge, on inscrira le violet qui résulte de leur mélange; de même au prolongement du rouge, on inscrira le vert, etc.

On peut encore diviser par la moitié chacun des secteurs obtenus et procéder d'une façon analogue : on obtient ainsi le bleu violet, le bleu vert, le jaune vert, etc.

Si maintenant nous voulons connaître la complémentaire d'une couleur, nous n'aurons qu'à nous reporter à la figure que nous venons de tracer. Aux deux extrémités de chaque diamètre on lira les couleurs réciproquement complémentaires. Nous trouverons ainsi le violet comme complémentaire du jaune, le rouge pour le bleu vert, etc.

Ces quelques notions sur les couleurs complémentaires suffiront à expliquer les phénomènes que l'on désigne sous les noms de contraste successif et de contraste simultané des couleurs.

III. — CONTRASTE DES COULEURS

1° Contraste successif des couleurs. — Si, après avoir regardé, pendant quelques secondes, un disque rouge placé sur une surface blanche, on enlève brusquement ce disque sans changer le regard de place, on aperçoit l'endroit occupé auparavant par le disque comme coloré en vert; le vert est justement la couleur complémentaire du rouge.

Inversement, le disque étant vert, la place occupée semblera colorée en rouge. Si le disque était bleu, on obtiendrait une teinte orangée, etc.

En se servant d'un disque noir et d'un fond grisâtre, l'endroit apparaîtra blanc; noir au contraire pour un disque blanc sur fond gris.

2° Contraste simultané des couleurs. — Le contraste simultané a lieu dans le cas de juxtaposition de bandes d'une même couleur, mais de tonalités différentes : par exemple, des bandes de couleur grise variant du gris clair au gris foncé. Chacune de ces bandes paraît plus foncée sur le bord en contact avec une bande plus claire; plus claire, au contraire, près d'une bande foncée.

Si l'on juxtapose des bandes de couleurs différentes, chacune de ces bandes tend à teindre de sa complémentaire la bande voisine. Si les bandes sont de couleurs complémentaires, elles s'accentuent mutuellement.

On voit par ces quelques notions le parti que peut tirer l'imprimeur intelligent du choix de ses couleurs. Les règles pratiques qui suivent ne sont que des applications des notions susdites.

IV. — APPLICATIONS

Le contraste des couleurs trouve des applications importantes dans les différentes combinaisons des couleurs pour impressions polichromes sur fonds blancs ou diversement teintés.

A. — **Impressions en deux couleurs.**

a) *Sur fond blanc :*

Vert vif (laque verte, nuance moyenne) et rouge vermillon ;

Vert vif et carmin ;

Vert vif et pourpre ;

Vert vif et brun chaud ;

Vert bleu (laque verte la plus foncée avec pointe de blanc) et orangé ;

Outremer et carmin ;

Outremer et marron ;

Outremer et brun chaud ;

Bleu clair et orangé brillant ;

Laque pourpre et jaune brillant ;

Cramoisi et jaune brillant.

b) *Sur fond jaune orangé pâle :*

Bleu vert vif et cramoisi ;

Outremer vif et marron ;

Outremer vif et bronze (jaune de chrome moyen mélangé d'un peu de laque pourpre) ;

Outremer vif et brun rouge ;

Outremer vif et rouge pourpre ;

Pourpre bleu et orangé ;

Pourpre bleu et carmin.

c) *Sur fond pourpre pâle :*

Pourpre rouge et outremer ;

Pourpre rouge et vert bleu ;

Pourpre bleu et cramoisi ;

Outremer et carmin.

d) *Sur fond bleuâtre pâle :*

Outremer et carmin ;

Outremer et pourpre rouge ;

Bleu foncé vert et marron ;

e) *Sur fond bleu pâle :*

Outremer foncé et rouge pourpre ;
Outremer foncé et carmin ;
Bleu foncé vert et carmin ;
Vert vif et rouge poupre ;
Bleu vif et rouge pourpre.

f) *Sur fond vert pâle jaunâtre :*

Vert vif et carmin ;
Vert vif et pourpre ;
Vert vif et rouge brun ;
Vert vif et marron ;
Vert sauge et rouge brun ;
Vert sauge et marron.

g) *Sur fond vert pâle brunâtre :*

Vert sauge foncé et carmin ;
Vert sauge foncé et pourpre ;
Vert sauge foncé et marron.

h) *Sur fond rose pâle :*

Carmin et outremer vif ;
Carmin et vert vif ;
Carmin et bleu pourpre ;
Carmin et bronze ;
Pourpre et bronze ;
Outremer clair et bronze ;
Rouge pourpre et vert jaune.

i) *Sur fond cuir foncé :*

Marron et bleu vert foncé ;
Marron et outremer foncé ;
Brun pourpre foncé et carmin.

j) *Sur fond brun clair :*

Carmin et pourpre foncé ;
Carmin et vert foncé ;
Carmin et noir ;
Marron et vert foncé ;
Pourpre rouge et vert foncé ;
Brun foncé et vert foncé ;
Brun foncé et noir.

k) *Sur fond vert moyen :*

Vert foncé et pourpre foncé ;
Vert foncé et marron ;
Vert foncé et carmin ;
Noir et carmin.

B. — **Impressions en trois couleurs.**

a) *Sur fond blanc :*

Carmin, outremer vif et pourpre ;
Carmin, vert vif et pourpre ;
Carmin, outremer et brun pourpre ;
Pourpre bleu, marron et jaune vif ;
Pourpre, orangé et bleu vert.

b) *Sur fond rose pâle :*

Carmin, outremer et bronze;
Carmin, pourpre bleu et bronze;
Carmin, pourpre et bleu vert;
Rouge pourpre, bleu vert vif et bronze;
Bleu de Chine vif, carmin et pourpre.

c) *Sur fond jaune :*

Carmin, outremer et brun pourpre;
Carmin, vert jaune et brun pourpre;
Carmin, vert jaune et pourpre;
Brun foncé, outremer et pourpre;
Employer l'outremer sur fond jaune *orangé*.

Dans les diverses combinaisons données ci-dessus, on peut remarquer que souvent une des couleurs contrastantes est la même que celle du fond dans un ton plus foncé.

Si l'on veut remplacer une des couleurs par un bronze métallique, il vaudra mieux conserver la couleur qui correspond dans un ton plus foncé à celle du fond.

Ainsi, étant donné une impression carmin et outremer sur fond rose pâle, on remplacera l'outremer par un bronze métallique.

III

LES ENCRES DE COULEURS

Nous avons dit précédemment que les couleurs fondamentales étaient : le rouge, le bleu et le jaune, dont les diverses combinaisons nous donneraient toutes les autres teintes. Mais il faut se garder de confondre les couleurs du spectre avec des couleurs matérielles, telles que les encres d'imprimerie. Certaines propriétés des premières se retrouvent bien dans les secondes, mais non pas toutes. Ainsi il y a analogie, jusqu'à un certain point, relativement aux résultats obtenus par les diverses combinaisons : mais le mélange des trois couleurs matérielles, loin de donner le blanc, produit un gris plus ou moins foncé.

Le blanc, en tant que couleur matérielle, est donc fondamental. Le noir, à la rigueur, peut passer pour le mélange des trois couleurs matérielles.

Nouvelle machine à retiration à grande vitesse (*Maison Alauzet*).

NOUVELLE MACHINE A RETIRATION

à grande vitesse

(Maison ALAUZET)

Machine à retiration à grande vitesse, modèle renforcé, avec mouvement de commande du dessous de marbre par un pignon se déplaçant latéralement, et supprimant l'ancien mouvement à joint de cardan, avec crémaillère à croissants aux extrémités.

Soulèvement des cylindres au moyen d'une pédale, permettant d'encrer sans imprimer.

Encrage mixte, commandé par crémaillère de chaque côté, avec tables en acier animées d'un mouvement de va-et-vient, et deux rouleaux chargeurs avec soulèvement mécanique et renversement pour dégager les toucheurs, soulevables eux-mêmes d'un coup de levier.

Distributeurs munis de rouleaux chargeurs en acier lisses.

Tables à encrer en fonte.

Encriers à déclenchement et avec volant pour les tourner à la main.

Prises d'encre avec cames étagées pour le réglage au moyen de volants à vis agissant sur les béquilles.

Taquets de marge spéciaux, à ressorts et mobiles pour éviter les variations de la prise de la feuille.

Receveur mécanique à pinces.

Coupe-papier circulaire, immobilisable à volonté.

Adaptation simple de l'appareil pour l'emploi du papier en bobine.

Réglage du mouvement du marbre à fin de course au moyen de quatre pompes à air.

Entraînement des bandes à galets par des crémaillères.

Arrêt instantané par frein au volant.

Fonctionnement en double jésus à 1 800 à l'heure.

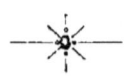

Dans la pratique, les teintes claires s'obtiennent par l'addition de blanc ou de vernis, les foncées par celle de noir.

Il y a donc cinq sortes d'encres indispensables pour le tirage en couleurs : le rouge, le jaune, le bleu, le blanc et le noir. Nous allons les étudier en détail sous le nom d'encres simples.

I. — ENCRES SIMPLES

1° Rouge. — Les impressions en rouge et noir sont d'un usage fréquent dans beaucoup d'imprimeries, principalement pour les travaux de ville, tels que : programmes de fête, menus, cartes d'adresse, factures, etc. ; sans parler même des travaux liturgiques qui sont plus spéciaux à certaines imprimeries.

Quelques lignes ou vignettes imprimées en rouge au milieu du noir égayent, rendent plus coquette une composition, en même temps qu'elles attirent l'attention sur certaines parties du texte, que l'on peut ainsi mettre en évidence.

Le rouge se marie très bien avec d'autres couleurs foncées : brunes, teintes photographiques, bistrés, bruns Van Dick, et surtout verts.

On fait beaucoup d'impressions en rouge et vert foncé (vert américain, vert russe).

On compte un grand nombre d'espèces de rouges ; les plus usités sont : le *vermillon* (cinabre, sulfure de mercure), le *carmin* (rouge de cochenille), le rouge *garance*, le rouge de *Fernambouc* ou du Brésil (laque, sulfure de mercure, de Venise, de Vienne, de Florence), le rouge d'*aniline* (fuchsine, rouge de Lyon), le rouge de *Saturne*, les *ocres* (rouge de France, rouge indien, rouge de Prusse), etc.

Par leur mélange, on peut en obtenir d'autres, comme : les rouges *cerise*, *pourpre*, *géranium*, etc.

Il est donc suffisant, pour les impressions courantes, d'avoir deux ou trois rouges : un vermillon, un rouge et un carmin.

L'essentiel, c'est que ces couleurs soient de bonne qualité, qu'elles couvrent bien et ne passent pas.

On aura bien soin de choisir une teinte appropriée à celle du papier employé pour le tirage. Pour un papier blanc, nous emploierons, par exemple, un vermillon additionné d'un peu de rouge cerise ou de laque géranium ; pour un papier teinté, nous prendrons encore du vermillon, mais en augmentant fortement la quantité de rouge foncé, ou même nous le mélangerons de carmin.

Pour les travaux destinés à subir l'action prolongée de la lumière, on évitera l'emploi du carmin, qui passe très vite, ainsi que celui d'autres rouges qui, au contraire, noircissent sous la même influence.

Les vermillons noircissent au contact du cuivre; il faut éviter de les employer pour le tirage des galvanos.

L'encrage du rouge demande des rouleaux presque secs, sans mordant.

2° Jaune. — Parmi les jaunes, on remarque : le jaune de *chrome* (chromate de plomb), qui noircit facilement ; le jaune de *Naples* (antimoniate de plomb), qui verdit au contact du fer ; les jaunes de *cachou*, de *curcuma*, de *gomme-gutte*, de *rocou*, d'*arsenic*, de *strontiane* (chromate de strontiane), de *zinc* (chromate de zinc), le jaune *indien*, etc.

3° Bleu. — Les bleus les plus employés sont : le bleu de *Prusse* (ferrocyanure de fer), qui donne des tons très riches et fournit beaucoup, mais a l'inconvénient de passer à la lumière ; le bleu d'*outremer* (artificiel), plus solide même que le bleu de cobalt (alumine de *cobalt*) ; le bleu d'*indigo*, très résistant aussi, etc.

On emploie, pour l'impression du bleu, des rouleaux un peu plus frais que pour le rouge.

4° Blanc. — Les encres blanches sont surtout employées, en typographie, pour obtenir des teintes claires par le mélange ; les plus employées sont : le blanc d'*argent*, le blanc de *plomb* ou de *céruse* (carbonate de plomb) et le blanc de *zinc* ou de *neige* (oxyde de zinc), etc.

Le blanc de *plomb* est le plus employé, parce qu'il couvre mieux, mais il noircit lorsqu'il est mélangé à certaines couleurs, comme le vermillon et quelques jaunes. Les blancs à base de plomb sèchent très rapidement.

On fait parfois des tirages en blanc pour des marques au moyen de vernis additionné d'un peu de blanc ; l'impression n'est visible que par transparence.

5° Noir. — Nous ne reviendrons pas ici sur l'étude de l'encre noire, déjà traitée dans la première partie ; qu'il nous suffise de dire que, pour obtenir de bons résultats dans les mélanges, elle doit être de très bonne qualité.

II. — ENCRES COMPOSÉES

A côté de ces encres, d'une teinte bien déterminée, il en existe une quantité d'autres, de teintes intermédiaires, soit naturelles, soient obtenues au moyen de diverses combinaisons.

Parmi les premières : le vert *malachite* (carbonate de cuivre), le vert *Véronèse* (arséniate de cuivre), le vert de *cobalt*, les *ocres* (argile coloré par l'oxyde de fer), les *terres de Sienne*, d'*Ombre*, de *Cassel*, le brun *Van Dyck* (ocre jaune colorée), etc.

Pour obtenir les autres, il suffira du judicieux mélange des cinq sortes simples : rouge, jaune, bleu, blanc, noir.

On fera bien, pour commencer, de n'opérer que sur de petites quantités, afin d'éviter une trop grande perte si l'on n'obtient pas de suite la teinte désirée. Il faut aussi avoir soin de faire l'essai de ses couleurs sur le papier même du tirage ; autrement on risquerait fort de ne pas obtenir le résultat cherché.

Fig. 33. — Le broyeur.

Il faut prendre garde de ne mélanger ensemble que des encres d'une sensibilité égale à la lumière, sous peine de voir la teinte obtenue se modifier rapidement.

Ces mélanges pourront être très utiles pour de petits tirages, d'autant plus qu'ils permettront l'utilisation de restes d'encres; mais pour des travaux plus importants, il sera plus simple et plus sûr de demander au fabricant la teinte voulue.

IV

ENCRES COMMUNICATIVES
ENCRES A DOUBLE TEINTE

Vu l'importance que prennent chaque jour les impressions commerciales aux encres communicatives, ainsi que le tirage des gravures aux encres à double teinte, le conducteur ne doit pas ignorer quelques notions indispensables concernant leur composition, leur usage et leur emploi.

I. — ENCRES COMMUNICATIVES

Les encres typographiques communicatives, à la différence des encres ordinaires, qui sont à base de vernis à l'huile, contiennent de la glycérine et ont la propriété de pouvoir se reproduire au copie de lettres, comme l'encre à copier ordinaire. Ces encres servent à l'impression des lettres d'avis, lettres de voitures, connaissements, cotes de valeurs, etc.

Leur emploi exige des soins particuliers. Il faut veiller à ce que les boîtes contenant l'encre soient hermétiquement fermées afin d'éviter le contact de l'air. Ne rien ajouter à l'encre, si ce n'est, lorsqu'elle est trop compacte, un peu de glycérine. On imprime sur un papier bien collé avec des caractères aussi neufs que possible.

La mise en train doit être très soignée, le foulage sec, les rouleaux disposés de façon à donner une touche très légère, le caractère bien couvert sans cependant être baveux. Le lavage se fait à l'eau pure. Après le séchage, il est nécessaire de satiner, un foulage creux empêchant l'encre de copier facilement.

Les rouleaux doivent être un peu durs et avoir une peau bien formee. S'ils sont neufs, il faut, après les avoir dégraissés plusieurs fois, avoir soin de les laver avec une solution d'alun à 5 %. Les encres communicatives étant solubles dans l'eau, les rouleaux doivent être lavés à l'eau pure et non à l'essence.

Les maisons Ch. Lorilleux, Lefranc et Laflèche et fils fabriquent des encres de différentes couleurs : noire copiant bleu, bleue copiant bleu, noire copiant violet, violette copiant violet, noire copiant rouge, noire copiant vert et verte copiant vert.

GRAVURE EN DOUBLE TEINTE

(*Lorilleux*).

Imprimé avec l'encre double-teinte 1646 de CH. LORILLEUX & Cie

II. — ENCRES A DOUBLE TEINTE

Les encres double teinte des maisons Ch. Lorilleux et Cie, Lefranc et Laflèche et fils, ont pour but de donner par un seul tirage une impression en deux tons différents.

Pour produire ce résultat, ces encres contiennent une composition chimique spéciale qui est le secret de la fabrication.

Leur emploi ne nécessite aucune disposition particulière et ne détériore pas les clichés; néanmoins on ne pourra guère obtenir de résultats satisfaisants sans l'emploi d'un papier couché de très bonne qualité.

Au sortir de la presse, l'impression ne présente rien d'extraordinaire. Mais, si on la laisse sécher entre maculatures, on voit peu à peu les demi-teintes se transformer et la double teinte apparaître.

Le résultat est complet au bout de quelques heures; on peut le hâter en exposant le tirage à une chaleur modérée.

L'encre double teinte se fait en plusieurs couleurs et convient surtout à la photogravure à contrastes accentués.

V

CONSEILS PRATIQUES POUR LES TIRAGES EN COULEURS

Pour obtenir une teinte bien uniforme pendant tout un tirage, il faut un bon réglage des couleurs, une parfaite distribution des rouleaux et l'attention constante du conducteur à surveiller la touche.

Le papier doit être bien égal, car les feuilles fortes recevraient une impression plus foncée que les minces, par suite de la différence du foulage.

On peut mettre à profit cette influence de la pression pour modifier légèrement certaines parties d'un fond dont la gravure serait trop uniforme ; on se sert de morceaux de papier de soie, superposés de façon à donner des pressions plus ou moins fortes, qui ont pour résultat des teintes différentes.

Il est préférable de n'avoir pas d'impression au dos de la feuille ; cette impression devra tout au moins être faite avec un foulage très léger, de façon à nuire le moins possible à la netteté de la couleur et à l'uniformité de la teinte.

Les encres de couleur étant assez longues à sécher, il est bon et même indispensable, pour un tirage soigné, afin d'éviter le maculage, d'intercaler, au fur et à mesure du tirage, des feuilles de décharge entre les feuilles tirées.

Pour les tirages en superposition de couleurs, on se sert d'encres spéciales transparentes. Il faudra donc, dans une commande, mentionner si les encres sont destinées à des tirages simples ou à des tirages en superposition de teintes.

L'impression des affiches demande aussi des encres spéciales, moins denses que les autres et d'un prix moins élevé.

Si l'on se sert de machines rotatives pour le tirage des chromos, il faudra employer des encres séchant très vite, afin d'éviter le maculage des feuilles qui se trouvent imprimées à plusieurs couleurs presque simultanément.

VI

DU BRONZAGE

Le bronzage est un genre d'impression tout spécial, offrant un aspect métallique. Ce genre devient de jour en jour d'un usage plus fréquent, surtout dans la confection des étiquettes et bibelots de réclames.

On trouve dans le commerce les teintes les plus variées : or pâle, citron, vert, orange, cuivre carmin, rouge feu, etc. ; argents de diverses nuances, etc.

Ce genre d'impression comporte deux procédés : le bronzage *aux poudres* et le *bronze direct*.

I. — BRONZAGE AUX POUDRES

Le bronzage aux poudres est, en même temps que le plus employé, le procédé qui donne les meilleurs résultats.

11

Machine en retiration (*J. Voirin*).

MACHINE EN RETIRATION

(J. VOIRIN)

Le type de machine si répandu en France a subi dans les dernières années de profondes transformations. Les imprimeurs, de plus en plus, en trouvaient la production insuffisante. Les établissements J. Voirin des premiers ont étudié et construit une machine en retiration nouvelle, à grande vitesse, qui peut imprimer, à la vitesse de 1 500 à 1 600 feuilles à l'heure, les travaux les plus soignés.

Les qualités essentielles qui permettent à cette machine de supporter ces très grandes vitesses sont la solidité et la précision.

Ses bâtis, ses entretoises, son marbre, ses cylindres sont extrêmement robustes. Pour donner une idée tangible de sa puissance, il nous suffira de dire que le modèle format double jésus pèse 8 000 kilos net, alors que le même format des anciennes machines ne pesait que 4 500 kilos.

Moyennant l'addition des chargeurs mobiles ou, mieux encore, de l'encrage commandé, cette machine imprime à la perfection les travaux de similigravure.

Une coupeuse automatique, à format variable, permettant l'emploi du papier en bobine, peut, à volonté, être adaptée à la machine.

On tire les gravures ou textes qui doivent être bronzés avec un vernis fort appelé mordant. Pour donner à l'impression plus d'éclat, on pourra teinter le mordant d'une couleur appropriée avec le bronze employé. Ainsi, pour du bronze argenté, on fera l'impression avec du vernis mélangé de blanc et d'une pointe de bleu; pour un bronze doré, on emploiera le rouge; pour du bronze jaune, un jaune, etc. Aussitôt après l'impression du mordant, ou plutôt concurremment, on procède au bronzage, au moyen de bourrons de coton, de morceaux de drap blanc très pelucheux, ou de molleton imprégnés de bronze en poudre, que l'on passe très délicatement sans appuyer sur l'impression. De cette façon le bronze prend bien uniformément.

Comme le bronze, à cause de son extrême division, se répand facilement dans l'air, s'introduit dans les voies respiratoires et peut causer des accidents, il faut, pour éviter ce désagrément, n'opérer qu'avec de très petites quantités à la fois et éviter les mouvements brusques.

Au fur et à mesure du bronzage, les feuilles sont placées les unes sur les autres. Au bout de quelques jours, quand le vernis est bien sec, on passe une brosse douce pour enlever l'excès de bronze non adhérent. Les impressions bronzées se font de préférence sur des papiers fortement glacés, ou mieux encore couchés; les papiers grenus ou duveteux conservent un peu partout des traces de poudre d'un effet désagréable.

Bronzeuse Marinoni. — Les imprimeurs qui exécutent couramment ce genre d'impressions ont tout intérêt à se servir de la machine à bronzer de Marinoni. Ils y trouvent une grande économie de bronze, un travail plus rapide et plus propre, et aussi moins d'inconvénients pour la santé des ouvriers.

Cette machine a un fonctionnement très simple. La feuille est margée, reçoit l'impression du mordant et passe ensuite dans un compartiment où se font mécaniquement le bronzage et l'époussetage.

II. — BRONZE DIRECT

On a inventé, ces derniers temps, un procédé de bronzage désigné sous le nom de « bronze direct ». La poudre est mélangée avec un mordant approprié, et ce produit est placé dans l'encrier comme une encre ordinaire ; mais, comme il est très siccatif, il faut employer des rouleaux secs. La distribution se fait alors d'une façon suffisante.

Ce procédé a plusieurs avantages sur l'ancienne manière : il est plus économique, plus rapide, pas malsain. Mais il est moins artistique : le bronzage n'a plus le bel éclat métallique qu'on obtient par la méthode ordinaire, et les finesses du dessin sont bien moins rendues.

Aussi ne convient-il guère qu'aux travaux courants, qu'il importe avant tout de faire vite et à bon marché.

VII

DES FONDS

Pour donner un caractère plus artistique à un tirage de fantaisie : menu, programme, réclame, etc., on peut recourir à l'emploi d'un fond bien approprié. La teinte généralement pâle, en rapport avec le sujet et les tons de l'impression, a pour effet de les faire ressortir davantage tout en les harmonisant.

On peut trouver chez les fabricants des clichés, zinc ou galvano, susceptibles d'être utilisés comme fonds ; on peut aussi se servir de combinaisons de vignettes, comme pour les billets de loterie, les billets de banque, etc. Souvent, il sera plus avantageux et plus expéditif de tailler soi-même le fond nécessaire dans l'une des matières dont nous allons parler.

On se sert surtout pour la confection des fonds :

du bois, du celluloïde, du carton, du linoléum, et enfin de plomb ou plutôt de matière de caractères.

I. — DIVERSES ESPÈCES DE FONDS.

Fonds en bois. — On obtient de jolis fonds de fantaisie avec des planches de chêne ou de tout autre bois. Ces fonds peuvent être unis ou veinés.

Si l'on veut un fond *uni*, on emploiera du bois dur (chêne, noyer ou poirier) et on le polira soigneusement au papier émeri et à la pierre ponce. On pourra même l'enduire d'une couche de silicate de potasse, qui fera disparaître toutes les petites rayures qui pourraient subsister après le ponçage.

Si l'on veut, au contraire, un fond *veiné*, on choisira un bois en conséquence et on en accentuera l'effet au moyen du procédé suivant : la surface du bois sera badigeonnée d'acide azotique qui attaquera les parties tendres. En passant ensuite une brosse à poils rudes, les parties brûlées disparaîtront et les veines et les nœuds du bois resteront seuls en relief.

On peut se servir soit de bois de la hauteur du caractère, soit de planchettes minces (de deux à trois millimètres) montées sur bois de cliché.

Ces planchettes, faciles à débiter, sont surtout employées pour les fonds de formes irrégulières. Après avoir préparé avec soin le côté de la planchette qui doit servir à l'impression, on reporte une épreuve du sujet, et on enlève à la scie à découper les parties inutiles. On fixe ensuite sur un bois de

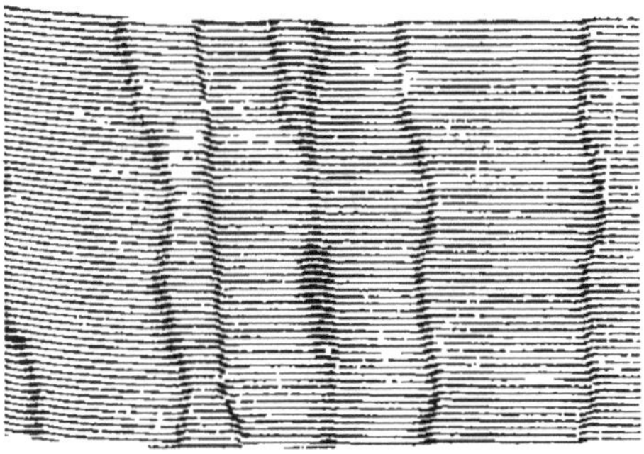

N° 1
Fond obtenu avec de la moire.

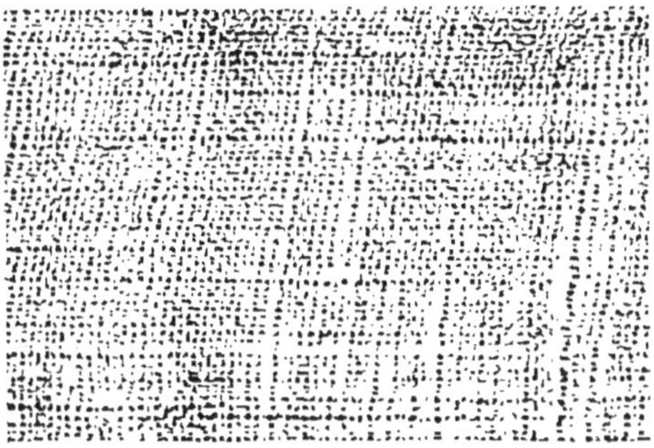

N° 2.
Fond obtenu avec un morceau de toile.

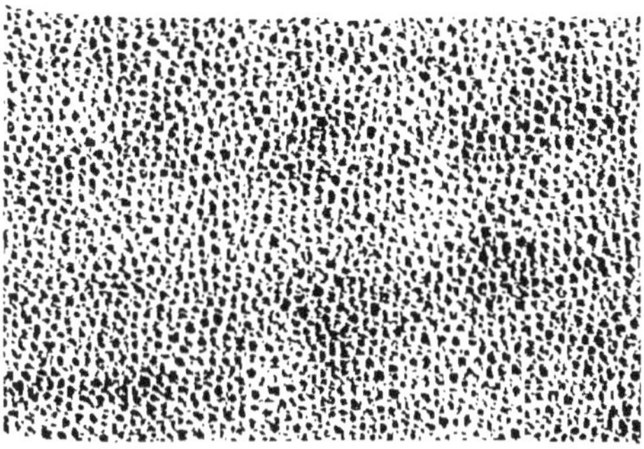

N° 3.
Fond obtenu avec du cuir chagriné.

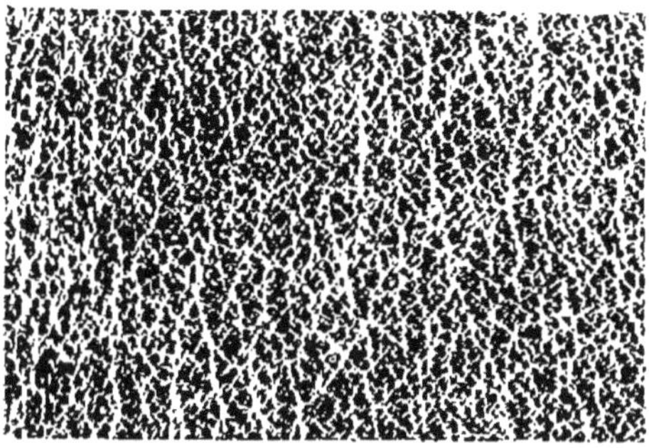

N° 4
Fond obtenu avec du maroquin.

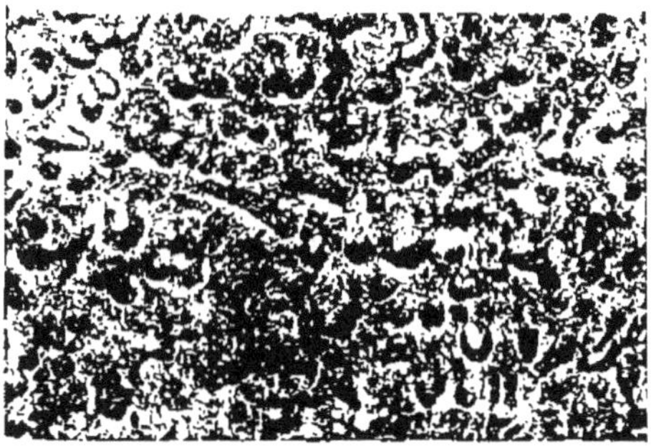

N° 5.
Fond obtenu au moyen du linoléum.

N° 6.
Fond obtenu avec une feuille de papier verré.

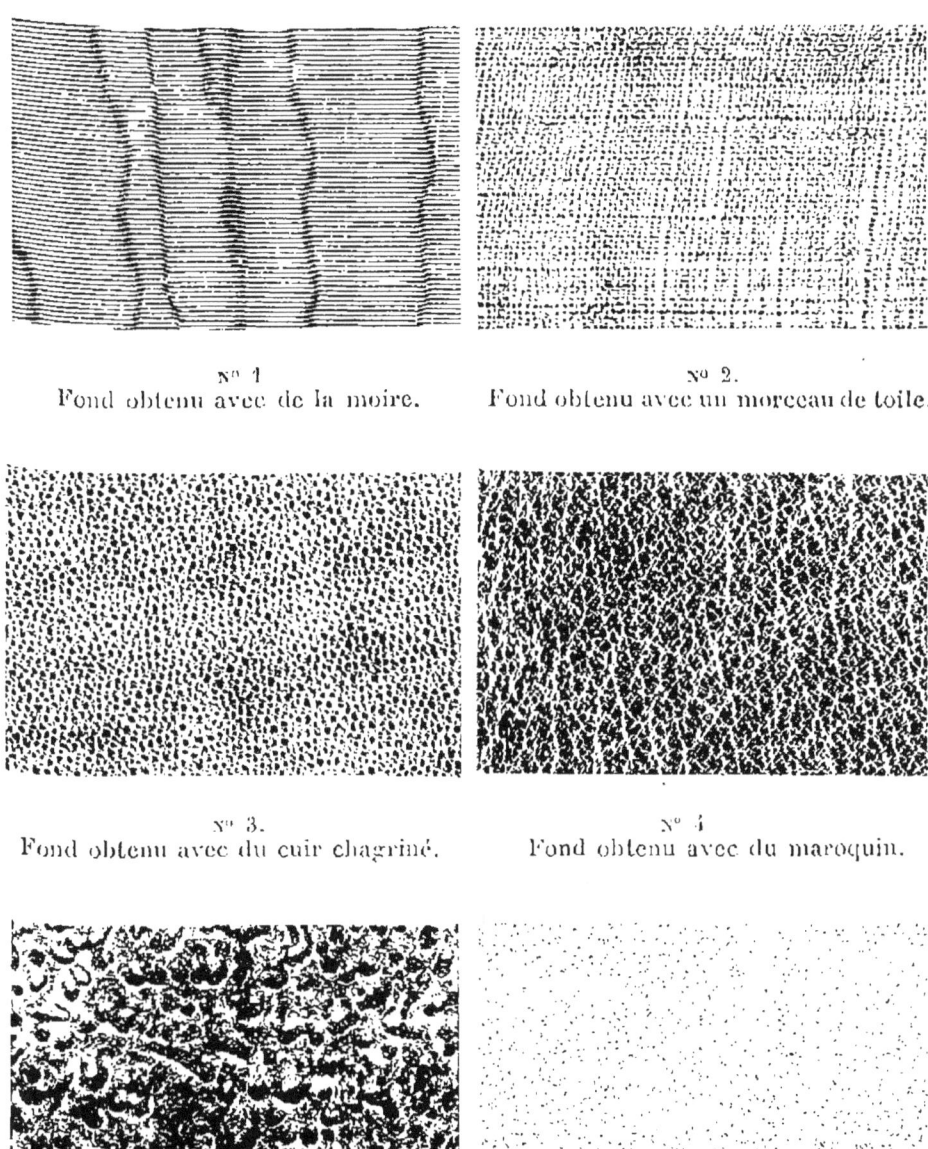

Fig. 34. — Fonds pour les tirages en couleurs.

cliché à l'aide de colle forte ou de quelques pointes. Les retouches sont faites au burin ou au canif, et le fond peut servir.

Fonds en celluloïde. — Le celluloïde se trouve dans le commerce sous forme de feuille d'un millimètre d'épaisseur et de la dimension de 50×60 centimètres, très polies sur une surface, légèrement rugueuses sur l'autre. Cette matière se travaille très facilement à la scie, au burin et peut donner plus de finesse au découpage que le bois. Mais le montage, le collage en particulier, sur le bois présentent de réelles difficultés ; ce qui fait que certaines imprimeries commandent leurs fonds aux fabricants et les reçoivent prêts à servir. Le procédé de fabrication est analogue à celui employé pour ceux en bois (lames minces).

Fonds de carton. — Le carton pour fond aura deux millimètres d'épaisseur. On peut, au besoin, coller plusieurs feuilles pour avoir l'épaisseur voulue.

On emploie soit le carton à satiner, soit le bristol. Le premier, plus dur à travailler, s'emploie pour les fonds réguliers, sans découpages ; le bristol convient mieux pour les fonds plus compliqués.

On monte son carton de la dimension et de l'épaisseur voulues sur un bois approprié ; on fait un report de la composition ; puis, à l'aide du couteau à découper, on enlève les parties inutiles. L'entaille se fait en biais, de façon à former un talus qui garantira l'adhérence du carton; elle devra être d'autant plus profonde qu'elle entoure un plus grand blanc, pour éviter les taches à l'impression. Dans les grands blancs on enlève même le carton à fond.

Le fond terminé, il est bon de l'enduire de deux ou trois couches de silicate de potasse, successivement et après séchage de la précédente.

On obtient des fonds de fantaisie en collant sur carton du papier chagriné, quadrillé ou gaufré : le relief se produit très exactement à l'impression. Avec du papier émeri, on aura un joli fond sablé.

Certains fournisseurs préparent des cartons très faciles à employer et qui deviennent très durs sous l'action du silicate. Ces cartons donnent plus de finesse, mais ils sont aussi plus chers.

Fonds en linoléum. — Le linoléum peut aussi servir à la fabrication des fonds. Il se découpe très facilement au canif et résiste bien à la pression. On le monte sur bois, et on le fixe à la colle forte.

Fonds de cuir, maroquin, etc. — Le cuir, le maroquin et beaucoup d'autres matières analogues peuvent aussi servir de fonds. L'imprimeur intelligent trouvera de lui-même le moyen pratique de les utiliser et les approprier.

Fonds de clichage. — Les fonds de clichage sont des plus variés. On les obtient soit par le clichage direct, soit par un moulage préalable. Papiers de fantaisie, tissus, dentelles, carton gaufré, etc., peuvent servir dans ce but. Il suffit soit d'en prendre empreinte, soit de les placer directement dans le moule où se coule la matière. On les façonne ensuite à la dimension voulue.

Voici une manière d'obtenir des fonds d'un très curieux effet : On graisse légèrement une surface plane, du marbre, par exemple; on pose dessus un châssis graissé également, et, après avoir projeté quelques gouttelettes d'eau, on coule dans ce cadre de la matière d'imprimerie. La plaque obtenue se trouve couverte d'aspérités de formes très variées. Avec quelques grains de gros sel, semés deci delà, on aurait un relief plus accidenté encore.

Ce même cliché peut, au moyen de diverses combinaisons, donner au tirage des effets très curieux. On peut tirer successivement deux teintes différentes avec déplacement du cliché, ou bien on imprime en rouge un premier fond uni; on superpose ensuite notre dernier fond imprimé avec mordant et bronze. Enfin on termine par un tirage au bleu de Prusse de ce dernier cliché avec déplacement. L'impression ainsi obtenne présente un bel aspect métallique, parsemé de taches rouges d'un très heureux effet.

II. — TIRAGE DES FONDS

Naturellement le tirage des fonds demande les mêmes soins que toute impression en encres de couleur. Il suffira des quelques conseils suivants :

On tirera d'abord les couleurs courantes opaques, puis les teintes légères et transparentes pour adoucir les contrastes trop dur.

Les blancs de zinc transparents et les blancs de magnésie sont indispensables pour l'adoucissement des teintes des fonds; ils sont préférables au vernis, qui jaunit la teinte, graisse, transperce le papier et fait mauvais effet, surtout pour les gravures fines. Au contraire du vernis, le blanc transparent conserve à l'encre sa compacité, tout en atténuant à volonté sa tonalité.

VIII

CONSEILS PRATIQUES

POUR L'EMPLOI DES ENCRES DE COULEUR

Nous avons donné précédemment les principes généraux relatifs à l'emploi des encres de couleur; voici maintenant quelques conseils pratiques concernant les différents sujets qu'un imprimeur peut avoir à rendre. Ces sujets peuvent se ramener à quatre groupes principaux : le portrait, la zoologie, la botanique et le paysage.

I. — LE PORTRAIT

Dans le portrait, nous comprendrons non seulement l'étude de la physionomie, mais aussi celle des vêtements, de l'ameublement, des scènes d'intérieur, et généralement de tout tableau où dominent les personnages.

1. Visage.

a) **Chairs.** — Pour femmes et enfants : blanc, mine de Saturne, un peu de vermillon et une pointe de bleu ou de noir. Pour hommes : blanc, terre de Sienne, mine de Saturne et une pointe de vermillon. Dans les parties ombrées, terre de Sienne brûlée avec un peu de noir d'Allemagne. Dans certaines parties, teinte légère de bleu de Prusse mélangé de beaucoup de blanc.

Chairs mortes, celles d'un Christ par exemple : un peu de mine, de terre de Sienne brûlée, du blanc et du noir.

b) **Cheveux.** — Blonds : terra-mérita en mélange avec stil de grain, terre de Sienne et un peu de blanc; dans les ombres, pointe de noir. Châtains : terre de Sienne brûlée et noir. Noirs : noir d'Allemagne et une pointe de bleu de Prusse ou d'indigo.

c) **Barbe, sourcils, moustaches.** — Mêmes couleurs que pour les cheveux.

d) **Yeux.** — Blanc de l'œil : mélange de cobalt et de laque et légère pointe de jaune de chrome. Prunelle : bleu de cobalt, de Prusse ou terre de Sienne brûlée. Paupières : supérieures, ajouter un peu de vermillon et de laque à la couleur chair; inférieures, plus grisâtres.

e) **Bouche.** — Laque orange dans les clairs,

carmin mélangé de mine ou de rouge de Saturne dans les demi-teintes. Lèvre inférieure : rouge de Saturne avec quelques tons violacés dans les ombres. Coins de la bouche : parfois carmin pur.

f) **Oreilles, nez, mains et autres parties nues.** — Tons déjà indiqués pour les chairs avec de légères modifications.

2. Draperies.

a) **Les velours** n'ont pour lumière apparente que leurs reflets ; la partie des plis brillante dans les autres étoffes reste mate dans celle-ci ; on ne rendrait pas l'effet du velours en éclairant les plis du côté de la lumière.

Velours jaune : laque, chrome ou terra-mérita ; dans les ombres, terre de Sienne mélangée de jaune de chrome, quelquefois de mine orange. Velours rouge : mélange de carmin et de mine de Saturne ; ajouter du carmin pour les demi-teintes, un peu plus de noir pour les ombres fortes. Velours bleu : bleu de cobalt et pointe de laque carminée, avec, pour les ombres, de l'indigo. Velours vert : bleu de Prusse mélangé de laque jaune, de terra-mérita ou d'un autre jaune, suivant la teinte.

b) **Draperies noires :** noir d'Allemagne, avec un peu de noir léger dans les ombres plus fortes.

c) **Broderies en or :** jaune de chrome, terra-mérita et pointe de mine de Saturne ; dans les ombres, terre de Sienne brûlée et un peu de brun rouge.

Machine "Deux Tours" (*J. Voirin*).

MACHINE " DEUX TOURS "

(J. VOIRIN)

Nous avons eu la satisfaction de voir fonctionner, dans une des plus grandes imprimeries parisiennes, une machine " Deux Tours " de marque " J. Voirin " dont le modèle a été présenté pour la première fois à l'Exposition du Cours-la-Reine.

C'est avec le plus vif plaisir que nous avons constaté que cette machine ne le cédait en rien à celles des marques étrangères les plus réputées, tant par son parfait fonctionnement que par sa vitesse et sa précision.

Elle exécutait, à la vitesse relevée par nous de 1 900 feuilles à l'heure, des travaux de similigravure en double jésus, imposés à plein marbre, et destinés à un magasine des plus luxueux.

Ce qui nous a tout particulièrement intéressé, c'est son mécanisme breveté de mouvement de propulsion du marbre établi sur un principe entièrement nouveau et d'une très ingénieuse conception. Étant données les très grandes vitesses auxquelles les machines du type " Deux Tours " sont destinées à marcher, leur durée dépendra surtout de la solidité et du bon fonctionnement du mécanisme du marbre ; nous pouvons affirmer avec certitude que celle des Établissements J. Voirin conservera ses qualités de précision et de repérage aussi longtemps que toutes ses autres machines, dont la durée presque illimitée est connue de tous les imprimeurs.

d) **Broderies d'argent** : bleu de cobalt mêlé de beaucoup de blanc; dans les ombres, noir mélangé d'un peu de noir d'Allemagne.

II. — ZOOLOGIE

La zoologie comprend : les mammifères, les oiseaux, les poissons et les insectes.

1. Mammifères.

Les mammifères présentent relativement peu de variétés dans les teintes. On ne rencontre guère que les suivantes : le blanc, le fauve, le roux, le brun, le gris et le noir.

Exemple : le *lion*. Teinte générale (roux gris légèrement jaunâtre) : jaune de chrome mélangé de terre de Sienne et pointe de noir; iris des yeux (jaune un peu verdâtre) : terra-mérita avec un peu de jaune de chrome et une pointe de bleu de Prusse, s'il est nécessaire; prunelle, cavité orbitaire, ombres et extrémités des poils de la queue : noir d'Allemagne avec pointe d'indigo.

Le mélange varié du jaune, du brun rouge, de la terre d'Italie, de la terre de Sienne calcinée, du carmin et du noir, fournira les nuances de presque tous les mammifères.

Pour quelques-uns, d'un gris plus ou moins ardoisé, mêler au blanc et au noir une légère pointe de cobalt.

2. Oiseaux.

Les oiseaux présentent des nuances aussi nombreuses que variées. Elles sont parfois brillantes et souvent remarquables par leur pureté. On trouvera plus loin, à l'étude des fleurs, un grand nombre de combinaisons de couleurs qui seront très utiles ici.

Citons comme exemple la jolie petite *perruche à tête grise* du Sénégal, variété assez commune à Paris, qui offre des nuances que l'on retrouve dans le plumage d'un grand nombre d'oiseaux exotiques.

Gris de la tête : mélange de blanc d'argent, de cobalt, de noir d'Allemagne et pointe de laque; cou et poitrine : mélange de cobalt et de laque jaune; dos, ailes et dessus de la queue : jaune de chrome et bleu de Prusse en mélange; épaulette : jaune de stil de grain, terra-mérita et un peu de laque jaune en mélange; ventre : mélange de jaune de chrome et de rouge de Saturne; plumes des cuisses et dessus de la couverture de la queue : jaune de chrome seulement; bec et prunelle : noir et pointe d'indigo; prunelle : mine orange; pattes : blanc, carmin et pointe de noir.

3. Poissons.

Certains poissons offrent les mêmes teintes brillantes que les oiseaux et les fleurs. On trouvera plus loin, à l'étude de ces dernières, diverses combinaisons de couleurs intéressantes.

4. Insectes.

Un grand nombre d'insectes revêtent de brillantes couleurs, notamment les *papillons* et les *coléoptères*. Parmi ces derniers, citons la cétoine dorée, que l'on trouve fréquemment dans les roses.

a) **Insectes à reflets verts.** — Dans les clairs : jaune mélangé d'une pointe de terra-mérita; dans les parties moins éclairées : jaune de chrome mélangé de rouge de Saturne; dans les demi-teintes : jaune de chrome, bleu de cobalt et un peu de carmin; enfin, dans les parties ombrées : laque jaune et bleu de Prusse.

b) **Insectes à reflets violets.** — Dans les clairs : violet léger composé de cobalt et de laque carminée; dans les demi-teintes : laque et bleu de Prusse; dans les ombres : laque et pointe de noir.

III. — BOTANIQUE

On comprend sous ce nom l'étude des fleurs, des feuilles et des branches. Les fleurs notamment offrant une variété infinie de teintes, nous nous étendrons plus longuement à leur sujet, et les combinaisons de couleurs que nous indiquerons pourront servir également pour les oiseaux, les poissons et les insectes de coloris plus éclatant.

1. Fleurs.

Rose commune : carmin ou laque mélangée de blanc léger dans les parties rose pâle, carmin pur pour le centre, ordinairement plus foncé; un peu de cobalt pour les reflets bleuâtres. Dans les espèces très foncées : carmin mélangé d'un peu de cinabre, de terre d'Italie, ou d'une légère pointe d'indigo, selon que la rose est d'un rouge vif, foncé ou violacé. Comme le carmin, ainsi que les laques, ont un ton un peu violacé quand on les emploie purs, on y ajoute presque toujours un peu de mine de Saturne. Fruit encore vert : stil de grain, bleu de Prusse avec une pointe de laque carminée. Fruit mûr : rouge mélangé d'un peu de jaune de chrome, s'il tire sur le jaune; cinabre ou carmin, s'il tire sur le rouge.

Roses de Provins panachées : fond des pétales : carmin et blanc léger mélangés d'une pointe de bleu de cobalt; pétales : carmin pur ou mélangé de cinabre dans les clairs, d'une pointe d'indigo dans les ombres violacées.

Primevère jaune : laque jaune dans les clairs; terre de Sienne calcinée dans les ombres; mélange de terre d'Italie ou de brun rouge avec un peu plus de mine pour les ombres plus fortes.

Primevère violette : bleu de cobalt et carmin; ou blanc, bleu de cobalt et carmin; forcer le blanc dans les parties très éclairées.

Primevère brun rouge : carmin et terre de Sienne calcinée; dans les ombres, mélange de terre d'Italie.

Primevère grise : laque, cobalt et blanc. Supprimer le blanc dans les fortes ombres.

Les **fleurs blanches** ne se travaillent que dans

les ombres, les parties blanches devant être données généralement par la couleur même du papier. Dans les ombres, varier suivant les nuances particulières à chaque fleur. *Jasmin, lis,* par exemple : mélange de blanc, de terra-mérita et de noir d'Allemagne.

Héllébore rose de Noël d'un blanc liliacé : blanc, bleu de Prusse, laque et noir en mélange dans les ombres.

Narcisse d'un blanc azuré : blanc, noir et cobalt en mélange.

Œillet rouge : mélange de laque carminée, de carmin et de rouge de Saturne, avec pointe d'indigo dans les ombres violacées.

Œillet chair pâle : laque, rouge de Saturne et blanc en mélange; forcer l'une ou l'autre de ces couleurs suivant la nuance plus ou moins foncée ou vive.

Jacinthe bleue : bleu de Prusse et blanc; ou mieux, cobalt et blanc léger dans les clairs; indigo ou bleu de Prusse dans les parties très ombrées.

Jacinthe gris de lin : laque, cobalt, blanc d'argent et noir en mélange.

Souci jaune : dans les clairs, jaune de chrome; mélange de minium ou de mine de Saturne dans les ombres.

Souci de la reine, de couleur plus ou moins orangée : jaune de chrome plus ou moins mélangé de mine orange ou de carmin.

Iris de Juze : mélange de laque ou de carmin, de cobalt et de blanc, avec le blanc en moins pour les parties foncées; pour la nervure jaune : jaune de chrome et stil de grain en mélange.

Rose d'Inde : jaune de chrome mélangé de terre de Sienne calcinée dans les ombres.

Renoncule pivoine : rouge foncé, laque, carmin et rouge de Saturne, ou mine orange mélangée de jaune de chrome ou de laque jaune, suivant la teinte plus ou moins vive.

Œillet d'Inde : jaune de chrome plus ou moins mélangé de cinabre et de carmin. Dans certaines variétés dites *mordorées*, terre de Sienne et carmin ou brun rouge et cinabre dans les ombres.

Anémone simple. 1° *Violette :* blanc, bleu de Prusse et carmin ; 2° *Rouge :* laque et minium purs ou mélange de minium et de carmin ; 3° *Citron :* laque jaune ou jaune de chrome mélangés d'un peu de rouge de Saturne.

Pivoine rouge : laque pure, avec quelquefois un peu de carmin ou de cinabre, plus rarement du rouge de Saturne.

Lis martagon : mine de Saturne mélangée à un peu de carmin ; forcer en carmin dans les parties ombrées.

Crocus jaune : dans les clairs, jaune de chrome ; dans les ombres, terre de sienne brûlée mélangée d'une pointe de carmin.

Crocus violet : blanc, carmin et bleu de Prusse ; pour les nervures, mélange de carmin et d'indigo ; pour les graines, laque jaune avec vert composé de terra-mérita et de bleu de Prusse dans les ombres.

Pensée : dans les fortes ombres, teinte légère de laque et de cobalt en mélange, forcer sur les ombres ;

La “ Danaïde ”. — Machine en blanc (*J. Voirin*).

" DANAÏDE "

Cette excellente petite machine en blanc a été présentée pour la première fois, par les Établissements J. Voirin, à l'Exposition Nationale du Cours-la-Reine à Paris, en juillet 1908.

Tous les imprimeurs connaissent le fini et l'excellence des machines sortant de cette consciencieuse maison, qui depuis de si longues années déjà a porté dans tous les pays du monde la renommée des solides qualités de la construction française.

L'apparition de la " Danaïde ", dont la conception et l'économie générale répondaient si bien aux besoins actuels de l'imprimerie, attira tout particulièrement l'attention de tous les praticiens. Aussi son succès dépassa de suite toutes les espérances de ses constructeurs, qui se virent obligés, pour pouvoir répondre à la demande, de créer un outillage très puissant et d'organiser des équipes spéciales pour la fabrication de cette machine qui se construit maintenant par très grandes séries.

Bien entendu, c'est l'acheteur qui bénéficie du principal avantage de cette construction en grand : *la réduction du prix de revient.* Pour un prix, que nous trouvons très modeste, il peut en effet faire l'acquisition d'une machine *Raisin, Jésus* ou *Double-Carré*, qui lui permettra l'exécution très soignée et extra-rapide (1600 à 2000 feuilles à l'heure) des travaux de luxe y compris la similigravure.

Comme succès oblige, les Établisssements J. Voirin se sont fait une loi de perfectionner sans relâche leur " Danaïde ", de façon à la maintenir constamment au premier rang dans la voie du progrès.

Voici quelles sont les caractéristiques de la " *Danaïde* " formats jésus et double-carré, modèle 1910 :

La machine repose sur un solide bâti de fond formant socle et avec lequel sont assemblés, par juxtaposition, les bâtis de côté. Le marbre, fortement nervé, est guidé par frottement dans toute la longueur des bâtis de côté et roule sur un train de six gros galets à joue.

Ces six galets sont commandés par crémaillère, ce qui assure un roulement parfait.

Le mouvement est donné au marbre par :

Le pignon de commande de grand diamètre qui engrène avec la roue manivelle puissante, large, laquelle actionne la *bielle motrice avec coussinet bronze et avec clef de réglage.* Celle-ci est reliée au marbre par l'intermédiaire de deux roues dentées engrenant avec deux crémaillères sur le bâti de fond et deux sous le marbre.

Dans le mécanisme de temps d'arrêt, les cames sont de très grandes dimensions ; les galets de la bielle d'arrêt sont en acier trempé, et son coussinet est en bronze.

L'encrage est cylindrique. — La touche est donnée par deux rouleaux de 82 m/m de diamètre supportés dans des coussinets réglables en hauteur par rapport à la forme, et latéralement par rapport à la table à encrer.

Ces coussinets sont en acier avec bague en bronze très facilement interchangeable. — Le mouvement de déplacement transversal de la table à encrer et des chargeurs peut se supprimer à volonté. — Un volant placé à l'encrier, qui est à rotation continue, permet de le nettoyer facilement.

L'encrier est embrayé par une manette placée à portée de la main du margeur.

La prise d'encre s'exerce par leviers articulés et élastiques avec came systématique permettant de régler la prise d'encre à volonté.

Un levier de prise d'encre est placé du côté du margeur pour lui permettre de régler le débit de l'encre sans arrêter la machine.

Sur demande, la machine est munie d'un rectificateur automatique de marge à double mouvement pour la retiration, appareil très pratique dont l'emploi se généralise de plus en plus. Les taquets de marge, en acier, sont réglables dans tous les sens et font partie du cylindre pour assurer un bon repérage, même quand la machine a pris de l'usure. Ces taquets portent des entonnoirs pour guider la feuille.

Un pince-feuille est disposé pour faciliter la mise en train et la pose du blanchet.

Le cylindre de sortie de feuilles, commandé par engrenage, est de gros diamètre.

Les leviers tendeurs de cordons de sortie de feuilles sont à contrepoids.

Les raquettes du receveur mécanique sont munies d'étoiles pour empêcher le maculage.

Un rangeur automatique de feuilles à trois palettes, d'un fonctionnement parfait, peut être ajouté à la demande.

parties claires : carmin pur mélangé d'un peu de blanc dans les parties très éclairées ; légère pointe de bleu de Prusse ou d'indigo dans les ombres fortes.

Tulipe. 1° *Jaune :* jaune de chrome pur ou plus ou moins mélangé de laque jaune ; 2° *Rouge :* carmin et rouge de Saturne, ou rouge de Saturne et cinabre, ou laque mélangée d'une pointe de mine orange ; 3° *Violette :* laque et bleu de cobalt dominant ou blanc mélangé de carmin dominant et de bleu de Prusse, mélangé dans les ombres de terre de Sienne calcinée ou de terre d'Italie ; 4° *Blanche :* ne travailler que les ombres, suivant la teinte.

Œillet de poète : comme la tulipe, mais en forçant sur le carmin.

Scabieuse rouge : laque avec un peu de cobalt pour le cœur.

Fleur de grenadier : vermillon ou cinabre, avec, au besoin, un peu de mine orange ; carmin dans les ombres.

Pied d'alouette. 1° *Bleu :* bleu de cobalt avec pointe de laque ; 2° *Rose :* laque rose, mélangée quelquefois d'une pointe de mine orange.

Violette : mélange de bleu de cobalt et de carmin dans les clairs ; laque et indigo dans les ombres.

Couronne impériale. 1° *Orange :* dans les clairs, jaune de chrome mélangé de mine de Saturne ; dans les ombres, terre de Sienne calcinée ou violet composé de beaucoup de carmin et d'une pointe de bleu de Prusse ; 2° *Jaune :* laque jaune et stil de grain ; dans les ombres, violet bleuâtre fait de bleu de Prusse et de carmin.

Dahlia. 1° *Jaune pâle :* jaune de chrome et blanc léger : dans les ombres, pointe de vert léger, préparé avec du terra-mérita et un peu de bleu ; 2° *Orangé :* jaune de chrome, terra-mérita et rouge de Saturne ; dans les ombres, violet composé de bleu de Prusse et de carmin ; 3° *Rouge* pourpre : mélange de laque et de carmin ; dans les ombres, violet ci-dessus ; 4° *Dahlia ponceau :* rouge de Saturne et carmin.

Quelquefois l'imprimeur doit tirer des **ébauches** de fleurs pour coloristes. Dans ce cas, il indique seulement le cœur et quelques parties ombrées ou plus foncées.

Prenons comme exemple la primevère jaune et quelques autres fleurs de la même couleur. Cœur et nervures des pétales : violet fait de bleu de Prusse et de carmin, avec une pointe de blanc dans les ombres faibles.

2. Feuilles.

Les feuilles sont ordinairement vertes ; mais cette couleur offre un grand nombre de nuances, non seulement dans les espèces différentes, mais encore sur la même plante. Aussi ne pouvons-nous donner ici que des règles générales.

La base de tous les verts est un mélange de jaune et de bleu ; mais, en faisant varier la quantité proportionnelle de ces deux couleurs, on obtient un grand nombre de nuances différentes, échelonnées entre le vert foncé où le bleu domine, et le vert clair qui contient surtout du jaune.

Selon l'espèce de bleu et de jaune que l'on mélange, le vert offre encore une série de nuances différentes. Par exemple, le jaune de chrome et l'indigo produisent une nuance plutôt terne, tandis que le mélange de la laque jaune et du cobalt donnent un vert très brillant.

Le mélange du jaune avec d'autres couleurs que le bleu produit quelquefois aussi des verts : par exemple, le jaune de chrome et le noir d'Allemagne; mais ce vert est terne et sans éclat. Cette troisième série offre peu de combinaisons.

La quatrième série, la plus étendue, renferme les verts composés de jaune, de bleu et d'une troisième couleur. Cette troisième couleur peut être du carmin, de la mine orange, du brun rouge, pour les feuilles vives comme pour les feuilles d'automne, mais en quantité plus ou moins grande. Dans la feuille morte, le vert finit même par disparaître presque entièrement, et c'est le jaune, la terre de Sienne, le brun rouge et le bistre qui dominent.

Les verts glauques, c'est-à-dire bleuâtres, comme la feuille de certains choux, de l'œillet des fleuristes, etc., s'obtiennent par le mélange du blanc et du bleu de cobalt avec une pointe de terra-mérita ou de stil de grain.

Pour les feuilles velues et blanchâtres, on emploie de l'indigo, les jaunes ci-dessus et beaucoup de blanc.

Voici d'ailleurs le tableau des verts les plus employés :

1° Jaune de chrome et bleu de Prusse;

2° Jaune de chrome et indigo;
3° Jaune de chrome et cobalt;
4° Laque jaune et indigo;
5° Laque jaune et bleu de Prusse;
6° Laque jaune et cobalt;
7° Stil de grain et bleu de Prusse;
8° Stil de grain et cobalt:
9° Terra-mérita et bleu de Prusse;
10° Terra-mérita et cobalt;
11° Noir d'Allemagne et jaune de chrome;
12° Noir d'Allemagne, indigo et jaune de chrome;
13° Terre de Sienne et bleu de Prusse;
14° Terre de Sienne et indigo.

3. Branches.

La couleur des branches ne varie guère entre les bruns gris verdâtres plus ou moins foncés. Quelques-unes sont blanches. Les jeunes rameaux sont verts comme les feuilles.

IV. — PAYSAGES

Les parties principales dans les paysages sont :
1° Les **ciels** : bleu de cobalt ou bleu de Prusse mélangé de blanc. Dans les deux cas, ajouter un peu de laque rose afin d'éviter la crudité, et une pointe de noir. L'indigo est employé pour les ciels de nuit, le jaune de chrome et la laque carminée en mélange pour les effets du soleil levant ou couchant. On peut aussi les remplacer par de la mine orange ou du rouge de Saturne. Pour les ciels vaporeux,

les lointains, arrière-plans : noir, brun rouge, blanc et bleu mélangés en diverses proportions, sans laisser dominer le noir. C'est ce qu'on appelle une teinte neutre. Composée de bleu de Prusse, de laque carminée, de noir et de brun rouge, elle convient très bien pour les ciels nuageux.

2o Les **eaux.** Dans un lointain : blanc et bleu de Prusse ou cobalt éteint d'un peu de noir. Plus rapprochées : dernière teinte neutre indiquée ci-dessus; en premier plan, bleu de Prusse et un peu de terre de Sienne calcinée en mélange. Quelquefois on ajoute une pointe de noir; d'autres fois, pour donner à l'eau plus de transparence et un ton légèrement verdâtre, on remplace la terre de Sienne par du stil de grain.

3o Les **terrains**, les **roches**, et généralement toutes parties recevant directement les rayons du soleil : vermillon ou mélanges appropriés à la couleur des objets avec vermillon dominant.

4o **Nature morte, terres labourées, feuilles sèches :** jaune de chrome, brun rouge et surtout terre de Sienne brûlée.

5o **Feuillage** des arbres, herbages, prairies, clairières des bois, et en général toutes parties vertes : laque jaune, jaune de chrome et terra-mérita, mélangés en diverses proportions de bleu de Prusse, de laque carminée, de terre d'Italie, de terre de Sienne, avec quelquefois une petite pointe de noir.

6o **Troncs d'arbres et branches :** mélange de noir ou terre de Sienne et de carmin ou de bleu de Prusse

7° **Terrasses.** Plus elles sont rapprochées, plus elles doivent être accentuées : dans les parties claires, avec des couleurs vives et franches, telles que jaune de chrome, laque jaune, verts frais et gais, etc.; dans les ombres, mélange de noir et de terre de Sienne brûlée, etc.

Les parties anguleuses des rochers, qui présentent des contrastes brusques de lumières et d'ombres, seront teintées : dans les parties claires, de tons chauds, par exemple : terre de Sienne, mine orange ou rouge de Saturne, etc.; dans les parties ombrées, mélange de noir, de terre de Sienne, de bleu de Prusse et de laque carminée; dans d'autres, tons bleuâtres ou verdâtres, etc.

En terminant ce chapitre, assez long pour l'ouvrier intelligent, nous ferons remarquer que si nous n'avons cité qu'un nombre restreint de couleurs, c'est que nous avons prévu les cas assez fréquents où l'imprimeur ne saurait avoir un assortiment complet de toutes les encres employées. Nous avons donc voulu le mettre à même de tirer partie du stock plus ou moins complet qu'il possède au moyen de mélanges judicieux.

Cependant l'expérience nous a convaincu que plus une teinte est composée, moins elle est franche et vive : le mélange des couleurs n'est donc qu'un pis aller; et, si on le peut, il y aura tout intérêt, pour la perfection du travail, à se munir d'un assortiment le plus complet possible des couleurs nécessaires.

Les combinaisons de teintes que nous avons indiquées sont quelques-unes de celles innombrables que nous offre la nature. Notre but n'était pas de dire tout ce que l'on pouvait dire, ni de mettre le conducteur à même d'exécuter un travail sans modèle. Non, mais seulement de lui faciliter la tâche et de l'aider dans ses recherches pour rendre fidèlement le modèle qu'il a sous les yeux.

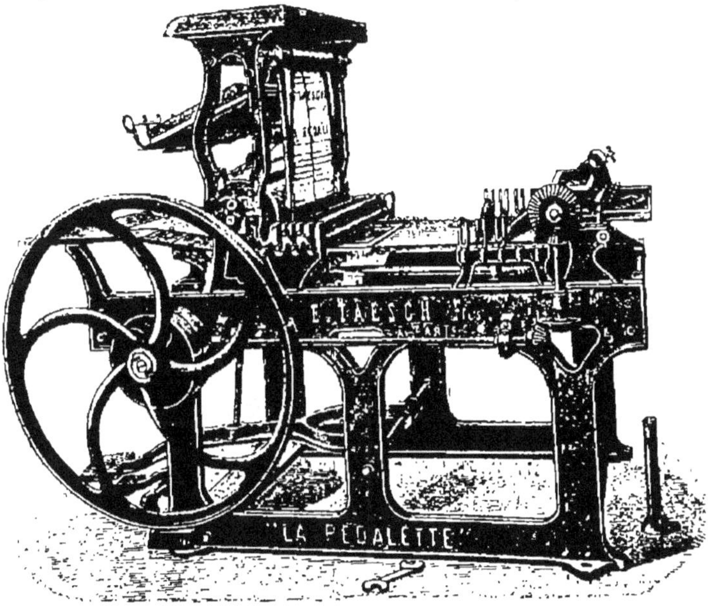

Fig. 35. — Pédalette (E. Taesch et Fils).
Cette machine ne nécessite qu'un très petit emplacement, et un seul ouvrier peut la conduire.

IX

SÉCHAGE, SATINAGE DU PAPIER

Les travaux un peu soignés ne doivent pas se livrer au client aussitôt l'impression terminée. Il est nécessaire de laisser sécher l'encre un ou plusieurs jours, suivant sa nature, pour éviter que les feuilles se décalquent les unes sur les autres au rognage ou au pliage.

Les impressions sur papier glacé ou frictionné, et surtout sur papier couché, sont très longues à sécher, le papier ne se laissant pas pénétrer par l'encre. Pour éviter le maculage, on ne devra pas empiler les feuilles par trop grande quantité, à cause de la pression produite, mais les étaler par petits paquets, et les manier toujours avec beaucoup de précautions.

Dans certaines maisons, on étend les feuilles par pincées sur des tringles de métal ou de fortes baguettes de bois suspendues horizontalement au plafond des salles de séchage, et que l'on a bien soin de protéger contre la poussière.

Pour les tirages de luxe en couleurs, on intercale les feuilles, à la sortie de la machine, dans des décharges, et on les étend ainsi au séchage. Le poids seul des feuilles suffirait en effet pour les faire se maculer. On désintercale un ou deux jours après.

Le *satinage* a pour but de faire disparaître toute trace de foulage, tout gaufrage du papier produit par l'impression. On intercale les feuilles une par une entre des cartons très lisses destinés à cet usage. Les cartons sont placés par jeux de vingt-cinq entre de forts plateaux de chêne, et le tout est mis sous la presse à satiner : c'est ordinairement une presse en bois avec vis de pression à volant; dans les ateliers importants, on se sert de la presse hydraulique ou du laminoir.

Pour procéder au satinage, il faut que l'encre soit bien sèche; autrement elle maculerait les cartons, et l'impression y perdrait aussi de son brillant et de sa netteté. Lorsque, dans les tirages en couleurs, on peut attendre que l'encre soit complètement sèche, on garantit les cartons par des décharges bien glacées.

Lorsque les cartons à satiner ont besoin d'être nettoyés, il ne faut jamais se servir d'essence de térébenthine; il suffit d'un bouchon de papier frotté énergiquement pour enlever l'encre sèche qui s'y est déposée; on saupoudre ensuite d'un peu de talc.

Ce nettoyage doit être répété assez fréquemment,

car l'encre qui sèche sur les cartons donne une poussière qui, au lieu de donner du brillant à l'impression, la rend mate.

Toutes les fois que l'on a des tirages en couleurs à passer au satinage, il faut avoir soin de bien talquer les cartons avec un morceau de coton ou de molleton, pour éviter que les feuilles soumises au satinage soient maculées.

Ces opérations du séchage et du satinage peuvent être faites à la machine, dans les grandes maisons qui ont suffisamment de travail pour alimenter ces outils supplémentaires.

La machine à satiner rend de grands services aux imprimeries importantes, grâce à sa production rapide et à ses bons résultats. Voici en quoi consiste son fonctionnement.

Le papier à satiner est amené entre deux cylindres de fonte chauffés à la vapeur, qui le compriment plus ou moins, suivant le résultat à obtenir. La partie inférieure de ces cylindres plonge dans une cuvette remplie de cristaux de carbonate de soude; à la sortie de la cuvette, le cylindre se trouve essuyé par un molleton saupoudré de savon Hudson entourant un sac de bonne toile plein d'éponges. Sur le devant de la première cuvette se trouve une lame de caoutchouc qui nettoie les cylindres.

Le chauffage des cylindres doit être d'autant plus intense que l'on veut obtenir plus de brillant. Cependant il faut éviter de trop chauffer les tirages en couleurs, l'excès de chaleur pouvant brûler le papier.

Quant aux menus travaux de ville en couleurs qu'il faut livrer de suite, il sera préférable, lorsqu'il n'y aura point de trous de pointures à faire disparaître après le tirage, de procéder au façonnage avant l'impression. Pour éviter le maculage, on rogne à la cisaille, et non au massicot, avec les plus grandes précautions. Le pliage surtout devra être fait très délicatement.

Dans les petits tirages, on peut encore, pour supprimer le maculage, talquer l'impression. Pour redonner ensuite à l'encre son brillant, on brosse énergiquement les feuilles, ou bien on les frictionne avec un tampon de coton ou de molleton.

X

PROCÉDÉ DES TROIS COULEURS

Un traité tant soit peu étendu sur l'imprimerie ne peut plus aujourd'hui passer sous silence le procédé d'impression dit " des trois couleurs ".

Ce procédé n'est pas nouveau d'invention, puisque au XVIe siècle on le trouve déjà indiqué, et au XVIIIe pratiqué couramment. Néanmoins, à comparer les résultats obtenus à ces époques reculées et ceux qui font aujourd'hui l'admiration des connaisseurs, on ne peut s'empêcher d'appeler cette rénovation d'un procédé anciennement connu, une véritable *recréation.*

C'est à l'exposition de 1878 que Ducos de Hauron présentait de premiers résultats sérieux, quoique un peu ternes, obtenus par ce procédé. Sur ces entrefaites, l'Allemagne et l'Amérique s'emparaient de l'invention et trouvaient le moyen d'en tirer meilleur parti que nous. Mais ce n'était là qu'un temps d'arrêt, et la France ne tardait pas à reprendre son rang, le premier, abandonné un instant.

On a pu juger de l'extension considérable qu'a déjà prise ce procédé, tant en France qu'à l'étranger, en visitant la section de l'imprimerie à l'Exposition universelle de 1900. Mais depuis cette époque que de progrès encore!

Notre but dans cette étude n'est pas d'entrer dans tous les détails de fabrication, non plus qu'énumérer toutes les opérations que comporte ce procédé; nous nous bornerons à résumer succinctement ce qui concerne le tirage des clichés typographiques trois couleurs.

Il n'est point de genre d'impression qui demande de plus grands soins et entraîne à plus de frais que celui-là. Sans parler de tous les préliminaires qui relèvent de la photographie et qui exigent, avec une main d'artiste, des soins et une précision extraordinaires, il faut que tout ce qui concourt à l'impression elle-même soit le plus parfait possible : outillage, clichés, encres, papier et même, et surtout, imprimeur.

Nous allons donner sur chacun de ces articles quelques conseils pratiques.

Outillage. — Pour obtenir des résultats satisfaisants dans le procédé des trois couleurs, il est de toute nécessité de se servir de machines irréprochables sous le rapport du repérage et de la distribution. Un bon repérage surtout est une condition absolument indispensable ; on peut à la rigueur obvier au défaut de distribution au moyen de chargeurs disposés avec intelligence.

Clichés. — Il serait trop long, et inutile d'ailleurs, d'exposer ici les détails de fabrication des clichés typographiques trois couleurs. Qu'il suffise de savoir que, grâce à différentes sortes de trames ou réseaux, on peut obtenir les demi-teintes du dessin. Les meilleurs résultats sont donnés par la combinaison suivante : le cliché jaune et le rouge sont tramés en une seule ligne à 45°, l'un à droite, l'autre à gauche, et le bleu est tramé complètement. Quand la trame est complète dans les trois, le moindre déplacement dans le repérage, et même parfois la seule superposition des teintes, produisent des moirés fort désagréables. Cet inconvénient n'aurait pas lieu si l'on substituait à la trame dite *américaine* une glace portant un grain de résine complètement opaque.

Rouleaux. — Les rouleaux employés devront être d'une pâte de bonne qualité et peu sensibles à l'action de la chaleur et de l'humidité. Il faut éviter avec grand soin les coutures et les aspérités. Pour cela on les fondra dans des moules d'une seule pièce, ou l'on aura bien soin tout au moins d'ébarber la couture au moyen d'un rasoir bien affilé.

Encres. — La question des encres est ici de la plus grande importance. L'imprimeur mettra tous ses soins dans un choix judicieux, se rappelant qu'une économie dans ce cas n'en serait pas une.

Les encres devront être très fines, très denses, très riches en matière colorante, et tout à la fois aussi douces et peu tirantes que possible : qualités très difficiles à rencontrer ensemble, l'encre dense ayant souvent l'inconvénient de se mal distribuer et d'arracher même l'enduit du papier couché, surtout dans les pâtes de qualité inférieure. L'imprimeur devra constamment surveiller son tirage.

Les encres devront aussi être transparentes, de façon à produire par leur superposition des teintes nettes et fraîches, et non ternes et sales.

Elles seront enfin très siccatives. Malgré une opinion qui prône le tirage à peu près simultané des trois couleurs sur des machines spéciales peu répandues encore, nous croyons pour le moment préférable de s'en tenir au tirage successif des couleurs, après un laps de temps suffisant au séchage parfait des vernis. Ce séchage demande naturellement plus ou moins de temps suivant la qualité des encres; mais il vaut mieux attendre plus que moins : le minimum serait de trois à quatre heures ; un jour entier serait préférable. Avec un séchage incomplet des vernis, on n'obtiendrait que des résultats tout à fait défectueux.

En principe, les couleurs employées doivent se rapprocher le plus possible des couleurs primaires. Cependant, pour produire certains effets plus artistiques, on peut les modifier un tant soit peu : par exemple, pour un paysage, le bleu tirera un peu sur le vert, tandis que pour un intérieur, le rouge sera légèrement violacé.

Papier. — Pour le tirage au procédé, on emploie ordinairement le papier couché, qui a l'avantage de conserver toutes les finesses de détail de la gravure sans exiger trop de foulage. On le choisira le plus blanc possible, et un peu tendre sans l'être trop, de façon à absorber plus facilement le vernis des couleurs superposées.

Registre. — Comme il a été déjà dit, le registre le plus impeccable est absolument indispensable ; les trames des différents clichés doivent se correspondre exactement. Pour cela, étant donnée une bonne machine sans déplacement, on fera l'habillage du cylindre très sec et l'on usera des pointures avec le plus de précision possible.

A propos du registre, nous devons signaler un nouvel appareil, le *Repéreur Studer*, de la maison Foucher, grâce auquel il est possible de faire le repérage exact des clichés de couleurs avant la mise sous presse : avantage énorme, qui représente pour une imprimerie un grand nombre d'heures pendant lesquelles les machines sont immobilisées.

Ce repérage, quel que soit le nombre des couleurs, se fait, au moyen de cet appareil, sans employer une feuille de papier ; d'où réelle économie. De plus, la durée du repérage est cinq fois moindre que par tout autre procédé employé jusqu'ici.

L'appareil se compose essentiellement d'un écran transparent, formé d'une feuille de celluloïde perforée régulièrement d'un très grand nombre d'ouvertures et tendue sur un châssis. Cet écran est fixé, par le moyen de deux charnières démontables, soit à un marbre spécial, soit à celui de la machine.

Pour se servir du *Repéreur Studer*, une première forme de clichés, que nous appellerons forme de base, étant placée sur le marbre et encrée, on abaisse l'écran et, au moyen d'un brunissoir, on imprime sur la plaque de celluloïde.

Ceci fait, on retire les clichés et on les remplace par ceux de la deuxième couleur, préalablement décloués de leur support et simplement posés dessus. L'écran abaissé, au moyen d'un petit outil que l'on introduit par les ouvertures ménagées, les clichés sont amenés rapidement à coïncider exactement avec ceux de la forme de base. On les cloue alors, sans relever l'écran, en utilisant toujous les perforations.

On procède de même pour la ou les couleurs suivantes.

Cette simple description suffira pour montrer au conducteur tout le parti que l'on peut tirer de cet appareil au point de vue de l'exactitude du repérage, de l'économie et de la rapidité de l'éxécution.

Le *Repéreur Studer* se fait dans les formats jésus et double-jésus.

Mise en train. — La mise en train doit être des plus simples. Inutile de faire pour chaque cliché un découpage analogue à ceux des gravures sur bois. On se contentera de coller sous le cliché lui-même un découpage des parties foncées de la gravure. Le papier carte de 30 à 35 kilos raisin convient très bien à cet usage. Comme il est déjà dit plus haut, faire l'habillage du cylindre très sec.

Tirage. — Le tirage des *trois couleurs* demande une bonne pression et peu de foulage. Il faudra donc se bien rendre compte que la pression dépend de la tension des ressorts du cylindre ou de son réglage, tandis que le foulage provient de l'habillage du cylindre et de l'épaisseur des découpages.

L'imprimeur devra sans cesse se rappeler, que dans ce genre de tirage, tout doit être irréprochable pour donner un résultat convenable ; le plus léger oubli rendrait le travail tout à fait défectueux. Son attention doit donc être de tous les instants et son soin extrême.

L'expérience a fait adopter pour la succession des tirages des couleurs l'ordre suivant : jaune, rouge, bleu ; il est de toute sagesse de s'y conformer. L'imprimeur aura bien soin de régler sa couleur à la lumière du jour ; autrement, la réussite serait de pur hasard, vu l'altération apparente subie par les couleurs à la lumière artificielle.

Enfin l'attention de l'imprimeur se portera constamment sur le réglage des encriers, le foulage, le registre, de façon à remédier au plus vite au

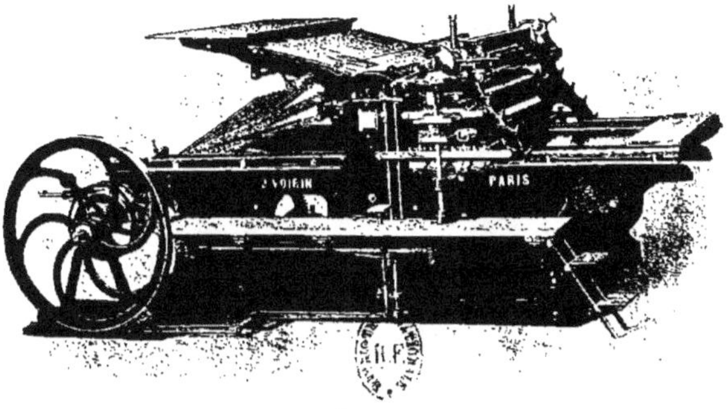

Machine chromotypographique à encrage cylindrique avec quatre rouleaux toucheurs (*J. Voirin*).

GRAVURE EN TROIS COULEURS

(*Lefranc*).

moindre accident, et empêcher des défectuosités irréparables.

L'imprimeur. — L'imprimeur appelé à faire des impressions en trois couleurs devra réunir trois qualités : être un artiste dans son genre, posséder parfaitement son métier et apporter dans son travail le soin le plus minutieux. Il devra en outre faire une étude approfondie des couleurs, pour se bien rendre compte des différents effets produits par la superposition des teintes et le mélange des encres.

TABLE DES GRAVURES

Fig. 1. — "Moderne". Machine en blanc (*Marinoni*) . . . VIII
— 2. — Serrage Marinoni à noix. 8
— 3. — Serrage Caslon 8
— 4. — Serrage Hempels (*Caslon*). 9
— 5. — Bloc à griffes mobiles (*Caslon*). 9
— 6. — Evier pour lavage des formes. Position avant le lavage 11
— 7. — Evier pour lavage des formes. Position pendant le lavage 13
— 8. — Presse à épreuves " Eclair " (*Caslon*) 14
— 9. — Rotative à quatre couleurs (*Marinoni*) 25
— 10. — Rotative à illustrations (*Marinoni*). 29
— 11. — Trempage au balai. 32
— 12. — Trempage mécanique 34
— 13. — Rotative à plieuses pour journaux de 4, 6 et 8 pages (*Marinoni*) 40
— 14. — Presse à bras, système Stanhope (Maison *Foucher*). 45
— 15. — Presse typographique du commencement du XVIe siècle. 51
— 16. — Machine réaction (*Marinoni*). 54
— 17. — Cales pour le serrage des formes sur les marbres (*Marinoni*) 62
— 18. — Rotative à retournement pour journaux de 4 pages 40 × 24 (*Marinoni*). 68
— 19. — Pédale Marinoni. 71
— 20. — Pédale Alauzet 74
— 21. — Le " Parfait ", numéroteur à pression (*Henri Chaix*). 77
— 22. — Châssis Derriey (*Henri Chaix*). 79
— 23. — Numéroteur à griffe (*Henri Chaix*). 80
— 24. — Pont de calibre (Maison *Foucher*) 83
— 25. — Position du couteau pour le découpage d'une gravure 86
— 26. — Gravure au trait tirée sans découpage. 90
— 27. — Gravure au trait tirée avec découpage. 91
— 28. — Gravure d'après un dessin au crayon 95
— 29. — Gravure d'après aquarelle rehaussée de gouache . 101
— 30. — Pointures. — Vis de pointure 108

— 31. — Pointure à coulisse 109
— 32. — Couleurs fondamentales et leurs complémentaires. 116
— 33. — Le broyeur 129
— 34. — Fonds pour les tirages en couleurs. 141
— 35. — Pédalette (*E. Taesch et Fils*). 161

TABLE DES GRAVURES HORS TEXTE

Gravure en quatre couleurs (*Malvaux*, Bruxelles).
L' " Universelle ", modèle 1908 (*Marinoni*).
La " Moderne ", modèle A (*Marinoni*).
La " Moderne ", modèle B (*Marinoni*).
Machine à retiration, modèle K (*Marinoni*).
L' " Universel ", margeur automatique (*Müller*).
La " Minerve ", série B (*S. Berthier et Durey*).
Nouvelle pédale " Héraklès " (*Voirin*).
Photogravure d'après photographie non retouchée.
— — — retouchée (*Caslon*).
Nouvelle machine en blanc à 2 tours du cylindre (*Alauzet*).
Nouvelle machine à retiration à grande vitesse (*Alauzet*).
Gravure en double teinte (*Lorilleux*).
Machine en retiration (*J. Voirin*).
Machine " Deux Tours " (*J. Voirin*).
La " Danaïde ", machine en blanc (*J. Voirin*).
Gravure en trois couleurs (*Lefranc*).

31229. — Tours, impr. Mame.

www.ingramcontent.com/pod-product-compliance
Lightning Source LLC
Chambersburg PA
CBHW070529170426
43200CB00011B/2368
* 9 7 8 2 0 1 1 3 0 6 5 4 8 *